SQVE·PO
NERVAE·F
P·M·DACICO
XVII·IMP·VI

PANORAMA OF THE

NIGEL SPIVEY AND MICHAEL SQUIRE
CLASSICAL WORLD

THE J. PAUL GETTY MUSEUM
LOS ANGELES

ACKNOWLEDGMENTS

A great many people, in both Cambridge, England, and
Cambridge, Mass., have contributed to shaping this book, and
we are indebted to all of them. The following also merit particular
thanks: Benedicte Gilman and Kenneth Lapatin at the Getty,
who read through various stages of the manuscripts and proofs;
Harold Mattingly, who cast his expert eye over the final set of proofs;
and Christopher Whitton, who helped draw up the timeline, and
aided the project in countless other ways besides.
At Thames & Hudson, Ian Mackenzie-Kerr, the designer,
masterminded many aspects of the book in addition to the complex
relationship between text and images; Pauline Hubner began
the collection of suggested illustrations, a process completed
by Sally Nicholls; above all, we are grateful to Emily Lane,
editor *sans pareil*.

NJS MJS
Cambridge, May 2004

On the endpapers: Detail from the inscription on Trajan's Column, Rome, AD 113.

On the half-title page: A lyre-playing satyr, depicted on the interior of an Attic
red-figure kylix by Epiktetos, *c.* 510 BC.

On the title page: Reconstruction of the Sanctuary of Apollo at Delphi, by Albert
Tournaire, who was involved in the École Française excavations at the site and
produced this painting in 1900 while those were still ongoing. He shows in the
centre the Temple of Apollo [431]; behind it to the left, the theatre; below it on
the right, the Stoa of the Athenians; and a host of treasuries and monuments
erected by various cities of the Greek world.

First published in the United Kingdom in 2004
by Thames & Hudson Ltd, 181A High Holborn,
London WC1V 7QX
www.thamesandhudson.com

Editor: Emily Lane
Designer: Ian Mackenzie-Kerr
Picture research: Pauline Hubner and Sally Nicholls
Production: Sheila McKenzie

First published in the United States of America in 2004
by Getty Publications, 1200 Getty Center Drive, Suite 500,
Los Angeles, California 90049-1682
www.getty.edu

Publisher: Christopher Hudson
Editor in Chief: Mark Greenberg

Library of congress Cataloguing-in-Publication Data
Spivey, Nigel Jonathan.
   Panorama of the classical world / Nigel Spivey and Michael Squire.
      p. cm.
   Includes bibliographical references and index.
   ISBN 0-89236-769-5 (hardcover)
   1. Civilization, Classical. I. Squire, Michael. II. Title.
   DE59.S67 2004
   938--dc22   2004007903

Printed and bound in Singapore by CS Graphics

CONTENTS

FOREWORD

NIGEL SPIVEY
MICHAEL SQUIRE

'A VIEW OF EVERYTHING': that is what the word 'panorama' literally means, according to its derivation from ancient Greek. This book surveys a past civilization, just one of many; yet it is naturally panoramic because the limits of the term 'Classical' cannot readily be fixed. As an epoch of Greek and Roman history, we allow it a span of just over a thousand years – from the notional date of the first Olympic Games in 776 BC until the official closure of the Olympic festival c. AD 393. But these are merely parameters of academic convenience. The 'Classical world' is not some sealed-off, distant object of historical curiosity, but an active presence, fluid in its boundaries of time and space.

Bearing that in mind, we have organized this volume thematically, exploring Greek and Roman antiquity not in terms of chronological periods (although the timeline at the back of the book, pp. 334–37, may be helpful along the way), but as a coherent package of various conceptual approaches. We begin with some of the 'big' questions: how individuals lived, loved, survived, and approached their deaths. We then proceed, in the following chapters, to investigate religion, myth, environment, politics, domestic life and economy, the associated realms of Dionysos and Apollo, and the Classical tradition in the visual arts. The final chapter returns to the knotty problem of this term 'Classical', and the ways in which the ancient world intersects with our own.

Time is not the only variable within our thematic survey: throughout, we have also been aware of geographical and cultural differences. While Classical antiquity is often considered as the basis for what some call 'the Western tradition', it encompassed great cultural and ethnic diversity. We have attempted to reflect that cosmopolitan aspect, and to salvage the significance of one 'buried' culture in particular – that of the Etruscans – within the ancient Mediterranean landscape.

Our access to the past is governed not only by current preoccupations (ideas of gender, sexuality, postcolonialism, and political affiliation among them), but also by our piecemeal reception of texts, monuments, and other relics down the ages. One minor issue is sufficient to make the point: spelling. Because so many Greek names have been handed down to us in Latinized form (first via Rome itself, and subsequently via Renaissance writers), it is impossible to devise any consistent rule for spelling Greek proper nouns; on the other hand, it seems perverse to Latinize all Greek spellings purely for the sake of editorial tidiness. The book's spellings are therefore simply those that seemed most familiar to its authors. As for the titles of ancient literary works, we have followed those of the Penguin Classics series wherever applicable, although all translations are our own unless otherwise stated.

For Classical scholars, the wealth of ancient textual and archaeological sources can be generous to the point of excess. We have tried to combine both types of evidence, emphasizing the visual, while allocating space for a number of Classical 'voices' to have their say in short excerpts. Doubtless there are important matters side-stepped, disregarded, or all too briefly abridged here. But our foremost concern has been to assemble a portable museum in which an array of artefacts and images are laid out for comparison and contrast.

Books and museums alike are sites of inspiration, insight and contemplation. If we have succeeded at all in constructing a 'museum without walls', it is largely due to the generosity of one institution, the Getty Museum in California (whose Antiquities collection will be reinstalled in Malibu in 2005), in providing so many illustrations. The assemblage of Classical antiquities at the Getty has its origins in the interests of an extremely rich and intensely private individual. Today, no museum in the world does more to make its collection accessible to the public. In similar spirit, we hope that this panorama may be a viewing open to all.

MORTALS: THE BODY IN CLASSICAL ANTIQUITY

FROM CRADLE TO GRAVE

'WHAT ANIMAL is it that in the morning goes about on four feet, in the afternoon on two, and in the evening on three?' This is one of the most notorious riddles ever posed. In Greek mythology, it was the question put to travellers who had the misfortune to meet a monster called the Sphinx, half-lion and half-woman [see fig. 584]. The Sphinx devoured anyone failing to work out the answer, and had notched up many victims before finally a young hero called Oedipus boldly supplied the solution: 'Human beings. As babies, they crawl about on hands and knees; when grown up, they walk erect; and in old age, they move with the aid of a stick.'

The Sphinx dropped dead with the right reply. As for Oedipus, his adventures were only just beginning. But for us, the riddle provides a succinct entry into the question with which our panorama of the Classical world begins: what was it like to be *alive* – to be born, to come of age, and to die?

Many people in Classical antiquity referred to the concept of Fate to help explain life's passage. 'The Fates' were often imagined as three sisters, daughters of the supreme god Zeus, spinning, measuring, and snipping the threads which were the allocated lives of human beings. They sang as they worked, and their lyrics were prophetic. Our word 'fate' comes from the Latin *fatum*, 'it is said', or 'decreed', and we have allowed the term 'fatality' to entail death. But Classical fatalism was not only a matter of doom. Fate assisted at the occasions of pregnancy, childbirth, and marriage. Fate could bring riches or ensure a speedy voyage. Ultimately it was the final reckoning, a summons that no mortal (from the Latin *mortalis*, 'subject to death') could shirk. But till then, all life was a 'gift from the gods'.

It is biologically possible for humans to postpone this destiny up to a maximum of about 110 years. In antiquity, as today, there were sporadic and unconfirmed reports of certain individuals reaching or even exceeding this limit; but generally it was thought that mortals might hope to reach the age of seventy before their time was up. One Classical compilation, ascribed to the 2nd-century AD writer Lucian, makes a list of persons who went beyond this expectation – the *Makrobioi*, or 'Long-lived Ones', who attained eighty years – many of them being writers and philosophers, whose superannuation might be considered a divine reward for blameless conduct. But potential longevity is not the same as average life expectancy. By contrast to modern Western societies, in the Classical world relatively few people were alive into their seventies. To celebrate a first birthday was a major achievement.

We deduce that from the firsthand evidence of cemeteries, where archaeologists may find the bodies of infants and children totalling up to half of all burials at a given site. Stillborn babies, or those who died in the immediately post-natal state, were probably not even accorded formal burial. Certain ritual and legal procedures suggest that the initial week after birth was the testing time for a baby and its parents, when disease or weakness was most likely to claim a victim: at Athens, for instance, it was customary not to name a child before the tenth day had passed.

1 opposite *The bronze* Diskobolos *by Myron of c. 450 BC, now lost, is recorded in several Roman marble copies, of which the most complete is this one, unearthed in 1781, known from its former owners as the* Lancellotti Discobolus. *This image of a discus-thrower has long epitomized the Classical ideal of male athleticism. Its genesis probably lies in a commemoration of victory in the pentathlon ('fivefold challenge') at one of the major athletic gatherings of 5th-century BC Greece.*

Gravestones in the Roman world often record the age of the deceased: from such monuments – admittedly the preserve of those wealthy enough to afford them – the average lifespans in ancient Rome have been estimated as thirty-four years for women, and forty-six years for men. If those statistics are right, we can understand why a 'veteran' of the Roman army was entitled to retire from active service after twenty years with a pension and, perhaps, an allotment of land. At Athens, a male citizen technically became an 'elder' at the age of thirty, when he was eligible to serve on the city Council. At Rome, the qualifying age for election to highest office in the Republican constitution, consul, was forty-two. Classical seniority, therefore, could be chronologically equivalent to our modern notion of middle age.

What follows cannot be a definitive typical Classical 'life-cycle': rather, an articulation of mortal existence as it might have seemed to the ancient audiences of the myth of Oedipus outwitting the Sphinx. First we crawl, then we walk, and finally we hobble. The middle part of that mobile progress is much occupied with the strategies of self-presentation and self-preservation that are dealt with in more detail throughout the rest of this chapter. So our attention will first be directed to the nature of the beginning – and the end.

Being born It was perhaps a piece of pure histrionics when the title-character of Euripides' play *Medea*, first performed in 431 BC, exclaimed, 'I'd rather stand in the front line of battle three times than give birth once' (*Medea* 250). But the comparison was not absurd. Carried out with an understanding of gynaecology more folkloristic than scientific, and in the absence of anaesthetics, the birth of a child was at best an excruciating agony for a woman, and at worst the cause of her death. The high degree of risk is reflected by the many cults of goddesses invoked for aid in birthpangs and delivery. These included Eileithyia (Roman Lucina), a deity specifically connected with pregnancy and its successful issue, and Demeter, the buxom female genius of all fertility and reproduction [150]. Leto, the mother of Apollo, and Artemis, Apollo's sister, were also often the focus of votive appeal. But above all there was Hera, consort of Zeus and supreme mother-goddess [571].

2 *Twin infants, tightly wrapped in swaddling clothes, suckle in the lap of a divine* kourotrophos *('nurturer of young men') figure. Limestone statue from Megara Hyblaea in Sicily, late 6th century BC.*

3 *A primary hope or purpose of marriage in Classical Greece: the production of male offspring. Detail of an Attic red-figure vase attributed to the Washing Painter, c. 430–420 BC. The vessel is a* lebes gamikos *– a vase specifically intended for the celebration of a wedding.*

4 *Marble relief on the Ara Pacis (Altar of Peace) in Rome, dedicated in 9 BC. The central figure is variously identified, as Italy, or Earth, or Peace (or perhaps she is the goddess Ceres): she is certainly symbolic of maternal fertility, peace, and plenty.*

5 *Baby sits in a terracotta high-chair, with mother or nurse in attendance. Interior of an Attic red-figure kylix (drinking cup) attributed to the Sotades Painter Workshop, c. 470–460 BC.*

Worshipped as Uni by the Etruscans, and Juno by the Romans, she was frequently envisaged as 'child-bearing', with a babe in her arms or at her breast.

Births took place at home, the only prop being a cut-away stool on which the woman might squat as she delivered her 'swelling one' (*embryon*). A jagged piece of pottery traditionally served to slice the umbilical cord. Despite our use of the word 'Caesarean' to denote the surgical resort of cutting open the womb – used allegedly for the premature delivery of the infant Julius Caesar in 100 BC – it is unlikely that such intervention was regularly available.

In gospel accounts of the birth of Jesus Christ it is said that the babe was immediately wrapped in 'swaddling clothes' or 'swathing bands'. This was common practice in antiquity, stemming from a belief that a newborn's limbs had such flexibility that they might be set crooked or distorted if not bound up straight in woollen strips. Votive images dedicated to the deities of childbirth indicate how comprehensive this packaging could be, enveloping the infant from top to toe, usually for the duration of a month or more [2, 8].

Breastfeeding was the normal mode of early nutrition [2], either by the mother or (in the case of wealthy families) by a wet-nurse. By the 4th century BC it had already been noted by Greek physiologists that the process of producing milk (*lactatio* would be the Latin term) was a natural female contraceptive, interrupting the menstrual cycle; so one effect of feeding a child at the breast, at least if sustained over several years, was to limit the number of pregnancies a woman could bear. Was this considered good or bad?

6 *Detail of a marble funerary stele of a boy, from Asia Minor, mid-3rd century AD. The inscription reads: 'In the year 244 in the month Hyperbertaios [23 August–22 September], Syntrophos and Spoude honoured their child, who lived two years [by erecting this monument].'*

7 below *Detail of a marble sarcophagus of a small boy, c. AD 110–130. The boy's image is displayed by two cupid figures.*

That question has to be asked, because there is a tension in the evidence we find about family size in Classical antiquity. On the one hand, children were generally regarded as a long-term investment. Adults cared for their children with a view to their children caring for *them* in years to come. On the other hand, family size could become unmanageable – in which case, it seems, the acceptable practice was to leave an unwanted baby exposed to the elements or the kindness of strangers. So often does such infant exposure supply the plot of a Classical legend (the stories of Oedipus, Telephos [442], and the twins Romulus and Remus [583] are three of the better-known ones), we might suspect the actual practice to have been common. But perhaps that is just the archetypal power of a satisfying myth.

Above all, however, it was a civic duty to have children and raise them as new blood for the citizen body. Nowhere was that obligation made more overt than in the Rome of Augustus, whose rule (27 BC–AD 14) was presented as a new 'Golden Age' of peace, prosperity and national regeneration. Legislation offered specific inducements for married couples to produce children; and an exemplary panel [4] on the Emperor's monumental Ara Pacis, or Altar of Peace, in Rome was complemented by verses from a leading poet at the Augustan 'court'. In the course of his *Hymn of the Century* Horace hails Eileithyia-Lucina, the genius of childbirth: 'Goddess, may you bring forth our successors, and prosper the Senate's decrees rewarding parents and marriage, for a new stock of boys and girls . . .'

So to bear children was both a private and a public requirement: childbirth was therefore an object of votive dedication in the sanctuaries; and the death of a child was an occasion for monuments [6, 7].

8 right *Etruscan terracotta statuette, c. 2nd century BC. This type of votive figure seems to show a swathed baby; but the adult features of the face, and the large hand, perhaps holding a pomegranate, suggest rather an adult 'reborn'.*

9 *Herakles attacks Geras, 'Old Age'. Detail of an Attic red-figure pelike (jar) attributed to the Geras Painter, c. 480–470 BC.*

Old age: a blessing – or a monster? In Greek legend, 'Old Age' figures as one of the nasty monsters that the hero Herakles must face – emaciated and bent over his stick, the antithesis of a standard young heroic physique [9]. And yet this monster's name, Geras, does not have wholly detestable associations. *Geras* otherwise denotes 'honour', 'reverence', 'privilege'. In Athens, men who reached the age of fifty-nine served one year as public arbitrators; thereafter they were officially *gerontes*: 'old men', indeed, but at least etymologically entitled to particular respect.

So was life's three-legged stage considered a desirable achievement, or a curse? The vignette given by Homer in the *Iliad* of his most senior campaigner in the Trojan War, Nestor, nicely captures the ambivalence of Greek attitudes to this dilemma. The old warrior is portrayed as indeed commanding respect when he speaks – but is then rather liable to ramble and reminisce, in the end dispensing advice that no one really heeds.

Generic images of the elderly become a feature of Greek art in the Hellenistic period (323–31 BC) [10, 11, 13]. It is hard to say whether these were intended to provoke sympathy or disgust among ancient viewers. We can be sure, however, that the old people of ancient Greece were rarely marginalized into 'homes'. Most could count on being supported by their own offspring – though a drastic law from Keos was said to have required that the over-sixties take poison, in order not to be a burden on the island's hard-pressed economy.

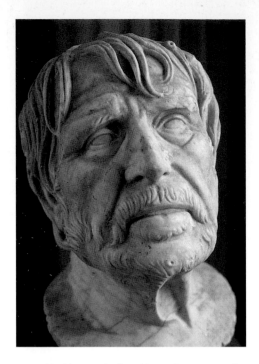

A more positive culture of respect for the elderly was fostered in the constitution of the Roman Republic. Here, as we have already noted, the most important public positions could not be sought before reaching a certain age; and there is no doubt that the distinctive 'veristic' portraiture associated with Republican Rome – featuring faces heavily creased by the furrows of experience and responsibility [280] – is partly due to the prevailing equation of age with wisdom. Much trust was placed in senior counsel, tradition, and 'the old way of doing things' – in the Latin phrase, the *mos maiorum*, the custom of elders or forebears [12].

One of the Republic's greatest statesmen was Cicero [261], who at the age of sixty-two dedicated an imaginary discussion, *On Old Age*, to Atticus, his longtime friend and correspondent at Athens. Cicero had recently been through what many Romans considered the most terrible of misfortunes, the loss of a grown child (his only daughter, Tullia, in 45 BC). His own life would be violently truncated just two

10 *Marble portrait of an old man: Roman copy of a type created in the 2nd century* BC, *possibly once intended to evoke the archaic Greek poet Hesiod, but subsequently taken as a generic image of careworn seniority (also mistakenly thought to represent the 1st-century* AD *Roman philosopher Seneca).*

11 The Drunken Old Hag: *marble copy of an original attributed to a sculptor called Myron of Pergamon,* c. 200 BC. *The woman holds a large* lagynos *(wine-jar): this has led some scholars to relate the statue to the cult of Dionysos, perhaps even to a festival of 'jug-carrying' (lagynophoria).*

12 *The* Barberini Togatus: *marble group showing a noble Roman (clad in a toga, a semicircular piece of cloth draped over the left shoulder) carrying two portrait busts (*imagines*) of his ancestors, c. 50 BC– AD 15. This statue unites three generations in one ensemble – and emphasizes the institutional respect in late Republican Rome for the family forebears.*

13 *The* Old Fisherman: *restored marble copy of an original created in the Greek East c. 200 BC, like the 'Drunken Old Hag' [11]. This too may be a votive piece, illustrative of humble piety – a fisherman bringing his catch to the temple. Pliny the Younger, writing in the 1st century AD, described a similar statue of a 'standing old man' thus: 'his bones, muscles, veins, and wrinkles appear like those of a living and breathing being – the hair is thin and receding, the forehead broad, the face shrivelled, the throat narrow, the arms limp, and the stomach sunken' (Letters 3.6).*

years after Tullia's death. But Cicero seems to have been philosophically preparing himself for the end. Using as his mouthpiece a former staunch Republican, Cato the Elder (who was said to have lived vigorously into his mid-eighties), Cicero admits that old age can come as a burden. But one by one he counters the factors supposed to make old age unpleasant. Retirement from activity, physical weakness, loss of libido, proximity to death – even if these are the characteristics of growing old, argues Cicero, they are not without their blessings.

It is a classic essay of consolation, and it ends with perhaps the single most consolatory sentiment of Classical philosophy: that human beings are not, ultimately, subject to the law of mortal decay. Our bodies perish – but what are bodies? As most Classical philosophers claimed: merely the temporary shelters for the better part of us – the soul.

Discussion of the theoretical nuances surrounding this doctrine of 'dualism', and of ancient notions of an 'afterlife', may be postponed (p. 236). We cannot guess what proportion of people in antiquity went to their deaths with the calm conviction of further existence famously manifested by Socrates after his condemnation to death by an Athenian court in 399 BC (p. 16). But we can pick up the traces of their collective and individual funeral formalities.

Death, the essential *rite de passage* Socrates' most famous pupil, Plato, once summarized the life's ambition of any citizen of his times (the 4th century BC). It was to be 'wealthy, in good health, and held in honour throughout Greece; to live to a ripe age; and, having buried one's parents beautifully, to be beautifully buried by one's own offspring, and sent off in great style' (*Hippias Major* 291d–e).

This wish-list is telling, especially in its final clause. A funeral marked by 'magnificence' constituted a sort of judgment on the value of a life: declaring that here was someone bound for dust, but whose reputation and esteem would solidly remain. And there is little doubt that when the stipulation is made to be buried 'beautifully', it is assumed that there will be the full range of funeral rites, with crowds of wailing mourners – and a grave not only made visible by an upright stone (*stele*) or some other 'sign' (*sema*) [14–20, 146, 324, 325], but also furnished inside: provisioned, that is, with gifts and supplies for the afterlife.

This assumption is highly significant for our knowledge of the material culture of the Classical world, for a simple reason. Most of the places where Classical people once lived have been obliterated, while many of the places where they were buried have stayed relatively intact. The haul from ransacked tombs

14 *Marble grave relief, probably from the Peloponnese, first half of the 1st century* AD. *A boy shakes hands with his grieving mother in a gesture of farewell.*

Socrates responds to his sentence of death:

Depending on how we look at it, we may hold on to the hope that death is a sort of bonus. For what happens to us at death is one of two things. Either the dead person just ceases to be, losing all senses in a sea of nothingness; or else, as many people believe, it is a change, a migration of the soul towards another place.

Well, if death is simply the end of our senses, then it is like a long dreamless sleep, and therefore a sweet prospect. If you can recall that rare night when you slept so deeply that you were undisturbed by dreaming – can you remember anything more pleasant? . . . Most of us can count such nights on the fingers of one hand; and if that is how death is, then I for one am looking forward to it – for then eternity will be like nothing more than a single night.

But suppose that death is, indeed, a journey to another place. Suppose the destination is as commonly imagined, and contains the spirits of all who have died. I ask you – what prospect matches that? Who would not want to travel to that other world where we are not subject to judgment from our so-called 'superiors' on earth, but the demigods of true justice in the afterlife – Minos, Rhadamanthys, Aiakos and Triptolemos? And think how much it would be worth, to have conversations with Orpheus and Musaeus, with Hesiod and Homer! I should be delighted to die, over and again, if this were so. I long to meet up with Palamedes,

and Telamonian Ajax, and other great individuals of the past who died as a result of unfair 'justice': I look forward to comparing my experience with theirs – that would be a very satisfying encounter. But above all it would be sheer pleasure to spend time talking to those inhabitants of the beyond in the same spirit of enquiry as I have practised here – trying to find out who is truly wise, and discovering those whose wisdom extended no further than their own imagining. . . . Certainly in that place, to ask questions is not deemed a capital offence. Over there – if what we are told is true – not only is everyone happier than us; they are immortal too.

And you who pass sentence on me: you too must face death with optimism, remembering the truth that so long as a man is good, no evil can befall him either in this world or the next. The gods do not cheat one who strives for goodness, and what is happening to me today was not a matter of chance. I see that it is appropriate for me now to take leave of life and be freed from trouble . . . So I harbour no malice towards my accusers, nor against those who have condemned me to death; although, since they meant to do me harm, not good, they can carry the blame for that. . . .

The time is up, and we must depart: I to die, you to live. Which of us takes the better path is unknown to all except God.

Plato, *Apology* 32–33

15 *Marble stele of Poseides, c. 275 BC. The deceased wears his hunting outfit; the painted outline of his pet dog is just visible. The small figure is Poseides' wife.*

amounts to an embarassment of riches, and the mentality which generated such riches may be hard for us to understand. How many of us, after all, anticipate being interred with a selection of our most precious personal possessions? In the 9th century BC a couple belonging to a small community at Lefkandi in the region of Euboea were buried not only with a scatter of prized drinking vessels, and other items of prestige and sentimental value such as weapons and jewelry: in an adjacent pit were the skeletal remains of four horses – presumably a chariot team, deliberately put to death to join their owners. It is not flippant to say that this is like the heirs of a multi-millionaire burying him with his best limousine, plus most of his assets.

Faced with this plenty, a science has evolved that is 'the archaeology of death'. Perhaps the most basic premise of this science is that the rank or social standing of individuals while alive will be reflected in the nature of their deposition when dead. Sometimes starkly so – at one cemetery in the Greek colonial settlement of Taras (modern Taranto), in South Italy, slaves were found buried with their leg-irons still attached. In 7th-century BC Etruria, a number of burials are classified as 'princely' not because we know anything about the actual political status of their occupants, but on account of the tomb's size and design, and the signal luxury implied by the objects laid out with the deceased.

It is not overly problematic to argue for a Classical concept of a 'community of the dead' in some ways mirroring the 'society of the living'. The archaeology of Etruria notably indicates that every centre of habitation has its accompanying *necropolis*, or 'city of the dead', whose overall layout and particular tombs are equally suggestive of familiar, domestic features – as if the dead were being made to feel perfectly 'at home' in their new surrounds. But we should be wary of resting too much faith in the notion that funerary remains are an accurate guide to social structure. We know, for example, that 'anti-sumptuary' legislation was periodically imposed in some Greek city-states, explicitly limiting the expense and showiness of a family funeral; while in Rome, certain elaborate tombs (such as the extraordinary monument erected by Marcus Vergilius Eurysaces, near the Porta Maggiore [101]) belong to individuals of relatively low social status (Eurysaces was a baker – albeit a successful one).

Most communities of the Classical world actively practised ancestor-worship, however, for which tombs obviously provided a focus. On one gravestone from eastern Greece [15] we see the deceased – a youngish man called Poseides – typically magnified by contrast to the accompanying figure of his wife. The increase of scale indicates his posthumous status as a figure to be venerated. But the inscription notched around the head of Poseides seems to convey a stream of his own anxieties regarding the monument as such, and is worth translating in full.

This is the memorial [*mnema*] of Poseides, son of Herakleides, a law-abiding man: he never wronged anyone. And anyone with the capacity to see and speak well, to him let the gods be gracious, and may he do no wrong. And if anyone should desecrate this memorial, or these plants or carvings, or should bring into this memorial any other body apart from mine, or those of my wife, my sons and my daughters; or if someone should take away this memorial to secure a debt, or should purchase it or assign it to others, or put another body into [the grave] without [Poseides] himself specifying as above in regard to the memorial; and if anyone should either vandalize or [use] physical force on this [monument], may Artemis Medeia and Ephesia and all the gods [punish] him and his descendants.

16 A prothesis ('setting-forth'). Detail of an Attic krater (a vessel used for mixing wine with water) in Geometric style that served as a grave-marker, attributed to the Hirschfeld Painter, c. 750 BC. The deceased lies on a funerary bier, while attendant mourners slap their heads in formal signs of distress.

17 Marble grave stele of Ampharete, from the Kerameikos cemetery in Athens, late 5th century BC. The accompanying inscription reads: 'My daughter's beloved child is the one I hold here, the one I held on my lap as we looked at the light of the sun while we lived, and I hold again now we are both dead.'

18 Paying respects at a grave stele. Detail of an Athenian white-ground lekythos (oil-flask), late 5th century BC. In democratic Athens, neglect of such duties was subject to state fines.

19 *Detail of an Attic marble funerary lekythos, c. 375 BC. The veiled and inclined head, and the half-clasped arms, are the indicators of bereavement.*

20 *A girl named Apollonia, represented on her marble funerary naiskos (shrine), c. 100 BC. She is shown with a dove and a pomegranate – both associated with Persephone and the Underworld.*

21 *Part of an* ekphora *scene – the processional escort of a body to the grave: fragment of an Attic funerary plaque attributed to Exekias, c. 540 BC.*

It is clear that the act of burial, however simple, was regarded as an essential rite of passage from this world to the next. Greeks, Etruscans, and Romans varied in the degree of imaginative detail they gave to their concepts of 'the Underworld' – often referred to by the name of its mythical overlord, Hades – but they largely shared in the belief that a person's body must be buried in order to make that transition. It might be enough to scatter a few handfuls of earth over a corpse, as made plain by the heroine of Sophocles' tragedy *Antigone*. But if that corpse were left utterly exposed, then it was, so to speak, a fate worse than death. A terrible limbo, when the immaterial essence of a person, the soul – Greek *psyche*, or Latin *anima* – had nowhere to rest.

The drama of deposition   Funerary ritual in the Classical world was essentially a 'three-act drama'. First there was an exhibition and tending of the dead body; then the transport of the body to the site of burial; finally, its interment. The first phase, known to the Greeks as a *prothesis*, or 'setting-forth', involved washing, anointing, and shrouding the corpse, and might last for several days, with the opportunity for family, friends, and members of the public to pay their respects to the deceased, laid out on a bier [16]. The second phase was the *ekphora*, or 'carrying-out', with the body trundled towards its designated cemetery place on a wagon, and a cortege following that would include mourners and musicians playing dirges [21]. A ritual lament was sung (for the Greeks, a *threnos*), mainly by women, and a standard gesture of sadness was for those in the procession to be slapping their heads. In Etruria and Republican Rome, professional mourners (*ploratores*) might be hired to raise the pitch of conclamation – our word 'histrionics' seems ultimately to derive from an Etrusco–Roman term for such affectation of grief – with women tearing their hair and scratching their cheeks. Finally there was the deposition. Both cremation and inhumation were practised throughout Classical antiquity, apparently according to convenience or personal preference; usually, cemetery space was ordered around family groupings.

Once the deceased was consigned to the community of the dead, the living could celebrate. In his account of the funeral conducted on the Trojan plain for Patroklos, Achilles' best friend, Homer describes (*Iliad* 23) a massive programme

22, 23 *Mummy portraits from Hawara in the Fayum, late 1st century AD. An inscription with the young woman identifies her as 'Demos' ('People'), aged twenty-four; it is likely that the sad-faced child buried with her (below) was her daughter.*

24 *Mummies as excavated by Sir Flinders Petrie at Hawara in the Fayum in 1911. Here the heads are made of a sort of papier-mâché.*

of athletic games – as if trials were being held to see who could replace Patroklos as a hero (see p. 36). To judge from their painted tombs, the Etruscans also arranged various contests around the occasion of deposition: such Etruscan 'funeral games' were thought by the Romans to be the origin of gladiatorial entertainment. On a gentler note, a meal might be taken in the precincts of the tomb, with the bereaved decked in garlands, toasting the memory of the deceased [99]. Items of food and drink were often left in the grave too, so the dead might share in this 'above-banquet' (*perideipnon*). And that was not the end of it; because, for years to come, the anniversary of this date would be marked with further attendance of the grave by descendants of the deceased. Liquid gifts of blood, wine or oil were poured at the tomb; in some places – the large Roman cemetery at Ostia, for example – it was customary to post pieces of solid food through tubes set into the ground.

The 'signposting' of graves was one of the earliest functions of Classical art, from *c.* 800 BC on. Over time, all sorts of statues and sculptured reliefs would be used for this purpose; but to begin with, painted images were set up as indicators of the mortuary zone. In the Dipylon zone of the Kerameikos cemetery of Athens, outsize ceramic pots were placed on top of burials, and modes of decoration developed to tell viewers why the vessels stood there. A vase-painting style that had been almost entirely dominated by geometric, abstract motifs therefore began to make specific figurative reference to the funeral drama [16]. Subsequently there would evolve not only a definite imagery of the rituals of death but also a repertoire of forms and gestures associated with ancestor-respect and bereavement. Even a fragment can eloquently attest this repertoire [19]: a piece of stone in the form of a vase known as a *lekythos*, customarily used for bringing a tribute of oil to the tomb, has carved on it the figure of a woman downcast in grief. Classical philosophers and physiologists defined grief as a particularly 'feminine' emotion; socially it was normal, at Athens and elsewhere, for women to take responsibility for the regular duties of tomb-cult.

Death in antiquity had a more immediate presence than it does today. Nowhere is this more striking than in the relics from several sites in Egypt, most notably the Fayum area of the Nile valley, where Egyptian, Greek, and Roman practices came together to produce the so-called Fayum portraits [22–24, 26]. It appears that mummified ancestors here were not only deposited in cemeteries, but for some while also stood upright in the entrance-halls to houses, as if prolonging their time above ground. The sense of proximity between the dead and the living was heightened by the remarkably vivid style of painting used to supply inserted 'masks' for many of the mummies.

25 *Etruscan bronze mirror, c. 400 BC. The reverse sides of Etruscan mirrors were often decorated with amorous or nuptial scenes – such as here, the betrothed Peleus and Thetis [cf. 187]. The reflective side was silvered.*

26 opposite *Portrait of 'Isidora' from Ankyronpolis (modern El-Hibeh), on the east bank of the Nile south of the Fayum, Egypt, c. AD 100–110. The subject – a Greek woman whose name appears to be painted on the shroud at the left – is decked in a gold-leaf diadem, plus quadruple pearl earrings, and a triple necklace of pearls and emeralds, with a central stone, perhaps a garnet or ruby.*

COSMETICS AND THE ART OF LOOKING GOOD

A face from Roman Egypt gazes out at us [26]. Her identity is uncertain, but one thing is for sure: she has dressed to impress. She wears a diadem, large earrings, and a triple necklace – all glitteringly rendered in gold paint and gold leaf. She will go to posterity looking her best.

The original Greek word *kosmetikos* has broader connotations than 'cosmetic' today. Certainly the art of make-up was among them: the famous queen of Egypt, Cleopatra, is reported to have written a treatise on that art. But *kosmos* generally entailed an order or arrangement of things. To be cosmetic with one's own body was to put it in order, arrange it for display. Some Classical voices – such as the man quoted in Xenophon's *The Estate Manager* (*Oikonomikos*; see p. 26) – denounce this as a form of fraud. Archaeology, however, indicates that the art of self-adornment was carefully practised at various social levels.

Of all the Classical artefacts preserved today in museum cabinets, jewelry is what causes most amazement with modern viewers [27–30]. Partly this is due to the intrinsic value of the materials used in its assembly; but even more striking is the finesse of craftsmanship. So far as we know, these craftsmen did not have the use of magnifying glasses. The delicacy of their 'micro-manipulative' handiwork is therefore almost incredible.

Fine jewelry was produced in Greece during the Mycenaean period (*c.* 1600–1150 BC). But a continuous tradition of fashioning elaborate jewels in both Greece and Etruria properly begins in the 9th century BC, stimulated by contact with Oriental expertise in the techniques of filigree and granulation. Filigree means the making of patterns with fine wire; granulation, creating patterns with tiny grains or spheres. Hot soldering is the basic method involved in both techniques, and gold the preferred metal (gold naturally 'granulates' when melted in minute quantities upon a charcoal block). Other modes of jewelry in Classical antiquity include enamel (coloured glass fused to metal), hammered gold leaf, various forms of inlaying, engraving or *intaglio*, and plating in gold and silver. But filigree and granulation cause most wonderment – perhaps because their ancient results remain so difficult to replicate.

In Etruria, where so many graves remained intact until modern times, enough evidence survives to show both the ceremonial and day-to-day utility of personal items of jewelry. Diadems would seem clearly to count as symbols of status; so too the large 'badges' of embossed gold usually referred to as 'pectorals'. Plaques and pendants, necklaces, amulets, hair spirals, earrings, finger rings, and bracelets may variously be judged as more or less 'essential luxuries'. But the most commonly found items might truly be counted as everyday necessities, for they are the pins, clasps and buckles (*fibulae*) that served to hold clothing together. An Etruscan fibula may take many forms, and can seem no more ornate than a modern safety-pin. The functional nature of the device did not however deter its frequent transformation into an intricately granulated item of personal prestige [27].

Etruscan burial customs also happen to have preserved a large quantity of hand-mirrors. To modern scholars, these bronze utensils are primarily of interest for the repertoire of mostly mythological scenes engraved onto their reverse sides [25]. But from the sheer quantity of artefacts either directly required for personal beautifying – including numerous little containers for perfumes, potions, and scented oils – or else illustrating the routines of self-embellishment, we can say that there was a thriving 'cosmetics industry' in the Classical world [31–35, 346].

27 left *Etruscan golden 'disc' fibula from Vulci, decorated with lines of fine granulation, 7th century* BC.

28 below *Centrepiece from a Greek diadem of gold set with garnets, 2nd century* BC. *The reef knot, known as a Herakles knot, originated in ancient Egypt, and became a very popular motif in Hellenistic jewelry.*

30 opposite *Golden hairnet designed to be worn over a bun at the back of the head, probably from Egypt, c. 220–100* BC. *The central image seems to depict the goddess Aphrodite with portrait features of one of the Ptolemaic queens of Egypt, Arsinoë II.*

29 right *Gold wreath from Vergina, late 4th century* BC, *part of the burial honours of a Macedonian king, thought by some to be Philip II and by others to be his son, Philip III Arrhidaios (half-brother of Alexander the Great). Though incomplete, it still weighs 714 grammes (25 ounces), and retains 313 leaves and 68 acorns.*

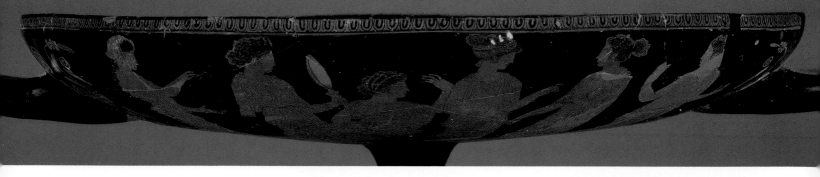

31 A group of women with mirrors and other items of self-adornment, depicted on an Attic red-figure kylix attributed to the Meidias Painter, c. 410 BC. The central seated figure is inscribed as kale ('beautiful').

A philosopher's view of female cosmetics. An Athenian, Ischomachos, is telling Socrates about his wife's experiment with make-up:

It happened one day, Socrates, that I saw her with her face all powdered. She had covered herself with white lead, so that she could look even paler than usual; and she'd rouged her cheeks with extract of alkanet [similar to the henna plant]. She'd also got some high-heeled shoes on, to make her seem taller. I said to her: 'My love, you are the one with whom I share my life. How would you like it if I pretended to have money and belongings that didn't really exist?' 'I'd hate it!' she cried. 'Well then,' I continued, 'do you like me to stand before you just as I am, with my natural countenance – or would you prefer it if I plastered my face in red lead, smeared rouge under my eyes, and presented myself to you as an impostor like that?' 'No!' she replied, 'It's you I want, not paintwork.' 'Then, dear wife,' I said, 'let us not deceive each other with displays that may fool everyone else. A bath, even a teardrop, gives the game away.'

Xenophon, *The Estate Manager* 10.2–12 (paraphrased)

Ischomachos goes on to instruct his young wife that the best way to keep a healthy complexion is to do plenty of vigorous housework.

32 Pyxis (perfume-jar) from Corinth, perhaps by the Chimaera Painter, c. 570 BC. During the 6th century BC, Corinthian potters supplied many such containers for perfumes and oils, decorating them in a busily 'Orientalizing' style itself suggestive of an Eastern origin of the vases' contents.

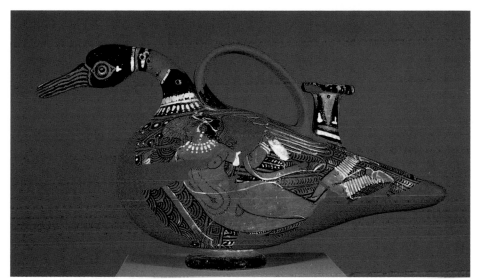

33 above *Faience alabastron (a flask used to hold precious oils and unguents) from the eastern Mediterranean, c. 200–100 BC. Faience is a compound of quartz, lime, and plant ash, mixed with water to form a paste that can be set in a mould and made to resemble alabaster or ivory.*

34 right, top *The minor goddess Psyche ('Soul') and cupids – little winged attendants of Venus – are shown confecting perfume on this fragment of a Roman wall-painting, c. AD 7. Similar scenes appear in the House of the Vettii at Pompeii [346].*

35 right, above *Etruscan red-figure askos (flask) in the shape of a duck, c. 350–300 BC. This small vessel would have contained perfume or scented oil. Winged female figures painted on each side are probably spirits associated with Turan – an Etruscan goddess similar to the Greek Aphrodite and the Roman Venus.*

Remnants of a late 1st-century BC poem by Ovid entitled *Facial Treatments* also suggest a wide range of organic substances used in female make-up, some still in use today (such as henna), others certainly not (such as white lead). The Latin satirist Juvenal mocked the sort of well-to-do women in Rome who developed distended earlobes from wearing huge pear-shaped pearls, and who clad their faces with layer upon layer of doughy creams and sticky poultices: the husband who tried to kiss such a wife would collide with a mask of grease (Juvenal, *Satires* 6.457–73). The voices of criticism here are male, and typically misogynistic. Yet we should remember that men, too, resorted to cosmetics. It was not uncommon, for example, to notice Roman men wearing wigs. But what differed about Classical male vanity was that it meant not dressing up, but stripping off.

Building the body beautiful No Classical city could call itself a city if it lacked a gymnasium. Usually located near the town baths, gymnasia were sociable places regularly visited by many citizens for the purpose of a daily 'workout'. The establishment of the more specialized *palaestra*, or wrestling-school, was also a common feature of urban design in the Graeco-Roman world. (In case this gives the impression of fanatical attachment to physical culture, it is worth adding that gymnasium or *palaestra* sites could double as places of intellectual activity.)

The term 'gymnasium' implies nudity: it was the place where one went unclothed or 'bare' (*gymnos*). As such, an element of self-display was built into the very concept of gymnastic participation. Thucydides in the late 5th century BC

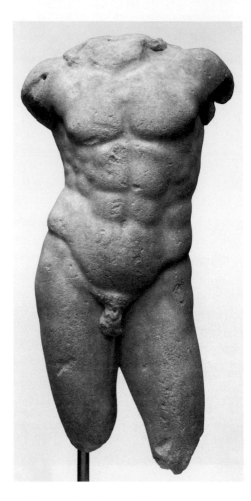

36 *Marble torso from Asia Minor, c. 1st century AD, after an original of the early 4th century BC. It probably represents a deity (Hermes?) or victorious athlete. The angle of the hips is characteristic of the bodily chiasmos ('diagonal tension') canonized by the sculptor Polykleitos c. 450 BC [37].*

noted that the practice of divesting for contest was peculiarly Greek, first instigated by the Spartans (*History of the Peloponnesian War* 1.7); from the beginnings of life-size Greek sculpture and *kouros* figures [393, 446, 453] it is clear that to be *gymnos*, at least for men, entailed no sense of shame. Taboos were attached to female nakedness in Greece, and for both the Etruscans and Romans there is evidence or more reticence on this matter. Our modern distinction between the naked and the nude is understood as follows: we are all born naked, but we can only pose nude. To be nude means to be naked and aware of it, or more precisely, aware of being seen naked by others. And this distinction is important to our present discussion. What emerges from the Classical gymnasium is not an ethos of perfect unselfconsciousness – but rather, in the phrase of one modern scholar (Larissa Bonfante), 'nudity as a costume'.

In the ideal Classical city, the paragon-citizen, whose voting rights originated from his availability for military service, kept himself in conspicuously good shape as a matter of political duty, not personal vanity. Yet the gymnasium ambience was also charged with the excitement of sexual selection. The obligation to practise combat sports in readiness for the battlefield faded, especially after the development of professional armies (pioneered by the Macedonians, in the 4th century BC). So Classical gymnasia became the sites of exercise for the sake of looking good. To generate erotic attention was only one motive: beauty was invested with morality; to *look* good was necessarily also to *be* good.

This connection of *kalos kai agathos*, 'beautiful and good', was already a common assumption when Socrates and his friends were philosophizing in Athens. Socrates – himself recognized as an exception to the rule, with his stout physique and pug-nosed features [369, 370, 546] – quibbled tirelessly to define goodness as an abstract virtue, but took it for granted that there was a general coexistence of the morally good and the physically beautiful (a compound saluted in Greek as *kalokagathia*, the joint nobility of appearance and conduct). According to this equation, what you saw was what you got. Ugliness implied a scurrilous, nasty-minded individual. A coward could be judged just by his shrinking shoulders. A telling literary instance of such physical determinism is provided by a minor character in the *Iliad*, Thersites. Thersites is the one who, early on in the story of the siege of Troy, tries to start a mutiny among the Greek forces. What is this war all about, he demands – a clique of aristocrats just pursuing their greed for glory and riches? Why don't we all sail home? But eloquent (and reasonable) as his protest might seem, Thersites is damned by being lame, hunched, fuzzily bearded, and 'pointy-headed' – in short, as Homer notes, 'the ugliest man that came to Troy' (*Iliad* 2.216). The aristocratic response is curt dismissal, with the threat to strip him of his cloak and tunic to expose his body in its full and shameful squalor of deformity, and to beat him (he gets the beating anyway).

One 5th-century BC Greek sculptor, Polykleitos of Argos, wrote a treatise about how to represent the ideal physique in bronze or stone, using a system of mathematical calculations. All we know of this text (known as the *Canon*) amounts to a few frustratingly enigmatic phrases, and no statue has yet been found that can be confidently called an original work of this artist. However, a fair notion of the Polykleitan project can be gained from the many copies or adaptations taken from his original bronze-cast pieces. One work, the *Doryphoros* ('Spear-carrier') [37], acquired particular fame as being constructed strictly according to the sculptor's *Canon*. It seems his measuring system was flexible insofar as it could accommodate variations of both age and gender; but that it sought harmony of parts even if that meant neatening up the natural anatomy of human beings into

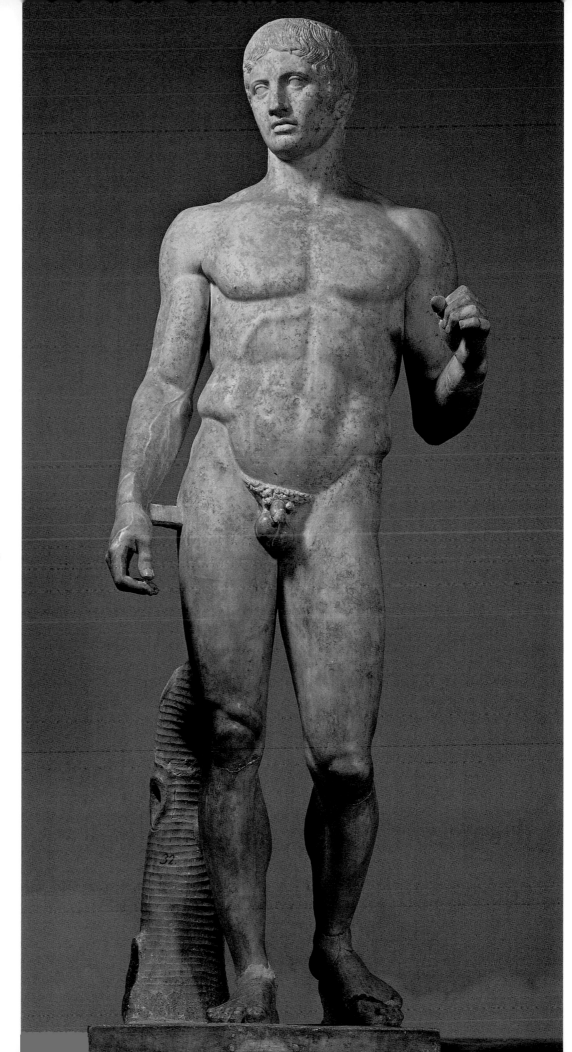

37 *Marble copy of the* Doryphoros *from Pompeii, after the mid-5th-century BC bronze original by Polykleitos. (The tree-trunk behind the figure, and the strut between his wrist and his hip, are necessary supports added for the marble version.) No work by Polykleitos directly survives, but his influence upon Classical (and subsequent) statuary was profound. In the absence of an inscription, whether the* Doryphoros *represents a heroized athlete or a heroized warrior (Achilles?) remains uncertain.*

38 *Athletes, on an Attic red-figure kylix signed by Pheidippos, c. 520 BC. The thin youth on the left seems about to start a race, while the thongs dangling from the hand of the plump boy indicate that he wants to box.*

39 *A boy with two javelins, and a discus in a sling, pours olive oil from his flask. Interior of an Attic red-figure kylix attributed to the Ambrosios Painter, c. 510 BC.*

impossibly geometric lines: 'aesthetically successful' in Polykleitan terms means a body dominated by qualities of tautness, symmetry, and balance.

Modern physiologists sometimes divide human bodily shape into three basic 'somatypes' – the endomorph (thin, attenuated), the ectomorph (plump, bulging), and the mesomorph (in between). An Athenian drinking-cup of the late 6th century shows us clearly the Classical preference for the mesomorphic [38]: beyond some 'good' athletes diligently practising with their javelins, we see the 'bad' forms of lanky youth and chubby youth providing the contrast. For young men, the pressure to aspire towards what would emerge as a more or less predictable 'Polykleitan' norm – broad shoulders, contoured thorax, firm waist, powerful thighs – was onerous, and pressed upon them by ubiquitous images of 'Mr Right'.

To judge from one surviving handbook of around the 3rd century AD, the *Gymnastics* attributed to Philostratos, regimes of exercise and diet could be followed very fussily. We also possess some testimonies regarding contests and incentives to motivate gymnasium attendance. The gymnasia of Greek-speaking communities in Hellenistic and Roman Asia Minor have yielded inscriptions that point to a range of institutional competitions that promoted outstanding bodily beauty, and encouraged related effort. One challenge was called the *euexia* ('good form'), evidently a test of body-building, with marks awarded for tone, definition, and symmetry. Another, the *eutaxia* ('good order'), stressed proficiency at military drills. Yet another perhaps recompensed the sheer sloggers: it was a prize for *philoponia*, 'love of training'.

The physical virtue above all was *euandria*: 'fine manliness'. This was the title of a male beauty contest regularly held at Athens from the late 6th century onwards, under the auspices of the Panathenaic Games. Young men would be nominated as representatives of their voting wards or 'tribes' (*phylai*), and subjected to various

tests of prowess (such as bareback riding) and appearance. Quite what were the criteria by which a prize-winning body was judged, we cannot say. But we do know the victors received substantial gifts – shields, or oxen, for example – and were greeted with multiple garlands, and had ribbons tied around their bodies. Beyond Athens there were other versions of this contest. One held at Elis, near Olympia, was called the *krisis kallous*, which might be paraphrased as 'the battle of the beautiful'; it was to the glory of the goddess Athena. Another, at Tanagra in Boeotia, was staged by the altar of the god Hermes Kriophoros ('the Ram-bearer'): here, the privilege granted to the boy showing most beauty was to carry a ram around the city walls in Hermes' honour. So there was a distinct votive element to these beauty competitions: human beauty was regarded as an insight into divine nature, and the sight of a beautiful person could be claimed as something which was pleasing to the eyes of the gods above.

Women were also involved in these rites of bodily appraisal. It is not clear to what extent, if at all, women frequented gymnasia in the Greek world; but there are some indications from Roman texts and images that female exercise-sessions were possible – among these a mosaic in Sicily showing several bikini-clad girls holding weights in their hands [40]. Whether for men or women, the Classical fetish for body sculpture might be thought to favour the young. But it is worth noting that the 'fine manliness' contest set up at Athens included senior categories, too. The bearded elders who prevailed here were granted the public triumph of being branch-carriers in a dedicatory procession to Athena. The branches they carried were young shoots of olive, a tree famous for its green and productive endurance over many, many decades.

40 *Detail of a mosaic pavement at Piazza Armerina, Sicily, 4th century AD. Something like this female gymnastic outfit (subligar, in Latin), made of soft leather, has been excavated from Roman London.*

43 *Fighting and athletics, on an Attic black-figure volute krater attributed to the Leagros Group, late 6th century BC. The upper band shows a scene of battle between gods and giants (the 'Gigantomachy' [cf. 458, 459]), while in the lower register we see various athletes with their trainers, and a central flautist providing musical accompaniment.*

opposite
41 left *The Delphi Charioteer: part of a bronze victory group dedicated at Delphi by Polyzalos, tyrant of Gela (a Greek colony in Sicily), who won the Pythian Games in 478 or 474 BC. The eyes are of glass and stone, the lips of copper, and the headband of silver. A four-horse chariot completed the original ensemble.*

42 right *Bronze head of a boxer from Olympia, mid-4th century BC. 'Cauliflower ears' and a corrugated brow were hallmarks of ancient boxing, which was done without padded gloves (and without timed rounds or weight categories either).*

ATHLETICS

Who can run fastest; who can jump longest; who can throw farthest: these are the sorts of contest we envisage when we refer to the particular sporting discipline of 'athletics', or 'track and field'. The Classical understanding of athletics was both more extensive and more precise. It was more extensive, because at the same meetings where running, jumping, and throwing were featured, there were also challenges of boxing, wrestling, mule-cart riding, chariot-racing, sprinting in armour, and other events. And it was more precise, due to the root-meaning of the very term 'athletics'. The Greek word *athletikos* denotes not simply the activity of competing for a prize (*athlon*) by physical effort and skill. It implies something of an ordeal, too: a struggle in which personal pain will be given and suffered. So the punishing tasks that Herakles had to perform (pp. 88–89) were known as *athla*, and the famous 'Twelve Labours' of Herakles amounted to a *dodekathlon*. The practice of athletics, then, was more than just a mode of keeping in good shape. It involved a fierce, almost warlike commitment to rivalry and victory [43]. 'Games' to us entail pleasure and diversion. Games to the Greeks were *agones*. For them, the ecstasy of winning was inseparable from the agony of strenuous participation.

According to Greek and Roman tradition, the first formal athletic meetings were established at the site of Olympia in 776 BC. Appropriately enough, the legendary founder of these 'Olympic Games' was Herakles. Olympia [47] was a prime location for the cult of Zeus and his wife Hera; and for all that ancient athletes were relentless in the quest to defeat all opponents, they were never allowed to forget that their activity was essentially religious. Victory (*nike*) could only be gained with the favour of Zeus, who was both depicted and worshipped at Olympia as Zeus Nikephoros, 'the Bringer of Victory'. The festival at Olympia was staged every four years, so it was possible to count according to 'Olympiads' until the late 4th century AD, when the Roman Empire was ruled by a Christian emperor who ordered an end to Olympia as an active shrine to Zeus. Right up to their closure, the Olympic Games were attracting competitors from all over the Classical world.

The Olympic Games were one gathering-point in a circuit (*periodos*) that included meetings at Corinth (the Isthmian Games), Nemea (the Nemean Games), and Delphi (the Pythian Games). The quartet were known collectively as the 'Sacred Games'; and they were constituted as 'Panhellenic' festivals, meaning

44 *The Athenian Treasury at Delphi, early 5th century BC. Built by the side of the 'Sacred Way' leading to Apollo's temple, this simple but striking Doric structure was decorated with metopes showing the deeds of Herakles and Theseus. It was later thought by some (Pausanias, Guide to Greece 10.11.4) to have been funded by spoils from the battle of Marathon in 490 BC.*

that any Greek – but only Greeks – could enter them. They were timetabled not to clash with each other, and there were some differences in their organization (for example the Pythian Games, in honour of the god Apollo, promoted trials of singing and other musical skills), but by the 6th century BC the developed schedule of major regional *agones* enabled some athletes to compete full-time. In addition to the four Panhellenic gatherings there were also numerous localized showdowns of physical prowess; and athletic contests were an integral part of regular ceremonies in a Classical city's religious calendar, such as the 'Panathenaic' festivals of Athens.

To win brought enormous public esteem, individual glory, and heroic renown (*kudos*); to lose was a matter for shame. At the Panathenaic Games, winners were awarded prizes of considerable cash value (see p. 40). But even at the 'big four' Sacred Games, where success was marked by a symbolic wreath of greenery (a crown of olive leaves at Olympia [58], of laurel at Delphi [56], and of wild celery and pine at the Nemean and Isthmian Games), prevailing athletes could hope for substantial reward. Beyond extravagant welcoming receptions, their home city might award pensions and free meals – not only to them, but also to their descendants. As early as the 6th century BC it is recorded that athletes from Athens who won an event at the Olympic Games were offered 500 drachmas – more than a year's salary for most workers. Victors might be further honoured with statues and poems of praise. In short, there was much at stake in being the best: which is why, in the history of the ancient Olympics, a number of fatalities are recorded – brought on by the pressure, ultimately, of trying too hard.

Inscriptions recovered from Olympia show that fastidious attention was paid to the enforcement of rules. We have some evidence, however, that cheating was not uncommon. When the travel-writer Pausanias visited Olympia in the 2nd century AD, he noticed many bronze statues of the god Zeus wielding a thunderbolt, of which each marked an accumulation of cash fines levied from athletes caught infringing the rules. This happened despite an obligation on all athletes, their trainers, and their family supporters, to swear by 'Zeus of the Oaths' that they would not dishonour the Games.

The temptation to cheat, and the determination to win even at fatal cost, were not only brought about by the lucrative consequences of victory. To win was a sacrosanct achievement, an overcoming of many difficulties to reach the summit of divinely blessed success. It also carried, at any Panhellenic venue, powerful political importance. The victorious athlete attested more than his personal prowess and dedication: he was the arch-representative of his city-state. This explains why the Greek colonies scattered around the Mediterranean took especial pride in sending strong teams to compete against cities of the 'motherland': their formidable athlete-delegates were proof of both economic prosperity in the colonies and military independence – not to mention a certain cultural satisfaction of 'new world' émigrés defeating 'old world' snobs. The so-called *Delphi Charioteer* is just one monument surviving from very many such symbols of colonial triumph [41]: it marks the victory in the chariot-race at the Pythian Games of 478 or 474 BC of Polyzalos of Gela. Polyzalos was the ruler of this colony in Sicily, founded in the early 7th century by pioneers (or outcasts) from Crete and Rhodes.

The Panhellenic Games were without doubt 'politicized', in particular those at Olympia and Delphi. A striking architectural feature within those sanctuaries is the presence of buildings known as 'treasuries' (*thesauroi*) [44]. Structurally they might seem discreet in size when compared with a temple. In function, however, they were bold and conspicuous. For the treasures they principally displayed were the spoils of war: arms, armour, and valuables lately seized from a defeated enemy –

often another Greek city-state, and quite feasibly one whose athletes would be present at the Olympic or Pythian Games. At Olympia, of the eleven Greek cities that erected such treasuries along the north side of the central sacred enclosure [47], most were overseas colonies: three from Sicily (Syracuse, Gela, Selinus), two from South Italy (Metapontum and Sybaris), one from the North African coast (Cyrene), and one from the eastern Mediterranean (Byzantium).

Excavation of the stadium at Olympia [46] suggests that even amid the space for spectators there were prominent war trophies erected. No one could forget that sport was, in its way, a sublimation of inter-state combat. In any case, the roots of athletics in military training were not entirely out of sight. In 520 BC the foot-race in armour became part of the Olympic programme: each entrant competed wearing a full-face helmet and carrying a large round shield (for a while he was also required to wear bronze shinguards).

This rationale for athletics was easily mocked. Athletes and their trainers became obsessed with the science and niceties of preparing for victory and breaking records. Prize-winning athletes became effectively professional, leading lives that were ever more bizarre in the eyes of ordinary folk: stories proliferate of caricature strongmen such as Milo, from the Greek colony of Croton in South Italy, who not only trained by walking around with oxen on his shoulders, but had the habit of eating entire animals too. But the martial justification of athletic contests helps to explain why women were mostly excluded from participating. At Olympia there was a minor separate gathering, held in honour of Hera, for unmarried women; and one Greek city (Sparta) notoriously fostered the involvement of girls in sport, wrestling included. Sparse evidence survives to prove that Etruscan or Roman women were actively included in formal games. The reported argument for female athletics at Sparta, prescribed by a 7th-century BC lawgiver called Lycurgus, itself carries a strongly civic (not to mention eugenic) cogency: 'if both parents are strong, their children should be stronger too'. But this was an exceptional attitude. Everyone else thought the Spartans were freaks.

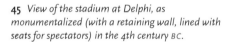

45 *View of the stadium at Delphi, as monumentalized (with a retaining wall, lined with seats for spectators) in the 4th century BC.*

The rise of sanctuaries suitable for the staging of athletic contests cannot be traced in Greece earlier than the 8th century BC. But the roots of formal 'agonistic' sport undoubtedly reach down into the earlier civilizations of the Aegean. The Minoan culture centralized at Knossos on Crete is famous for its wall-paintings of acrobats somersaulting over bulls; at other Minoan sites less spectacular images of boxers have also been found. At any rate, Greeks in the 8th century assumed that the practice of athletics had an epic pedigree. Homer, whose *Iliad* and *Odyssey* are thought to have been composed between the mid-8th and mid-7th centuries BC (see p. 111), gives two clear vignettes of such 'old-time' sporting customs. In the course of his sea-borne wanderings, Odysseus finds himself in Phaeacia, where he is taunted by local aristocratic youths to join their games. Thousands of spectators are there to see tests of wrestling, boxing, running, and jumping. Odysseus, though exhausted from his travels, is stung by the insinuation that he is no more than a bourgeois merchant sailor, obsessed with making profits from his trade (Homer's world is one where only the nobility have the leisure to devote themselves to sport). He rises, picks up the biggest available discus, and without even bothering to remove his cloak, sends the enormous weight humming through the air a distance far exceeding the best efforts of everyone else. Never one to resist verbal triumph, Odysseus invites all comers to take him on at any event they choose. There is awed silence: he has proved the point. 'A man gets no greater glory while alive than what he achieves with his feet and his hands' (*Odyssey* 8.147–78).

The games described in the *Iliad* are generated by a special occasion, the burial of Patroklos. The relish with which Homer follows the contests – which have generous prizes on offer – may be savoured in his account of the start of the chariot-race (*Iliad* 23.365–71) [cf. 187]:

> The charioteers all shook their reins, and shouted to their horses; and off they went, galloping inland over the plain. From under the horses' chests the dust rose up like a cloud or tornado, and their manes flowed full in the windstream. One moment the chariots were thundering close to the all-giving earth, the next they were jolted high in the air. Yet the drivers stayed upright in their chariots, each man's heart pounding with the strain to be first . . .

Olympia   The sanctuary of Olympia [47] lies in a fertile plain once bisected by two rivers, the Alpheus and the Kladeos. Subsequent to the closure of the site, in AD 393, and a powerful earthquake, these two rivers joined and flooded the plain, leaving a thick layer of alluvial silt over the monuments, the stadium, and other buildings. Preliminary investigations by a French team in 1829 located the Temple of Zeus, where the widely famed image of Zeus by Pheidias was once housed [126]. A longer-term German project was commenced in 1875 and is still continuing. Among the early finds of this excavation were the marble pedimental sculptures of the Temple of Zeus, carved around 460 BC, which were immediately hailed as notably 'Severe' in style [391]. The colossal Zeus had been moved in late antiquity; but the workshop where Pheidias is supposed to have made the statue has been discovered, along with many traces of the complex process whereby a colossus of gold and ivory ('chryselephantine') was constructed.

The archaeology of Olympia suggests that the sporting festival developed out of a rustic custom – perhaps an annual occasion, timed around the harvest season, when livestock was exhibited and traded. Thousands of bronze figurines have been found from the 8th century, most of them in the form of horses or steers [cf. 450]. It was not until the early 5th century that the athletic contests became codified into

46 *The covered* krypte *(tunnel), at the entrance to the stadium of Olympia, late 3rd century* BC. *Much of Olympia's infrastructure was financed by endowments during the period of Macedonian and Roman rule over Greece.*

47 *Model of the Olympia sanctuary as it would have appeared around the 2nd century* AD. *Dominant within the enclosed Altis, or sacred 'grove', is the Temple of Zeus, c. 460 BC [cf. 126, 140, 391], which stood near a mound believed to contain the remains of the mythical hero Pelops. The small buildings top right are treasuries. Both stadium and hippodrome lay away to the far right.*

a five-day calendar of ritual and events; and even then, those making the journey to Olympia could expect few visitor facilities. The athletes – many of whom would have travelled long distances – simply camped rough by the rivers, accompanied by their trainers and supporters. Baths were not provided before the late 5th century. The stadium [46] was simply a banked oval enclosure, with eventual capacity for about 40,000 spectators. When seating was installed, it was reserved for officials and civic delegates – the ancient version, it seems, of corporate hospitality.

Over time, Olympia became the athletic venue *par excellence,* controlled by a small local state, Elis, but attracting competitors and visitors from all over the Greek world. The official victory lists for the Olympic Games show a clear demographic shift in the origins of champion athletes. Between 600 and 300 BC they came primarily from the Greek mainland (the Peloponnese in particular) and from Greek colonies in the west. From 300 BC to AD 400, by contrast, there was relatively sparse success for competitors from mainland Greece and the western colonies: the winner's podium was dominated instead by representatives from cities of Asia Minor and the eastern seaboard, and Alexandria in Egypt. Eventually Olympia's Panhellenic status was undermined, as powerful foreigners began to intrude upon the Greek world. So in the 4th century BC Philip II of Macedon, the father of Alexander the Great, was not only allowed to enter for the chariot-race (which he won), but also to build, within the sacred precinct of Zeus and Hera, a chapel glorifying himself and his ancestors. Later, it was largely due to Roman sponsorship that the facilities at Olympia were extensively enlarged and upgraded; the cost to the integrity of the Games, however, is signalled by the story of what happened in the year AD 67 when the Emperor Nero took part in a race for ten-horse chariots. Nero had not much experience of chariots; he fell off, and failed to finish the race. Yet he was awarded victory; for which, we are told, he reimbursed the race officials handsomely (Suetonius, *Life of Nero* 24).

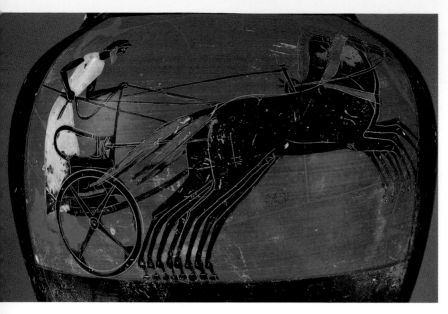

48 *A charioteer in white* chiton (a woollen tunic) *driving his four-horse team. Detail of a Panathenaic amphora attributed to the Kleophrades Painter, c. 480 BC. This type of vase, painted in the black-figure technique, was established as the distinctive prize for the Panathenaic Games of Athens [59]. Though many thousands were regularly produced, and their images were predictable, these olive-oil jars could be transformed by artists of high calibre into memorable studies of athletic endeavour. The Kleophrades Painter was one of the most inventive vase-painters in early 5th-century Athens.*

49 above right *A moment of excitement for spectators and danger for the riders, as one chariot overtakes another on the inside: fragment of an Athenian red-figure* hydria (water-carrier) *attributed to the Pioneer Group, c. 520 BC.*

The athletic disciplines The most prestigious contest of the Olympic Games, and probably the most exciting to watch, was chariot-racing [48, 49], which took place in the Hippodrome, a rectangular area where further horse-and-jockey races were also organized – riding bareback, without stirrups.

The *pentathlon* or 'five-fold challenge' followed: running, jumping, discus-throw, javelin-throw, and wrestling. For the jumping, athletes evidently gained momentum by holding metal weights in their hands. The discus began as a stone platter and evolved into bronze; its weight varied, and it seems to have been thrown from a fixed-feet position on an elevated base [1, 55]. As for the javelin, it was shaped from elder-wood, and partly bound up by a cord which the thrower used to give extra pull and spin on the shaft at the time of release [50]. Music might be played to the pentathletes while they performed, 'psyching them up' as we should say [43].

Wrestling was a separate event, for which fighters covered themselves in fine dust; three throws, falls, or lifts off the ground were required to win a bout. No categories of body weight were distinguished, which is why Classical depictions of wrestlers always show hulking men [53, 54]. Boxing, too, favoured the hefty; and since no gloves were worn, only tightly wrapped leather thongs, serious damage was routinely inflicted, especially about the face and ears [42, 60]. But of all the combat sports in ancient athletics, none seems more intimidating than the *pankration*,

50 *A sequence of the javelin throw – one of the five disciplines of the pentathlon – depicted on an Attic red-figure kylix attributed to the Carpenter Painter, c. 515–510 BC. Extra spin was imparted by winding a length of cord around the shaft and looping this onto the forefinger.*

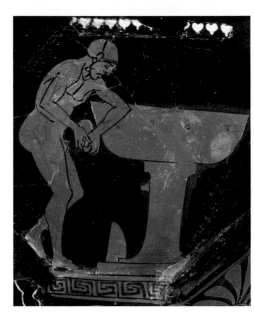
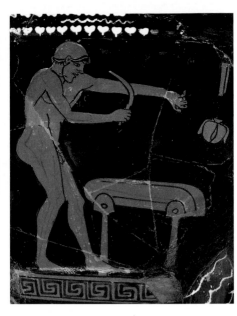

51, 52 *Two athletes depicted on an Attic red-figure kantharos (wine-cup) attributed to the Foundry Painter, c. 480 BC. One is shown at a basin, squeezing a sponge; another scraping himself with the curved metal tool known as a strigil.*

the 'all-power contest' [461]. To say that any kind of violence was permissible in this competition is not quite true: referees were supposed to penalize biting and the gouging-out of eyes. But to kick, strangle, smite, and otherwise beat one's opponent into submission or death was a highly esteemed art, and some statues of prize-winning pankratiasts were venerated as magical touchstones of strength.

In the Olympic programme there were running races over various distances, with dashes such as the 'double-pipe' (*diaulos*) up and down the stadium – the stadium at Olympia [46] measuring 192 metres (630 feet), the one at Delphi [45] a little less – and the furthest, simply known as the *dolichos*, 'the long one', probably involving twelve lengths of the stadium. (Though the Greeks kept the 'stade' as unit of measurement, there appears to have been no standard length for athletic stadia.) The race in armour at Olympia was a sprint over two lengths of the stadium. Nothing like a modern marathon was part of any ancient games, probably because specialized messengers or couriers did 'day-running' on a professional basis.

All of this activity at Olympia happened within a stone's throw of the sacred precinct of Zeus and Hera [47]. Punctuated by prayers and sacrifices – a hundred oxen were slaughtered at the altar of Zeus on the third day of the Olympic festival – the sequence of athletic contests was brought to a close with a night of feasting within the sanctuary.

53 *Wrestlers engage over a prize cauldron, with referee gesticulating in the background. Detail of a Panathenaic amphora attributed to the Swing Painter, c. 540–530 BC.*

54 *Detail of wrestlers on a bronze bowl from Roman Gaul, late 1st century AD.*

Celebrating victory Prizes for athletic victory at the various sporting festivals ranged from wreaths [56] to cloaks, silver cups, and lumps of solid metal. At the Panathenaic Games, large quantities of olive oil were on offer: at one point in the 4th century, for example, the first runner home in the men's stade-race received over 100 jars of oil – equivalent to some 4,000 litres (880 gallons), and with a market value of about $75,000–$100,000 in modern terms. The Panathenaic prize jars – of a double-handled shape known as an *amphora* – have long since lost their valuable contents; but they remain the most numerous relics of sporting success in the Classical world [59]. Their decoration was kept to a more or less predictable formula over several centuries. On one side they carried an appropriate image of athletic exertion [48]; on the other, an icon of Athena, the patron goddess of Athens, in stridently spear-rattling pose [57]. During the 5th century, inscriptions were added to this side of the vessel, giving the name of the *archon*, or city magistrate, who had organized the games, which were part of a civic birthday-rite celebrated with much pomp every four years ('the Greater Panathenaia'); and on a lesser scale, but always in late summer, each intervening year.

To win a particular event often earned the right to be added to an honorary roll-call of distinguished athletes, inscribed for public display. But more lavish bids for undying fame could be made by the commission of a commemorative piece of poetry or statuary – usually at the behest of the victor's family or city. If poetry, this would take the form of an *epinikion*, or 'epinician ode' – a hymn of victory that normally commenced with a salute to the strength, skill, and commitment of the athlete concerned, but then widened its scope to dwell upon the athlete's fine ancestry, to make parallels with the venerable heroes and demigods of myth, and to expound a general moral lesson about the virtues of rigorous training, self-control, and sheer determined 'effort'. The delivery of an *epinikion* could be a grand affair, with a large chorus marshalled to chant it loudly at the homecoming of the victorious athlete. A number of such poems from 6th- and 5th-century Greece have survived whole, or in fragments, to give clear proof that some of the most accomplished lyricists of the day – Bacchylides, Ibykos, Pindar, Simonides – were in demand for victory verse.

The poets, in turn, faced competition from other artists – the makers of statues, some of whom would travel to the pre-eminent athletic gatherings and set up workshops on the spot, ready to produce commemorative pieces. The epinician poets dug deep into the Greek vocabulary for all words to do with brightness, glory, lustre, and shine. The sculptors settled on bronze as their favoured medium [58], to similarly flashing and burnished effect. One 5th-century sculptor, Myron, was

55 *Bronze statuette from South Italy, c. late 6th century BC, depicting a* diskophoros *(discus-carrier).*

56 *Gold laurel wreath, c. 300–100 BC. Though probably deposited in a tomb, this garland evokes in particular the prizes on offer at the Pythian Games in honour of Apollo at Delphi.*

57 *A striding figure of Athena on a Panathenaic amphora [48], c. 480 BC. The winged horse on her shield is a device favoured by the Kleophrades Painter.*

58 *Life-size bronze figure of an athlete crowning himself, c. 300 BC. The wreath he held up was of olive, perhaps indicating victory at the Olympic Games.*

59 *A Panathenaic amphora, attributed to the Painter of the Wedding Procession, 363–362 BC. Winged Nike crowns a victorious boxer.*

60 *Marble bust of a pugilist (or possibly Herakles) from Alexandria, 2nd century BC.*

From Pindar's salute *to the victor of the chariot-race at the Isthmian Games (in 458 BC?):*

If a man strives with all his soul towards true excellence, stinting neither in expense nor hard work, then it is right for us to recognize that honour, and offer in tribute the proud hymns of praise, banishing all thoughts of envy. What does it cost the poet to devise sweet phrases in return for incalculable hardships, and construct a monument for all to share? Rewards for labour are variously prized, each to his own choice – the shepherd, the ploughman, the hunter of fowls, or the one who finds food from the sea: all of us try to keep sneaking hunger at bay. But whoever reaps the rich harvest of glory in games or in war is owed that welcome, most precious prize: fame – the widespread praise from fellow-citizens and strangers alike.

Pindar, *Isthmian Ode* 1.41–52

61 *Runners are depicted in the Tomb of the Olympics at Tarquinia, c. 500 BC, though to date no stadium has been located in Etruria.*

famed for capturing athletic actions in his monuments to victors, and numerous marble copies of his *Diskobolos*, or 'Discus-thrower', were made for Roman admirers of this work [1]; he also, we are told, cast a statue of a runner in full flight, 'just as he was, straining for the victor's crown'. Other sculptors, such as Myron's contemporary Polykleitos, preferred to make studies of athletes standing in balanced repose [37], or crowning themselves with a wreath (as in his *Diadoumenos*, literally 'boy binding his hair'). Inscriptions on the bases of these statues left viewers in no doubt as to how such images were to be regarded. The following lines, attributed to Simonides, accompanied a statue of one Theognetos, winner of the boys' wrestling at Olympia in 476 BC: 'Know what you see when you gaze upon this: it is Theognetos, boy-champion of Olympia, who skilfully steered his course to victory in the wrestling ring. Most beautiful to behold, most formidable to challenge, here is a youth who crowned the city of his good forefathers.'

Athletics in the Roman Empire   As we have noted, Greek colonists in South Italy and Sicily were among the keenest participants at Olympia and the other Panhellenic Games. To what extent the neighbouring peoples of Italy adopted the practice of athletics from those colonists is uncertain. The graves of Etruscan aristocrats have often been found to contain gymnastic equipment (such as strigils – 'body-scrapers' [52] – and oil flasks), and sometimes with painted decoration that shows wrestling, chariot-racing, and other sports [61]. The Etruscans also liked to collect Panathenaic prize vases – presumably secondhand, since no Etruscan would ever have been able actually to compete at Athens. Games were probably held in the Homeric style at funerals of certain important individuals, with combat sports prominent. As for the Romans, their own collective pastimes might overlap with certain events of Greek athletics [54], as might their myths [62]; but they also indulged a more formal adoption of Greek ideals of physical culture. Statues of Greek champion athletes, for example, were routinely installed in the niches of Roman bath-complexes.

The function of athletic prowess as part of the Greek definition of a hero never faded. On the contrary, it gained fresh currency in the later Roman Empire, when periodic campaigns of persecution against Christian believers were conducted. In the emotive literature of Christian martyrdom, the faithful who provided fatal entertainment in Roman arenas were hailed as 'athletes of Christ'. They were volunteers for extreme pain, reminding us, again, that 'athletics' derives from the Greek verb *athleuo* : 'I struggle, I contest – I suffer'.

62 *Mosaic of Dares and Entellus, from Roman Gaul , c. AD 175. This evokes a 'prize fight' described in epic detail by Vergil (Aeneid 5.362–484). The setting is funeral games, held by Aeneas in Sicily on the first anniversary of his father's death. A contest is staged between Dares, an overconfident young Trojan, and Entellus, an elderly local pugilist, which ends only when Aeneas stops the contest, afraid that the younger man will be killed. Dares turns away, bloodied; Entellus wins the bull – and fells it with a blow of his fist.*

63 *A young man dries himself after the bath. Detail of an Attic red-figure kantharos attributed to the Foundry Painter, c. 480 BC [cf. 51, 52].*

64 *Detail of a 'sea-creature' mosaic from a Roman villa at what is now the spa of Bad Vilbel in the Rhineland, c. AD 175. Aquatic myths and evocations were a natural choice of decoration for the bathing ambience.*

65 *A public latrine at Ostia, 3rd–4th century AD. A channel of running water below the seats conducted waste away.*

BATHTIME

It is an often overlooked fact that the engineering effort behind Roman aqueducts [251, 252] derived predominantly from the urban need for clean water to bathe in, not clean water to drink. The Romans derived some hydraulic techniques and design features of bath-buildings from Greek colonists in South Italy, and also from their Etruscan neighbours; but the fully developed complex of baths (*balnea*, or *thermae*: for reasons which will soon become evident, always in the plural) remains a distinctly Roman phenomenon – both architecturally and culturally [66–69].

In the Classical world at large, bathing tended to be a communal process. Toilets, too, were often shared facilities. There may have been separation of the sexes (certainly in Greek households and cities); but regular bodily functions and intimate personal hygiene presented social occasions at which it was normal to gossip and chat. A central latrine in the Roman port town of Ostia [65], for example, could accommodate at one sitting (so to speak) some twenty-five people, all in full view of each other – and sharing, too, wet sponges on sticks in lieu of toilet paper.

With the exception of courtesans – who might avail themselves of the public fountain-houses created at Athens and in other Greek cities during the 6th century BC – Greek women would have washed at home. For Greek male citizens, the facilities of the gymnasium or *palaestra* normally included showers and large tubs, and so bathing was usually done after the daily workout, prior to dinner [63]. But how did these practices develop into the Roman art of bathing virtually for its own sake? The answer to that question probably lies in the Italian region of Campania, settled variously by Greeks, Etruscans, and Romans. It was, and still is, a territory rich in hot springs and therapeutic mineral waters – the benefits of simmering volcanic activity – and this natural feature was exploited by local builders of villas and towns. So, by the 1st century BC, we find at Pompeii two urban bath-complexes in place, both exhibiting what would come to be some standard features of Roman imperial design.

66 The 'Great Bath' at Roman Bath (Aquae Sulis), part of a thermal spa established in the west of England during the 1st century AD. The pool, fed by local springs, is lined with lead sheeting. Formerly (c. AD 200) the roof was vaulted.

As hinted above, one did not take 'a bath' in these surrounds, but rather a sequence of baths. The connected central parts of the so-called Forum Baths at Pompeii contain a changing-room (*apodyterium*), a cold room (*frigidarium*), warm room (*tepidarium*), and hot room (*caldarium*). The principle was clearly akin to the modern understanding of a 'Turkish' bath: that is, plunging into water of different temperatures, and alternately opening and closing bodily pores. Exercise areas were routinely provided, and often also a dry heat chamber (called a *laconicum* or *sudatorium*, 'sweat-room'). Eventually, an imperial establishment such as the Baths of Caracalla in Rome [67–69] could accommodate not only a large number of bathers, but other activities too – shops, lecture-halls, and concert-rooms.

Roman bath-complexes were technically made possible by the invention of concrete – a compound of stone chippings, sand, and mortar which can withstand high levels of heat and humidity – and the use of concrete for domed ceilings, effective for controlling levels of moisture and temperature. Clay pipes and flues ran around the walls, conducting hot air generated by the underground 'hypocaust' – a basement furnace system fuelled by brushwood. These were the key engineering features that lay behind veritable palaces of keeping clean, whose interior surfaces might be clad in fine stone (such as alabaster) and further decorated with mosaics and displays of statuary. Many baths, in Rome and throughout the provinces, were built as the result of imperial largesse, or some other individual benefaction: but they were public amenities, with charges for entrance kept minimal. No other type of building is more diffused throughout and characteristic of the Roman Empire.

67 *The Baths of Caracalla, Rome, constructed in AD 212–217. The pillars of the central bath complex now provide the backdrop for open-air operas.*

68 *Plan of the Baths of Caracalla. Entrance was from the north-east side, where the first water feature was the* natatio – *an open-air swimming pool (1). The sequence of progress then includes the changing-room (apodyterium, 2), wrestling area (palaestra) or exercise space (3), plunge baths and steam bath, hot room (caldarium, 4), warm room (tepidarium, 5), and cold room (frigidarium, 6).*

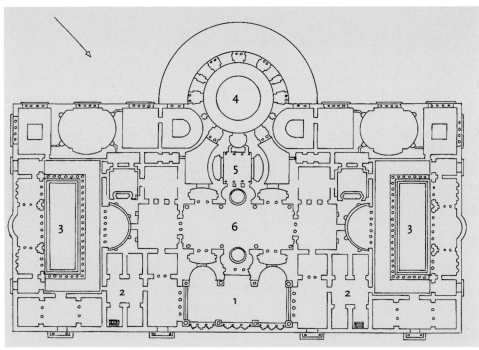

69 *Artist's impression of the frigidarium of the Baths of Caracalla. Following a precedent set during the time of Trajan* (AD 98–117) *by the architect Apollodorus of Damascus, the* frigidarium *has effectively become a large basilica, or public hall.*

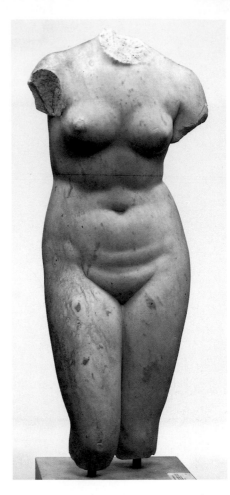

70 Marble torso of Aphrodite, Roman copy of a Hellenistic original of c. 200 BC. The pose is of the Medici Venus type [cf. 479].

71 Marble sculpture of sleeping Cupid, c. AD 50–100. The winged, curly-haired messenger of love rests on the lion skin of Herakles; just visible is the strap for his quiver full of arrows.

EROTICS

> To me he seems like one of the gods – even more fortunate than a god, if that's not blasphemous – the man who sits straight before you, gazing on you and hearing your sweet laughter. As for me, Lesbia – I take one look, and all my senses are snatched. I lose the voice in my mouth. My tongue thickens. Nerves of flame snake through my limbs, my ears go deaf with their own pounding; and the lights of my eyes are plunged into darkness . . .

The fifty-first song of the Latin poet Catullus, who lived in the first half of the 1st century BC, is a studious composition. He modelled its structure and sentiments upon a much older Greek lyric well known to have been written by Sappho – one of the few female authors who survive from Classical antiquity, and a woman whose verses often celebrated lovers of her own gender (our word 'lesbian' is derived from the name of Sappho's home island, Lesbos). Yet despite their undisguised literary heritage, these lines by Catullus have the ring of raw experience. They voice the physiology of the lovestruck. That furnace beneath the ribcage. The wobbly knees. The churning, consuming hunger for union. Romans spoke of Cupid, 'Desire', and imagined him as a mischievous little boy armed with either a torch or bow and arrows [71]. Greeks similarly pictured their Eros, 'Love', as a youth [556, 567] – the son of Aphrodite – and no less disposed to make sport with mortals. No one is to be deceived by the smiling angel. An exquisite agony is what Catullus reports; brought about entirely by this cute little, fierce big power of love.

Catullus is often referred to as a 'love poet'. The extent to which Classical poetry could be categorically predictable in its form and subject is indicated by the existence of a word to denote a particular type of poem as 'the lament of a lover outside the closed door of his loved one' (*paraclausithyron*): given this level of formality, therefore, it would be rash to use the love-poems of Catullus as the basis for constructing an account of the love-*life* of Catullus. Nonetheless, we can approach the topic of erotics in the Classical world with the confidence of knowing that it was a topic much discussed in Classical times. And not only a topic of poetry, but an object of religious cult, philosophical debate, artistic representation, and civil justice. Love and sex were not matters for shameful secrecy or whispered confessions. On the contrary, there was a willingness to acknowledge the carnal side of human existence that for centuries later would embarass the scholars of Classical art and literature. Prior to the 20th century, this was an aspect of antiquity mostly kept hidden from general knowledge.

How far the freedom to talk about sex equates to a modern state of 'sexual permissiveness' was questioned by the influential 20th-century French historian and philosopher Michel Foucault. Broadly, he made the following key distinction between 'sexuality' in the Graeco-Roman world and 'sexuality' in the ensuing Christian cultures of the West. Sex in Classical times was subject to certain social laws and conventions, but it was not associated with sin or evil, nor abuse – either of self or of others. Christianity introduced, as Foucault phrased it, new 'techniques of the self', encouraging the disregard of one's own body, and transforming sexual motivation into the impulse of not pride, but guilt.

Terminology supports this basic contrast. Classical Greek has its word for 'love', *eros*, often indicative of what we would call 'lust'; with another word, *philia*, signifying gentler, non-sexual affections. Neither word satisfied the early Christian evangelists writing in Greek. They settled for an entirely different term, *agape*. 'God is love', claims a key Christian scripture: *ho theos agape estin* (1 John 4.8).

A mythical theory about the healing power of Eros, *as contributed to Plato's dialogue on the topic of love, the* Symposium:

We humans totally underestimate Eros. Of all the divine powers, he is the one who cares most for our happiness. Let me tell you how things once were, and you will understand why.

When lord Zeus first fashioned us, we humans looked quite different from our present shape. We were, in a word, duplicate. Or at least, doubled in most respects. Two heads. Four arms. Four legs. A single torso; but two sets of genitals attached. Mostly these double humanoids had both male and female parts, but not all of them were like that: some were double man, some double woman. At any rate, those who wanted to reproduce just did it automatically. Well, we were very happy that way. We went cartwheeling around, immensely pleased with ourselves. Too pleased for our own good. We thought there was nothing that we couldn't do. . . . We planned to take heaven by storm. That was when the Olympian divines grew alarmed. They held a council, to discuss our turbulent behaviour. And Zeus gave the order – to have us sliced in half. Cut us down to size. See how we liked that. Any more nonsense, and he'd do the same again. Have us hopping. For a while he was tempted to get rid of us altogether: but then who would be left to worship him and the other gods? So it was that we were each of us weakened by a drastic split. We were stitched up and rearranged, of course. Apollo did the surgery, and he did it neatly as he could. But we could never again continue our own kind as we wished, independently; and forever after we have suffered from the wound.

All of us remain like tallies, or symbols, of our former selves. And so it is deep in our nature, now, to roam around in search of the missing part – our *other half* – to be fused as once we were.

This craving, this anxiety to be restored whole again: this is the primal repair we call Love.

Plato, *Symposium* 189c–193d
(abridged and paraphrased)

Agape connotes regard, esteem, interest, and concern. It is removed from carnal desire. When Christian men and women in the Roman Empire gathered for communal meals of fellowship or 'love-feasts', they used the same word. At an *agape* there should be not the slightest suggestion of amorous bonding.

The sexual continence associated with Christianity should not imply, however, a Classical or 'pagan' culture of easy erotic abandon. What both Greek and Roman writings acknowledge is the extreme physical impetus of 'falling in love'. Sometimes the god Eros was shown with a hammer, for he was understood to strike hard. To be smitten by desire could be a form of painful fracture; at any rate, Eros was hard to resist. As Catullus knew, the Latin word for 'being in love' (*amans*) was very close to going 'out of one's mind' (*amens*). A poet could exploit the bittersweet delirium brought about by Eros: several times in the verses of Sappho we find surrender to the pell-mell coercion behind the urge to love, and grievous recognition of the abysmal 'yearning' laid open by desire. 'Eros shook my heart, like a gale in the mountains tipping the oaks' (*Ode* 47); 'You came, while I was aching for you; you cooled my heart, so overheated with the want of you . . .' (*Ode* 48). But for philosophers, the actions of Eros could appear as dangerous subversions of individual well-being and social equilibrium.

So we find, almost at the outset of Plato's *Republic* – the early 4th-century dialogue in which Socrates and his friends attempt to define the ideal society, a state where philosophers are kings – the following report of a brief encounter with one of the most distinguished minds of Classical Athens, the playwright Sophocles. Sophocles lived to a fine old age. As one of Socrates' company recalls, 'I was with Sophocles when someone once asked him: "Sophocles, how goes it in bed these days? Are you still up to intercourse?" "Don't mention it, man," replied Sophocles. "It's with deep relief that I've at last broken free of that – like escaping from some crazed and savage overlord"' (Plato, *Republic* 329c).

Elsewhere in Plato's writings we find erotic compulsion listed among the ills endemic to humankind. Other Classical philosophers were similarly suspicious of the potential hostility of Eros to the powers of reason and self-control. Diogenes, the 4th-century founder of the sect known as the Cynics (see p. 237), drastically exemplified his own resistance to Eros by masturbating himself in full public view in the marketplace of Athens. True, he and his followers were called Cynics ('Dogs') on account of their shamelessness; and it was at the heart of Diogenes' teaching that natural needs should be satisfied either immediately and openly, or else not at all. But here his message was censorious. If Paris had channelled his erotic eagerness for Helen into a simple act of masturbation, argued Diogenes, then the entire Trojan War would never have happened . . .

But if only the power of love could be harnessed for wholly positive ends? That is one of the questions addressed in perhaps the most eloquent and influential philosophical discussion of love ever composed, Plato's *Symposium* (dated *c.* 384 BC). The *Symposium*, purporting to record an amiable gathering between Socrates and his friends (see p. 255), begins with a salute to love as, indeed, a tremendous and overwhelming force in mortal affairs. 'If a state or an army could be made up of friends united by love, it is incalculable how well they would organize themselves', muses Phaedrus, one of the opening contributors to the debate. Paris may have caused war by acting on the spur of compulsive desire; but from the same epic of Troy came the example of Achilles, an outstanding hero not merely because of his bravery in combat, but because he went into battle for the sake of love. Achilles had been primed with the divine foresight that, if he killed the Trojan prince Hector, then he himself would die. But what drew Achilles into

72 A youth offers cash to a woman holding a mirror. Interior of an Attic red-figure kylix attributed to the Briseis Painter and Brygos, c. 480–470 BC.

73 Two male lovers entwined. Interior of an Attic red-figure kylix, c. 480 BC.

battle was the fact that his most beloved companion, Patroklos, was killed by Hector. With Patroklos gone, Achilles had no care of a peaceful old age: he would rather lose his own life, and rejoin his lover in the Underworld.

We talk of 'love at first sight'. Is that a kind of recognition? Another participant in Plato's *Symposium*, supposedly the comic dramatist Aristophanes, argues to that effect: he relates a curious fable to explain how we are all, quite literally, searching for our 'other halves' – a myth which may underpin the modern romantic notion that everyone has a certain 'perfect partner' or 'destiny'. But of all the various views and theories aired in the *Symposium*, none has had more influence than the division of love into two types of experience. One of Plato's protagonists visualizes this as a double existence of Aphrodite, the goddess of love. In one form, she is Aphrodite *Pandemos*, 'to all people' – 'Popular Love', therefore. In another form, she is Aphrodite *Ourania*, 'Heavenly'. This is the love that generates noble aspirations, the passion for honour and goodness. In such a sense, one can truly 'love' a piece of music, a poem or a landscape.

It was an Italian scholar in the 15th century, Marsilio Ficino, who coined and diffused the phrase 'Platonic love' (*Amor Platonicus*). Ficino devised a treatise 'On Love' that was part-imitation and part-translation of Plato's *Symposium*, at the same time collecting related thoughts of subsequent 'Platonist' philosophers. And so the concept of a 'Platonic relationship' has passed into modern parlance, denoting love or affection 'of a purely spiritual character, and free from sensual desire'.

Plato's successor Aristotle would neatly define the essence of friendship as 'one soul in two bodies'. Much of Classical philosophy was concerned with the way in which a soul or spirit dwelt within the human body, like some invisible lodger: for Socrates and Plato, it was everyone's immortal portion. Was it utterly transcendent of carnal urges, or were there certain ways in which the soul interacted with flesh, blood, and bones?

This is not the place to pursue such metaphysical dilemmas. But no survey of Classical erotica would be fair if it did not draw attention to the primary source of moral scruple about erotic gratification in pre-Christian Greece and Rome. Socrates likened the onset of sexual desire to a team of stallions. The sheer dynamic horsepower of love was never denied: but virtue could be won by not getting carried away.

Sex and the Athenians No man or woman in Classical times ever talked about his or her 'sexuality'. Certain sexual practices might become subject to gossip, jokes, disapproval, or scurrility; and some individuals seem to have been defined according to their particular preferences for modes of erotic gratification. But there was no talk of 'gays' and 'lesbians' as distinct types, however much men and women engaged in sex with partners of the same gender (which is all that our word 'homosexuality' entails, deriving as it does from the Greek *homos*, 'same' – the opposite of *heteros*, 'different'). Nor, for that matter, does any Classical person ever seem to have thought in terms of maintaining a 'sex life' – that is, putting his or her erotic activity into some neatly defined compartment of regular existence. So how should we go about searching for 'norms' of sexual behaviour in Classical antiquity?

Merely to make a category of 'Classical antiquity' here is dangerous, because within that category, the social organization of sexual behaviour differed both locally and over time. But one city does offer us especially generous evidence, in both words and images, about how its inhabitants conducted themselves sexually. This (no surprise) is Athens – more specifically, Athens during the 6th to 4th centuries BC. For various reasons, Athens in that period gave rise to prolific words

74 right *Masturbating youth and tippling hetaira (courtesan). Detail of an Attic red-figure kylix by Phintias, c. 510 BC.*

75 *A pederastic embrace. Interior of an Attic red-figure kylix attributed to the Carpenter Painter, c. 515–510 BC. Usual courtship rituals are here reversed, as the younger* eromenos *(beloved) draws his older* erastes *(lover) towards him.*

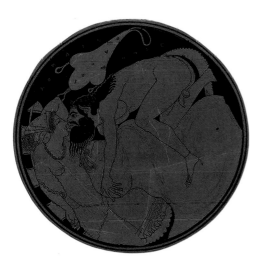

76 *A satyr creeps up on a sleeping maenad; above the pair is a wineskin. Interior of an Attic red-figure kylix by Onesimos, c. 500–490 BC. The inscription above the maenad explains the satyr's erotic interest: 'the girl is beautiful'.*

and prolific images, many of which have survived. Since, as we have already noted, sex was not a taboo subject, we can expect the Athenians to reveal themselves even in this 'private' respect.

And they do. Most prominent among the many types of testimony (including some highly informative recorded law-suits) are the thousands of Athenian painted vases that show sexual activity [72–80]. Of course there is no telling how many of these scenes are the products of fantasy; and we can fairly suppose that some of them would have been considered in 'bad taste' by some of their ancient viewers. But from these images, it is possible to create the following summary of sexual customs prevalent in Athens, say, at about the time the Parthenon was being raised (447–432 BC).

(1) Most sexual activity happened not between men and women but between men and adolescent boys. A man might be married, and care for his wife; but that did not preclude him from having relationships with younger men. This was the practice of pederasty (*paiderastia*, 'boy-loving') – and it was perfectly respectable, so long as proper procedures were heeded. For example, a man seeking to make the acquaintance of a boy whom he fancied should first ask for the consent of the youth's father; meetings were to occur in designated places; and only certain toys or pets were appropriate as gifts of courtship – among them hoops, and live hares [78, 437], cockerels or deer. The relationship could be quite cerebral ('Platonic', no less), an educational experience for the younger man. When it was sexual, the 'beloved' (*eromenos*) was passive to his senior 'lover' (*erastes*). Anal intercourse almost certainly happened [79], but perhaps more often practised was copulation between the thighs, from front or rear.

(2) Athenian women of civic status – that is, the wives of male citizens – kept their sexual activity very discreet. It is never depicted on vases nor described in literature. This modesty may even have extended to keeping clothes on during marital intercourse – whose purpose was chiefly procreation, not recreation. No reliable contraceptive devices were available; in any case, the expectation was that children should be produced to prosper and fortify the city. For some women, there were occasions in the religious calendar of Athens – namely, festivals of the god Dionysos – that may have blessed the resort to dildoes, and possibly some mutual stimulation among women only. (The Greek verb *lesbiazein* connotes a range of oral sex acts.) Whether his wife was 'good in bed' or sexually contented was a concern unlikely ever to have troubled the regular citizen of Classical Athens.

78 Pederastic courtship: a youth is offered a pet hare by his older admirer, on an Attic red-figure pelike attributed to the Triptolemos Painter, c. 460 BC.

(3) Both male and female prostitution were legitimate in Athens. In the early 6th century the lawgiver Solon, it appears, had instituted a number of subsidized public brothels, staffed by women who could be regarded as the 'common possessions' of all citizens. By coincidence, the area of Athens known as the Kerameikos, where the pottery-producing workshops were situated, was also where the 'sex trade' operated. So Athenian vase-painters had, as it were, a subject close to hand. Many of the vases they decorated were intended for use at a drinking-party, or symposium (see p. 254); and it was customary to hire women to provide entertainment and sexual favours at a symposium. To describe such women as 'prostitutes', however, is slightly misleading. They were called *hetairai*, meaning simply 'female companions'. They were socially marginal, with tenuous legal rights. But they were educated in music, dancing, and recitation; and they could drink wine, while holding company at table with the men of the city – concessions not made by those men to their own wives and daughters. Perhaps the term 'courtesan' more subtly conveys what the *hetaira* offered. How often a symposium at Athens developed into an orgy of group sex involving *hetairai* it is impossible to say. It may be enough to note that a pejorative term existed for prostitution, *porneia* (*pornai* were mostly female slaves, working from brothels, who solely offered casual sex); and when coupled with the Greek word 'to draw', *graphein*, gives us the concept of 'pornography': not a particular category in ancient moral discourse, but a concept literally relevant to the image of Aphrodite.

79 Interior of an Attic red-figure kylix attributed to the Foundry Painter, c. 470 BC

80 right Detail of a fragmentary Attic red-figure kylix attributed to Onesimos, c. 500 BC.

81 *The* Mazarin Venus, *Roman marble copy of a statue of Aphrodite made c. 200 BC. The dolphin sporting alongside recalls the marine birth of the goddess, who was widely venerated by ancient seafarers at coastal cult sites around the Mediterranean.*

'The business of Aphrodite' In Greek mythology, the story of the birth of Aphrodite, goddess of love, is a sensational mix of sex and violence. As first related in Hesiod's 7th-century BC cosmological poem, the *Theogony*, Gaia (the Earth [98]) became weary of the rough advances from her partner Ouranos (the Heavens). She provided one of her many children, Kronos, with a sharp flint sickle, and as Ouranos fell into a post-coital doze, the boy lopped off his father's genitalia and flung them far away. Where the amputated 'members' of Ouranos dripped blood, the Furies of revenge, giants, and wood-nymphs sprang up. The testicles of Ouranos finally plunged into the ocean, causing a 'white foam' to fizz up amidst the waves. This foam rolled as surf to the island of Cyprus, where it took an immortal shape – the lovely Aphrodite, whose very name recalls her origin as 'foam-born' (*aphrogenea*) [512].

As Hesiod testifies (*Theogony* 200), Aphrodite was also called *Philommedea*, 'genital-loving'. That partly derived from her bizarre birth, but it was a title which also paid unashamed homage to Aphrodite's divine function. Her sprightly companions were Love and Desire; she herself was the high patroness of 'sweet whisperings' and all business immediately below the navel. So it happens that Aphrodite confers her own name upon erotic activity. She becomes both a verb, ' to make love' (*aphrodisiazein*), and a noun, 'the things of Aphrodite' (*ta aphrodisia*) – which can mean anything from kissing to copulation.

Because of her marine associations, Aphrodite was a favoured cult for sailors, who sometimes worshipped her as Aphrodite Euploia, 'Aphrodite of the Fair Voyage'. Aphrodite herself may derive from Astarte, a 'Mother Goddess' or fertility figure of much older tradition in the East, particularly venerated by the Phoenicians (whose homeland is roughly equivalent to modern Lebanon). In any case, where Greeks and Phoenicians shared trading posts around the Mediterranean basin, it was usual for Aphrodite to be paired with Astarte. And both goddesses presided over a mode of adoration that may seem, to modern eyes, somewhat squalid.

'Sacred prostitution' is how it is conventionally described. A sanctuary would be staffed by 'priestesses' who, as vicars of the goddess, dealt in her attributes. Those making pilgrimage to a temple of Aphrodite could expect – with due payment, prayers, and sacrifice – to share in Aphrodite's gift of sex. One such sanctuary, evidently frequented by Phoenicians, Greeks, and Etruscans alike, is the shoreline site of Pyrgi, a little to the north of Rome. Here, rows of small cubicles were provided for the 'acts of Aphrodite'. Across the Mediterranean was the Greek settlement of Knidos, clinging to the Ionian coast of Asia Minor. Knidos, it seems, was the first Greek state bold enough to set up an image of Aphrodite naked: a marble statue made by Praxiteles *c.* 360 BC, it showed the goddess as if caught while washing herself [83]. By Roman times, it is reported, boatloads of tourists were travelling to Knidos simply to see the piece. Even this sculpture, which eventually gave rise to numerous other representations of Aphrodite undressed or half-draped [70, 81, 84–86, 556, 579], had its proper sacred space, in an elegant little circular temple, designed so that visitors could walk around and appreciate her beauty from all angles [82]. Nearby, couches were installed, amid fragrant bushes: those paying homage to the goddess had somewhere to practise her arts.

Another sanctuary of Aphrodite was particularly notorious by the time of the early Roman Empire. This was her temple at Corinth. Located on high ground above the city – an eminence known as 'Acrocorinth' – the site was staffed by an estimated one thousand 'priestesses'. It was a by-word for sexual licence: one colloquial Greek euphemism for the act of fornication was therefore *Korinthiazomai*, 'to Corinth'.

82 *Reconstruction of the Sanctuary of Aphrodite at Knidos after c. 200 BC, showing the statue of the goddess in the centre of the circular colonnade. (A copy of the temple was constructed in antiquity as a feature of the Emperor Hadrian's villa at Tivoli.)*

83 *The* Aphrodite of Knidos, *Roman copy after an original by Praxiteles, c. 360 BC. 'The finest statue by Praxiteles, indeed the finest in the world, is the Aphrodite that many have sailed to Knidos just to see' (Pliny the Elder,* Natural History *36.4.20).*
  The water jar at her side explains Aphrodite's nudity: she is preparing to bathe. More ambiguous is the hand gesture: Aphrodite's very attempt modestly to cover her genitals only serves to draw our attention to them.

84 *Marble statuette of Aphrodite in 'Sandalbinder' pose, 1st century BC or 1st century AD.*

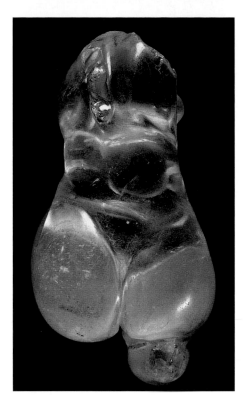

85 *Rear view of 'Crouching Aphrodite' statuette in rock crystal, perhaps from Roman Egypt, 1st century BC.*

86 *Marble statue of 'Crouching Aphrodite' (with clutching Eros figure), from Asia Minor: copy of an original type created c. 200 BC.*

Venus, sex, and 'The Nature of Things' To the Romans, the Greek Aphrodite more or less equated to their Venus; and for Romans around the time of the birth of Christ, Venus had recently gained fresh importance in the pantheon of deities. For the first Roman emperor, Augustus, not only traced his own genealogy to the goddess: he was making sure that his claimed line of divine descent was impressed upon public consciousness by featuring repeatedly in art and literature [286]. The 'Julian family' (*gens Iulia*) to which Augustus belonged – his great-uncle and adoptive father was Julius Caesar – asserted that their kinship could be traced back to Aeneas, the mythical pioneer of Rome's foundation [222]. Aeneas, in turn, was the result of an extraordinary coupling between a shepherd, Anchises, and Venus herself. But a single family could not annexe completely a goddess whose power was saluted throughout the Latin-speaking world with such cult titles as *Genetrix* ('Mother', or 'Originator') and *Victrix* ('Prevailer', or 'She-Victor'). Venus to the Romans represented a subtle and ultimately matchless power. This was best symbolized, perhaps, in the tale of how Venus, goddess of love and charm, could even overcome Mars, the god of war and strife – for all that he was bristling with heavy weapons.

It is with the image of Venus subduing Mars that one of the finest pieces of Latin poetry begins: *On the Nature of Things*, by Lucretius (a contemporary of Julius Caesar). In a dedicatory overture, Lucretius calls upon Venus to work her magic over Mars: for when she does so, the world finds respite from conflict, and then the poet's voice does not have to compete with the clangor of war. But before we deduce from this that Lucretius believes in the Latin motto *Amor vincit omnia* – 'Love conquers all' – we had better see how he subsequently deals with erotic compulsion in his account of the universe.

... Love with phantoms cheats our longing eyes,
Which hourly seeing never satisfies;
Our hands pull nothing from the parts they strain,
But wander o'er the lovely limbs in vain:
Nor when the youthful pair more closely join,
When hands in hands they lock, and thighs in thighs
   they twine,
Just in the raging foam of full desire,
When both press on, both murmur, both expire,
They grip, they squeeze, their humid tongues they dart,
As each would force their way to t'other's heart—
In vain; they only cruise around the coast,
For bodies cannot pierce, nor be in bodies lost:
As sure they strive to be, when both engage,
In that tumultous momentary rage;

So tangled in the nets of love they lie,
Till man dissolves in that excess of joy.
Then, when the gather'd bag has burst its way,
And ebbing tides the slackened nerves betray,
A pause ensues; and Nature nods a while,
Till with recruited rage new spirits boil;
And then the same vain violence returns,
With flames renewed th' erected furnace burns.
Again they in each other would be lost,
But still by adamantine bars are crossed;
All ways they try, successless all they prove,
To cure the secret sore of lingering love.

Lucretius, *On the Nature of Things* 4.67–92
translated by John Dryden
(from *Sylvae*, 1685)

87 *Roman bronze wind-chime (tintinnabulum) in the shape of a flying phallus, from Pompeii, before* AD *79. These good-luck charms were evidently a common sight, hanging in the doorways of houses and shops.*

88 *Detail of a wall-painting in the House of the Centenary at Pompeii, c.* AD *62–79. Erotic themes in the Pompeian repertoire of domestic decoration were, naturally, usually reserved for the bedroom (cubiculum) of the house.*

On the Nature of Things is the most complete statement we possess of the Classical philosophy known as 'Epicureanism', which advocated that a primary aim of human endeavour was to find and take pleasure in the world (see p. 237). It soon becomes clear, however, from the way in which Lucretius affirms Epicurean tenets, that pleasure is understood not as some transport of delight, but rather as freedom from nuisance and discomfort – the state of tranquillity that the Greeks termed *ataraxia*. Insofar as love can be a tumultous experience, the good Epicurean must regard it suspiciously. So when Lucretius analyses the supposed pleasures of sex, in book 4, he gives his readers little cause for cheer. Eros is like an itch: scratching only makes it worse. Or, in the more elegant phrasing of Dryden's 17th-century translation:

> Love, and Love alone of all our joys
> By full possession does but fan the fire.
> The more we still enjoy, the more we still desire.

Love may even have been the end of Lucretius: tradition tells that he experimented with a love-potion, which threw him into a frenzy he could only escape by suicide.

89 *Sexual encounters painted on the walls of an apodyterium (changing-room) of the Suburban Baths at Pompeii, c. AD 62–79. The painted boxes with Roman numerals referred to real boxes that lined a shelf below, in which bathers stored their clothes. Each bather was invited to remember his 'locker' by a different sexual act – I, 'woman-riding'; II, 'rear entry'; III, fellatio; IV, cunnilingus; etc.*

90 *Terracotta decoration of a rhyton (drinking horn), from Delos, 2nd century BC: an erotic symplegma ('coupling' or 'entwining') in miniature.*

'The Art of Love' The Greeks were morally haunted by fears of sensual self-abandon: lack of self-restraint was a barbarian trait. In the 4th century BC, a Greek historian called Theopompos had the following observations to make about sexual habits among the Etruscans: that their women spent much care on their bodies, but were also hard drinkers, accustomed (worse still) to drinking with men – leading to a state in which it was normal to make love at any hour, and quite openly: so that if someone called at an Etruscan house, they would find its occupants at some 'act' without any shame or embarassment. So loose were the bonds of Etruscan wedlock, says Theopompos, that all babies were reared as a common responsibility (he is quoted in Athenaeus, *Intellectuals at the Table* 12.517d–518b).

Had Theopompus lived several centuries later, he might have been similarly shocked by some of the ways in which the Romans, too, indulged an apparently lax attitude towards the pleasures of the flesh. It was in the early Imperial period (around the year 1 BC) that Ovid published his poem entitled *The Art of Love*, an urbane guide to fornication that ran counter to the official Augustan policy of encouraging Romans to respect the coherence of marriage and 'family values'. The overt and irrepressible glee with which Ovid instructed his readers in techniques of flirtation and more may have contributed to his own eventual disgrace, in AD 8, when he was banished to a remote place of exile on the Black Sea; though it says something about the Augustan ambience that some suppose Ovid's crime to have been simply that he saw (and perhaps wrote about) an impromptu striptease display, at a party, by one of the Emperor's close female relatives.

Once banished, Ovid did nothing but beseech, without success, for his return to civilization. His poetry of complaint can seem tedious, but one can understand his sense of hurt. For if he had been over-salacious in his celebration of love, it was by mistake, not criminal intent. And what was there in his writing that was not already abundantly in evidence – on painted walls, on finger rings, on drinking cups, cameos, lamps, and more besides – to demonstrate that Romans took unabashed delight in amorous diversions?

This is clear enough from the sites of Pompeii and Herculaneum, caught as they were in the year AD 79 by a volcanic eruption. Whatever the strictures on sexual comportment emanating from the Emperor and his court, it looks as if inhabitants of these provincial towns enjoyed their sex, at all social levels – or at least enjoyed the freedom to depict it, and make it a prime topic of their graffiti.

The wall-paintings of houses here give plentiful testimony of a shameless acceptance of, literally, 'the art of love', with numerous scenes (especially in bedrooms) of all sorts of sexual congress [88]. This was not a case of hidden or private imagery for connoisseurs of the erotic. Some of the most adventurous sexual vignettes are to be found in a public building used daily by both men and women, the so-called Suburban Baths in Pompeii. Threesomes, foursomes, various entries and excitements are depicted on the walls of the changing-room here [89]. One scene shows a naked woman on a couch, spreading her legs to receive cunnilingus from a diminutive man (or dwarf), whose height perfectly positions him to render the service. It is not uncommon, in Classical art, to find images of women performing fellatio on men: so is this a rare and deliberate inversion of the norm – and if so, as some commentators suppose, was it done for comic effect? Yet the inscribed records of Pompeian brothels tell us that gigolos were available, offering cunnilingus for the price of several 'asses' (a small coin) – the cost of a snack or cup of wine. So these people saw the funny side of sex, or else perhaps recognized that the sex-needs of a woman might equal those of a man. Either way, the art and artefacts of Imperial Rome attest a widespread delight in the visual expression of erotic pastimes.

The language of love As Ovid put it: 'Love is a sort of military service' ('militiae species amor est': *The Art of Love* 2.233). Ovid styled himself as a veteran campaigner, and accordingly laid out his poetry like a field manual on warfare, detailing all sorts of stratagems for the attainment of victory. If the poet, for example, felt himself to be the typical *exclusus amator* – 'shut-out lover' – then his efforts to gain entrance could readily be described as a drawn-out exercise of siegecraft. The victorious lover might hoist his standard, seize 'booty', celebrate a triumph – and so on. As a poetic analogy this could be effective (if rather predictable). As a sign of relations between sexual partners it is clearly disturbing – at least, to modern sensibilities. Do the metaphors of besieging, ambush, attack, and conquest imply an association of sex with violence that was often enacted? If the Greek and Latin streetwise jargon for sexual activity is to be taken as further indication, we might fear so. Consider the following lists of Classical euphemisms for the male and female genitalia:

M		F	
corn-cob	shaft/stake	garden	gate
ram/crowbar	ploughshare	crack	hollow
oar/boat-pole	sword	sea-shell	rose
point	spear	pit	fig
handle	sickle	dish	bush
meat	baton	oven	mousehole

The obvious conclusion from such language – most of it to be found in the surviving scripts of Greek and Latin comedy – is that in heterosexual relationships the woman was essentially soft, passive, and receptive, while the man was hard, aggressive, and probing. At a broader metaphorical level, the most pervasive Classical image of the female body likened it to a field which needed to be ploughed and sowed by the well-tempered tools of the male: invariably, then, reference was made to Earth (in Greek, Gaia or Ge [98]). Male writers on 'the science of women' – which is what 'gynaecology' literally means – hardly refined this widespread acceptance of female passivity by their diagnoses of certain conditions peculiar to women. To become 'hysterical', for example, was deemed a feminine tendency, brought on by a loose and wandering uterus (for which the Greek is *hystera*):

A sultry encounter. *Ovid starts off recumbent – but soon goes on the offensive:*

In summers heate and mid-time of the day
To rest my limbes upon a bed I lay,
One window shut, the other open stood,
Which gave such light, as twincles in a wood,
Like twilight glimps'd at setting of the Sunne,
Or night being past, and yet not day begunne.
Such light to shamefast maidens must be showne,
Where they may sport, and seeme to be unknowne.
Then came *Corinna* in a long loose gowne,
Her white neck hid with tresses hanging downe:
Resembling fayre *Semiramis* going to bed
Or *Layis* of a thousand wooers sped,
I snatcht her gowne: being thin, the harme was small,
Yet striv'd she to be covered there withall.
And striving thus as one that would be cast,

Betray'd her selfe, and yeelded at the last.
Starke naked as she stood before mine eye,
Not one wen in her body could I spie.
What arms and shoulders did I touch and see,
How apt her breasts were to be prest by me.
How smooth a belly under her wast saw I?
How large a legge, and what a lustie thigh?
To leave the rest all lik'd me passing well,
I cling'd her naked body, downe she fell,
Judge you the rest, being tirde she bade me kisse;
Jove send me more such after-noones as this.

Ovid, *Love Affairs* (*Amores*) 1.5
translated by Christopher Marlowe
(*All Ovids Elegies: Liber Primus, Elegia 5, c.* 1600)

the recommended remedy for 'wombiness' was penetration by the stabilizing, 'disciplined' male member.

In a play called the *Lysistrata*, written in the year 411 BC by the Athenian comic playwright Aristophanes, a fantasy is imagined in which the women of Athens attempt to stop war by staging a sex strike. It is the nearest that any Classical source comes to anticipating the modern plea of 'Make love, not war'. But again we can turn to the poetess Sappho, for the most succinct expression of an alternative voice. This is Fragment 16 in the Sapphic collection:

> Some say a formation of cavalry is the most splendid sight on the dark earth; some claim it is a line of infantry, others prefer ships. But I say: it is always one's beloved.
>
> I think of Anactoria . . . Her swaying gait, her face with flashing eyes – they are what I want to see – not the chariots of the Lydians, or some marching-men in armour.

Rape: myths and realities   Many Classical myths centre upon some act of sexual violence or violation. Call it 'rape', 'abduction' or 'ravishing': did such stories provide a sanction for this forcible abuse?

The Trojan War itself was deemed to have been caused by a beautiful woman – Helen [91], whose face 'launched a thousand ships'. Helen was minding her own business as the dutiful wife of Menelaus, King of Sparta, when she became nominated as the prize in the Judgment of Paris (see p. 113). Paris accordingly 'abducted' her from Greece to Troy. But then, what to make of the origins of Helen herself? Her mother Leda was a mortal married woman, to whom the god Zeus (Jove, or Jupiter, to the Romans) took a passing fancy. Zeus descended upon Leda in the form of a swan, and (as it is usually euphemized) 'ravished' her [575]; Leda subsequently produced a huge egg, from which hatched Helen in all her matchless pulchritude.

Another myth tells how Zeus carried off a princess called Europa from the shores of Phoenicia: on that occasion the god appeared in the shape of a bull, apparently docile; but once Europa had clambered upon its back, it charged away with her [94, 95], over the sea to Crete, where the girl was to bear at least two sons by Zeus (and would give her name to an entire continent). By making these episodes of divine sexual assault so bizarre, Greek mythographers perhaps intended to distance the actions of Zeus from the harmful realities of 'rape'. Alternatively, if Zeus chose not to transform himself on such occasions, could his victim count herself lucky, to

91 *Helen seeks sanctuary as Menelaus advances to recover her as his rightful property. Detail of an Attic red-figure bell krater attributed to the Persephone Painter, c. 440–430 BC.*

92 The shepherd boy Ganymede, wearing a rustic 'Phrygian' bonnet, offers a kantharos to the eagle about to abduct him. Engraved jasper gem, 2nd century AD.

93 Zeus, seated by an altar, holds out his own kylix to be filled by Ganymede. Interior of an Attic red-figure kylix signed by Douris, c. 480 BC. (The exterior of this cup shows Zeus pursuing the boy.)

be chosen as if for a sort of immaculate conception, or 'sacred coupling', as the Greeks understood it? Such may have been the understanding, for instance, of the visitation by Zeus to Alkmene [413], a queen of Thebes, resulting in the birth of Herakles, the Classical hero and saviour *par excellence*.

But it was not a blasphemy to envisage the gods as prey to the same erotic turbulence that could rock the knees of mortals. When Zeus became inflamed with passion for a boy called Ganymede, it was enough to say that Ganymede was a youth of all-surpassing prettiness – possessed of good looks that were, so to speak, 'out of this world'. In the story of how Zeus seizes Ganymede to become his 'cup-bearer' and *eromenos* (our word 'catamite', meaning the passive partner of male homosexual intercourse, comes from the Etrusco–Latin rendering of the Greek *Ganymedes* into *Catamitus*), Zeus may cause a breeze to swirl the boy up to Olympus, or else swoop down himself in an eagle's guise [92, 93, 212]. But many Classical artists were content simply to show Zeus as the archetypal pederast, claiming his prize with energetic glee [568]. Who was going to stop him?

And yet, for all that Eros caused aggression in heaven as on earth, rules of conduct were in place. So it was necessary that Ganymede's father profit handsomely (as Greeks would have seen it) from the loss of his son, by receiving from Zeus an amazingly fine breed of horses, or a golden vine. With women, Zeus might do as he pleased: but in the law-courts of Athens, any man following the example of Zeus risked severe punishment. The offence was *moicheia*, usually translated as 'adultery', but more precisely meaning 'sex without a guardian's permission'. Not all women came under such male stewardship – prostitutes, slave-girls, resident aliens were among those left out – but an Athenian citizen could invoke the law if advances were made upon his wife, his sister, his daughter, or his widowed mother; and if he kept a live-in mistress or concubine (as many Athenian men seem to have done), she too was protected.

To the citizen coming across rape or adultery *in flagrante*, the legal entitlement was immediate homicide. Alternatively, a financial settlement might be levied; and some sources suggest various modes of corporal humiliation too. But one thing is dismayingly obvious, to sensibilities of the 21st century: there was no particular sympathy for the *victims* of sexual molestation. If a woman of Classical Athens was subject to what we should deem 'rape', it was either not an offence at all (if she was an *hetaira*, foreigner, or suchlike); or else it was a crime against the man who 'owned' her.

The situation in Rome was not much different. 'Debauchery' (*stuprum*), when inflicted upon a 'respectable' woman, demanded redress primarily on account of the insult to her family. Latin mythology contains one of the most egregious examples of predatory machismo ever scripted, the so-called 'Rape of the Sabine Women', in which Rome's pioneer-founder, Romulus, invites a neighbouring tribe (the Sabines) to a festival, with the plot of making a wholesale capture of females to increase his new foundation's populace. For a more 'plausible' story of a woman's dilemma in the event of rape, however, we might heed what befalls the Latin noblewoman Lucretia, in an episode of Roman legendary history set in the late 6th century BC. Lucretia, we are told, was assaulted in her own bedroom by the son of Tarquin the Proud, the Etruscan king ruling Rome at that time. It would prove a turning-point in Rome's political fortunes, for the manly vengeance required of Lucretia's husband and father and their friends eventually led to the expulsion of the Etruscan tyrants from Rome. Lucretia herself proved an exemplary figure, but with dismal implications for the female sufferance of sexual outrage. She killed herself, lest it ever be said she lost her virtue complacently.

Sextus Tarquinius . . . was welcomed graciously, for no one suspected his plans. After dinner, he was conducted to a guest-room. He was burning with desire. As soon as it seemed that everyone was in bed and the coast was clear, he crept along to the sleeping Lucretia with his dagger drawn. He held his left hand to her breast and hissed: 'Keep quiet, Lucretia; this is Sextus Tarquinius. I have a sword in my hand: utter one word, and you die.' The girl started out of her slumber, realized no help was nearby, and immediately feared for her life. Then Tarquinius began to state his love for her, pleadingly, but mixing entreaties with threats, trying from every angle to cajole some affection from her. But as she held out against him, and seemed unmoved even by the prospect of dying, he added to death the taint of disgrace. Once she was killed, he said, then he would strangle a slave and lay that naked body beside hers, so it would seem that she had been caught in some act of squalid fornication. With this menace, Lucretia's stubborn chastity was broken, and lust prevailed as if by force. Then reckless Tarquinius rode off, exultant at having overcome a woman's honour.

Lucretia, weeping at the calamity, sent an identical message to her father at Rome and her husband at Ardea: that each should come with a trusted friend, and come quickly, too: for a terrible thing had happened. [Her father] Spurius Lucretius came with Publius Valerius, the son of Volesus, and Collatinus [her husband] arrived with Lucius Junius Brutus, with whom he happened to be journeying towards Rome when the messenger caught him. They all found Lucretia sitting aghast in her bedroom. Fresh tears brimmed when she saw her kinsmen. 'Are you all right?' asked her husband. 'Not in the least', she said. 'What can be right, when a woman's integrity is gone? Traces of another man, Collatinus, are in your bed. But it is only my body that was taken; the heart of me is innocent, as death is my witness. Each of you hold up your right hand and swear that the adulterer shall not go unpunished. It was Sextus Tarquinius who was here last night and who repaid our hospitality with his invasion. When he took his pleasure he ruined me – and he will have ruined himself, too, if you are real men.' Those present pledged their faith, in turn; and they tried to console her, wretched as she was, with reassurances that the blame lay not with her, but with the perpetrator of the deed – that guilt resided with the mind, not the body, and that without intent there was no culpability. 'You', she said, 'concern yourselves with what is owed to *him*. As for me, I *do* discharge myself from any crime: but not from the punishment. No one, ever, is going to take Lucretia as the precedent for being shameless.' She had a knife concealed in her gown: she pointed it to her heart, and collapsed, fatally, onto the wound she made.

Livy, *History of Rome from its Foundation* 1.58

94 *Europa carried off by the bull. Detail of a Paestan red-figure kalyx krater by Asteas, c. 340 BC. Above her floats the personification of Pothos, 'Longing'.*

95 *Europa and the bull, flanked by cupids, in a mosaic from the Romano-British villa at Lullingstone in southern England, mid-4th century AD. An inscription next to the image (not seen here) playfully relates the myth to an episode in Vergil's Aeneid. Image and text together could therefore boast an understanding of Graeco-Roman ('European') myth, despite the villa's location on the fringes of the Roman Empire.*

One does not have to be a doctrinaire feminist to paint a dark and damning picture of erotic behaviour in ancient Greece and Rome. Even those who would make rationalizing apologies for the mythology of rape – saying that it served as a metaphor for marriage – must concede that sexual coercion was a practice that went largely unquestioned in the Classical world. (It is significant that when the 5th-century Greek 'Sophist' Gorgias composed a speech in which a case is made for Helen's innocence – the *Encomium of Helen* – it was as an exercise of rhetorical skill, not moral reasoning.) But it would be wrong to suppose that no Classical couple ever loved each other with tenderness, humour, gentle consent, and mutual respect. One of Aphrodite's epithets, after all, was as 'the goddess of sweet whisperings'.

96 *Boeotian terracotta statuette-group,
c. 500–475 BC: a woman feeding hen and chicks
– a typical genre scene from terracotta workshops
located at Tanagra, east of Thebes.*

DIET

'Wouldn't you agree that the supreme good consists in being able to live without absolute need of food?' This question occurs in the course of an imaginary gathering described in 'The Banquet of the Seven Wise Men' (written in the late 1st or early 2nd century AD), and may seem like an idle speculation, given its context. But for the author (Plutarch) and his readers, the hypothesis – which is attributed to the semi-legendary Athenian lawgiver Solon – was not wildly eccentric. The soul was immortal. What nourished the soul could not possibly be any substance cultivated in fields and cooked in pots. So did wisdom truly lie in some ultimate transcendence over the pangs of hunger and thirst? One of the symposiasts, Cleodorus, takes up the intellectual challenge of living without dependence on food. His answer (Plutarch, *Moral Essays* 158) may be paraphrased as follows:

> As soon as we suppress the importance of food to our lives, we are in effect saying that the table, too, is an item we can do without. But the table is a sacred item of furniture: it is the altar of the deities who preside over friendship and hospitality. Take away food, and you rip out the heart of domestic existence, the hearth. Take away food, and all agriculture becomes a waste of time, leaving the world like a wilderness. The bonds of humanity are forged in the sharing of food and drink; so too are our tributes to the Sun, the Moon, and all our beneficent gods. Sacrifice, first fruits, and libations are due to them: how else should we thank them for meeting our needs? You say the soul is nourished by other pleasures, arguably more elevated than food? Of course! There is no more basic nor natural satisfaction than that of feeding oneself. And just think what a gladsome and shameless indulgence it is, to sit down to lunch with company. Making love, by contrast, must be done by night, or in shadows. We know which is our primary source of happiness: the pleasure that can be taken openly, without disgrace.

The sacral aspect of this apology for enjoying food is significant. For in ancient Greece it was undoubtedly the case that most people's normal *diaita* ('mode of

99 *Detail of the Tomb of the Leopards, Tarquinia, c. 480–470 BC. Etruscan painted tombs often feature such scenes of convivial dining – though whether these reflect typical socializing, an ideal afterlife, or a particular* perideipnon *(funerary banquet), is not always clear [cf. 406]. Here one of the reclining figures holds up an egg, and a slave between the two couches flourishes an* oinochoe *(wine-jug).*

opposite
97 left *The departure of Triptolemos from Eleusis. Detail of an Attic red-figure* dinos *(jar) attributed to the Syleus Painter, c. 470 BC. Entrusted with grain – and the art of its cultivation – by Demeter and Persephone [150], Triptolemos is despatched in a winged chariot to spread the knowledge of arable farming around the the world.*

98 right *The goddess Gaia Pantaleia, 'All-providing Earth', seated to receive a sacred branch offered by Dionysos; he holds a strand of vine foliage, and has a leopard at his feet. Detail of an Attic red-figure* kalyx krater *by Syriskos, c. 470–460 BC.*

living') was simple, predictable, and predominantly vegetarian. Meat and cakes and other special dishes were reserved for religious occasions. Admittedly, such occasions were regular and numerous. But when the heroes of Homer sit down each night to huge steaks roasted on spits [cf. 100], they are in the world of wishful thinking. Homer is closer to daily realities when he salutes barley-meal as 'the marrow of humankind'. Grain was the prime form of sustenance; meat a festal indulgence, inextricably associated with the logic of sacrifice (see pp. 96–98). Domesticated animals and birds were of course raised [96], but did not figure in everyday consumption: nuts, fruits, and assorted pulses were the common supplements. Within the modern menu of global cuisines, there is abiding respect for 'the Mediterranean diet', whose principal constituents – olive oil, wine, and grain (most familiar today as bread, pizza, or pasta) – were established in Classical antiquity. (No one should think that dietary habits in this part of the world have gone unchanged for centuries, though: among foods unknown to ancient Greeks and Romans are tomatoes, rice, potatoes, coffee, and sugar.)

The olive tree with its silver-green foliage seems to have claimed the Mediterranean as its natural habitat [229–31], though its origins in agriculture probably belong in the Near East. Both olives and the oil pressed from them were major items of Classical trade, and evidently provided the main source of (polyunsaturated) fats in the daily diet. There is no evidence for ancient anticipation of the division into fats, carbohydrates, and proteins; but physiologists didrecognize idirect links between nutrition and health, and olive oil was valued as a rich source of both energy and flavour, not to mention its various other culinary, household, athletic, and cosmetic uses.

100 *Roasting meat on spits on a flaming altar. Detail of the Ricci Hydria, an East Greek black-figure vase of the late 6th century BC.*

The Classical mythology and protocols surrounding wine are discussed elsewhere in this book (see pp. 253–59). Here perhaps it is enough to note that wine could serve as a fluid intake often safer than water, or as a means of making brackish water palatable; and that while wine was very much the liquid of parties, festivals, and libations, it was also a daily staple. Most Greek men began their day with a piece of bread dipped into undiluted wine; when Jesus instituted wine as a symbolic element of the Christian communion, he chose a beverage generally accessible to the poorest members of society, and doled out to Roman soldiers as part of daily rations. That is not to say, however, that wine was not subject to connoisseurship. Despite the problems of wines 'travelling well' in large clay amphoras, there was much talk in certain circles of regional characteristics. The Aegean islands of Naxos and Thasos, for example, were renowned for their sweet muscats, while the bitter dryness of Corinthian wine was deemed 'suitable only for making criminals confess'. Among the Greeks it was usual practice to drink wine quite soon after first fermentation. The Romans preferred theirs aged – in amphoras sealed with pitch – so snobbery about particular vintages also arose.

Wine, like oil, was produced in the Near East long before the Greeks; and the same is true of the third constituent of the Mediterranean food triad, bread. But again we are indebted to Classical relics and writings for a veritable 'culture' of this dietary staple, with 'celebrity bakers' appearing in Athens in the 5th century BC.

101 *Detail of the tomb of M. Vergilius Eurysaces (the 'Tomb of the Baker'), Rome, late 1st century BC. Eurysaces was a freedman of Greek origin. Though the monument was mainly intended for his wife, he heroizes his success as a pistor (baker) – his fortune made by supplying the army. Relief friezes show all the stages of producing bread, and the holes represent wall-ovens [cf. 355].*

102 *Two men dress the carcass of an animal, probably a goat or a small deer: Roman wall-painting, c. AD 50–75. On a raised tray nearby are a bulb of garlic and other foodstuffs – perhaps bread, fruit, or olives.*

An extensive range of loaf shapes and textures is attested, using both yeasty and unleavened dough from flour derived mostly from barley, spelt, and wheat. In the city of Rome, around the time when Augustus – then known as Octavian – took control of Egypt from Cleopatra and Mark Antony (30 BC), there were no less than 329 bakeries [cf. 355], with an ethnic bias of the profession leaning heavily upon immigrant Greeks and Gauls [101].

Greek myth quaintly told that the know-how of arable farming and grain-processing had been entrusted by the goddess Demeter, in the course of her 'Mysteries' at Eleusis, to a young hero called Triptolemos, who from an airborne chariot diffused that knowledge around the world [97, 150]. By the time of the early Roman Empire, 'bread and circuses' could epitomize the twin defining features of low-class urban existence (see Juvenal, *Satires* 10.81). But of all the elements of the Classical diet, none was more prone to political and economic fortune than bread. When Augustus seized Egypt, he kept the country as his personal province, for one overriding pragmatic reason. The fertile valley of the Nile produced large quantities of grain. It could be exploited as the Emperor's own bread basket, which he might share with the populace of Rome – so long as they supported him.

The rise of gastronomy One of the largest surviving works of Classical literature is the fifteen-volume compendium known as the *Deipnosophistai* by Athenaeus, a Greek author based in Egypt around AD 200. *Intellectuals at the Table* is how the title might be translated: it purports to be a discussion, over a banquet lasting several days, between several men of learning interested in food (evidently), poetry, and sex. Classical scholars have mainly used the book as a source of quotations from lost Greek plays and poems. But it is also a monument to the Classical culture of sensuous consumption. 'Gastronomy' literally means the laws or science pertaining to the stomach (*gaster*), and Athenaeus tells us that there was once a poetic treatise whose topic was just that – *Gastronomia*. Athenaeus' citations of Athenian comedy, from Aristophanes to Menander,

103 *Interior of a South Italian red-figure 'fish plate', c. 300 BC.*

104 *A man carrying a fish, apparently a tuna. Detail of an Attic black-figure kylix attributed to the Theseus Painter, late 6th century BC.*

make it apparent that by the 5th century BC food had already become a key indicator of social identity. He also conveys the names and reputations of many famous chefs and food-writers over centuries – and though it is piecemeal, his information enables us to follow trends of taste and sophistication in the Mediterranean ambit. In the Hellenistic period, for instance, it seems that a chef made his mark by devising ever more ingenious dishes from fish. Archaic Greeks had been suspicious of seafood, but by the 3rd century BC there was much prizing of sea bream, mullet, conger eel, turbot, squid, and shellfish; and 'fish plates' are a familiar ceramic find from the time [103].

Should one eat to live, or live to eat? Athenaeus quotes some Greek historians highly critical of aristocratic lifestyles among the Etruscans, allegedly given over to the luxury of gargantuan meals twice a day. Scenes from painted Etruscan tombs half-confirm this image [99, 406], and the Romans would make a stereotype of the 'plump Etruscan' (*pinguis Tuscus*). But the temptation to make a status symbol of the 'well-loaded table' was almost irresistible, if Etruscan society had anything like the Roman system of convivial obligations.

Dinner (*cena*) was the main meal for Romans, beginning around four in the afternoon and continuing beyond nightfall. It began with a *gustatio* or sequence of *hors d'œuvres*, followed by several main dishes known as *fercula*, 'carried on trays', from the kitchen, and ending with a dessert course of fruit and nuts. Two factors combined to make this meal a potentially gruelling or gluttonous experience. One was the social hierarchy whereby a powerful man or *dominus* attracted 'clients'. The Greeks had reserved a special term, *parasitoi*, 'around-fooders', for those who ate at someone else's expense, earning their food by flattery. With the Romans it was a more formal reciprocity. The master received votes, favours, and daily 'salutations' from his clients. The clients gained not only meals but perhaps also financial handouts, legal assistance, and suchlike. At dinner, clearly, it was incumbent upon the master to show largesse – and his guests might well be ravenously ready to do justice to the spread.

Reports of greedy Romans deliberately vomiting halfway through a meal in order to make space for yet more dishes are more the stuff of modern fantasy than ancient practice. Yet what did it mean to be masters of the world, if Romans could not command the best of the world's delicacies? Once they controlled Asia Minor (from the 2nd century BC onwards), they had access to the 'spice routes' of Arabia, India, and China. So it is that in the best-known surviving culinary manual from Rome, the treatise *On Cookery* ascribed to Apicius, there is hardly a recipe that does not feature herbs and ingredients from beyond the Mediterranean – cardamom, cinnamon, cloves, ginger, nutmeg, pepper, and many more.

For a once presumably solid man, Apicius himself remains a shadowy figure: in fact his name is given to several different gourmets at Rome, not just the chef of the 1st century AD; and the cookbook seems to be a 4th-century concoction. Notoriety has gathered around some of the more unfamiliar (to us) propositions contained in the book – stuffed dormouse, ragout of flamingo tongues, calf's brains braised in cumin and ginger. But the 470 recipes collected in the Apician 'corpus' still stand at the head of the Western tradition of gastronomic literature.

Vegetarianism   Did people in Classical times go on 'diets' in the usual modern sense of the word – that is, to lose weight? It was not unknown. One medical handbook composed by Galen in the late 2nd century AD was entitled *The Slimming Régime*, and contained much scrupulous advice about the properties of various herbs, vegetables, and other foods. But the ascetic or self-denying tradition of

105 *Wall-painting from the House of Julia Felix at Pompeii, c. AD 70. Recovered in excavations of 1755–1757, this 'still life' study evokes an abundance befitting the extensive 'estates' (praedia) attached to the living quarters of Julia Felix.*

Classical philosophy was more concerned with establishing moderation as a core dietary precept, not a remedy or penance. It is in this context that we encounter the first Western advocate of vegetarianism, Pythagoras.

Pythagoras is mostly known today for his geometrical theorem regarding right-angled triangles. But up until the 19th century his name was synonymous with abstinence from meat. For Pythagoras, teaching through the mid-6th century BC at the Greek colony of Croton in South Italy, this principle stemmed directly from the doctrine of reincarnation and 'migration of the *psyche*' (p. 236). He purportedly believed the human soul could occupy an animal's body, and that all animals were therefore part of humanity's fellowship. Fish, birds, reptiles, and mammals alike were related.

Because animal sacrifice was such an integral aspect of most Greek, Etruscan, and Roman cult practices [158], with worshippers normally expected (and expecting) to join the 'communion' of partaking in meat offered to the deities, vegetarianism must always have been an eccentric personal choice in Classical antiquity. Pythagoras, however, was only the first in a line of philosophers teaching the moral and physical virtues of a vegetarian diet. And perhaps it is no accident that the most eloquent of Classical voices on the subject was Plutarch, who served as a priest of Apollo at Delphi in the late 1st and early 2nd centuries AD. Plutarch has left descriptions of animal death and dismemberment that are both visceral and credible. As a priest, it was a sight (and sound) he knew only too well.

106 *Bronze statuette of Asklepios, c. AD 100–150. By the side of the god is a coiled snake – one of his symbols of healing power.*

MEDICINE

Throughout Classical times, the internal structures and workings of the human body remained mysterious. This is not to say curiosity about such matters was lacking. The origins of Western clinical medicine can be definitively located in Greece, in the 5th century BC. But a simple catalogue of what was *not* known about human physiology by someone deeply interested in the subject – the 4th-century Greek philosopher Aristotle – soon gives us the measure of the mystery. Aristotle knew nothing of bacteria, sterilization, antibiotics, or the immune system. Without a microscope, there was no way he could have recognized cell tissues, let alone genetic structures. He had no inkling of how the brain connected to the body as a central nervous system; the function of the heart in pumping blood around the body was likewise utterly obscure. The science of anatomy scarcely existed. The elements of organic chemistry were unidentified. Given this level of ignorance, we may wonder how it is that our basic vocabulary of healthcare – concepts such as 'clinic', 'surgery', 'pharmacy', 'therapy', and 'medicine' – is rooted in Classical practice.

Yet Aristotle himself is said to have lived to the age of sixty-two (before succumbing to a disease of the digestive tract): as we have seen, longevity was not an impossible hope for him and his contemporaries. Diet, exercise, and environment contributed to an individual's well-being. Nor should we underestimate the health benefits of the Classical slave economy – benefits to the owners, of course. Chores regarded as dirty, dangerous, and wearisome were routinely delegated to a sub-species of humanity (see pp. 216–18), enabling slave-owners to pursue less 'stressful' lives.

Greek practitioners commonly referred to themselves as *technitai*, 'craftsmen', masters of various and particular skills. One doctor might specialize in gathering roots from which to extract drugs, poisons, and antidotes (the Greek word *pharmaka* can mean all three); another might dedicate himself to cauterization, the flesh-sizzling technique of sealing wounds and removing unwanted growths with hot iron. As today, there were alternative styles of healthcare on offer in the medical marketplace.

In the years 430–427 BC a plague spread through various of the Greek city-states. This is how the historian Thucydides described its onset in Athens:

> People in good health were all of a sudden attacked by violent heats in the head, and redness and inflammation in the eyes, the inward parts, such as throat or tongue, becoming bloody and emitting an unnatural and fetid breath . . . internally it burned so that the patient could not bear to have on clothing or linen . . . The bodies of dying men lay one upon another, and half-dead creatures reeled about the streets and gathered round all the fountains in their longing for water. (*History of the Peloponnesian War* 2.59)

This disease attacked the strong and weak alike. Among its first wave of victims were the doctors who visited the afflicted, because it was highly contagious; but, as Thucydides notes, 'supplications in the temples, divinations, and so forth were found equally futile', and were discontinued.

A few years later, the same inexplicable malady visited Phigaleia, deep in the Peloponnese; thanksgiving for the city's eventual relief was rendered in traditional ways, the most durable of which must be the exquisitely poised Temple of Apollo Epikourios ('the Helper'), set up in the mountains of Arcadia, at Bassae [170–72]. But, just as the disastrous epidemic of the 'Black Death' across medieval Europe gave rise to modern urban health programmes, so the plague chronicled by

107 *Reconstruction of the terraced Asklepieion on Kos, as embellished in the 1st century AD with a benefaction from a man named Xenophon, physician to the emperors Claudius and Nero.*

Thucydides seems to have galvanized medical care around Greece in the late 5th century. It is from this period that we notice a widespread expansion of the cult of Asklepios [106], with major centres developed at Epidauros in the south of Greece; on the island of Kos [107], close to the coastline of Asia Minor; and at Lebene in Crete; later joined by an important dormitory-temple near to the citadel of Pergamon, in Anatolia. In direct consequence of an outbreak of plague at Rome in 293 BC, the cult was also instituted there.

The Asklepios sanctuary, or Asklepieion, at Epidauros constitutes the archetypal health-centre of Classical antiquity, and presents to this day the aspect of a tree-shrouded convalescent haven [108, 109]. Like most other ancient healing cults,

108 *Foundations of the colonnaded rotunda of the Thymele (hearth) building of the Asklepieion at Epidauros, c. 360 BC. The ritual function of this circular structure, or tholos, once roofed over and elaborately decorated, remains obscure. Below ground, six concentric rings form a maze, perhaps leading to an altar where libations were poured to the deities of the Underworld; it is also speculated that the sacred snakes of Asklepios were kept here.*

109 right *The Sanctuary of Asklepios in the valley site of Epidauros contained a temple to the god and several other shrines; also covered walkways, athletic facilities, baths, hostels, and a small theatre; a much larger theatre [417] lies slightly further away (right). The outline of the Thymele [108] is visible in the foreground.*

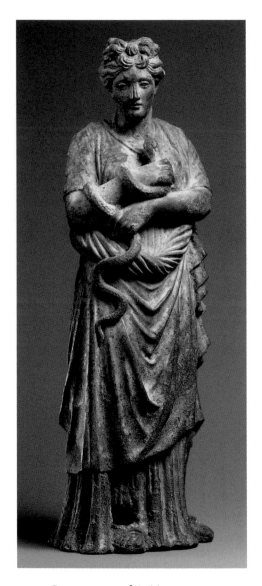

110 *Bronze statuette of Hygieia, c. AD 100–150. Hygieia, Health personified, was deemed a daughter of Asklepios; she holds one of her father's therapeutic serpents.*

it was situated by a source of good spring water, here rising in the lap of a secluded valley. Its prime focus of worship was the Temple of Asklepios, monumentalized around the year 370 BC; baths for physiotherapy and other exercise facilities (including a stadium) may also be seen at the site. The best-preserved remain is the late 4th-century theatre [417], whose presence at the sanctuary reminds us of the 'purgative' justifications of Classical tragedy and comedy (see p. 260). But the most interesting structure at Epidauros is one about which we can only speculate. Beneath what was once an elegant circular colonnade lies a subterranean maze arrangement [108]. Was this where offerings were made to powers of the Underworld, the so-called 'chthonian' deities? Were patients sometimes left to wander in the maze – and did they, if they reached its inner core, find themselves in a pit infested with snakes? For we know that the snake was seen as both the symbol and messenger of Asklepios, and that a number of harmless yellow snakes were set loose in the precincts of Epidauros. Some scholars even wonder if the maze might not have served as a sort of shock-treatment for certain psychiatric cases.

Dogs also roamed the sanctuary, and visitors with flesh wounds were evidently encouraged to let these dogs lick the afflicted parts, for they were believed to have curative power (modern research, as it happens, has indeed proved the presence of antiseptic agents in canine saliva). The cures on offer at Epidauros were not entirely folkloristic remedies or forms of faith-healing. Pilgrims were accommodated in cubicles, and each patient expected to be visited in a dream by Asklepios, revealing the path back to health. Beyond this sacred protocol, however, lay the application of pharmaceutical drugs and remedies, and some surgical intervention. Scalpels, lances, and other instruments have been recovered at Epidauros: it is clear that the priests of Asklepios not only expounded but also enacted the god's instructions.

The expansion of Epidauros from the 4th century onward into Roman times, and the spread of similar sites around the Mediterranean world, says something of the efficacy of available treatments. To some pilgrims these sanctuaries served like spa resorts, offering an annual rest-cure. One prime literary source for Asklepiad procedures is Aelius Aristides, whom the cynical might characterize as a full-time hypochondriac. He seems to have spent most of his life (in the 2nd century AD) in the Asklepieion of Pergamon, addicted perhaps to the radioactive waters that are a local speciality.

Yet these places were also locations of serious research. The Asklepieion on Kos [107] was home to the methods and theories we group around the name of Hippocrates, traditionally saluted as the 5th-century BC pioneer of clinical practice – that is, literally, the art of healing as learned at the bedside (see pp. 74–75). Pergamon, for its part, determined the career-choice of a youth called Galen, who in the latter half of the 2nd century AD emigrated westwards to Rome and eventually became court physician to the Emperor Marcus Aurelius.

Galen is our single most important source for medical science in Classical antiquity. He gained his apprenticeship tending to the wounds sustained by Pergamene gladiators. Galen owed much to his Hippocratic predecessors, but made many advances too, especially in the field of human anatomy (despite the fact that the dissection of human corpses was periodically taboo in the Classical world, and only performed publicly at certain medical schools in Alexandria around the 3rd–2nd centuries BC). But above all, Galen was a vigorous and comprehensive author, making it his business to rid the medical profession of all quackery, and assemble a critical, copious, and coherent system of information about how human beings functioned (or not, as the case might be).

'Surgery' *comes from the Greek and Latin words for healing 'by hand'. The lack of anaesthetics is implicit from the following piece of advice to would-be surgeons from the compiler of a medical handbook in Rome in the early 1st century* AD.

Your surgeon ought to be a young man, or at least not too far from youth. He should have a hand that is strong, firm, and never prone to shake; and he should be as quick to use his left hand as his right. His eyesight must be keen and sharp, his spirit intrepid. And he must have compassion only to the extent of wanting to heal. He must not be moved by a patient's shrieks into operating too hastily, or cutting less than is needed. No howlings of agony should sway him from doing what has to be done.

Celsus, *On Medicine*, from the *Proemium* to book 7

What Galen collected amounts to an essentially holistic view of human health. The titles alone of Galen's many tracts (e.g. *A Beginner's Guide to Bones* and *On the Uses of the Parts of the Body of Man*) make it plain that he believed in empirical investigations. But underpinning his detailed analyses of human physiology was a concept of bodily constitution that had no basis in experimental probes. Accepting a philosophy already formulated by Hippocrates and others, Galen conceived of the body as a receptacle to four cardinal fluids. These were the moistures or 'humours' of blood, phlegm, yellow bile, and black bile, which within a healthy person were more or less equally distributed. The preponderance of one humour in a given body produced a certain personality or temperament: if it were blood, the individual was generally 'sanguine', or cheerful; if phlegm, 'phlegmatic' – slow-moving and imperturbable; if yellow bile, 'choleric' – quick-tempered, irritable; and if black bile, then prone to gloom, and usually 'melancholic'.

Hardly anyone now ever resorts to the Classical doctrine of the humours. Throughout the Middle Ages in Europe, however, it was widely invoked both in medical diagnosis and for the purpose of popular and literary characterizations. Those who delve into the works of Galen will find that the humours in turn connect to a complex system of subsidiary fluids and internal mechanisms or 'souls' that required regulation and equilibrium; and that the entire scheme derives from a quadruple classification of cosmic elements (fire, air, water, earth) and their defining properties (respectively hot, cold, moist, and dry).

The cult of Asklepios   Asklepios – or Aesculapius, as he was known to the Romans – occupies the mythical basis of Classical medicine: founding father, patron saint, hero, first practitioner, and divine parent, all in one. His badge was a snake, often shown curled round a staff. Whether he had any historical existence no one in antiquity could be sure: legendarily he was supposed to have learned his healing arts from a wise Centaur (half-man, half-horse) called Chiron. At least two of the daughters of Asklepios were worshipped as divine personifications, Hygieia ('Health') [110] and Panacea ('All-healer'); while many practising doctors claimed to be, actually or spiritually, his descendants.

In one version of his myth, the healer-hero himself came to a drastic end. Tempted by a handsome fee, he managed to restore to life one person already

112 *Marble votive relief from Athens, late 4th century BC. An offering from one Lysimachides to a hero-doctor called Amynos, whose shrine was on the western slope of the Acropolis, it is evidently a plea – or thanksgiving – for the cure of varicose veins.*

The incubation rite, *as described in a comedy by Aristophanes of 388 BC. The title character, Ploutos ('Wealth'), has been guided to the sanctuary of Asklepios by Karion and others. Karion tells his wife how it happened.*

KARION: So, into the temple precincts we went, and laid out honey-cakes and offerings on the altar, to be licked by the flames of Hephaistos. Then we tucked Ploutos up in bed as instructed, and found beds for ourselves, too.

WIFE: So – who else was in the god's waiting-room?

KARION: Old Neokleides was there – claims his sight's gone, though he's still the sharpest-eyed thief in the business. Lots of others; everything you can imagine wrong with them. Well, the temple priest snuffed out the lights and told us all to switch off too. No fidgeting, no chatting, and absolutely no getting out of bed, whatever racket we heard. So we all obeyed. But I couldn't sleep. There was this tempting bowl of stew, beside some old woman's head, and I was dying to crawl over to it. Just then I looked up, and saw the priest was hovering over the cakes and figs we'd left on the holy altar. He was doing the rounds himself: passing from altar to altar, consecrating the offerings – by popping them in his bag. That must be the rightful thing to do, I thought: so I made for that bowl of stew.

WIFE: Naughty man! Weren't you fearful of the god?

KARION: Only in case he got there first, in those garlands of his, and beat me to that supper. Well – I was just following the priestly example, wasn't I? Anyway, the old crone heard me prowling towards her, and she stretched out her hand. So I made a hissing sound, and gave the hand a little nip, like the sacred snakes are supposed to do, and she quickly drew back and dived under her covers, and wet herself with terror, mewing like a kitten. I set about her stew and gulped down as much as I could.

WIFE: No sign of the god even then?

KARION: In a bit. This'll amuse you. Just as he came, I felt a rumbling in my guts – and I let rip the most enormous fart.

WIFE: Ugh! He must've been disgusted!

KARION: His daughters sure were. One blushed, and Panacea veered away, holding her nose. I'm not made of frankincense.

WIFE: What about his holiness?

KARION: Didn't bat an eyelid.

WIFE: You're kidding. You mean he's got no sense?

KARION: No, no. But they're part of his business – bowel movements.

WIFE: How gross.

KARION: Well, I got scared then, and covered my head, while he padded about among all the patients, examining every ailment. He had an assistant with him, carrying a stone pestle and mortar and medicine chest.

WIFE: A stone chest?

KARION: Not the chest, silly –

WIFE: So how come you saw all this, you brute, when you just said your head was covered up?

KARION : My cloak's full of holes, isn't it? See? Well – for Neokleides, he mixed a poultice, chucking in three cloves of garlic from Tenea, mashed up with fig-sap and sea onion and all soused with best Sphettian vinegar . . . then he flips up the eyelids of the poor man, and pastes that lot on the inside, just to make it really sting. Neokleides sits bolt upright with a yell, ready to flee; but the god only laughs, and tells him to sit tight in his anointment. 'At least', says he, 'we'll keep you from shooting your mouth off at the next Assembly.'

WIFE: Now that's a god who cares for the city.

KARION: Then he came to our Ploutos. He had a look at his head, then he pulled out a nice clean napkin and wiped around the eyes. Panacea produced a scarlet cloth to shroud the patient's face and head and then the god made a sort of cluck-clucking noise – and these two huge snakes came creeping out from under the altar –

WIFE: Great heavens!

KARION: – and . . . well, it looked like they sort of wriggled under the cloth, and licked at his eyelids – and no sooner had they done that, my dear – well, no sooner than you could put away ten cups of wine – Ploutos jumped up, and he could see! I gave an instant round of applause. The god and the serpents disappeared into the shrine. I woke the master, and you can imagine how everyone around Ploutos jumped up to congratulate him, and we all stayed awake till daylight. O Asklepios – I can't praise him enough, for restoring Ploutos to sight – and making Neokleides completely blind!

Aristophanes, *Ploutos* 653–747

113 *Marble relief dedicated to the hero-doctor Amphiaraos, from a sanctuary at Oropos in Attica, first half of the 4th century BC. This scene offers a synopsis of clinical and incubation treatment for a damaged shoulder. A youth is tended by a physician; then, while asleep, he is visited by a snake that hovers over the same shoulder.*

certified as dead; but that was a presumption of immortality, and it earned Asklepios the fatal punishment of a thunderbolt from Zeus. His followers were thereby warned.

The cult of Asklepios flourished nonetheless, with first traces to be located in a northern region of Greece, Thessaly. Most deities of the Classical pantheon were credited with powers of healing, and there were countless localized votive shrines believed to have therapeutic qualities. It was common practice for pilgrims to leave at such shrines small *memoranda* of their reason for being there – an image or model of some distressed or dysfunctional body part (internal organs included) [112, 115, 116, 152]. But the Asklepiad sanctuaries were marked by their monumental development. This happened largely as a result of the pressure upon visitors to stay in cubicles or dormitories for the rite of 'incubation' [113], an experience related with due banter by the Athenian playwright Aristophanes; and incubation in turn depended upon a general credence in the symbolic importance of dreams. A writer from the late 2nd century AD, Artemidoros, made an almanac of such symbols: to peruse his collection is to appreciate that the Classical 'reading' of dreams was not in any sense the precursor of modern (Freudian) psychoanalytical theories of the subconscious, concerned with the salvage of buried traumas from the past, but rather a repertoire of premonitions about the future.

Hippocrates and the 'Hippocratic Corpus' Hippocrates [114] was, as far as we can gather, a master-physician who travelled widely from his base on the island of Kos, teaching and practising, during the second half of the 5th century BC. He did not, as was claimed in antiquity, 'separate medicine from philosophy'. His achievement lay rather in pioneering an empirical system of observing how illnesses and traumas arose and developed – at least, that is what we would surmise from the documents collectively known as the 'Hippocratic Corpus'.

Not a single page of this literature can be proven to be the authentic composition of Hippocrates himself. And not all of it adds up to a consistent body of medical intelligence. But whoever browses through this 'Hippocratic' literature – probably mostly written down in the late 4th and 3rd centuries BC – soon appreciates that its authors were not content to blame disease upon heavenly malevolence. Plenty of pragmatic advice is retailed: how to deal with head wounds, treat an epileptic patient, resolve gynaecological problems, and so on. But much of the Corpus is pure observation. Factors of climate, demography, heredity, local ambience (including political régime), and seasonal weather-patterns are prominent areas of discussion. What a patient eats and drinks is studiously noted, likewise how a patient sweats and sleeps; and intense scrutiny is given over to the colour, texture, and odour of what the patient excretes. The Corpus includes an extensive sequence of case-studies, entitled *Epidemics*, of which the following brief and typically terse entry may give a general idea of the Hippocratic system (*Epidemics* 7.6).

> Sister of Harpalides, four or five months pregnant: swellings about the feet, as if water-filled. Circles of eyes also puffed up, and entire body swollen, symptoms similar to dropsy. Dry cough. Upright breathing [*orthopnoea*] only, asthmatic and choking occasionally while sat up in bed. Unable to lie prone; could only sleep propped up. Became almost without sensation. Foetus seemed motionless for a long while, as if dead in womb. Patient then improved. Breathing problems persisted for some two months, but patient took beans with honey, a honey-based linctus, and concoction of Ethiopian cumin in wine. Amelioration. Began to cough productively, bringing up a good deal of fused white phlegmatic matter. Normal respiration resumed. Gave birth to a baby girl.

Insofar as it has a happy ending, this is an unusual Hippocratic case-study. Otherwise the content and style of reportage is typical of the Hippocratic 'art': an impartial, open-minded, and thoroughly earnest effort to understand the causes and find the remedies of disease. It was underpinned by a pledge of vocation known as the 'Hippocratic Oath' (also preserved in the Hippocratic Corpus) – whose key ethical tenets inform Western medical practice to this day.

The archaeology of faith healing The Hippocratic Oath implies a binding, pseudo-familial fellowship among those doctors who signed up to its promises. The very existence and terms of the Oath imply suspicion of medical practitioners whose competence and scruples went unattested. Yet for all the rational intent of the Hippocratic method and its followers, no voices of atheism were raised. An element of 'believe and be healed' was always there. It is not clear how far the doctors of antiquity believed in what we would call the 'psychosomatic' factors of illness and recovery – the effect of a person's mentality upon his or her state of health. But rationalism in medicine evidently entailed no secular crisis. Even for Galen, the blessing of sound health remained an object of prayer to higher powers.

114 *Marble portrait of Hippocrates, after c. 300 BC. There were various 'schools' of medicine in Classical antiquity, sometimes rivals in the marketplace for patient care; but Hippocrates was unmatched in his reputation for devising a holistic approach to afflictions and disease.*

115, 116 *Examples of 'body-part' votives from the Gallo-Roman sanctuary of Sequana at the Sources of the Seine in France. In both cases, probably dedications made in hope of improved eyesight. Poor eyesight was only one of the maladies which Sequana was reputed to cure in the 1st and 2nd centuries AD; others apparently included paralysis, enlarged thyroid glands, and disorders of both male and female genitalia.*

We appreciate this soon enough from the accounts of how one cult figure in the Roman imperial province of Judaea drew large crowds not only because of his preaching, but by the fame of his remarkable healing gifts. Blindness, deafness, epilepsy, leprosy, and lameness were among the chronic conditions reported as cured by Jesus Christ, seemingly without recourse to any drugs or treatment whatsoever. (In common with Asklepios, his climactic feat was restoring a man presumed dead, Lazarus.) The local tradition that certain maladies were a form of possession by evil spirits would gloss these healing 'miracles' of Jesus as episodes of exorcism. Beyond Judaea, however, and before the 1st century AD, claims of healers with a curative touch were not unknown. One archaic Greek philosopher credited with such magical power was Pythagoras, whom we have already encountered as a guru of vegetarianism. A number of Roman emperors fostered the rumour of having a 'thaumaturgic' (wonder-working) presence. Not long after the time of Christ, an itinerant Greek sage called Apollonius, from Tyana in Cappadocia (modern Turkey), journeyed as far as India, gaining a reputation for clairvoyance and amazing acts of first aid: from his biography (by Philostratos), it is tempting to suppose that Apollonius absorbed from Central Asia the practices of faith-healing that would be subsequently characterized as 'Shamanism'.

The material remains of 'believe and be healed' survive from sites all around the Classical world, mostly in the form of objects dedicated *ex voto* ('out of prayer'). France, or the former Roman province of Gallia Transalpina ('Gaul Across-the-Alps'), is where one of the best-preserved ancient sites of votive healthcare has been excavated. This was the sanctuary of a Celtic goddess called Sequana. Sequana personified the River Seine, at whose wellsprings in Burgundy her cult was located; in a typical act of religious compromise, the Roman administrators of this area arranged a divine partnership, whereby the Celtic Sequana 'married' the Graeco-Roman Apollo, and indigenous worship continued in more or less its customary ways.

Devotees at Sequana's shrine evidently partook of the limpid waters rising there and channelled into drinking-fountains and basins for total immersion. Over several centuries, these visitors left behind them dedicatory offerings whose excavated total runs into thousands. A few were items of personal jewelry – gold rings, clasps, and suchlike. Some were statues or reliefs representing a pilgrim carrying a gift or tithe to Sequana. But most were images of isolated parts of the human frame, carved or cast, in wood, stone or bronze [115, 116]. Heads, eyes, arms, fingers, intestines, genitals, legs, feet – there is virtually no bodily component missing from this poignant depot of afflictions.

II HIGHER POWERS:GODS AND HEROES

117 *Marble statue of Tyche (Fortune) c. 100 BC. The Greek goddess became particularly important in the later Hellenistic world. As well as presiding over an individual's fate, she directed the destiny of a city – hence her 'city wall' crown.*

118 opposite *The Pantheon in Rome, as rebuilt by the Emperor Hadrian in c. AD 118–125 [cf. 180], was dedicated to 'all the gods' – an all-inclusive monument to a coherent Roman, and Greek, religious pantheon. At ground level, niches held statues of various deities. The zone above was adorned with porphyry pilasters and blind windows surrounded by patterns in marble veneer (in the 18th century they were replaced, but two bays – on the right, here – were later restored to the old design). The coffered concrete dome, with a central circular opening, was originally clad in gilded bronze, plundered in 655 by the Byzantine Emperor.*

HOW FAR the local priesthood at the Sources of the Seine (p. 75) practised what we would term 'pharmacy' is open to debate. Whatever medical treatment happened there, we can be sure that it was diligently accorded Sequana's divine sanction. Priests were on hand to dispense suggested courses of convalescence (and to relieve the faithful of their precious offerings), but it was a deity who presided over activities. This introduces an important aspect of ancient attitudes towards mortals and immortals: where the modern tendency is to segregate the 'religious' from the 'secular', in Classical antiquity religious rituals framed birth, death, and every aspect of private and public life in between.

PANTHEONS AND PAGANS

If we can be sure of one thing about Graeco-Roman religion, it is that it was a much messier affair than later writers, and many modern scholars, have often suggested. Certainly, the Classical world was tolerantly polytheistic: the worship of one divinity by no means excluded that of another. But we tend to conceive of a rather staunch Classical pantheon consisting of twelve Olympian deities (named after their supposed residence on Mount Olympus in Macedonia): Zeus, Hera, Athena, Apollo, Artemis, Poseidon, Aphrodite, Hermes, Hephaistos, Ares, Demeter, and Dionysos. We tend to think of these Greek deities as having straightforward Roman equivalents: Jupiter, Juno, Minerva, Apollo, Diana, Neptune, Venus, Mercury, Vulcan, Mars, Ceres, and Bacchus. And we tend to ascribe to each Greek and Roman god a handful of specific roles, to list divinities in pairs of specific associations – Zeus and supremacy, Hera and marriage, Athena and wisdom, Apollo and poetry, Artemis and hunting, Poseidon and the sea, Aphrodite and sex, Hermes and communication, Hephaistos and manual workmanship, Demeter and harvest, Dionysos and wine, and so on.

But such a static breakdown of Graeco-Roman polytheistic religion does less than justice both to the cohesiveness of the religious system and to the diversity of conceptions of the divine within Classical antiquity. The Greek goddess Hera, for example, might eventually have influenced Roman conceptions of 'Juno', but the two goddesses were not one and the same. While Etruscan gods came to be conceived in conjunction with Greek modes of representation, the Etruscan goddess Uni could be fluidly conflated not only with the Greek Hera and the Roman Juno, but also with the Phoenician goddess Astarte (a set of inscribed gold tablets from Pyrgi attest the connection in the 5th century BC). What is more, ancient polytheism could expand in all directions. It is difficult to reconcile the multitude of other ancient deities with a central Olympian group: Eros (Sexual Desire), Tyche (Fortune) and Nike (Victory), to name just a few examples, were not abstract notions, but personified divinities in their own right, with their own cults and schemes of visual portrayal [e.g. 117]. Add a selection of antiquity's many other divinities, such as Asklepios [106] (his attribute of the staff coiled with a snake is still used in pharmacies and clinics today), Hades (the word could refer to the god of the Underworld and to the Underworld itself), and Hekate (a goddess associated

119 *Bronze statuette of Athena Promachos ('First in Battle'), with inlaid silver eyes, c. 50 BC–AD 25. The figure was probably displayed in a Roman domestic shrine, but it evokes a statue type crafted by Pheidias in the second quarter of the 5th century BC: the original (and colossal) Athena Promachos was erected on the Athenian Acropolis and funded by Persian booty after the battle of Marathon. The goddess strides confidently forward; originally she brandished a spear in her right hand and a shield in her left. A vigilant griffin crouches on top of her helmet, and her scaly protective 'bib' (aegis) is adorned with the head of the Gorgon Medusa.*

with witchcraft); combine this with the Hellenized, and later Romanized, cults introduced from the Near East and Egypt, like those of Sarapis, Mithras, and Isis; include also the various cults of Hellenistic rulers and Roman emperors, not to mention Roman local spirits (Lares) that protected family and state, household gods (Penates), and the spirits of the dead (Manes); and it soon becomes almost impossible to sustain any single theological scheme for understanding the flexible, pluralistic, and divergent forms of Classical conceptions of the divine.

In antiquity, the nature of the gods was a question open to constant interrogation, debate, and negotiation. Greek and Roman authors had no problem satirizing their gods, laughing at their domestic quarrels on Mount Olympus, and characterizing their behaviour as unreasonable: immortals, after all, were not subject to the ethical rules governing human behaviour. Unlike many religions today, there was no sacred scripture that could give definitive answers to 'theological' questions. Herodotus (*Histories* 2.53.2) in the 5th century BC claimed that Homer had established the epithets and attributes of the Classical gods for posterity, but different philosophical schools attributed, and denied, to the gods different degrees of cosmic significance. That led Cicero, writing *On the Nature of the Gods* in around 45 BC, to open with the complaint: 'So diverse and contradictory are the opinions held even by the most learned scholars on this matter, that they constitute strong evidence that philosophy has its origin and root in ignorance' (1.1).

To complicate issues further, Classical cults were diverse not only in the number and types of their gods, but also in the variety of ideas with which any one deity could be associated. Each god might embody paradoxes and contradictions. The goddess Athena is an excellent example [119–22]. One of Athena's capacities was as guardian of Athens, a role enshrined in the Archaic wooden statue of her as Athena Polias on the Acropolis. While the Parthenon (that is to say the Temple of Athena Parthenos, or Athena the Virgin) is her most familiar temple today [482], it was only one among her many sanctuaries. Athena shared another with Hephaistos in Athens (both divinities were connected with craftsmanship); another was dedicated to Athena Nike ('the Victorious'); and yet another worshipped her as Athena Hygieia ('of Health'). Athena's multiform cultic identities went hand in hand with the way in which she bridged 5th-century Athenian ideas of gender. At the quadrennial festival in her honour, the Greater Panathenaia (see p. 40), her association with the feminine craft of weaving was celebrated with the presentation of a cloak woven by a number of selected Athenian adolescent women (*parthenoi*). The images on that cloak did not parade any feminine subject: instead, like the statue of Athena Parthenos in the Parthenon itself [122], they celebrated the goddess's mythical capacity for masculine warfare (the same association that was monumentalized in the statue of her as Athena Promachos on the Acropolis [119]). When we stop to think of antiquity's strict segregation of gender roles, this image of Athena as a warrior maiden, a contradictory hybrid of the masculine and feminine realms, should strike us as curious indeed. How should we even begin to make sense of it?

Since the 1950s or so, one way has been to adopt a 'Structuralist' approach. According to this anthropological method (championed by a French school rooted in the methodologies of Claude Lévi-Strauss) every aspect of a divinity must be studied at once. Instead of a single meaning, we look for a 'network of expressiveness' – a circle of stories, aspects, and rituals revolving around some core idea. According to one story, Athena was born asexually from the head of Zeus after he had swallowed Metis, or 'Cunning' [560]. Many Structuralist interpreters have combined this story (and others) with the various rituals and cults performed in

120 *Marble head of a statue of Athena, wearing her customary helmet with upturned visor, from Pergamon, second half of the 2nd century BC. Pergamon saw itself as the reincarnation of Classical Athens and therefore treated the city's eponymous deity with special reverence.*

121 *Athena and Herakles on an Attic black-figure cup by Nikosthenes, c. 530 BC. Athena wears a helmet and wreath; Herakles, behind, is dressed in a lionskin and holds a club.*

122 *above right Reconstruction of the lost chryselephantine (gold and ivory) cult statue of Athena Parthenos by Pheidias erected in the Parthenon on the Acropolis in Athens c. 440 BC. Our knowledge of this huge statue (some 12 metres/ 40 feet tall) stems from later marble copies and a description in Pausanias' Guide to Greece (1.24.5–7). Athena, the paradoxically female patron of a deeply patriarchal city, is presented as a masculine warrior, wearing a helmet, equipped with a spear and shield, and holding a Nike, or Victory. But as the prototypical Athenian 'Virgin', she wears the modest garb of the citizen's wife, the Doric peplos. Three related myths (the battles between the Greeks and Amazons, giants and gods, and Lapiths and Centaurs) were depicted on her shield and sandals, and the story of Pandora appeared on the base of the statue.*

Athena's honour, and have seen this *metis* aspect as a central key for unlocking all of the goddess's various cultic roles. Athena, they conclude, embodied cunning craftwork, cunning warfare, and cunning tricks, making her a popular choice of protectress for all manner of heroes, from Odysseus to Herakles [121, 140]. Of course, that sort of approach works better for some deities than for others. But its weakness lies in the reduction of dynamic and indefinable entities to a sort of formula: there is usually no straightforward way of codifying a Classical deity's complex characteristics and meanings, nor of reconciling Classical myths about their gods (themselves as much exploratory as explanatory) with religious cults. If there was a central core idea that encompassed the totality of a deity, it was never stable: it was prone to change according to time and place, and also to cultic occasion.

Eager to probe beyond such chronological and geographical diversities, other scholars have returned to an earlier way of making sense of Classical divinities:

For Pliny the Younger, in his official capacity as governor in northern Asia Minor in AD 110, Christianity constituted a civic offence (crimen) and a fault worthy of punishment (culpa). Pejoratively dismissed as a 'superstition', even an insanity (amentia), Christianity was proving an administrative headache: its inflexible, intolerant, and self-defining belief in a single god and human saviour, in addition to its antisocial refusal to take part in communal Roman cults, threatened to undermine the social hierarchies and cultural fabric of the imperium Romanum (not least the political supremacy of the emperor). It required a prompt, authoritative, and final solution, as Pliny reports to the Emperor Trajan:

I have pursued the following policy towards those denounced to me as 'Christian'. I interrogated them as to whether or not they were Christians. If they confessed to it, I asked them a second time, and then a third, threatening them with a penalty. If they persevered, I ordered their execution, since, whatever their story, I have no doubt that their persistence and inflexible obstinacy should certainly be punished . . . As for those who denied that they were, or had been, Christians, I thought it right to discharge those who invoked the gods after me, paid homage to your image (which I had ordered to be brought to me for this purpose, along with images of the gods) with incense and wine, and cursed Christ. It is said that true Christians cannot be coerced into performing any of those actions . . . While the spread of this superstition has infected the cities, villages and even rural plains, it seems possible to suppress and cure it.

Pliny the Younger, *Letters* 10.96

The Emperor replied, applauding the governor's action: Christians who became supplicants before 'our gods' (diis nostri) should be pardoned. In other words, the explosive threat of otherness which early Christianity posed to contemporary religious practice could be defused by two actions: first, through re-subscribing to communal Imperial Roman cults; and second, by acknowledging the intrinsic sacredness of the cultic image.

scrutinizing the origins of each god and goddess, searching for an archaeology of cult in Greek prehistory, and looking to the Near East for sources and parallels. This is no easy task, and it has the obvious flaw of presupposing that Classical cults developed in a linear manner. Still, the Bronze Age remains of 'Minoan' Crete (so called after its legendary ruler, King Minos) and 'Mycenaean' Greece (Mycenae was the most powerful of a number of civic strongholds on the Greek mainland in the 2nd millennium BC [198–200]) have sometimes yielded some clues about the earlier histories of later religious symbols, myths, and rituals. When Michael Ventris deciphered the Mycenaean writing system known as 'Linear B' in 1952, it was with great excitement that scholars perceived deities like 'a-ta-na po-ti-ni-ja' as anticipating Athena, or 'po-se-da' as Poseidon.

Following the precedent set by Max Müller in the 19th century, other scholars have probed prehistory further in their search for an 'Ur-religion' – an ultimate set of cults from which all Classical (and many other) religious ideas supposedly descended. Again, the search has been dominated by etymological analysis: the linguistic relationship between the Greek 'Zeus', the Indic 'Dyaus pitar' and the Roman 'Diespiter' or 'Jupiter', to give one example. Linguistics aside, we should note that the ongoing debate between those who support an 'Aryan' model and those who argue for an 'Afro-Asian' origin of ancient Mediterranean gods channels into a much larger controversy, most famously fuelled by Martin Bernal's *Black Athena: The Afroasiatic Roots of Classical Civilization* (1987). Bernal's comments on the Eastern origins of Greek and Roman gods form part of his larger conspiracy theory – that from the early 19th century onwards, Eurocentric scholars have dramatically underrated the influence of non-European cultures on the formation of the 'Classical' world.

A floating and flexible pantheon, a diverse and shifting characterization of the gods, and a hazy and controversial set of origins: ancient cults seem set to frustrate modern analysis. It remains very difficult to find a way of entering the study of Classical pantheons without simultaneously compromising their rich (almost chaotic yet somehow coherent) complexity. For us, the concept of religion entails a set of personal beliefs and creeds in which a divinity has pride of place; it is something that we think, feel, and live out. In the Classical world, however, religion was generally much less a theology or metaphysical faith than a set of practices – practices that were instituted on a public as often as on a personal level.

There is, however, a more positive side to interpreting the pluralistic nature of Graeco-Roman cults. The way in which Classical religions constantly incorporated, assimilated, and engulfed different gods itself testifies to the inherent flexibility of ancient polytheism. The gods could be many things to many people. The 5th-century Athenian philosopher Socrates – at least, as Plato characterized him – showed little unease in reconciling his own theories of a 'divine spirit' (*daimonion*) with contemporary concepts of the divine. The 1st-century BC Latin philosopher-poet Lucretius could likewise expound a philosophy of rational enquiry that did not encroach on the existence of the gods or reject religious worship outright. Alternatively, deities might be interpreted allegorically, as personifications of broader truths: this was how a number of early Christian writers justified clinging on to the cultic myths that had been fundamental to Classical art and literature, but the idea was also rife hundreds of years earlier (the allegorization of mythical figures is ridiculed, for example, in Plato's *Phaedrus* 229e).

Graeco-Roman religious practice, as Herodotus recognized, served as a means of affirming group solidarity. A shared reverence for the temples and trappings of the gods, a shared duty of avenging any dishonour to those gods, and a shared

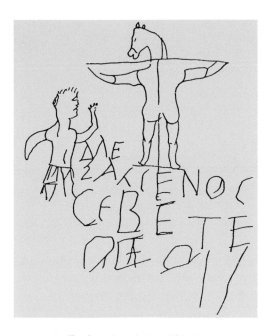

123 *Graffito from the Palatine Hill in Rome, late 1st–early 3rd century AD, showing a man worshipping an ass-headed figure suspended on a crucifix (seen from behind). The Greek inscription apparently reads 'Alexamenos worships god'. If, as seems likely, the graffito parodies the story of Christ's crucifixion – ridiculing the very basis of Christian cultic devotion – it is one of the earliest testimonies to the disjunction between ancient polytheism and Christian beliefs.*

124 *An Eastern sanctuary to the Egyptian mother goddess Isis, depicted in a wall-painting from Herculaneum, third quarter of the 1st century AD. Note the exotic palm trees and sphinxes in the background, and the African flute-player and ibises (Isis's sacred birds) in the foreground. A priest, dressed in typical long white robes and with shaven head, stands at the top of the stairway of the temple, displaying the sacred vessel of water from the Nile. On the right, another priest shakes the musical instrument associated with Isis, the sistrum; on the left a masked priest performs a sacred dance. A fourth priest attends the altar in the foreground. In the centre a man conducts a choir of initiates who stand on either side of him.*

The cult of Isis became especially important between the 1st and late 2nd centuries AD, promising its followers a new sort of individual salvation. Its popularity is reflected in the 2nd-century novel by Apuleius, the Metamorphoses *(more commonly known as* The Golden Ass*): 'you shall live blessed in this world,' the goddess promises the novel's protagonist, Lucius; 'and when your allocated span of life is completed and you descend to the Underworld . . . you shall perpetually worship me as one who has been favourable to you' (11.6).*

practice of sacrificing to them, Herodotus implies, were central to Greek definitions of 'Greekness' (*Histories* 8.144.2). Within the increasingly, and perhaps menacingly, cosmopolitan world of the expanded Hellenistic period, religious practice became an even more explicit way of exerting a collectively Greek character. Take the case of the kingdom of Alexandria, the new Greek colony founded in the late 4th century BC on the alien shores of Egypt. Egyptian gods were worshipped alongside Greek deities and increasingly influenced Alexandrians' notions of their inherited Greek pantheon; but when the Alexandrian-Greek poet-cum-scholar Callimachus wrote about the gods in his *Hymns* (in the 3rd century BC) he completely expunged those Egyptianizing influences, and stressed a more staunchly Hellenocentric tradition of Greek religion, closely bound to the literary texts of Archaic Greece. It may have been considerations like these that motivated Pausanias, a Greek in the Roman Empire, to embark on a nostalgic tour around the sanctuaries and cultic relics of Greece in the 2nd century AD (see p. 186): for Pausanias in Roman Greece, as for Callimachus in Greek Alexandria, religious cults constituted a key means of negotiating and affirming cultural identity.

Pausanias was writing at a time when a number of different cults and expanded 'mystery' religions – each with its own initiations, priest-conducted ceremonies, and offers of salvation – competed in their promises of providing the ultimate communal and individual spiritual experience within a fragmented Roman Empire. In that period (which has come to be called the Second Sophistic, approximately late 1st–mid-3rd centuries AD) aggressive cultic rivalry was accompanied by a degree of religious syncretism: different cults 'borrowed' aspects from rival cults, fusing what was distinctive about their own rites with the characteristic stories and iconographies of their competitors. The ultimate winner in that competition would eventually be Christianity (sanctioned within the Roman Empire by the Emperor Constantine after the Edict of Milan in AD 313), a cult that was quick to damn practitioners of rival sects as 'pagans'. But initially the subversive religion that grew up around Jesus, an itinerant preacher in Judaea, was only one of many cults that preached a message of personal redemption, and it was prey to misunderstanding and ridicule [123]. Much more popular, in the 1st–2nd centuries at least, was the cult of Isis [124].

For later Christian writers, the relationship between Christianity and the Graeco-Roman cults that preceded it could be painted in starkly contrasting colours: it is a narrative of persecution (begun by Nero, who blamed the sect for the great fire in Rome of AD 64), and survival against the odds. In chapter 40 of the *Apology*, composed at the end of the 2nd century AD, the North African Christian writer Tertullian complains that Christians had become the scapegoat for every sort of human misfortune: 'if the Tiber rises to the walls of Rome, or the Nile fails to rise to the fields, or if the sky stands still without rain, or if the earth moves, or if there is famine, or plague, the cry is immediate – "Christians to the lions!"' Rome's ideological clash with Christianity in fact only served to fan the sect's theological flame, strengthening its sense of communal identity and furnishing local churches with saints and martyrs – literally 'witnesses' to the faith – who followed the message of the Christian Gospels and 'turned the other cheek' (Luke 6.22).

IMAGINING AND IMAGING THE DIVINE

The urge to represent higher powers in visual form was perhaps the single most unifying aspect of Graeco-Roman cults. It is often an unnerving fact that the majority of ancient objects familiar to us today originally had particular, and all too often overlooked, cultic contexts. Even one of antiquity's most famous icons, the naked Aphrodite, ultimately stems from a cult image of the goddess by Praxiteles installed in the 4th century BC at her sanctuary in Knidos [82, 83]. The qualities of an artefact, too – qualities which might constitute for us mere classifications of size or medium – were usually not without cultic importance. One general rule seems to have been that the bigger and finer the image of the god – like the colossal 5th-century BC statues of Zeus at Olympia [126] and Athena Parthenos in Athens [122], both chryselephantine (made of gold and ivory [cf. 258]) and created by the sculptor Pheidias – the more effectively it embodied the deity. There was an enduring sense that visual representations of the gods were the gods themselves: images had an intrinsic force and a divine power; they could actually *do* things (pp. 286–89). In book 6 of the *Iliad*, a statue of Athena is described as moving (she physically nods, denying Trojan supplications). Pausanias (who, like many other ancients, often called images by the name of the deity itself, without any mediating term like 'statue', 'painting', 'image', etc.) has many stories to tell about how statues of deities actively intervened in human life. And a number of Classical writers bear witness to the practice of chaining down statues to prevent them from running off. Images, in short, were powerful things. That intrinsic power made them one of the best means of imagining, negotiating, and experiencing the power of the gods.

Herodotus thought it very odd that the Persians had no need for statuary, temples, or altars, 'for they do not believe that the gods share the same nature with men, as we Greeks imagine' (*Histories* 1.131.1). As Herodotus implies, the drive to depict the gods was closely bound up with their anthropomorphic (literally, formed 'in human shape') conceptualization. In Homer's epic poetry, the gods act, speak, and look like humans; in Athenian drama (especially the tragedies of Euripides), they could appear on stage to set a scene or give divine guidance; and they

125 *Fragment of a Buddhist schist relief from Gandhara, 1st century AD. According to Apollonius of Tyana, who travelled to India in the 1st century AD (as recorded by the 2nd-century AD writer Philostratos: see p. 75), Greek anthropomorphism was something to be highly applauded. He also approved of local cults in India which, he claimed, styled their gods in the Greek mode. Apollonius' claim is perhaps corroborated by this fragment from the Gandhara region of the Indian subcontinent (reached by Alexander the Great c. 327 BC): Vajrapani, the guardian of the Buddha, is decked out in a lionskin like the Greek Herakles, and holds a thunderbolt, evoking Greek representations of Zeus.*

126 *Reconstruction of the colossal chryselephantine statue of Zeus by Pheidias in the Temple of Zeus at Olympia, c. 435 BC. The figure (some 14 metres/ 45 feet high) sits wearing a mantle and olive wreath, holding a winged Victory in his right hand and in his left an eagle-crowned sceptre. The shallow pool, made of dark limestone and filled with olive oil, reflected light onto the cult statue and ensured that its ivory remained soft. This reconstruction is based partly on numismatic evidence and other later depictions, and partly on literary descriptions of the statue (e.g. Pausanias,* Guide to Greece *5.11). Those literary accounts stressed the statue's capacity for animation, suggesting that it might suddenly stir, nod, or even rise up. The 1st-century BC geographer Strabo went so far as to express his concern that 'if Zeus were to stand up straight, he would unroof the temple' (Geography 8.3.30).*

recurrently figure alongside humans on pots, relief sculptures, and free-standing statues throughout the ancient Mediterranean (and even as far away as parts of the Indian subcontinent, where a handful of images have been taken as proof of the influence of Greek iconographic schemes on representations of local gods [125]). For some scholars, Greek anthropomorphism even provides an explanation for the rise of naturalistic artistic styles in late 6th- and early 5th-century Athens: in a social context where the gods were imagined in human form, and where images of those gods were required for all manner of different cultic rituals, there must have been a competitive drive to craft increasingly lifelike images of them.

Reputedly, not all ancients approved of anthropomorphism. One 6th-century BC philosopher, Xenophanes, regarded Homer's humanizing of the divine as ridiculous. All races, he sceptically points out, make their gods in their own image, including all that is 'shameful and blameworthy' in mankind. The Ethiopians say that their gods are black and snub-nosed; the blue-eyed and ginger-haired Thracians claim that their gods have blue eyes and ginger hair; so if horses had gods, they would draw them with four legs, cattle in the shape of cattle, and so on.

'Reputedly' is an important qualifier here. Xenophanes' sentiment is in fact preserved in the writings of a 2nd-century AD Christian intellectual, Clement of Alexandria (in his *Exhortation to the Greeks*, chapter 4). Although a similar

Ephesus, on the western coast of Asia Minor, had a long history as a sanctuary to a Mother Goddess who later became associated with Artemis: its cult centered around the famous wooden image of the Ephesian Artemis which had reputedly fallen from the heavens. The reproduction of that image [127] furnished Ephesian craftsmen with a profitable trade, which was threatened when St Paul, probably between AD 54 and 56, preached the alternative message of Christianity.

Now at that time there arose a great disturbance about the Way of the Lord. For there was a certain silversmith, named Demetrios, who made silver shrines for Artemis and provided considerable income for the craftsmen. He gathered together the craftsmen, along with workmen in other trades, and spoke as follows: 'Gentlemen, you know that our prosperity depends upon this, our business. And you see and hear, too, how this man, Paul, has converted and misguided a large crowd of people – not only from Ephesus but also from all of Asia. He says that gods made by human hands are not gods at all! We are in danger, then, not only of our trade falling into disrepute, but also of the temple of the great goddess Artemis being discredited; furthermore, we risk that the goddess herself will be robbed of her divine majesty – the majesty which the whole of Asia, and the world, reveres!'

Acts of the Apostles 19.23–27

Faced with their fury, Paul was forced to flee the city. But although the craftsmen won the battle, they did not win the war: Ephesus, claiming to be the site of St John's tomb, eventually became a site of Christian, rather than Artemisian, pilgrimage.

127 *Marble copy of the statue of Artemis worshipped at Ephesus, 2nd century BC. The globules on her chest – most probably breasts, but alternatively identified as eggs or bulls' scrota – evoked the exotic goddess's super-fertility.*

sentiment was attributed to the 6th-century Ionian philosopher Heraclitus, such unorthodoxy seems only to have characterized an eccentric intellectual fringe. But for Clement, Xenophanes' concept of the divine was satisfyingly akin to the Christian: according to one fragment (fr. 23), Xenophanes even postulated a single great deity, 'supreme among gods and men, unlike mortals in body or in mind'. And for Clement, as for most early Christian writers, the question of the cultic role of the statue – of how, if at all, Christianity could be squared with the pagan tradition of imagining the divine both anthropomorphically and through images – was at the forefront of theological debate.

The battle that Christianity came to wage upon pagan cults eventually centered precisely around these issues of the cult image. From the outset, Christianity was a religion of the 'word' (*logos*) rather than the image (*eikon*). The 'New Testament' was not just the means by which Christianity triumphed in its diffusion of its 'Good News' (or 'Gospel') across the Mediterranean world; it was an ideology of written Revelation ('in the beginning was the Word, and the Word was made flesh', as the evangelist John has it). While images served to make Christian myths and messages known, they would be reduced to the role of illustrations, subservient to a fixed, indelibly inscribed, textual reference-point. Today, the sabotaged Classical cult statue, with its mysterious pagan power defused by a cross chiselled on the forehead, may be seen all around the Mediterranean. One way of undermining the credibility of a pagan religious cult, as early Christians realized, was to undermine the power attributed to its cult image. If pagan images could not be stripped of their associated divine power, they could, at least, be 'baptised'.

But was Christianity really so fundamentally different from the cults that initially existed alongside it? Certainly, there were a number of crucial differences: not least Christianity's intolerance of other cults, adherence to a sacred scripture, and all-important emphasis on personal redemption. And we should, of course, be wary of thinking of too uniform an early Christian community. In terms of visual imagery, however, early Christians do not seem to have been at all adverse to appropriating 'pagan' iconographic schemes [128]. As Jás Elsner has demonstrated, Christian imagery emerged from the 2nd century AD out of a multi-cultic and multicultural melting-pot of inherited visual languages. In terms of iconographic forms, the images with which early Christians surrounded themselves differed little from those used in other Greek and Roman cults: what changed was the new variety of ways in which those images could be interpreted.

128 *Detail of the sarcophagus of Junius Bassus, AD 359. On the upper tier are scenes of the arrest of St Peter, Christ enthroned between SS. Peter and Paul, and Christ brought before Pilate; below are Adam and Eve in the Garden of Eden, Christ's entry into Jerusalem on Palm Sunday, and Daniel in the lions' den. The two central scenes of Christ triumphant clearly adopt Classical iconographic schemes. The depiction of Christ enthroned, complete with a personification of the heavens at his feet, is a Christian adaptation of the Roman imperial donatio motif, as though Christ were an emperor handing out gifts to his conquered peoples. The entry into Jerusalem takes up the triumphant adventus ('arrival') motif [cf. 314], although Christ rides a humble donkey rather than a horse.*

129 *Wall-painting depicting St Paul (whose bald head and pointed beard cast him as a sort of Greek philosopher), in the Catacomb of Praetextius outside the walls of Rome, 3rd century AD. Because of their belief in literal resurrection, Roman Christians in the 2nd–5th centuries AD chose to bury rather than cremate their dead, constructing elaborate underworlds, later called catacombs, outside the walls. At around the same time, the tombs of early Christian saints and martyrs came to be regarded as sacred, just as the tombs of Greek heroes had been venerated.*

HEROIC INTERMEDIARIES

While the issue of representing Christ was subject to complex theological debate, early depictions of the paradigmatic lives of Christian saints and martyrs were less controversial [129]: though in closer harmony with the divine, saints did, after all, occupy an indisputably human sphere; and images of them could purportedly inspire viewers to emulate their virtues. That mediating role of Christian saints, as well the way in which their relics were piously venerated, provides one of the best examples of Christianity's adoption and adaption of Graeco-Roman religious practice. For the notion of the Christian saint was rooted in one of the most endemic elements of ancient religion: the hero.

The definition of the Classical hero was inherently flexible. The term was not reserved for the warriors whose glory came to be universally renowned in epic poetry: any powerful mortal who was seen to have transcended the limits of human achievement seems to have been eligible for appropriate acknowledgment, tomb-worship, and propitiation. The hero occupied the middle ground between the realms of gods and men: heroes were at once human and superhuman. While so much of Graeco-Roman cultic practice seems to have been concerned with defining and bridging the gulf between the human and divine sphere, heroes offered a particular paradigm of interaction.

Perhaps the most influential model for negotiating the gap between common men and heroes was articulated in the *Works and Days*, a poem attributed to Hesiod – one of antiquity's earliest, most important, yet most enigmatic poets, writing in the early 7th century BC. In Hesiod's 'golden' age, humans existed in perfect harmony with the gods: 'they lived like gods without grief in their hearts, without toil and sorrow; wretched old age did not rest upon them, but with ageless hands and legs they delighted in banqueting and were beyond the reach of all evils' (lines 112–15).

There followed a 'silver' age – an age of simpletons who forgot to sacrifice to the gods and were punished by Zeus accordingly. In the third, 'bronze', age, the race of man destroyed itself through its eagerness for war. The fourth age, however, was in every way more noble: it was characterized by its 'god-like race of hero-men who are called demi-gods' and who fought at Thebes and Troy. An unbridgeable distance separated them from today's mortals, 'for now, indeed, is a race of iron, and men never cease from labour and grief by day, and from death by night, and the gods will continue to bestow troublesome cares upon them' (lines 176–78).

When was the heroic age? Homer certainly puts it in the past. When the doughty Hector picks up a gigantic rock and tosses it across the Trojan plain, the rock's size is quantified with a brief aside to the world in which the poem was composed: 'nowadays two of the best men of the people could scarcely have heaved it from the ground onto a wagon' (*Iliad* 12.447–48). That fourth, heroic, generation, in contrast to the fifth, was quite literally larger than life. It was an age of supermen.

It seems likely that the composition of Homeric poetry (pp. 110–11) was itself the product of a new obsession with heroic ethos. In book 12, the poet of the *Iliad* actually allows the character of Sarpedon to forecast, rather self-consciously, his own heroization back in Lycia after his glorious death in battle. There can be little doubt that many of the heroes named and described in epic poetry had already received special cultic attention throughout the Mediterranean world, with different city-states laying claim to different heroic ancestors. It also seems likely that the discovery of the tombs and relics of the heroes of that bygone age acted as a catalyst for the process.

Heroes who had not received their due of honour and sacrifice could express their displeasure by terrorizing an individual or community, almost in the manner, we might say, of a poltergeist; by contrast, heroes who had been appeased could come to the aid of a community, so that Theseus was said to have miraculously fought for the Athenians at the battle of Marathon in 490 BC. Heroes were the 'powerful dead', chthonian (literally 'earthy') beings whose worship was centred around their supposed tomb (*heroön*); although usually associated with the realm of the dead, they might intervene, for better or worse, like the gods, in human affairs.

There is no such thing as a 'typical' Classical hero. Different communities furnished different heroes with different degrees of honour, reverence, and

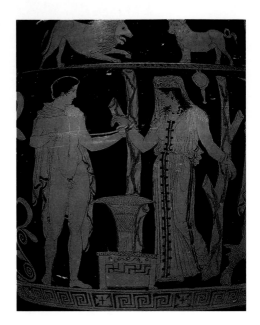

130, 131 *One of Perseus' exploits involved rescuing the princess Andromeda, who was the daughter of Kepheus, King of Ethiopia, and his wife, Kassiopeia. Kassiopeia had boasted that her daughter was more beautiful than the Nereids (sea nymphs), and in punishment Poseidon sent a monster to ravage Ethiopia. It could be appeased, Kepheus learnt, only by the sacrifice of his daughter. But Perseus intervened at the crucial moment . . .*

Above, Andromeda is prepared for sacrifice: she stands beside a wool-basket and chest, the typical attributes of the good wife (see pp. 212–14). Detail of an Apulian red-figure volute krater attributed to the Sisyphus Group, c. 410–400 BC.

Right, Perseus wrestles with the monster: he wears winged sandals and a winged hat, and Eros kneels on the monster's back, reminding us of the hero's motivation. Detail of an Apulian red-figure loutrophoros *(literally a 'bath-bringer', used to carry the water in which a bride bathed before her wedding, and also as a grave-marker) attributed to the Metope Group, c. 340–330 BC.*

132 top left *The Gorgon Medusa, from the western pediment of the Temple of Artemis at Corcyra (modern Corfu), c. 600–580 BC. Her eyes bulge, her tongue protrudes, and snakes dangle from her head and clasp her waist. The small figure to the right is Chrysaor [cf. 134].*

133 top right *Medusa fleeing before Perseus, depicted on an Attic black-figure kyathos (a cup with a single vertical handle) attributed to the Theseus Painter, c. 510 BC.*

134 above left *The decapitated Medusa (right) with one of her Gorgon sisters; the mythical creatures Pegasus and Chrysaor are emerging from Medusa's neck in the form of winged horses. Detail of a Pontic black-figure amphora attributed to the Tityos Painter, 530–510 BC.*

135 above right *Perseus holding Medusa's head. Roman sardonyx cameo, c. 25 BC–AD 25.*

importance, and even cultivated different stories about the same heroic figure. Still, some heroes are more typical than others. For instance, Perseus (whose exploits were among the most popular themes of painted pottery from the 7th century BC), like most heroes, was credited with divine ancestry, born from the union of immortal Zeus and mortal Danae. His heroism was to the benefit of mankind: armed with a cap for invisibility, winged shoes in which to flee, a sickle to decapitate the beast, and a bag in which to carry away her head, Perseus beheaded the Gorgon Medusa, who turned all that looked upon her into stone [132–35, 569]. As with many other mythical heroes, Perseus' exploits included a love interest and the rescue of a damsel in distress – in his case Andromeda, who was to be sacrificed as a peace-offering to a sea-monster [130, 131]. The heroic feat of Perseus' decapitation of Medusa, as taken up in the visual arts, framed all manner of rituals, be they funerary [207] or associated with the Greek symposium. And artists' attempts to articulate the monstrosity of Medusa and her Gorgon sisters ever more effectively should be understood as partly motivated by a drive to evoke the magnitude of Perseus' feat ever more heroically.

136 *Herakles' first Labour, wrestling with the Lion from Nemea. Detail of an Attic black-figure kylix attributed to the Phrynos Painter, c. 550 BC.*

137 *Herakles' second Labour: helped by his nephew Iolaos, he slays the Hydra of Lerna near Argos, who had multiple heads that re-grew whenever one was cut off. Detail of a black-figure hydria attributed to the Eagle Painter, c. 525 BC.*

138 *Herakles' third Labour, ridding Arcadia of the Erymanthian Boar, depicted on an Attic black-figure amphora attributed to the Leagros Group, c. 510 BC. Athena stands on the left. Eurystheus, King of Tiryns, who had imposed the Labours on the hero, cowers in a giant storage jar below the huge beast.*

One hero, more than any other, did receive universal acclaim: Herakles (Herkle in the Etruscan tradition, Hercules in the Roman). As stories of his feats proliferated and expanded, Herakles became the most god-like hero of them all, presiding over the physical training and general education of the young (young men, that is) who might aspire to follow his example. Invocations, cults, and literary texts endowed him with Olympian honours; and images explored the deeds that manifested his godliness [136–40]. Herakles' wide acclaim made him an important emblem at the Panhellenic athletic sanctuary at Olympia, where sculpted metopes of his twelve heroic feats (*athloi*, or labours) adorned the Temple of Zeus [140]. Those Labours contributed to the universality of his heroism, leading him all over the known world (including most of the regions from which athletic competitors had travelled) – the Peloponnese, Thrace, Crete, Italy, the Hesperides, and even the most universally human land of all, Hades, the realm of the dead. While Christian saints might have been heroic in the Classical sense, we should note that Classical heroes were by no means saintly in the Christian meaning of the word: their behaviour could encompass a whole spectrum of moral values, not all of which were to be applauded. Herakles proved no exception: according to one set of myths, he was so angered at Apollo's refusal to grant him an oracle after his treacherous murder of a figure called Iphitos that he stole the god's tripod from his sanctuary at Delphi [cf. 557]. That was a gross impiety to be expiated only by a sentence of three years in slavery: even Herakles, we mere mortals should be encouraged to learn, was prone to err.

Visually, Herakles could be depicted in a variety of ways: he could be a bulky muscular figure, following a lost statue-type by Lysippos made in the second half

139 opposite *Herakles' tenth Labour, to confront the three-bodied giant Geryon and steal his cattle, depicted on an Attic black-figure amphora attributed to the Painter of Berlin 1686, c. 540 BC. The eagle flying towards Herakles foretells his victory.*

140 right *Herakles' eleventh Labour, on a marble metope from the Temple of Zeus at Olympia [47], c. 460 BC. Herakles had been ordered to fetch the golden apples of the Hesperides. In one version of the story he goes there himself. In another, he persuades the Titan Atlas, who holds the heavens on his shoulders, to perform the errand, and, until Atlas' return with the apples – the scene depicted here – the hero relieves him of his burden. Athena, on the left, lends Herakles her customary help.*

141 *Herakles, with lion skin and club flung over his shoulder, rests from his Labours for a moment to urinate. The subject was chosen for an engraved gem, 2nd century AD.*

of the 4th century BC, of which over eighty reproductions are known [142], a slender youth, his head draped with a lion skin [143], or the sort of Hellenic beauty so beloved by the Emperor Hadrian [144].

Attitudes towards Herakles' heroism could be just as varied. Certainly, he exercised his supremacy over all manner of beasts and ghouls – be they lions, Centaurs, cattle, birds, horses, or untamed Amazons – but his conduct was not immune to criticism (or to comic deflation [141]): one story, for instance, has the hero slaughter his wife, Megara, and children in a fit of madness. Images of Herakles often raised ethical questions. On an Attic amphora dating to around 510 BC, Herakles' Labour of the Erymanthian Boar [138] is juxtaposed with a scene, on the other side of the vase, depicting a hoplite's valiant departure for war. Are we to make an association between parallel acts of heroism – one set in heroic times, the other within the contemporary world? If so, another Attic amphora, of around 540 BC, perhaps prompts a very different kind of reading [139]. Herakles sports two of his trademarks, the skin of the Nemean Lion and a club (his customary primitive weapon). The subject of his attack is ostensibly Geryon, a three-bodied outlandish ogre. But Geryon, with his three pairs of legs and three heads, is here depicted as three armed hoplites: far from piously exalting Herakles' feat, this image might then seem to problematize his heroism, presenting it as potentially incongruous with contemporary Athenian values. What is more, the tripod emblazoned on one of their shields reminds us of Herakles' transgression against Apollo at Delphi. Worthy as Herakles might be, within the world of this amphora's production his brute heroism was not without its problems.

142 above *Bronze statuette of Herakles with inlaid silver eyes, c. AD 40–70. This follows the type known as the* Weary Herakles *or* Farnese Hercules, *a colossal statue created by Lysippos in the second half of the 4th century BC.*

143 above, centre *Etruscan bronze statuette of Herkle, late 4th–early 3rd century BC.*

144 above, far right *Marble statue of Herakles known as the* Lansdowne Hercules, *from the villa of Hadrian at Tivoli, c. AD 125.*

145 opposite *Marble bust of Commodus as Herakles, from the Esquiline Hill in Rome, c. AD 190. The Emperor is depicted complete with club and lion skin, holding the apples of the Hesperides [cf. 140] in his left hand. Below, next to cornucopias and signs of the zodiac, kneels a subjected Amazon: she refers both to Herakles' ninth Labour (when he collected the girdle of Hippolyta, the Amazon Queen) and to Commodus' imperial conquests of barbarian tribes.*

The constant interrogation of Herakles' heroism did not prevent powerful rulers from adopting him as their *alter ego*. In political terms, the ambiguous category of the hero was particularly useful for staking a claim to superhuman power while allowing for some degree (albeit a fudged one) of distinction between man and god. Thus Alexander the Great, like other Macedonian kings before him, could validate his claim to rule by boasting descent from Herakles. By the time of Commodus' rule in Rome (AD 180–192), the boundaries between hero and ruler had become so blurred that it is hard to know whether the Emperor is posing in the guise of Herakles or Herakles in the guise of Commodus [145].

The 4th century BC saw a major change in ancient delineations of the hero. By the early part of the century, heroes were no longer necessarily figures from the mythological past: instead, heroic status was slowly opened up to incorporate the newly deceased. This shift, of course, was not an entirely new development – at least, not in Athens. Although there is little interpretative consensus about the Temple of Athena Nike, of the late 420s, its frieze does seem to commemorate a recent Athenian military victory in heroic mode; one interpretation of the still more controversial Parthenon frieze [488], carved some time around 440 BC, reads it as depicting heroized Athenians who had fought at Marathon half a century before. Even earlier in the 5th century, there had arisen a sort of hero-cult of Athenian democracy's personal 'tyrannicidal' heroes, Harmodios and Aristogeiton (pp. 172–74). One way or another, though, the traditional category of the hero expanded dramatically in the 4th century. And one medium more than any other seems to have affected that change: funerary monuments.

146 *Marble grave stele found in the River Ilissos, Athens, third quarter of the 4th century BC. The deceased stands in relaxed heroic nudity; an old man (his father?) gazes pensively towards him, a dog sniffs the ground where its master once trod, and a hunched young boy (a slave?) despairs at his feet.*

147 *Reconstruction of the Mausoleum at Halicarnassus, built in the mid-4th century BC. Mausolus was* satrap *(governor on behalf of the Persians) in Caria; he chose Halicarnassus as his capital, adorned it with monuments, and seems to have been worshipped there after his death in 353 as its founding hero* (oikistes). *His grand sepulchre, attributed to the Ionian architect Pythios and crafted by Greek artists, combined Greek architectural styles and subjects (such as the Ionic colonnade, and friezes depicting Amazons fighting Greeks and Centaurs fighting Lapiths) with Eastern elements (including the high podium and plinth, imitating Persian royal tombs, and the pyramidal roof which perhaps alluded to Egyptian precedents, so wonderingly described by Herodotus in the previous century).*

While the erection of such monuments was no new phenomenon either – at least not in Athens – the practice was dramatically renewed from the last quarter of the 5th century. Thousands of stelai survive from this period onwards, from all over the Greek world; the deceased were placated with sacrificial offerings – in many cases, the same sorts of offerings that older heroes had previously received at their tombs. But what interests us here is the way in which a grave stele could actually perform some sort of heroizing apotheosis of the deceased, making them, as it were, *super*human. Take one of the most famous of all, a monument found in the bed of the Ilissos at Athens [146] and dated to the third quarter of the 4th century BC. While we do not know the name of the individual commemorated, we can be certain that his pose and idealized nudity present him as no ordinary mortal: he is endowed with a sort of ancestral heroic presence. He stares out at us, as if asking us to aspire to his bulky 'Polykleitan' physique and to pay due respect by worshipping accordingly.

It was perhaps only a short step to a new kind of extravagantly heroizing sepulchre, most famously the mid-4th-century Mausoleum at Halicarnassus (modern Bodrum in Turkey) [147, 537]. Representations of Mausolus and his wife Artemisia adorned the base of the podium, and an elaborate charioteer group crowned the top. Below, excavations have revealed a vast deposit of bones of

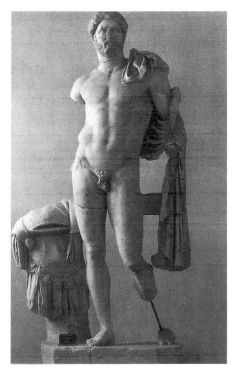

148 *Marble base of the column of the Emperor Antoninus Pius, erected after his death in AD 161 by Marcus Aurelius and Lucius Verus. Antoninus Pius – holding an eagle-crowned sceptre (like the Olympian Zeus [126]) – and his wife Faustina ascend to heaven on the wings of a genius, between two eagles (Zeus' sacred birds). A personification of Rome sits on the right below, and a personification of the Campus Martius (the area in Rome where the deceased emperor was ceremonially deified) reclines on the left, holding the obelisk that had been erected there by the Emperor Augustus.*

149 *Marble statue of Hadrian, from the Asklepieion at Pergamon, c. AD 130. The bearded Emperor stands in Classical Greek pose – that of Polykleitos' Doryphoros [37] – but with Roman military regalia at his side. An inscription confirms what his nudity suggests: this is 'the god Hadrian'. Following Augustus, Roman emperors seem to have been treated as living gods in the Eastern provinces; in the West, however, they were deified only after their deaths. So it was that Vespasian could declare from his deathbed in AD 79: 'alas, I think I am becoming a god' (Suetonius,* Life of Vespasian 23*).*

animals, whose sacrifice was presumably the focal point of Mausolus' funeral (true to the tradition of the very greatest Homeric heroes). The Mausoleum took its place among the Hellenistic Seven Wonders of the Ancient World, and inspired the Roman emperors Augustus and Hadrian to build their own rival 'mausolea'. Its use of a funerary monument to heroize, even deify, the deceased also came to be developed in a variety of ways. In Rome, columns bearing sculpted representations of the deeds of an emperor [314, 466, 469] and crowned with his image were one literal means of deification, as they projected the honorand into the heavens. When on the base of one such column Antoninus Pius was depicted ascending into heaven with his wife Faustina [148], a very real kind of apotheosis, from man to god, was being enacted upon his death.

By the time of Antoninus Pius, the deification of the emperor already had a lengthy history, going back at least as far as the deification of Julius Caesar (in 42 BC, after the appearance of the *Sidus Iulium*, or Julian comet, which was deemed to confirm his ascension to the heavens). Just as hero cults had served to foster a local civic identity, the cults of the emperor exerted a unifying force on the diverse cultic and cultural practices of the lands over which Rome held sway, enshrining the city and its political leader as the ultimate referent within the Empire (which explains why the Christian refusal to recognize the emperor's divinity was so menacing in the 2nd and 3rd centuries: see p. 80). With the cults of the Roman emperors, as with those of Hellenistic rulers, it is difficult to decide where, if at all, we should draw the boundaries between political adulation and religious worship. Did the grand marble statue of Hadrian erected in Pergamon during the Emperor's lifetime (*c.* 130 AD) [149], and inscribed with the words 'the god Hadrian', predominantly serve as a cult image, or a political statement? Is it fair to make that sort of 'religious'/ 'secular' distinction? And given that cults of the emperor were as diverse and multiform as the provinces over which Rome held sway, was the phenomenon of deifying Hadrian during his lifetime, demonstrated by this inscription at Pergamon, paralleled elsewhere? Suffice it to say that by the 1st century AD, the concept of the hero seems no longer to have been able to contain imperial aspirations for all-out power.

150 *Marble relief from the Sanctuary of Demeter and Kore at Eleusis, c. 440–430 BC. The annual Eleusinian Mysteries had become well established by the end of the 6th century. The rites were open not only to male citizens, but also to female, non-Greek, and slave initiates; they seem to have revolved around the notion of cyclical renewal. Here Triptolemos, the boy who taught humanity how to grow grain [97], is shown naked, standing between two female figures: on the left is Demeter, holding a sceptre and wearing a matronly Doric peplos [cf. 566]; on the right is her daughter, known as Kore or Persephone, who holds a torch and wears a less austere, and more revealing, Ionic chiton.*

151 *Group of votive terracotta statues and statuettes, from a sanctuary at Ayia Irini on the north-west coast of Cyprus, c. 700–550 BC, reassembled in the Museum of Mediterranean and Near Eastern Antiquities, Stockholm. Over two thousand votives were found, arranged in a semicircle around a central altar: despite variations in size and subject, it is clear that the power of these objects lay in their formulaic iconographic repetition.*

CULTIC PERFORMANCE

Throughout the Classical world, there was an enduring sense that, when it came to cultic worship, actions spoke louder than words. That is not to say that words were unimportant. A large variety of elaborate hymns, formulaically charting the place of birth, titles, and powers of a deity, survive from antiquity. But as divine superintendents over human existence, deities required something more: they expected regular acts of devotion. 'You will find that those who followed the gods had every success', the 1st-century historian Livy summarized (*History of Rome from its Foundation* 5.51.5); 'those who disregarded them were visited with misfortune.'

The problem is that it is often very difficult to reconstruct the meanings and even the practical structures underpinning Classical acts of cultic performance. In antiquity, just as in the contemporary world, the most routine rituals received the least degree of textual record, never mind analytical investigation. A number of religious ceremonies defined themselves around their clandestine ineffability, not least the famous 'Mysteries' honouring the goddess Demeter and her daughter Persephone at Eleusis in Attica [150] and other cults imported from the Near East. It is also hard to compare the different cultic rituals of the ancient Mediterranean: while many central religious rites remained more or less the same in different parts of the Classical world, and at different times, the social, political, and cultural forces that gave them their meaning differed widely.

Nowhere is this difficulty better illustrated than in the field of votive offerings. Sanctuaries throughout the Mediterranean have yielded thousands of gifts and artefacts dedicated to their various gods and goddesses. Enshrined in museums, these individual objects – be they humble terracotta maquettes [164] or elaborately wrought bronze sculptures – soon become detached from their original dedicatory

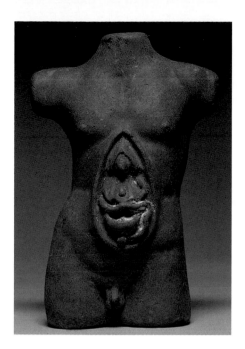

152 *Terracotta votive offering, probably dedicated at an Etruscan healing sanctuary in the hope of healthier bowels, 4th century* BC.

153 *Bronze statuette dedicated in Thebes, c. 700–675* BC. *The inscription announces it as an offering to Apollo, but if a helmet was attached (as the hole on the forehead suggests), the image is unlikely to have represented the god.*

'An art of trade *between gods and men':* *Socrates' definition of conventional* hosiotes *(a word incorporating ideas of 'holiness', 'piety', and the 'observance of divine law') neatly encapsulates the idea of reciprocity around which ancient cultic activity revolved. Socrates critically summarizes Euthyphro's argument that in order to receive the gods' blessing one must offer them prayers and sacrifices. The official charge brought against Socrates by the Athenians in 399* BC, *which led to his execution, was one of 'impiety' (specifically introducing new gods and corrupting the young, see p. 230). Plato's* Euthyphro *perhaps shows one way in which Socrates challenged current religious norms: piety, he argues, is not an external act of devotion but an internal value, the means of perfecting an individual's soul.*

EUTHYPHRO: I am simply arguing that holiness is knowing how to say and do what the gods find pleasing – namely, prayer and sacrifice. Such things offer salvation to private families and public states. The opposite of what the gods find pleasing is impiety, and impiety overturns and destroys everything.
SOCRATES: . . . What are you arguing 'holy' and 'holiness' to be? Are you saying that it is some science of sacrifice and prayer?
EUTHYPHRO: Yes, I am.
SOCRATES: And sacrifice entails giving gifts to the gods, and prayer entails asking the gods for something?
EUTHYPHRO: Exactly, Socrates.
SOCRATES: So, according to your argument, holiness would be a science of asking the gods for things and giving them things?
EUTHYPHRO: You understand my argument perfectly, Socrates. . . .
SOCRATES: And would not the proper way of asking be to ask for things that we need from them?
EUTHYPHRO: Of course.
SOCRATES: And would not the proper way of giving be to give them in turn things that they happen to need from us? After all, to give someone something that they have no need for wouldn't be scientific giving.
EUTHYPHRO: That's right, Socrates.
SOCRATES: Then holiness, Euthyphro, would be an art of trade between gods and men.
EUTHYPHRO: Trade, yes, if that's what you like to call it.
SOCRATES: But that's not what I like to call it – that is, unless it happens to be true. . .'

Plato, *Euthyphro* 14B–14E

contexts; the glass case has a tendency to deceive us into treating the relics of acts of piety as *objets d'art*. But when brought together again *en masse*, as the statues and statuettes from the sanctuary at Ayia Irini in Cyprus are displayed in Stockholm [151], they make an impression that may well daunt the modern mind. Scholars choose to restore, classify, and date such objects; they search for an artist, workshop, and consumer; they sometimes look beyond an individual artefact to find artistic comparanda. The objects, however, prompt a more immediate question: what did it mean to make a votive offering in the first place?

One answer lies in the reciprocal logic that underpinned ancient acts of piety. Gifts to the gods (whether crafted images, foodstuffs, or animal sacrifices) commemorated an earthly reward already received, or sought one in the future. As an expression of thanks, Demeter could be acknowledged with the offering of first fruits at the harvest; after victory in war, booty could be stacked up for a god in gratitude for help; and initiatory rituals (marking the passage from puberty into adulthood) were also frequently accompanied by material offerings. Alternatively, as a supplication, offerings could be made on a conditional basis, to request some sort of divine intervention: at antiquity's many healing shrines (see p. 75), particularly from the 4th century BC onwards, there survive hundreds of miniature body parts, each presumably associated with some hoped-for miraculous cure [115, 116, 152]. A small bronze votive statuette from early 7th-century Thebes [153] neatly encapsulates this rhetoric of mutual reciprocity: 'Mantiklos offers me as a tithe to Apollo of the silver bow ' runs its inscription; 'in return, Phoebus [Apollo], give me some pleasing favour.' The Latin motto *do ut des*, 'I give so that you may give', best summarizes the principle.

It is tricky to decide why certain sorts of votive offerings were chosen for specific occasions – if indeed the choice was deliberate. Typical of this dilemma are the statue-types so popular in Greece between the late 7th and the early 5th centuries BC, to which modern interpreters, for want of more specific titles, have given the name *kouros* and *kore* ('young man' and 'maiden') [154, 446, 453]. Here, as elsewhere, we cannot be certain whether such votives were erected as images of the dedicator, the deity receiving the dedication, or even a sanctuary's resident priest or priestess; in fact, those ambiguities probably struck ancient viewers too, although a figure's attributes might once have helped [156]. The presence of an inscription may not necessarily clarify the situation: an Etruscan figure [155] may be explicitly dedicated to Selvans, a god associated with woodlands (who would come to be Latinized as the Roman god Silvanus), but that need not mean the statue depicts the god.

Some votive offerings were apparently chosen purely on the grounds of their showiness, asserting social muscle as much as perpetuating a prayer to the gods. The greater the expenditure and time invested, the greater both the god's delight and the dedicator's prestige. That is not to say that the dedicator needed to be a private individual. On the island of Delos in the late 7th century BC, the citizens of neighbouring Naxos erected a colossal marble image of Apollo outside his sanctuary; its inscription proudly read, 'I am of a single stone, statue and base' [cf. 255].

This same ostentatious aspect of ancient religious ritual also applied to the central rite of ancient cultic performance – animal sacrifice. Although the rites (and the terms used to describe them) differed throughout the Classical world, the overall practice seems to have been more or less the same. First came the sacrificial procession (*pompe*, in Greek), when a domestic animal – a cow or bull [158], goat, pig, or sheep – was driven towards the altar. (In the official rites of

154 *Painted plaster cast of the* Peplos Kore, *dedicated on the Athenian Acropolis c. 530 BC – a potent reminder that Classical sculptures and buildings were once painted in bright polychrome colours. She is named after her garment, a long robe worn pinned on the shoulders and belted.*

155 *Inscribed Etruscan bronze statuette of a youth, last quarter of the 4th century BC. The inscription reads: 'Avle Havrnas gave this for [or in] the* tuthina *[probably referring to a rural village] of the father to Selvans of the boundaries' – perhaps for a good harvest. It might be easier to identify the subject if the figure's attribute (in its left hand) had survived.*

156 *Etruscan bronze statuette of a bearded man, c. 480 BC. The figure wears a* tebenna *(an Etruscan precursor of the Roman toga [284]). If it originally held a sceptre in its clenched left hand, it may have represented Tinia, the supreme Etruscan deity, comparable to Zeus.*

Roman state protocol, the set trio of sacrificial animals – sow, sheep, bull – constituted a processional motif often recorded in Roman imperial relief sculpture, the *suovetaurilia*.) Prominent in this procession was a figure, generally female, carrying a basket containing the slightly curved sacrificial knife; by the altar, another figure, usually a senior bearded male, stood ready, with a handwashing basin at his side. Depictions of the throat-slitting that happened next are rare: Greeks and Romans seem to have been squeamish about the actual moment when animals, especially pigs, sense their imminent death with agitated squeals. The first spurt of blood was caught in a special bowl; then it was a matter of butchery. Following the protocol canonized in the myth of Prometheus (see p. 354), the portion reserved for divine consumption – consigned to the flames on the altar – consisted of the meat-stripped thighbones plus the sacrum and tail of the sacrificed animal. For the mortal attendants, what remained were the flesh and precious entrails, to be roasted on spits at the altar and consumed at a communal feast.

157 *A man and a woman standing on either side of an outdoor altar, on an Attic red-figure oinochoe attributed to the Richmond Painter, c. 440 BC. The woman (right) holds a jug of the same shape as the one on which she appears, perhaps indicating that it was itself used for pouring sacrificial offerings.*

158 *Marble relief showing Marcus Aurelius presiding over a sacrifice in front of the Capitoline Temple [178], c. AD 180. The Emperor stands beside a tripod filled with incense: his veiled head casts him as pontifex maximus (high priest), a title held by the emperor following the precedent of Augustus. Beside him stands a young assistant, or camillus, and behind, next to the bull, is a flamen (priest) with characteristic spiked hat [cf. 290]. A piper plays, and a victimarius, on the right, holds a sacrificial axe.*

159 *Detail of a scene in the Tomb of the Augurs, Tarquinia, c. 510 BC. While the* haruspex *was a soothsayer who divined the will of the gods by examining the entrails of sacrificial victims, the augur did so by interpreting natural phenomena like lightning, the flightpaths of birds, and the significance of comets. The augur in this Etruscan tomb carries a special crook-staff (*lituus*) that gives him a particular religious and political status. Although he has also been seen as a referee in the adjacent wrestling contest, he seems here to be reading the flightpath of birds – an omen either of the outcome of the wrestling match, or else of the allocated lifespan of the deceased who now occupies the tomb.*

The choice of sacrificial victim depended partly on the wealth and showiness of those performing the sacrifice. In the fourth *Mimiamb* by the 3rd-century BC Greek poet Herodas, we encounter two low-born women making a sacrifice to Asklepios; their limited financial means allow them only to offer a chicken, but they hope that, Asklepios willing, next time they may be able to afford something more substantial. Certain deities were, for particular reasons, offered animals not eaten by humans (dogs for Hekate, horses for Poseidon). As for human sacrifice, despite the occasional reference in Classical mythology (e.g. the story of Iphigeneia – where, as elsewhere, it is presented as an act of transgression) and the controversial archaeological claims for the disposal of infants at the Etruscan site of Tarquinia, it appears to have been strictly taboo.

Sacrifice in Greek sanctuaries was mostly an act to gain divine favour (propitiation) or to purify oneself of wrongdoing (expiation). Roman sacrifice, inheriting something of the Etruscan discipline of 'haruspicy', incorporated additional aspects of divination. A special priest (*haruspex*) would inspect the entrails, especially the liver [160], of the victim for information about the attitudes of the gods towards the sacrifice, what actions should be taken, and what the future might hold. That was just one of many ways in which the Romans, like the Greeks and Etruscans, sought to foresee the future: others included the consultation of oracles (pp. 273–74), astrology, and the interpretation of dreams and omens [159].

160 *Bronze model of a sheep's liver from Setima, near Piacenza (hence known as the 'Piacenza Liver'), c. 100 BC. Bearing forty-two Etruscan inscriptions, it functioned as a sort of map of the heavens and was probably used as a tool for interpreting the entrails of sacrificial animals.*

A PLACE FOR THE GODS

Animal sacrifices to the gods were performed on altars located not within temples but outside in the open air. It was not the presence of a monumental building that designated a particular space as holy, but rather the consecration of the land that the altar occupied, the *temenos* (the word is Greek, referring to a space 'cut off' from ordinary use). Within the boundaries of the *temenos* was the *hieron*, the 'holy place' or 'sanctuary'.

Sanctuaries were not of fixed design. There were small 'urban' altars in the heart of a city, such as the 6th-century BC Altar to the Twelve Gods in the Athenian Agora [302:14]; 'extra-urban' sanctuaries located in the rural environs of the cities that dominated them, like the Argive Heraion dedicated to Hera; and 'inter-urban' sanctuaries, like the Panhellenic sites at Delphi, Olympia [47], Isthmia, and Nemea, or the yet-to-be-found pan-Etruscan sanctuary of *Fanum Voltumnae*, whose festivals attracted participants from all over their respective worlds. Some sanctuaries were humble affairs. Others were so large as to require further spatial distinctions between the inner sacred area and the surrounding buildings that comprised the larger sanctuary – hotels, stadiums, and theatres, for instance. Others still, in fact the vast majority of larger sanctuaries (including the cosmopolitan Etruscan sanctuary at Pyrgi), had altars to more than one deity: Delos was not unusual in being famed as a sanctuary to Apollo while also housing sanctuaries to gods and heroes including Artemis, Leto, Hera, and the Dioskouroi.

Our word 'temple' derives from the Latin term for a sacred space, *templum*. The *templum* was a quadrangular area consecrated by special priests (*augures*). In addition to sacrifice and worship, other activities were ordained to take place in it, not least the meetings of the Senate (reflecting how Roman politics were as much a religious as a political affair). Like the Greek *hieron*, the *templum* was both more and less than what we think of as a temple: more, in that it was a sacred space subject to its own rules and conventions (which could offer sanctuary, for instance,

161, 162 *The remains of the Temple of Mars Ultor in Rome (right), and a model showing its original appearance (above). The temple of 'Mars the Avenger', dedicated in 2 BC, was ostensibly built to fulfil Augustus' vow in 42 BC, on the eve of the battle of Philippi, to build a temple to Mars commemorating his revenge upon the assassins of his adopted father, Julius Caesar. It was the crowning feature of the Forum of Augustus (see p. 191), flanked by two colonnades and exedras (themselves once lined with statues of the founding figures of Augustan Rome). Today the only substantial remains are the back wall, the steps, podium, and three Corinthian columns of the temple, and parts of the walls that enclosed the two exedras.*

163 *This fragment of an Apulian red-figure krater, 380–370 BC, depicts a Doric temple of Apollo in which a colossal statue of the god, holding a bow and sacrificial plate [cf. 393], is visible through the open cella doors. Outside, the god himself (this time also identified by an inscription) is shown playing his lyre.*

164 *Terracotta offering from the Sanctuary of Hera at Perachora, mid-8th century BC. It probably represents an early mud-brick temple of the goddess, with a single inner room and thatched roof; alternatively, it might depict a domestic dwelling, as Hera was entrusted with the protection of the home.*

to runaway slaves and criminals); and less, because although in the grandest examples the altar might be framed by a marble temple, colonnaded courtyard, and gateway [161, 162], the space was not defined by monumental buildings.

So what were temple buildings for? Unlike churches and mosques, Classical temples were not places for congregation. (It is significant that the early Christians did not build temples as their sites of worship, but appropriated a different sort of Classical building type – the basilica – which had served for official meetings, could hold a large number of people, and was not tainted with pagan associations.) Classical temples usually housed a cult image of the god, acting as a 'home' for that deity (the Latin word for a temple building, *aedes*, 'dwelling', nicely conveys the point) [126]. On special festivals, the doors could be opened so as to enable the deity to witness the acts of piety in which the worshippers outside were engaged [163]. A temple also functioned as a treasury for the offerings to the god, all displayed for anyone admitted inside to admire. The Parthenon went one step further. The late 4th-century BC scholar–historian Philochoros records how 44 talents (some 1,144 kilogrammes) of gold were invested in the drapery of its statue of Athena Parthenos [122]; the metal was placed on the statue in conveniently removable sheets so that the temple doubled as a sort of glorified fiscal reserve, funding state expenditure in times of emergency.

Publicly funded temples were a source of local pride – and inter-city competition. Greek temples of the 6th century BC betray something of that rivalry: if the Ephesians, in around 550, could dedicate a temple with a surface area of 6,017 square metres (64,767 square feet), then the temple-builders at Samos were sure to trump their neighbours by making theirs 6,038 square metres (64,933 square feet). Every aspect of the temple could be exploited in the competition: architectural scale and finesse, the size and detail of its adornments outside and image inside, and presumably also its painted colours.

Early temples seem to have been diverse in form, and substantially different from later canonical examples. The motivation for their development in the 8th century BC seems to have been the need for a *cella*, the inside room housing the image of the god – a revolution presumably effected by the novel import of large-scale statues in this period. Different temples addressed that need differently, but a votive offering found at the Sanctuary of Hera at Perachora on the Gulf of Corinth, made of clay and dated to the mid-8th century BC [164], gives some idea of what an early temple might have looked like.

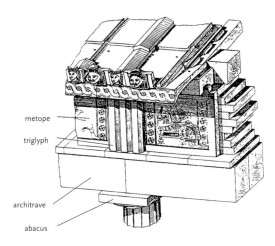

metope
triglyph
architrave
abacus

165 *Reconstruction of the entablature of the Temple of Apollo at Thermon, third quarter of the 7th century BC. The walls were made of mud-brick, but the roof was tiled rather than thatched (foreshadowing the shift towards monumental temples in stone). Above the wooden architrave, a frieze of metopes [166] and triglyphs was inserted, anticipating the Doric order.*

166 *Part of a painted terracotta metope from the Temple of Apollo at Thermon. The ornate rosette patterns and rendering of human figures suggest Corinthian artists. An inscription identifies the figure on the right as Chelidon (later known as Philomela), the mythical maiden who was raped and mutilated by her sister's husband, and who exacted her revenge by feeding him his son.*

167–69 *The three main architectural orders: Doric, Ionic, and Corinthian. Greek Doric has no base. In other respects, the elements are the same: above the shaft is the capital, on which rest the architrave, frieze, and cornice (together called the entablature).*

In later Roman times there also developed the Composite order, which superimposed Ionic volutes on the Corinthian capital.

Early temples were made of wood and mud-brick. The changeover to monumental stone was gradual, with masonry coming into use at the beginning of the 7th century BC. Beyond that our knowledge consists of a series of insecure surmises, ranging from the plausible to the probable. The early use of wood perhaps conditioned the later use of stone; the exploitation of stone was possibly influenced by quarrying and working techniques witnessed in Egypt; and it was probably initially introduced into Greece by Corinthian architects, a suggestion based on the pioneering temples erected in Corinth itself (such as the Temple of Apollo), at nearby Isthmia (the Temple of Poseidon), in Corinthian colonies like Corfu, and elsewhere in the Mediterranean – Thermon in Aetolia (in north-west Greece) being the prime example [165, 166] – where the painting techniques betray Corinthian hands.

Apart from surviving remains, our understanding of ancient sacred buildings derives chiefly from a treatise entitled *On Architecture*, written by a practising Roman architect named Vitruvius during the early reign of Augustus in the late 1st century BC (p. 191). Today, following Vitruvius, temples are classified according to three main architectural styles: Doric, Ionic, and Corinthian [167–69]. Conservative and formulaic as Classical architectural forms may seem, there was always scope for originality through innovative details. In simple terms, Doric temples have sturdy columns, with unadorned circular capitals cushioning a plain upper band, or architrave; above that architrave are triglyphs (rectangular blocks with vertical grooves) and metopes (which could be left unadorned, or painted [166], or sculpted in relief [140]). Ionic is more ornate: columns are slimmer, with moulded bases, and capitals are enriched with scrolls at the sides or corners; above the architrave is a continuous frieze. The Corinthian order, which became popular in the later Hellenistic and Roman periods, is characterized by its rich capitals, adorned with sprouting acanthus foliage that clusters into smaller volutes as the block passes from round to square. The three categories were not mutually exclusive: the Parthenon combined Doric and Ionic, as did the Temple of Apollo at Bassae [170–72], where the Ionic frieze appears on the *inside* wall of the cella (and where the Corinthian order seems to have made its debut).

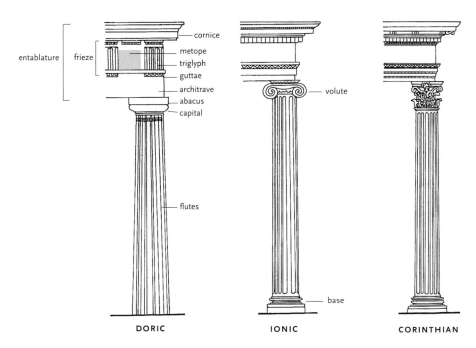

entablature — frieze

cornice
metope
triglyph
guttae
architrave
abacus
capital

volute

flutes

base

DORIC   **IONIC**   **CORINTHIAN**

170 *View of the Doric Temple of Apollo Epikourios ('the Helper') at Bassae, in south-west Arcadia, supposedly built by Iktinos (who is also credited with the Parthenon in Athens) in the late 5th century BC. According to Pausanias, it was dedicated by the nearby city of Phigaleia in thanks for deliverance from plague (Guide to Greece 8.41.7–9).*

171 below *The temple at Bassae drawn by C. R. Cockerell, the English architect who excavated it after finding fragments of the carved frieze in 1811. He shows the Doric peristyle and remains of the cella walls [cf. 172]; in the foreground he has arranged parts of the frieze, the sole Corinthian capital, and one of the distinctive Ionic capitals.*

172 opposite *Cockerell's reconstruction of the interior. The Bassae temple was unusual in being oriented north–south, and unique in at least two respects: there was a side door to the cella, which probably also functioned as a light source (the skylight is a fanciful addition); and the frieze [555] was displayed on the inner rather than outer wall of the cella, above tall Ionic attached columns. Note the single Corinthian column at the rear – the earliest one known. It is placed where the temple's sacred image would usually have stood: the statue of Apollo probably faced the side door so as to command a view of the surrounding landscape.*

173 *Reconstruction of the Doric Temple of Zeus at Agrigento (Greek Akragas) in Sicily, begun c. 480 BC. Between the columns, giant figures nearly 8 metres (25 feet) tall, which only partially survive, once appeared submissively to support the architrave.*

Those architectural differences went hand in hand with the cultural diversity of the Classical world: the experimental styling of temples was simultaneously a concession to collective homogeneity and an assertion of local individuality. This is clearly the case with some of the best-preserved temples in Magna Graecia ('Greater Greece'), that part of South Italy and Sicily colonized by Greek city-states from the 8th century BC onwards. What better way to demonstrate mid-6th-century affiliation to, and yet independence from, the Greek motherland than to alter the evolved proportions of the Greek Doric temple and give it exactly twice as many columns along its length as along its width, as does the Temple of Hera – misleadingly termed the 'Basilica' – at Paestum (Greek Poseidonia) [174]? Or, with the huge early 5th-century 'Olympieion' at Agrigento (Greek Akragas) – so huge, in fact, as to have remained unfinished after the city was sacked in 406 BC – to monumentalize both Greek and Italic affiliation by setting its 'Greek' columns into an 'Italic' continuous wall, and then adding giant figures [173]? Or again, with the late 5th-century temple at Segesta, to change the standard proportions of the Doric metopes, making them longer than they are high, thus giving the building a uniquely squat aspect [175]?

The monumental temples in durable stone that we know today did not become the norm everywhere in antiquity – especially in Etruria, where the earth predominantly yielded soft tufa rock rather than limestone and marble. The result is that little Etruscan sacred architecture has survived. Still, a possible reconstruction of a late 6th-century temple at Veii, north of Rome, should make us wary of

174 *Two of the three surviving Doric temples at Paestum (Greek Poseidonia) in South Italy, both made out of local travertine but originally covered with stucco to give the impression of marble: the squat 'Basilica', really a Temple of Hera, of the mid-6th century* BC *(left), and another Temple of Hera, mistakenly considered a Temple of Poseidon, of the mid-5th century* BC.

175 *The Doric temple at Segesta in Sicily, begun in the last quarter of the 5th century* BC, *remained unfinished in antiquity. Work was never begun on the cella, the columns remain unfluted, and, around the three surrounding temple steps (the 'stylobate' and 'stereobate'), the bosses to which ropes were attached to hoist the large blocks into place remain unsmoothed.*

176 *Reconstruction of the Portonaccio Temple at Veii, c. 500 BC. This Etruscan temple, probably dedicated to Menerva, a goddess comparable to the Greek Athena and Roman Minerva, is distinctive for its frontal pronaos (deep porch) with two rows of wooden columns, its central flight of steps (Greek temples were built on a continuous three-stepped podium), and the figures on its gabled roof [177].*

177 above right *Terracotta statue of Apollo from Veii, c. 510 BC. Representing Apollo clothed, with windswept drapery – not naked, as in Greece – accentuated the figure's sense of movement and position on the roof of the temple.*

178 *Model of the Capitoline Temple, dedicated to Jupiter Optimus Maximus ('Best and Greatest'), Juno, and Minerva, on the summit of the Capitoline Hill in Rome. The first temple on the site was built in Etruscan style, and the Tuscan three-roomed cella suited the dedication to three deities. According to tradition, that temple was begun by the Tarquin kings, who summoned artists from 'all over Etruria' (Livy, History of Rome from its Foundation 1.56.1); inaugurated in the first year of the Republic (509 BC), it was Rome's foremost religious monument, and was later copied in many cities of the Empire [cf. 298]. The Capitoline Temple was periodically rebuilt during its long history: this model reflects its final Corinthian form, sponsored by the Emperor Domitian in the early 80s AD.*

dismissing Etruscan cultic architecture as 'provincial'. The impact of the Veii temple [176], like that of other temples in Tarquinia and Orvieto, was enhanced by its position on a high plateau, in addition to its tall podium. The elaborate roof decoration, in hollow terracotta, looked down upon worshippers from all sides. Terracotta may have lacked the enduring prestige of marble or limestone, but its lightness made possible a quantity of rooftop figures [e.g. 177], and thereby visual narratives, quite unparalleled in Greece.

The reconstruction of the Portonaccio Temple at Veii is again largely indebted to Vitruvius: according to him, temples of the 'Tuscan' order were adorned with columns only at the front, and had their cella split into three separate rooms. That Etruscan design was influential on much Roman sacred architecture. One of the oldest, biggest, and once most famous of Roman temples, the Capitoline Temple that crowned the Capitoline Hill and derived its name from it [178], was also originally marked by a high podium, three rows of columns at the front, and a single frontal row of steps, similar to the temple at Veii. But the Capitoline Temple had attached columns on the sides of the cella wall, foreshadowing later Roman compromises between native Italic and Greek forms [cf. 179].

One of the most imitated of Roman temples is also the most unusual: the Pantheon, or temple to 'all the gods', in Rome [118, 180]. Crowned with a perfect hemisphere (the height of the inner dome, placed on a cylinder, is equal to half its diameter), the circular interior marks a complete break with Greek models: although the Greeks, and the Romans after them, did build circular buildings, some of which had cultic functions [e.g. 82], those buildings generally had a wooden conical roof, and none of them was built to this scale, made possible by Roman engineering in concrete. As the sun moves round the Pantheon, natural light enters the wide opening in the vault (its *oculus*, or 'eye'). But the immediate survival of this temple, like others, is deceptive: today it is crowded with images drawn from Christian theology, following its conversion into a church in AD 609; in antiquity it echoed to the shrieks of animals dragged to sacrifice, and outside altars hummed with flies round coagulated blood.

179 *The Temple of 'Fortuna Virilis', Rome, c. last quarter of the 1st century BC. The design fuses Greek architectural elements with an Etruscan ground-plan: like the temple at Veii [176], it has a deep porch, high podium, and frontal steps; unlike that, however, it is made of marble, with Ionic columns, and its steps run almost the full width. Whereas columns usually adorned only the front of Etruscan temples, here half-columns on the outer wall of the cella give the impression of a Greek peripteral temple, surrounded by columns on all four sides.*

180 *The Pantheon in Rome, given its present form by the Emperor Hadrian c. AD 118–125. The honorific inscription naming Agrippa as the original sponsor (he had built a structure on the site in 27 BC) was one of several ways in which the building disguised its radical innovativeness with a bow to Augustan traditionalism: the combination of a rectangular classical porch with a monumental circular drum [118] is typical of Hadrian's fusion of Greek classicism with Roman architectural innovation.*

III MYTH IN THE MAKING

181 *A rhapsode (literally, a 'song-stitcher'), perhaps a competitor in the four-yearly Greater Panathenaia in Athens, depicted on an Attic red-figure amphora attributed to the Kleophrades Painter, c. 490 BC. He stands on a platform (inscribed with the words 'you are beautiful'), wearing a loosely draped himation, or cloak, and with extended right arm resting on a staff. The beginning of his poetic recitation is etched beside his mouth, in the manner of a speech bubble: 'as once in Tiryns . . .' (Tiryns was a Bronze Age settlement just south of Mycenae, associated with a number of mythical heroes.)*

182 *opposite The Judgment of Paris – the story that lay at the heart of the whole cycle of myths about the Trojan War and its aftermath – on an Attic red-figure pelike attributed to the Painter of the Wedding Procession, c. 360 BC. Paris, in rich Oriental costume, sits between Athena and Aphrodite (right) and Hera and Hermes (left). A small Eros tugs at Aphrodite's himation, while the goddess holds a veil to her face in feigned modesty.*

The vase is unusual not only for its use of several colours, but for its raised relief areas and golden highlights: this is the 'Kerch Style', named after the area in the Crimea where many such vases were found.

YEAR AFTER YEAR, artists find fresh inspiration in the mythical stories that permeated and framed every aspect of Classical antiquity. New spins on age-old myths supplement the vast numbers of existing plays, operas, and films that have drawn upon them, by all manner of writers and in all manner of genres – from Seneca to Ted Hughes, Jean Anouilh to Bertolt Brecht, Jean Racine to Richard Strauss. Classical myths are reinterpreted to reveal new cultural truths: psychoanalysis continues to forage in them for an understanding of the human condition (following the precedents of Sigmund Freud and Carl Jung); the visual arts go on mining them for what they might have to say about our relationship with the Classical past; even our language engages with them on a daily basis ('narcissistic', 'tantalize', and 'Europe' are just some of the many words that derive from those stories). Classical myths, in short, continue to provide ways of contemplating, questioning, and expressing every kind of human emotion and thought. This leads us to a series of questions: why should we be affected by (or even remotely interested in) the plights of Oedipus, Medea, or Odysseus? Why do we still keep on returning to such myths to express our concerns, thoughts, and fears? Why do we not just deal in the plain, objective language of scientific prose rather than the mysterious and poetic metaphors of Classical mythology?

MYTHS ABOUT MYTH

The earliest but perhaps most satisfying answer is provided by Aristotle in the 4th century BC. While discussing the differences between historical prose and the poetic tragedies that dealt with mythical stories, Aristotle arrived at the conclusion that poetry is intrinsically more valuable than history (*Poetics* 9.1–8). Poetry tells of the kinds of things that *might* happen – the universal tendencies of human nature, existential issues of life and death. History, by contrast, is bogged down in particular details – the questions of 'who', 'when', and 'where' that stagnate in the classroom. As T. S. Eliot put it in 1923 (discussing another adaptation of a Classical myth, James Joyce's *Ulysses*), myth is 'a way of controlling, of ordering, of giving shape and a significance to the immense panorama of futility and anarchy which is contemporary history'. So Classical myths persist into modern times, just as they persisted in the ancient world, because of their potential to defy specifics of time and place: new concerns constantly reanimate, reinvigorate, and remodel millennia-old stories.

At the same time, it is this fluidity of Classical myths that the modern world usually finds most difficult to grasp. The quick-fire questions on television quiz-shows, typically chosen from a selected canon of literary works, give the impression that those myths comprise some sort of factual reference system, with single 'right' and 'wrong' answers: 'according to Greek myth, who was X's father?', 'how did Y die?', 'where was Z born?'. Only rarely do we think to challenge the encyclopaedic (even biblical) sanctity with which these myths have been handed down to us. But the single most important thing to grasp about Classical myth is that it was always a matter of Classical *myths*; every story had a whole range of different versions and

183 *Bronze statuette, probably from Crete, first quarter of the 7th century BC. A young companion accompanies an older man holding a lyre. A number of epic bards were characterized as blind – Demodokos in the* Odyssey, *the poet of the Homeric Hymn to Apollo, and, according to later ancient tradition, Homer himself – and so it is tempting to see this older figure too as a blind poet, in need of a young companion to steer his path.*

184 *Marble bust of Homer, a Roman copy of a type probably created in the late 2nd century BC. The flesh hangs in heavy folds over the bones, the forehead is creased in stern contemplation, and beneath the high brows are sightless, narrow eyes; but the idealizing deep carving and the long shaggy beard cast animating shadows over the visionary's portrait, and the undulating surface hints at a lively inner world of poetic imagination.*

outcomes, at least as vast as the chronological and geographical spans of this book. Myths were constantly remodelled and even reinvented, with the potential radically to redefine and challenge how Classical cultures constructed their past, present, and future. At the same time, because of each myth's evolution over a long period (like the Classical deities in the last chapter, a number of stories have been traced back into the 2nd millennium BC), to play with mythical traditions was a tradition in its own right. So myth was – and is – a means of cultural innovation that also firmly roots the present in the past.

In antiquity, myths were everywhere. Authors reveal how they were on everybody's lips as parables to entertain, theorize, and understand the complex powers of the gods; and material culture likewise shows how myths were drawn, painted, and sculpted into all aspects of daily life. Nevertheless, 'myth' remained an ambiguous and multifaceted category. The Greek word *mythos* had a wide range of meanings, from 'word', 'report', and 'speech' to 'story', 'fiction', and 'fable' (from the Latin *fabula,* from which we derive our idea of the 'fabulous'). So it is that when Thucydides came to introduce his history in the late 5th century BC, he made a point of contrasting his purportedly objective account with the fabulous and 'romantic strain', *to mythodes,* of other writers (*History of the Peloponnesian War* 1.22.4).

The origins of mythical tales are blurred and problematic. What we can be sure of is that legendary clangs of battle, wondrous heroes, and the amazing feats of the gods were the stuff of the earliest epic poetry (composed in dactylic hexameters, with six metrical 'feet' in each line), sung by travelling minstrels or 'rhapsodes' ('song-stitchers'). While archaeological excavation has yielded a number of possible depictions of bards [181, 183], we know very little about the actual poets and performers. Perhaps more promising are the occasional clues in epic poetry itself. In the *Hymn to Apollo* (which used to be attributed, along with the other so-called *Homeric Hymns,* to the most renowned epic poet of all, Homer), we are perhaps given some hints about a context for at least one form of poetic performance. The occasion seems to be a particular cultic festival in honour of Apollo, probably on the Cycladic island of Delos (legend had it that it was on this barren and otherwise unpromising island that Leto gave birth to Apollo and Artemis: see p. 251).

Just as this hymn has been attributed to Homer, so too has its poet, characterized as blind and from the island of Chios, been connected to that

185 *Detail of a marble relief of the apotheosis of Homer, by Archelaos of Priene, found on the Appian Way in Rome, c. 200 BC. Homer sits with his two poetic creations, the* Iliad *(holding a sword) and the* Odyssey *(holding a ship's ornament), kneeling on either side of his throne. Inscriptions name the figures performing the sacrifice as Myth, History, Poetry, Tragedy, and Comedy; at the far right, clustered together, are Human Nature (portrayed as a child), Excellence, Memory, Trustworthiness, and Wisdom. Two further personifications, Chronos ('Time') and Oikoumene ('The inhabited world'), stand behind Homer, one crowning him with a wreath: Homer's epics will last for all time and be known the whole world over.*

The early composition *of poetry was a competitive business, and bards were expected to travel between different city-states.*

But come, Apollo and Artemis, bestow your favour; and farewell to you, all you maidens. Remember me after this, whenever some earth-dwelling man, some much-suffering vagabond, should come here and ask: 'Whom do you consider, maidens, to be the sweetest singer to wander here? In which singer do you delight the most?' Then answer all together: 'It is a blind man, who lives on rocky Chios, whose songs are the greatest and will last for ever.' And I will carry your fame, as far as I wander over the Earth, to the well-inhabited cities of men. Thus will they believe me also, since this declaration too is true: I will never cease hymning far-shooting Apollo, who bears the silver bow, whom Leto of the beautiful locks bore.

Homeric Hymn to Apollo 165–78

most renowned (though also most enigmatic) crafter of epic verse. The ancients constructed their own archetypal identity for the shady figure of Homer which satisfyingly coincides with the description in this hymn: he was old and bearded; his brows were furrowed; and although he was blind, with gaping eye sockets, his insightful 'sixth sense' remained all-penetrating [184].

A whole mythology soon developed around Homer, with cities competing for the prestigious claim of being his place of birth. Whether in fact 'Homer' was one man or many, the poet of both the *Iliad* and the *Odyssey* or of neither, a real figure or a posthumous construct (some of these questions have been debated for over two thousand years), here is a sure example of the folly of attempting to disentangle, and perhaps even to distinguish, history from myth. At best, we must satisfy ourselves with three more or less agreed-upon deductions. First, Homer was widely credited in antiquity with composing both poems [185]. Second, while a general consensus now places the date of that composition somewhere between *c.* 750 and *c.* 650 BC, scholars continue to debate exactly how derivative our 'Homeric' texts are from 'pre-Homeric' oral poetic traditions, and how fixed they were before and after they were written down. Third and finally, the context for such poetry seems to have been public performance. The epics were not, originally at least, texts for private reading: instead, they evolved as bards adapted for each successive poetic recitation the portions that they had committed to memory. The writing down of the poems and their division into twenty-four books were later developments – developments associated with the advent of literacy in Greece.

By the 6th century BC poetic competitions had become *de rigueur* throughout the Mediterranean. It was Athens that developed one of the most renowned forums for musical and poetic *agones*, which occurred alongside contests in other fields as part of the city Panathenaia (see p. 40) [181]. One tradition has it that they were initiated by Peisistratos, the tyrant of Athens who died in 527 BC. If so, there seems to have been more to his parade of Homeric epic than a dilettante delight in things poetic: it was said that Peisistratos claimed descent from the Neleids of Pylos; Neleus was the father of Nestor; and it is perhaps no coincidence that Nestor is treated so sympathetically in our text of the *Iliad*.

186 *Scene of the Judgment of Paris on a Euboean black-figure amphora, c. 570–560 BC. Hermes, wearing his customary hat and carrying a special staff, reaches out to grasp Paris' hand; behind him stride the three goddesses.*

THE *ILIAD* AND THE *ODYSSEY*

The *Iliad* takes as its main theme the epic quarrel between Achilles (a brilliant young warrior from Thessaly) and Agamemnon (King of Mycenae and leader of the Greek armies). At the beginning of the poem, Agamemnon abducts Achilles' favourite handmaid, Briseis [189]; Achilles, seeing this as a humiliating affront to his heroic valour, sulkingly withdraws from battle, to the dramatic detriment of the Greek fighting force. The poem is concerned with the various efforts and events (ultimately the death of his beloved companion, Patroklos) that entice Achilles back into the fray. Although the *Iliad* deals with only fourteen days of the Trojan War, which was famously fought for a full ten years, it uses the story of Achilles' wrath to treat a miscellany of interrelated themes, stories, and myths which in turn deposited a bank of tales that could be elaborated in later texts and images.

But when they saw Helen walking upon the wall, they quietly uttered winged words to each other: 'No reproach is it for the Trojans and well-greaved Achaeans to suffer prolonged troubles over a woman such as this one. To gaze upon her is as wonderful as to look upon some immortal goddess. But regardless of her appearance, let her still be shipped back so as not to remain here in Troy and be a grief to us and our children hereafter!'

Homer, *Iliad* 3.154–60

Who hailed her Helen? He could foresee fate,
He bullseyed this spear-spouse, this murder-married date –
This *Hellen*, Hell-en! She wreaks hell for ships,
Turns men and cities into hellish wrecks!
An apt exchange: from bed to gore-war HELL . . . !

Aeschylus, *Agamemnon*, lines 681–92

Was this the face that launched a thousand ships,
And burnt the topless towers of Ilium?
Sweet Helen, make me immortal with a kiss!
Her lips suck forth my soul: see, where it flies!
Come Helen, come give me my soul again.
Here will I dwell, for heaven be in these lips,
And all is dross that is not Helena.

Christopher Marlowe, *Dr Faustus*, Act 5, scene 1

187 opposite *Detail of an Attic black-figure volute krater, known as the François Vase (after the excavator of the tomb near Etruscan Chiusi where it was found), signed by Kleitias as painter and Ergotimos as potter, 580–570 BC. This vase combines a complex pictorial evocation of a number of Greek myths with careful labelling of every person and thing, from heroes and gods to inanimate objects like fountains and seats.*

Of its six friezes, which cover both sides of the mixing bowl, three are shown here. The largest one takes up the story of the marriage of Peleus and Thetis, the parents of Achilles: the gods make their way to the banquet; Dionysos faces out in the middle, characteristically bringing an amphora of wine. The frieze above shows the funerary games which Achilles staged in honour of Patroklos (see p. 36). In the uppermost frieze, Peleus and Meleager are about to spear the Calydonian Boar sent by Artemis.

As is typical of the misogynistic myths of the Greeks (and other patriarchal societies), the Greek offensive against Troy was ultimately thought to have stemmed from female folly: in this case, three women – and an apple. But this was no ordinary apple: it was fashioned from gold and inscribed with particularly fateful words – 'for the most beautiful woman'. Nor were these three ordinary women: they were goddesses – Hera, Athena, and Aphrodite. To determine the apple's rightful owner, the goddesses collectively called upon Zeus; but he knew better than to adjudicate the divine feud, and dispatched them to consult a Trojan prince named Paris [182, 186]. Each goddess attempted to win Paris' favour through bribery: Hera promised imperial power, Athena military victory, and Aphrodite the love of the most beautiful woman on earth. For any respectable Classical hero – at least any respectable male warrior in the *Iliad* – Aphrodite's offer would have been the least attractive; but Paris was not a traditionally valorous figure, and he duly voted Aphrodite supreme. He was instructed to collect his prize in person. Her name, Aphrodite now revealed, was Helen, and she was to be found on the other side of the Aegean in Sparta. But there was a catch. Helen was already married – and not just to anyone, but to Menelaus, King of Sparta and brother of the lordly Agamemnon. Paris' subsequent abduction of Helen, after being welcomed and entertained by her husband, was a grave offence that was avenged by the Greek campaign against Troy, the recovery of Helen, and ultimately the destruction of the Trojan city and its inhabitants.

If Greek myths were messy, they were also complexly interrelated. Thus the apple that would eventually lead to the Trojan War and Achilles' death had been thrown by Eris (Strife) at the wedding of Peleus and Thetis [187] – who were to be the parents of Achilles.

Amid the graphic scenes of battle, interventions of the gods, countless acts of intrigue, and narrative twists and turns, the *Iliad* also gives us a vivid sense of the events that precede and succeed the poem's actual plot. We catch numerous glimpses of Helen, and we piece together the previous history of her relationship with Paris, which ultimately remains ambiguous (was she passively abducted? did she wilfully elope with him to Troy? to what extent was either party a free agent, rather than the puppet of the gods?). At the same time, the *Iliad* also points forward to later stories about its heroes and the destiny of Troy: although the poem does not narrate Achilles' death, nor the downfall of Troy and its inhabitants, it is driven by a particularly fatalistic sense of destiny.

188 *Achilles, restraining a horse with his right hand
and holding a shield in his left, prepares to drag the
body of Hector, attached to his chariot, in the dust
around the walls of Troy: Roman sarcophagus, last
quarter of the 2nd–first quarter of the 3rd century
AD. The desecration of Hector's body (narrated in
books 21–22 of the Iliad) was Achilles' most extreme
form of vengeance on the valorous Trojan prince
who had killed Patroklos: Achilles is here shown
stepping on the body as he mounts his chariot.
Three sides of this sarcophagus take up tales drawn
from the life of the Greek hero – a wistful way,
perhaps, of associating the life of the deceased (who
was represented, with his wife, on the lid) with that
of the Greek hero par excellence.*

189 *Mosaic floor showing the abduction of Briseis,
2nd century AD. Achilles sits in his tent in pensive
grief, leaning on a lyre and staring off into the
distance. To the left stands Patroklos, and to the
right the bearded Phoenix (the childless émigré from
Thessaly commissioned by Peleus to mind Achilles
in Troy). Briseis – of whom only part of the head
survives – is being led off by two heralds to the camp
of Agamemnon; she turns towards Achilles with a
parting glance.*

190 *Scenes of the sack of Troy, on the interior of
an Attic red-figure kylix, signed by Euphronios (as
potter) and attributed to Onesimos (as painter),
c. 500–490 BC. In the centre, the Greek warrior
Neoptolemos – the son of Achilles – strikes the old
white-bearded Trojan king Priam (defended in vain
by his daughter Polyxena), using as his weapon the
lifeless body of Priam's grandson Astyanax. Above,
Cassandra is seized by the hair: she clutches a statue
of Athena to claim sanctuary, but her nudity signals
her feminine desirability and vulnerability, thereby
alluding to the story of her rape by the 'Lesser' Ajax
[cf. 205, 220].*

Ancient artists took up the challenge of conveying that tragic drive in painting
and sculpture [e.g. 188]. On an Athenian drinking cup, an early 5th-century painter
ventured to bring the narrative action of the *Iliad* to its terrible climax. On the
exterior, one side shows Briseis being led away from Achilles (in book 1), the other
the duel between Hector and Ajax (in book 7); but what awaits the viewer upon
draining the cup is a graphic summation of where all these events are leading [190]
– the murder, rape, sacrilege, butchery, and infanticide which will accompany the
sack of Troy. Nothing, and no one, is spared.

In many ways, the *Odyssey* tells a very different story. Set in the aftermath of
the Trojan War, concerned in every sense with a post-Iliadic world, it narrates the
wanderings and homecoming of its hero, Odysseus. Back in his kingdom of Ithaca,
Odysseus' wife, Penelope, and his son, Telemachos, await his return. Twenty years
have passed since Odysseus departed to Troy, the kingdom is descending into
chaos, and Penelope is under increasing pressure to marry one of her bullying,
and now impatient, suitors. She uses a variety of guiles to postpone action, such
as promising to marry a suitor only after completing a woven shroud that she is

191 *Odysseus and the Sirens, on a Paestan red-figure krater attributed to Python, c. 340 BC. Two Sirens, represented as half woman and half bird, attempt to lure Odysseus and his shipmates to their deaths. But Odysseus had instructed his sailors to block their ears with wax and tie him to the mast of his ship: he alone therefore can hear the Sirens' song, but he cannot succumb to it.*

Odysseus greets the shade of Achilles, *who tells him that a heroic death, although regarded as glorious by the living, is not preferable to a more humble but protracted life on earth.*

'For I have not yet . . . set foot on my homeland. My troubles have been endless. But you, Achilles! No man past or future can ever be more utterly blessed than you. Before, when you were alive, we Argives honoured you as we do the gods. And now that you are here, you rule mightily over the dead! So grieve not at all in death, Achilles.' So I spoke, and straightaway Achilles answered: 'Do not console me about death, shining Odysseus. I would rather be a common hired labourer – a servant to a man with no property and humble income – than be king over the lifeless dead.'

Homer, *Odyssey* 11.481–91

192 *Telemachos and Penelope, on an Attic red-figure skyphos (drinking cup), the name-vase of the Penelope Painter, c. 440 BC. Telemachos addresses his mother, who sits with veiled head bowed; beside her is the shroud on which she works while waiting for Odysseus' return.*

making for her father-in-law – unpicking by night her day's work at the loom [192]. Telemachos sets out on a journey of his own, visiting and questioning some of the *Iliad*-renowned warriors who fought alongside his father. All the while Odysseus himself is beset by trials and traumas – ferocious storms and devastating shipwrecks, wrathful gods, weird beasts, and amorous enchantresses (epic heroes must expect epic adventures). At one point, in a 'flashback' speech delivered to the people of Phaeacia, who eventually supply him with the means to return to Ithaca, Odysseus narrates some of these adventures, including his encounters with the giant Polyphemos, the cannibalistic one-eyed Cyclops (see p. 124); with Scylla [212] and Charybdis, the one a canine-bodied monster, the other a deadly whirlpool; and with the Sirens whose sweet voices lull mortal sailors away from their ships [191]. In the end, Odysseus returns to Ithaca, reveals himself to his son, and together with him affects a particularly bloody revenge on Penelope's suitors: eventually, too, Odysseus and Penelope are reunited as husband and wife.

The relationship between the *Iliad* and the *Odyssey* has fascinated critics for millennia. It seems as if the *Odyssey* speaks to and through the *Iliad*, discussing and debating its ideas of heroic valour. In book 11, Odysseus' adventures have taken him to the Underworld where he meets the ghostly shades of a number of figures, among them the hero Achilles. But this Achilles is a changed man. No longer does he stand by his decision to die in heroic youth rather than aged mediocrity. One reading might be that it is the Odyssean struggle for life, rather than the Iliadic privileging of heroic death, that is here applauded: if so, the *Odyssey* perhaps promotes a different code of heroism from that of the *Iliad*, one which is as much about endurance, cunning, and craftiness (the Odyssean virtue of *metis*) as it is about military valour.

193 *Detail of the inscription on 'Nestor's Cup', found at the Euboean colony of Pithekoussai (modern Ischia), last quarter of the 8th century BC. The inscription, incised over the painted decoration, is among the earliest in alphabetic script known from the greater Greek world. The complete text reads something like this: 'I am the cup of Nestor, good to drink from; whoever drinks this cupful will straightaway be seized by desire for fair-crowned Aphrodite'. Epic by metre (at least in part), it may also have been epic by allusion, perhaps recalling the heavy gold-studded cup which, according to Iliad 11.632–37, Nestor alone could raise when full.*

194 *View of the megaron (hall) at 'Nestor's Palace' at Pylos, in the Peloponnese, built in the 14th century BC and destroyed by fire in the 12th century BC. The palace was wistfully named by archaeologists after the Homeric elder who ruled Pylos for three generations (in antiquity, however, a number of Greek sites claimed to be the 'sandy Pylos' of Homeric epic). Here we see the area of the throne room, reached at the far end through a wide portico and vestibule from an interior court: in the centre is a large hearth, once framed by four columns which supported a second storey; a royal or priestly throne stood at the centre of the left-hand wall. In the foreground, in a separate space, are the remains of large pithoi, or storage jars.*

EXCAVATING HOMER

These brief descriptions of the *Iliad* and the *Odyssey* cannot do justice to the complexities of the poems, their subsequent impact across ages and continents, and their profound influence on Western literature. Nor can they convey the shadow that epic poetry has cast upon our understanding of ancient material culture. And not only material culture: one scholar (Barry Powell) has even argued that the Greek alphabet was concocted for the urgent purpose of writing down Homer's tales (and certainly some of the earliest surviving instances of Greek writing seem 'Homeric' by allusion or metre [193]).

During the later 19th and 20th centuries, it was Homeric poetry that directed many of the efforts of early Classical archaeologists. Heinrich Schliemann [196], a German millionaire-cum-archaeologist, used it as guide to unearth 'Priam's Troy' and as ultimate source for understanding the treasures found at 'Agamemnon's Mycenae' [198–200]. Schliemann's projects have long been subject to criticism, controversy, and a mythologizing of their own. Most famous is the story that while excavating at Mycenae he telegraphed Athens, claiming to have 'gazed upon the face of Agamemnon'. What Schliemann had in fact discovered was a number of golden death masks in six 'shaft graves' that he collectively termed 'Circle A' [195, 200].

195 *Gold funerary mask interpreted by Schliemann as a representation of the visage of Agamemnon. It is said to have been found on the skull of a king buried in Shaft Grave V in Circle A at Mycenae [200], 16th century BC. (Its unusual eyes, nose, and moustache, however, have led some scholars to suggest that it is a forgery.)*

196 *Enchanted with Homeric epics, Heinrich Schliemann set out to prove that they were not just the stuff of poetic fantasy, but had a historical basis that could be authenticated by archaeological excavation (at Mycenae, Troy, Tiryns, and Orchomenos).*

197 *Sophia Schliemann wearing 'Priam's gold'. Ten years after retiring a millionaire in 1863, partly from trading gold dust in California, Schliemann struck gold in Troy (modern Hissarlik in Turkey). He dressed his young Greek wife in the treasure – which included two gold diadems, earrings, and necklaces – and later illegally smuggled it out of the country.*

More sophisticated archaeological techniques eventually deflated any association between Homer's Agamemnon and the Mycenaean death-mask: the gold is now dated to the 16th century BC, at least three centuries earlier than any 'historical' Trojan War; and some even conjecture that the 'Mask of Agamemnon' is a forgery that Schliemann himself commissioned. Still, we should not underestimate the immense gratification in finding apparent confluences between literary and material evidence – unearthing something connected with the very origins of Western literature.

Schliemann *tells the King of Greece the momentous news of the gold found in Circle A at Mycenae. In doing so, he allows himself a degree of romantic embellishment (albeit supported by a reference in the 2nd-century AD writings of Pausanias): these were not the lavish tombs of any ordinary Mycenaean royal family, Schliemann surmises, but those of Agamemnon, the Homeric king, and his wife, Clytemnestra, who, legend had it, murdered Agamemnon upon his return from Troy.*

With great joy I announce to your Majesty that I have discovered the tombs which the tradition proclaimed by Pausanias indicated as the graves of Agamemnon, Cassandra, Eurymedon, and their companions, all slain at a banquet by Clytemnestra and her lover Aegisthus.

I found in the tombs a huge treasure of archaeological objects of pure gold. This treasure alone is sufficient to fill a large museum, which will be the most brilliant in the world and which in time to come will draw tens of thousands of visitors to Greece from every land. Since I am working merely out of a disinterested love of science, I ask nothing in return for this treasure, which with boundless enthusiasm I hand over untouched to Greece.

With God's help, Your Majesty, may these treasures constitute the cornerstone of unlimited national wealth.

Heinrich Schliemann, telegram to King George of Greece, 28 November 1876

198 *The 'Lion Gate' at Mycenae, c. 1250 BC.*

199, 200 *The 'Treasury of Atreus' at Mycenae, c. 1250 BC (above), and Grave Circle A at Mycenae, c. 1600 BC, enclosed by a large defensive wall c. 1300 BC (right). Schliemann began his excavations at Mycenae, north of Argos in the Peloponnese, in 1876: his discoveries would prove so important that the site would lend its name to the 'Mycenaean' period of the Greek Bronze Age (the late Helladic period, c. 1600–1150 BC). Schliemann focused his attention on the citadel's graves. These included six shaft burials – rectangular trenches dug into the ground, walled with rubble and roofed with wood – in Circle A, and a number of chamber tombs created by cutting a corridor into the side of a hill. The most spectacular of the latter is the 'Treasury of Atreus'; a long passage leads through a lintelled door to a corbelled, beehive-shaped chamber.*

Whether connecting the Mycenaean 'Lion Gate' [198] with the *Iliad*'s tendency to compare its heroes to lions, or reconstructing the social layout of 'Nestor's Palace' at Pylos [194] with the Homeric poems in hand, this game of pairing archaeology and Homeric texts has proved particularly addictive; and perhaps nowhere more so than in the sphere of early Greek iconography.

Despite this chapter's use of images to 'illustrate' the stories of the *Iliad* and *Odyssey*, any specific association between epic poetry and surviving ancient images (especially, but not exclusively, those of the 8th to early 6th centuries) remains deeply controversial. In the *Iliad* and the *Odyssey*, artistic objects are generally defined by their material value – that is to say, the honour they bestow upon their owner. But one passage in the *Iliad* provides a particularly useful way to begin thinking about the relationship between epic poetry and the visual arts: in book 18, Thetis has commissioned no less a craftsman than the god Hephaistos to fashion armour for her son Achilles [585]; before she delivers it to him [201], we hear how Hephaistos decorated Achilles' new shield with a number of elaborate images. What follows is an equally elaborate verbal evocation of the shield, which incorporates the whole world into its imagery – all describable emotions, actions, and times.

But this verbal description of a work of art, or *ekphrasis*, is no simple process, and the passage should in fact alert us to the very different narrative modes of word and image. Words can narrate the stories on the shield in a single linear sequence: the poet can use time ('first this happened, then this, then that') to transcribe the images into an ordered and chronological narrative. Pictures, by contrast, do not work in this sort of temporal framework: were we actually to view the imaginary shield, our eyes would survey all its images in one glance.

201 *One of the Nereids (sea nymphs) helping Thetis carry the divine armour crafted by Hephaistos across the seas to Achilles: detail of the interior of a painted marble* lekanis *(footbath) from South Italy, c. 325–300 BC. She rides an obliging sea dragon and carries a golden shield.*

The shield of Achilles, *as described in book 18 of the* Iliad, *is made up of five concentric bands, with the constellations represented in its central section. The second band depicts two contrasting cities: the one described here is at peace (in stark and poignant contrast to the setting of the* Iliad), *while the other is at war, with scenes of siege and ambush. The marvel of the divine workmanship is ascribed to the lifelikeness of the shield's figures: it is as though the images come to life.*
The appreciation of artistic realism surely foreshadows the development of naturalistic art in late 6th- and early 5th-century BC *Athens.*

First of all Hephaistos wrought a great and sturdy shield, elaborating every part of it. Around it he cast a shining, glittering, three-part rim, and from that he hung a silver strap. The shield had five bands, and on each Hephaistos used his talent and skill to forge numerous cunning designs. On it he wrought the earth, on it the heavens, on it the ocean. On it he crafted the unrelenting sun, the full moon. On it he represented all the constellations that crown the sky: the Pleiades, the Hyades, the mighty Orion, and the Bear . . . He also decorated it with two fair cities of mortal men. In one there were weddings and banquets; people were leading the brides from their chambers through the city by the light of flaming torches; and a great bridal song arose. Young men danced and whirled; among them flutes and lyres made music, and married women stood each beside her door in wonder at the sight. The people, however, collected together in the Assembly, for a dispute had arisen and two men were arguing about the penalty for a murdered man: one, addressing the people, swore that he had paid the full amount; the other refused to accept any of this as true. Both agreed to abide by the verdict of an arbitrator. The people were cheering both parties, supporting both sides. Heralds kept them in order as the Elders sat on polished stones in a sacred circle, holding in their hands the staffs of the loud-voiced heralds. They would rise up and pronounce judgment to each in turn. In their midst lay two golden talents to be given to whoever should utter the most righteous judgment among them.

Homer, *Iliad* 18.478–508

202 *Drawing of the scene on the neck of a late Geometric Attic oinochoe, c. 750 BC: sailors surround a capsized warship. The central seated figure has been identified as Odysseus (who alone survives such a sea-storm in Odyssey 12.403–25). But are the surrounding figures drowning, or swimming? Each still manages to grasp the ship, or at least another sailor who has managed to do so. Whatever we decide, this image adds a new level of dramatic narrative complexity to the Homeric verbal description.*

The recognition of this fundamental difference must make us very wary of postulating too straightforward an influence of epic poetry on the visual arts. Verbal narratives and pictorial 'narratives' are necessarily different, and to postulate too close a relationship between the two media would be to underplay those essential differences.

Despite that *caveat*, many scholars do continue to pair epic poetry with early figurative representations in a whole variety of different ways, as their responses to a fragment of a late Geometric krater from the Dipylon region in the Kerameikos cemetery at Athens nicely exemplify [204]. The fragment's upper zone presents an early depiction of battle. This is certainly war at its grimmest: the two armies (characterized by their different body-shapes) are fighting beside the stacked bodies of the dead. One, at the centre of the upper frieze, is shown resisting attack from both sides; another (on the far right) falls from his chariot; yet another has been shot in the head with an arrow. Such scenes were probably thought appropriate for the funerary context in which these vases were used, reflecting an idealized mode of death and personal military glory. But is this an Iliadic story? The fact that the fragment does not recall any specific surviving poetic reference need not exclude the possibility (later inscribed names, attributes, and iconographic formulae could all be used to connect, in whatever sense, images like these to famous epic events); and some ancient viewers, like modern scholars, may have made an association between this image and an epic text. So it is that an Attic Geometric bowl showing a man and woman about to embark on a ship [203] has predictably been associated

203 below *On a late Geometric Attic krater, of the second half of the 8th century BC, a staffed warship, powered by two banks of oarsmen, looks set to pull out to sea. On the left a man grasps a woman by her wrist, in a seemingly coercive manner (she stands with her feet together in defiantly static pose). Is this Paris abducting Helen from Sparta? The pair have also been identified as Jason and Medea (in which case the ship is the renowned Argo) and as Theseus and Ariadne. In an age before identifying labels and attributes, interpretative ambiguity seems to have been unavoidable.*

204 right *Drawing of a fragment of a late Geometric Attic krater from the Dipylon cemetery in Athens, attributed to the Dipylon Master, third quarter of the 8th century BC. The upper band shows a vivid scene of military action. In the lower band three figures march into battle, carrying shields of a distinctive (so-called 'Dipylon') shape. At the far left is the controversial silhouette of 'Siamese twins'. But do these images evoke a specific mythological or poetic episode? Or are they highly stylized, but essentially generic, scenes?*

with the myth of Paris and Helen (among others); and a shipwreck on a wine jug [202] has been related to an episode in book 12 of the *Odyssey*. But such interpretations tell us as much, if not more, about our own ways of approaching ancient material culture as they do about what these images might originally have meant: these are the stories that are most familiar to us modern viewers, and we are more prone than ancient viewers to 'read' material culture through text-tinted glasses.

The lower zone of the Dipylon fragment [204] raises two further questions. The first is prompted by the appearance on the extreme left of a pair of warriors whose silhouettes are so close, with two pairs of legs but seemingly only a single torso (as in as many as thirteen other instances), that some have argued they are physically joined together. As it happens, surviving epic texts also make reference to a pair of conjoined twins: a fragment of Hesiod's *Catalogue of Women* and three passages in the *Iliad* name them (after their two parents) as the Aktorione-Molione. But can we be sure that this is not just an early pictorial convention for depicting one person behind another? And if the figures are indeed the Aktorione-Molione, why are they in this scene? They do not seem to be the chief subject, and their actions here cannot easily be reconciled with their descriptions in the *Iliad*.

A second feature of this lower zone has prompted debate about what the visual arts might contribute to our understanding of the cultural climate behind the genesis of Homeric epic. This is an elongated shield in 'figure of eight' shape (known as the 'Dipylon shield', because it appears on a number of pots from the Dipylon cemetery). This does not resemble any ordinary piece of armour that can be dated to the 8th century BC: instead, it appears to hark back to a shield type used much earlier, in the Mycenaean period, which may have been known to the 8th century through the rediscovery of ancestral graves and the development of hero cults. The shield, then, might help us to contextualize the emergence of Homeric story-telling: we may discern in its archaizing form a symptom of the intense interest in the heroic past that also lay behind the production and content of epic poetry (see p. 86).

ΕΡΜΗΣ ΠΡΙΑΜΟΣ ΑΧΙΛΛΕΥΣ

205, 206 *Marble 'Capitoline Iliac Tablet', signed by a certain Theodorus, probably early 1st century* AD. *Tablets like this may have served as votive offerings, teaching aids, or mythological prompt-sheets – 'teach yourself' guides to the canon of Greek literature.*

Minutely detailed images of the Iliad, arranged in horizontal friezes according to the poem's twenty-four books, could here be 'read' alongside a synopsis of the text in Greek (on the tall stele centre right). An inscription associates the large scene on the left with a (now lost) work by the early 6th-century BC *lyric poet Stesichoros. Its theme is the Ilioupersis, or sack of Troy. To the right of the city gates, Cassandra is seized by the 'Lesser' Ajax, and above them, to the left, Neoptolemos grasps Priam by the hair [cf. 190, 220]. In front of the gates Aeneas, wearing a Phrygian cap, carries his father Anchises on his back, and leads his son Ascanius out of Troy by the hand [cf. 221, 222]. Some of Aeneas' subsequent adventures are depicted below.*

Even in an object like this one, where image and text are juxtaposed, 'illustrations' were not required to follow the Homeric text to the letter. In the scene of Priam's ransom of Hector's body from Achilles (above), for example, Hermes is conspicuously represented inside Achilles' tent and in divine garb (notice his winged helmet), whereas in the Iliad he remained outside the tent and took on a mortal guise (24.457–71). When it came to evoking stories in a pictorial medium, after all, visual artists have always had a degree of 'artistic licence'.

The one-eyed giant Polyphemos is holding Odysseus and his companions captive, and Odysseus forms a plan to stop him from devouring the Greeks one by one: he will get the giant blind drunk before physically blinding him. Note some of the specific details of the story (as recounted by Odysseus to the Phaeacians): the olivewood stake, the five assailants, and the interior setting of the cave.

To my mind, the following plan seemed best. The Cyclops' great green olivewood staff lay beside the sheep pen. He had cut it down so that when it was dry he could carry it with him. As we looked at it we thought it to be the size of the mast of a broad, black merchant ship, which has twenty oars and crosses the great sea; such was the length and breadth of it to look upon. I went up to it, cut off about a fathom's length, and handing it to my comrades instructed them to shave it down. They made it smooth while I, standing by them, sharpened the point and immediately took it to the blazing fire to harden. Then I laid it well away, by hiding it beneath the dung that lay in huge piles around the cave. And I told the others to cast lots as to which of them should dare lift with me the stake and twist it into the Cyclops' eye, whenever sweet sleep should descend on him. And those who were chosen by lot were those whom I myself would have wanted to choose: they were four, and I myself was the fifth.

Homer, *Odyssey* 9.318–35

207 *Amphora from Eleusis, Attica, the name-vase of the Polyphemus Painter, second quarter of the 7th century BC. The neck evokes the story of Odysseus' blinding of the Cyclops Polyphemos, here a seated giant. Below that, a lion attacks a boar. On the belly is a depiction of Perseus' beheading of the Gorgon Medusa [cf. 132–36]: he rushes off to the right, protected by Athena and pursued by two skirted Gorgons, presumably Medusa's sisters, who stare out at us with arms outstretched and heads shaped like contemporary tripods (their ears and hair become protruding 'handles' in the shape of snakes and griffins).*

The tension between early Classical art, myth, and poetry can best be sensed in the earliest appearances of Polyphemos, the giant Cyclops encountered by Odysseus in book 9 of the *Odyssey*. One example occurs on the neck of a 7th-century Protoattic funerary amphora from Eleusis [207]. As in the Homeric narrative, Polyphemos is drunk at the moment of his blinding (he holds a skyphos in his right hand), and the use of outline as opposed to black silhouette for one of the figures probably signals some special protagonist (Odysseus himself?). But other pictorial details do not coincide so neatly with the Homeric account: there are only three assailants, as opposed to five; the weapon is a spear rather than a massive olive staff; and there is no hint of the cave setting. Those salient details might lead us to think that the artist had no specific knowledge of the Homeric narrative. But does this sort of detailed sleuthing constitute a valid methodological approach?

Not, perhaps, after we have taken three issues into account. First, it is very unlikely that our surviving texts of the *Iliad* and *Odyssey* are the same as the oral poems circulating between the 8th and 6th centuries, which were themselves subject to temporal and geographic variations. This is not mere philological nit-picking: if our Homeric texts are the final products of the late 6th century, how can we even begin to compare them with earlier pictures, searching for correspondences of detail? Second, even if our Homeric texts had remained static throughout antiquity, and even if artists could have consulted them at any stage, there is no reason to suppose that those artists would have followed the poetry faithfully. Evidence for the independence of images from verbal narratives is provided by the marble plaques referred to as *Tabulae Iliacae*, or 'Iliac Tablets', which summarize the story of the *Iliad*, book by book, in both words and pictures [205, 206]: here images are unambiguously set against verbal summaries of the *Iliad*; and yet the visual illustrations of the story still stray from the letter of the text. Third and finally, the elements of the story of a heroic protagonist blinding a giant are not unique to the story of Odysseus and Polyphemos, still less to the specifically Homeric rendition of the tale; anthropologists have demonstrated that 'hero-blinds-one-eyed-monster' stories are found the world over, from Norway to Hawaii, from the Celts to the peoples of New Guinea. So who is to say that the artist of the amphora from Eleusis was not thinking of some tale about a flesh-creeping monster heard at his mother's knee rather than any Homeric version? Just how do we determine how 'Homerically' an image might have been interpreted in an age before Victorian notions of pictorial 'illustration' – when pictures were not required to follow the details of a text verbatim? How gauge the level of engagement, interaction, and flirtation between literary and visual – as opposed to mythical and visual – media?

One way out of these dilemmas is to follow the lead of the 20th-century art historian Ernst Gombrich. Gombrich argued that epic poetry's influence on figurative art should be charted in general rather than specific terms. Homeric epic, he claims, was poetry of the emotions: once again, the Homeric description of the Polyphemos tale provides a nice example. In the Homeric version, our repugnance at the brutality of the Cyclops is softened by a touch of tender sympathy. After Polyphemos has been blinded, Odysseus must devise a way to escape the cave. A crucial detail in the Homeric story is that Polyphemos is a shepherd: each morning he brings his sheep out from the cave to pasture; so if Odysseus and his men could hide underneath the animals as they leave, they might evade the avenging anger of the sightless ogre. What makes the Homeric scene so remarkable is Polyphemos' address to his favourite ram, under which Odysseus hides [208]. 'What's delaying you? You're usually the first out of here', he fondly asks (*Odyssey* 9.447–60). 'You must be waiting behind in grief for your blinded master; if only you could talk and tell me where he is hiding!' Here we find suspense, irony, and pathos: to apply Gombrich's argument, this is story-telling not concerned just with *what* happened, but *how* it happened. The story of Odysseus and Polyphemos could have been dealt with in a few lines, with a handful of matter-of-fact details; but Homeric poetry rather chose to impersonate, to dwell on the emotions, to compare one action or feeling to another, to challenge and complicate our initial response even to a vicious, gargantuan, and hideous brute.

For Gombrich, this Homeric drive for telling the 'how' of myth was not only an original departure within the world history of poetry: it also inspired an original departure within the world history of art, as visual artists too brought their figurative representations to life. Eventually, Gombrich suggests, it was this drive towards animated and descriptive narrative that set Classical art on an evolutionary course towards 'naturalism'.

Attractive as Gombrich's theory might at first appear, closer scrutiny reveals a number of problems. Gombrich assumes that Homeric epic was born from an indigenous Greek source, distinct in style, if not in substance, from Near Eastern epics. But modern scholarship rather emphasizes the affinities between Greek and Near Eastern poetry, from the Mesopotamian *Epic of Gilgamesh* to the Old Testament. And can we really imagine, as Gombrich seems to have done, an early setting where poets and painters could interact? In what social or performative context could a poet influence a painter? Can we be sure, for that matter, that a humble craftsman could even have understood the weird Ionian dialect of Homeric poetry? Even more damning is the fact that if artists were aware of the stories of the

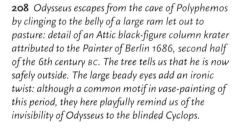

208 *Odysseus escapes from the cave of Polyphemos by clinging to the belly of a large ram let out to pasture: detail of an Attic black-figure column krater attributed to the Painter of Berlin 1686, second half of the 6th century BC. The tree tells us that he is now safely outside. The large beady eyes add an ironic twist: although a common motif in vase-painting of this period, they here playfully remind us of the invisibility of Odysseus to the blinded Cyclops.*

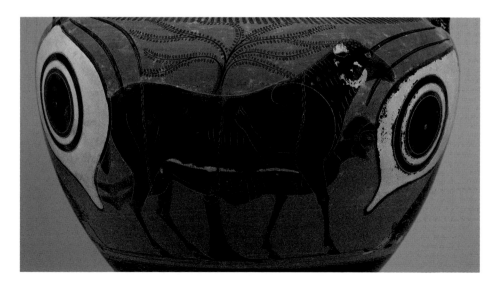

209 *The blinding of Polyphemos depicted on an Etruscan pithos, c. 625 BC. Odysseus and two companions hold a wooden stake (note the swelling end of its trunk): Odysseus may well be the figure on the right who grasps the stake with one hand, perhaps twisting it (cf. Odyssey 9.384). Polyphemos is shown seated at the far left, human size; the amphora in front of him alludes to his drunkenness.*

Iliad and *Odyssey*, they most often seem to have turned their back on them in their work: surviving images do not reflect a significant range of stories from the poems, nor is there a sustained number of representations of any single Homeric episode.

A lot of space has been devoted to the issue of Homeric influence on the visual arts. This is partly because this question has so thoroughly engrossed scholars. But it is mostly because the specifics of the debate nicely pinpoint a more general problem in approaches to ancient mythology: it is often thought that we can understand an image that we assume to 'illustrate' a myth just by identifying its subject. For this we look to any external source that might provide a clue, often disregarding the malleable aspect of Classical myths that made – and continues to make – them a living and exploratory tool, rather than merely the stuff of encyclopaedic reference books. The debate over influence has also tended to eclipse more interpretative issues about how to make sense of archaeological objects as *objects*: how a myth functioned within the context of a particular artefact; what the juxtaposition of two or more myths might have meant; how visual evocations of myths differ from representations in other media. Perhaps most importantly, it has blinded a number of interpreters to the fact that what is often classified as a single myth, or cycle of myths, actually had a variety of meanings within the different cultures of the ancient Mediterranean.

'GREEK' MYTH ABROAD

In fact, the Eleusis amphora [207] raises a number of these issues. A preoccupation with its 'Homeric' Polyphemos scene has sometimes distracted scholars from examining the amphora's two other decorative bands. Collectively the three bands seem to be concerned with what one scholar (Robin Osborne) has termed 'sensory deprivation'. On the body of the amphora, Perseus has decapitated Medusa (see p. 87) and is pursued by her two Gorgon sisters: according to the myth, anyone who cast eyes upon her was turned to stone, so as viewers we too should be literally petrified upon looking at the scene. Between this and the Polyphemos image, a lion attacks a boar – an epic simile turned into a picture? some sort of aristocratic metaphor? or an embodiment of devouring mortality?

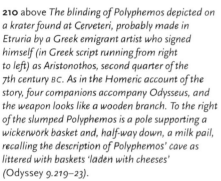

210 above *The blinding of Polyphemos depicted on a krater found at Cerveteri, probably made in Etruria by a Greek emigrant artist who signed himself (in Greek script running from right to left) as Aristonothos, second quarter of the 7th century BC. As in the Homeric account of the story, four companions accompany Odysseus, and the weapon looks like a wooden branch. To the right of the slumped Polyphemos is a pole supporting a wickerwork basket and, half-way down, a milk pail, recalling the description of Polyphemos' cave as littered with baskets 'laden with cheeses' (Odyssey 9.219–23).*

211 above right *The blinding of Polyphemos depicted in the Tomb of Orcus at Tarquinia, last quarter of the 4th century BC. Polyphemos is portrayed as a grotesque giant with a huge head. His single large circular eye, surrounded by eyelashes, is vastly out of proportion with his big nose, moustachioed and grimacing mouth, and bearded chin. The stake is plainly made of sharpened olive wood – to the left, we can just make out the remains of a branch that sprouts from the bark, covered with olive leaves*

The grey, rectangular illusory door behind the giant's right arm is an interesting touch: while alluding to the detail that the entrance of Polyphemos' cave was closed, it also evokes the openings that often adorned Etruscan tombs, perhaps as liminal passageways to the nether-world of the dead.

These three sets of images might not add up to much if we did not happen to know one significant archaeological detail: this amphora functioned as a coffin for an adolescent boy. The juxtaposition of scenes seems to relate to the epic formula of 'living and seeing the light of the sun' – that is to say, the convention of defining life as an ability to see, and death as the loss of the senses. The conjunction of myths on the coffin-cum-amphora, then, might not have been a random (nor any sort of 'literary') choice, but part of a larger meditation on issues of life and death.

This funerary interpretation of the Polyphemos myth may find little corroboration in the Greek world; but something interesting was happening in the Etruscan reception, and redefinition, of the Polyphemos myth at around the same time. One of the earliest Etruscan images of the Cyclops myth appears on a gigantic terracotta pithos dating to around 625 BC [209]. We must resist the temptation to re-enter the debate about how 'Homeric' this image is, although Odysseus does seem to be twisting an actual branch, with a pointed tip, into the giant's eye. From the 7th century onwards, the story of Polyphemos apparently appealed to the Etruscans: it appears again on a krater made in Etruria by a Greek artist who signed his name as 'Aristonothos', literally 'Best Bastard' [210]. Here, as in the Homeric text, the cave of the Cyclops is littered with dairy paraphernalia, and beside him stands a pole holding a milk bucket (perhaps artists working in Etruria had a more literal-minded attitude to Greek poetry than their Greek counterparts?). A later wall-painting in the Tomb of Orcus in Tarquinia gives us the Etruscan names of Polyphemos and Odysseus [211]: Cuclu and Uthuste. But its sepulchral context also hints at a far more important aspect of the myth's meaning in Etruria. The funerary context of this wall-painting, as well as of numerous urns and Greek vases featuring this myth, surely directs us to postulate that some sort of eschatological metaphor is working behind the Etruscan understanding of this story. This was not simply a tale about Odysseus and his exploits: it was a story of blinding which provided an allegorical way of envisioning death.

For the most celebrated adaptation of the myth of Polyphemos, we must leap forward in time to the turn of the millennium. The scene is a grotto in Sperlonga (Spelunca in Latin) [212, 213], now a favourite seaside resort on the coastal highway

212, 213 *Reconstruction of the grotto at Sperlonga as it appeared in the early 1st century AD (right), and a view of it as it survives today.*

The triclinium was set into a rectangular basin. Beyond it, in the centre of an artificial pool, the monstrous Scylla attacked the ship of Odysseus (B); her lower body consisted of dogs that pounced upon the Homeric crew. To the left (A), a warrior supported a dead comrade (the 'Pasquino Group', here perhaps representing Odysseus carrying the body of Achilles). To the right (D), a group showed Odysseus and Diomedes stealing the Palladium (the sacred image of Athena) from Troy. Behind, tucked away at the back of the grotto in a recess (C) that evoked Polyphemos' own cave, Odysseus and his men were shown blinding the Cyclops [214]. Above the cave (E) was a coloured marble statue depicting Ganymede's abduction by the eagle of Zeus. An inscription chiselled on the outrigger of the Scylla group names its artists as Athenodoros, Hagesandros, and Polydoros (see p. 138).

Ten lines of Latin hexameters were found on a plaque, perhaps added in the late 3rd century AD, which was probably once displayed on the rear wall of the Sperlonga grotto. Although the right side of the inscription has broken away, making reconstruction at times uncertain, it clearly set the cave's sculptural programme against the potential of poetry to narrate mythical stories.

If Mantua were able to resurrect its divine poet-priest [Vergil], he would be amazed at the tremendous work and admit defeat before our cave. And as for the treachery of the Ithacan [Odysseus], the flames and the blinded eye of the semi-beast who was oppressed with sleep and wine alike, the grottoes and restless waters, the Cyclopean rocks, the savagery of Scylla, and the ship's prow broken in the whirlpool – he himself would confess that he could not [express] these things in a poem, not as vivid [representations] moulded [by the] artist's [hand]. Only [the artifice and artistic skill] of Nature surpasses that [hand]. Fortunate indeed is Faustinus [to craft] this [cave] for his masters.

The 'Faustinus' inscription
at Sperlonga

between Rome and Naples, but once part of an elaborate Roman villa complex. A dining room (*triclinium*) was attached through a series of pools and channels to a natural cavern. At some stage in the villa's long and complicated history, it seems to have belonged to the Emperor Tiberius. According to Tacitus (*Annals* 4.59) and Suetonius (*Life of Tiberius* 39), one of Tiberius' dinner parties here in AD 26 ended in disaster when the cave collapsed, almost killing the Emperor. In 1957, many thousands of fragments of sculpture, like the pieces of some vast three-dimensional jigsaw puzzle, were found in the cave, including pieces of a group depicting Odysseus – Ulysses, to the Romans – and his companions blinding Polyphemos [214]. This was only one of several sculptural groups that took up Homeric (or otherwise epic) themes: it was accompanied by at least three other large groups and an eclectic hotch-potch of other finds (including a tantalizing ten-line Latin inscription).

To understand how this new Roman setting at Sperlonga played upon Greek myths about Polyphemos, we need first to consider how such stories were filtered through the Hellenistic literature of the 3rd and 2nd centuries BC, especially in the city of Alexandria. Hellenistic myths used to be discussed in terms of a dramatic change from a vibrant Greek cultural force to a body of quaint surviving tales that gratified only the collecting, cataloguing, and classifying habits of élite and scholarly connoisseurs. This was a transformation, it was argued, from stories that were actually 'believed' to mythological fancies that served only to furnish learned poetry with academic and literary embellishments. The 3rd and 2nd centuries were seen as an age of 'mythography': writers who collected myths revolving around a common theme, place, or name were thought merely to have been interested in flaunting their learning. Certainly, the era does seem to have been characterized by a delight in the more obscure aspects of Greek myth (poems like Lycophron's *Alexandra*, composed probably in the early 2nd century BC, were crammed full of bafflingly enigmatic mythological references). Today, however, it is accepted that Hellenistic treatments of myth constituted much more sophisticated ways of exploring the relationship between the poets' own Alexandrian present and the Greek past.

Imagine the atmosphere in which most of these poets were writing. The Ptolemies, rulers of Alexandria, had founded a great library. Its size was unprecedented, and it was crowded with oppressively canonical texts: whatever the poets might choose to write, it had all been done before. One response was to develop a

214 *Plaster reconstruction of the Polyphemos group at Sperlonga. The fragmentary marble original probably dates from the first quarter of the 1st century AD, although some scholars argue that it copied an earlier Hellenistic group, perhaps made at Pergamon or on the island of Rhodes. The muscular giant sprawls against a rock in drunken slumber (the only substantial parts to have survived are his head, left leg, right lower leg, and fragments of both arms). Odysseus, closest to Polyphemos on the left and wearing a conical cap, directs three companions in the act of blinding. Two help him to wield the huge stake, while the third figure, in the foreground on the right, drags a large wineskin (the source of Polyphemos' drunkenness).*

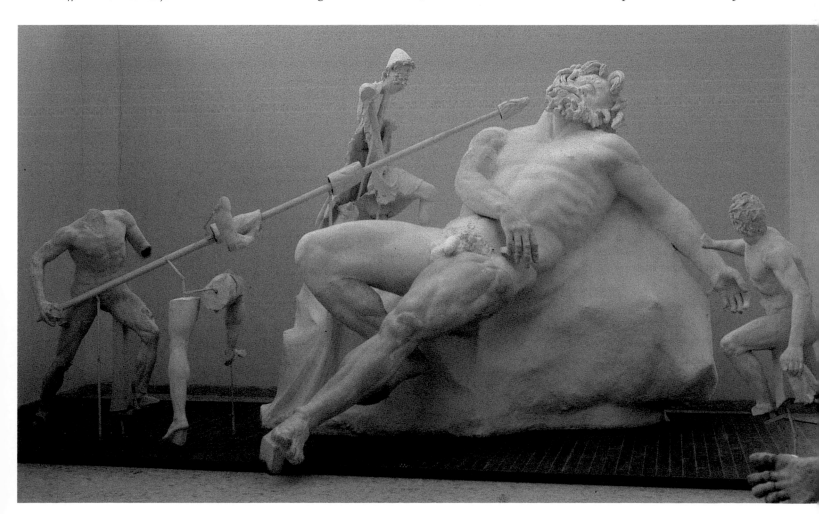

215 *Marble* Barberini Faun, c. AD 50, *probably after a Greek sculpture made c. 200 BC. The pointed ears, animal skin, and panpipes all help to identify the sprawling figure as a satyr, innocently duped by potent wine. The Sperlonga Polyphemos statue [214] seemingly evoked this statue type's pose, heavy musculature, and drunken subject.*

216 *Marble* Dying Giant. *The giants, sons of Gaia (Earth), took up arms against the Olympian gods, and thus stood as archetypes of brutish barbarism [cf. 458, 459]. This statue is thought to relate to a set of figures of a giant, Amazon, Persian, and Gaul, all on the brink of death, erected by the Attalid kings of Pergamon in Athens in the 2nd century BC (the 'Lesser Attalid Group'), which were frequently imitated in Roman marble sculptures. The tilting head and the schema of the legs, as well as the bushy beard, bestial tufts of body hair, and heavy muscular proportions, all foreshadow the iconography of Polyphemos at Sperlonga [214].*

new form of poetry, taking myths and tracing their history back through time in an implicit search to find their cause (or 'aetiology', to follow the title of the most famous collection, Callimachus' *Aetia*, or *Causes*).

The story of Polyphemos, too, was treated in this sort of 'before they were famous' manner. In his eleventh *Idyll*, written in the 3rd century BC, Theocritus made constant and ironic allusion to Polyphemos' later cannibalistic encounter with Odysseus; but that Homeric Cyclops seems far removed from this shepherding country bumpkin, the rustic who pines after his beloved sea-nymph, Galatea. Educated Romans knew their Theocritus, and enjoyed a Latin version too (in Vergil's ninth *Eclogue* lines 39–43). This is the bucolic Polyphemos whom we also encounter in a number of Roman wall-paintings [217].

Might not the Polyphemos sculpture at Sperlonga hint at this same rustic figure? The giant as reconstructed [214], with his outstretched legs and tilted head, recalls two particular types of Hellenistic sculpture with very different associations. The first is preserved in the *Barberini Faun* [215]: an appealing, rustic satyr has over-indulged himself with wine and, rather provocatively, stretches out for a nap. The second is the type of the *Dying Giant* [216], one of a clan who had dared to threaten the Olympian order, but who now lies conquered.

So has our Sperlonga Polyphemos, then, been beguiled by wine, a gullible provincial akin to the rustic Polyphemos of Theocritus? Or does he resemble a giant – a savage threat to civilization, like the Homeric monster? Doubtless those were questions that were set up to direct table-talk in the *triclinium* at Sperlonga. Viewers seem to have enjoyed the rich ironies of encountering Polyphemos in this dining setting: the prototypical bad host is introduced into the context of a civilized dinner party; the consequences of alcoholic over-indulgence are demonstrated to the guests as they themselves drink; and the theatrical display in stone probably mimics the performance of Homeric mimes during dinner. Whatever the precise workmanship of this Polyphemos group (discussion has largely centred on the rather vain question of whether the Sperlonga sculptures are 'Greek originals' or 'Roman copies'), it is clear that this is not just a 'passive', 'parasitic', 'purely derivative' representation of a Greek myth. Instead, the Sperlonga sculpture cleverly played upon a number of different Greek associations, no less than this specifically Roman dining context, to produce a thoroughly original experience for its viewers: so original, in fact, that the subject became a sort of imperial signature-tune, to be further played upon, in ever-new and creative versions, in the residences of later 1st- and early 2nd-century Roman emperors.

217 *Polyphemos and Galatea, in a wall-painting from the rich Roman villa at Boscotrecase north of Pompeii, last quarter of the 1st century BC. The bucolic Polyphemos sits in the centre with a set of panpipes in his right hand and his shepherding staff put aside. He stares across the dreamy landscape at Galatea (bottom left), who rides on the back of a dolphin (emphasizing the differences between the realms of Polyphemos and his beloved). As if explicitly to remind us that this lovelorn romantic is the same fiendish Polyphemos that we encounter in Homer, just above him, on the right, we see a later episode in the myth: the blinded Cyclops throws a rock at the departing ship of Odysseus (cf. Odyssey 9.480–90, 536–42).*

The combination of two stories in a single composition parallels various Hellenistic and Roman literary attempts to foreshadow the later destiny of Polyphemos while treating his earlier naïve and unrequited love for Galatea.

The love-sick Polyphemos *woos the stubborn Galatea: the pastoral enticements that Theocritus' Cyclops can offer, however, seem more appropriate to a gentle shepherd than a monstrous cave-dweller. There is particular irony in Polyphemos' reference to his ewes' milk and cheese-crates here; for these are the very things that Odysseus describes in his famously less amicable encounter with the Cyclops.*

I know, fair Galatea, why you avoid me. It's because of the shaggy brow that stretches over my whole forehead, isn't it – the long, single brow from one ear to the other, the single eye beneath, and the broad nostril above my lip? Well, I might be such a man, but I still tend a thousand cattle; I still farm and drink from them the purest milk; and

I do not lack cheese in summer, autumn, or bitter winter – my crates of cheese are always heavy! I can play on the pipe as no other Cyclops can, as often in oppressive night I sing, my sweet little honey-apple, of you and me. And for you I rear eleven collared fawns, for you four bear cubs.

Theocritus, *Idyll* 11.30–41

218, 219 above and opposite *The Trojan Horse and scenes of the subsequent sack of Troy, on a pithos found on Mykonos, second quarter of the 7th century* BC. *The square portholes in the wheeled wooden horse on the neck allow us to see what the Trojans presumably could not – Greek warriors poised to storm the city. Some soldiers remain seated, dangling swords, shields, and helmets; others,* *having already disembarked, set off on the brutal expeditions recounted episodically below (the latter have also been interpreted as Trojan soldiers, suspicious of events). Note the difference in armour between the figures in the upper frieze and the lower three bands: when assailing innocent women and children, warriors have no need of protective shields . . .*

220 *Drawing of the sack of Troy on the shoulder of an Attic red-figure hydria attributed to the Kleophrades Painter, c. 480–475 BC. The hydria's large upper handle is indicated at the top, its two smaller handles at the sides. Working anticlockwise from the upper handle, we see Aeneas with his father Anchises and his son Ascanius; the rape of Cassandra, who clings to a statue of Athena [cf. 190] but is seized by the 'Lesser' Ajax [cf. 190, 205]; the murder of Priam; a Trojan woman (Hector's wife Andromache?) resisting capture; and the rescue of Aithra (the mother of Theseus, who was abducted and taken to Troy as Helen's maidservant).*

The painter has used every available space to evoke a melée of scenes, interrupted only by the hydria's upper handle. The complex overlap of figures also reinforces the sense of tumultuous disorder, disarray, and disturbance that is recounted in the individual episodes.

TROJAN ASPIRATIONS AND ROMAN RECEPTIONS

Rather than unoriginally following Greek precedents, the Romans imbued the Greek myths in both art and literature with new cultural, religious, and political significance. While so many Greek myths were concerned with the creation of the universe, Roman myths most frequently revolved around the foundation of the Roman world and the *Imperium Romanum*. Greek stories were transformed into ways of framing distinctively Roman concerns. Nowhere is that process more evident than in the Roman appropriation of the myth of the fall of Troy.

We have already seen one Greek artistic representation of the sack of Troy, attributed to an Athenian vase-painter named Onesimos [190]. In fact, the pot ended up at Cerveteri in Etruria, where, as we have seen, versions of Homeric and other Greek tales were circulating with local twists of meaning, and probably in the Etruscan language. Somewhat earlier is a terracotta pithos from the Cycladic island of Mykonos which functioned, like the Eleusis amphora [207], as an ornate receptacle for human remains [218, 219]. Around its huge neck is the vessel's largest scene: the Greeks manage to enter Troy by hiding in a hollow wooden horse (the ruse is recounted by Demodokos in book 8 of the *Odyssey* and we know that it was told in several other epic poems that have not survived [cf. 205]). The Trojans believe the horse to be a gift from the gods, until the Greeks, who can here be seen through small windows in the side, jump out and ransack the city. The subsequent scenes of conquest are depicted in a series of snapshots, roughly organized into three horizontal zones on the jar's belly.

Later Greek representations of the sack of Troy tended to isolate a number of specific incidents (which may or may not find precedents on the belly of the Mykonos pithos). On the shoulder of a red-figure hydria [220] we can discern one Greek invader, the 'Lesser' Ajax, seizing the Trojan royal prophetess Cassandra; Neoptolemos striking the Trojan king, Priam, who holds the mutilated corpse of

221 *Aeneas and Anchises on an Attic black-figure amphora attributed to the Class of Cambridge 49, c. 510 BC. Aeneas escapes Troy, guiding his son Ascanius by the hand and carrying his father Anchises on his back. The old man turns round to catch a final glimpse of the city.*

222 *Aeneas and Anchises on a silver denarius commissioned by Julius Caesar, c. 48–46 BC. Aeneas is shown naked and highly heroized. Displaying both filial and religious* pietas, *he carries his father and also holds the Palladium – the sacred image of Minerva which he rescued from Troy, and which could supposedly be seen in the Temple of Vesta in Rome at this time. The image of Aeneas also boasts of Caesar's ancestry, which could, Caesar claimed, be traced back to Venus via Aeneas, her son.*

his grandson Astyanax in his lap; and a Trojan lady, perhaps Andromache (the wife of Priam's son, Hector) picking up some domestic instrument as the only weapon left for her defence. This is city-sacking at its most spiteful and piteous: notice how the statue of Athena points her spear vainly at Cassandra's assailant, while a palm tree bends sympathetically over a crouching woman. Some modern viewers have understandably thought that the scene, painted in Athens in the aftermath of the city's own invasion by the Persians in 480–479 BC, might reflect a new-found awareness of the plight of the defeated.

But amidst these scenes of desolation – of bodies oozing blood, sanctuaries violated, age dishonoured – there are glimmers of hope: these take the form of two scenes of rescue. On one side of the hydria's upper handle comes the rescue of Theseus' mother, Aithra, by two Greek soldiers. On the other, we can see an elderly man hoisted onto the shoulders of a young warrior, an iconographic scheme which recurs on both Greek [221] and Roman [222] artefacts: here is an early testimony to the piety of the Trojan prince who would later develop into one of antiquity's most renowned household names – for this is Aeneas carrying his aged father, Anchises, from the sacked city of Troy. Aeneas does appear in the *Iliad* and in later poems, tragedies, and mythographies: he was said, for example, to have fought hand-to-hand with the great Greek warriors Diomedes and Achilles (although in both instances he was only saved by the divine intervention of Aphrodite – his mother – and Poseidon). Even in the *Iliad*, a specific destiny seems to have been reserved for him: as Poseidon makes explicit (*Iliad* 20.293–308), Aeneas had been fated to escape Troy and establish a new kingdom. That kingdom, or so the Romans would claim, was Rome.

For the Romans, the myth of Aeneas provided an especially resonant and versatile set of stories. While Aeneas had his own function in Homeric poetry and subsequent Greek literature, he was also a decidedly non-Greek character – a cameo Trojan hero who held his own against the 'A-list' of his Greek counterparts. What better metaphor than Aeneas, then, for Rome, with her empire beginning to encroach upon various Greek cities in the 3rd century BC, and subsequently coming into ever closer cultural contact with Greek literature, art, and mythology? The myth of Aeneas (who would found the city of Lavinium, over which his son Ascanius ruled before establishing Alba Longa [225], from which Romulus would in turn found Rome) enabled the Romans to negotiate some sort of shifting balance between an affiliation with, and hostility towards, Greece. In turn, the myth of Troy and Aeneas provided a framework for other civilizations to pitch their relationship with Rome, not least in Etruria from the 4th century BC onwards. With the Romans aligning themselves with the mytho-history of Aeneas and Troy, Etruscan nobles could conversely take the side of Greek heroes: a tomb at Vulci nicely captures the mythically pitched rivalry, framing scenes of contemporary

223 *Scenes from the* Aeneid *in a mosaic from a Romano-British villa at Low Ham in south-west England, probably mid-4th century* AD. *By drawing on Classical myths, especially those drawn from the* Aeneid, *local dignitaries could affirm an emphatically Roman identity, despite living on the fringes of the empire [cf. 95]. This mosaic brings together several scenes from books 1 and 4. On the right we see ships arriving at Dido's kingdom in Carthage. At the top is Venus with Cupid, whom she has disguised as Aeneas' son Ascanius so that he might arouse in Aeneas and Dido a 'living love' (*Aeneid 1.721): *and indeed, on either side of them, Aeneas and Dido meet each other's longing gaze. Next, on the left side, we see Dido and Aeneas behind Ascanius, setting off on horseback to a hunt. The story comes to a climax at the bottom, with the couple's embrace. The central panel foretells the episode's outcome: Venus is flanked by two cupids, of which the animated one holds an erect torch while the more sombre one holds his torch to the floor, a motif that signals imminent death – the suicide of Dido, on a funerary pyre, after Aeneas had abandoned her.*

224 *Achilles killing Trojan prisoners in revenge for the death of Patroklos (cf. Iliad 23.175–77): detail of a wall-painting from the François Tomb at Vulci, third quarter of the 4th century BC. Etruscans and Romans, at war in this period (Vulci was conquered by Rome c. 280 BC), were evidently taking sides in the epic of Troy. Here, two Etruscan demons – the winged Vanth, and blue-faced Charun – assist the Greeks in the despatch of 'Roman' Trojans: the deceased, named as Vel Saties, could thus envisage a mythical exaction of revenge beyond the grave.*

Etruscan–Roman opposition with a heraldic image of the Greek Achilles slaughtering Trojan prisoners [224].

It was in the time of the Emperor Augustus that the story of Aeneas was most definitively recast, in the form of Vergil's *Aeneid*. So influential was Vergil's treatment of the story that it becomes almost impossible to trace alternative versions of the myths that it treats. The *Aeneid* rapidly became the 'set-text' of schoolboys, the standard against which contemporary and later poetry was judged, and the inevitable butt of literary and visual parody. In short, it became a Roman literary classic – Rome's answer to the Greek *Iliad* and *Odyssey*. Before the *Aeneid* had even been finished (tradition has it that Vergil died in 19 BC before completing the work, ordering his manuscripts to be burnt), Vergil's contemporary, Propertius, foretold the birth of something 'greater than the *Iliad*' (*Elegies* 2.34.66). Indeed, the *Aeneid* is a poem acutely aware of its Homeric derivations. In its opening phrase, 'Arma virumque cano', for instance, *arma* (arms) roughly corresponds to the subject-matter of the *Iliad*, *virum* (a man) to the opening lines of the *Odyssey*, and *cano* (I sing) to the recitation of Greek epic, and perhaps also to later Greek cyclic epics.

The *Aeneid*'s canonical literary status endured throughout antiquity [551] and has long loomed large over Western literature. But what must originally have struck the *Aeneid*'s audiences is the poem's insights into the contemporary world. True, this was a poem set in a time (and place) before even Romulus and his settlement of seven hills by the River Tiber. Nevertheless, its backdrop was clearly the political territory of Augustan Rome. In the world of the *Aeneid*, just as in the Rome of Augustus, national interest triumphs over personal desires: so it is that Aeneas must abandon his beloved Dido, Queen of Carthage, for the public good of the 'new Troy' [223] (unlike Augustus' political nemesis, Mark Antony, and Antony's Egyptian queen, Cleopatra). For both Aeneas and Augustus, too, dutiful piety towards the gods is presented as the foremost virtue. Vergil's rendition of the

Now turn your eyes here and look upon this people – the Romans that belong to you. Here are Caesar and all the descendants of the Julian family who are destined to pass under the great sphere of heaven. Here is the man – this is the very man himself – whom you hear so often promised to you: Augustus Caesar, son of a god, who will again establish a golden age amid the fields which Saturn once ruled in Latium. He will expand his empire beyond the Garamantes and Indians. His land will extend beyond the stars, beyond the paths of the year and sun, where sky-bearing Atlas spins on his shoulders the sphere of earth that is joined with blazing stars. As he draws near, the kingdoms of Caspia and the Maeotic lands now shudder at the prophecies of the gods; the quaking mouths of the seven-bodied Nile are panicked and confused. Truly, Hercules has not travelled over so much of the Earth . . . nor has victorious Bacchus who, guiding his chariot with reins made from vine leaves, drives his tigers down from the high peak of Nysa.

Vergil, *Aeneid* 6.788–805

Aeneas story is clearly an example of a myth in the service of the state. But it is a testimony to the creative vitality of the *Aeneid* that scholars today are divided over just how pro-Augustan the poem really is: does its manipulation of numerous Augustan political ideas, symbols, and language amount to an uncompromising celebration of the new political status quo? Or would that reading be incompatible with the poem's more tragic, melancholy, and even downright damning moments?

The relationship between Roman art and the specifically Vergilian shaping of the Aeneas myth remains disputed. Contenders for the prized title of 'Vergilian' include a miscellany of images, from a supposed relief of Aeneas sacrificing a sow to the Penates (household gods) on the Ara Pacis in Rome (see pp. 182–83) to a number of Pompeian wall-paintings depicting the deserted Dido. But perhaps the best-known association between a piece of visual art and Vergil's *Aeneid* involves a marble group now in the Vatican Museums, perhaps dating to the beginning of the 1st century AD: the *Laocoön* [226]. It was Laocoön, a Trojan priest, who declared that he 'feared Greeks even when they came bearing gifts' ('timeo Danaos et dona ferentes': *Aeneid* 2.49), warning his countrymen that the Wooden Horse was a trick. The gods did not take kindly to his attempted subversion of divine schemes: they dispatched a pair of snakes to devour the priest's children before turning upon Laocoön (who was busy preparing a sacrifice by the shore). 'He stretched out his hands to untie the knots,' Aeneas continues the story (*Aeneid* 2.220–24), 'drenched to his priestly headband with blood and black venom. All the while he raised hideous screams to the heavens, like the roaring of a wounded bull when it flees the sacrificial altar and has shaken from its neck a poorly aimed axe.' Whatever other connection we may postulate between the Vergilian and sculptural rendition of the story, they share an acute interest in the artistic rendering of pain. The sculpture's emphasis upon Laocoön's physical agony has caused much debate since the 18th century about the aesthetic decorum of representing emotional extremes; and comparisons between the story's verbal and sculptural rendition also founded a framework for thinking about the differences between verbal and visual media – not least by the German philosopher and dramatist Gotthold Ephraim Lessing, who centered *Laokoön*, his 1766 essay on the 'limits of painting and poetry', around the group.

225 *The four walls of a tomb on the Esquiline Hill in Rome, c. 40–30 BC, took up the story of Rome's foundation in continuous narrative. This scene shows the founding of Alba Longa by Aeneas' son Ascanius: the city wall is under construction, overseen by a seated figure whose turreted crown recalls Hellenistic images of Tyche [117], and who is probably a personification of the city. It was at Alba Longa that Rhea Silvia, a Vestal Virgin impregnated by Mars, bore the twins Romulus and Remus. They were cast into the Tiber, but washed ashore and suckled by a she-wolf, then discovered by a herdsman. They built a new settlement, named Rome after Romulus.*

But, as with the sculptures at Sperlonga, scholars have been bound to ask: is the *Laocoön* a Roman marble copy of a Greek bronze original? Can we attribute it to a school of sculpture comparable with that of the Great Altar of Zeus at Pergamon [458–60]? Perhaps even to the artists of the Sperlonga groups [212, 214]? This last question has been fuelled by a possible correspondence between a second inscription at Sperlonga (this time on the Scylla group) naming the artists as Athenodoros, Hagesandros, and Polydoros, and a fortuitous literary reference by the Roman encyclopaedist Pliny the Elder (*Natural History* 36.37). Pliny recorded this same trio, or at least three Rhodians with the same names, as the creators of a marble *Laocoön* group displayed in the palace of the Emperor Titus (near to where the *Laocoön* was discovered in 1506).

In the case of the *Laocoön* group, however, these questions of authorship may amount to something more than the dry and technical pedantry of scholarly attribution: they perhaps point to an ideological antithesis between Greek and Roman responses to the myth of Laocoön. For we might have expected Greek viewers to receive this sculpture's subject rather unsympathetically: this is what happens if you cross the gods – the fair retribution for opposing Greek invasion and ultimately for Helen's adultery. For the Roman viewer, however, the myth of Laocoön was more likely to raise a lump in the throat: here was a Trojan 'ancestor', here a symbol of a lost homeland – the promise of a new Troy and (by association) the legacy of Aeneas fulfilled by Augustus. Of course the reception of any image can never be drawn in such stark and diametrically opposed colours. But the myth of Laocoön may have struck the statue's Greek artists, or at least its later Roman owner, as interesting precisely because of the way in which it threw up such questions about the cultural appropriation of Greek myth. To put it another way, then, perhaps the sculpture embodied for its viewers, and in the starkest terms, the very malleability of Classical myths.

So the *Laocoön* sculpture brings us back to the observations with which this chapter opened: the endless evolution of myth; its intrinsic ability to be moulded so as to debate a variety of issues; its tireless plasticity over time, place, and cultural context. Just as Athenian tragedy could uproot the Homeric heroes from Troy and resurrect them on stage to discuss (albeit often implicitly) peculiarly contemporary and democratic concerns, so too could Attic vase-paintings transform Homer's hardened fighting crew into an Athenian democratic jury [268], or mythical stories of change be metamorphosed into a metaphor for understanding Augustus' transformation of the political and cultural landscape of Rome (in Ovid's *Metamorphoses*, an epic rival to the *Aeneid*, published two decades or so after Vergil's poem). Given that plasticity, it is misguided simply to pair 'mythological' image and story together, and still more to concentrate on finding a myth's pristine 'original' version. For material culture (especially, but not exclusively, in conjunction with other sources) allows us to explore something far more rich, nuanced, and interesting: the application of a myth, the ways in which it could constantly be reapplied, and how (and why) myths were – and still are – made to mean something in new and ever-changing cultural contexts.

226 *Marble statue of Laocoön and his two sons entwined in the crushing coils of two serpents, sent by the gods (Minerva, in the Aeneid; Apollo, in an earlier tradition) to punish the Trojan priest for his warning against the Greeks.*

For all its celebrity, the statue's date remains uncertain. It is now generally thought to be a virtuoso reproduction (perhaps in the early 1st century AD) of an early 2nd-century BC bronze original, produced in Rhodes or Pergamon. Pergamon was close to Troy and ideologically connected with the doomed city through Telephos, her mythical founder [cf. 460]: one local myth even had the

Greeks attack Telephos' kingdom after mistaking the city for Troy; and what greater allegory of that city's potential pseudo-Trojan fate at the hands of a growing Roman military threat than Laocoön?

At the very least, we can be certain that this was a statue widely known in antiquity, and widely associated with the Aeneid in the greater Roman world. When, in the early 5th century AD, the illustrator of a codex of Vergil's poems needed a set of images to accompany the text of the Laocoön episode in the Aeneid, he chose precisely this schema to evoke the priest's despairing anguish.

IV MANIPULATING NATURE

CLASSICAL MYTH-MAKING was comprehensive. It extended characterization to elements of the natural world. Water and rocks, winds and weather, growth and decay – little escaped the web of mythology. Every roll of thunder, every earthquake or volcano, was a message from the gods; and all stories, however fantastic, had locations that were plausible and definite. No 'description of the earth' (*geographia*) was complete if it did not say where Perseus had rescued Andromeda, Troy once stood, and Odysseus wandered. If Polyphemos lived on Sicily, then the huge rocks he hurled after the departing Odysseus must still be visible – and there they were, sure enough: several outcrops prominent off the coast of Syracuse . . .

The Classical investment of landscape with myth may be rationalized as an act of taming or familiarizing what seems wild and bewildering. But beyond these stories, how did the ancient inhabitants of the Mediterranean deal with the realities of their environment? This chapter offers a summary of four aspects of such 'ecological' interaction: agriculture; gardens and landscapes; the exploitation of natural resources; and (as a further sort of such exploitation) the rise of particular arts, crafts, and technologies.

MANAGING THE COUNTRYSIDE

It was a genteel metropolitan writer, Virginia Woolf, who declared about 1930: 'Peasants are the great sanctuary of sanity . . . when they disappear, there is no hope for the race.' The fact is that, in 21st-century Greece and Italy, the peasants at last have all but disappeared from the landscape. In some areas (Tuscany is one [229]) their homesteads have been colonized by well-to-do refugees from urban stress, souls hankering for the 'sanity' – though not the sanitation systems – of the peasant mode. But the originals are gone, and their loss is lamented only by romantic outsiders.

'Do you know the land where lemons bloom?' hymned the 18th-century German writer Johann Wolfgang von Goethe – one of so many northern Europeans whose Classical enthusiasms were underpinned by affection and preference not only for the light and warmth of Italy and Greece, but also for the apparently easy and timeless rhythms of rural Mediterranean existence. Goethe, along with painters such as Nicolas Poussin and Claude Lorrain a century earlier, played a major part in elevating a landscape staffed by peasants into the category of 'the picturesque' – eventually a sunlit southern place of escape from the agrarian and industrial revolutions spelling the end of 'green and pleasant' land elsewhere.

The peasants deserted this scene because, of course, it never did support an 'easy' life, and they (or their children) were not inclined to pass up motor cars for mules and videos for candlelight. To describe the Mediterranean peasant mode as 'timeless', however, could be forgiven – at least until the mid-20th century, when great demographic shifts took place in the region. Carlo Levi, an Italian writer exiled by Mussolini's Fascist régime to deepest Lucania in 1935, could claim that the pattern of lives of tenants and smallholders in this region of South Italy had hardly altered over two thousand years: hence the title of his autobiographical

227 opposite *Detail of a wall-painting from Herculaneum, c. AD 75: a bough of green peaches by a glass of water. Such 'nature-studies' in Roman domestic decoration were evocative of the 'gifts of hospitality' (xenia) provided by a generous host.*

account, *Christ Stopped at Eboli* – though Levi sensed that the ancient Romans and Greeks (who colonized nearby Metapontum) had not made much impact, either.

Western hankering or nostalgia for the lost peasant lifestyle is compounded by the fact that 'the Mediterranean diet' has conquered our tables and tastebuds. The essential daily rations of a rustic underclass are now purveyed expensively in restaurants and prescribed for health and longevity. But beyond romanticism and fashions in food there is also a range of sound scholarly reasons for trying to recover evidence for ancient rural settlement. To posterity, the glories of 'Classical civilization' may consist largely in the monuments of cities; but ancient sources agree that no city was independent of its immediate hinterland – the essential circumference of supportive countryside that the Greeks termed a *chora*. Broadly sketched, the shift from a pastoral, herding, nomadic mode of agriculture to arable cultivation had occurred in most parts of the Mediterranean by the early 1st millennium BC. When in the course of his travels the Homeric Odysseus wants to signal that a people are 'civilized', he calls them 'bread-eaters' (*sitophagoi*), meaning that they are settled in one place, raising the wheat that makes the bread. To grow wheat means clearing, tilling, fertilizing, and sowing a certain piece of land. It means houses instead of tents, and fixed boundaries instead of seasonal grazing lands. In short, arable farming is the necessary prelude to the *polis*.

228 *Images of ploughing, sowing, and hunting are gathered on an Attic black-figure kylix by Nikosthenes, late 6th century BC. Generally, however, Greek artists paid little attention to depicting agicultural activity – or the countryside as a 'landscape'.*

229 *A typical view of Italy's 'green heart', in Tuscany. On fertile slopes formed in the Pleistocene period – two million years ago – the Classical agricultural staples of grain, vines, and olives still dominate the pattern of cultivation in this part of the world.*

As we shall see in Chapter VI, there was a traditional bias in the Classical economy towards subsistence farming; and the systems of Greek democracy and Roman Republicanism were equally founded upon the basic political unit of the small-scale, self-sufficient landholder. In Classical art and archaeology, the importance of all those living 'beyond the acropolis' tends to go unnoticed, because such figures in the landscape were rarely a subject of interest to artists; and because with their frugal habits these people typically left little of worth behind them. Certain Marxist-inclined historians have sought to redress the resultant imbalance, even arguing for a 'class struggle' in the ancient world. But it is not obligatory to be Marxist in order to appreciate that the peasants of the Classical world must be acknowledged as its basic and indispensable providers.

There are several ways of recovering the realities of both subsistence farming and 'industrialized' agriculture in the Classical world. To begin with, we possess a certain quantity of 'wisdom literature' about estate management from Greek and Roman authors. There is also the ethnographic approach – feasible, at least, so long as a few peasant communities survive, since it entails making historical deductions from their presumed 'changeless' lives. And then there are two relatively recent developments of archaeology. One is the science of 'environmental archaeology' – the analysis of floral and faunal remains, including pollen samples and bones. Another is the practice of 'field survey' – an efficient way of collecting large quantities of archaeological data without actual excavation (see pp. 146–48).

To find the rules of farming cast in the form of poetry may strike us as peculiar. But this was a particular literary genre of the Classical world – to be distinguished from 'pastoral', which is a much more whimsical mode, evocative of shepherds singing and piping to while away the tedium of watching their flocks. Admittedly, the first example of the 'agronomic' genre, the *Works and Days* poem attributed to the early 7th-century BC Boeotian bard Hesiod (see pp. 85–86), is more of a gloomy and reproachful sermon on the virtues of hard graft than a practical guide to daily tasks. Yet even if indebted to Near Eastern traditions of finger-wagging homilies, it has a tone of authentic experience. A more studious text, it seems, was produced by the 5th-century BC philosopher Democritus of Abdera. This has not survived, but it may have influenced sections of Xenophon's *Estate Manager* (*Oikonomikos*) that describe the good running of an Athenian estate *c.* 400 BC. Members of Aristotle's Peripatetic school (see p. 236) were actively interested in the botanical and biological science behind agricultural practice. We also know that a detailed manual of farming ways was circulating in North African Carthage prior to the Roman destruction of that city in 146 BC. Whether inspired by Greeks or Carthaginians, however, the Romans added their own didactic texture of 'down to earth' advice to an existing canon of smallholding lore. The arch-Republican Cato the Elder is credited with a handbook of the first half of the 2nd century BC written in a markedly gruff, staccato Latin, just as one might imagine a Roman farmer speaking. ('What's the first secret of good farming? Good ploughing. Next best? Just ploughing. And third? Muck-spreading.' *On Agriculture* 61.) Varro, Columella, and eventually Palladius (in the 5th century AD) continued the tradition in prose. But even when the Augustan poet Vergil adds his contribution in regular hexameter verse, the result is practical. A beginner to bee-keeping, for instance, could do worse than follow the instructions given in book 4 of Vergil's *Georgics*.

So what, in general, does this literature tell us? Without exception, it assumes a property of about 24– 30 hectares (60–75 acres). 'Praise a large estate, but stick to a small one' was the Roman motto (Vergil, *Georgics* 2.412), meaning that a modest farm managed well was more efficient than some uncontrollably large estate. Slaves or staff are also assumed, but not in great numbers. The principle of what in Greek was called *autarkeia*, self-sufficiency, underpins everything. The virtuous landowner works hard not only because he has to, but also because it befits him not to delegate the many and varied tasks. And these tasks are many and varied because *autarkeia* demands that no farmer specialize in his productivity. 'We have a little of everything': this is the slogan tagged to the system of Mediterranean 'polyculture' idealized and outlined from Hesiod onwards. Grain, grapes [241], and olives [230, 231] are the three primary crops, supplemented by nuts, figs, and other fruits (cf. pp. 63–65); a few fowl [96] and animals – including a goat for milk and cheese, and perhaps a team of oxen for ploughing [228, 232] – are the usual extent of livestock.

Accordingly, what the 'wisdom literature' principally provided was a sort of memorable almanac of seasonal reminders and instructions. When to plough (with crop rotation, there might be three or four ploughings per year); how to read the night skies for good harvesting opportunities in early summer; on which chalk slopes young vines should be planted; and so on. If a proprietor were only devoted to grain, he might have had some breaks in his year; if just olives – tough, low-maintenance trees – he might also take leave. But the polyculture system meant that there was always something to do.

230 *A scene of the olive harvest on an Attic black-figure amphora attributed to the Antimenes Painter, c. 520 BC.*

231 *Detail of olive-gathering from a Roman mosaic from North Africa, 2nd century AD. Tunisia was the prime oil-producing area of the Roman Empire: olive plantations were established there also as a means of settling nomadic communities to the land.*

232 *A ploughman with two yoked oxen: Etruscan bronze statuette-group from Arretium (modern Arezzo) in North Italy, c. 430–400 BC.*

In Roman literature, *peasants were a byword for moral integrity and laborious stamina. The following lawsuit is typical of residual 'Republican' faith in diligent landholding – its moral being that 'the best fertilizer is the proprietor's watchful eye'.*

Gaius Furius Chresimus, a freedman, became deeply unpopular on account of making better returns from his smallholding than neighbouring proprietors got from their much larger estates. He was rumoured to be poaching crops from others by some kind of wizardry. Eventually he was formally accused by the magistrate Spurius Albinus. When the time came for his appearance in court, fearing that he might indeed be judged guilty, Chresimus hauled all his farm implements before the jury, and furthermore produced as evidence his farm-labourers – thickset individuals and, by Piso's report, to a man evidently well cared-for, and decently clothed. The implements were of solid iron – tough mattocks, hefty ploughshares – and some sleek oxen were also displayed. As the defendant declared: 'Well, you see before you the extent of my magic potions [*veneficia*]. Alas, what I cannot produce for the court to witness is all the midnight toil, the getting up early, and the sweat of my brow –' Unanimously, he was acquitted.

Pliny the Elder, *Natural History* 18.41–43

The question of how far Classical 'wisdom literature' tallies with the traditional patterns of subsistence agriculture as observed by modern scholars and anthropologists is complicated by considerable variations of climate and terrain within the Mediterranean region. How smallholders cope with the mountainous aridity of the southern Peloponnese – where thin layers of soil can only be cultivated by terracing – must be different from the strategies suitable to the rich alluvial tracts of Tuscany and Umbria. But studies of post-antique peasant conditions in Boeotia confirm that in terms of its scope and techniques, the polyculture described by Hesiod in the early 7th century BC continued more or less unaltered for over two millennia. And this polyculture lies at the heart of the *longue durée*, the 'long-term process' influentially imposed upon Mediterranean history by the French scholar Ferdinand Braudel and the so-called *Annales* school of modern historians.

233 *Excavating a farmstead, near the Etruscan site of Tuscania.*

234 *Fieldwalking in Etruscan territory, again near Tuscania. The deep-ploughing machinery of modern arable farming has brought traces of many ancient sites to the surface. Though these traces may only amount to a scatter of rooftiles and coarse pottery, mapping their density has enabled archaeologists to gain some insight into levels of rural population and land exploitation throughout Classical antiquity.*

'BEYOND THE ACROPOLIS'

It was in 1826 that a German landowner, J. H. von Thünen, put forward his model of 'the isolated state': a city surrounded by radial zones or bands of agricultural activity. Since then, the combination of bulk transport systems with the tendency of modern cities to lose their central 'isolation' in suburban sprawl (Los Angeles is a good example) means that we have largely lost sight of the traditional rapport between a city and its supportive agricultural hinterland. In Classical times, however, this was an essential dependency. When an architect proposed to make a mountain in the form of Alexander the Great, cradling a city in his hand, Alexander liked the idea; but regretfully he had to turn it down – because the city had no encircling agricultural territory (Vitruvius, *On Architecture* 2.1).

The archaeological discipline of field survey has illuminated the extent of that dependency. Pioneered by J. B. Ward-Perkins and others after the Second World War, field survey came about as a direct result of mechanized agriculture and urban expansion in the Mediterranean. Ward-Perkins, himself based in Rome, realized how many ancient sites were coming to the surface in the Roman Campagna – the *ager Romanus*, or agricultural hinterland, of ancient Rome – as Italian farmers began to use tractors with heavy ploughing equipment, and new roads and towns around Rome were built. There was no time to excavate all these sites, still less the resources to do so. But if they could be logged, and the deposits of surface material collected or sampled, at least some record might be made.

At its most basic, field survey may be (and has been) done by one man and a dog – strolling around the country, noting what ancient remains and marks on the landscape there are to be seen. More scientifically, it requires teams of walkers to comb a certain stretch of terrain, preferably after deep ploughing in late summer or early autumn [234]. Various refinements of method have been tried on this basic technique, and its results are not infallible. But the principal revelation of field survey in Classical lands is without doubt. There *was* life 'beyond the acropolis'; the Classical countryside was populated far more densely than we should otherwise have imagined. Thanks to field survey, the peasants of Greece, Etruria, and Rome are no longer 'people without history'.

Numerous areas of the Mediterranean have been subject to field survey. In Greece, meticulous work has been done in Boeotia, Nemea, the southern Argolid, and Crete; also on the islands of Keos and Melos. Studies in Italy include the *chora* of the Greek colony at Metapontum, the Biferno valley, the surrounds of Gubbio in Umbria, the Phoenician–Roman site of Nora in Sardinia, and several areas of southern Etruria. A large-scale survey – also making use of aerial photography – has been conducted around Roman sites in Libya. On the Iberian peninsula, surveying the valley of the Guadalquivir has revealed much about settlement patterns in the province known to the Romans as Baetica.

Where excavation is possible in the course of survey, it may not bring much to light: rudimentary structures of farmsteads, relics of agricultural activity and food-processing – grinding-stones, storage jars, and suchlike. But the gathering and analysis of material dragged to the surface by heavy modern ploughs enables a mapping-out of land-use and settlement density in a particular area over centuries – or even over millennia, if records are kept of finds from prehistoric times up to the Middle Ages. So, for example, a survey around the minor Etruscan centre of Tuscania showed that in the 6th century BC small farmsteads were densely distributed within a radius of some 6 kilometres (about 2^1/$_2$ miles) around the town, with sites more intermittent further outwards [233].

235 *Artist's impression of how the* latifundium *at Settefinestre might once have looked. As developed in the 1st century BC, the Roman* latifundium *was a large-scale combination of agricultural, industrial, and commercial enterprises, with residential possibilities too.*

A scatter of coarse pottery and roof or hypocaust tiles may be enough to indicate a 'site' in this kind of archaeological reconnaissance. It is not always easy to determine from superficial evidence whether such sites were properly inhabited, or simply served as barns or shelters for workers who 'commuted' to them from dwellings inside city walls. Levels of rural habitation would have fluctuated for various social, historical, and economic reasons. But field survey should make us cautious about accepting stories of disaster and depopulation in the Classical countryside. For instance, one ancient account of a major land reform pressed controversially past the Roman Senate by Tiberius Gracchus in 133 BC relates that Tiberius was motivated by having seen, on a journey through inland 'Tyrrhenia' (Etruria), large tracts of land desolate except for labour-gangs of immigrant slaves (Plutarch, *Life of Tiberius Gracchus* 8). Yet field survey of the same area indicates that in the mid-2nd century BC it was a dense patchwork of smallholdings.

Where field survey reveals a multiplicity of small farming units, we are reassured of the widespread Classical agricultural philosophy of 'small is beautiful'. But determining the socio-economic status of those small units remains problematic. There is little doubt that the Spartan hinterland was mostly occupied by serfs or 'helots'; but in the countryside of Attica, for example, it is unclear how many inhabitants were 'hired hands' or *thetes* – the lowest class of free individuals. In the Roman world, even a relatively humble smallholder might possess some slaves – Columella, in his 1st-century AD treatise *On Farming* (1.6.8), advises keeping them in stalls, alongside the herds – but how far did the prejudice against large estates prevent the rise of slave-staffed *latifundia* (industrial farms)? Certainly, there were parts of Italy and the Empire where huge, grain-producing estates were established after the 2nd century BC. South Italy, Sicily, and North Africa were notorious for them: Pliny the Elder (*Natural History* 18.35) claims that at one point, half of colonized Africa was in the hands of just six landlords. But perhaps the most intensively explored *latifundium* is the site of Settefinestre [235], located just inland of the Tuscan coast by the Roman colony of Cosa. Grain was not the sole product here: rooms and equipment for the processing of grapes and olives suggest polyculture on the grand scale, with the estate extending to over 125 hectares (300 acres). A workforce of numerous slaves is assumed, partly on the basis of a series of *cubicula* (simple sleeping quarters) excavated near the processing rooms. But the adjacent residence seems sufficiently elegant to imply that the proprietors also lived on the site.

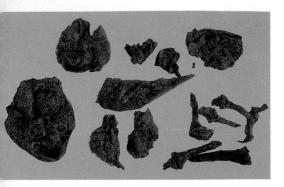

236 *Carbonized ancient remains of grapes plus stalks and pips, recovered from the Etruscan site of Cerveteri.*

On account of its residential desirability, Romans might have counted Settefinestre not as a *latifundium* but rather as a *villa*. Quite how to translate the term 'villa' still vexes archaeologists: 'house in the country' is probably the safest covering phrase, though that may cover anything from (in modern terms) a cottage to a mansion. Some Roman villas were built along corridors, others around courtyards; some were tranquil retreats for wealthy city-types, others rural factories. This diversity may be less evident in Italy; but throughout the provinces of the Roman Empire, villas provide a key index of 'Romanization' (cf. pp. 195–96), as indigenous people followed colonists in appropriating land and practising the virtues preached by Cato, Columella, Vergil, *et al.*

The process of colonization might appear to have dramatic consequences for land-use. The survey around Metapontum demonstrated that Greeks colonists operated a linear system of land division in both the city and its surrounding hinterland. More emphatic still would seem to be the Roman practice of 'centuriation': partitioning land into a matrix of regular blocks, with one unit of measurement being the *iugerum* – derived from what could be ploughed by two yoked oxen in a day, 240 by 120 Roman feet: about $^1/_2$ hectare, or $^2/_3$ acre. (Settefinestre, exploiting a 'wine boom' in the 1st century BC, was a property of 500 *iugera*: its size was certainly great when we remember that just 2 *iugera* formed an *heredium*, the standard allottment of land to a colonist – typically, a Roman soldier reaching 'veteran' status.) But the overall effects of Roman occupation upon non-Mediterranean landscapes such as Britain have been exaggerated. It is true that Roman settlers introduced some new crops and plant varieties – including olives, figs, and vines – to north-west Europe, and influenced the native landscape with certain imported techniques (such as drainage of wetlands by ditch-digging). However, the existing cereal types (mainly spelt wheat, emmer wheat, and barley) stayed in cultivation; and patterns of animal husbandry continued very much as they were already established. Agricultural practices became more intensive – not least because there was an army to feed – but there were no radical shifts in agricultural method.

We can assert this continuity thanks to environmental archaeology. By microscopic analysis (of pollen grains) and macroscopic analysis (of plant and bone debris, usually preserved either by charring [236] or by waterlogged conditions), this science is able to piece together delicate profiles of land-use and agrarian habits (not to mention local patterns of diet and disease, too). The inconspicuous trophies of palaeobotany – the study of ancient plants – are never likely to find display-space in a museum. But they are truly the miniscule components of the basis upon which Classical civilization was founded.

LANDSCAPE AND GARDENS

Peasants are insignificant figures in the pages of Greek historical writing; equally so in Greek art. It follows, perhaps, that Greek artists were not much interested in depicting the places inhabited by peasants. Certainly there are remarkably few evocations of the countryside in what survives of Greek painting and sculpture. A few trees and other leafy features are found on the Telephos frieze of the Great Altar of Pergamon, and Greek idiom took from Persia the concept of the *paradeisos*, a pleasant hunting-park; but no aesthetic enthusiasm for landscape as an artistic subject in its own right can be registered before the Romans.

'A picture representing natural inland scenery.' That is how the Oxford English Dictionary defines a 'landscape'. In the art of Egypt, Greece, and the ancient Near East there is nothing that properly equates to this modern understanding of a

237 *Detail of a wall-painting in the House of the Golden Bracelet (also known as the House of the Wedding of Alexander) at Pompeii, c. AD 40–62. 'Room 32' of this house once offered a rich painted garden to those within, featuring typical Mediterranean flora – oleander, laurel, viburnum, camomile – and birdlife (here, a thrush amid roses).*

238 *Mosaic from Praeneste (Palestrina), east of Rome, c. 100 BC. An imaginary panorama of the River Nile – from its rise in African heartlands to the cities of the delta. Depicting the fertile watercourse at the time of annual inundation, this mosaic may once have decorated a cult space of the goddess Isis, who at Praeneste was associated with the town's protective deity, Fortuna.*

pictorial landscape. Elements of flora and topography, if they appear at all, supply a basic setting – no more. The professional painters of stage-sets for the Classical Greek theatre, whose work was in demand from around the mid-5th century BC onwards, are presumed to have experimented with large backdrops in receding perspective (see p. 290), but this is only supposition. So the first recorded notice of an artist specializing in landscapes is made by Pliny the Elder, writing in the 60s and 70s AD.

Pliny names one 'Studius' (who may also be transcribed as 'Ludius') as the pioneer of painting walls with 'most agreeable scenes' of villas and porticoes, set in manicured gardens; along with 'groves, woods, hills, fishponds, canals, rivers, coasts – whatever could be wished – with people strolling about . . .' (*Natural History* 35.116–17). It is clear from Pliny's phrasing that this Studius based his pictures very much upon a countryside that had itself been carefully 'landscaped' (Pliny uses the term *topiaria opera* to mean such contrived or ornamental cultivation), and which then served as much for retreat and recreation as for the rural economy. Pliny locates the artist as working during the rule of Augustus, a period in which the consolations of rustic escape were eulogized by poets close to the Emperor, such as Horace and Vergil. Studius most likely worked for patrons imbued with that poetic dream of pastoral ease. And Pliny specifically tells us that the artist did it with a whimsical sense of humour. Whether the people incorporated in these landscapes of Studius were amorously wandering, goading donkeys, stalking wildfowl, or harvesting grapes, no one here was overexerted. The purpose of such painting was to conjure the perfectly 'pleasant place' (*locus amoenus*).

Nothing survives on ancient Roman walls that is actually signed by Studius. However, his manner may be deduced from Roman frescoes and mosaics from around the time when he is reported as making his name [465]. Before his day, in fact, a certain taste for panoramic vistas was already part of Roman interior decoration. At its most expansive, this pretended to encompass, on the space of a single wall or floor, the entire valley of the River Nile. In the foreground of the best-known of such 'Nilotic' views [238, 239] there are urban structures that seem to stand for 'civilization'. Temples, shrines, kiosks, and groves host various pursuits, including picnics and fishing parties, as our gaze travels upstream from the busy delta. The seasonal event that is celebrated here is the Nile's annual breaching of its banks. Priests, bureaucrats, and punting marsh-dwellers are among the local people shown greeting the September inundation, with its promise of burgeoning crops. The synopsis is sprinkled with details of local flora and fauna; as the river is followed to its first cataract and beyond, its gentler features (such as lizards, ducks, and waterborne lotus blossoms) give way to more peculiar or threatening sights – crocodiles, warthogs, hippopotamuses, and farther off, as the terrain turns rocky, giraffes, big cats, and Nubian tribesmen stalking antelope and cranes.

239 *Detail of the lower right corner of the Nilotic mosaic seen opposite: an embankment with dovecote and reed enclosure, and diverse river traffic – a warship, a merchant vessel, and one fisherman in his canoe.*

240 *Detail of the Ara Pacis in Rome, 13–9 BC. Acanthus scrolls dominate the mixed foliage of the Altar of Augustan Peace: their vigorous growth suggests a 'Golden Age'; and the plant itself was hallowed by its association with the god Apollo.*

241 *A vintaging figure – a follower of Dionysos, perhaps Priapus – in a grape arbour: detail of a Roman plaster relief, 1st century AD.*

This mosaic, with its instructive scatter of labels (in Greek), is a form of 'geography'. In the later history of European colonization, a certain nexus would develop between landscape art, the making of maps, and laying claims to land; perhaps the Roman viewers of this piece already had inklings that Egypt would come under Roman control (as it did, after the death of Cleopatra in the year 30 BC). But it seems that the work of Studius and others was not directed towards justifying imperialism, nor giving lessons in the fauna of the Upper Nile. What their genre supplied was essentially idyllic.

'Idyll' derives from the Greek word *eidyllion*, 'little image'. In antiquity the term was annexed for a type of versifying that evoked life in the countryside, in particular life as viewed through the eyes of those whose task was keeping the flocks. As it happened, the port-metropolis of Alexandria, at the mouth of the Nile, was where the literary fashion for such 'bucolic' or 'pastoral' evocations developed. The poetry of certain learned mock-goatherds at Alexandria, notably Sicilian-born Theocritus in the 3rd century BC, would become canonical favourites in Western literature. In direct homage to the *Idylls* composed by Theocritus, Vergil supplied his Latin audience with a sequence of *Eclogues* ('Selections'), so fostering the taste for landscape animated by idling pipers. Like Theocritus, Vergil allowed rough and illiterate rustics to sing exquisitely – even the mythical one-eyed monster-herdsman Polyphemos, who is imagined lovesick for a sea-nymph, Galatea (see p. 131).

The terms of seduction offered by Vergil's Polyphemos (*Eclogues* 9.39–43) are similar to those of Roman landscape-painting at this time [217]. The architect Vitruvius – writing, like Vergil, in homage to Augustus – noted how Roman interior decorators had created a world of 'groves, mountains, sheep, and shepherds' (*luci, montes, pecora, pastores*: *On Architecture* 5.2). A generic name would be attached to this idealized place, which was 'Arcadia'. It was taken from an area of central Greece whose inhabitants legendarily enjoyed their music and dancing, undisturbed by war and toil. 'Et in Arcadia ego' goes the phrase: 'Arcadia for me, too' – apparently a claim upon the absolute happiness of lounging about in meadows and joining the supposedly carefree existence of a country swain: yet death lurked there as well.

This was an art that not only presented a fairer creation than was known, but rendered it sacrosanct. Many landscapes painted around the time of Augustus have been referred to as 'sacro-idyllic' precisely because they contain, amid the slopes and sheep-pens, tokens of rural piety: altars and shrines, not neglected, but freshly decked with garlands. Arcadia is not merely the green refuge from urban stress. It preserves the age-old rapport between people and their deities – the 'spirits of the place'.

That this ideology flowered in the age of Augustus is no coincidence. The man who put an end to the Roman Republic artfully presented his rise to autocracy not as political revolution but as restoration (see pp. 178–84). So his new 'Golden Age' (*aurea aetas*) of peace and prosperity retrieved a long-lost 'Age of Gold' when Saturn ruled and there were no cities (Hesiod, too, knew of some such carefree primal state: see above, p. 85). No one cut down trees for building boats; no one hammered metal into weapons. There were no boundary-stones or fences; cattle offered milk of their own accord. So the gods were honoured, and everyone was happy. The lower friezes of Augustus' Ara Pacis, packed with profuse, unstoppable vegetation [240, 287], show just one of the many ways in which official art and literature under Augustus conspired with this ideal.

Livia, the wife of Augustus, must have had something like Arcadia or the Golden Age in mind when she commissioned a master-painter like Studius to decorate the dining-room of her villa outside Rome on the Via Flaminia,

242 *Mosaic from the Emperor Hadrian's villa at Tivoli, c. AD 130. A scene of goats by a stream, with the statue of a robed divinity – perhaps a young Dionysos – making it 'sacro-idyllic'. It is a romanticized image of the countryside that Hadrian sought to realize in his palatial complex at Tivoli, east of Rome.*

'Ad Gallinas Albas' ('Place of White Chickens') [243]. It is, as we instantly understand, a 'natural' or at least horticultural scheme. Why did Livia need pictorial reminders of bird life, fruit, and flowers, when they were there, as it were, on her doorstep? But if we look closer at what her painter devised, we see that it is much more than a record of some garden at its prime. It is not Nature, but Nature 'improved' – Nature rendered impossibly perfect.

Two low boundaries set the distance for our view. Trained close to the second fence are flowers and shrubs: roses, chrysanthemums, periwinkles, and poppies. Beyond is a tangle of laurel, oleander, myrtle, and assorted fruit trees; and beyond that is a thicket of oak, pine, and cypress. To the casual glance, this simply collects a profusion of growth – the sort of unbridled abundance that Livia might have wanted as symbolic of the gilded peace promoted by her husband's steady rule. But it is more than that. Everything is in blossom, and also ripely laden. The quince and the pomegranate, which bear fruit in late autumn, are there with blue periwinkles that flower in early spring, and close by are the lavender poppies of early summer.

243 *Detail of the north wall of the 'Garden Room' of Livia's villa 'Ad Gallinas Albas' ('Place of White Chickens') at Prima Porta, to the north of Rome, c. 20 BC. This decorative fantasy – designed for a subterranean room probably used for dining in hot weather – mixes botanical accuracy with seasonal disregard. Beyond a low wicker fence and a further balustrade (with a pine tree in a recess), a profusion of fruit and flowers again evokes an Augustan 'Golden Age'.*

244 *The Villa dei Papiri at Herculaneum, as recreated to form the original Getty Museum at Malibu in California. The oil magnate J. Paul Getty (1892–1976) saw affinities between himself and the supposed ancient owner of the Villa dei Papiri (L. Calpurnius Piso); the comparable climates of coastal California and the Bay of Naples have certainly favoured the development of an authentically 'Roman' hortus at Malibu, surrounded by a peristyle.*

Birds alight amid these breeze-bent bushes: what can be spotted of their variety includes quail, thrushes, orioles, and nightingales. As this is a year depicted without seasons, it takes no count of migratory needs. Things can all happen at once, and immediately nearby: such is the virtual reality of art.

Yet the art of landscape should not be regarded as entirely artificial. Many Romans took their gardening seriously. Prime evidence for that has come from Pompeii, where it has been estimated that almost 20 per cent of the excavated town was given over to ornamental gardens or fruit, vine, and vegetable plots [245]. Because Vesuvius erupted at a time when gardens and orchards were blooming (August), plenty of seeds were preserved, allowing close identification of varieties. The examination of root cavities left in the lava has also enabled precise reconstructions of some garden layouts. The present appearance of surrounds at the Villa dei Papiri reconstructed by the Getty Museum at Malibu in California conveys a very credible impression of how a luxurious Roman garden once looked [244].

The peristyle enclosures of such sites as the House of the Faun in Pompeii were clearly designed as fragrant retreats – pockets of tranquillity within the urban whirl, offering walkways to soothe the spirit. The concept of *rus in urbe*, 'the country in the city', was also vigorously embodied in the extension of the word 'garden' (*hortus*) to what we should call an allotment, nursery, or 'market garden': a highly productive unit of land inside or on the edge of city boundaries. The *horti* at Pompeii not only produced vegetables, herbs, and salads, but also nuts, olives, grapes, and soft fruits – with at least one establishment also producing flowers for perfume.

Roman wall-paintings *of landscapes and panoramic city-views [238, 465] typically depend upon the perspectival device of* trompe-l'œil – *the 'eye deception' of foreshortening – so as to confer depth upon two-dimensional space. This was a valuable trick in the often rather cramped surrounds of a Roman house. But what would the truly rich householder do if there were few constraints on space and spending power? The actual landscaping commissioned by the Emperor Nero for his megalomaniac Domus Aurea (Golden House) near Rome's Palatine Hill perhaps reveals the dream behind many paintings of grandiose and idyllic views:*

The house . . . was so extensive, it had a three-aisled, mile-long portico. And there was a lake in the grounds, almost a sea, with buildings all around, looking like cities; and beyond, a countryside variegated with tilled fields, vineyards, grazing-lands, and forests, all stocked with a multitude of herds and wild beasts . . . When he came to dedicate the completed palace, Nero's only comment of approval was that at last he could begin to live like a human being.

Suetonius, *Life of Nero* 31

Subsequent emperors built landscaped parks and palaces that rivalled the Domus Aurea in scale – like Hadrian's villa at Tivoli [242] – but they did so outside the city walls of Rome.

245 *The garden of the House of Loreius Tiburtinus (also known as the House of D. Octavius Quartio) in Pompeii was landscaped between* AD *62 and 79. In an attempt to evoke the grounds of grand rustic villas, it occupied even more land than the house, and was shaded by chestnut, pear, pomegranate, and fig trees. This is the view from an upper terrace, which contained a nymphaeum complete with double masonry couches for al fresco dining. The water course, which takes up the full length of the garden, was interrupted by two elaborate fountains and bridges; it was originally flanked by walkways and statues (among the latter Dionysos, river gods, exotic animals, and a hermaphrodite).*

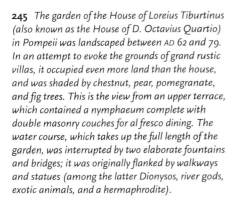

246 *View of the Roman quarries at Simitthus (in modern Tunisia), opened c. 27 BC and active until the 3rd century AD. The stone exploited here was* yellow *marmor Numidicum (Numidian marble). The Romans are estimated to have quarried some 700,000 tonnes from this site.*

247 *Detail of a lion carved in Numidian marble, 1st century AD. The richly hued striations of this tawny North African marble made it particularly suitable for representing an exotic African animal – of the ferocious sort imported to Rome for circus entertainment.*

NATURAL RESOURCES

Metal, stone, water, and clay: these were the primary natural materials exploited in Classical antiquity. Where other resources occurred – such as gum-mastic on the island of Chios – they might form a particular element of the local economy. The general importance of metals is obvious enough from archaeological parlance, given that most of the period understood as 'Classical antiquity' falls into what archaeologists call the Iron Age – roughly the 1st millennium BC. And the intensity with which precious metals might be extracted is nowhere more evident than in Attica, at the silver mines of Laurion, near Cape Sounion: up to twenty thousand slaves may have been working here during peak operation in the 5th century BC.

To describe the entire range of technologies devised for working metal deposits and other natural resources is beyond our present scope. It is daunting enough simply to glance at the first book of Pliny the Elder's *Natural History*, which outlines the author's project of itemizing 'the nature of things' (*rerum natura*). Book 37, for instance, will tell of gems and other precious stones: Pliny proudly informs us that this volume alone contains 1,300 'facts, inquiries, and observations'. He was compiling, as it were, an inventory of what the Roman Empire actually or potentially had in its possession; and in the course of this imperialist catalogue, he provides abundant information about how Greeks, Romans, and certain other civilizations harnessed what the earth offered. In many cases, archaeological investigation substantiates what Pliny reports: so we can trace, for instance, a 'supply line' from a certain object displayed in ancient Rome [247] to its provincial earthly origin as a raw material [246]. But one resource above all may illustrate the ingenuities of Classical engineering: water [248–54].

No one in antiquity writes about water more lovingly than Sextus Julius Frontinus, who was appointed curator aquarum, in charge of Rome's water supply, by the Emperor Nerva in the late 1st century AD. Here he eulogizes the public benefits – and imperial prestige – connected to an efficient urban water system. Frontinus was as good as his word: it has been calculated that Rome around AD 100 received more fresh water per head of population than modern New York.

Thanks to the care of Nerva, best of rulers . . . the city feels itself in better health, what with so many new water-works – reservoirs, fountains, basins. Equally better-off are the private consumers, to whom the Emperor has increased concessions: those who once siphoned their supplies in fear of acting illegally can now openly take water by imperial permission. And no surplus is wasted: the city's appearance is renewed and bright, the air clearer, and the causes of unhealthy air – which earned Rome such a bad reputation in the past – removed.

Frontinus, *On the Water-Supplies of Rome* 2.88

248 top *Two women by a fountain with a lion-head waterspout: fragment of a limestone relief from a funerary building in Greek Taras (modern Taranto), South Italy, c. 300 BC.*

249 above *Limestone waterspout from a building, in the form of a lion head, from South Italy, mid-5th century BC.*

250 left *A woman holding a large amphora by its handles: detail of an Apulian red-figure krater perhaps by the Sarpedon Painter, c. 370 BC.*

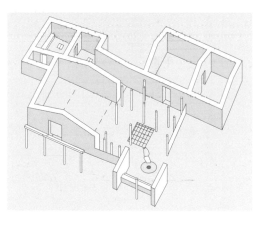

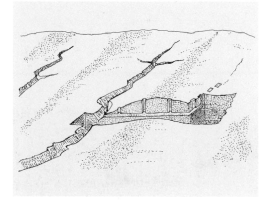

251 left *View of the Roman aqueduct at Segovia in Spain, c. AD 100. This bridge – built of granite blocks without mortar or clamps and over 800 metres (2,600 feet) long, with 118 arches – brought water from a source 17 kilometres (some 10 miles) distant. Like other aqueducts in the Empire, it also stood as a monument to Rome's power and munificence.*

252 above *The Pont du Gard aqueduct near Nîmes (Roman Nemausus) in the south of France, c. 19 BC: nearly 50 metres (370 feet) in height, it is one of the most spectacular feats of Roman engineering. Romans explicitly contrasted such structures with the 'useless' monuments of the Egyptians and Greeks (Frontinus, On the Water-Supplies of Rome 16).*

253 right, above *Axonometric drawing of the Etruscan House of the Impluvium at Roselle in Tuscany, 6th century BC. A series of slanting roofs conducted water into the central sunken pool. This was a technique of domestic water conservation that would have an enduring history, in the form of the Roman impluvium [cf. 338].*

254 right *Diagram showing the workings of an Etruscan cuniculum (water tunnel). Two river-valleys are connected by an underground conduit; well-shafts then give access to water for the intermediate terrain.*

CRAFT SPECIALIZATION

It has been made clear that land cultivation in the Classical world was generally regarded as a worthy, even gentlemanly, occupation. In the course of Xenophon's *Estate Manager*, Socrates says that farming (*georgia*) is something that would complete the happiness of any well-contented man. Apart from its gratifying productivity, he argues, it also provides 'discipline for the body so as to be in shape for all those activities befitting a free man'. This distinctly contrasts with a previous allusion, in the same text (4.2–3), to those other forms of manual exertion which are industrial and physically debilitating. A 'free man' would have nothing to do with such 'banausic' labour.

'Banausic' is understood to denote any work that involved furnaces or fires. More widely, it can be used to categorize anyone who is a 'crafter-by-hand'. Socrates condemns this sort of work because it tends to be sedentary and done indoors, and is therefore 'effeminizing' to the body and even injurious to the soul. It is also so absorbing that it leaves no time for a man to attend to 'his friendships and the political community'. Some cities, Socrates remarks – approvingly – therefore legally forbade their citizens to follow such trades.

True enough, it seems that some Greek city-states did indeed restrict manufacturing jobs to slaves or other non-citizens. Apart from their serf-population of helots, the Spartans had *perioikoi* – Greeks deemed belonging to Sparta, but without political rights. As for Athens, it was a matter of practice, not statute, that so much banausic work was assigned to 'metics' (*metoikoi*), 'alien residents', whose status lay somewhere between slavery and citizenship. This is not to say that citizens were not involved: certain distinguished Athenians are known to have been associated with such crafts as leather- and metal-working, probably as the foreman or owner of a particular 'workshop' (*ergasterion*). But the recorded rates of pay for skilled artisans in 5th- and 4th-century Athens – ranging from several obols to one and a half drachmas per day – are enough to confirm the general low esteem for craftsmanship of all sorts. The owner of an *ergasterion* may have made good money. But at a time when, for example, a cavalry horse could cost as much as 1,200 drachmas, his workers must be reckoned to have been paid a 'minimum wage'.

255 *Unfinished marble statue in situ at Apollonas on the island of Naxos, c. 6th century BC. Because transport was difficult and costly, Greek sculptors in the Archaic period tried as much as possible to work on the stone at its quarry. Here we see how far they had shaped a colossal image – probably of the god Dionysos – before a crack appeared in the marble, and the project was abandoned. (The inhabitants of Naxos were justifiably proud when they had erected a colossal marble image of Apollo, 'of a single stone', at Delos: see p. 96.)*

On the far left is the head, clearly bearded, and on the far right the roughed-out feet and plinth; in places it has been carved within 1 or 2 centimetres (less than an inch) of its intended surface. The statue is immense – it would have been 10.66 metres (35 feet) tall.

256 *The interior of a bronze-casting workshop, depicted on an Attic red-figure kylix known as the Foundry Cup, the name-vase of the Foundry Painter, c. 490–480 BC [cf. 445, 585]. On the left, two crouching figures operate a kiln; on the right, the statue of an athlete has already been cast: before its head (lying on the floor between the craftsman's feet) can be joined to the body, an interior core must be knocked out. Hanging on the wall are various tools of the bronze-worker's trade.*

Inside the cup [585], Hephaistos, the smith-god, is shown handing the arms he has crafted for Achilles to Thetis: for all their grime and toil, the vase suggests, bronzesmiths could still look to a divinity as their patron and rival.

So, as with the rural peasants, we should not expect to find much documentary evidence for the urban artisans of Classical antiquity. In Roman times some improvement of status may be registered, with evidence for the formation of craft-guilds, or *collegia* (by tradition ascribed to one of the legendary Tarquin kings of Rome, Numa Pompilius) – not quite 'trade unions', but fraternities of specialized workers such as blacksmiths, cobblers, dyers, and fullers. Mythologically, the 'patron saints' of such craftsmen bear witness to their reputation – loaded with a mixture of scorn, awe, and suspicion. Hephaistos, the smith-god, might produce amazing objects like the shield of Achilles (p. 119) [585], or be paired with Charis, 'Grace'; but he was also a lame outcast among the Olympians, embittered and begrimed. Prometheus, stealer of fire from Zeus, was hideously punished for his theft, and punished again for his ingenuity with clay (for the story, see Hesiod, *Works and Days* 47–89). And Daedalus, creator of the first 'lifelike' statues (see p. 294), and credited with all sorts of useful inventions – tools, plumb-bobs, glue – had an ambivalent reputation too. His spectacular resort to flying was brought on by the need to escape an angry patron; whether he should be respected for skill or denigrated for trickery was a choice imposed by the Classical respect for beautiful things – and disdain for making them.

One scholar (Pierre Vidal-Naquet) has described artists and craftsmen as the 'secret heroes' of the Classical world. This book is conspicuously illustrated with their heroic efforts. How such efforts were judged by contemporaries is a question addressed in Chapter IX, where a Classical 'history of art' is outlined. As we shall see (p. 284), while the Greek *techne* and Latin *ars* both carry several nuances of meaning, it should be remembered that there was effectively no distinction made in antiquity between 'art' and 'craft'. A relatively small number of skilled 'craftsmen' became what we should call 'famous artists'. For the rest, as far as status and reward were concerned, there was little difference between specializing as a maker of bronze door-hinges or as a carver of marble reliefs.

This is made abundantly clear by epigraphic records relating to the organization of a workforce to build the Temple of Asklepios at Epidauros in the 4th century BC. Specialist craftsmen came from all over the Greek-speaking world, and we assume that to have been standard practice. Greek *technitai* were remarkably itinerant, not only around the Mediterranean but beyond: their marks, for example, have been

found on the Mausoleum at Halicarnassus [147] and on the masonry of the Persian cities of Susa and Persepolis. King Darius I may have compelled Greeks to work for him, but equally they may have volunteered, as they did when offering their services in the West. (It is a basic truth of both 'Etruscan art' and 'Roman art' that those who produced it were predominantly of Greek ethnic origin.)

Passing their expertise from father to son, Greeks around the Mediterranean were the acknowledged virtuosi of making things by hand, even if there were certain fields of expertise set aside, such as large-scale terracottas (in which Etruscans excelled [177]) and mosaics (some scholars consider the use of myriad coloured pieces, or *tesserae*, to have been a distinctly Roman development [238, 239]). 'Secret heroes' of the Classical world, then: like the toilers in the fields, these craftsmen, for all their heroic efforts, largely go unsung in ancient literary texts. But by looking at their handiwork closely we appreciate that their secret labours attained levels of technical excellence that remain unparalleled today.

257 *Limestone statuette (the* Auxerre Kore) *probably from Crete, c. 640–630* BC. *Early Greek stone sculpture was influenced by the monumental traditions of Egypt – but also indebted to the practice of carving in wood. Archaic wooden statues of deities, known as* xoana, *do not survive; we know, however, that they were still being venerated in Greek sanctuaries in the mid-2nd century* AD.

258 *Part of a chryselephantine statue – perhaps of Apollo – from Delphi, 6th century* BC. *'Chryselephantine' means a composite of gold and ivory: here the head is carved ivory (blackened by fire), and the hair is of hammered gold. Such statues were always the most splendid objects of any shrine where they were placed [122, 126], reflecting a Greek sentiment that the gods were best represented using the most precious raw materials available.*

259 *Remains of the clay 'jacket' of a bronze kouros statue found in the Athenian Agora, mid-6th century BC. Most ancient hollow bronzes were made by the 'lost wax' technique, a complicated process involving a clay model, a thin layer of wax over that, and cladding over the wax (the 'jacket'). Molten bronze was poured in, replacing the wax, which flowed out through specially designed channels (hence 'lost wax'). The outer mould was then removed, and the parts of the bronze statue put together [256]. Fine details were sculpted with a chisel, and the surface of the bronze smoothed.*

260 *The 'Hermes of Praxiteles', showing the god Hermes teasing an infant Dionysos with a bunch of grapes, from Olympia, probably 3rd century BC. Many of the 'masterpieces' of Greek sculpture were originally crafted in bronze; but Praxiteles, active in the mid-4th century BC, was renowned for his work in marble. This statue's attribution to Praxiteles stems from a reference by Pausanias (Guide to Greece 5.17.3); a modern consensus, however, classes it as a later, albeit close, copy.*

V POLITICAL ANIMALS

MAY 1787: in the Assembly Room at Independence Hall, Philadelphia, the congregated 'Founding Fathers' are deliberating over the articles of their new constitution. Only recently freed from the rule of King George III of England, these American delegates have been called upon to devise a form of government that would combine, in varying degrees, the participation of the people, the government of a selected few, and an executive overseer to uphold the constitution. What sort of political system, they ask, would make for 'a more perfect Union, establish Justice, insure domestic Tranquillity, provide for the common defence, promote the general Welfare, and secure the Blessings of Liberty to ourselves and our Posterity'?

In forming their responses to such questions, those early delegates found a whole library of political precedents in the Classical world. 'Mankind is by nature a political animal', stated Aristotle (*Politics* 1253a): just as bees instinctively take their place in the hive, fish swim in schools, and birds form into flocks, human beings intuitively construct their own systematic units of social organization. For Aristotle, that unit was the *polis* (and his 'political animal' was literally a 'creature of the *polis*'). Usually translated, not altogether satisfactorily, as 'city-state', *polis* denotes the self-contained, sovereign unit of the Greek city and its hinterland (*chora*: see p. 142). This concept developed from the late 9th century BC, as scattered, semi-nomadic dwellings were gradually rejected in favour of communal civic sites, complete with temples, public buildings, and planned urban spaces. It was part of a process that the ancients themselves called 'coming together to live' (*synoikismos*) and associated with the organized colonization of the lands that framed the Mediterranean. 'Greece' did not exist, but 'Greekness' (*to Hellenikon*) did: it was made up of a series of *poleis*, each with its own historical sense of community and laws and customs. Although the nature of our sources makes it harder to analyse the political make-up of Etruria (attempts largely depend on the interpretation of Etruscan tombs), we can be sure that Etruria too did not exist as any sort of nation-state in our sense of the word, even if we believe Roman claims that twelve Etruscan cities formed some sort of federal league that met at a sanctuary in Velsna (probably modern Bolsena).

With the onset of vast imperial expansion, initially undertaken by Alexander the Great in the late 4th century BC and after him by numerous Hellenistic rulers and eventually the powers of Rome, conceptions of what the Classical polity meant were set to change. New 'mega-cities', like Alexandria in Egypt and then Rome itself, brought with them new ideas about what political life entailed, where civic power lay, and how different cities, even kingdoms, related to one another. Nevertheless, reflection about good government and civic values marked all times and places of antiquity. And it is with some of those reflections – about civic origins, the visual languages of political power, the organization of urban space, and the centrality of warfare to social definitions of the Classical self – that this chapter is concerned.

261 opposite *Marble portrait thought to represent Cicero, 40–30 BC. The Roman politician, orator, and polymath Marcus Tullius Cicero provided a role-model for the aspiring statesmen of late 18th-century America, who prized the cool and rational outlook manifested in his writings. Cicero presented himself as opposed to political and moral corruption, and his four speeches against his political rival Catiline, when he was consul in 63 BC, projected him as the national hero of the Roman Republic.*

FOUNDING FATHERS: DEMOCRATS AND REPUBLICANS

We are prone to use an ancient word to describe the system that emerged from the deliberations of America's founding fathers: democracy. 'Democracy' comes from the Greek term *demokratia*, meaning 'rule of the people' – a state where power (*kratos*) is not in the hands of one man (*monarchia* or *tyrannia*), or of the nobility (*aristokratia*), or of any other selected few (*oligarchia*), but of the masses – the *demos*, or *hoi polloi* ('the many'). Like the word itself – as many have been keen to stress – the institutionalized practice of democracy is also Classical: it is usually thought to descend from democratic Athens (or, more specifically, the constructed 'Golden Age' of the city in the 5th century BC, under the leadership of Pericles [262]). In the revolutionary institutions of Athens, originating in reforms made some 2,500 years ago, a global community of states has continued to find (or mythologize) an ancient soulmate to their values of 'people power' and to be inspired by the legacy of this supposed 'Greek miracle'.

In some ways this idolization of Athenian democracy is at odds with the values that underpin our own modern democratic systems. Once slaves, women, foreigners, and youths under the age of twenty (together reckoned to approximate as many as 200,000 out of a 5th-century population of 250,000), not to mention the city-states coerced into the Athenian empire in the 5th century, are excluded from the democratic franchise, it becomes difficult to sustain any lofty ideal of 'votes for all'. But within this limited suffrage, Athenian democracy worked by the

262 *Marble portrait of Pericles, probably a Roman copy of a sculpture reputedly made by Kresilas c. 425 BC. While Thucydides might have been exceptional in presenting Pericles in unreservedly flattering tones, the statesman's portrait acknowledged, at the very least, his military strengths: it presented him as an ever-ready general, with helmet tipped back.*

*A **speech** purportedly delivered by Pericles in the winter of 430 BC supplies us with one of the most idealistic visions of Athenian democracy, the prototypical form of 'government of the people, by the people, for the people' (as Abraham Lincoln would implicitly style American democracy after Athenian mode in the Gettysburg address of 1863). The Athenian system centered around eleutheria (liberty in the public and private sphere), isonomia (equality before the laws and a right to political participation), and isegoria (freedom to speak one's opinion). Freedom of speech was perhaps the most cherished ideal of all: in the Athenian Assembly (Ekklesia), all citizens could raise and debate issues of concern so that speech (logos) was the essential precursor to action (ergon).*

The occasion for Pericles' oration was the state burial of those who had died in the first campaign of the Peloponnesian War (431–404 BC) fought between Athens and Sparta. It is recorded here by Thucydides: how much of its craft is due to Pericles himself, and how much to Thucydides' perspective of what Pericles could, might, or should have said, is not known. We can be certain, however, that throughout the speech an implicit contrast is established between the ways and institutions of Athens and those of her arch-enemy, Sparta. 'As a city,' Pericles unambiguously concludes, 'I say that we are the school of all Greece.'

Our constitution does not copy the laws of our neighbours: we ourselves are a model for, rather than an imitation of, others. We have the name 'democracy' because our administration is in the hands of the many instead of the few. As concerns the laws, we afford equal justice to all men in their settlement of private disputes; as concerns status, advancement in public affairs depends on an individual's reputation – reputation not of his class but of his virtue; and as concerns poverty, no man is held back by obscurity of rank so long as he can serve the city well . . . People are concerned with their private and public affairs at the same time; even those who are concerned with their own affairs are well informed about political matters. For we Athenians alone regard the man who is unconcerned with such things not as non-meddlesome, but as useless. We decide upon affairs for ourselves, or at least ponder on them so as to form a sound understanding: instead of regarding debate as a hindrance to action, we think it a hindrance not to be instructed by debate before the time comes for necessary action.

Thucydides, *History of the Peloponnesian War* 2.37.1–2.40.2

263 *Marble statue of George Washington by Horatio Greenough, 1840. Washington, the first president of the United States, was presented in a Classical guise, just as the new republic constructed itself in the image of Classical institutions. Lord Byron had even called Washington 'the Cincinnatus of the West', after the legendary Roman political leader who vanquished his nation's enemies and then returned to his humble home and harvest – a noble image of incorruptible power.*

Greenough's statue, commissioned in 1832 to mark the centenary of the President's birth, depicts him as a sort of seated Zeus [cf. 126], with stern facial expression and incongruously naked body. As such, it mirrors the dilemma that faced political figures in Rome [279]: how could native visual languages be reconciled with Greek associations between nudity and manly power?

direct participation of all citizens (*politai*) in governmental decision-making, whereas modern democracy usually relies on passive representation rather than active involvement. An Athenian citizen might have been baffled to hear our representative democracy called an inheritance of his direct *demokratia*. He might even have dismissed those modern individuals who fail to perform their civic duties and boycott the ballot box as 'idiotic': in Greek, *idiotes* meant 'private' or 'self-minded', not interested in public policy, and therefore, in democratic Athens, 'freakish' or 'strange'.

For the American Founding Fathers, however, chief among them George Washington [263], Roman 'republicanism' was a closer ideal than Athenian democracy. Just as the Roman Republic (or *res publica*, literally meaning the 'public affair') supposedly followed the expulsion of a Roman monarch, the constitution of the United States was established after a revolution against an English king. Whereas the newly founded Roman Republic was said to have despatched three delegates to Greece to study their laws and political practices and disclose their findings to the Republic's founding fathers (Livy, *History of Rome from its Foundation* 3.31.8), the American legislators turned to the political precedents of Rome itself. According to the 2nd-century BC Greek historian Polybius (*Histories* 6.11–18), the stability of the Roman Republic could be explained by its tripartite model of government, which brought together the merits of democracy, aristocracy, and monarchy. First, there were the Roman people whose votes and meetings (at assemblies, or *comitia*) regulated the election and agenda of the Senate; then there was the elected Senate of noble dignitaries, which made the decisions about the day-to-day running of the state; and finally there were the chief magistrates – two consuls, who topped the Republic's pyramid of power. Since no single branch of government held absolute power, instability that might lead to revolution (what Polybius and earlier Greek political theorists called *stasis*, meaning a faction, or civil war) could be avoided. The people's political involvement would not descend into mob rule or demagoguery; the governmental privileges of the aristocracy would not remain unchecked by the people; and presidential consuls were prevented by their short terms of office from sliding into tyranny. So appealing was this Roman Republican model to the Founding Fathers that they consciously fashioned their new state as the reborn (and Christianized) Rome of Cicero [261].

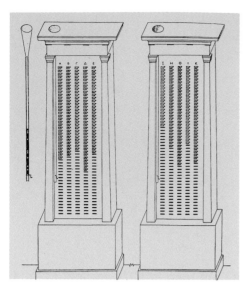

264 *Reconstruction of a* kleroteria, *an allotment machine used to select jurors and magistrates, which made sure that late 5th- and 4th-century Athenian elections were thoroughly random. Each eligible citizen's bronze tag, inscribed with his name and tribe (phyle), would be inserted into a vertical row (ten in all, one for each tribe). Black and white balls were funnelled into a hollow bronze tube beside the machine. Each crank of a lever caused a ball to fall at random and line up with a horizontal row of inscribed plaques. A white ball meant that the corresponding ten citizens were chosen as jurors; a black ball, that they were dismissed. To elect ten annual magistrates (archontes) only one white ball was used among many black.*

265 *Bronze ballot used in the Athenian law-courts, inscribed* psephos demosia *('public ballot';* psephos *literally means 'bean' or 'pebble'). All private and public grievances in Classical Athens were tried before randomly selected juries of between 201 and 2,501 citizens over the age of thirty. Each juror was given two bronze ballots: one with pierced, and one with solid 'axle'. After hearing both sides of the case, jurors placed a ballot into a box (holding it by the axle for a secret vote). Ballots with pierced axle like this one – signalling a 'hole' in the argument – found the accused guilty; those with solid axle called for acquittal.*

Ancient models of government, or at least later interpretations of them, have been used to justify a whole range of modern political systems (pp. 320–23): the Roman Empire acted as an explicit paradigm for both the 19th-century British Empire and Mussolini's Fascist régime in Italy; Karl Marx believed that his ideal socialist republic was the real heir to Roman Republican values; and the rigorous disciplinarianism of ancient Sparta has been approved by all manner of different political theorists, from Niccolò Machiavelli to Jean-Jacques Rousseau and Adolf Hitler. As Thomas Jefferson wrote to John Adams in 1813, 'the same political parties which now agitate the United States have existed thro' all time: whether the power of the people or that of the *aristoi* should prevail were questions which kept the states of Greece and Rome in eternal convulsions, as they now schismatize every people whose minds and mouths are not shut up by the gag of a despot.'

MYTHOLOGIZING POLITICAL ORIGINS

The ways in which modern states have taken to mythologizing their own civic origins are themselves paralleled in antiquity. Perhaps the most enlightening examples are the myth-histories that grew up around the institutions of one particular Greek *polis*: Athens. Even now, it remains very difficult to extricate the historical institutions and practices of democratic Athens from the mythologized stories with which the new political system framed that 'founding moment'.

On an institutional level, the machinery of Athenian democracy seems to have been put in place by a citizen named Kleisthenes in 508–507 BC. Kleisthenes is credited with having reorganized Attica into a new bureaucratic system of local municipalities, or demes (*demoi*), with their own form of local government; 139 in total, these constituencies also formed the basic building-blocks for larger-scale

Writing the history *of any city is problematic – especially when that city, like Rome, was capital of a world empire. But that did not deter Livy – Titus Livius – from creating a monumental history of Rome in 142 books, of which some 35 survive mostly intact. Ab Urbe Condita (literally 'from the foundation of the city') chronicled the rise of Rome in a long chain of development, from the fall of Troy right up to political events in living memory. It fused the foundation-myths of heroic time with the real-time historical figures whose actions were still resonating around the Augustan city, breaking down distinctions between civic 'myths' and 'objective' political histories. Despite problems of historiography and scope, Livy suggests, such histories are worthwhile precisely because by studying former Golden Ages the reader can consider which civic values the contemporary world should admire, and which vices it should condemn.*

Were I to write down the achievements of the Roman people from the foundation of their city, would I produce something that was worth the effort? I do not really know. And even if I were to know, I still would not say 'yes'. For I realize that this enterprise is both old and hackneyed. New writers always believe that they will either produce greater accuracy in terms of events, or alternatively that they will surpass the crude attempts of a previous age by the erudition of their writing style. But however it will turn out, it will nevertheless be sufficient for me to have myself contributed (as much as I can) to recording the deeds of the foremost people of the world; and if my own reputation is obscured by so great a crowd of writers, I would be consoled by the honour and stature of those who eclipse my light . . . It is this that chiefly makes the understanding of events salutary and profitable: you can perceive documents of every sort of example laid out for you as on a shining monument. From these you may select for yourself, and for your public state [*res publica*], something to emulate. Furthermore, from these you may select something – whatever is as shameful in conception as it is in consequence – to avoid.

Livy, *History of Rome from its Foundation* 1.1–3, 10

political organization. The demes were divided into 30 *trittyes*; these were in turn divided into 10 new *phylai*. Each *phyle* – usually translated as 'tribe' – comprised one *trittys* from the city of Athens itself, one from around Attica's harbour (the Piraeus), and one from her inland countryside. Every Athenian citizen belonged to a tribe, and each tribe was named after a mythological figure [299]. All aspects of political life seem to have revolved around them, from the organization of the army and navy to the selection of jurors and constitutive membership of the Council (the *Boule* of 500 men, 50 from each tribe). Kleisthenes does not seem to have made any significant constitutional change to the make-up of the pre-existing Assembly (*Ekklesia*), which would eventually emerge as the centrepiece of Athenian democracy – where the citizenry would gather to debate the political issues of the day. (The origin of that Assembly was attributed to a still more mysterious Athenian politician-cum-poet of the early 6th century BC, Solon, who later came to be mythologized into yet another democratic founding father.)

If these seem rather complicated achievements, another reform attributed to Kleisthenes in antiquity was much simpler: ostracism. The act of ostracism could be performed once a year. It provided an opportunity for the populace to expel any individual whom they disfavoured – be it through fear of tyrannical aspirations, political rivalry, or plain spite. The citizen's task was straightforward enough. He had merely to scratch the chosen name onto a potsherd, or *ostrakon* (several thousand *ostraka* have been found in the area around the Agora, or marketplace, in Athens [266]). If a minimum of 6,000 votes were amassed, the citizen with the most votes had no channel for appeal; he had ten days in which to leave Athens, and he was prohibited from returning for ten years – long enough, supposedly, for his hot ambitions to turn cold. But, in the wrong hands, ostracism could itself prove a heated political weapon: 190 *ostraka*, for instance, all inscribed with the name of Themistocles (ostracized in the late 470s BC, according to Thucydides) but bearing the distinctive handwriting of a few individuals, seem to reflect the manipulative

266 *Examples of* ostraka *found in the Athenian Agora. Three bear the name of Themistocles – one of eight men who we can be sure were ostracized between 487 BC (when the first ostracism took place) and 416 BC.*

Since magistrates in democratic Athens were randomly selected, the canvassing that accompanied ostracism was perhaps the closest Athens came to a fiercely fought modern election. But where elections today vote candidates into power, ostracism elected citizens out of the public sphere: such was the Athenian fear of demagoguery.

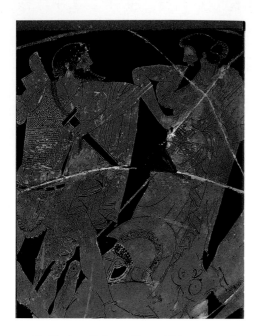

267 The brawl between Ajax and Odysseus over the arms of Achilles, on an Attic red-figure kylix signed by Douris, c. 480 BC.

268 below left An imagined democratic solution to the quarrel, on the other side of the cup painted by Douris [267]. The scene is presided over by – who else, given democracy's Athenian origins? – Athena. Votes in the form of pebbles are being cast for Ajax and Odysseus: the pile of Odysseus, on the left, is larger, and he raises his hands in delight.

269 below right The final tragic outcome of the dispute, depicted inside an Attic red-figure kylix attributed to the Brygos Painter, c. 490 BC. After losing the contest, Ajax has impaled himself on his sword, and his concubine Tekmessa covers his body with a shroud.

scheming of a group of Themistocles' political opponents. Those citizens who had not yet made up their minds were perhaps subject to the same forms of vote-canvassing that the modern world witnesses, and might, quite literally, be given a helping hand: Athenian citizens who could not read or write – surely a significant percentage – might quite easily have been deceived into ostracizing Themistocles instead of the person whose name they had asked to be inscribed on their *ostrakon*.

Beyond this basic analysis, it soon becomes very difficult to pinpoint the exact origins of Athenian democracy: the search for a revolutionary, original, definably 'democratic' moment has to give way to an evolutionary, mythically coloured model. For however we decide to judge the matter, Athenian literary and visual traditions shrouded that 'founding moment' with legendary narratives of their own. A whole array of ancient myths was reinscribed with democratic significance. Take the quarrel over the armour of Achilles after his death, between Odysseus and the 'Greater' Ajax (as opposed to the 'Lesser' Ajax, who raped Cassandra [190]). In the most frequent versions of the story, the brawny Ajax, considering himself the rightful heir to the divinely crafted armour (p. 119), is outwitted by the brainy Odysseus. On a cup dating to around 480 BC we see the fight between them [267]. But on the other side [268], the Homeric heroes are shown, rather anachronistically, as if *they* had initiated the democratic 'founding moment', as each casts his vote with a pebble in the manner of a democratic jury. Ajax holds his head in despair at seeing his heap of votes so small; but this, as we should say, is a 'democratic decision'. Inside another cup with similar images on the outside we see the outcome: Ajax, defeated, has committed suicide [269]. Even democracy cannot satisfy all.

One of the earliest legends about democracy's founding moment revolves around two Athenian 'Tyrannicides', Harmodios and Aristogeiton: they were credited with ending the tyrannical dynasty founded by Peisistratos, who on his death in 527 BC had been succeeded by his two sons, Hippias and Hipparchos. At the Panathenaic festival of 514 BC, Hipparchos was assassinated. Both assassins were punished: Harmodios was killed instantly, and Aristogeiton was later captured, tortured, and killed. Historically speaking, we should note that Harmodios and Aristogeiton did not put an end to the Peisistratids: they only assassinated Hipparchos, and not his brother, Hippias, who continued to rule for several years, becoming even more fiercely tyrannical; and when he was eventually

270 The Tyrannicides, *from the villa of the Emperor Hadrian at Tivoli: a marble copy of the bronze group attributed to Kritios and Nesiotes erected in the Athenian Agora in 477 BC. On the left stands Aristogeiton, the protective older lover, and on the right Harmodios, dagger in hand. But where is the murdered tyrant? In some ways the viewer, standing in their line of attack, is assimilated to that role. So it is that Harmodios and Aristogeiton's act is presented not as a one-off assassination, but as a continuous and aggressive commitment to the democratic cause. Woe betide the tyrant.*

271 *Detail of the* Tyrannicides *motif on a marble throne from the Theatre of Dionysos in Athens, early 4th century BC. The motif quickly became a sort of logo for the Athenian democracy. The Theatre of Dionysos was where the City Dionysia – a festival honouring Athenian civic pride as much as its presiding deity, Dionysos – was held (see pp. 260–62).*

being deposed, in 510 BC, it was thanks to the military might of the Spartan army in coalition with another Athenian family, the Alkmaionids. That must have been a 'founding moment' that the people of Athens, in the context of 5th-century rivalries between Athens and Sparta, most likely wished to forget.

The story of the Tyrannicides was soon elaborated into an urban myth of political intrigue, homoerotic devotion, and self-sacrifice. Thucydides presents the two as motivated not by a heroic desire to eliminate tyrants but by a personal vendetta. In the first place he claims that Harmodios joined in the conspiracy because Hipparchos had dishonoured his sister; in the second, that Aristogeiton and Harmodios were lovers and that Hipparchos had attempted to seduce Harmodios (*History of the Peloponnesian War* 6.54–59). Indeed, Thucydides himself seems to have been sensitive to the romantic fantasy underlying such democratic appropriations of an essentially non-democratic foundation legend: 'by relating the story at length,' he declares, 'I shall demonstrate that neither the Athenians nor other peoples give any accurate account of their own tyrants and this event' (6.54.1).

Whatever its motive, the deed was soon immortalized in a bronze statue group commissioned for the Athenian marketplace, supposedly made by Antenor in 509 BC. It is clear that the group very quickly became a talismanic icon for the new political régime: it presented the origins of Athenian democracy as deeply revolutionary, something associated with Athenian democratic standards of group bravery (no less than homoeroticism) and individual panache. When the Persians stormed Athens in 480–479 BC, they reputedly chose this group as a trophy to

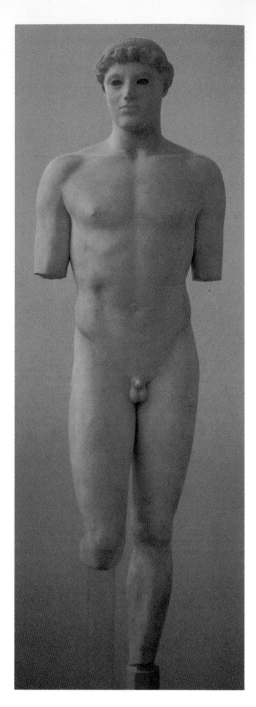

272 *Marble statue known as the* Kritian Boy, *c. 480 BC. According to one interpretation, this represents Athens' founding hero, Theseus; to another, it once stood on a surviving inscribed base and commemorates a certain Kallias, victor in a Panathenaic foot-race. Either way, the sense of movement and introspective contemplation, together with the turn of the figure's head (so that he does not return the viewer's gaze), marked a new departure in Greek art, bound up with the artistic and cultural developments of late 6th- and early 5th-century BC Athens. The statue's sobriquet stems from a 19th-century attribution to Kritios, one of the sculptors to whom the second* Tyrannicides *group is attributed [270].*

mark their annihilation of Athens and democracy. In 477 BC the Athenians replaced it with a copy, attributed to the sculptors Kritios and Nesiotes (itself copied in Roman times [270]), and that in turn was reproduced by other Greek *poleis* as a symbol of the origins of their own democracies. On the island of Chios, for example, a 4th-century inscription instructed the keepers of the marketplace to adorn their local *Tyrannicides* sculpture with garlands and to keep it 'heroically shining'. What is more, when one of antiquity's other 'tyrants', Julius Caesar, was assassinated in Rome in 44 BC, the Athenians reputedly erected bronze images of Brutus and Cassius at the group's side, intimating that those Romans had emulated this Athenian democratic example (Dio Cassius, *Roman History* 47.20.4). Indeed, the iconography of this democratic founding moment resonated throughout Athenian visual culture – from a representation of Theseus in allusive Tyrannicide pose on a metope of the Temple of Hephaistos in Athens to images of athletes on the amphoras awarded to victors of the Panathenaic Games, and a throne in the Theatre of Dionysos [271].

STYLING CIVIC POWER

In democratic Athens the state of the art and the art of the state were inexorably connected. Philosophically speaking, this 'politicized aesthetic' is a well-documented phenomenon. The German antiquarian Johann Joachim Winckelmann [498] in the 18th century was the first to forge an ideological connection between the Classical 'perfection' of Athenian art and the circumstances under which it was created, namely the artist's individual 'liberty'. Why were 6th-century iconographic schemes abandoned? How do we explain the heightened Athenian sense of artistic experimentation? What drove artists to make their representations more 'lifelike'? For Winckelmann, as for a number of more recent scholars, it was Athenian democracy that provided the explanation. Take the case of a relatively small early 5th-century statue, the *Kritian Boy* [272]. In terms of apparent connections between Athenian democracy and artistic naturalism, the sculpture is almost too good to be true. Discovered on the Acropolis, where it seems to have been piously buried some time after 480 BC, it has been interpreted as being as revolutionary as the age of democracy in which it was produced. Like earlier *kouroi* [446], the figure stands with his arms at his side and one leg forward; but there is a new sense of organic movement: the boy's weight is not distributed evenly, making the left hip higher than the right, and his head is slightly turned to one side.

Despite the artistic innovations that coincided with the foundation of democracy, Athens feared the political abuse of images. Notice how the statues erected in connection with democracy's 'founding moment' were not of Kleisthenes, or of any other early associate of the new political organization. Instead, they commemorated a pair of men who posed no political threat in terms of ancestry or individual political ambition, and who, now they were dead, could not exploit their quasi-cultic status as tyrant-slayers to any political end. On one level, we should associate this phenomenon with Athenian democracy's very real fear, already encountered in the context of ostracism, that an individual might tyrannically preempt the say of the populace. On another, it is connected with an important point about the function of images in 5th- and 4th-century Athens: they served to commemorate, promote, and immortalize. Art was potentially dangerous to democracy because public images of an individual could endow him with a sort of public power. When it came to funerary monuments, for instance, the Athenian democracy seems to have had fairly strict rules about what was acceptable piety towards the dead and what constituted shamelessly self-aggrandizing displays of individual wealth (p. 17).

273 Bronze head of Demosthenes, inscribed with his name, last quarter of the 1st century BC. However Demosthenes' portrait may have related to his actual physiognomy, it evokes a man who gave his life over to public political service: his brow is wrinkled, his eyes downcast, and his expression is steeped in brooding contemplation for the public good (almost in the manner of a Greek philosopher). In his speeches, a number of which survive, Demosthenes repeatedly spoke out against the growing power of Macedon under Philip II and his son, Alexander the Great.

274 Gem engraved with a portrait of Demosthenes, signed by a carver named Apelles, inset into a gold ring, last quarter of the 1st century BC. Over fifty portrait busts of Demosthenes survive from the Roman period; so too do a large number of portraits in other media, especially from the late 1st century BC. Roman clients seem to have admired not only Demosthenes' thundering political oratory, but also the visual evocation of his ethical gravitas – akin, in some ways, to their own Republican portraits [e.g. 280].

One of the most effective ways in which Pericles' opponents attempted to discredit him in the third quarter of the 5th century BC, or so we are told, exploited this fear of images to political end. When Pericles was supervising the building programmes on the Acropolis, they accused his sculptor, Pheidias, of incorporating his likeness into the shield of the Athena Parthenos (the colossal gold and ivory sculpture [122] that stood in the Parthenon). The charge brought against Pheidias – for which he was reputedly imprisoned – was (according to the early 2nd-century AD biography by Plutarch) *blasphemia*: the sculptor had bestowed on Pericles an iconic privilege that was reserved for the gods. The public display of an image of a living and active citizen (unlike Harmodios and Aristogeiton) constituted a blasphemy against the Athenian democracy, and nearly all extant portraits of Athenian democratic figures are correspondingly posthumous constructions: surviving images of the orator Demosthenes [e.g. 273], for instance, probably derive from a portrait by Polyeuktos erected in the Agora in 280 BC, a generation after his death. In fact, most of the images of Athenian statesmen that survive today have been filtered through a rationalizing Roman lens: they served as a learned 'who's who' within the libraries of Rome's rich and famous (like the Villa dei Papiri at Herculaneum) and spoke of the owner's cultural pretensions.

According to the Greek historian Arrian (writing in the 2nd century AD), it was the Macedonian king Alexander the Great who returned the original *Tyrannicides* sculpture to Athens. This was a shrewd move: Alexander could appear to restore Athens to the acme of its democratic glory, while subsuming that glory under his own personal fame.

The ways in which Alexander manipulated and mass-produced a personal political image [275–78] must have seemed a strange innovation to Athenian viewers. Alexander and his 'Successors' (*Diadochoi*) paraded his image across the many territories that he had conquered: it appeared in statuary, in reliefs, in paintings, and especially on coins. Specific artists are even said to have been exclusively commissioned to depict him in different media – Lysippos in sculpture, Apelles in paint, and Pyrgoteles in gem-engravings – and his portrait demanded adoration, literal worship (*proskynesis*). Like his expansionist foreign policy, Alexander's sophisticated use of art in the service of power probably owed much to the precedent of his father, Philip II of Macedon. Nevertheless, Alexander's projected image was a

'**Some men are born great**, some achieve greatness, and some have greatness thrust upon them', or so Malvolio is made to believe in Shakespeare's Twelfth Night. *But, in the wake of Alexander and the world rulers that succeeded him, we might want to institute another category: those who manipulate visual languages of power so as to convey themselves as great among their subjects. In the 20th-century cultural historian Daniel Boorstin's cynical rephrasing, 'some men are born great, some achieve greatness, and some hire public relations officers' . . .*

Accounts of Alexander's appearance relished the irony that such a powerful ruler was, in the flesh, rather short and unimposing. Stories even grew up that Alexander's subjects (indeed on one occasion the mother of Alexander's opponent, Darius III of Persia) mistakenly prostrated themselves before his more impressive companion, Hephaistion. For a successful autocrat, however, the propagation of a convincing image has always been more important than 'real-life' appearances. For Cicero, Alexander's worldwide fame had little to do with the propagation of his image; for Plutarch, Alexander was closely involved in the process. At any rate, the posthumous fusion between the 'real-life' appearance of Alexander and his portrait, as a 4th-century anecdote about Caracalla (Roman emperor AD 211–217) demonstrates, reveals how successful that artistic bestowal of 'greatness' really was.

When Alexander himself wanted to be painted by Apelles and sculpted by Lysippos rather than by anyone else, it was not for the artists' sake. He probably thought, rather, that their art would glorify him as much as it would them. The images that those artists made of his body are well known even to the ignorant. But even if there were to be no such images, the glorious would still be glorious.

Cicero, *Letters to his Friends* 5.12.7

After Lysippos had created his first Alexander, staring upwards with face turned towards the heavens (just as Alexander himself was prone to staring, gently inclining his head sideways), someone wrote this fitting epigram:

This bronze statue seems to behold
    Zeus and say
'I over the earth as you, Zeus, over
    Olympus hold sway.'

Therefore Alexander ordered that it would be Lysippos alone that would sculpt his representations. For only Lysippos, he thought, developed his character in bronze and gave physical expression to his spiritual excellence. The other sculptors, by contrast, merely desired to imitate how Alexander turned his neck to one side and represent the melting languor of his eyes: they did not do justice to his manly, lion-like air.

Plutarch, *Moral Essays* 335A–B

After Caracalla had inspected the body of Alexander of Macedon, he demanded that he himself be called 'Alexander' and 'the Great'. In doing so, he was encouraged by the lies of his sycophants to the extent that, adopting a pitiless brow and twisting his neck towards his left shoulder (for he had noted these features in Alexander's countenance), he proceeded to persuade himself that their facial features really were very similar.

Sextus Aurelius Victor,
On the Caesars 21.4

278 *The Alexander Mosaic, from the House of the Faun in Pompeii, 2nd century BC. The subject is probably the battle of Issus in 333 BC: Alexander appears on horseback on the left, routing the Persians, led by Darius III, who has wheeled round his chariot in flight. The glory of the victor and the pathos of the vanquished are evoked in equal measure: note, for instance, in the bottom right corner, how the stricken face of a fallen Persian warrior appears reflected in his shield.*

opposite
275 top *Marble portrait of Alexander, c. 320 BC. Identified on the grounds of its mass of leonine hair, upturned eyes, and twist of the neck, this head once formed part of a larger monument – perhaps the elaborate tomb of a courtier who was keen to associate himself in death, as in life, with the all-powerful ruler.*

276 centre *Alexander, depicted as an Egyptian pharaoh, with Ammon, the supreme Egyptian deity, in a granite relief at Luxor in Egypt, completed c. 320 BC.*

277 bottom *Alexander has Ammon's attribute of ram's horns on a tetradrachm issued by Lysimachos, his successor as ruler of Thrace, c. 290 BC.*

novel departure. It tapped into the iconographic schemes that had formerly been the preserve of the gods, with its unbearded youthfulness, 'lion's mane' hairstyle (thick hair roughly swept back with a centre parting, or *anastole*), tilted neck, and charismatic 'melting gaze' (as if in touch with a divine inspirational force – an *enthousiasmos*). Alexander, his portrait manifested, was larger than life: he could not be contained within the confines of the Greek *polis*. As the continuous restyling of that image by later Hellenistic kings demonstrates, 'Alexander' would also become a power even larger than his image, transcending any single mode of iconographic representation.

So influential was Alexander's image in the Hellenistic kingdoms that sprang up after his death that it is extremely difficult to determine which portraits date from Alexander's own time and which represent later monarchs [362, 520]. Alexander himself died young – from excessive drinking, an unrelated illness, or the poison of some scheming companion. His 'Successors' divided his kingdom among themselves: Ptolemy in Egypt, Seleukos in Asia, Antigonos in Macedon, later Attalos in Pergamon, and so on. And to further their chances of holding on to those kingdoms, they produced images of their own political power that drew on the quasi-mythical origins of Alexander.

Alexander exerted a much wider iconographic influence on posterity: he initiated a new alignment between power and artistic styles. Just as the *Tyrannicides* became a symbol for expressing democratic allegiance among 4th-century Greek *poleis*, so the iconography of Alexander was used by his dynastic successors to symbolize their own autocratic modes of power. What followed was a new degree of self-conscious reflection about what artistic styles meant. Rulers were prompted to

279 *The 'Pseudo-athlete' from Delos, c. 100 BC. The statue demonstrates a seemingly unlikely fusion of Greek and Roman styles, combining Greek Polykleitan prowess with the austere features of a Roman portrait. It was found in the courtyard of a merchant's house on the island (which was famous for its slave trade, from the Greek East to Rome).*

contemplate how iconographic styles might be harnessed to reflect, and affect, their political status within the new power structures of their kingdoms and the Hellenistic world at large. Given the unprecedented size of the empires of Alexander and his Hellenistic 'Successors', these styles could not be uniform: the traditions that gave Alexander's image meaning at Luxor in Egypt [276], for example, were not the same as those operating in Greece.

Hellenistic styles in turn exerted a two-way influence on Roman culture – an influence of both fascinated absorption and disdainful rejection (see p. 302). In the words of the Augustan poet Horace (*Epistles* 2.1.156–57), 'conquered Greece has conquered its rough victor and brought its arts to rustic Latium'. As the Roman Republic extended its power over the world, it seemed to witness its own 'native' styles being infiltrated by the Hellenic cultures of the lands it had subdued, first via Etruria and then, in the 2nd century BC, from Greece itself. Now we might see this distinction between 'native' Roman and 'foreign' Greek as misconceived: Greek visual culture had, after all, in many respects informed and fused with Etruscan uses of visual culture in a two-way process of cultural exchange for several centuries; besides, Rome by no means reckoned itself synonymous with Etruria. Nevertheless, for Roman viewers in the 1st century BC, the dichotomy seems to have appeared very real indeed. Just how 'Roman' was Rome? Could its civic past be reconciled – could it even compete – with the iconographic styles and associated *luxuria* of the Hellenistic world? And would embracing those styles undermine Rome's own civic conceptions, ancestral traditions (*mores maiorum*), and military bravado?

The 'identity crisis' that ensued is reflected in late Roman Republican political portraits. On one hand, a staunch conservatism rejected Greek influences and drew politicians back to 'native' styles – 'warts and all' depictions which scholars have called 'veristic' [280]. On the other hand, Hellenistic images of kingship, with all their associations of individual power, attracted those Roman dignitaries who wanted to propel themselves into the contemporary public sphere [281]. Some of the images that resulted from this stylistic culture-clash may now appear rather absurd. Who was the client of the 'Pseudo-athlete' from Delos, commissioning an image that presented him as a nude Hellenistic warrior king in body, but a Roman Republican senator in mind [279]? Could Pompey really mythologize himself as Alexander the Great, his thick hair brushed into a leonine mane, while also posing as a Roman Republican with wrinkled brow, double chin, and puffy cheeks [282]?

It is tempting to draw an association between the political success of Octavian (who effectively became the first Roman emperor when he received the title of 'Augustus', or 'Consecrated one', in 27 BC) and his fusion of such seemingly divergent 'Roman' and 'Greek' visual languages. Augustus presented his state as a restoration of the old political *status quo* – the *res publica restituta*. Initially he appeared as 'first among equals' (*primus inter pares*), holding the consulship like any other prominent political figure in the Republic; but, exceptionally, Augustus continued to hold that office year after year from 31 to 23 BC, and he sealed his power by declaring himself the tribune-hero of the people in 23 BC (this was the event from which Augustus counted his years of office as *princeps*, or 'first citizen'). The statue of Augustus discovered at the villa of his wife Livia at Prima Porta [cf. 243] provides one of the best-known examples of how he – or Livia – manipulated artistic styles to embody political meanings [286]. Perhaps a later marble copy of a bronze original, it is a highly Hellenized image: it recalls Polykleitos' *Doryphoros* [37], which had been adapted by Hellenistic sculptors (most famously Lysippos) as a prototype for images of Hellenistic kings [e.g. 283]. So for Roman viewers the sculpture must have come complete with associations of immeasurable majesty and power.

280 *Marble portrait of a Roman statesman, late 1st century BC. Republican portraits have been called 'veristic' on the grounds that they captured a 'true to life' photographic likeness: brows are furrowed, heads are balding, and the whole face is creased with age-exaggerating wrinkles. Portraits, however, always reflect deeply rooted values: in these images, the individual's cultural and political gravitas is projected through the features of late middle age, not idealized youth and beauty as in Greece. In Republican Rome, after all, candidates for the office of consul had to be at least forty-two years old.*

281 *below left Bronze portrait of a political figure, from Asia Minor, 1st century BC. The image is comparable to the portraits of Alexander the Great [275] and his successors in its mass of short hair, soft modelling of the face, and turn of the head. The subject may be the ruler of an eastern Mediterranean country; but because such Hellenistic images were first used to style Roman civic power during this period, it has also been interpreted as the Roman legislator Sulla.*

282 *below right Marble portrait of Pompey, styled 'the Great' in conscious imitation of Alexander, c. 55 BC. This bust is perhaps the most famous Roman Republican attempt to combine the mannerisms of Hellenistic ruler portraits with Italic veristic traditions.*

The Prima Porta statue [286], however, is not simply a Hellenistic ruler portrait. For one thing, the gesture of Augustus' right arm alludes to a specifically native representational trope, the *adlocutio* (or oratorical 'address'), seen for instance in an Etrusco-Roman bronze portrait dated to the early 1st century BC [285]. For another, his costume is very distinctive. He does not wear the standard Roman toga, or the footwear that might have marked him as an equestrian or senatorial figure [284]. Instead, he is shown with bare feet, associating the figure with depictions of gods and heroes. His breastplate, sculpted in relief with its own narrative of military and cosmic prowess, taps into specifically Roman modes of military representation. If we were in any doubt as to Augustus' divine aspirations, the small Cupid that tugs on his leg provides a veiled visual reference: Augustus claimed descent from the

283 *Bronze statuette of a ruler, late 2nd century BC. This recalls a lost type of bronze sculpture of Alexander the Great, crafted by Lysippos in the late 4th century BC. The subject is displayed in the full glory of his nudity, which is if anything emphasized by the piece of drapery that hangs over his left shoulder. He originally held a lance in his left hand [cf. 462].*

284 *Bronze relief group of two magistrates wearing togas and sandals, mid-1st century AD. The toga was a roughly semicircular piece of white woollen cloth worn over the tunic, draped over the left shoulder [cf. 12]: patterned with different colours and stripes to indicate different offices and social initiations, it became synonymous with free-born Roman citizenship – so much so that Vergil called the Romans the gens togata, or 'togate race'.*

285 *Bronze statue of Aulus Metellus, early 1st century BC. The statue (known as the Arringatore, or orator) interestingly combines Etruscan and Roman features. The orator's name is Roman, as are his dress and gesture of addressing his fellow statesmen (adlocutio); his name, however, is inscribed in Etruscan script. Unlike Hellenistic political portraits, where the quasi-divinity of the subject is evoked by the display of the naked body [283], he is dressed in toga and boots.*

286 right *Marble statue of Augustus from the villa of Livia at Prima Porta, perhaps copying a bronze original made after 20 BC. The portrait subtly fuses Roman and Greek iconographic styles: his adlocutio gesture is Roman [cf. 285], but his pose and coiffure recall the Doryphoros of Polykleitos [37]. Unlike images of Hellenistic monarchs [283], Augustus is not naked, but clothed in military attire; and yet the curious hip-mantle wrapped around his arm does recall a frequent motif of nude Hellenistic ruler portraits; his cuirass, moreover, shows off the muscular physique below. It depicts a bearded Parthian king returning the military standards that the Romans (under the generalship of Crassus) had lost at the battle of Carrhae in 53 BC. That event was in reality a matter of diplomacy: here, however, it is given full divine and cosmic significance, witnessed by a number of allegorical figures – Earth, Sun, Moon, and Heaven. The figure of Cupid at his feet alludes to the way in which Augustus, like Julius Caesar before him, claimed descent from Venus.*

MVNI[ ]PII IX P·M·
AN·XVIII

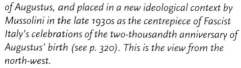

287 *The Ara Pacis in Rome was commissioned by the Senate to celebrate Augustus' return from Spain in 13 BC and the supposed end of military conflict. The monument was moved from its original site, reassembled next to the mausoleum of Augustus, and placed in a new ideological context by Mussolini in the late 1930s as the centrepiece of Fascist Italy's celebrations of the two-thousandth anniversary of Augustus' birth (see p. 320). This is the view from the north-west.*

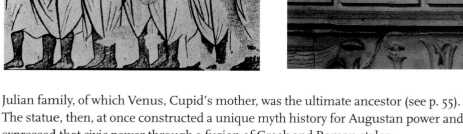

288 above *Water-carriers in procession on the frieze from the Parthenon in Athens, c. 440 BC.*

289 above right *Members of the Etruscan Apuna family, accompanied by priests holding staves and trumpets, process in honour of the deceased: detail of a wall-painting in the Bruschi Tomb at Tarquinia, 3rd century BC.*

Julian family, of which Venus, Cupid's mother, was the ultimate ancestor (see p. 55). The statue, then, at once constructed a unique myth history for Augustan power and expressed that civic power through a fusion of Greek and Roman styles.

Under Augustus, as under all effective despots, artistic styles were not just harnessed as a passive medium to express a political content: stylistic allusions could themselves summon up a whole spectrum of associations so that the medium became the message. For the Augustan viewer, that message, simply put, was that Rome ruled the world; and Augustus ruled Rome. Roman culture brought together, in a constructed 'Golden Age' of Augustan rule, all that was to be cherished in artistic (as in literary) traditions. This, at least, is one way of interpreting what is perhaps the most famous monument of Augustan Rome, the Ara Pacis Augustae,

290 *Detail of the religious procession on the south frieze of the Ara Pacis. Two figures are taller than all the rest: Augustus, second from the left, in profile and laurel-crowned, and Marcus Agrippa, Augustus' favoured administrator, at the far right, with veiled head. Priests (flamines) wearing their distinctive leather caps with metal spikes [cf. 158] attend Augustus who, as pontifex maximus (high priest), was probably shown in the act of preparing a sacrifice. The scene is highly idealized – not least because Agrippa had died almost three years before the altar was dedicated.*

or Altar of Augustan Peace. The Ara Pacis was dedicated in the Campus Martius, the electoral assembly-place, in 9 BC. It consists of a small central altar table on a raised platform encased in elaborately decorated walls [287]. On the east and west sides, flanking the entrances, are scenes associated with the civic origins of Rome: on the west side we see Aeneas and Romulus, on the east Rome and Italy (or Earth, or Peace – in some ways identification seems less important than appreciating the fecundity and stylistic allusions of the iconography [4]). Two huge processions adorn the south and north sides: the former depicts the extended imperial family [290], the latter a further consort of priests, magistrates, and senators. Below on all sides are elaborate patterns of floral scrolls [240] and fantastic fruits, testimony to the concurrent blossoming and maturation of Rome under Augustus.

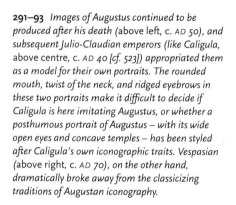

291–93 *Images of Augustus continued to be produced after his death (above left, c. AD 50), and subsequent Julio-Claudian emperors (like Caligula, above centre, c. AD 40 [cf. 523]) appropriated them as a model for their own portraits. The rounded mouth, twist of the neck, and ridged eyebrows in these two portraits make it difficult to decide if Caligula is here imitating Augustus, or whether a posthumous portrait of Augustus – with its wide open eyes and concave temples – has been styled after Caligula's own iconographic traits. Vespasian (above right, c. AD 70), on the other hand, dramatically broke away from the classicizing traditions of Augustan iconography.*

294 *Marble portrait of Livia, Augustus' wife, c. AD 10. Her face is idealized in a classicizing mode and her features are softly modelled; her hair is arranged into a wide frontal roll (nodus).*

'Neoclassicism' is a word that has been used to characterize the stylistic language of the Ara Pacis. Classicizing drapery and idealized faces (also evident in images of Livia, Augustus' wife [294]) abound, prompting inevitable comparison, among scholars at least, with the east pediment of the Parthenon, just as this religious and civic procession seems to draw on that of the Parthenon's frieze [288]. But we might more appropriately substitute a different term, 'cosmopolitanism', since the altar actually comprises an amalgamation of different styles. The togate procession was a common subject in Italic art [289], and the combination of shallow carving to render spatial depth with deeper carving for figures in the foreground was a feature of Hellenistic reliefs. The interior of the enclosure was sculpted to look like wooden boards, adorned with the paraphernalia of Roman sacrificial ceremonies – including sacrificial bowls (*paterae*) and bulls' skulls (*bucrania*) – evoking much earlier, temporary, wooden altars that were erected in Republican times. And for all its apparent allusions to the styles of Athenian democracy, the Ara Pacis stresses a Roman religious aspect in the traditional caps and woollen cloaks worn by the priests (*flamines*) [290]. Like the acanthus leaves on the exterior, which themselves draw on Greek, Persian, Etruscan, and Pergamene styles, and the sculpted fruits on the interior, all symbolic of natural harmony, Augustan Rome evidently presented itself as embodying the simultaneous florescence of all those different stylistic traditions.

In turn, the visual styles with which Augustus framed himself and his state could be adopted or rejected by his imperial successors as a means of mythologizing, legitimating, and fashioning their own forms of civic power. We do not know what Caligula (emperor AD 37–41) 'really' looked like, but his portrait [292] clearly cast him as the iconographic heir of Augustus [291]. By contrast, a portrait of Vespasian (emperor AD 69–79) [293] evokes a very different myth history for his principate. Gone is the idealized, smooth-faced, Augustan youth (which had perhaps been discredited by the turmoil and corruption that marked the end of the Julio-Claudian dynasty): instead, Vespasian has returned to older veristic styles [cf. 280], complete with their associations of reinvigorated Republican values. While Vespasian's motto, 'Res publica restituta' ('the Republic restored'), surely alluded to an Augustan maxim (p. 178), his radically different image physically embodied the message of an institutional return to the ancestral traditions, or *mores maiorum*, of the Republic.

SITUATING THE CITY

So far, our analysis of the Classical city has focused on its constituents – its political animals (and their keepers). This is how the ancients themselves seem to have communally defined their city: as the Athenian commander Nikias reminded his despondent troops in Sicily in 413 BC (according to Thucydides' *History of the Peloponnesian War* 7.77.7), 'the *polis* is its men, it does not comprise walls or ships without men in them'. Even the language used to describe different *poleis* reflected that communal definition. While in Greek the names 'Sparta', 'Athens', and 'Thebes', for example, were used to refer to a place when travelling to and from it, or indicating a location within it, it was much more common to use terms that alluded to the living creatures of those *poleis* – not 'the laws of Sparta' but 'the laws of the Spartans', 'the constitution of the Athenians', 'the ships of the Thebans', and so on.

Inevitably, however, we are bound to ask: what did a Classical city look like? Modern travellers who have wandered around the remnants of Classical Mediterranean cities usually form their own impressions of some of the essential constituents. Greek and Roman urban centres – like modern Western cities – are marked by certain recurrent types of structure: religious (such as sanctuaries and temples), administrative (from council buildings to governmental offices), juridical (law-courts), commercial (shops and stores), and buildings dedicated to other communal activities and amenities (gymnasia, *palaestra*, theatres, amphitheatres, baths, inns, etc.). Many of those categories come together in two of the most familiar sites in an ancient Mediterranean city: the *agora* (the 'marketplace' or central civic area of a Greek city) and the *forum* (a Roman open square). The distinctions between categories were also fluid: temples were simultaneously 'religious', 'communal', and in some senses 'administrative' buildings

295 *Detail of a Roman relief of a small town, found in Lake Fucino near Avezzano, east of Rome, 2nd century AD. Like most Roman and Greek towns, the settlement is surrounded by a defensive wall; here we see an open gate, leading to a straight street. The buildings, many with two or three storeys, are laid out on a grid plan. At the top, second from the right, is a basilica.*

Analyses of the layout *of the Greek* polis *have almost always privileged the model of Athens. In a moment of great prophetic insight, Thucydides gave one explanation as to why that should be: through successive monumental civic building programmes, the Athenians inscribed a larger-than-life image of themselves into our history books. When examining their tremendously expensive and elaborate schemes, not least the Parthenon and the Propylaia (entrance gate) erected on the Acropolis in the third quarter of the 5th century BC [482], we might almost think that this was a self-consciously pursued policy; later in his* History of the Peloponnesian War, *Thucydides has Pericles say that Athens is the 'school of Greece' (cf. p. 168), the model that all other* poleis *would follow. And the truth is that the material remains of Athens are more substantial than those of any other Greek* polis *[300], and our fascination with Athenian literature and democratic ideologies has led us to scrutinize them more carefully than those of most other city-states. As Thucydides warns us, though, we should be wary of interpreting them as a straightforward reflection of her power.*

Just because Mycenae was small, or because any other town of that age now seems insignificant, it would be inaccurate to use this as evidence to discredit what the poets proclaim (and tradition maintains) about the size of the Trojan expedition. Take the case of the Spartans. If their city were to be abandoned so that nothing survived but the temples and building foundations, I imagine that as time went by future generations would be very reluctant to believe that the power of the Spartans matched their renown. Although the Spartans occupy two-fifths of the Peloponnese, preside over the rest of it, and have many other allies besides, their city is not compactly laid out; it lacks monumental temples and buildings, and it is organized (in the old Greek fashion) by village. For these reasons, Sparta would seem less powerful than it actually is. If the same thing were to happen to the Athenians, however, we would conjecture from the appearance of their city that their power was twice what it really is . . .

Thucydides, *History of the Peloponnesian War* 1.10.1–2

296 *Scene on a fragment of a Roman wall-painting, third quarter of the 1st century BC. Illusionistic cityscapes were a favourite subject of the 'Second Style' of Pompeian wall-painting [cf. 465], as fictive panels became windows to an imagined world. This one includes a temple and human figures.*

297 *Nilotic landscape on a fragment of a wall-painting, c. AD 70. Roman wall-paintings often depicted Egyptian scenes [cf. 238, 239], especially after Egypt had become a province of Rome following Mark Antony's defeat at Actium in 31 BC. Subjects range from the exotic to the humorous, incorporating fantastic buildings (the humble thatched hut on the right contrasts with the elaborate architecture in the background), strange monsters (such as this crocodile), and mythical black dwarfs, named pygmies (such as the one who manœuvres a small raft along the flooded River Nile here).*

(pp. 99–107). For us, it is usually difficult to match up the remaining rubble with ancient descriptions of the hustle and bustle of civic centres. There are, of course, a few exceptions: the towns preserved by the eruption of Vesuvius in AD 79, which were sensationally rediscovered in the 18th century (initially Herculaneum, then Pompeii [298] and some smaller villas and farmsteads), are perhaps the most renowned example.

In building up a tourist's conception of the ancient city, modern travellers were foreshadowed (and influenced) by a number of ancient travel writers. Pausanias, writing his ten-volume *Guide to Greece* around the middle of the 2nd century AD, defined cities precisely in terms of their religious and public buildings (temples, governmental offices, gymnasium, theatre, agora, and fountain); as his narrative makes its way from Attica to Delphi – combining the monuments he might really have seen with an imaginative landscape of a past, pre-Roman Greece – the reader builds up some idea of what, to Pausanias at least, Greek cities looked like. Earlier authors too exploited travel writing as a means of reflecting on the Greek polity, especially in implicit contrast to cities in Egypt. During an account of a journey there, Herodotus pondered how the Egyptians lived in a topsy-turvy mirage of a Greek *polis* (*Histories* 2.35–36), where rivers, for example, flood not in winter but in summer. For Herodotus, as for later literary and visual artists [297], illusionistic portrayals of the Egyptian city comprised *thaumata*, or 'sites of wonder'. But those *thaumata* were by no means analogous to the physical and metaphysical constituents of the Greek *polis* and Roman *urbs*.

298 The Forum, Pompeii, with Vesuvius in the Distance, *by Christen Købke, 1841. Goats grazing in the distance, lizards basking in the mid-afternoon sun, vegetation romantically creeping over fragmentary columns, all under a bright still sky: the looming slopes of Mount Vesuvius remind us of the cause of the city's ruin, the volcanic eruption of August AD 79. Pompeii offers an unparalleled view into Roman provincial attitudes towards civic space, the physical zoning of different urban activities, and the development of a provincial cityscape over time (not least the buildings earmarked for reconstruction following an earthquake in AD 62). The forum, seen here from the south-east corner, was developed in the 2nd century BC, and dominated by a central temple of Jupiter, the Capitoline Temple (named after the temple in Rome [178]), at its north end. By the 1st century AD several structures serving the cult of the imperial family had been constructed along its east side. At the south-west corner, next to the Temple of Apollo, there was a large three-aisled basilica, which served as a centre for trade, commerce, and civic administration.*

Given that each *polis* was a self-contained political unit, it should come as no surprise that there was no universal way of organizing urban space. The Piraeus (the harbour district of Athens), Miletos in Asia Minor, and Olynthos in northern Greece were all organized according to a considered, rectangular, gridiron plan [295], traditionally attributed to a political theorist and town-planner from Miletos named Hippodamos. But in Sparta the emphasis on war-like bravado and divide-and-rule techniques of government rather than monumental self-aggrandizement has left modern archaeologists guessing even as to precisely where the civic centre was situated. The spatial organization of cities also changed with time: the 9th-century communal settlement at Zagora on the Cycladic island of Andros, with its close-packed community of small houses, bears little resemblance to the rectilinear city layouts of the 5th and 4th centuries. Some might think this lack of a universal model rules out any attempt at an analysis of ancient civic planning. We can be sure, however, that throughout the Classical world city planning reflected, and itself contributed to, the different communal ideologies and traditions of each *polis*. As ever, it is Athens that provides the best example.

Aristotle seems to have connected the very arrangement of the Athenian city with its fervour for democracy: 'a citadel suits an oligarchy', he argued, 'and a level plain suits a democracy' (*Politics* 1330b). That 'level plain' was the Agora. If the Athenian Acropolis was the focus of the city's cultic, ritual and patriotic practices, the Agora was the centre of day-to-day civic life [299–302]. In a literal sense, the two areas were

299 *Monument of the Eponymous Heroes, on the west side of the Athenian Agora, c. 330 BC. The sill of the railing seen here surrounded an inner stone base which supported ten statues of the heroes after whom the city's tribes (phylai) were named. Below each statue a citizen could find announcements, conscription lists, upcoming legislation, and other official information relating to his tribe.*

conjoined: a major street (the Panathenaic Way) connected them, metaphorically presenting the awe-inspiring monuments of the Acropolis as the culmination of the democratic values paraded in the Agora. Like the Acropolis, the Agora (as with every agora in Greece) was a kind of sacred space, or *temenos* (see p. 99): entering it was prohibited to the likes of certain criminals, pregnant women, and the seriously ill.

All aspects of city life were laid out for the Athenian citizen in his open Agora. Political buildings were clustered together alongside cultic and commercial structures to form an integrated and open display of shared civic power. In the Agora were located, in addition to the market stalls and stores, the official notice boards [299]; the *Bouleuterion*, where the democratic Council (*Boule*) of the five hundred met; the *Metroön*, where archives, standards, and records were housed; and the *Strategion* (or military headquarters), the magistrate offices, and the mint.

It is probably within this public nature of civic space that we should understand the vogue for one of the most popular architectural forms – the *stoa*. This was a colonnaded portico that provided both shade and protection; its architectural origins are difficult to pinpoint, but it seems to have developed out of the shelters constructed in religious sanctuaries. In the late 5th century the Athenian Agora had

four monumental stoas, whose grand architectural order gave something of the status of a temple to these otherwise civic structures. But more than that, each stoa was inherently accessible: its open colonnades were a place not for confidentiality but for the public discussion of all manner of political, even philosophical, problems. One group of philosophical thinkers, under the leadership of Zeno, were labelled 'Stoics' precisely because they conducted their discussions in the public shade of the Stoa Poikile, or Painted Stoa (see p. 238).

Today the Agora is an archaeologically messy, chaotic, and cluttered site, scattered with monuments that date from the 6th century BC (and earlier) to a time beyond the latest periods of antiquity. Most postdate the zenith of Athenian political, economic, and military power, posing a puzzling dilemma for modern visitors: how to reconcile the increase of public building programmes in the Agora with Athens's loss of political influence?

300 above *View of the Agora, Athens, in the late 20th century, with the Acropolis in the distance. (The buildings visible there are the Parthenon – built 447–432 BC – on the right, and the slightly later Erechtheion on the left.) The ancient Agora is today a landscaped national park in the heart of the modern city. Excavations were begun in 1931 by the American School of Classical Studies at Athens and have continued ever since: that involvement has remained a symbolic way of expressing a connection between American democracy and its supposed descent from democratic Athens. In 1956 the School reconstructed the Stoa of Attalos, on the left [301].*

301 *Looking along the ground floor of the Stoa of Attalos, originally erected in the mid-2nd century BC. While providing Athenians with shade and shelter, this commercial centre also associated its dedicator, Attalos II of Pergamon, with the cultural achievements of Athens.*

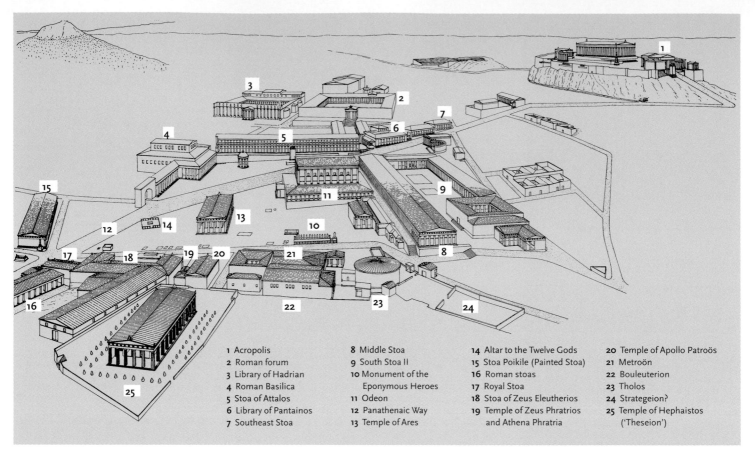

1 Acropolis	8 Middle Stoa	14 Altar to the Twelve Gods	20 Temple of Apollo Patroös
2 Roman forum	9 South Stoa II	15 Stoa Poikile (Painted Stoa)	21 Metroön
3 Library of Hadrian	10 Monument of the	16 Roman stoas	22 Bouleuterion
4 Roman Basilica	Eponymous Heroes	17 Royal Stoa	23 Tholos
5 Stoa of Attalos	11 Odeon	18 Stoa of Zeus Eleutherios	24 Strategeion?
6 Library of Pantainos	12 Panathenaic Way	19 Temple of Zeus Phratrios	25 Temple of Hephaistos
7 Southeast Stoa	13 Temple of Ares	and Athena Phratria	('Theseion')

302 *The Athenian Agora, as it appeared* c. AD *150 (north is at the left). By then its architectural development reflected Athens' status as both a subordinate city within the Roman province of Greece and a renowned centre of culture and learning. The Panathenaic Way (12) still led through the Agora to the Acropolis (1), but it was now flanked by a number of Roman monuments: the Basilica (4, to the east of the gateway), the large Odeon (11, originally built by Agrippa, used as a sort of lecture hall), and a handful of temples (like the Temple of Ares, 13) which were removed from their original locations in Attica in Augustan times and reconstructed in the Agora, as if to concentrate the cultural heritage of Athens within her central civic space. Perhaps most significantly of all, the old Agora's commercial activities were relocated to a new Roman forum to the east (2), begun by Julius Caesar in the 50s BC, but only completed by Augustus c. 11–9 BC. In the second quarter of the 2nd century AD, the Emperor Hadrian also built a library (3) to the north of the forum, one of his many benefactions to the city.*

To answer that question, we need to think about how an ancient civic landscape could be manipulated to articulate new hierarchies of power. In democratic Athens the Agora was a shared, communal, public space: it generated a sense of people-power. But following the subordination of Athens to the grand empires of Hellenistic kings and Roman rulers, new architectures of power were conspicuously stamped onto her civic centre: buildings such as the stoa sponsored in the mid-2nd century BC by Attalos II, King of Pergamon [300, 301], and from Roman times the Odeon of Agrippa, the Basilica, and the Library of Hadrian all cast new shadows of authority over the Athenian civic landscape [302]. The open space of the democratic Agora was soon closed off on all sides, flanked by new structures, and filled with imposing monuments that ostensibly paid homage to the cultural achievements of Athens while imperially subsuming them. Under Augustus, a new marketplace had been completed on its eastern side [302:2], transforming the old Agora into a Greek cultural relic. While the administrative buildings of the earlier democracy still stood (and remained in use, to some extent, in an affected semblance of Athenian self-determination), and although the city had been spared the annihilation of its civic space, those who frequented the Agora from the 1st century BC on must have been in little doubt that Athens now belonged, in no unequivocal terms, to Rome.

In asserting individual power through the organization of civic space, the Roman world seems to have built on an array of Hellenistic models. In Egypt, the Palace of the Ptolemies was the crowning feature of Alexandria's civic landscape, and other monuments, from the museum and library to the Tomb of Alexander the Great, were all positioned to emphasize its magnificence. At Pergamon the whole city was constructed hierarchically: to reach the palace of the ruling Attalids required a physical and metaphorical ascent up the slopes of the citadel. These cities, in other words, manifested a new degree of self-conscious consideration about how power could be aligned with urban space. Many of them were also built from scratch – according to Plutarch, Alexander the Great founded no fewer than seventy new cities. Even allowing for a degree of exaggeration, it is clear that by the 3rd century BC, time, effort, and money were being expended on creating mega-cities on a scale that the Classical world had never previously witnessed.

Of all the Hellenistic mega-cities that emerged, we might expect Rome to have been the largest and most monumental. Certainly, by the 1st century BC public infrastructure was developed almost in proportion to Rome's imperial expansion abroad, with new roads, temples, bridges, and aqueducts. By the 1st century AD, urban expansion was so conspicuous that Pliny the Elder could muse that 'if the universe of our Roman buildings were heaped up and amassed into a single pile, the size of that stack would rise high above us; it would be as though some other universe – all unified into one place – were being described' (*Natural History* 36.101). But that large-scale monumentalization of Rome was a relatively late phenomenon, closely bound up with the struggles for power that marked the last century of its Republic. Simply put, the funding of public buildings was a way of flaunting the power of the benefactor. Pompey could immortalize his name by constructing Rome's first stone theatre in the Campus Martius in 55 BC, and Sulla could build a new Senate house to complement his political reforms some time around 81 BC. This was not, as in the Hellenistic world, a rivalry between different cities: the civic space of Rome became a kind of battlefield on which the civil wars of the Senate could be physically acted out, as individual citizens competed over who could adorn the city with not only the biggest and best, but also the most significant and ideologically loaded buildings.

Within that battle of building programmes, as within the war of images (see pp. 246–49), it was Augustus who emerged as the ultimate victor. He gave his ties with Julius Caesar monumental form by completing Caesar's plans for urban improvement (including the Julian Basilica, the Saepta, and the Forum of Caesar), while also ensuring that his own structures surpassed those of his predecessors.

According to Suetonius, writing around AD 100, Augustus could boast that he had 'inherited a city of brick and left it a city of marble' (*Life of Augustus* 28.3). But Augustus' urban building programme was no venture in mindless marbleization. With much greater subtlety, it embodied the ideologies of his rule. When the Forum of Augustus [161] was constructed alongside the old Roman Forum [303], which had long been the centre of the Republic's commercial, civic, religious, economic, and political life, the decision seems to have embodied the idea of restoring the Republic. But just as Augustus marketed his state as an improved and restructured Republic, his forum was at once subservient to the old Forum (and political ideal) of the Republic and superior to it. Unlike that cluttered and unfocused space, the Forum of Augustus gave the old Republican political order a new spatial order. And unlike the old Forum with its tufa and limestone constructions, Augustus' was built of marble – and not just white marble, but an array of different sorts and colours imported from all over the Roman world, including northern Italy, Greece, Africa, and southern Asia Minor. The display of such bold new materials, amassed from the colonies over which Rome now held sway [e.g. 246, 247], itself manifested the extent of Rome's global supremacy. And the crowded images of Rome's mythical founders in the Forum of Augustus (Mars, Venus, Romulus, and Aeneas among them), all juxtaposed with images of the imperial family, signalled that it was Augustus who was responsible for that supremacy: this was sure visual testimony to Augustus' title of *pater patriae*, 'father of the fatherland', officially conferred in 2 BC.

For Vitruvius, *writing under Augustus, the discipline of architecture was more than a physical science of practical engineering: it was a way of bringing together the subdisciplines of philosophy, natural science, history, and even medicine and astronomy. While drawing on a number of earlier books on the subject that no longer survive, Vitruvius was aware of the political significance of urban infrastructure: in his preface, he presented his ten-volume* On Architecture *as being of special significance at a time when Augustus was extensively remodelling Rome.*

I saw that you were concerned not just for the welfare of the whole community and the establishment of the Republic, but also to provide [the Republic] with public buildings. Thus through your initiative the state was enriched with provinces, and at the same time its majestic imperial power was reflected in the pre-eminent authority of its civic constructions . . . I began to write this for you because I observed that you have built extensively, that you continue to do so, and that in the future you will ensure that posterity will remember your public and private works alongside your other distinguished achievements. I have drawn up definitive rules to enable you, in observing them, fully to realize the quality of the projects that you initiate, now and in the future. For I have disclosed all the principles of the discipline in these volumes.

Vitruvius, *On Architecture* 1.1–3

On his death in AD 14, Augustus left an autobiographical summary of his 'achievements' (Res Gestae Divi Augusti) to be read in the Senate. It survives in later copies which were displayed in three different provincial cities. In it he lists an array of building programmes and especially emphasizes his restoration of cultic buildings, thereby marketing his principate as a return to Republican modes of piety. But the Res Gestae itself testifies to the power-potential of reorganizing urban space, for its text was originally inscribed on bronze pillars at the entrance to the Emperor's mausoleum – both manifesting and contributing to Augustus' monumental achievements.

I restored the Capitol and the Theatre of Pompey, each at enormous expense and without any inscription of my own name. I restored aqueducts that were in many places collapsing from age; and I have doubled the 'Marcian' water by diverting a new spring into its course. I have completed the Forum Julium and the basilica, located between the Temple of Castor and the Temple of Saturn – constructions begun and carried forward by my father [Julius Caesar] . . . When consul for the sixth time, and in accordance with the Senate's decree, I restored eighty-two temples of the gods. No temple that was at that time in need of repair was excepted.

Augustus, *The Achievements of the Deified Augustus* 20

303 *Remains of the Roman Forum, seen from the west. From left to right, the buildings are the Temple of Antoninus and Faustina (erected in AD 141), the Column of Phocas (dedicated in AD 608), the Arch of Titus (after AD 81 [318]), directly in front of the Arch the circular Temple of Vesta (AD 190s; home to the fire that symbolized the perpetuity of the State, guarded by the Vestal Virgins), and three columns of the Temple of Castor and Pollux (inaugurated in AD 6).*

The area of the Forum was first paved as a marketplace in the late 7th century BC. It was successively monumentalized during the Republic and Empire, and now stands, in ruins, as an evocative archaeological theme-park of faded grandeur.

304 *Part of the scale model of Rome in the early 4th century AD, made for the 'Augustan Exhibition of Roman Culture' in Rome of 1937–1938 (see p. 320). By the time of the Emperor Constantine (AD 306–337) Rome had become a sprawling capital city, cluttered with imperial civic monuments. At the upper left, near the bank of the Tiber and just west of the Capitoline Temple [178], stands the Theatre of Marcellus (dedicated in 13 or 11 BC); in the foreground is the Circus Maximus, which had probably occupied this site since the 7th century BC, but which was repeatedly rebuilt and in this form was sponsored by Caracalla (emperor AD 211–217); the Colosseum [426, 427] lies on the right. Between it and the Capitoline Temple lie the various buildings of the Republican and Imperial Forums.*

305 *The Porta Nigra, or Black Gate, at Trier in Germany. The 3rd-century AD military commander Postumus, breakaway emperor of the 'Gallic colonies', chose Augusta Treverorum as his capital and adorned it accordingly with public buildings in Roman style, which probably included this fortified gate.*

Augustus' reshaping of the urban centre of Rome cast him as the grand master of all things: of peace (in the Ara Pacis); of war (among the numerous spoils brought to Rome, an obelisk from Egypt was erected in the Campus Martius [148]); of time (that obelisk itself functioned as a sundial); of religion (eighty-two temples were restored in his name in one year alone); and even of death (Augustus began the construction of his mausoleum long before his death). So much so, in fact, that while Augustus' imperial successors continued to build new structures (including forums, arches, markets, baths, and temples), they must have found it almost impossible to rival his initiatives in spatial power-parading. One megalomaniac alternative was pursued by Nero, as he took over much of Rome's civic space to build a lavish palace, the gigantic Domus Aurea, or Golden House (p. 157). That space was later restored to the people of Rome, through the building of the Colosseum [304, 426, 427] (named after a colossal statue of Nero that had stood nearby) and public baths, in an ideological gesture extended by Vespasian and Titus. A later alternative, taken up by Hadrian, was to supplement and upstage the buildings of Augustus, for example by erecting a rival mausoleum (now the Castel Sant'Angelo) and substantially redesigning the Pantheon [118, 180].

If Rome was the metropolis par excellence [304], how did the civic infra-structure of its provinces compare to its own? Not very closely – at least, if we take at face value the accounts written by citizens living in Rome. According to them, the acquisition of colonies (begun in the 4th century BC with a handful of trading and defence posts at Italy's key seaports such as Ostia and Terracina) embodied an asymmetrical relationship of domination and passivity: Rome was the centre, the provinces its periphery; the process of 'Romanization' actively brought them 'culture', 'humanity', and 'civilization'. Occasionally there were signs that the process was being reversed – that the provincial manners of barbarians were filtering into Rome: in Juvenal's third *Satire* (published in the early 2nd century AD) the character Umbricius presents himself as the last 'true' Roman in a city contaminated by the ways of foreigners.

306 *View of the Great Colonnade at Palmyra in Syria, mid-2nd century AD. The city, a trading junction between East and West, displayed its ties with Rome in large stone temples, a Roman theatre, and not least this huge Corinthian colonnade: its columns are over 9 metres (some 30 feet) in height and fitted with brackets which originally held statues of distinguished citizens. But Palmyra also maintained an Eastern identity: Parthian gods, for example, were worshipped in its Roman temples.*

In some ways, the civic infrastructures and urban organizations of provincial communities in the Empire might seem to have embodied that literary, paternalistic, and staunchly imperial model of Romanization [306]. Although modes of urban planning differed widely, streets were often laid out on a grid just as in Rome, and certain kinds of Roman structure certainly became *de rigueur* throughout the Empire: forums, temples, sewers, porticoes, baths, fountains, etc. Temples to Roman gods and the cults of the emperor could serve to enshrine Rome as a cultural absolute: at Baalbek in the Lebanon (Roman Syria), for instance, the huge 1st-century AD Temple of Jupiter, bigger even than the Parthenon in Athens, paraded Roman architectural styles, values, and gods as the city's ultimate cultural determinant. In constitutional terms, urban structures could even play a part in upgrading *municipia* (provincial towns) into more prestigious centres: within this cultural hierarchy, with Rome at the top, there was much room for aspiration, with different cities being endowed with differing degrees of monumental favour [305].

But archaeological investigations of *municipia* (especially, though not exclusively, in Roman Britain), coupled with our own post-colonial perspectives, can suggest an alternative narrative about the process of provincial Romanization. Changes in urban infrastructures can be read as the product of a two-way exchange, a means of asserting cultural status. On the one hand, works in Roman style, such as the art and villas commissioned by local élites [e.g. 223], were a means of displaying the patron's social aspirations within the framework of the Empire. But on the other, indigenous modes of building and urban organization still flourished alongside Roman models. In Britain, at Calleva Atrebatum, or Silchester [307], a forum was built almost immediately after the site became a Roman 'city-state' (*civitas*); but that forum was originally built of wood, in accordance with native practice, and it seems to have been instigated by the indigenous inhabitants of the town rather than the imperial power. So not all aspects of Romanization were part of a forced process; and not every instance of Roman urbanization need amount to more than a superficial affectation, rather than profound adoption, of Roman precedents. In provincial public building programmes, then, as in other spheres, we should perhaps see, instead of Roman literary concoctions of a dominant Roman and subordinate local culture, a more cosmopolitan and dialectical exchange of forms and styles.

307 *Aerial view of excavations of part of Calleva Atrebatum (Silchester). Unlike many other cities in Roman Britain, the site was abandoned at the end of the Roman occupation in the 5th century AD, and never substantially resettled: as a result, its foundations remained more or less intact. An amphitheatre was built outside the walls in the second half of the 1st century AD, but new large stone walls were called for to defend the area by the early 3rd century. In addition to the gridiron street plan, other Roman urban features included a bath complex, basilica, and forum. But native Iron Age designs existed alongside, and even fused with, their imported counterparts: thus a pair of rectangular Roman temples were built of both wood and stone, and other temples seem to have been polygonal and apsidal, ignoring more standard Roman practices.*

308 *The triumph of Romans over barbarians, on the Ludovisi Sarcophagus, mid-3rd century AD. The central figure on horseback – presumably a portrait of the deceased – stares out into the distance, and surveys his military feats with a sweeping gesture. Around him, his fellow-Romans, dressed in tunics, plumed helmets, and cuirasses, beat their barbarian enemies (shown with customary pointed Oriental caps, baggy trousers, and thick hair) to the ground.*

CITIZEN RIGHT AND MILITARY MIGHT

The word *municipium* literally means the 'undertaking of duty'. Throughout antiquity, that definition of civic life was a very important one: to be part of a Roman *municipium*, just as to be a citizen in a Greek *polis*, entailed certain obligations. And for male citizens, the primary duty was military.

The association between citizen right and martial might resonated throughout the Classical world. Civic power was the preserve of those who fought for it: those who did not, namely women and slaves, were largely excluded from the political sphere. A magistrate in the Roman Republic, according to Polybius' *Histories*, had to perform ten years of military service before being allowed to compete for office; Augustus' *Achievements* presents the emperor's power as bound up with military strength, prowess, and manliness (the literal meaning of the Latin *virtus*, from which our word 'virtue' derives); and images of later emperors consistently associate imperial power with military conquest [314]. It was as a result of this military tradition that Alexander took his army from Macedon to the Hindu Kush, and Rome expanded from a local shantytown on the banks of the Tiber in the 6th century BC to an intercontinental empire by the 1st century AD. For the Greeks and Romans, military service was more than just a civic ideal: it constituted a way of life. Military experience, or at least a semblance of it, was essential for political advancement, and imperial conquest underpinned trade and wealth. War, in other words, was not only the basis of prestige and status [308]. It was also a very real means of acquiring land, materials, and slaves.

The close nexus between military and political power can be traced far back into the history of the ancient Mediterranean. In the *Iliad*, war is presented as a way of displaying the personal glory, valour, and excellence (*aristeia*) that legitimated an individual's right to rule: Homeric heroes therefore conducted their battles through a series of one-to-one confrontations, dismounting from their chariots to fight.

309 *Detail of a Mycenaean krater from Cyprus, first half of the 13th century BC. Whatever their historical role in Greece during the late 2nd and early 1st millennium BC, chariots loom large in Homeric descriptions of war – functioning as vehicles that transport the heroes around the battlefield. Charioteers were also a favourite subject on Mycenaean jars such as this one, where they often seem to have had a funerary significance. Here a tall male figure in silhouette stands at the back of the chariot, holding a long sword; in front of him are three charioteers; and in front of them is another man, seemingly riding a horse – a practice not well documented in the Greek world until after the Bronze Age.*

This Homeric model of war was a concept that could be revived and venerated throughout antiquity: Alexander the Great, for example, was reputed to have visited Troy *en route* to Persia (and world domination), made offerings to the individuals who had fought there, and carried his Homeric texts with him wherever he went. Historically speaking, however, the rise of the Greek *polis* brought with it new ways to conceive of war: military conduct, like political control, evolved into a more communal affair. One infantry formation manifested and brought about that change more than any other: the phalanx [310].

The phalanx, from the 6th century onwards, became an egalitarian ideal. In forming a phalanx, soldiers placed their lives in each other's hands. Holding their spears in their right hand and their shields in their left, so as to defend their neighbour, armed foot soldiers, or hoplites, would fight in cohesive lines. Each line's fate was sealed only when their collective defence was penetrated by the enemy and dispersed: an individual soldier had little hope of survival against the onslaught of the opposing collective troop. It is interesting that this communal formation did not

In Athens the stage was one site where the civic value of war could be simultaneously questioned, challenged, and reinforced. Athenian comedy produced during the Peloponnesian War often treated the theme of peace and the fantastic ways in which it might be achieved (most explicitly in The Acharnians, Peace, and Lysistrata, all by Aristophanes). But, perhaps more than any other Athenian playwright, it was Euripides who potentially challenged Athenian attitudes to war. His Trojan Women treats the end of the Trojan War from the perspective of the women conquered – Cassandra, Andromache, and Hecuba among them. At this time the savagery of war must have been an especially prominent theme in Athens: a year earlier, the city's harsh treatment of the Melians had received stern criticism, and in the year of the play's first performance, 415 BC, the Athenians voted to send a military expedition to Sicily, which ultimately proved disastrous.

In this extract, Cassandra takes up the theme of the civic value of war and 'beautiful death' (kalos thanatos), contrasting how the Greeks and Trojans have respectively benefited from the Trojan War. The chief gain, as Cassandra sees it, is heroic renown, or kleos. As is typical of Athenian tragedy, it is possible to interpret her words on more than one level. After all, despite the apparent logic of Cassandra's argument, another character will shortly remind us that 'Apollo has deranged her mind' . . .

Contrast the Trojans. First there are those who died for their country, and that is the greatest glory. As for those killed by the spear, their corpses were carried home by their loved ones, found earthly enclosure in their native land, and were prepared for burial by the hands of those who should rightfully do so. And as for those Trojans who did not die in battle, they lived day

after day with their wives and children – pleasures denied to the Greeks. As for Hector's 'wretchedness', as you deem it, hear now the truth. Hector died after achieving the greatest renown among men: the cause was the coming of the Greeks; if they had stayed at home, he would not have manifested his excellence. Moreover, Paris married Helen, the daughter of Zeus: if he had not married her, he would have had a marriage at home that no one would have heard of. So while the sensible man should avoid war, when war is inevitable the man who dies a heroic death is a crowning glory for a city, while the man who dies ignobly is a disgrace to her.

Euripides, *The Trojan Women* 386–402

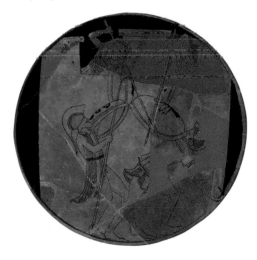

310 above *Detail of a Protocorinthian olpe (squat jug) known as the Chigi Vase, c. 650 BC, showing a phalanx engagement. A pipe-player accompanies two Greek phalanxes into war: the soldiers are decked out in crested helmets, shields, and bronze greaves and cuirasses.*

311 above right *Armed warriors and youths prepare their horses for battle: detail of an Attic red-figure kylix attributed to the Nikosthenes Painter, c. 510–500 BC.*

312 *A city under siege: two hoplites attack its crenellated walls, while another two defend it. Interior of an Attic red-figure kylix attributed to the Kleomelos Painter, c. 500 BC.*

313 right *Triremes – warships with three banks of oars – carried 170 oarsmen and 30 or so officers and armed hoplites. At the prow was a bronze ram, used to sink other ships; on the deck, hoplites would engage in battle with soldiers on other triremes at close quarters. (This is a recent reconstruction, the* Olympias, *built to celebrate the 2500th anniversary of democracy in 1993 – counting from Kleisthenes' reforms of 508–507 BC.)*

catch on everywhere. The fact that (despite some Roman literary attestations to the contrary) the Etruscans seem not to have adopted it reveals something of the differences between the Greek *polis* and the Etruscan city. For the Etruscans, the army, like government, was less a collective affair than something organized and mobilized on a clan or familial basis (what the Romans would call *gens*).

The diversity of military modes in different times and places can therefore help us to reconstruct different civic attitudes. In 5th-century Athens, the prime fighting force was seaborne. Rowing ships, called triremes after their three banks of oars [313], could ram enemy fleets and ensure the safe passage of food and supplies across the Mediterranean. Like the affairs of state, they were powered by (and provided a good source of employment for) the *demos*. The 'Old Oligarch', despite his professed disapproval of Athenian democracy (p. 169), had to concede that it was somehow right for the *demos* to wield governmental power at home, for it was they who, by manning the navy, ensured Athens's power abroad. Other *poleis* attached greater significance to the cavalry (although fighting on horseback was

not intrinsically suited to the islands and rough terrains of Greece). In the Classical world, equestrian warfare was the preserve of a wealthy élite who could afford a horse and the necessary equipment; even on pots from democratic Athens such aristocratic associations were flaunted, implying the social aspirations of the owner [311]. In Macedon, cavalry forces were largely made up of the royal court of *hetairoi* (or 'companions') of the king, and to fight on horseback was a status symbol that bespoke political influence.

'War is father of all': the grim dictum of the 6th-century BC philosopher Heraclitus might serve as a motto for much of Classical history. Wars recurrently provided a framework for considering the past in relation to the present. Thus Herodotus constructed the history of Greece as revolving around her military engagements with Persia in 490 and 480–479 BC; Thucydides presented the Athenian conflict with Sparta (the Peloponnesian War of 431–404 BC) as the war to end all wars; and Hellenistic and Roman writers subsequently composed elaborate histories centred on Alexander's military campaigns and Rome's seemingly cosmic conquests in Europe, Africa, and Asia.

Images played an essential part in the construction of that Classical military tradition: depictions of war functioned as a status symbol, a display of individual and collective valour, and a marker of an individual's integration within (or preeminence over) society. In Rome, images glorifying war were publicly displayed on arches that were themselves erected to commemorate military triumphs [317, 318, 467]; and throughout the provinces, for instance in the modern-day towns of Orange in France and Adamklissi in Romania [315], triumphal monuments served to remind the conquered of their subjection. In the private sphere, iconographies of war could also be replicated in miniature [316].

In the Greek *polis*, too, images of war abounded. The various ceramic and metallic wares used in the symposium, for example, paraded models of military valour to which all male citizen-warriors who attended were expected to aspire [322, 323]. Helmets [321], along with other pieces of armour, were taken to sanctuaries and given to the gods as thank-offerings. Even the aesthetics of male physical beauty were bound up with concepts of masculine military valour: the young men decking themselves out in the paraphernalia of battle on a white-ground lekythos [319, 320] are each described as *kalos* – both physically and spiritually attractive.

314 opposite, left *Detail of the Column of Trajan, erected in Rome in* AD *113 to celebrate the Emperor's victories in Dacia (modern Romania). Trajan approaches his troops on horseback and greets them with raised arm: the gesture alludes to the* adventus *motif, traditionally marking an emperor's return to Rome after victory abroad; here, however, Trajan is represented on campaign, and the gesture alludes to his forthcoming success.*

315 opposite, right *In Dacia itself the same Roman victory was commemorated in a humbler trophy monument, erected at Adamklissi in* AD *109, this time crafted by local artists out of rubble faced with limestone sculpted in shallow relief.*

316 right *Silver cup from Boscoreale, north-east of Pompeii, c.* AD *10–20. This brought the glory of war – the stuff of public monumental reliefs – into the home. Tiberius (emperor* AD *14–37) is shown in triumphal procession after victory in battle: he rides in a chariot, a crown of laurel held over his head.*

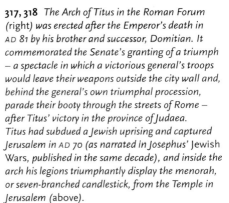

317, 318 *The Arch of Titus in the Roman Forum (right) was erected after the Emperor's death in* AD *81 by his brother and successor, Domitian. It commemorated the Senate's granting of a triumph – a spectacle in which a victorious general's troops would leave their weapons outside the city wall and, behind the general's own triumphal procession, parade their booty through the streets of Rome – after Titus' victory in the province of Judaea. Titus had subdued a Jewish uprising and captured Jerusalem in* AD *70 (as narrated in Josephus' Jewish Wars, published in the same decade), and inside the arch his legions triumphantly display the menorah, or seven-branched candlestick, from the Temple in Jerusalem (above).*

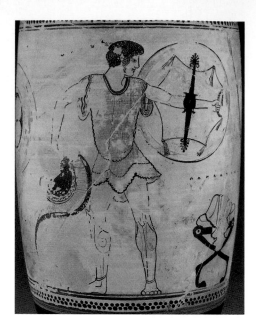

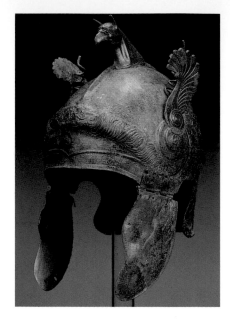

319, 320 *above and centre Two figures on an Attic white-ground lekythos attributed to Douris, c. 500 BC: the youths (named, and called kalos, or 'beautiful', in the inscriptions) arm themselves for war. One proudly holds out his shield and helmet, the other stands naked with a spear and sword.*

321 *above right   South Italian helmet, c. 350–300 BC. This type, with hinged cheekpieces and openings for the ears, was developed in Chalkis (on the island of Euboea); it became very popular in the Greek colonies in South Italy, and later in the Roman world.*

322 *A warrior putting on his greaves, with his helmet, shield, and spear ready to hand: detail of an Attic black-figure kylix attributed to the Heidelberg Painter, c. 550 BC.*

323 *Bronze statuette of a fallen Greek youth, c. 480–460 BC, probably once attached to a bronze krater.*

This oil-flask was most probably used or offered in a funerary context, and funerary monuments provide some of the most frequent depictions of citizens cast as warriors. The man whose image is inscribed with the name Philoxenos [325] may have died in old age, of natural causes or disease, but a military mode of representation was chosen for his public memorial – just as the woman inscribed as Philomene is here presented as his humble, compliant wife in the private world: Philoxenos is going to war to protect both his *polis* and his home. Another stele, depicting a hoplite pressing forward into battle [324], conveys the point unambiguously: 'I, Pollis, the beloved son of Asopichos, speak, having not died a coward in the line of battle . . .'

War is always, anthropologists inform us, a ritual of group communality and group opposition. On one hand, it generates state solidarity: citizens are brought together to fight for a single cause, be it defence or conquest. On the other, that cohesiveness is dependent upon conceiving of the enemy in hostile terms: opponents must be stereotyped, dehumanized, and associated with the opposite of everything held dear by the community; they must be turned into a caricature of the 'Other'. Whatever the universal applicability of that model, it does help to make sense of much Classical iconography. As we have seen, a warring ideal was central to defining, and legitimating, the place of an individual within society. But war also created another sort of social cohesiveness by instituting and reinforcing an ethnic

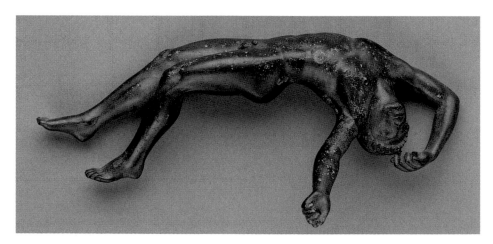

324 *Detail of the inscribed marble grave stele of a man named Pollis, from Megara, c. 480 BC. The deceased is represented in full military glory, and (rather fancifully) heroically nude [cf. 320]: he advances into battle with shield raised and spear poised; a sword hangs at his left side. Such funerary monuments are one of the most important sources for reconstructing ancient societies' cultural ideologies – the values that the deceased took to the grave.*

325 *Inscribed Attic marble grave stele, c. 400 BC: Philoxenos, wearing a cuirass and helmet and holding a shield in his left hand, bids farewell to his wife, Philomene.*

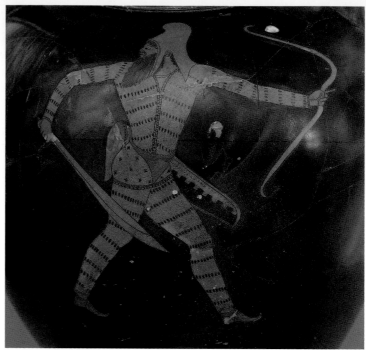

326, 327 *Two sides of an Attic red-figure amphora attributed to the Berlin Painter, c. 480–470 BC. One shows a hoplite, lunging into battle, decked out in greaves, cuirass, and Corinthian helmet; the other a fleeing barbarian, sporting his wily weapon, the bow.*

328 *Attic mug in the shape of an African man's head, c. 510 BC. This mug, used at the symposium (Dionysos is shown on the rim with two satyrs), probably paraded the African as a symbol of exotic, even Dionysian, beauty. The inhabitants of Greek city-states seem to have encountered relatively few black Africans. While Greeks and Romans did define themselves in antithesis to 'barbarians' (whose ethnicity was primarily constructed around costume and attributes), they do not seem to have defined race in modern racialist terms of skin colour.*

antithesis between a constructed 'us' and 'them'. By the late 6th century BC Greeks had already imposed that polarity on the world: on 'our' side there were Greeks, and on 'their' side there was everyone else, subsumed under the label *barbaroi* (perhaps mocking the curious 'bar-bar' sounds of non-Greek languages). This antithesis finds neat expression in an Attic red-figure amphora of the early 5th century BC [326, 327] – the time of one of the most enduring Athenian 'inventions' of the barbarian, Aeschylus' *Persians*. On one side we see a standard image of a Greek citizen-warrior. He is prepared for manly direct combat, with greaves on his legs, a cuirass to protect his chest, and, pushed back on his brow, a helmet. On the other side is his nemesis, a strange 'foreigner' (to pin him down as specifically Scythian or Persian would be to go against his iconographic reduction to a stereotyped caricature). This antitype clutches a bow and arrow, a sinister weapon which, unlike the shield and spear, allows attack from a distance; he is also dressed in an effeminate tunic, spotted trouser suit, and weird pointed slippers.

Even for Athenian democratic viewers, then, political power was by definition an exclusive privilege. Not everybody had the right to a civic role. Images of the disenfranchised, the enslaved, and the subjected served to boost the ego of a community of dominant Greek male citizen viewers. That attitude might now be termed 'racist'; Athenian writers (most explicitly Aristotle) deemed it entirely 'natural'.

Greek modes of representing the citizen in antithesis to the barbarian had an enduring legacy in the later Classical world (and, as Edward Saïd has demonstrated in the context of the West's construction of 'the Orient', in our own). Early Christians expended much effort in attempting to eliminate this distinction, arguing that it was irrelevant in the eyes of the Judaeo-Christian God. But the typecasting of the barbarian continued in Latin literature as an effective means of discrediting an opponent, soliciting public condemnation, and stressing 'civilized' Roman ways. And the Roman iconography of the barbarian, complete with straggling beard, contorted face, and alien apparel (most notably trousers) [308], owed more to stylized Greek modes of representing the Other than it did to any interest in what that Other 'really' looked like.

329 Detail of the Column of Marcus Aurelius in Rome, completed c. AD 193 [466]. The monument commemorated the Emperor's military victories over the barbarians in the Danube area, between AD 172 and 175. Compared with Trajan's Column [314], it portrays the barbarian cause with a new degree of drama, emotion, and pathos, as in this detail of the plight of a German woman and her child during the sack of their village: the Romans, with their costume and scraggly beards, look more 'barbarian' than their captives (note, for example, the woman's classicizing drapery). That new-found uneasiness about war, with innocent victims shown helpless against the armed brutality of Roman victors, might have had something to do with Marcus Aurelius' own Stoic philosophy (recorded in his Meditations), concerned with the moral consequences of human action.

330 Hadrian's Wall stretched from sea to sea, symbolically separating Roman Britain to the south from the wild Celtic tribes beyond. There were small fortifications every Roman mile and larger rectangular garrisons at five-mile intervals. Here we see the wall stretching off into the wilderness, to the west of the fort known as Housesteads (ancient Vercovicium).

But Roman attitudes to ethnicity were in fact too complicated to be squared with any single Greek model. For one thing, of course, Romans were themselves non-Greeks: appropriating the Greek concept of 'barbarianism' must have brought with it at least some jarring awareness of that irony. For another, within the Roman Empire, who exactly was the barbarian? In the Roman world, there were different degrees of ethnic 'otherness', just as ethnic 'Romanness' itself was a woolly concept [329]. On one hand, elaborate fortifications (such as Hadrian's Wall in Britain [330]) acted as monumental boundary-markers between the Roman Empire and the outside world: such boundaries (limites) drew a clear line between 'insiders' and 'outsiders' and were vehemently guarded against military attack. But on the other hand, the inhabitants within the borders, whether in North Africa or Gaul, were hardly unified under the name 'Roman'. Conversely, some of those that we might deem to have belonged to outsider groups, including Jews and Christians (most famously St Paul), were – legally at least – Roman citizens. In short, Roman concepts of ethnicity and cultural identity were much more fluid, metropolitan, and multicultural than Greek. 'How much greater an achievement it is', Pliny the Elder observed in the 1st century AD (Natural History 7.117), 'to have extended the boundaries of Roman thinking than of the Roman Empire.' Whatever else we may commend or disdain in Classical antiquity, that might today resonate as a sentiment of laudable intent.

VI OIKOS AND ECONOMY

331 *Excavating for papyrus fragments at Oxyrhynchus, c. 1897.*

332 opposite *Trade amphoras from excavations at the ancient quayside of Pisa at San Rossore, c. 1st century BC [350, 351]. The cargo capacity of a Roman merchant vessel at this time averaged between 5,000 and 10,000 such amphoras (stacked horizontally in the ship's hold). Remains of fruit and nuts were found in the submerged wrecks at Pisa, but primarily the amphoras were used for transporting wine.*

RUBBISH, quantitatively, is one of the great products of civilization. Of course it is not supposed to survive: burned or decomposed, it rarely does so. But one settlement of the Classical world has bequeathed to us a rubbish dump of remarkably fine preservation. This is the site of Oxyrhynchus in Egypt, known to its 11,000 or so Greek-speaking citizens as *Oxyrhynchon polis*, 'City of the Pointy-Nosed Fish'. Some 150 kilometres (a hundred miles) south of Cairo, connected by a natural inlet to the River Nile, Oxyrhynchus indeed owed some of its prosperity to a fishing industry, with a local species of sharp-snouted fish also venerated in the city's temples. Once it had proper perimeter walls, and colonnaded streets within. But while all these crumbled away over the years, the ancient piles of urban waste, banked up on the outskirts of town, were covered in a sealing layer of desert sand – and remained quite undisturbed for century after century.

No rain fell on these mounds by Oxyrhynchus; and they lay beyond the Nile's irrigated floodplain. So their hoards of trash stayed dry and did not rot. One substance above all was kept intact by such conditions: papyrus, the plant-based material that served as writing-paper throughout Egypt and in other parts of the Classical world. Towards the end of the 19th century, local people realized that whatever was scribbled on the piles of papyrus pieces around Oxyrhynchus was of interest to Western scholars, and began to offer scraps for sale. It did not take long for the British military governors of Egypt to facilitate an archaeological mission there in 1897, delegated to two young Oxford graduates called Bernard Grenfell and Arthur Hunt. Over the next few decades, a continuous campaign of excavation retrieved around 50,000 papyrus documents once consigned as trash [331].

'Papyrology' – the reading and interpretation of such documents – has become, thanks largely to the abundant Oxyrhynchus finds [e.g. 384], a specialized branch of Classical scholarship. And it is fair to describe its primary aim – or at least, the principal motivation for the labours of Grenfell and Hunt – as the recovery of fragments of Classical literature. The inhabitants of Oxyrhynchus, after all, had maintained a full-size theatre, and had studied the 'Classic' authors at school: so it happened that their waste-paper mountains included scraps of otherwise lost works by the Athenian playwrights Aeschylus and Sophocles, lyrics by Sappho, and other such precious literary relics. But these were relatively unusual items amid the Oxyrhynchian detritus. Passages of great literature are far outweighed by the mass of what we should describe as bureaucratic paperwork: bills, lists, statements, reminders, tax deeds, solicitations, and so on; not to mention lawsuits, love letters, classroom exercises, complaints about builders not finishing their work, wills, wedding invitations, and much more.

The finds from Oxyrhynchus give a new meaning to the phrase 'junk mail'. Whoever sifts through this waste paper, however, will not only be moved by its peculiar salvage of myriad persons and events from oblivion. What is also striking is how many of the documents relate to the possession of land and associated property (houses, livestock, crops, and suchlike). A good number of papyri relate to people evidently desperate to own or lease some kind of shelter or field. Some

scrolls tell us about the 'liturgies' encumbent upon a landowner – the compulsory obligations to serve as some kind of state official, or contribute to public funds; many others pertain to the revenues generated from the possession of land. Overall, the Oxyrhynchus finds confirm what we believe to be true of the Roman Empire generally, and perhaps of the Classical world at large: that landholding was the pre-eminent source of personal prosperity and status. It was a burden too: land was the principal basis of taxation. Yet it was what everyone wanted.

By most modern definitions, the economy of the Classical world was pre-capitalist. At least, there were no stock markets, nor any centralized credit institutions. As we shall see, money-lending for interest was practised, if subject to periodic state regulation; and 'trading' took place both locally and overseas, though its protagonists, like 'banausic' craftsmen (see p. 162), were subject to general disdain from the educated élite. But without doubt ultimate financial security lay in property; and managing one's own property was esteemed as the best mode of generating wealth (cf. pp. 144–45). That is why so many people of Oxyrhynchus were so pathetically desperate to have their share of property; and that is why any discussion of the ancient economy must begin at home.

HOUSE AND HOME

The Greek word for 'home' or 'household' is *oikos*. Our word 'economy' derives from the Greek *oikonomia* – 'household rules', literally, or the principles of domestic efficiency. (Only in the 17th century did the English use of 'economy' come to denote the science of financial affairs.) So Classical economic activity, in the original sense of *oikonomia*, was centred within the household; and Aristotle voiced a Classical truism when he defined houses, *oikoi*, as the fundamental components of the *polis* (*Politics* 1253b).

This does not mean, however, that we find a wealth of information from Classical writers about the organization of domestic space ('domestic' comes from a Latin word for 'home' or 'household', *domus*). Manuals on the practical aspects of estate management, as we have seen (pp. 143–44), formed a certain genre of Greek and Roman literature. But the principles of running a household were rarely deemed worthy of dedicated discussion – perhaps because then, as now, it was

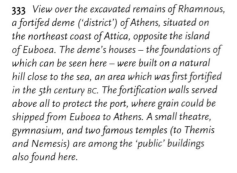

333 *View over the excavated remains of Rhamnous, a fortifed deme ('district') of Athens, situated on the northeast coast of Attica, opposite the island of Euboea. The deme's houses – the foundations of which can be seen here – were built on a natural hill close to the sea, an area which was first fortified in the 5th century BC. The fortification walls served above all to protect the port, where grain could be shipped from Euboea to Athens. A small theatre, gymnasium, and two famous temples (to Themis and Nemesis) are among the 'public' buildings also found here.*

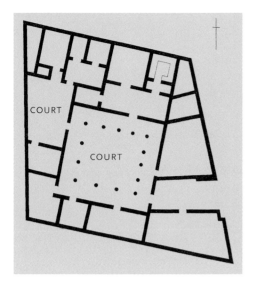

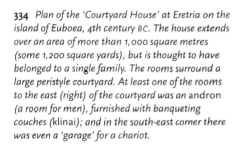

334 *Plan of the 'Courtyard House' at Eretria on the island of Euboea, 4th century BC. The house extends over an area of more than 1,000 square metres (some 1,200 square yards), but is thought to have belonged to a single family. The rooms surround a large peristyle courtyard. At least one of the rooms to the east (right) of the courtyard was an* andron *(a room for men), furnished with banqueting couches (*klinai*); and in the south-east corner there was even a 'garage' for a chariot.*

335 *Restored remains of the two-storeyed courtyard in the House of the Hermes on the island of Delos, 2nd century BC. The house was built into the slope of the hill (on the left); rooms at ground level included a dining room and bath; on the upper level seen here, a peristyle gave a view out over the surrounding area; there was originally also a third floor, though not above the peristyle.*

The colonnaded central space evoked the architecture of public buildings, especially that of the gymnasium (an effect criticized by Demosthenes as early as the 4th century BC: see p. 189). Its design, incorporating both open and covered spaces, also lies behind the atrium of the Roman house [338].

largely women's work, unpaid and taken for granted. An exception to this tendency is a composition of *c.* 400 BC by Xenophon, *The Estate Manager* (*Oikonomikos*), a dialogue in which an affluent but prudent Athenian called Ischomachos reportedly describes to Socrates how he has trained his wife to be an efficient steward of his family domain (see p. 26). In what follows, Xenophon's short text provides some essential points of reference.

More generous is the archaeological record. In fact Classical archaeologists have often been remiss in the search for dwelling-places, because the material from such sites is intrinsically likely to be mundane – items of everyday utility instead of glittering treasures (with notable exceptions [336]). But several excavations have been particularly fruitful in yielding information about domestic structures and conditions. From the Greek world, the outstanding site remains Olynthos, a city in the Chalkidike peninsula of northern Greece, abandoned after being sacked by Philip II of Macedon in 348 BC, and subject to several seasons of investigation by D. M. Robinson and teams from the University of Mississippi in the 1920s and 1930s [337]. In Etruria, the Swedish School at Rome brought to light the inland settlements of Acquarossa and San Giovenale, both relatively small in size, but providing key glimpses of how family units subsisted in a community. Then, for a poignantly detailed picture of households in the early Roman empire, we have those places abruptly buried by Mount Vesuvius in AD 79 [338]. Estimates vary as to how much warning of disaster came to the inhabitants of Pompeii and Herculaneum; but clearly many of them were caught by the fumes and lava of the volcanic explosion before they had time to make a systematic evacuation of their homes.

'Hives of activity': that phrase might be applied to houses in Greece, Etruria, and Rome as revealed by archaeology; and Xenophon's Ischomachos begins his outline of domestic principles with an appeal to the beehive as a model of the nuclear household. Nature, he tells his young wife (aged just fifteen), has ordained that the queen bee stay within the hive; so a woman's place is at home. The queen bee stays inside, but her role is far from trivial. She supervises the ordering of the hive, the rearing of the young, and the assignment of tasks to worker bees. So the good wife must see to all interior matters, bring up new offspring, and organize the workers – the family's slaves.

336 *Detail of a luxurious banqueting couch in bronze, with silver inlaid decoration, from a Roman house at Amiternum, north-east of Rome. Most domestic furniture was made of wood, and consequently has not survived. Bronze fittings such as this are relatively rare and, because of their expense, can only have decorated the richest houses. In its shape this clearly resembles a couch made of turned wood, although the young god (probably Dionysos) at the bottom of the armrest and the elaborate wreathed head of a mule at the top better suit the medium of bronze.*

337 below *Reconstruction of a 4th-century BC house at Olynthos. Beyond the inner front door is an open courtyard. Typically, the andron with its couches was located at a street corner – lower left – with windows allowing passers-by to glimpse the extent of hospitality.*

338 opposite *The House of Menander at Pompeii, 1st century AD, with a basic layout conserved from the 3rd century BC. The grandiose scale of this residence can be assessed from this view of its* atrium, *or reception hall; a skylight in the roof allowed water to collect in the sunken pool (*impluvium*) [cf. 253]. The* tablinum *beyond has been converted to give open access to the* peristyle, *a courtyard surrounded by columns.*

339, 340 *Details of an Attic black-figure lekythos attributed to the Amasis Painter, c. 560 BC. One side (above) shows a woman with spindle and distaff, and two women folding cloth; the other (above right) shows women weaving at a tall loom, whose warp threads are held by loom-weights. The vase may well have formed part of a wedding set.*

341 *Terracotta spools from a grave at the Etruscan cemetery of Casale del Fosso near Veii, 8th century BC. Items of domestic use were often deposited in Etruscan tombs; they do not, however, necessarily entail that the deceased was female.*

342 opposite *Detail of a terracotta relief from Locri in South Italy, c. 460–450 BC. A woman stows a robe or blanket in a carved chest. Behind her is a cushioned chair; above, assorted domestic items: wool basket, handled mirror, lekythos, and a high-stemmed two-handled kantharos.*

About the Classical institution of slavery we shall have more to say later. For now, it is important to underline the positive slant given by Xenophon to female domestic responsibilities. Women's lives in antiquity are sometimes imagined to be nothing but confinement and drudgery. Certainly the structure of the *oikos* was enclosed – not so much as a garden fence to gossip over – and women were excluded from very many public offices and occasions. What Xenophon says about women being naturally intended to operate indoors as 'the weaker sex' must offend modern Western sensibilities. But in *The Estate Manager* this homely stewardship is presented not as subjection – rather as a partnership, a division of labour, or a pooling of resources. An oft-quoted passage of the text (9.5) refers to a specific part of the house as being 'the women's quarters' (*gynaikonitis* – lockable, it seems, from outside), yet it is also quite clear that the wife was deemed mistress of the entire premises. To say that she 'ruled the roost' may be putting it too strongly (and mixing metaphors). Still, she is distinctly acknowledged here as 'law-upholder' (*nomophylax*) or chief executive officer within the household.

The question of how far Greek houses were divided into 'male' and 'female' areas has caused much scholarly discussion. Literary references suggest that there were such divisions, sometimes demarcated by floor level (many houses were two-storeyed buildings [335]). The analysis of utensils, storage pots, and other domestic objects found *in situ* in the houses of Olynthos, however, points to considerable flexibility of room-use under one roof. Archaeology bears witness to the habitual reservation of one room as the particular 'men's place' (*andron*) where symposia would be held (see p. 254): this can be identified, for example, in the layout of one carefully excavated house at Eretria on Euboea [334]. Otherwise, domestic activities seem to have been carried out in various parts of the familial enclosure.

What were these 'domestic activities'? Beyond the predictable chores of cooking [344], cleaning, folding linen [339, 342], fetching water [248], and so on – and in addition to the supervising of slaves, who in affluent homes will have performed some of those tasks – Xenophon's *Estate Manager* indicates the central importance of two female responsibilities: storing food and making clothes. The former required skills of estimating consumption, budgeting for shortfalls and surpluses, and perhaps also controlling accounts. The latter, textile production [339–41],

343 *View along the Via dell'Abbondanza in Pompeii, 1st century* AD. *The large openings front what remains of shops. Raised basalt blocks provided crossing-points for pedestrians so that they could avoid wading through the raw sewage that stagnated in the street; carriages could also travel this main thoroughfare, and their wheel ruts can still be seen.*

344 *Bronze cooking pots as left on the hearth of the House of the Vettii, Pompeii, in* AD *79.*

was as much a symbolic vocation for Greek wives as it was a mode of economic enterprise. Girls were taught to spin and weave at an early age. Even if the mistress of the house could afford to delegate work at the loom, she should nevertheless be skilled at it. Mythologically, it had been Athena's command to the women of Athens that they assume the role of Arachne (whom Athena defeated in a spinning contest and transformed into a spider), and fashion not only clothes for their families but also gorgeous robes and hangings to adorn the images of deities. In other stories – of Penelope, the wife of Odysseus [192], for example, or in the Latin tale of Tanaquil – spinning and weaving are significant of female virtue. And on Greek vases, the images of this sort of work are surely as much prescriptive as descriptive: *this*, they seem to say, is how the good woman keeps busy.

Both food storage and the activity of making clothes at home leave distinctive archaeological traces. Terracotta storage jars – *pithoi* in Greek, *dolia* in Latin – may be up to 2 metres (6½ feet) tall, with capacities rising to over 1,000 litres (more than 200 gallons). These could be sunk in the ground for extra coolness [194]: commonly their contents were liquid (wine, oil, honey), but they were equally suitable for dry goods (notably wheat and barley grain). As for spinning and weaving, distaffs – the cleft sticks on which bundles of shorn wool were fixed – are rarely encountered; but the circular spindle-whorls that helped to tease out a thread to be wound about a spindle are very common finds, as are spools [341], and the small ceramic oblong lumps that served as loom weights (holding taut vertical 'warp' threads in place, while a weave was made horizontally [340]). A single loom might require anything from a dozen to forty-odd of these weights: in houses at Olynthos, clusters of this range (and greater, indicating several looms) have been found in all but the men's rooms and washrooms.

The main communal area of a typical Greek *oikos* was either an inner courtyard or a covered corridor [334, 337]. Ideally houses were oriented so as to be shady in summer but catch the maximum of low winter sunlight: therefore the open courtyard might be a pleasant place in which to work throughout the year. And while it is true that for some well-to-do citizens of Greek cities this courtyard space might eventually (from the early 4th century BC onwards) become a haven of tranquillity (see p. 232), the fact remains that most households functioned as small centres of craft and industry. Many houses at Olynthos had rooms which fronted onto the city's streets and demonstrably served as shops or workshops. The modern dichotomy of 'work' and 'home' can hardly have existed: certainly not for women.

There are some sites – the little island of Delos is one [335] – where the transition from Greek to Roman domesticity appears almost unmarked. This is not surprising, because Roman houses, and Etruscan houses too, were similarly conceived as economic units. Excavators of Marzabotto, an Etruscan town laid out on a gridiron plan by 5th-century BC colonists in the Apennine mountains, labelled one part of the settlement as an 'industrial quarter', where metalworking took place: but in fact all the dwellings of Marzabotto were quasi-industrial, if textiles and pottery-making are counted. And the substantial evidence from Pompeii and Herculaneum makes it very plain that urban life in Roman Campania was also founded upon the Latin house, which could double as both residence and shop or workshop. So bakers lived hard by their ovens and flour mills [345], carpenters by their benches, wheelwrights near their anvils. And so certain houses must have been piquant places of habitation. Some at Pompeii were given over to the manufacture, for example, of the strong condiment called *garum* (a fish sauce). Another local industry was the fulling of cloth – which, although a sort of cleansing process, called for quantities of human urine as a caustic agent. But, as the Emperor Vespasian once quipped, *pecunia non olet* – 'money doesn't smell'. One of the many surviving graffiti from Pompeii reads *salve lucro!* – 'hail to profit!'; and a burgeoning ethos of the small and home-based business has been invoked to explain the later Republican trend, at Pompeii and Herculaneum alike, for street-facing rooms to be converted into shops (*tabernae*) [343] – as at Greek Olynthos.

It may be observed here that the Roman urban house was ideally constructed on an axis between the private and the public, with a central hall, or atrium [338],

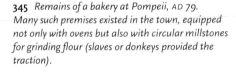

345 *Remains of a bakery at Pompeii, AD 79. Many such premises existed in the town, equipped not only with ovens but also with circular millstones for grinding flour (slaves or donkeys provided the traction).*

346 *Detail of a wall-painting in the reception room of the House of the Vettii at Pompeii, AD 62–79. With a daintiness typical of the 'Fourth Style' of Pompeian painting, a cupid is shown extracting oil to make perfume or medicine. The House of the Vettii appears not to have doubled as industrial premises, but rather provided a richly decorated retreat for the two freedmen brothers, Aulus Vettius Restitutus and Aulus Vettius Conviva, who appear to have purchased the property after the earthquake of AD 62.*

serving to receive those entering off the street by a *fauces* or 'throat-passage'. Local politics, business, and social affairs were all conducted either within the atrium or in quarters leading off from the atrium – notably the *tablinum*, which in turn gave access to an enclosed colonnaded space, or peristyle [338]. In a provincial ambience where the high-ranking individual (*dominus*, or *patronus*) dispensed favours and cash to supporters (*clientes*) who came regularly to the house to give their 'greeting' (*salutatio*), we should not be amazed by the splendours of interior decoration within these houses. Visitors were expected; and visitors could expect to find upon the walls of the property signs of its owner's wealth, power, and status. The subjects of such wall-paintings were full of clues (myths [217], landscapes [465], and so on). But even the pigments of the paint said something of economic significance. Cobalt blue, for example, was well known to be a very costly colour.

A relatively rich householder in Pompeii might prefer not to maintain a noxious fulling installation in his home, but instead commission pictures of cute little cupid-figures doing the work. Whether the householders of Pompeii were by local standards 'rich' or 'poor', however, is perhaps beside the point when discussing the actualities of 'work'. For at Pompeii, as elsewhere in the Classical world, most work was done by slaves.

SLAVES IN THE CLASSICAL ECONOMY

Iconographically, the ancient slave body – the principal labour force of Classical antiquity – is virtually invisible. Slaves were objects; but not objects of art – and when they do appear, they are shown as the possessions and minions of their masters [348]. Archaeologically, too, this large population has left very few traces. Slaves were usually buried without ceremony; they had few possessions to take to any kind of grave (though some, as we have noted, were shackled even in death: p. 17).

This is the melancholy overture to a topic which can still embarrass the teachers and upholders of 'Classical civilization'. How can we regard as 'civilized' any society that treated great numbers of human beings as mere instruments of manual labour? And how can it be that for all the supposed moral and intellectual 'wisdom' of Classical writers and philosophers, not one of them – not even Socrates or Plato – ever so much as queried the blatant creation and exploitation of a menial underclass?

It is hard to find answers to those questions, and impossible to devise an apology for such ancient ethical myopia. Slavery was simply a blind spot in the worldview of thinking individuals. Even Xenophon's Ischomachos, so 'proper' in his dealings with his wife, and proud of his loving rapport with her, assumes that the slaves within their household are at his disposal for sex (*The Estate Manager* 10.12–13): he is their master, they his possessions. Elsewhere, in his essay *On Revenues*, Xenophon shows no qualms about suggesting that the city of Athens install sufficient slaves in the mines for 'each citizen of Athens to be maintained at public expense' (4.33).

Aristotle, the Classical philosopher most deeply concerned with making a system of ethics, likewise demonstrates solid indifference when discussing slavery as an institution (*Politics* 1254a17–1254b39). He defines a slave as 'an animate article of property', to be treated more or less like an animal. Briefly he wonders if a feasible alternative to slavery might lie in devising machines to do their work. But Aristotle merely confirms the mentality of idiomatic Greek usage, which classified a beast of burden as a *tetrapodon*, 'four-footed thing', and generically regarded the slave as an *andrapodon* – 'man-footed thing'. The unpalatable core truth about ancient slavery is that it depended – like the Nazi Holocaust – upon the categorization of certain

347 *Another detail of a wall-painting in the House of the Vettii shows the cupids working as busy little goldsmiths. Elsewhere in the house they may be seen engaged in fulling – which has been suggested as the proprietors' source of wealth.*

humans as a sub-species: 'a tool that talks' (*instrumentum vocale*) is how Varro described the Roman slave in the 1st century BC (*On Farming* 1.17).

We can still proceed to outline something of the function of slaves within the domestic economies of Greece and Rome. The deployment of slaves in agriculture and mining has already been mentioned (pp. 147 and 158 respectively). But how did they operate within the basic unit of the the ancient economy, the household? And what was the economic importance of the ancient 'slave trade' itself?

The case of Olynthos may be invoked again. As noted above, Olynthos was abandoned by its inhabitants after being taken by the Macedonians in 348 BC: it was abandoned because those inhabitants who were not killed were sold off into slavery. Immediately we are made aware that Classical slavery was not racially determined. In practice, many slaves may have been of foreign origin; but the division of humankind into the free and the enslaved had no clear ethnic basis.

Precisely what prices the captured Olynthians fetched on the slave market is not known. Typically, a slave sold at Athens in the 4th century BC was worth between 150 and 300 drachmas, with skilled artisans commanding higher prices. Once purchased, of course, the slave was an owner's property, and therefore had to be fed, clothed, and accommodated at the owner's expense. This was not tantamount to 'employment', although some slaves were evidently able to make a little money, perhaps sufficient eventually to buy themselves freedom. Still it is important to remember that while slavery was undeniably demeaning, most urban slaves probably lived in close domestic proximity to their masters; and that while discipline of slaves was generally strict, slave-owners had no economic interest in the neglect or abuse of their staff. Xenophon's Ischomachos made sure his slaves were educated, and rewarded for good work. An efficient household, after all, depended upon an honest and willing workforce.

This consideration is enough to make us regard with suspicion some ancient tales of slave maltreatment – the tradition, for instance, that the Roman plutocrat

348 *An old man followed by a slave: detail of an Attic red-figure amphora, the name-vase of the Painter of the Copenhagen Amphora, early 5th century BC. To represent a slave as a diminutive or stooping figure was a typical way of delineating his/her servile status in the imagery of the ancient Mediterranean world [cf. 146, 406].*

Vedius Pollio, friend of the Emperor Augustus, used to punish his slaves by throwing them into a pool of carnivorous fish (Seneca, *On Anger* 3.40). Even with the recurrent boosts to their supply from war and conquest, slaves were never such disposable items. Specialized slave-traders operated around the Mediterranean, where known centres of the trade included Ephesus and Delos; and trade, it seems, was always brisk (Strabo, writing at the time of Augustus, says that the daily turnover in slaves at Delos could reach 10,000 per day: *Geography* 14.5.2).

Only a small number of slave revolts are known in Classical history. None of them, so far as we can judge, aimed at abolishing the institution of slavery: these were simply slaves seeking their own emancipation. The story about Pollio may be psychologically credible in this respect, because he was the son of an ex-slave – a slave who had escaped not by rebellion, but through the process of 'manumission'.

Manumissio – 'sending away from the hand's authority' – was the Latin term for discharge from servile bondage. It could be purchased, or otherwise 'earned' as a reward for diligent service. Sometimes it took the quaint form (recorded at Delphi) of being sold off or 'promoted', as it were, to divine supervision. The practice of this release-process is not so clear among the Greeks as it is in the Roman world, where a significant number of 'freedmen' (*liberti*) are known from various sources [e.g. 101]. Would Pollio have bullied his slaves because he himself had servile origins? Perhaps; Latin literature has some memorable vignettes describing the behaviour of 'slaves-made-good', none more florid than Trimalchio, the central figure of fun in the boisterous 1st-century AD sketches by Petronius usually entitled the *Satyricon*.

Trimalchio makes no attempt to conceal his servile origins: on the contrary, the first painting to be seen on the threshold of his house showed him in the slave-market, prior to lessons in book-keeping skills. He exults in the prodigious wealth and property he has since acquired. Boastful, vulgar, and culturally clumsy (see p. 259), Trimalchio shows stereotypical features of the 'newly arrived' in high society; and his slobbering greed recalls the Aristotelian view of slaves as on a par with domesticated beasts. Yet Trimalchio's ascendancy to power is caricature, not fantasy. The biographical pictures on his wall showed him led away from the slave-market by Mercury, the god of crossing boundaries. Like many actual citizens of the Roman Empire, Trimalchio had succeeded in negotiating the greatest boundary in Classical ideology – the distinction between slavery and freedom.

TRADING ABROAD

Analysed in modern economic terms, the Classical slave-trade may be defined as a redistribution of people around the Mediterranean. And we know that in later historical periods of slave-trading, sea transport played a key role in such 'redistribution'. This brings us to the question: what levels of overseas trade existed in Classical antiquity?

An answer based only upon the earliest Classical literature would be sceptical of much business in this sphere. The Archaic Greek bard Hesiod styled himself as an authentic farming man: he was, he claimed, tending his flocks on the slopes of Mount Helicon when the Muses diverted him to poetry (*Theogony* 22–23). Whatever the truth of this tradition, Hesiod certainly voices prejudices against long-distance trade that are characteristic of land-based tenants and proprietors in the Classical world. We learn not only that Hesiod's father had tried to be a seafarer, and came to no good by it, but also that Hesiod's brother Perses was similarly tempted by the adventures and riches of trading abroad (*Works and Days* 618–94). The poet admits that his own marine experience is slight – a transit across the Euripos strait to Euboea: very slight indeed – but that does not prevent him from

349 *Marine archaeologists at work on the wreck of a Greek merchant vessel off the coast of Cyprus, during investigations in 1967–1969.*

evoking all the ruinous powers of the 'loud-roaring sea'. There is, he says, only one proper time for men to go sailing, and that is high summer, and they should hurry home before autumn storms gather. Plainly to take such risks is for the greedy and foolish: for Hesiod (and his audience of aristocratic proprietors) there were better things to do on dry land – not least, harvesting the crops.

Homer, too, viewed seaborne merchants with suspicion (singling out the Phoenicians for particular scorn). The dream of his hero-mariner Odysseus is to cease travelling and settle down to manage his kingly estates on Ithaca.

Such influential literary expressions of disdain for mercantile activity, compounded by the general and pervasive Classical faith in land as the optimum form of capital investment, have encouraged some historians to deny any similarity between today's complex and 'globalized' trading systems and the operation of ancient economies. This is the 'primitivist' view of the ancient economy. If, as we

surmised (pp. 143–45), there was a widespread practice of self-sufficiency and local markets, why should we expect to uncover substantial inter-continental or trans-Mediterranean commerce? There is no doubting that the logistical risks of trading abroad were real enough. Pirates, treacherous waters, storms, and other freaks of the weather: Hesiod did not invent these perils at sea. Yet the very victims of such dangers also testify most eloquently to volumes of mercantile activity – *prexis*, as the Ionian Greeks called it – that we should never have imagined.

'Marine archaeology' is the name of the science, and its revelations occur on an almost annual basis [332, 349–53, 567]. Important finds in the last few decades include wrecks from Bon Porté, off the south coast of France, El Sec (Majorca), and Porticello, in the Straits of Messina; not to mention the underwater exploration of important ancient harbours such as Caesarea and Alexandria. The techniques of such research were pioneered in the 1960s with a Bronze Age vessel off Cape Gelidonya on the south coast of Turkey by George Bass, founder of the Institute of Nautical Archaeology in Texas. Since 1945, over a thousand ancient shipwrecks have been located in the Mediterranean and Black Sea.

Who can tell what proportion of ancient sea-journeys ended in disaster? To judge from ships excavated on the sea-bed, however, the vessels' owners (*naukleroi*) were typically plying complex, shrewd, and varied routes. Take, for example, a wreck investigated off the island of Giglio, in the Tuscan archipelago. This was a boat that capsized around 580 BC. It seems to have set out from the Ionian coast of the eastern Mediterranean, carrying storage jars or amphoras from Phoenicia and Samos. One stop *en route* was probably made at Corinth, perhaps the point at which a number of small perfume or unguent bottles (*aryballoi*) [353] were taken aboard, along with other goods from the Peloponnese (including a fine Corinthian-style helmet [352]); then the ship made its way across to Etruria in the west, where at

350, 351 *Views of excavations at the Roman riverside wharf of San Rossore, Pisa. Discovered in 1999, this site has so far yielded the remains of eleven capsized vessels, including (below) a 2nd-century AD merchant craft with a keel length of 14 metres (46 feet). Some of the boats were evidently loaded with products from the Bay of Naples; further destinations were very likely ports along the south coast of France and the Iberian peninsula.*

352, 353 *Two items recovered from the Giglio shipwreck, c. 580 BC: a Corinthian-style helmet with incised decoration, and a Corinthian-made aryballos (a flask for perfume or oil).*

some port it took on at least 130 Etruscan amphoras containing olives, pitch, and wine. It must have been heading for the south of France – perhaps Massalia, ancient Marseilles – when it sank; going down with not only the pots aboard, but also a quantity of ingots and finished metal products, and some 'prize possessions' of the time – a silver drinking service, a boxwood writing tablet, a set of musical pipes . . .

We should remember that certain substantial but perishable types of freight – including timber, textiles, grain, and slaves – will not show up in underwater wreckage. But we can presume that carrying mixed cargoes was one way for a merchant to spread his risks. A mid-5th-century BC lead sheet from Pech Maho on the Languedoc coast inscribed in Greek and Etruscan contains details of reciprocal obligations involved in the embarcation and delivery of goods. The 'carriers' are unlikely, however, to have put up their own capital. From Athenian court records of the 4th century BC dealing with particular 'commercial lawsuits' (*dikai emporikai*), it is clear that mercantile voyages were funded by loans, usually from family and friends. The average sum was around 3,000 drachmas; and however steep the interest rates may have been, some ancient sources imply that profit margins could be very large. In the mid- to late 1st century BC Diodorus Siculus, for example, asserts that traders reaching the Gaulish settlements on the south coast of France could reckon on exchanging one jar of wine for one slave (*Library of History* 5.26.3) – a remarkable testimony to Celtic thirst. Writing some four centuries earlier, Herodotus (*Histories* 4.152) was aware of an entrepreneur from the island of Aegina, one Sostratos, who had made an unparalleled fortune by trading in the western Mediterranean. In Etruria, a number of amphoras have been discovered with the letters 'SO' or 'SOS' scratched on their bases – very plausibly marked as goods transported by a certain 'Sostratos'; and from excavations at Gravisca, the port-depot serving the Etruscan city of Tarquinia, a stone anchor has been recovered bearing a prayer to Apollo for safe passage, in Aeginetan Greek – dedicated by 'Sostratos'.

Gravisca was the sort of place that the Greeks would have described as an *emporion* or *emporikos oikos* – a dedicated 'trading-post'. A little way down the coast lay another such site, Pyrgi, whose associated temples catered for Etruscans, Greeks, and Phoenicians. Greek and Phoenician traders also had similar bases further westwards, with at least one Spanish town, Ampurias, still indebted by name to its ancient *emporion* status; while over in the east, important ports of call for traders in the Archaic period included Al Mina on the Levantine coast, Naukratis in the Nile Delta, and the Aegean island of Chios.

The notion that trade fosters international cooperation is relatively modern. It remains hard to judge how far patterns of trade determined the process of Greek and Phoenician colonization around the Mediterranean basin; and some trading relationships may have been quite impersonal. (Herodotus describes how some Phoenician merchants, bartering with a tribe of north-west Africa, unload their goods on a beach, and retire to their ships while the indigenous people assess how much gold they think those goods are worth. Without exchanging a word, both sides act scrupulously and to mutual satisfaction; *Histories* 4.196.) What archaeology does indicate, however, is that plenty of Greeks paid no heed to the warnings of Homer and Hesiod: the potential gains of cross-Mediterranean trade evidently outweighed the risks.

One basic economic factor underpinned the development of Classical seaborne trade. Despite its hazards, transport by water was by far the most cost-effective means of moving goods and people in antiquity. The quantification of relative logistics in Archaic Greece is difficult, and further complicated by the fact that a favoured vessel of Archaic traders seems to have been the *pentekontor*, with an

354, 355 *above and above right Stone reliefs from Ostia, c. 2nd century AD. Whether used for shop signs or sarcophagi, such images illustrate the extent to which individuals identified themselves with a particular trade. The shopkeeper (above) sold groceries and livestock: fowl are suspended beside her; far right are two rabbits in cages; the man far left is holding a piglet. In addition to these local goods, she also has two pet monkeys, exotic imports from overseas. The relief of a baker (above right) shows him with two different kinds of round bread for sale, below two circular ovens in the wall [cf. 101]. Grain was a crucial, albeit less exotic, import.*

'engine' of fifty rowers who all needed feeding and rewards. But from the more abundant evidence from the Roman Empire it has been calculated that transport overland was something like thirty times more expensive than transport by sea. Where rivers were navigable, they were just five times the cost of going by sea – which explains why, for example, the geographer Strabo, writing at the end of the 1st century BC, considered transalpine Gaul such an attractive imperial territory: it had a readymade infrastructure of arterial rivers.

Such stark advantages of waterborne transport may surprise anyone who thinks of the Romans as indefatigable builders of long straight roads. But the roads were primarily for troops on the march. Archaeology, again, conclusively demonstrates that for supplies of goods and foodstuffs, whether military or civilian, the traffic was predominantly boats and barges. The Roman invention of a concrete that could set in water facilitated the development of artificial harbours and river-ports. In turn, heavy-keeled ships were constructed that could take cargoes of up to 1,000 tonnes and more.

The principal bulk to be shifted around the Empire was grain. One computation of the amount of imported grain required by imperial Rome estimates it at some 150,000 tonnes per annum. So the laughable reputation of the Emperor Claudius is greatly redeemed by his commission of Portus, a major new harbour for Rome just north of Ostia at the Tiber's mouth. Further docking facilities for large freight consignments to Portus were subsequently made possible thanks to an artificial lake sponsored by Trajan; while in Egypt and North Africa – the main sources of

LMVNATIVM·C·F·PLANCVM·ITALICEI
ET·GRAECEI·QVEI·DELEI·NEGOTIANTVR

356 *Inscription from the 'Agora of the Italians' on Delos, 1st century BC. Found in what may have been the main marketplace for slave-trading on the island of Delos, it records the dedication of a statue of a Roman administrator, L. Munatius Plancus, by grateful Greek and Italian businessmen.*

the grain – monumental harbours at Alexandria, Carthage, and Lepcis Magna testify to the volume of shipments.

The harbour-town of Ostia, subject to excavation since the 19th century, yields signs of many sorts of trade that connected Rome not only with her imperial provinces, but also – via the 'Silk Road' traversing Asia – the Indian subcontinent. And we only have to consult the recipes attributed to the Roman gourmet Apicius (see p. 66) to see that there must have been substantial traffic in spices from the East – peppercorns, saffron, and much more. The most pervasive evidence of trade around the Roman Empire, however, besides surviving inscriptions [356], comes from pots. Because such enormous quantities of pottery survive in the archaeological record, the typologies created for its classification are daunting to the non-specialist – and there is no space even to summarize them here. But some ways in which pots can illuminate economic history may be briefly indicated.

Roman transport amphoras, like those used by the Greeks and Etruscans, were large oval cylinders that could be hermetically sealed with lids and pitch [332].

In a ship's hold, they would be stacked horizontally, protectively wrapped in straw. The barrels and sacks that may have accompanied them are gone, but the amphoras are tough survivors. *En masse*, one such container may look very like another. But there were variations of shape, which have duly been ordered into modern categories. 'Dressel 1', for example, is an elongated form used for carrying wine; 'Dressel 20' a more globular jar typically reserved for olive oil. These were strictly utilitarian objects. However, that did not prevent their makers from marking them with some symbol of fabrication, or a producer of their contents 'labelling' his ware in similar fashion. So we find, for example, that a Tuscan-based wine-producer called Sestius, stamping his amphoras with the letters 'SEST', was part of a trading pattern that extended along the coast of France to the Iberian peninsula, and up the Rhone valley, penetrating further inland as far as Basel to the east and Poitiers to the west. (The same Sestius has also been suggested as a likely owner of the *latifundium* of Settefinestre [235].)

The 'fine' ceramics used on household tables throughout the Roman world are also obdurate witnesses of overseas trade – despite being delicate, and intrinsically unsuitable for travelling long distances. It may be that consignments of cups and plates and so on travelled 'piggy-back' with other loads, such as timber or metals. Nevertheless, although every region of Rome's empire had its own localized pottery-producing capacities, certain centres of production supplied markets far afield. In southern Gaul, for example, there were kilns making a reddish-glazed and relief-decorated pottery (*terra sigillata*), sometimes misleadingly called 'Samian ware', whose products during the 1st century AD travelled not only around the provinces – including Germany, Britain, and North Africa – but also back to the source of prototypes, Italy. An individual drinking-bowl from one of these Gaulish factories at La Graufesenque (near Millau in Aveyron) [357, 358] may be analysed according to the finesse and interest of its relief decoration – later phases of production show a marked decline in technical standards – but what could be a better sign of economic success for such pots than finding a crate of them at Pompeii?

357 *A bowl of 'Samian ware' from La Graufesenque in the south of France, 1st century AD. Southern Gaul and the Moselle Valley were the primary sources of this distinctive pottery – not the Greek island of Samos.*

358 *View of pottery-producing kilns at La Graufesenque.*

359 *Silver tetradrachm (four-drachma piece) of the Greek colony of Akragas (modern Agrigento), Sicily, c. 510–420 BC. The bird is identifiable as a white-tailed sea-eagle, a bird sacred to Zeus.*

A MONETARY SYSTEM?

Tradition has it that the first gold and silver coins in the world were minted in thezkingdom of Lydia under the rule of Croesus (*c.* 560–547 BC). As the Greeks legendarily knew him, Croesus was extremely rich, and a benefactor, too, who endowed the great Temple of Artemis at Ephesus. Under that temple a deposit was found of almost a hundred circular stamped pieces of electrum, produced in Lydia around the time of Croesus. Electrum, or 'white gold', is a natural alloy of gold and silver that could be extracted from sources close to the Lydian capital, Sardis. Soon electrum gave way to units of gold or (more often) silver, these being easier, perhaps, to assess in terms of their solid value as 'bullion' – precious metal measured in absolute blocks of weight. In Mesopotamia, Egypt, and other pre-Hellenic civilizations, bullion had served as a standard form of currency.

The first coins minted by Archaic Greek *poleis* could probably be stored or bartered as if they were bullion; that is, as if they were worth their weight in silver. But it did not take long for those city-states to realize not only that coinage might accrue a purchasing power over and above the worth of its original metal, but also that these miniature hard-wearing discs might carry considerable symbolic value.

To say that coins – *nomismata* to the Greeks, meaning things 'in currency' or legally sanctioned – constituted an early sort of 'mass medium' may be an exaggeration. Yet they were soon loaded with motifs and messages which clearly had civic and collective importance. So the colony of Akragas (modern Agrigento), in Sicily, aligned itself to the mainland cult of Zeus by issuing coins with the image not only of an eagle but more specifically of a sea-eagle (Zeus across-the-water) [359]; in South Italy Poseidonia (Roman Paestum) paraded an image of Poseidon [581], its tutelary deity. The polity of Ephesus, 'trading' on the reputation of its cult of Artemis [127], marked its money with a bee [360], an insect sacred to Artemis, and a palm tree [361], probably referring to the birth of the goddess under a Delian palm. The abstract prominence of such sacred or mythological emblems encouraged a sense of political identity, of course, and by signalling state authority, also encouraged public faith in the metallic purity and economic steadiness of the coinage. So the imagery on Athenian coins remained almost changeless over centuries: a helmeted head of the city's goddess on one side, and Athena's special bird of wisdom, the owl, on the other – perhaps accompanied by some further iconographic token, such as an outline of the *Tyrannicides* group; or an amphora and a wreath of olive leaves, signalling olives as the chief cash crop of Attica.

Not all Greek cities immediately followed the fashion: the Spartans (predictably) shunned coins until the 3rd century BC. And in Italy, where the Greek colonial cities were pioneers of monetary exchange, indigenous peoples preferred to stay with systems based on metal ingots measured by weight, such as the 'dried branches' of solid bronze favoured in Etruria and early Rome. Livy (*History of Rome from its Foundation* 6.60.6) says that senators of the archaic Roman Republic had to drag their bullion of *aes rude* ('roughcast bronze') around in carts. But the symbolic potential of coinage proved particularly irresistible in two political spheres of the Classical world. First the Hellenistic monarchs; then the Roman emperors.

Perhaps no autocrat had ever needed numismatic emblems of his charisma more keenly than Alexander the Great, whose features still retain talismanic powers in some parts of the world today. In Bactria and Arachosia (Afghanistan), Alexander issued coins despite the fact that the local economies were not monetary. In this policy, as with many other aspects of his conquests, Alexander could rely upon precedent set by his father, Philip II, who had used coins to emphasize the quasi-divine legitimacy of his dynastic rule in Macedon and beyond. With his seizure of Persia in the 330s BC, Alexander also had massive amounts of precious metal at his disposal. Those of his generals who created their own kingdoms after his death lost no time in issuing monetary signs of a 'right to rule' thanks to Alexander [277].

So we find the ex-Macedonian Antiochos I of Seleucia – a territory sometimes called 'Syria', though its capital lies east of modern Syria, in the plains of the Tigris and Euphrates – unashamedly minting a portrait that emulated the royal posture and headgear of Alexander (head slightly uplifted, wearing a diadem) [362]; and on the reverse, the legend 'Basileos Antiochou', 'of King Antiochos', inscribed beside

360, 361 *Silver tetradrachm of Ephesus, 4th century BC. On one side is a bee, symbolic of the goddess Artemis, with the Greek letters* epsilon *and* phi *spelling 'Eph' for Ephesus; on the other side, a stag (also sacred to Artemis) reclines by a palm tree, presumably referring to the one on Delos where Artemis was born. 'Karno' is thought to be the name of the magistrate then responsible for minting-standards at the city.*

362, 363 *Silver tetradrachm of King Antiochos I of Seleucia, c. 280 BC. A regal portrait on one side; on the other, the words 'Basileos Antiochou' frame an image of the god Apollo, an arrow in his hand, sitting upon the 'navel' (omphalos) of the world.*

an image of the god Apollo [363]. So what belonged to Antiochos? The portrait head? The coin itself? The image of the god? Or the god himself? Users of the coin were probably intended not to be clear on such questions. Like Alexander, Antiochos cultivated a divine or semi-divine style of rulership, which made him the heaven-sent 'saviour' (*soter*) of his subjects.

The Roman conquest and absorption of Macedonian-controlled territories meant that by the time of the battle of Actium (31 BC) Greek coinage was out of currency. But the victor of Actium, Octavian, more or less followed the lead of the Hellenistic monarchs in his own numismatic strategy. Diadems were eschewed. Rome was, after all, ideally still supposed to be a Republic. So on his early issues of the principal Roman unit of currency, the silver denarius – worth 10 bronze 'asses' originally, 16 later (after 140 BC) – Octavian wears instead of a crown a laurel wreath, symbol of victory [364]. But the laurel was also Apollo's special tree, and young Octavian was not shy of identifying himself with the god (see p. 249). It was a divine association that he would confirm on coins issued throughout his rule under the name of 'Caesar Augustus', after his deified 'father', Julius Caesar (see p. 93).

Augustus actually stored substantial quantities of gold in the form of *ex voto* offerings to temples of Apollo. But the pairing, on regular coinage, of his image with symbols or attributes of Apollo somewhat undermines one of the well-known precepts of Jesus Christ (issued not long after the death of Augustus), 'Render unto Caesar that which is Caesar's' (Mark 12.15–17). For Jesus to pick up a Roman denarius and decide from its image (*eikon*) that it counted as 'that of Caesar' (*ta Kaisaros*) rather than 'that of God' (*ta tou Theou*) may have fobbed off a group of trouble-stirring Pharisees; but the original numismatic message suggestively identified imperial power with divine.

That episode is also logged in Matthew's Gospel (22.21), with more than a hint of the author's self-justification, since Matthew was himself a tax-gatherer, in the business of collecting tariffs due to Caesar. Locally recruited tax-collectors and 'tax-farmers' (*publicani*) – individuals who contracted with government for the right to

364 *Silver denarius of Octavian (the future Augustus), c. 30 BC. In the image wars between Octavian and Mark Antony, coins were powerful weapons; while Antony associated himself with Dionysos, Octavian was shown as the laurel-crowned earthly embodiment of Apollo.*

365 *Silver denarius of Faustina the Younger, daughter of the Emperor Antoninus Pius and wife of the Emperor Hadrian, c. AD 161. By the 2nd century BC, the silver content of Roman coins was substantially reduced.*

gather revenues – were key operators within the Roman provincial administrations; and they were highly unpopular among the Jewish communities of Judaea, where they were perceived as collaborators with an occupying army. As, indeed, they were. The basic economic logic of the Roman Empire was that the emperor himself was its richest individual; he was therefore not only the commander (*imperator*) of the army, but ultimately its chief paymaster.

The need to finance a large army had been a primary reason for the adoption of coinage at Rome (during the wars against Hannibal and others in the 3rd century BC). By the mid-2nd century AD, something like three-quarters of the total imperial budget – estimated at around 225 million denarii – was being spent annually on maintaining armed forces of over 400,000 men. Vast quantities of coins were put into circulation merely by military operations. (A legionary soldier at the time of Septimius Severus received an annual *stipendium*, 'weight', of some 600 denarii.)

Some emperors distributed periodic handouts of coins to the civilian population. The subdivision of the basic silver denarius into lesser units of bronze (notably the sestertius, worth 4 asses, with the as in turn composed of smaller denominations) meant that coinage served the daily purchasing needs of people at all levels of society. Because of its ubiquitous utility, coinage remained the most effective way for an emperor to circulate images not only of himself, but of members of his family [365–67]. Yet for all this flow of currency in the Roman Empire, a cluster of historical factors warn us against characterizing it as a proto-modern 'monetary economy'. Throughout the centuries of Roman imperial rule there was a general state of 'low liquidity, or short cash supply' – even when, in the 'Golden Age' of Augustus, a new high-value coin of gold, the aureus (worth 25 denarii) was introduced. Supplies of official coinage were continually stretched by the demands of empire, resulting in forgery, inflation, and repeated debasements (the denarius, solid silver under Augustus, had lost most of its silver content two centuries later). Moreover, the absence of a dependable banking system meant that the safest thing to do with savings was generally to bury them – hence the 'hoards' so eagerly sought by modern hunters with metal-detectors.

We have noted that the word 'economy' has Greek roots. The words 'money' and 'monetary' are of Latin origin, deriving from the place where coins were once minted at Rome – the Temple of Juno Moneta (usually taken to mean 'the warning Juno'). We may also note that our term 'interest' comes from the Latin verb *interesse*, 'to come between'. There was moneylending in the Roman world, officially (after 88 BC) subject to a maximum interest rate of 12 per cent. But whether the term 'monetary economy' can be applied to any part or period of the Classical world is debatable. Some historians argue that the 'decline and fall of the Roman Empire' was indeed the climax of a fundamental failure among the Greeks and Romans to create fiscal policies that balanced assets against credits and debts; and that the Roman Empire ultimately taxed itself out of existence. But rather than analyse such hypotheses further – fiscal policies in the modern world are perplexing enough – perhaps we can conclude this section by recapitulating the core faith of the Classical economy. It is here paraphrased from the opening remarks of *On Agriculture*, written *c.* 150 BC by Cato the Elder (see p. 144) – speaking on behalf of all believers in the tradition of Mediterranean subsistence farming:

> Yes, making money through trade can be more profitable – so long as you accept the risks; and the same goes for money-lending – if only it were honourable. That was the attitude of our forefathers, which they cast in law by making the penalty for usury double the penalty for theft. Their accolades for upright citizens were invariably reserved for the 'good farmer' or the 'model smallholder'. True, I count the trader as a hard-working type, and one striving to make good; but, as I say, trading is a dangerous, sometimes calamitous career. It is from those who work the land that the sturdiest men, the most resilient soldiers derive. Farmers are the most respected and least resented members of society: no livelihood is more stable than theirs, and no job gives more satisfaction to those who do it.

366, 367 *Bronze sestertius of Marcus Aurelius, c. AD 180. This issue is posthumous, on one side hailing the emperor as 'divus' (deified), and on the other alluding to the four-storey funeral pyre of Marcus Aurelius, with the legend that his deification ('consecratio') was sanctioned by senate decree.*

VII PHILOSOPHY AND EDUCATION

'THE UNEXAMINED LIFE IS NOT WORTH LIVING'

I T WAS the Anglo-American philosopher Alfred North Whitehead who sweepingly declared – in the early 20th century – all Western philosophy to be 'a series of footnotes to Plato'. Whitehead also put it another way: whichever path of enquiry modern philosophers might take, they always meet Plato coming back in the opposite direction. So Western philosophy was not only invented by the Greeks: they are also claimed to have explored its limits.

'Love of knowledge' is what *philosophia* literally means. Systematic pursuit of intellectual questions and logical argumentation were the signs of this love, a passion exemplified by no one more than Socrates [369, 370, 546]. Socrates used to say that he was without wisdom (*sophia*), but was curious to find out which of his contemporaries truly possessed it. That he proved a nuisance to political authorities in Athens may be judged a predictable consequence of that curiosity. (In fact the double charge eventually brought against him by an Athenian court in 399 was that he had 'introduced strange deities' to the city, and 'corrupted the youth'.) His death (see p. 16) was – as he surely intended – a martyrdom that only increased and fortified his disciples; and the most devoted of those disciples was Plato [373], whose many writings feature Socrates in dialogue.

How much of Plato's elegant prose gives us Socrates *verbatim*, or how far Plato uses Socrates as the mouthpiece for his own ideas, is debatable. Socrates was a tireless talker, Plato no mere scribe. Yet it is clear that Socrates himself did much to 'set the agenda' of philosophy in the sense understood today. His method was 'dialectical' – putting up questions, trying their answers. Xenophon preserves a list of some typically 'Socratic' questions. 'What is pious? What is impious? What is honourable? What is shameful? What is just? What is unjust? What is self-control, and what is foolishness? What counts as courage, and what as cowardice? What is a state, and what does it mean to be a statesman? What is government? By what right do some men rule over others?' – and so on (*Memorabilia* 1.1.16).

Plato, and Aristotle after him, would extend the scope of philosophy beyond the ethical and political topics that preoccupied Socrates. But there is no doubt that Socrates both personified and pioneered the ideal of the 'examined life' (*bios theoretikos*), and established the philosopher's vocation as essentially interrogative. ('The unexamined life is not worth living for a human being', as cited in Plato, *Apology* 38a.) Socrates set himself apart from those who sold their wisdom like a commodity, the so-called 'Sophists' or 'Wise Ones' who earned large sums of money by teaching various 'life skills' to the young men of Greek cities – especially the art of oratory, which was a highly valued commodity in the law-courts or democratic assembly. As one prominent Sophist, Protagoras, pointed out, every argument has two sides – so cleverness consisted in being able to argue a case either way, with equal fervour and application. Another successful Sophist, Gorgias, used a fluent and persuasive speech (the *Encomium of Helen*) to argue that nothing was more powerful than a persuasive speech. Socrates disdained the practice of charging a drachma per head for such 'exhibitions' (*epideixeis*) of intellectual wizardry. He refused to accept the Sophists' assumption that all

368 *Marble head of a philosopher, carved in the 3rd century AD and reworked in the 5th century. 'Pagan wisdom' is embodied in such portraits – even when (as in this case) the identity of the particular philosopher remains obscure to us.*

369 opposite *Wall-painting of Socrates seated, from a house at Ephesus, second half of the 1st century AD. Here, the name 'Sokrates' above the figure was hardly necessary: his blunt 'satyric' features [370] were part of his enduring cult reputation.*

370 *Marble portrait of Socrates: Roman copy of a type probably created in the 4th century BC, not long after the philosopher's 'martyrdom'.*

371 opposite   Seven Sages *mosaic from Torre Annunziata near Pompeii, c. 100 BC. This image of philosophers and scientists in discussion – holding their scrolls, and with a globe in the foreground – may derive from a painted evocation of Plato's Academy.*

individuals were primarily motivated by self-interest; and he judged that the Sophists' own self-interest clouded their claim to teach 'virtue' (*arete*).

The Socratic method was more critical than practical, and its aims were quite unworldly. While he was manifestly rigorous in his discussions, Socrates was not combative in the manner of the Sophists. He regarded the search for truth as a communal endeavour among friends. Above all he was, as we should say, 'idealistic' about human nature. In book 2 of Plato's *Republic*, we find Socrates and his friends discussing how someone would behave if he found a ring that made him invisible. Those around Socrates, as most of us might, presumed that some mischief would ensue. But Socrates was steadfast. A good man with the power of invisibility would continue to do good. No-one, Socrates believed, wanted to do evil – not if they thought about it; not if they had knowledge. Goodness was not a state of innocence. It came from knowing things – which in turn came from asking questions. That was why, he said, 'the unexamined life is not worth living'. Or to cite Plato's baseline belief: 'Every soul is deprived of truth against its will' (*Republic* 413a).

Socrates never claimed to offer a 'world view' or dogma. His method was his message. In this sense there is little more to say about him. Two aspects of his influence, however, deserve further notice.

One concerns his physical appearance. Socrates was notoriously an exception to his own rule that beauty was a sign of goodness (see p. 28). Bald, pug-nosed, stocky, and pot-bellied, he seemed even to his dearest admirers like some kind of satyr [369, 370, 546]. Yet he also showed astonishing levels of physical resilience, and had proved conspicuously brave while on active military service. It followed that by appearing so atypical and 'out of place' (*atopos*), the person of Socrates seemed to embody the extraordinary nature of his insight and authority. 'Bearded egghead' is an abrupt way of describing the 'Socratic look' as it has been identified down the centuries (including, for instance, the biologist Charles Darwin); yet there is a certain sameness about all subsequent portraits of Classical philosophers that has prompted one scholar, Paul Zanker, to speak of a 'mask of Socrates' that any Greek or Roman with intellectual aspirations (or pretensions) – including early Christian saints [129] would wear. Looking at a bearded sculptural type, we can say that the subject is unquestionably a philosopher [368], though which one we cannot be sure.

The second feature of Socratic influence is more oblique. We know that Socrates himself was proud that he could 'philosophize' in the marketplace, while on a military campaign, or anywhere. It was Plato who created a dedicated precinct for seeking knowledge in the Athenian suburb known as the Academy [371]. (There was already a gymnasium here, by the burial site of an obscure Bronze Age hero called Akademos.) But before Plato's 'Academy' became eponymous to the endeavour of 'higher education' generally, the Socratic insistence upon the value of the 'examined life' had furthered a particular trend in Classical domestic architecture. One examined one's life in an enclave of tranquillity: away from the crowds, detached from the hurly-burly of everyday democratic politics, but with a coterie of chosen friends, sharing a preference for 'the sovereignty of the good'. For some Athenians, the best place for such contemplative activity was at home – or rather, at a home with an inner recess congenial to gentle perambulation and discussion. So we find appearing in the age of Socrates the first urban 'peristyle houses' – houses with an inner colonnaded courtyard [cf. 334]. These were havens for those citizens who had free time at their disposal. The Greek word for free time or 'leisure' is *schole*. And so we see where our 'schools' and 'scholars' come from. You go to school, you become a scholar – because you have no more pressing claim upon your time than the pursuit of knowledge.

The text of the Hortensius, *Cicero's dialogue about the value of philosophy, does not survive intact. But there is no doubting the force of its message upon the young Augustine in* AD 373:

[In my late teens] I began reading the textbooks of rhetoric. It was a discipline in which I wanted to become eminent – a damnable desire, inflated with all the zest of human vanity. But in the course of this study I came across a certain text by Cicero – the Cicero whose style is so widely admired (his content not so). This book of his, called the *Hortensius*, is an exhortation in praise of philosophy. And it utterly changed my life. It directed my prayers to you, Lord; it charged me with new resolves and ambitions. All my former useless hopes disgusted me. With an amazing energy in my heart, I now craved the immortality of wisdom, and began to rise up and address myself to you . . . My God, how I burned for you then . . . for with you is wisdom. The Greeks call this love of wisdom 'philosophy' – that was what set me on fire, ardent to leave the things of earth . . .

St Augustine, *Confessions* 3.4.7

THE 'SCHOOLS' OF CLASSICAL PHILOSOPHY

The pivotal importance of Socrates in the history of Classical philosophy is reflected by the fact that the Greek philosophers before his time are often labelled as 'the Pre-Socratics'. This is more a term of chronological convenience, and should not imply a close intellectual fraternity amongst Greek thinkers from Thales (born in the late 7th century BC) to Democritus (born in the mid-5th century BC). However, Socrates himself was able to identify a cluster of questions and speculations that characterized philosophy when he was a young man – and which were largely put in the background when he himself reoriented the philosopher's vocation.

It is a significant anecdote about the first acknowledged Greek philosopher, Thales of Miletos, that he fell into a ditch while gazing at the stars (Plato, *Theaetetus* 174a–b); also significant is the legend that another Pre-Socratic, Empedocles of Sicily, died when he leapt headlong into Mount Etna's volcanic crater. The Pre-Socratics were interested in the nature of the universe, the elemental fabric of

372 The School of Athens: *fresco by Raphael in the Stanza della Segnatura in the Vatican, Rome. Commissioned in 1508–1509 to decorate the private library of Pope Julius II, Raphael created a fantasy scene, bringing together very diverse Greek 'intellectuals' – including Pythagoras (left foreground, writing, next to a diagram of musical harmonies), Diogenes (reclining on the steps), and Euclid (right foreground, bending down to demonstrate a geometrical theorem) – and integrating them with traditions of post-Classical learning. Central to the composition are the figures of Plato (with long white hair and beard, holding his Timaeus) and Aristotle (holding his Ethics); Plato points upwards, to his lofty realm of transcendental 'Forms', while Aristotle points downwards, interested in more 'earthly' affairs.*

the world as divided between earth, air, fire, and water; they tended to be prophetic figures, trailing scattered testimonies to their social eccentricity. Few of them left treatises that survive beyond fragments; some evidently only ever issued gnomic utterances. The reported sayings of Heraclitus from Ephesus, for example, range from deeply enigmatic phrases ('Night and day are one') to nuggets of folkloristic good sense ('Donkeys would rather have garbage than gold') and explicit denunciations of religious practices ('You might as well pray to a brick wall as to a statue').

Pre-Socratic philosophers had neither microscopes nor telescopes – so their earnest musings about particles of matter and the composition of the galaxy might seem rather laughable today. In their time, however, some of them gained devoted disciples. One was Pythagoras. Mathematics was of central importance to him: he taught that numbers (*arithmoi*) were built into the nature of all things, so that everything could be expressed numerically, including the ultimate philosophical

373 *Marble portrait of Plato, probably a Roman copy of an original 4th-century BC type attributed to Silanion. The rapport between Plato and Socrates remains hard to quantify. It may be sufficient to note that many of the titles of Plato's works relate to characters with whom Socrates speaks.*

Central to Plato's philosophy was the doctrine of ideal 'Forms' – crudely summarized, that all material and discernible things (whether a table, an animal, or an idea) reflected a perfect essence that existed independently in an immaterial universe, that of the Forms. The theory is most famously expressed in the 'Allegory of the Cave' in the Republic (514a–518d): there human beings are compared to 'prisoners' in a cave, who mistakenly take the shadows projected by things to be reality itself.

goal of 'attunement', or *harmonia* (see p. 281) . But Pythagoras offered his followers more than a single 'big idea'. From his oral instructions (*akousmata*) a doctrinal package of 'Pythagoreanism' can be partly reassembled, and it shows a nice internal logic. For instance, Pythagoras believed in reincarnation – the process whereby an individual soul inhabits one body after another. Once, we are told, he stopped a man from whipping a dog because in the animal's yelping he recognized 'the soul of a friend'. Souls, he maintained, were resident in all living creatures. If that were so, then butchering a cow could be tantamount to murder – and Pythagoras duly preached vegetarianism (p. 67).

Vegetarianism would never become a widespread practice in the Classical world. But the reasoning by which Pythagoras advocated abstention from meat was based on a recurrent and often central feature of Classical philosophy: the belief that mortal beings possessed 'souls'. The Greek word for 'soul', *psyche*, filters into everyday modern parlance through terms such as 'psychology' and 'psychiatric'; the Latin equivalent, *anima*, is also behind our words 'animal' and 'animated'. Such etymology is sufficient to suggest that the Classical concept of a soul is something like an 'inner self' or spirit that essentially gives life to moribund or temporary matter. As we have previously noted, in antiquity there was little physiological comprehension of how the human brain functioned. Commonly it was understood that the faculty of intelligence and consciousness was located in the chest (where the voice came from). Essentially, however, the soul must remain elusive to describe. The soul was that which invested a body with life. A body could die; the soul, being the very principle of life, was 'beyond the physical' – or even 'immortal'.

Creating separate entities of 'soul' and 'body', or 'mind' and 'matter' is sometimes referred to as 'dualism'. It would be too much to claim that every Classical philosopher was a 'dualist'. However, one way of outlining the various schools or sects after Socrates is to compare their teachings about the nature of the soul. Metaphysical speculation was not the only scope of philosophy post-Socrates. But Socrates and Plato together made 'the immortality of the soul' a central premiss of philosophical enquiry; it was a concern that no successor could evade.

The direct intellectual descendant of Plato was Aristotle – who died in 322 BC, one year after the demise of his most famous pupil, Alexander the Great. His school at Athens was the Lyceum, which enclosed a covered walkway or *peripatos* – giving the name 'Peripatetic' to the Aristotelians. Aristotle has been cited often enough throughout this book, for his range of interests was vast, and no Classical philosopher was more lovingly adopted and adapted by Christian thinkers throughout the Middle Ages – meaning that Aristotle's writings have generally survived well, and have influenced certain areas of modern philosophy – notably logic – *ad nauseam*.

Some of Aristotle's sayings betray his Platonic pedigree regarding the soul (for instance, his nice definition of close friendship as 'one soul in two bodies': cf. pp. 49–50). But otherwise Aristotle tends to depart from Plato in allowing regular interaction between mind and matter. Biology and the classification of species were two of Aristotle's key endeavours. Aristotle developed a way of thinking about the world in terms of 'universals' and 'particulars', whereby an abstract or collective concept (such as 'beauty' or 'flower') was necessarily expressed in some 'particular' form (such as 'a beautiful orchid'). It followed that organic bodies were not just temporary shelters for roving souls, but imprinted and individualized by them.

Aristotle's teaching on this topic was the subject of furious dispute among his medieval commentators; but it provides a certain link to a philosophical sect that

374 *Diogenes, founder of Cynicism, with Alexander the Great: detail of a restored Roman marble relief, c. late 2nd century AD. Known as 'the dog' – hence the creature above him – Diogenes legendarily lived in a large storage jar in the Agora of Athens. When Alexander the Great paid him a visit and asked what he could do for the beggarly philosopher, Diogenes is alleged to have replied, 'You can stop blocking my sunlight.'*

375 *Marble bust of Epicurus, late 1st century BC, perhaps once part of the decoration of a Roman house. The stern features of the philosopher suggest that his teachings were not synonymous with 'hedonism'.*

developed in Athens towards the end of the 4th century BC, Epicureanism. Its founder, Epicurus [375], held that the soul was composed of atoms, and died when the body died. There was, accordingly, only one life for human beings; and their duty was to make it as happy as possible while it lasted. To indulge earthly pleasures before this absolute end eventually gave the Epicureans a reputation for sensuality and hedonism – the Roman poet Horace expressing this consequence of Epicureanism most succinctly in his motto *carpe diem*: 'seize the day' (*Odes* I.II.8). Predictably, critics of this attitude misrepresented it as a deplorable sort of hedonism, compounded by ungodliness (Epicurus taught that the universe came about by accident, not divine creation). But the Epicurean ideal of living in a state of 'freedom from disturbance' (*ataraxia*) could equally be achieved by a discipline of simplicity and self-denial. If one had little in the way of wealth and possessions, then one had little to worry about.

This kind of insouciance or unworldliness certainly characterizes the philosophical movement which flourished in various parts of the Mediterranean in the late 4th and 3rd centuries BC, Cynicism. It was hardly a 'school': those who identified themselves as 'Cynics' would have scorned the notion of fixed premises, lectures, and libraries. Instead, taking their example from the eccentric figure of Diogenes, they went around as vagabonds, ostentatiously disrespectful of social norms. Diogenes, from whose sobriquet 'doglike' (*kynikos*) the group gained its name, had been happy to live in an old pithos, or storage jar [374]. Rich tales were attached to Diogenes' austere mode of existence and direct methods of exemplifying his core message of self-sufficiency (*autarkeia*); it seems life was never dull when the Cynics were around. We are told, for example, that a group of them in Athens made a practice of eating tulips before a meeting of the Assembly: disgesting tulips (it seems) causes spectacular flatulence, and so these Cynics were able to fart loudly throughout the most pompous speeches of important politicians.

376 *Bronze equestrian statue of Marcus Aurelius, c. AD 180. This image is one of very few ancient statues believed to have stayed on view in Rome throughout late antiquity and the Middle Ages, and it has often been taken as a stereotype of imperial power. The irony is that, to judge from his* Meditations, *Marcus Aurelius himself was painfully conscious of his own transience – and set little store by his status as emperor. Although this statue's scale and pose (with extended hand, as if addressing his subjects) betray his political power, the face takes up the 'mask' of the Greek philosopher.*

It may be a short move from the attitude we understand as 'cynical' to the state of mind we call 'sceptical'. In fact the ancient Sceptics were a product of the Athenian Academy during the late 4th century BC. Their dogma was the fallibility of all dogma. Like Socrates, they doubted that anyone was truly wise. Unlike Socrates, some Sceptics could therefore assert that all philosophy was a waste of time, and we should get on with enjoying ourselves. Others (notably one called Carneades, who was in charge of the Academy at Athens in the mid-2nd century BC, and also took his teachings to Rome), shaped Scepticism into a delicate system of making judgments on the basis of probability. We might not *know* anything for certain; but by weighing up competing claims, and on the basis of what has happened in the past, we can at least act for the best.

In the second half of the 1st century AD another Greek philosopher came to Rome. His name was Epictetus, and he was an ex-slave. One of his experiences as a slave had been to endure torture by his master. Epictetus remarked: 'If you continue with this, you'll break my leg.' The torture went on, the leg was broken; and Epictetus, in the same calm voice, remarked: 'There. What did I tell you?' The practical implication is that he will now be unfit for work. The philosophical significance is that he was a Stoic. A Stoic knew how to suffer extremes of pain with dignity.

Epictetus, in whose influential *Discourses*, published by Arrian, that anecdote is to be found (3.24), was not himself the most original of Stoic thinkers. Stoic doctrines emerged, again, from Athens, *c.* 300 BC, with Zeno, who taught in the precincts of the Stoa Poikile, or Painted Stoa, in the Athenian Agora [302:15] – whence the name 'Stoicism'. Kleanthes and Chrysippos were also articulate protagonists of the Stoic faith in an unalterable, divine-ordered cosmos, and a world where wisdom consisted in 'freedom from passion' (*apatheia*) – the renunciation or rational suppression of fear, anger, desire, and distress. Subsequently, a prolific and versatile Syrian-born writer called Posidonius did much to make a system of Stoicism that was attractive to the Romans. If one can make such cultural generalizations, Stoic values may be said to have fitted conveniently with the Roman sense of doing one's 'duty' (*officium*). Cicero was a sympathizer, and Seneca a distinguished adherent. But no Roman Stoic is more engaging than the Emperor Marcus Aurelius [376], whose notes 'To Himself' (or *Meditations*, as they are usually titled) were composed mainly while he was on campaign north of the Danube in the late 2nd century AD. Even for an emperor, military service was filled with discomfort, weariness, and pain. So Marcus reminds himself, repeatedly, that these are passing afflictions. Whether in wretchedness or luxury, the body has not long on earth. 'You are nothing but a little soul dragging along a corpse, as Epictetus said . . .' (*Meditations* 4.27). But for all that this 'little soul' (*psycharion*) was encumbered by moribund flesh and bones, and Marcus treasured it as a refuge – his 'inner citadel'.

Marcus wore a beard: he looked the part of a Classical philosopher. His predecessor Hadrian had been the first Roman emperor to cultivate this Greek 'academic' image – to put on 'the mask of Socrates' [149, 531]. Hadrian was himself an active protagonist in the epoch of scholarly and philosophical enthusiasm known as the Second Sophistic, when rhetoricians and lecturers travelled around the Roman Empire enjoying celebrity status. In the 3rd century AD, Diogenes Laertius collected the lives of distinguished philosophers up until the Second Sophistic, making it clear how much this or that philosophical 'movement' or intellectual trend depended upon a single personality. The stars of the Second Sophistic may have been quibbling over minor refinements of what had gone before – adding, we might say, only further pedantic footnotes to Plato. But the development of Classical philosophy was still active, as demonstrated by the school that gathered around Plotinus [540] and Porphyry in Rome during the mid-3rd century. They are termed 'Neo-Platonists'; but in the eloquent discourses by Plotinus on the life of 'the mind' (*nous*) we find a psychological introspection that Plato never broached.

As it happened, the work of Plotinus made Plato's thinking useful to Christian theologians; Plotinus, too, would be echoed loudly in the subsequent literature of Christian 'mysticism' – the tradition of achieving spiritual ecstasy by 'becoming one' with the divine. It was a robustly Christian emperor, Justinian, who in AD 529 finally closed down the Academy and the other schools of philosophy at Athens. Thanks largely to a cross-cultural love of learning in the Arab world, the texts of 'pagan wisdom' were not all consigned to oblivion. But the indebtedness of Christianity to the Classical philosophical tradition was already marked. Aurelius Augustinus, or 'St Augustine' – perhaps the most influential thinker of the early Western Church – admitted that his own Christian conviction had come from reading Cicero (p. 233). And just five years before the closure of the Academy, Boethius, a high-ranking official at the court of Theodoric, the Ostrogothic king of Italy, drew deeply upon Classical sources for his semi-poetic dialogue *The Consolation of Philosophy*. Boethius wrote this while in prison and awaiting execution for suspected involvement in an anti-royal plot. His situation was truly Socratic; and the Christian Boethius had no qualms in reaching for Socrates, Plato, and Aristotle as a 'Holy Trinity' of inspirational enlightenment.

PAIDEIA AND THE PRINCIPLES OF CLASSICAL EDUCATION

Educare is a Latin verb which literally means 'to lead forward'. This is a crucial fact of etymology for those who believe that *education* is fundamentally a project of developing an individual's potential, rather than driving individuals into herds. It should not imply, however, that Classical systems of education were models of liberal enlightenment. Generally it is true that schools for young people (or rather, young males) in Greece and Rome were intended to produce 'good citizens'.

377 *A schoolroom scene, on a sandstone relief from Neumagen In Germany, c. AD 200. A boy arrives at class and finds his two contemporaries already at work, reading from papyrus scrolls. A 'Socratic' beard distinguishes the master (*magister*) here.*

379 Terracotta statuette of a woman carrying a child on her shoulders, from Boeotia, c. 500–474 BC. Typical of the so-called 'Tanagra' style of figurines, this seems a generic image of daily life [cf. 96]. The woman may be mother or nurse.

But the requirements of good citizenship might be very remote from the ideal of producing alert and inquisitive minds. At Sparta, for instance, boys from the age of seven were taken from their homes and put into military-style barracks whose disciplinarian régimes would make any modern juvenile detention centre or boot camp seem soft. What served the Spartan *polis* was an army of unswervingly drilled and obedient warriors, not masters of geometry.

Aristotle probably voiced a common opinion in antiquity when he described children as essentially irrational. In Athens, as at Sparta, these irrational creatures were tended mainly by their mothers till they were seven. They had toys – dolls, miniature carts and animals [378, 380] – and little else to do but play at home and be suckled and fed like burgeoning livestock. That stage or element of straightforward rearing was referred to as *tropheia*. Then came *paideia*. Though it literally connotes no more than being a child (*pais*), *paideia* entailed more than 'upbringing'. To translate it as 'education' is also inadequate. According to Plato, *paideia* was principally the schooling in moral sensibility or *arete* (*Laws* 643e). Not long after Plato, however, *paideia* came to entail whatever things of value that could be stored within the mind – 'knowledge', 'understanding', and 'culture'.

In Homer's *Odyssey*, it happens that when Odysseus goes off to take part in the expedition to Troy, he entrusts an old friend called Mentor with the running of his household. When the French writer François Fénelon composed his 1699 romance *Télémaque*, elaborating the tale of Odysseus' son Telemachos, the role of Mentor as counsellor was enlarged, and the word 'mentor' gained currency as a generic term for a senior advisor. Children in Classical Greece, however, might have been more likely to associate Homer's Mentor with the type they knew as a *paidagogos* – the elderly man whose job it was to take them to school and back. Though it was a servile role, this was quite literally a 'leading forth' to the world of learning.

'Schools' as institutions did not exist before the advent of literacy in Greece – which happened between the late 8th and early 6th centuries BC. By contrast to Etruria, where it was very much a case of 'restricted literacy' – the skills of reading

and writing confined to an élite group of priests, magistrates, and aristocrats – education in the Greek alphabet soon became relatively normal for citizens and artisans. Slaves might also be included: from the Roman world, in particular, there are clear instances of slaves being rather more literate (and numerate) than their masters. It is not so clear to what extent girls were admitted into the classrooms (which would surely have been segregated). We know however that at least some female teachers existed: one of the Fayum portraits from Graeco-Roman Egypt defines a lady called Hermione as a *grammatike* – meaning a professional scholar or instructor of reading, writing, and arithmetic.

With the *grammatike* or *grammatistes* children practised their letters and numbers on writing tablets [385]. They also learned lines of poetry [381]: the epics of Homer were 'set texts' by the mid-6th century BC. In keeping with the rhapsodic tradition, music and lyrical recitation were also taught (by a *kitharistes*) [382];

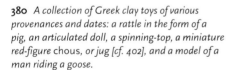

380 *A collection of Greek clay toys of various provenances and dates: a rattle in the form of a pig, an articulated doll, a spinning-top, a miniature red-figure chous, or jug [cf. 402], and a model of a man riding a goose.*

381 *right   A boy reading from a scroll: fragment of an Attic red-figure kylix attributed to the Akestorides Painter, c. 470–450 BC. The text appears to be part of the poet Hesiod's* Catalogue of Women.

382 *below   A 'school room' scene, on an Attic red-figure kylix signed by Douris, c. 480 BC. We see one boy, at the left, having a lesson in the art of playing the aulos (pipes); another in the art of writing, from a master using a stylus and wax tablet. The mature bearded figure on the right turns round on his stool to witness the proceedings. Note the lyre hanging on the wall.*

383 *opposite   Three boys playing a game of knucklebones (in principle similar to marbles): detail of an Attic red-figure chous attributed to the Painter of Boston 10.190, c. 440–430 BC. The jug was very likely produced for the Anthesteria festival [cf. 402], when on a day called 'Jugs' (Choes) three-year-old boys were formally admitted to their father's extended family group.*

and, of course, there was physical training, which came under the supervision of a *paidotribes* (whose title, 'boy-rubber', implies that he showed apprentice wrestlers how to oil and dust themselves for sparring). In all these activities, discipline was strictly enforced by corporal punishment. Floggings were routine, and parents expected no less. 'Aristotle played the taws / Upon the bottom of a king of kings', in the lines of W. B. Yeats ('Among School Children'): even young Alexander the Great could expect no leniency from his distinguished tutor.

Formal examinations were not conducted, and no qualifications awarded. With competitive occasions so frequent in the sporting and theatrical religious calendar of Greek city-states, there were numerous opportunities for prize pupils to make their mark. Plato, in both the *Republic* and his *Laws*, argued vigorously for a curriculum of subjects that focused exclusively upon what was deemed useful for the good of the *polis*. His dialogue *Timaeus* lays particular stress upon what Plato regarded as the core mathematical sciences of arithmetic, geometry, astronomy, and musical theory – later grouped as the 'fourfold discipline' (*Quadrivium*) of medieval European universities. But since schools in Plato's Greece tended to be private initiatives, funded by fees from their pupils, anyone could set up a particular programme of intellectual and physical instruction. Contemporary with Plato, for example, was Isokrates at Athens, whose school (established *c.* 390 BC) followed the Sophists in laying special emphasis upon learning the tricks of rhetoric.

In the second half of the 4th century, Macedonian conquests carried Greek as a language far beyond the Greek mainland, islands, and colonies. Leaving aside the moot issue of how closely 'Macedonian' and 'Greek' were linguistically related, we can accept that the use of *koine* (common dialect) Greek as a language of convenience, as a sign of cross-ethnic 'communality', is the prime defining feature of the Hellenistic period. Literacy in the Greek language was not only a cultural acquisition, but had clear commercial value. This may explain why there was a marked development of 'state education' from the 4th century onwards. To judge from a number of reported or surviving decrees – notably from Delphi, Teos, Miletos, and Rhodes – schools were established by the process of 'euergetism':

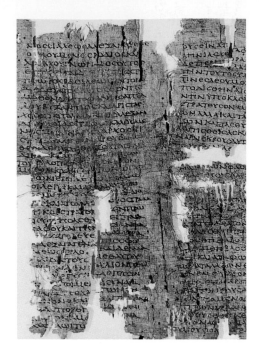

384 *Names of early directors of the great library at Alexandria founded by Ptolemy I in the late 4th century BC, on a papyrus fragment from Oxyrhynchus, 2nd century AD. The poet Apollonius of Rhodes and the mathematician and geographer Eratosthenes are among those listed. Prior to its mysterious destruction (probably during the 1st century BC) the Alexandrian library is thought to have contained almost half a million volumes.*

private benefactions for public good. A wealthy citizen or a generous ruler would endow a capital fund to pay the stipends of teachers, presumably making it possible for children to be educated if their parents could not otherwise afford it. At Miletos *c.* 200 BC a teacher's annual salary was fixed as 480 drachmas – a modest honorarium, sufficient for basic subsistence. *Plus ça change.*

Though Classical authorities disagreed over the relative importance of physical education, the location of a school was generally as an annexe or integral part of a city gymnasium. In these precincts, too, libraries came to be established. The grandest expressions of 'book-treasuring' (*bibliophilia*) happened at Pergamon (promoted by the Attalid ruling dynasty) and at Alexandria (under the sponsorship of the Ptolemies). Alexandria claimed the largest collection of texts, attracting scholars from all over the Greek-speaking world [384]: this was the library that would eventually be burnt down (quite when, and whether by accident or not, we do not know). But Pergamon became virtually synonymous with manuscripts. Our word 'parchment' derives from the type of animal membrane stretched and treated for writing which was known in Latin as *pergamenum*, or (later) *pergamentum*. The Romans inherited all these manuscripts when the last of the Attalids, Attalos III, made his will *c.* 133 BC – bequeathing, indeed, the entire kingdom of Pergamon to Rome.

The cultural centrality of such institutions as the library at Pergamon was not undermined by the Roman conquest of Greece and the Hellenistic kingdoms. 'Conquered Greece has conquered its rough victor' observed Horace (*Epistles* 2.1.156: see p. 178), meaning that the ideals and products of Greek *paideia* effectively came to dominate 'high culture' at Rome. To be literate in Greek as well as Latin was an admirable aspiration in the eyes of Cicero; to spend time at Athens was regarded rather like a 'finishing school' for the sons of Roman nobility. For all that distinguished Republican figures such as Cato the Elder had previously made a point of not delegating their children's education to anyone – the good Roman *paterfamilias* should take it upon himself to impart everything from spelling to javelin-throwing [378] – teaching was already a profession largely assigned by Romans to Greeks, even at the domestic and elementary level. Pedagogues and private tutors were usually of Greek ethnic origin; and if not slaves, then maintained in genteel poverty.

385 *Roman school materials: a writing tablet with pen ledge and bronze inkwell, from Vaison-la-Romaine, France, 1st–2nd century AD, and a book (far right) that belonged to an inhabitant of the Fayum in Egypt called Theodorus. In provinces such as Gaul, the cultivation of* eloquentia – *literacy and rhetorical skills – was germane to the process of 'Romanization' (see p. 196). One of the most celebrated 'Sophists' of the 2nd century AD, Favorinus, came from Arles in the south of France.*

Many children in the Roman world only ever went to a 'primary school' (again, on reaching the age of seven), where a *magister* or *litterator* taught them basic alphabet and arithmetic skills [377, 385]. At ten or eleven, they were set to work in some sort of trade. Those pursuing secondary schooling continued with a *grammaticus*, who would develop their faculties of literary and oratorical expression, their appreciation of language and literature, and their range of general knowledge. Finally (after fifteen) – and particularly for boys aiming to follow a legal or political career – there was the *rhetor*, who specialized in the art of verbal expression. The first Latin handbook of this discipline, the *Rhetoric addressed to Herennius*, was produced in the early 1st century BC; subsequently it was an imperially appointed professor of rhetoric, Quintilian, who in his *Education of an Orator* (*Institutio Oratoria*) of c. AD 95 showed how being 'skilled in speaking' (*peritus dicendi*) ultimately defined 'the good man' (*vir bonus*).

Quintilian's own writing is charged with moral sensibility. He may be cited, for instance, as one of the very few Classical writers on education to deplore the practice of flogging students for their misdemeanours. But the systematic training in Latin rhetoric was in any case closely bound up with ethical and judicial issues. Two particular exercises of this schooling deserve mention, *controversiae* ('controversies', or 'debatable topics') and *suasoriae* ('deliberations', or 'advisory speeches'). For a *controversia*, the instructor would give his pupils some kind of dilemma – such as: 'Is evidence given by a man under torture admissible in court?' – and get them to argue for (*pro*) and against (*contra*), using suitable sequences of logic, historical case-studies, and so on. A mock-vote might be held at the end of the class session, to judge who had assembled the most powerful argument. A *suasoria* involved perhaps more literary artifice, but would again be presented by declamation. It generally required the student to put himself in a certain historical situation, and meet the demands of a public-speaking occasion. For example: imagine you are the Carthaginian commander Hannibal. You are about to lead thousands of weary and apprehensive troops across the Alps – plus a number of even more apprehensive elephants. What would you say to your men, to encourage them across the mountains?

So the Roman education system acknowledged that an empire was not built on military genius alone, but also on the skills of negotiation and the power of address.

VIII DIONYSOS : APOLLO

A PHILOSOPHER'S POLARITY

DIONYSOS: orgiastic frenzy, excess, mania. Apollo: order, restraint, control. This is the polarity made famous by the German philosopher Friedrich Nietzsche in his essay *The Birth of Tragedy* (1872). On one side is raw nature, spontaneous and wild – the realm of Dionysos. On the other is the cool, calm, and collected cosmos of Apollo, the god of 'nothing in excess'. Dionysos provides escape from our sense of individual self ('ecstasy', literally 'standing outside of oneself'); Apollo, the god of prophecy and the sun (hence his epithet 'Phoebus', the 'Bright'), provides illusion and insight – literal and metaphorical enlightenment. 'It is by those two art-sponsoring deities, Apollo and Dionysos,' Nietzsche surmises, 'that we are made to recognize the tremendous split, as regards both origins and objectives, between the plastic, Apollonian arts and the non-visual art of music inspired by Dionysos.'

From a historical perspective, Nietzsche's polarity is mistaken in a number of details; and it is somewhat confused by the fact that Apollo was never a particular patron of sculpture, nor Dionysos the divine president of music (that was chiefly Apollo's role, see pp. 277–81). Nietzsche's opposition between the two gods is also embroiled within a larger philosophical discussion about the nature, and our understanding, of things: so the Apollonian becomes a byword for representational art, phenomena (most explicitly sculpture and painting) empirically perceived; while the Dionysian symbolizes a numinal force – something unmediated, bypassing physical form, that puts us in touch with the very essence of things. Still, there is more to Nietzsche's polarity than mere 19th-century abstraction.

Here, for example, is how it surfaced in the world of Roman politics in the mid-30s BC. Rome's empire stretched across the boundaries of the known world, offering wealth, power, and prestige to its prospective rulers. Julius Caesar had been assassinated, and his assassins dealt with by a powerful triumvirate (three-man alliance) established in 43 BC: it consisted of Octavian, Julius Caesar's adopted heir who would later become known as the Emperor Augustus; Mark Antony, the genius of military strategy; and M. Aemilius Lepidus, who was soon ousted from power. In the subsequent two-man race for supremacy, Octavian and Mark Antony each needed an organized iconographic campaign – a set of related symbols for quick identification, a metaphor that worked to each man's own advantage, and an *alter ego* that could be reconciled with his projected ideology.

One solution revolved precisely around the polarity discussed by Nietzsche. On coins [536], in sculptures, and in personal appearance, Antony played a swaggering Dionysos in opposition to Octavian's graceful Apollo. Emphasizing the god's associations with rebirth and salvation, Antony offered renewal and regeneration to the Roman Republic. Dionysos (who was himself associated with Asia Minor) had already served as a model for a number of Near Eastern Hellenistic rulers, and Antony's siding with the East – both through the reportedly florid 'Asiatic' style of his oratory and his infamous affair with Cleopatra – served to heighten the allusion.

386 *Marble statue of Apollo, 2nd century* AD. *The image imitates the late Archaic/early Classical styles of the first quarter of the 5th century* BC *(note the hair, arranged in rows of snail-like curves on Apollo's forehead [cf. 272]), which may have given it an air of sacred venerability.*

387 opposite *Bronze head of Dionysos, early 1st century* AD. *Dionysos (Bacchus to the Romans) is represented as a beardless youth wearing a wreath of twisted ivy. His irises, now lost, were probably made of stone or glass and inserted into the silvered eye sockets so as to give the image a startlingly lifelike appearance.*

388 *The bearded Dionysos wearing a crown of ivy and a leopard skin, and holding a kantharos in his right hand, on an Attic red-figure amphora attributed to the Kleophrades Painter, c. 500 BC. The god dances in a vine arbour, colourfully rendered in purple paint.*

389 *The continuous painting that adorned all four sides of a room in the Villa of the Mysteries just outside Pompeii, c. 60–50 BC, still eludes interpretation: one reading understands its subject as a commemoration of a wedding, another as an allegory of Dionysian cultic initiation. In this detail we see Dionysos resting in the lap of a woman (perhaps Ariadne, his mythical bride [440, 558]). On the left sits the elderly Silenus, accompanied by two young satyrs: one stares intently into Silenus' pot, while the other, shedding his yellow cloak, holds a theatrical mask of a silenus above the real Silenus' head.*

390 *Marble relief of a mortal receiving Dionysos into his home, c. 40–30 BC. The stumbling and drunken god is accompanied by satyrs; one carries his thyrsos (a wand wreathed in ivy and vine-leaves topped with a pinecone); others play the aulos (a pipe played in pairs) and the cymbals. Masks under the couch allude to Dionysos' connections with the theatre. This is one of several similar reliefs from private contexts, which may have proclaimed their owners' affiliation with the Dionysian Mark Antony.*

Octavian, by contrast, posed in the guise of Apollo: his symbols alluded to Apollo's attributes, such as the sphinx, tripod, and laurel leaf [364], and his house, on the Palatine Hill next to the Temple of Apollo which he dedicated in 28 BC in thanks for the god's favour, further fudged the boundaries between the two. In Octavian, his images suggested, were order, constancy, and stability, and by implication political harmony and peace; here was leadership with divine backing; here was youth and rejuvenation (portraits of the type depicting the youthful Octavian were produced into the Emperor's old age). 'Apollo reigns', proclaimed Vergil in his fourth *Eclogue*.

Dionysos versus Apollo: *Mark Antony, characterizing himself as Dionysos, celebrated Bacchic bibulousness in a lost tract,* On His Own Drunkenness; *according to Plutarch, in 41 BC he entered the city of Ephesus in Asia Minor dressed as the god:*

Women dressed as Bacchants and men and boys as satyrs and Pans led the way before him. The city was full of ivy, Bacchic wands, harps, pipes, and flutes. They hailed him as Dionysos, the Beneficent Bringer of Joy. He was indeed such a god to some; but to the majority he was Dionysos the Wild and Savage. For he took property away from the nobility and gave it to sycophants and scoundrels.

Plutarch, *Life of Antony* 24.3–4

Octavian, meanwhile, characterized himself as an Apollonian figure, and even dressed up as the god at a private 'fancy-dress' dinner party (Suetonius, Life of Augustus *7). That association led Propertius, in a poem written to celebrate Octavian's dedication of the Palatine Temple of Apollo, to imagine Apollo addressing Octavian as if he were the god, using language and formulas usually reserved for divine hymns (see p. 94). The context is Octavian's final showdown with Mark Antony, at the battle of Actium in 31 BC.*

Then Apollo said: 'Augustus, saviour of the world, sprung from Alba Longa, recognized as greater even than your Trojan ancestors, conquer now by sea! For you already control the land. My bow fights for you, each arrow here on my shoulder supports your side. Set your country free from fear – the country that relies on your protection and has laid her public prayers at your prow ...! Antony's forces are rowing their insolent way too close to Rome! The shame that, while you are leader, Latium's waves should suffer the sails of a king ...! Though their prows bear Centaurs that threaten you with rocks, you will see that they are just hollow planks and painted horrors. For it is the cause that makes or breaks the soldier's strength: if the cause is an unjust one, shame itself discharges the soldier's weapon!

The time has come! Launch your ships! It is I who ordain the time of battle, and it is I who will guide the Julian prows with my laurelled hand!

Propertius, *Elegies* 4.6.37–54

Dionysos received early cultic status in Italy (the 6th-century BC *Homeric Hymn to Dionysos* tells how the god first revealed himself to Tyrrhenian sailors). He was known to the Etruscans as Fufluns or Pachies, names probably mimicking the cultic shrieks of his followers. The Romans appropriated a Greek title for Dionysos, Bacchus (again imitating his cultic cry), and associated him with their god Liber – the deity who was liberated, and who promised liberation, from the rules that governed natural and social life.

Although the cult of Apollo seems to have developed fairly late in the history of Rome, and Apollo himself was never aligned with a native Roman god, as happened with other Greek deities, Octavian presented the Dionysian Antony as strange and foreign, degenerate, and inebriated with his own *luxuria*. Antony was an Eastern and 'non-Roman' force: to wage war with him, Octavian's campaign made out, was to do battle with a foreign enemy, not a fellow Roman citizen.

For all their differences, Apollo and Dionysos were, Classical legend had it, half-brothers fathered by Zeus. Dionysos was the son of Zeus and Semele: ever jealous of her husband's affairs with mortal women, Hera persuaded the pregnant Semele that she should ask Zeus to reveal himself to her in full divine glory; just as Hera had planned, Semele was consumed by lightning at the revelation. But Zeus rescued the embryonic Dionysos from Semele's womb, planted him in his own thigh, and nurtured him to term. Being born both of a woman and of a man, the product of sexual intercourse and asexual reproduction, gave Dionysos his particular capacity to transcend boundaries: he was simultaneously young and old, masculine and effeminate, man and beast. The story of his birth perhaps also explained his association with the afterlife: as one literally born twice, he promised

391 *Marble figures of a Centaur and Apollo from the west pediment of the Temple of Zeus at Olympia [cf. 47], c. 460 BC. Apollo stood supreme in the centre of the pediment, unperturbed by the chaotic scenes on either side of him, as the unruly Centaurs, drunk after attending a wedding feast hosted by the Lapith king, turned their attention to the Lapith women.*

392 right *Wall-painting of Apollo, last quarter of the 1st century BC. This image of the youthful god, with his quiver on his back and his lyre in his left hand, is thought to have come from the house of the Emperor Augustus on the Palatine Hill in Rome.*

393 *Bronze statue of Apollo from the Piraeus, the port of Athens: probably an 'archaizing' 1st-century BC imitation in the style of a kouros statue made c. 530–520 BC. In the* Homeric Hymn to Apollo *(lines 447–450) the god is presented as a man in the prime of youth, with broad shoulders, flowing hair, and a taut muscular body, leading to the belief that all kouroi [e.g. 446] represented Apollo. This statue – originally with a votive bowl in his right hand and a bow in his left – almost certainly did.*

his followers triumph over death and many other transformations besides – through intoxication, ritual madness (what the Greeks termed *mania*), and theatrical impersonation. Dionysos' characteristic instability may also account for the diversity of his visual forms. He could take the appearance of a bearded elder [98, 255, 390, 580], or give up his senior semblance for a crown of myrtle or ivy, a vineyard, and the mischievous company of his followers [387–89, 558]. Whatever his guise, Dionysos' power could not be denied: the stronger the human resistance, the more drastic its consequences – as when, in Euripides' *Bacchae*, King Pentheus of Thebes refuses to recognize Dionysos' divinity, and is punished by being torn limb from limb by the Theban women, whom Dionysos had possessed.

The jealous Hera also plagued Apollo's mother, Leto. When the time came for Leto to give birth, no land would receive her for fear of Hera's rage. Eventually, she persuaded the barren island of Delos to accommodate her, and Apollo was duly born (together with his twin sister, Artemis). Apollo presided over law and order, including the spheres of prophecy, purification, archery (but not war), healing, poetry, and music; and he presented young male citizens with a model (and a body) to which to aspire. The iconography of Apollo is significantly more consistent than that of Dionysos: he is nearly always young, athletic, and handsome, and his ideal corporeal proportions reflected the metaphysical harmony within [386, 392, 393]. The west pediment of the Temple of Zeus at Olympia is perhaps the best example: the imposing figure of Apollo contrasts with the chaotic scenes around him, as Centaurs turn their bestial attentions to the wives of their Lapith hosts; Apollo has not yet re-established order, but his calm and dignified pose marks him out as the antithetical force to their transgression [391].

394 *Attic red-figure volute krater and stand attributed to the Meleager Painter, 390–380 BC. On the neck of the vase are three pairs of male symposiasts. The central left figure has put down his lyre to play kottabos, a flirting game in which a participant spins his drinking cup on his finger and flicks drops of wine at his fancied target. On the stand is a frieze of gods, satyrs, and maenads in ecstatic revelry. The krater imitates grander metal vessels: note its black-glazed fluted body, and the olive wreath and African heads in relief on the shoulder.*

395 *Silver oinochoe, second half of the 4th century BC. It has recently been argued (by Michael Vickers and David Gill) that painted pottery originally developed as a cheap imitation of expensive silverware, like this wine-jug decorated with floral patterns. Black paint, it is suggested, originally imitated tarnished silver, the red-figure style copied gold relief imagery, and purple and white colours reproduced the effects of copper and ivory.*

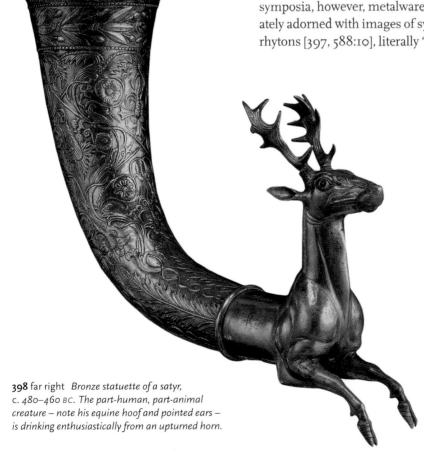

396 *Marble sarcophagus of Maconiana Severiana, early 3rd century AD. Three satyrs crush grapes in a large wine vat with a spout in the form of a lion head, while two others bring further grapes in baskets. On the right a maenad dances, holding a cymbal in her left hand. The sarcophagus has further Dionysian scenes on the front [440].*

397 below *Silver gilt rhyton in the shape of a stag, from the eastern Mediterranean, late 1st century BC. Such vessels usually contained unmixed, and therefore very potent, wine (in this case, drunk from a spout between the legs of the stag). Its stimulating effect is suggested by the spirited expression of the stag, with head erect, inlaid glass eyes wide open, and veins protruding.*

398 far right *Bronze statuette of a satyr, c. 480–460 BC. The part-human, part-animal creature – note his equine hoof and pointed ears – is drinking enthusiastically from an upturned horn.*

WINING, DINING, AND DIONYSIZING

One of the best-recorded realms of Dionysos is the institutionalized Greek drinking party, or *symposium* – literally a 'drinking together'. It probably developed out of an aristocratic system of poetic patronage, but quickly became synonymous with Greek culture: as early as the 8th century BC, the Old Testament prophet Amos characterized and condemned the Greeks as a people who 'drink wine in bowls and anoint themselves with luxurious anointments' (6.6).

The goings-on of the symposium are best seen in surviving Athenian painted pottery, and a number of vase types were explicitly, though not exclusively, associated with it. Concentrated wine was stored in an amphora [404, 407, 588:1] and mixed with iced water in a krater, a large vessel [394, 588:4] (to drink it neat was a social *faux-pas* that characterized the non-Greek peoples of Macedonia and Thrace). It was served from the krater with a specially designed jug, an oinochoe [157, 588:5]. For drinking, a variety of shapes were available: the kylix, a rounded shallow cup on a short stem [399, 588:6, and see 404]; the skyphos, a squat, mug-shaped vessel [588:8]; and the kantharos, with two distinctive, high-reaching handles [388, 588:7]. For the grandest symposia, however, metalware seems to have been preferred [395], often appropriately adorned with images of symposiasts; and in the eastern Mediterranean, metal rhytons [397, 588:10], literally 'horns', were the favoured drinking vessel.

399 *Six symposiasts recline under luxurious twisting vines around a central Gorgon head, on an Attic black-figure kylix attributed to the Lysippides Painter and Andokides (as potter), c. 520 BC. All are crowned with ivy wreaths, a common indicator of a symposium scene; one holds a lyre, another a rhyton, and the others cups like the one on which they are portrayed.*

Pliny the Elder *was interested in the subject of wine and how it was produced. But he wholeheartedly condemned those who abused it.*

All this hard toil, labour, and expense produces something which corrupts the human mind and begets madness; something which causes thousands of crimes; something which is so seductive that a large proportion of mankind knows nothing else worth living for . . . Many drunkards never wake early enough to see the sunrise, and consequently they shorten their lives. A pale face comes from drinking, as do sagging cheeks, sore eyes, and shaky hands that spill the contents of vessels when they are full. The immediate punishment of drunkenness is disturbed sleep and restless nights; its greatest reward, perverse sexual wantonness and delight in doing wrong. The next day, the breath smells of the wine-jar's rim, everything is forgotten, and the mind feels dead. That's what they call 'living one's life as though there's no tomorrow': but whereas through death we will all lose our past, these men, through drinking, sacrifice their future also!

Pliny the Elder, *Natural History*
14.137–42

An Attic kylix dating to around 520 BC is typical of Athenian sympotic imagery [399]. It depicts six men reclining [cf. 405], four of them drinking from cups just like the one on which they figure. There are no women here: the symposium was a masculine realm, usually held in the *andron*, or men's quarters, of the house (see p. 212). Mothers, wives, and daughters were by definition excluded, but *hetairai*, female 'companions' (see p. 52), were not: they provided music [433], poetry, educated banter, and – perhaps most importantly – sex. The host's slaves would pour out the wine, but participants might also bring their own minions (such as the lithe youth who holds an improvised urinal up to his revelling master on an Attic red-figure chous [402]). The foliage that surrounds the figures is probably symbolic of the Dionysian aspect of the ritual, and should not be taken to suggest an outdoor setting: the symposium was usually celebrated indoors, in a room with couches (*klinai*) arranged around its sides and a large krater at its centre.

Why is the centre of this kylix neatly filled by the motif of a Gorgon's head? While there may have been an aesthetic motive (the head neatly fills the cup's central space), there seems also to have been a symbolic meaning. The head would only have become visible after the cup had been drained; and given that the image of the Gorgon occurs elsewhere in association with liminal spaces and transitions (cf. pp. 126–27), it is likely that it is here related to the rising disorder that comes with drinking. Such plays upon the structural space of drinking cups, relying upon the different perspectives of the viewer to form (often unexpected) narrative sequences, are common on Attic vases used in the symposium, reminding us that ceramic vessels were designed for use – for handling, caressing, playing – rather than the museum's display case. So it is that the drinker, upon emptying his cup, may be vehemently reminded of the consequences of overindulgence [400].

Three of the men on the late 6th-century kylix [399] are pubescent, the other three older (their seniority is indicated by their beards). We cannot tell if the three

400 right A post-symposium scene, on the interior of an Attic red-figure kylix attributed to Onesimos, c. 490 BC. An adolescent has put aside the paraphernalia of citizen duty (the stick raised for voting in the Athenian Assembly), and stoops to comfort his vomiting older lover. Both men still wear their garlands from the symposium.

401 far right A garlanded boy, dancing provocatively and holding a kylix in his left hand, depicted on the interior of an Attic red-figure kylix attributed to Makron, 480–470 BC. The inscription calls him kalos – beautiful. Traditionally a master of ceremonies would present such a cup, also inscribed with the specific name of an individual, to an invited youth at the symposium as an expression of his erotic interest. The person who commissioned this cup, however, seems to have kept his options open.

402 On this Attic red-figure chous attributed to the Oionokles Painter, c. 470 BC, a boy-servant waits while his master urinates into a wine-jug, which is playfully shaped like the vessel from which the viewer is about to pour his drink. This special form of small jug was used for a drinking contest during a three-day Athenian festival of Dionysos, the Anthesteria [cf. 383].

403 Satyrs and maenads on an Attic red-figure kylix attributed to Nikosthenes, c. 510–500 BC. The aroused satyrs, one holding a wineskin, another a drinking horn, are chasing the maenads, who only halfheartedly resist their advances. Like humans, satyrs are bearded and stand upright; unlike them, they have pointed ears, curly tails, and grotesquely large penises: satyrs therefore became a favourite means of contemplating where the lines should be drawn between acceptable and unacceptable behaviour at the Athenian symposium.

older men are 'chatting up' the youths, but such pederasty was common enough at the symposium. Hosts went to extreme efforts to win the affections of prospective boyfriends, inscribing drinking-cups with their name, for instance, then adding the word *kalos* ('so-and-so is beautiful') [401]; the symposium even had a special flirtatious drinking game, called *kottabos* [394, 408]. It is this homoerotic aspect of the symposium that Athenian writers describe over and above any other, and it was the symposium's associations with homoerotic courtship that must have led Plato to use it as the setting for Socrates' most famous philosophical discussion of love. In the *Symposium* (c. 384 BC; see p. 49), the usual protocols of courtship, whereby the older lover (*erastes*) wins the affection of his beloved youth (*eromenos*), are subverted: the young Alcibiades chases after the older, squat, and unsightly philosopher Socrates. As the evening (and drinking) progresses, Alcibiades' tactics become more and more desperate, while Socrates remains true to the idea of what, in modern parlance, we call 'Platonic love'. The comic theme of the pug-nosed older citizen and the youthful beauty was popular in Attic sympotic pottery too: a red-figure amphora attributed to the Berlin Painter depicts on one side a handsome youth holding a kylix [404], epitomizing adolescent nimbleness and beauty (his dancing, muscled body is exaggerated by the natural curvature of the amphora), while on the other side is a much older, fatter, and balding man. It is an antithesis – between the young and

404 *On an Attic red-figure amphora attributed to the Berlin Painter, c. 480 BC, a lithe youth holds a kylix in his left hand and dances, the clothing draped around his arm only emphasizing his nudity. The reverse of the same pot depicts his fat, balding, middle-aged admirer.*

The Greek symposium *provided a forum for a variety of songs, from the musical recitals performed by skilled* hetairai *[433] to the raucous drinking songs that typically accompanied the procession that followed it. A number of lyric songs, typically about drink and sex, were also set in the symposium. Although hugely influential in antiquity (recast into Latin verse, for example, by the Roman poet Horace), only a few fragments of ancient Greek lyric survive today. The following passage by the 7th-century* BC *poet Alkaios (from Mytilene in Lesbos), translated by John Easby-Smith, gives some idea of their contents.*

Let us drink, and pledge the night!
Wherefore wait the torches' light?
   Twilight's hour is brief.
Pass the ample goblet round,
Gold-enwrought, whereon is wound
   Many a jewelled leaf.
Sprung from Semele and Zeus
Dionysos gave to us
   Care-dispelling wine.
Pouring out the liquid treasure
With one part of water measure
   Two parts from the vine.
Mix it well, and let it flow,
Cup on cup shall headlong go,
   While we drink and laugh,
While we sing and quaff.

based on Alkaios, fragment 346

sexually desired, and the old and sexually desiring – that was central to the courting rituals of the symposium.

So far, we have looked at the symposium in terms of its social agenda – its organization, ideologies, and sexual protocols. But it was also a cultic ritual, framed at its opening and close with hymns, prayers, and libations to Dionysos. To participate was to join Dionysos' mythical cohort: images recurrently cast symposiasts in the guise of satyrs and sileni – wild hybrids of man and beast – who accompanied the god along with his female followers, maenads or Bacchants [403]; symposiasts would also round off their proceedings by forming a rowdy procession, like satyrs, in honour of Dionysos, the *komos*.

Because of the wealth of visual material from 5th-century Attica, it is easy to form a rather static image of the symposium across time and space. Certainly, it was one of Greece's most celebrated exports throughout the Mediterranean. But this is not to say that other cultures uncritically adopted it: instead, they reconciled it with their own social customs, traditions, and rituals of drinking and eating.

From a Greek perspective, we might hesitate to classify images of Etruscan dining scenes as symposia [406]. Unlike the Greeks, the Etruscans evidently consumed food at these gatherings, and also allowed women to participate – a sign of Etruscan licentiousness, according to Theopompos, a 4th-century BC historian whose comments are preserved in Athenaeus' *Intellectuals at the Table*, and to Diodorus Siculus in the mid- to late 1st century BC (*Library of History* 5.40). On incised mirrors, painted tombs [406], and sarcophagi [448], men lie together with

405 *Bronze statuettes of symposiasts from northern Greece, third quarter of the 6th century* BC. *These three reclining figures probably once adorned the rim of a large bronze krater used at the symposium for mixing wine. Although each man reclines on one elbow, with cloak wrapped round his waist, all are rendered differently: the first holds a drinking horn, the second gesticulates as if in deep conversation, and the third strokes his belly.*

406 *Wall-painting in the Tomb of the Shields, Tarquinia, last quarter of the 4th century BC. At the Etruscan, as opposed to Athenian, 'symposium', respectable women seem to have been admitted. In this image, a bejewelled wife sits next to her reclining, wreathed, husband; the figure on the left, probably a slave to judge from her diminutive stature, holds a fan to both participants. Note also the food on the table in front of them – another distinctive feature of the Etruscan drinking party.*

Interpretation of the function of such scenes is tricky. Did they play on the dual capacities of Dionysos as a god associated with both resurrection and wine (like the Egyptian god Osiris before him, and Christ after him)? Did they depict the funerary meal that accompanied the laying out of the deceased's body? Or were these images intended to summon up a vision of the 'heavenly banquets' of the afterlife? In this tomb, of Larth Velcas, the ancestors of the deceased (identified by inscriptions) are assembled to take part in a perpetual banquet.

407 *Attic black-figure amphora attributed to the Antimenes Painter, c. 520 BC. This amphora, with its epiphanic beaming visage of Dionysos, was brought to Etruria from Athens and ultimately used not as a vessel for holding wine but as an ossuary at the Ripagretta cemetery in Tarquinia.*

women on couches, although only rarely (as in the Tomb of the Whipping in Tarquinia) are couples represented in erotic activity. This leads us to two related questions. First, why did the Etruscans choose to adopt Greek sympotic iconography at all? And second, what lay behind their adaptations of that iconography?

To answer the first question, we only need to consider the Etruscan cultural investment involved in imitating an Attic ritual. The Etruscans were assiduous collectors of Attic sympotic ware (it is estimated that over 80 per cent of all surviving Greek painted pots are from Etruscan contexts), and just as in Athens, Etruscan drinking gatherings functioned to celebrate a shared aristocratic ideology, to bond convivial peer groups. As regards the second question, we must beware of adopting too imperialist an attitude to Etruscan culture – of maintaining a model of active Greek and passive Etruscan interaction in which the Etruscans (like other non-Greek peoples) become indiscriminate consumers of Greek cultural products.

In Etruria, almost all surviving representations of the symposium come from funerary contexts, an Etruscan phenomenon connected with Dionysos' shared drinking and afterlife associations. Greek writers emphasized the relationship between those two realms too ('Dionysos is Hades', the 6th-century Ionian philosopher Heraclitus declared; and the Greeks in the South Italian colonies frequently drew upon the afterlife connotations of Dionysos [408, 409]. But the Etruscans capitalized on the ambiguity between Dionysos' drinking and funerary spheres with special enthusiasm, appropriating foreign, Attic visual culture to their own native funerary rituals. It is consequently the interpreter's delicate task to decide where, if at all, to draw the line between 'Etruscan' and 'Greek' readings of such images. An Attic amphora with representations of Dionysos on both of its sides nicely makes the point [407]. The object may have been produced in Athens with an Athenian symposium in mind, but add a locally produced lid, then place inside it not wine but an individual's ashes (together with some suitably small prized possessions), and finally bury it in a hole in the ground: as a result, the significance of the object clearly shifted with its new context. Its images, in other words, did not have the same meanings in Etruria as they may have had in Athens.

408, 409 *The paintings in the Tomb of the Diver at Paestum in South Italy (named Poseidonia by its Greek settlers), c. 480–470 BC, testify to the ancient association between the Dionysian realms of the symposium and death. The symposiasts on one of the inner sides (above) are garlanded, drinking from* Greek kylixes and playing kottabos [cf. 394]. The imagery of the lid (below) suggests the special funerary significance attributed to such sympotic scenes in South Italy: an individual (the deceased?) plunges into a blue lake, perhaps an allegory of the soul's descent into the realm of the dead.

410 Triclinium *in the House of the Cryptoporticus in Pompeii, c. 40–30 BC. The Roman* triclinium *consisted of three large connected couches, covered with cushions, each of which could accommodate three people. The host's family would recline on the left couch, the most favoured guest on the right of the middle couch. The ledge in front of the couches was for placing cups, and the table for the mixing-bowl. In the foreground, attached to the masonry couches, further seating (rather than reclining) space has been added, perhaps for children. The grandest houses had both outdoor and indoor dining-rooms, designed for summer and winter use: this one was suited to the former.*

The tireless Christian evangelist *whom we know as St Paul had special difficulty in conveying the meaning of the Christian 'eucharist' (literally the 'giving of thanks') to the 1st-century AD Greek citizens of Corinth. For the Corinthians seem to have treated the Christian celebration as an excuse for the festive drinking and dining that characterized the Greek symposium and Roman convivium.*

When you meet, it is not really to eat the Lord's Supper at all. For when the time comes to eat, each of you goes ahead with your own supper: one man goes hungry, another man gets drunk. What! Surely you have houses in which to eat and drink? Or do you despise God's church and make those who have nothing feel ashamed? What can I say to you? Should I praise you for this? Absolutely not! For I received this from the Lord, and I also handed it on to you: the Lord Jesus, on the night on which he was betrayed, took bread; when he had given thanks he broke it and said: 'This is my body – it is for you: do this in memory of me.' Similarly, after supper, he took the cup, saying: 'This cup is the new covenant sealed in my blood: do this, whenever you drink, in memory of me.' For whenever you eat this bread and drink this cup, you proclaim the Lord's death until he comes. Whoever of you, therefore, should eat the bread and drink the wine of the Lord in an unfitting manner will be guilty of profaning the Lord's body and blood.

St Paul, First Letter to the Corinthians 11.20–34

The Romans too were influenced by the idea of the Greek symposium. Many Roman lyric poems, especially those of the 1st-century BC poets Catullus, Tibullus, Propertius, and Horace, have symposium-like settings. Just how 'realistically' we should read them is again a subject of dispute. The symposium probably struck Roman authors more as a literary construction – bound up with the Greek literature that they so eagerly imitated – than as something actually experienced, still less something necessarily implicated with the cult of Dionysos. Like the Etruscans, the Romans combined the Greek drinking party with an elaborate dinner (*cena*), which took place in a specially designed *triclinium* [410]: they termed it the *convivium*. The occasion was a formal and hierarchical affair (see p. 66); it also often formed the backdrop for cultural and literary discussions, as is evidenced, for example, by Tacitus' *Dialogue on Orators*, Athenaeus' *Intellectuals at the Table*, and Plutarch's *Sympotic Questions* (the latter two written in Greek, and only too aware of the similarities and differences between the Roman *convivium* and Greek symposium).

Inevitably, the Roman *convivium*, like so many other aspects of Roman life, became the subject of burlesque satire. One such occasion is the episode of Trimalchio's dinner party in Petronius' *Satyricon* (see also p. 218), where Encolpius (the narrator) and his younger boyfriend show up at a grandiose party hosted by Trimalchio. Many of the jokes come from parodying famous sympotic literary moments, as when Socrates' lofty philosophical conversations in Plato's *Symposium* are mirrored in the vulgar ramblings of former slaves. Formerly a slave himself, Trimalchio is now, thanks to an inheritance from his master, extraordinarily wealthy; and wealth, Trimalchio thinks, is for flaunting. Trimalchio's failed attempts to show off his learning are almost as nauseating as the grotesque food served by his countless slaves, and his party finally ends on a macabre note when Trimalchio acts out his own death and funeral. Once again, the dining room and funerary chamber become one.

Christian commentators deplored the drunkenness and sexual promiscuity of the symposium. In some ways, though, the symposium in honour of Dionysos and the community celebrations centred on the body and blood of Christ were very similar. To early converts to Christianity, the character of Jesus, who commemorated the Last Supper on the night before his crucifixion, must have struck a strangely familiar note – perhaps as another transformation, or 'mask', of the pervasive Dionysos, whose cup, in the end, offered life everlasting.

411 *An actor, depicted on an Apulian* situla *(water bucket with swinging handle) attributed to the Konnakis Painter, c. 360–350 BC. The exaggerated mask, tights, and short padded tunic mark him as an actor in a farcical* phlyax *play (the name probably comes from the Greek verb* phlein, *'to swell', referring to the actors' well-padded costumes).*

ACTING OUT DIONYSOS

Wine was one form of Dionysian transformation, but drama was a more literal means of 'ecstatic' release, made possible by the adoption of a new *prosopon* (a 'mask' – or, in Latin, a *persona*). The world of the theatre, like that of the symposium, especially in Athens, was one in which the frameworks governing social behaviour could be brought into question, even momentarily subverted and undermined. And just as it was Dionysos who presided over the raucousness of the symposium, it was Dionysos who directed the theatre's realm of misrule.

The origins of drama are complex (ancient tradition linked its development to a shadowy 6th-century figure named Thespis), but it is important to register just how firmly rooted in Dionysian cult Athenian drama was. In the fourth chapter of his *Poetics*, Aristotle argued that tragedy – literally a 'goat song', perhaps alluding to an early award of a goat as a prize, or else to its performance during a goat-sacrifice to Dionysos – descended from 'satyr-like activity'. And some say that tragedy's poetic meter (the iambic trimeter) can be traced back to the *dithyramb*, the dance-hymn in honour of Dionysos. Today we are used to plays that are produced for entertainment, for repeated performance, and usually in the evening. But the original context of Athenian drama was a religious one: staged during the daytime, performances formed part of cultic celebrations in honour of Dionysos, notably the City Dionysia.

Although the City Dionysia was only one occasion for dramatic performance in Athens (the Rural Dionysia and the Lenaea were two others), it was Dionysos's most important annual celebration. As a preliminary, a statue of the god was led to the Theatre of Dionysos [416], on the southern slope of the Acropolis. On the first day, there was a great procession in which participants would parade huge phallic figures, sacrificial animals, and other offerings to the sacred precinct of Dionysos. This was located beside the theatre, although the theatre itself was also considered part of the god's sacred space: the chorus danced around a central altar to Dionysos, and it was the priest of Dionysos who supervised the theatrical proceedings.

The dramatic performances occupied days two to five of the festival. On the second, third, and fourth days, a single playwright was called upon to produce no fewer than three tragedies (which were not always as closely thematically

*In his **Poetics**, written in the 4th century BC and destined to become one of the Western world's most influential pieces of literary criticism, Aristotle attempted to explain how Athenian tragedy could exert such a powerful effect on its audience. After discussing the constituents of tragedy, he argued that the most important element is the plot: a good tragedy will deal with the protagonist's reversal of fortune (peripeteia) and his recognition (anagnorisis) of his overbearing insolence (hybris).*

The successful representation of the downfall of the protagonist (literally, the 'first actor') should elicit two emotions from the members of the audience: first, their pity for the character on stage; and second, their fear that the character's ruin might befall them too. The result was katharsis: although Aristotle's meaning remains contested, it
seems that the audience could be beneficially 'purged' (in an almost medical sense) of its fears – either through rationally understanding how this downfall could occur, or by seeing represented on stage its worst emotional fears and thereby ridding itself of them.

Since the plot of the best tragedy should be complex, not simple, and should represent fearful and pitiable events (for that is what characterizes the art of tragedy), it is obvious, first of all, that good men must not be shown passing from good fortune to bad. For that does not arouse pity or fear; it repels us. Second, a wicked man must not be shown passing from bad fortune to good. That is the least tragic situation of all: it would have none of the required elements because it fails to arouse human

sympathy, as well as pity and fear. Third, a tragedy should not show a wicked man passing from good fortune to bad. Although such a plot might arouse human sympathy, it does not arouse pity or fear. For we only feel pity for the *undeserving* victim of misfortune; and we only feel fear if that person is *similar* to ourselves . . .

So, then, we come to the man between these extremes: someone who is not pre-eminent in virtue and justice; and yet someone who passes into misfortune not through any villainy and vice of his own, but through some sort of miscalculation [*hamartia*]; someone who is highly thought of and blessed by fortune, like Oedipus, Thyestes or other illustrious men of such lineage.

Aristotle, *Poetics* 13.2–5

413 above *A scene from a phlyax play, on a Paestan red-figure krater painted by Asteas, c. 340 BC. Zeus (the old man carrying a ladder) embarks on a night-time visit to Alkmene (the richly dressed woman who peers out of her window). Hermes (identified by his hat and wand) holds out a lamp to help Zeus see where he is going. The union between Zeus and Alkmene, by which Herakles was conceived, was a perfectly serious story, but here it is sent up as an episode of slapstick buffoonery. The scene is typical of phlyax plays, which took up stories from myth and everyday life and comically deflated them.*

connected as the sole trilogy that survives today, Aeschylus' *Oresteia*); each day's set of tragedies was followed by a satyr-play, when the stage would be transformed with the subversive antics of satyrs. Satyr-plays were more than just light relief: they were an integral part of the Dionysian ritual, and even 'high-brow' tragedians were expected to turn their hand to the genre. Only one complete satyr-play survives, Euripides' *Cyclops* (probably produced in 412 BC), in which Odysseus comes face to face with Dionysos' attendant, Silenus, and his gang of frolicsome satyrs. Here the much-debated act of Odysseus' blinding of Polyphemos is neither a display of heroism nor a tragedy of aggression against a sympathetic foe: it merely allows everyone to get back to having a wild, drunken, and generally raucous time.

On the sixth day, after the three days of tragedies and satyr-plays, five comedies were staged. Eleven such plays, written by Aristophanes, survive, all of them characterized by their own different forms of social ridicule, irreverent buffoonery, and uninhibited language. The word 'comedy' comes from the Greek word *komos* – the term also used to describe the revels and processions that followed the symposium (p. 256), but which probably originally referred to a phallic dance sanctioned by Dionysos; in the hands of the 4th-century BC Greek colonists of South Italy, comedy evolved into an even more far-fetched farce, the *phlyax*, with ever more burlesque outfits, grotesque masks, and padded tunics [411, 413]. Comedies often delighted in subverting the theatrical conventions of tragedy, as one krater from the South Italian colony of Apulia demonstrates [412]. A figure dressed in tragic costume, labelled 'Aigisthos' (Agamemnon's cousin, who adulterously usurped his wife and the Mycenaean throne, and with whose fate several tragedies dealt) has just entered the stage from the left. He scratches his head in bafflement – as well he might, for it seems that he has emerged on a comic stage, faced by a burlesque chorus of jeering phallus-clad men.

Dionysian festival as the City Dionysia undoubtedly was, it was also a civic occasion. During the proceedings, adolescents whose fathers had been killed in battle were presented with hoplite armour purchased at state expense. The Theatre of Dionysos had enough space to seat all male citizens (slaves were certainly excluded, and women may well have been too); and since the festival was held

Of all creatures that have spirit and mind, we women are the most wretched species. To begin with, we must hand over money and buy a husband; we must accept a master over our enslaved body. But there is a more painful offence than this wrong. A great risk lies in this matter: will that man be good or bad? For women have no recourse to any reputable divorce, nor is it possible to choose our own husband . . . But the argument does not hold true for you as it does for me. You have your city, your father's home; you find delight in life and have the company of your friends. I am alone, without a city, and insulted by the husband who stole me from a barbarian land. I have no mother, no brother, no relation at all all to shelter me from this ruin.

Euripides, *Medea* 230–37, 252–58

in March, when the seas could safely be traversed after the winter, a number of foreign ambassadors were also invited. The City Dionysia was therefore a celebration of an Athenian way of life, a proud consideration of what it meant to be an Athenian citizen. Although tragedies ostensibly dealt with the themes and events of the heroic past (to the extent that Plato called Homer the 'first of the tragic poets'), they were recast in such a way as to deal implicitly with contemporary civic concerns. They might problematize the relationship between the private life of the household (*oikos*) and the public world of the city (*polis*); they might question the social distinctions between man and woman, Greek and barbarian, or citizen and foreigner; and they might challenge the Athenian zealousness for war (see p. 198), devotion to the gods, or even democracy. But the overriding cause of celebration seems to have been that Athens was a city stable enough to call her own public and private ideologies into question. She could interrogate her deepest values and not only survive the doctrinal affront, but emerge all the mightier from the challenge.

In some ways, the theatre's civic aspect made it strikingly similar to some of the city's other public spaces. Here, as in the Athenian law-courts, a variety of contests (*agones*) were waged. On one level, there was the contest between the characters and ideas within each play; on another, the literal competition between the three playwrights, each striving for victory (the winner was decided upon by a democratic jury of ten men, one from each Attic tribe). In the theatre, as in the democratic Assembly that met on the Pnyx, powerful words were bandied about in such a way as to compel the audience to sit, listen, and decide whose arguments were most valid. No wonder, then, that the word used of the dramatic playwright and director was the same as that used for teacher (*didaskalos*).

So theatre formed part of an Athenian democratic citizen's civic education. That probably explains why performances were staged at public expense – or rather, at the expense of three wealthy *choregoi*. As part of a special democratic system of taxing the rich, or 'liturgy', these men landed the bill for training the twelve-man (later fifteen-man) chorus of each tragedy; should his set of tragedies be judged victorious, the *choregos* would share the credit with the playwright and might construct a self-celebratory monument on the Athenian 'Street of the Tripods' [414].

The remains of Greek theatres all over the Mediterranean world testify to the speedy and far-reaching export of Athenian drama. The best-preserved examples stagger us with their size and acoustics [417]; and calculating a theatre's audience capacity is now a standard way of estimating a city's ancient population in Graeco-Roman times. But the remnants of the earliest surviving Greek theatres, like that at Thorikos in Attica, suggest rectilinear, rather than extended semi-circular, plans, and the grand stone theatres that we are so accustomed to seeing today (not least the Theatre of Dionysos with its row upon row of marble seats [416]) are usually later refashionings of what were originally humble wooden structures. Common to even the earliest theatres, however, was the *orchestra* floor where the chorus (who commented on the dramatic action rather like an operatic chorus) would sing and perform their dances [415–17]. It was reached from two side entrances, called *parodoi*. Behind the *orchestra* was the *skene* (from which we derive the word 'scene'): literally a 'tent' connected to the stage by a central door, this was originally a humble hut where actors might change costumes; soon, however, it became a multi-storey stone building. The *skene* could be appropriated into each tragedy's particular setting, whether as the royal palace from which news of the violent ends of the royal family comes (in Sophocles' *Oedipus the King*); or a watch-tower in Mycenae (in the opening of Aeschylus' *Agamemnon*); or as the heavenly platform from which the gods could look down on human affairs (in Euripides' *Electra*).

414 *The Lysikrates Monument in Athens, erected in 334 BC. This small structure with engaged Corinthian columns commemorates the sponsorship of a successful chorus of boys in 335–334 BC by the* choregos *Lysikrates. It stood on the 'Street of the Tripods', which was lined with such monuments, all erected at private expense.*

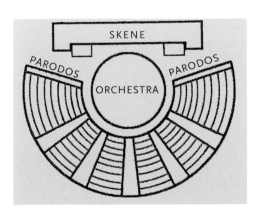

415 *Schematic drawing of a typical Greek theatre. The auditorium comprised an extended semi-circle, divided by stairways into a number of wedges. The layout centred on the circular* orchestra, *a dancing space for the chorus, which also contained a small altar to Dionysos. Both the chorus and the audience entered and exited through two* parodoi *('ways in'). Behind the orchestra was the* skene. *By the 4th century BC, a raised stage in front of the* skene *(the* proskenion*) was used, supported by a row of columns [cf. 412].*

When studying plays as texts – and texts without staging directions – it is easy to underestimate the visual power of Athenian drama; but we should remember that 'theatre' literally means a 'place for seeing'. Because of the actors' use of masks, which both exaggerated a character's features and drew explicit attention to the 'becoming other' that this Dionysian activity involved, even those in the back rows could share in a play's visual, as well as spoken, aspects. The spectacle was made all the more vivid by elaborate stage-painting (*skenographia*: see p. 290) and a number of special effects – like the *mechane*, a crane that could hoist actors into the realm of the gods (the process of theatrical apotheosis), as when Medea is triumphantly carried away by the chariot of the Sun at the end of Euripides' play. A rolling platform called an *ekkyklema* was also employed to reveal the results of events that had happened off-stage. Sophocles' *Electra* used this device to particular effect when Aegisthus unveils it expecting to find the body of Agamemnon's son, Orestes. In a moment of great theatrical suspense, we witness his reaction upon seeing instead the murdered body of his lover and co-conspirator, Clytemnestra.

The works of the three tragedians that we have mentioned – Aeschylus (*c.* 525–456 BC), Sophocles (*c.* 496–406 BC), and Euripides (*c.* 485–406 BC) – became established early on as the dramatic classics of antiquity. Sophocles is said to have produced the greatest number of plays (around one hundred and twenty) and to have won the most prizes; only seven of his plays have survived. The same number of tragedies by Aeschylus survives, although he is thought to have written between seventy and ninety. Euripides seems to have been less popular in his own day, at least in Athens; but out of an output of around ninety plays, nineteen have come down to us. These tragic poets soon assumed celebrity status. In *The Frogs* (performed in 405 BC), Aristophanes has Dionysos go down to Hades to bring the recently deceased Euripides back to Athens. Dionysos finds a feud going on between Euripides and Aeschylus as to whose tragic poetry is better (Sophocles has modestly awarded Aeschylus the title and refuses to intervene), and, after being called upon as an adjudicator, ultimately decides in favour of the older dramatist: Athens is in such a bad way, Dionysos surmises, that only the proper morality of Aeschylus' tragedies could restore her to her former righteous path.

In Aristophanes' Frogs we see Euripides and Aeschylus arguing for the title of the greatest playwright and possession of the throne of tragedy. Each embarks on an elaborate parody of the other: here, Euripides mocks Aeschylus' fondness for using long compound words, while Aeschylus retorts criticizing Euripides' 'soap-opera' delight in turning the great mythical heroes of the past into beggars and cripples. In doing so, Aeschylus' language illustrates the very features that Euripides sends up:

EURIPIDES: Don't you tell me to give up my throne: I will do no such thing! Hear me say it: *I* am the better artist!
DIONYSOS: You hear him, Aeschylus: what's your riposte?
EURIPIDES: Oh no, he'll be all pompous and aloof at first – the old razzle-dazzle trick he used to play in his tragedies . . .

DIONYSOS: Let's not go over the top, my dear fellow.
EURIPIDES: . . . But I can see through him, yes, I've long known what he's like: a crude versifier of self-satisfied strophes, his mouth unbridled, incontinent, and uncontrollable, the height of bombastiloquent pomposity!
AESCHYLUS: Ha! That's what you say, is it, you spawn of Mother Bumpkin? *You* say that of *me*! Why, you gossip-gathering, beggar-staging, stitcher-together-of-rags: you're going to regret every word!

Aristophanes, *The Frogs* 830–843

After four hundred lines or so of squabbling, Dionysos hits upon a different idea: each tragedian speaks a line of verse into a pair of scales to determine whose poetry is the weightier.

416 *Theatre of Dionysos, Athens. Situated on the southern slope of the Acropolis, the theatre was originally constructed of wood in the 6th century BC, and rebuilt in stone in the 4th century BC. The surviving remains date from late Hellenistic and Roman times, when the circular orchestra was transformed into an elongated semi-circle. The front row was made up of special marble seats which were reserved for priests and dignitaries [271].*

417 *Among the best-preserved Greek theatres is that at Epidauros, built in the late 4th century BC. The site [109] was famed in antiquity as a sanctuary of the healing god Asklepios, hosting a festival of athletics and drama, called the Asklepieia, every four years: indeed, the presence of the theatre here recalls Aristotle's theory of tragic katharsis – the idea that tragedy could 'cure' an audience of its inner anxieties. The theatre itself could accommodate around 14,000 people in its 55 rows of limestone seats, and the near-perfect acoustics offered by its extended semi-circular plan meant that speech in the orchestra could be heard even in the back rows. The special altar of Dionysos is still preserved in the centre of the orchestra, but only the foundations of the skene remain.*

418 above *An* aulos *player stands between two dancing men who are both dressed as cockerels (and wear large strap-on phalluses), on an Attic red-figure calyx krater attributed to the Painter of Munich 2335, c. 415* BC. *Some have seen this image, especially because of its date, as an illustration of Aristophanes'* Birds, *in which the chorus is composed of twenty-four different types of bird. Cockerels do not, however, appear in that chorus, but they do feature in Aristophanes' first version of* The Clouds, *performed in 423* BC.

If relatively little survives of the work of Aeschylus, Sophocles, and Euripides, even less remains of the new form of comedy that arose in late 4th-century BC Athens, particularly associated with the figure of Menander [423]. It is clear, however, that this 'New Comedy' relied on a different form of humour from the slapstick comedy of Aristophanes. It finds a modern parallel in the sitcom – the comedy of manners, concerned with fictional private lives and centred on recognizable, stylized, human types. Before the relatively recent discoveries of one of Menander's plays and parts of others in fragmentary papyri, and the

419 right *Terracotta figurine of a seated comic character, from South Italy, early 3rd century* BC. *He sits grinning and cross-legged, with his chin resting on his hand in a manner associated with the plotting slave. He wears sandals, leggings, and a long-sleeved costume; his thick hair, attached to his mask, is swept back in rolls.*

420 far right *Terracotta hanging oil-lamp in the shape of a comic actor, from Egypt, late 2nd century* BC. *His pose, attire, and gesture are similar to those of the other figurine [419], but his mask has a more furrowed brow. This figure, however, has been integrated into a novelty lamp, suspended from the ring above his head.*

421 above *Mosaic from the so-called Villa of Cicero in Pompeii, signed by Dioskorides of Samos, c. 100 BC, depicting three musicians and a slave boy, all in comic masks. The same composition appears in a large 3rd-century AD mosaic from Mytilene, where it is one of a set of theatrical scenes surrounding a portrait of Menander.*

422 above right *Fragment of a Roman wall-painting, third quarter of the 1st century BC. A large theatrical mask of Herakles and a number of his attributes (club, quiver, and lion skin) are set in an elaborate trompe-l'œil architectural vista.*

423 *Bronze portrait of Menander, first quarter of the 1st century AD. The image perhaps stems from the statue by the sons of Praxiteles erected outside the Theatre of Dionysos after Menander's death.*

development of scientific methods of deciphering them in the late 20th century, this form of comedy was almost entirely reconstructed through the lens of Roman adaptations. New Comedy was particularly influential on two 2nd-century BC Roman playwrights, Plautus and Terence, and a number of Pompeian wall-paintings and mosaics also took up some of its more famous scenes (imagery from the theatre became *de rigueur* in Roman dining rooms, another fusion of the Dionysian spheres of theatre and dining) [421, 422].

'All the world's a stage': the sentiment predates William Shakespeare by some two millennia, first attributed to a 4th-century BC philosopher named Anaxarchos. By extension, all mortals could be envisioned as actors. Perhaps the greatest impact New Comedy had on the 4th and 3rd centuries was precisely this sort of conceptual typecasting: the world, like the stage, could be conceived as a motley collection of different personas. Descriptions of theatrical masks provided one means of classifying human character (some are preserved in Julius Pollux's 2nd-century AD *Onomasticon*, or *Encyclopaedia of Terms*, 4.133–42); another was the collection of *Characters* observed in the marketplace, humorously sketched by a former student of Aristotle, Theophrastus, and paralleled in the visual arts by terracotta figurines of stock dramatic characters from comedies (like the scheming slave, plotting mischief with hand raised to his chin [419, 420]).

Wall-paintings, mosaics, and statuettes are only three of the ways in which the visual arts commemorated and mimicked the theatre in antiquity. Some pots, such as a late 5th-century Attic krater [418], appear to document known theatrical scenes: the two dancing chorus members decked out in elaborate bird costumes have been interpreted as alluding to *The Birds* or to *The Clouds* of Aristophanes, performed in 414 and 423 BC respectively. In other cases, while one may associate an image generally with the comic theatre on account of costume and gesture, it may be impossible to work out which lost play – if any specifically – is depicted.

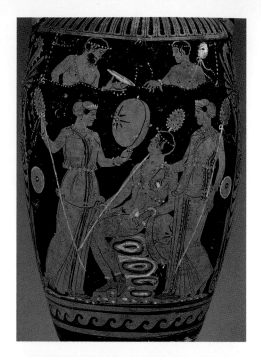

424, 425 *Two sides of a Campanian red-figure neck-amphora attributed to the Caivano Painter, c. 340 BC. On one side (top) are three satyrs and two maenads; on the other (above) is the dramatic story of Kapaneus holding a torch and climbing the battlements of Thebes (most famously told in Aeschylus' Seven Against Thebes). Although neither scene is explicitly taken from the theatre (certain non-theatrical elements are added, like the quadriga and winged Nike), there are hints that theatre provided the inspiration, especially in the lower scene: note, for example, the theatrical double doors [cf. 412], the way in which Kapaneus turns round to face the audience, and the exaggerated detail of the fortification's grained wood.*

The theatre's cultic connection with Dionysos continued to be displayed in South Italian painted vases, where quasi-dramatic scenes were the single most popular subjects [424, 425]. (Like the vases made for the Athenian symposium which ended up in Etruscan tombs, these pots were also often used in funerary contexts.) But the 4th century BC saw the emergence of theatres largely detached from the conceptual world of Dionysos, like the theatre at Epidauros [417], constructed in the sanctuary not of Dionysos but of Asklepios.

The most significant shift came in Roman times, when Greek theatres were adapted for various *spectacula* involving animals and gladiators. The Athenian priests of Dionysos were particularly distressed at this apparent 'secularization': most disturbing of all was the spillage of blood on the robes of those in the front row, where the priests themselves sat (cf. Dio Chrysostom, *Thirty-first Discourse* 121). To prevent animals from leaping into the audience nets were erected, and traces of supporting poles can still be seen in the outer *orchestra* of the Theatre of Dionysos.

The city of Rome had many theatres. All were free-standing (Greek theatres were usually built into the hillside), with auditoriums that were precisely semicircular. The Theatre of Balbus could accommodate some 6,000 people, the Theatre of Pompey 12,000, and the Theatre of Marcellus [304] around 10,000. Dramatic performances of sorts did continue on the Roman stage – not only 'pantomimes', but also a number of Latin comedies and tragedies (like the lost *Medea* of Ovid and *Thyestes* of Varius Rufus, and perhaps the surviving tragedies attributed to Seneca). But the total audiences in the city's theatres came nowhere near the 50,000 people that could be seated – quite apart from standing room – within the 76 arcades of the Colosseum, dedicated in AD 80 [426, 427]. This amphitheatre (literally 'theatre in the round') was a worthy rival to the biggest and best arenas of the modern world.

Oval theatrical structures on a smaller scale were common throughout the Roman world. Among the earliest is the provincial amphitheatre at Pompeii [430], erected between 80 and 70 BC, soon after the Roman colonization of the town, which could seat some 20,000 spectators; as various surviving graffiti and advertisements around Pompeii suggest, its games (*ludi*) could boast the most familiar names in gladiatorial combat. In their time, gladiatorial and animal combats seem to have been valued for the physical and martial prowess they displayed, and spectators perhaps aspired to emulate such skills. More than that, the games played a key role in defining what it meant to be Roman; perhaps this is why their imagery was especially popular on the fringes of the empire [428, 429]. The images, no less than the games that they idealized, served to form a cultural bond between the deserts of North Africa and the dominant cultural power of Rome.

The opening games *of the Colosseum in Rome in June AD 80 attracted spectators from every corner of the Empire, and were commemorated with a book of epigrams by the poet Martial. If in Athens the Greek theatre honoured its divine superintendent, Dionysos, the Roman amphitheatre bestowed a sort of cultic status on its imperial sponsor – in this case, Titus.*

What race is so remote, what race so barbarous, Caesar, that it does not have someone in your city watching the games? The Thracian farmer has come from Orphic Haemus; the Sarmatian, nourished through drinking horses' blood, has come; as has the man who has discovered the Nile and drinks from its first streams, and the man lapped by the waves of the farthest Tethys. The Arab has sped his way, as have the Sabaeans; the Cilicians have been sprayed by their own showers [of exported saffron]. The Sygambrians have come with their hair tied up in a knot, and the Ethiopians with their hair tied in a different fashion.

The sound of the peoples may be diverse: but it is united in calling you, Titus, the true father of the fatherland.

Martial, *On the Spectacles* 3

426, 427 *The Colosseum, Rome, begun by Vespasian and completed by Titus in* AD *80. Designed like all Roman amphitheatres as a complete oval, it was the grandest in the city and in the Empire, and held a variety of spectacles, such as gladiatorial combats, hunts, and even naval battles. It was built on the site of the artificial lake in the grounds of Nero's Domus Aurea – an imperial gesture of handing back power to the people (see p. 195).*

The building was constructed of concrete and faced with travertine limestone. On its exterior, an arrangement appeared for the first time that was to have an enduring legacy: the three arched storeys display the three main architectural orders, in ascending sequence of delicacy – Doric for the lowest tier, Ionic above that, and Corinthian at the top. Below the arena's original timber floor, which was covered with sand (harena, in Latin), was an elaborate two-storey system of passages, drains, and cages which was used, among other things, to stage-manage the release of animals. Above the arena was a retractable awning that shaded spectators from the midday sun [cf. 430].

428 right *Mosaic from El Djem, Tunisia, late 2nd century AD, showing a barbarian prisoner eaten alive by wild beasts – the sentence of damnatio ad bestias.*

429 below *Floor mosaic from Smirat, Tunisia, 3rd century AD. This commemorates a set of venationes (hunts) sponsored by a certain Magerius, who appears top right – upside-down). The composition is arranged to be seen in a way that suggests the spectator's viewpoint in an amphitheatre. Four bestiarii (hunters) fight four exotic leopards; all are named in the inscriptions. Diana, goddess of the hunt, appears centre left, and Bacchus on the right (upside-down): in the middle stands a boy holding money-bags for the hunters. The motivation for Magerius' generosity is preserved in the inscription: 'hoc est habere, hoc est posse' – this is money; this is power.*

430 opposite *The amphitheatre of Pompeii, built in the 70s BC, depicted in a wall-painting from the House of Actius Anicetus in Pompeii, third quarter of the 1st century AD. The subject seems to be a a riot between local people and the townsfolk of Nuceria that took place in the amphitheatre in AD 59: participants inside and outside the arena are throwing stones and wielding swords. Note the awning at the top, shading the seats.*

431 *The Doric Temple of Apollo at the Panhellenic sanctuary of Delphi [cf. 557]. The first temple was destroyed by earthquake or fire in the mid-6th century; it was then twice rebuilt, and the surviving columns date to the mid-4th century BC.*

A league of representatives from different Greek city states administered the sanctuary, and between the 6th and 4th centuries BC four 'sacred wars' were waged against states deemed guilty of 'sacrilege' of this sacred space of Apollo.

'KNOW THYSELF': APOLLO AND COSMIC HARMONY

Less than a decade after Nietzsche had published his *Birth of Tragedy* in 1872, French archaeologists began excavating what literary sources indicated to be the central ancient sanctuary of Apollo: this was the site of Delphi, high up in the slopes around Mount Parnassus, overlooked by the looming crags of the Phaedriades [ill. pp. 2–3; 431]. With one million francs at their disposal, the permission of the Greek Government to displace the inhabitants (and post-classical remains) of the modern town of Kastri that got in their way, and a range of romantic preconceptions about what they might find, the École Française set to work.

It is always difficult to gauge how earlier peoples might have responded to the natural world around them. But Delphi's wild remoteness – its sudden, spectacular emergence from the winding mountain-passes by which it is approached – coupled with the various origin-myths which later attached to it demand that we make some attempt. Even with the aid of modern archaeological science, the beginnings of Apollo's Delphic cult remain obscure. Greek myths came up with their own ways of explaining the sanctuary's origin: according to the most popular version, Apollo appropriated the sacred ground of Delphi from Gaia, the earth goddess. The *Theogony* of Hesiod tells us that Gaia was born from Chaos; and the *Homeric Hymn to Apollo* tells how Apollo won her sanctuary after defeating its guardian, the Python (hence Apollo's epithet, 'Pythian'). So the myth served to characterize Apollo as a god who defeats the world's primitive, dark, and disorderly cosmic forces and subordinates them to his celestial cause; and perhaps the juxtaposition of the impressive cultural monuments of Apollo's sanctuary and its wild setting served to heighten the visitor's sense of savagery subdued.

Gnothi seauton, 'Know thyself': that was the proverb attached to Apollo's cult at Delphi. According to tradition, it was inscribed (together with the words 'Nothing in excess') over his temple there. For centuries, Western thinkers have turned to the phrase as an inspired anticipation of their own philosophical tenets. For Socrates, whom the Delphic oracle declared to be wisest among men, it meant accepting the relativity of human knowledge (Socrates concluded that only he was 'wise' enough to acknowledge his own ignorance); for English Romantic poets like Shelley and Byron, it pointed to the individual's 'inner voice' that brought understanding and guidance; and for Sigmund Freud, it involved the psychoanalytical examination of the inner self – the search for the 'true you'. In the context of our analysis of the polarized realms of Apollo and Dionysos, however, the motto provides a neat means of synthesizing the antithesis between the two gods. If Dionysos offered ecstasy, a chance to experience 'otherness' (as through drinking, acting, madness, and death), Apollo promised a sort of inner knowledge. And it is in that context that we should probably understand the Delphic oracle over which he presided.

Oracles were one of the Classical world's most respected forms of divination, and Apollo's oracle at Delphi seems to have been the most respected of all. Like Apollo's other oracles throughout the Mediterranean, it could offer guidance to any individual, family, or state that sought the god's advice, by hinting at the universal order and fated destiny of things. Questions could be asked on a variety of issues: whether a city should go to war, how to be cured of disease, or even whose hand should be sought in marriage. After a consultation tax had been paid, and an initial sacrifice made, the enquiring supplicant would hope to be accepted into the inner temple, where a second sacrifice was offered and a question put to the Pythia. This female spokesperson for Apollo, who sat (probably unseen, in the depths of the

432 *Marble statue of a Muse, probably from Aphrodisias in Roman Asia Minor, c. AD 200. The Muses were the divine acolytes of Apollo and presided over music, literature, drama, and intellectual pursuits. Canonically there were nine, each associated with a specific branch of the arts. The leaning pose of this statue, together with her pensive, otherworldly gaze, correspond to images of both Polyhymnia, Muse of hymns and pantomime, and Melpomene, Muse of tragedy [cf. 576].*

Herodotus *tells how Croesus, king of Lydia in the 6th century BC, tested the authority of the world's different oracles. Having concluded that the oracles of Apollo at Delphi and of Amphiaraos at Oropos (in Boeotia) alone could be trusted, he decided to follow their counsel on military matters.*

When the Lydians arrived at their destination, they handed over the offerings and inquired of the oracle, saying: 'Croesus, King of the Lydians and of other peoples too, considers these oracles to be the only true ones for mankind. He has given you offerings as befit your knowledge, and now asks whether he should attack the Persians and whether he should make an alliance with any mortal army.' Such was their inquiry, and the same answer came from both oracles: if Croesus attacked the Persians, they told him, he would destroy a great empire. They also counselled him to discover who were the most powerful of the Greeks and to make them his friends.

Herodotus, *Histories* 1.53

*As Croesus later found out (*Histories *1.91), however, the great empire whose destruction the oracle foretold was not the kingdom of Persia: it was his own.*

temple) on a tripod in a permanent and perhaps drug-induced trance, would then boom her answer. Her nonsensical pronouncements were shaped into verse by a *prophetes*, or interpreter. Though these secondary answers were more comprehensible than the weird initial responses of the Pythia, they were usually at best enigmatic and at worst downright ambiguous riddles: to make sense of them called for a degree of individual soul-searching – of 'knowing oneself'.

The sequence of chaos to order, darkness to light, ignorance to knowledge is a recurrent one in the myths, rites, and images that surrounded Apollo. One way of understanding the ritual of having Apollo's prophets interpret the ramblings of the Pythia is to see it as symbolic of Apollo's ordering presence – a re-enactment of Apollo's victory over the dark forces that had ruled Delphi before him; another way, that the Pythia's utterances were not gibberish at all, but rather a divine vision of Apollo's cosmic understanding – something too sublime for human comprehension. In any case, those who abstained from repeating the process of enlightenment and self-critically thinking over Apollo's answers – or worse, turned their back on his predictions – did so at their peril.

Most famous is the story of Sophocles' tragedy, *Oedipus the King* (originally performed in the second half of the 5th century, perhaps between 430 and 425 BC). The Delphic oracle had warned Laius, King of Thebes, that his son would be his assassin. Desperate to escape this fate, Laius ordered that the infant Oedipus be abandoned to die on Mount Cithaeron; but the child was rescued and taken to the King of Corinth, who brought him up as his own. Suspecting that he was illegitimate, Oedipus proceeded to consult the oracle: 'you are destined to couple with your mother', it ordained; 'you will bring into the light a breed of children unbearable to look upon; and you will kill your father who gave you life' (lines 791–793). Terrified, Oedipus did not return to Corinth, fleeing instead to Thebes. On his way, he was almost thrown off the road by a chariot and, in anger, killed the old man and his entourage who were riding in it; forgetting the incident, and proceeding to rid Thebes of the Sphinx (see p. 8), he married the widowed queen of Thebes, Jocasta, and became king (*tyrannos* – a word loaded with negative connotations in 5th-century democratic Athens). Plague struck Thebes, and another oracle declared that it would only cease when the former king's killer was banished. From the various testimonies delivered on stage, the characters gradually piece together what the audience have known from the onset (dramatic irony at its finest); then comes the sudden moment of enlightenment, as Oedipus realizes the terrible truth about himself – that Jocasta is his mother, and that the old man whom he killed on his way to Thebes was none other than his father, Laius.

433 *A woman playing a* barbitos, *seen on a fragment of an Attic red-figure kylix attributed to Douris, c. 460–450* BC. *The* barbitos *had longer, more curvaceous arms than those of the* kithara, *and produced a lower-pitched sound; it was popular in the 6th and 5th centuries* BC. *Given her Oriental head-dress, the musician is most probably a* hetaira, *or female 'companion', at a symposium.*

For Oedipus, the revelation proves so terrible that he stabs out his eyes: the man famed for his far-sightedness in solving the Sphinx's riddle, but who had been blind all along as to his own identity, has no further need of them in his quest for self-understanding. As for us, the audience, the chorus sums up the precariousness of human fortune – the 'infernal machine' of fate over which Apollo rules – in the last lines of the play: 'call no man happy until he is dead'.

It must have been a small conceptual step in antiquity to move from Apollo as the god of order, control, and enlightenment to Apollo as god of harmony in an extended sense – that of music. The Classical world credited music – at once sensual and metaphysical – with a living force, and Apollo (together with his associate goddesses of science, poetry, and music, the Muses [432, 576]) presided over it with special enthusiasm: this explains one of his most frequent attributes, the lyre [392, 439]. The *paean* was Apollo's cult hymn in archaic Greece and it was reputed to have been so powerful that it could even cure physical sickness and disease, reinvigorating the body and restoring it to its natural order. In the right hands, like those of the mythical poet Orpheus [434], music could tame even the most savage beasts; its strains could move animate beings and inanimate objects alike, even break the laws of nature (as when Orpheus' song persuades the powers of the Underworld to release the soul of his beloved Eurydice [578]).

Fragmentary surviving musical instruments, a handful of musical notations, and a number of inscriptions and images pertaining to performance are all that remains today. Nevertheless, it is clear that music penetrated every sphere of Greek and Roman life – be it military (keeping rhythmic time for marching [310] or rowing, and leading Roman soldiers into battle with *tubae*, or trumpets), religious (using music to bridge the gap between mortals and gods), and private (music was performed at weddings, funerals, and symposia [433]). 'Let me not live without music' declares the chorus in Euripides' *Herakles* (line 676); few people did.

As early as the 3rd millennium BC, a number of 'harpist' statuettes from the Cyclades testify to the cultural importance of music [436], and small clay statues and colourful wall-paintings from Minoan Crete and Mycenaean Greece evoked and commemorated its ritual performance. In the *Odyssey*, itself probably once performed to musical accompaniment, we experience the lays of two fictional bards, Demodokos and Phemios (see p. 110); and in the *Iliad* even the macho Achilles seeks solace in his lyre (*Iliad* 9.185–89) [189]. This practice of singing to stringed accompaniment was called *kitharoidia* [435]. The *kithara* was only one, albeit the most popular, form of lyre: its basic component was a wooden box (originally a tortoise shell [439]); to this were attached two curved arms which

437 *A scene of courtship between older lovers (erastai) and their younger 'loved ones' (eromenoi): detail of an Attic red-figure cup by Douris, c. 480 BC. The lyres suspended in the background, alongside athletic equipment, indicate that the boys are all the more eligible for being well educated musically. (The seated boy on the left has a hare in his lap – a gift from his admirer.)*

Well-bred Roman schoolboys, and even more so girls, were also expected to have a degree of musical competence: so it was that in Rome's Secular Games of 17 BC, the poet Horace selected and trained the sons and daughters of the nobility to sing his *Hymn of the Century*. In Rome, there seem even to have been early guilds (*collegia*) of musicians, each dedicated to particular sorts of musical instruments. To represent the performance and paraphernalia of music on the walls of their mansions [435], or on their elaborate glass drinking implements [438], was a way for the Empire's aspiring rich and powerful to flex their intellectual, cultural, and social muscle. On the other hand, to more conservative Romans, music might be perceived as symptomatic of Greek decadence and regarded with due disdain: so when Tacitus reports rumours that Nero greeted the great fire of AD 64 with a lyric performance about the burning of Troy (a scene made famous by Peter Ustinov in the 1951 film *Quo Vadis?*), he does so with more than a whiff of criticism of the Emperor's Hellenic degeneracy (see *Annals* 15.39).

438 *Cameo glass skyphos, last quarter of the 1st century BC–first quarter of the 1st century AD. A wreathed satyr plays the kithara, as two half-draped women look on: one, leaning against a krater, sips from a wine-bowl; the other, also holding a wine-bowl, sits on a rocky outcrop.*

Cameo glass [cf. 473] was relatively rare in antiquity, because of the time and labour involved in its production: first coloured glass had to be covered with opaque white glass; then parts of that white layer were carved away to reveal the coloured surface beneath, and the remainder incised in relief.

Music's role within the education of the young only partly accounts for its association with Apollo. For a fuller explanation, we must briefly turn our attention to the principles of Greek mathematics, and in particular to the followers of the 6th-century philosopher Pythagoras. Besides his famous geometric theorem and musings on vegetarianism and reincarnation (pp. 67, 235–36), he was credited with one of the first analyses of musical pitch. According to Pythagoras and his followers (most notably, a 5th-century philosopher from Croton in South Italy named Philolaos), the spheres of mathematics, cosmology, and music were inexorably connected: musical harmony was a reflection of the cosmic *harmonia* with which mathematics too was concerned. Divide a musical instrument's string into sections using a bridge to produce a musical octave, fifth, and fourth, Pythagoras discovered, and the length of that string corresponds to the pitches produced in an orderly ratio (*tetraktys*) – 2:1, 3:2, 4:3. In music, in mathematics, and in the order of the universe, everything fitted together and could be charted in a coherent set of proportions and formulae. Apollo presided over all three spheres: one tradition even had it that Pythagoras was Apollo's son.

Listening to music was a serious, and ethical, pastime; not until Ptolemy's influential tract on *Harmonics*, written in 2nd-century AD Alexandria, did music become a science of the ear as much as the soul. Plato and Aristotle – both influenced by the tracts of the 5th-century philosopher Damon (now lost) – agreed that when listening to music our souls undergo change; and different types of music (classified by Plato into seven modes) could mould the listener's soul in a variety of ways. Some musical forms, Plato argued, could generate noble qualities, like strength, restraint, and courage. Others induced effeminacy, frivolity, and melancholy: they could have deleterious consequences for society's laws and values, and consequently posed a moral threat to Plato's ideal political order.

439 *Apollo, depicted on the interior of an Attic white-ground kylix from Delphi sometimes attributed to the Pistoxenos Painter, c. 470 BC. The god holds a lyre in his left hand – note its tortoise-shell base – and pours a libation with his right. He is crowned with laurel, and wears a himation over a peplos (a strange costume for a male, as opposed to female, figure). At the left is a raven, one of the birds sacred to Apollo.*

Something of the power of music is explained in book 2 of one of Plato's later works, the Laws, *by his protagonist, an Athenian visitor in Crete. Although Plato, like Pythagorean philosophers before him, seems to have been sympathetic to the view that music reflected a greater cosmic order (especially in his* Timaeus*), he disapproved of its 'mimetic' quality. Certainly, musical harmonies echoed the very structures of the universe – the so-called 'harmony of the spheres', the pitches made by heavenly bodies as they whirl around their orbits at different speeds – but they did so in a sensual way which, if abused, might permanently mar an individual's soul. Given its stirring effect, Plato concludes, music has to be carefully censored by the state so as not to corrupt the young.*

ATHENIAN: So, does it do someone any harm if he enjoys depraved dancing movements or songs? And, conversely, does it do him any good if he enjoys dances and songs of the opposite kind?
CLINIAS: Yes, presumably it does.
ATHENIAN: And is it not probable – or even inevitable, in fact – that the result will be the same as when someone who lives amidst the evil ways of corrupt men ends up not hating their customs, but rather condoning and adopting them? Will he not condemn his depravity only in jest, as if it were a mere dream? Surely it is inevitable that this man, in his delight, will grow into the habits that he enjoys, whether good or bad, even if he were ashamed to praise them explicitly. But what greater blessing, and what worse curse, could we say would inevitably happen to us than this?
CLINIAS: I don't think there is one.
ATHENIAN: So do we imagine that, wherever laws are fairly laid down . . . concerning the instruction and entertainment of music, poets should be granted this licence? Will poets be allowed to instruct the children of law-abiding citizens and young men in choirs whatever form of composition, rhythm or lyric they enjoy composing? Should it be left to chance whether the effects prove to be a virtue or a vice?
CLINIAS: How could that not be illogical!
ATHENIAN: And yet that is the current situation in virtually all states – all, that is, except Egypt.

Plato, *Laws* 656 A–D

440 *Marble sarcophagus of Maconiana Severiana, early 3rd century* AD *[cf. 396]. An inscription on the lid declares that it was dedicated by the deceased girl's senatorial-class parents; framing the inscription on either side are images of satyrs, maenads, and panthers. The front of the sarcophagus displays a scene of Dionysian revelry: Dionysos stands half-draped in the centre, supported by a satyr holding a* thyrsos, *while around him satyrs and maenads play the* aulos *and cymbals.*

The reclining female figure on the right, whose veil is lifted by Pan, is Ariadne. The myth of Ariadne, who was abandoned while asleep on the island of Naxos by Theseus but rescued by Dionysos, was a favourite image on Roman sarcophagi from the 2nd century onwards. The story had a number of religious and spiritual connotations, not least as an allegorical hope for the deceased's afterlife with Dionysos. Ariadne's face has been left unfinished: sarcophagi were often bought ready-made and customized by incorporating a likeness of the deceased.

In fact, Plato's strictures about music serve to bring us back full circle to Nietzsche's ideological dichotomy between the battling forces of Dionysos and Apollo. For not all forms of music were associated with Apollo: Dionysos had his own train of musical followers, and it was primarily their instruments that Plato would banish from his ideal republic on the grounds that they sounded (and induced) discordance, dissonance, and excessive emotion.

If Apollo's delight was the melodious and restrained lyre, Dionysos' instrument, at least by the 4th century BC, was the rousing, versatile, and dramatic *aulos* (*tibia* in Latin). The *aulos* was a cylindrical pipe, sounded with a reed (a cross between the modern oboe, clarinet, and flute), and played in pairs [390] – not to be confused with the *syrinx*, the 'panpipes' associated with Pan, the rustic god of shepherds and fertility [441, 579]. It was played in all manner of Dionysian rituals – at the theatre (accompanying the chorus of an Athenian drama [418]), Bacchic mysteries, and the symposium – perhaps because, in keeping with Dionysos' association with transformation, it was notorious for distorting the face of the musician as he or she puffed into it [440]. When the Phrygian satyr Marsyas fatally challenged Apollo to a music-making contest, he naturally chose to play his melody on the *aulos*, the antithetical instrument to Apollo's lyre. The rhythmic fervour of cymbals, the tambourine, and drums could also be connected to Dionysos and his primordial realm; and given that Dionysos also presided over the passage from life to death, the playing of such instruments made an appropriate subject on Roman sarcophagi [440].

To put it another way, then, different musical instruments could actually bring the very different, antithetical forces of Dionysos and Apollo to life. In music, as in the world at large, on one side could be found Dionysian discord; on the other, Apollonian harmony.

441 *Marble group of Pan and Daphnis (a mythical Sicilian herdsman credited with the invention of pastoral music), usually considered to be a Roman work derived from an earlier Hellenistic sculpture of the 3rd–2nd century* BC. *Pan was originally a rustic deity, associated with the Peloponnesian region of Arcadia, who was worshipped in a number of sacred caves. He resembles satyrs, but unlike them he is horned, cloven-hoofed, and has shaggy goat's legs. In this group, Pan instructs the young boy how to play the instrument associated with him, the panpipes. The Greek variety (as in this statue) had pipes of equal length in which wax was placed to produce different pitches; the Roman version usually had stepped pipes. Given Pan's associations with insatiable lust, and his connections with the realm of Dionysos in the Hellenistic period, it is no surprise that this music lesson has strong erotic overtones . . .*

IX THE CLASSICAL TRADITION OF ART

THIS BOOK is a sort of portable museum. We have woven a text around a set of Classical images from a variety of times and places; and we have offered a thematic framework for interpreting their many subjects, styles, and contexts. But in a museum, as in any illustrated catalogue, such images can easily, albeit anachronistically, become *objets d'art*. It seems fitting, then, to include here some assessment of the role images played in Classical antiquity; to offer a general ancient consensus about the ways in which 'objects of art' were considered; and to explore, along the way, how their various functions, and styles, developed over time.

As we have already noted (p. 163), there was no linguistic resource in either ancient Greek or Latin for distinguishing between our (admittedly sometimes blurred) categories of 'art' and 'craft'. The Greek and Latin terms *techne* and *ars* (from which we derive 'technique' and 'art' respectively) encompassed a wide spectrum of meanings: a Greek sculptor might be praised for his *techne*, but so too might a cobbler, doctor or bricklayer. Nor was there anything about the lifestyle of a sculptor or painter that set him apart from other craftsmen. So when, in the 2nd century AD, Lucian whimsically toyed with the idea of becoming a sculptor, he claims that a female personification of Sculpture visited him in a dream: with typical wit, Lucian characterizes her not as a gentle muse, but as an unkempt, stammering, and conspicuously masculine-looking foreigner. Sculpture is followed by Education, who summarizes the livelihood of the sculptor thus (*The Dream* 9):

> You will be nothing but a workman, doing hard physical labour and investing the entire hope of your livelihood in it. You will be obscure, earning a meagre and ignoble wage, a man of low esteem. You will be deemed lowly, reckoned cheap by public opinion, and you will not be courted by friends, feared by enemies, nor envied by your fellow citizens: instead, you will, quite simply, be a workman and one of the common mob, always cowering before the distinguished, serving the articulate, living a dog's life at the mercy of your superiors. Even if you should emerge a Pheidias or a Polykleitos and produce numerous marvellous works, so that all praise your art, there is nobody who, if he had any sense, upon looking at you would pray to be like you. For this is what you will be: a common workman, a handyman, and a manual labourer.

This hardly tallies with modern romantic notions of the inspired artist and creative 'genius'. Admittedly Lucian's vision is not representative of attitudes during the whole of antiquity: some artists did acquire a sort of celebrity status (and Pheidias, for example, was well connected with the political circles of 5th-century BC Athens). But for the most part, they were invisible manual workers, dedicated to a life of grime and grind. As for the product of their labour, it was never 'art for art's sake'. So how, then, *did* antiquity envisage the visual?

442 opposite *Wall-painting from the Basilica at Herculaneum, 1st century AD. Probably derived from a Pergamene original of the 3rd–2nd century BC, this Roman copy of an 'old master' scene shows the discovery of the infant Telephos – mythical founder of Pergamon – by his father Herakles. Telephos, whose name means 'suckled by a deer', can be seen in the foreground; the naked Herakles stands before a personification of Arcadia, the pastoral land where Telephos was abandoned by order of King Aleos. Auge, the daughter of Aleos, had given birth to the child, and had been banished [460]. Comprehending the myth behind this image was doubtless part of the painting's appeal to Roman connoisseurs of Classical art.*

CLASSICAL *AESTHETIKA*

The modern category of such a topic would be 'aesthetics', an academic discipline which arose in the mid-18th century, itself indebted to the doctrines of ancient Greek and Roman philosophical treatises: the term takes its name from the Greek word *aesthetika,* meaning 'those things which are perceived by the senses', as opposed to things that are thought of or 'known' by the brain. The aesthetic experiences undergone by an audience at the theatre were carefully analysed by Aristotle, as evident from his surviving lecture-notes, the *Poetics* (see p. 260). But no equivalent theory of response in the visual arts has come down to us from Classical antiquity. Philosophers might use the making of art as a metaphor, and rhetoricians and epigrammatic poets often turned to it to make stylistic analogies with their 'crafting' of words. We also know that individual artists and architects left instructive guides to their work – so the 5th-century BC sculptor Polykleitos detailed his rules for making the perfect human figure in his *Canon,* and various architects (including the builders of the Parthenon) prescribed their formulae for success. A minor literary tradition of art appreciation did exist, and gained popularity in the Hellenistic period when artists like Xenocrates (writing in the 3rd century BC) compiled their own accounts of the history of art. Very little survives today (Vitruvius' *On Architecture* is the only complete professional treatise on the visual arts, specifically buildings, to have been handed down to us: see p. 191), but snapshots and summaries are preserved in the works of later writers who compiled and preserved the traditions about the development of *techne* in sculpture and painting. The most famous example is Pliny the Elder's encyclopaedic *Natural History,* published *c.* AD 80. Pliny's Roman readership included collectors of art and connoisseurs who were keen to have information about the paintings and sculptures they owned.

But we can still assert that the science of aesthetics went unheeded. The focus of ancient interest was primarily fixed upon technical virtuosity – viewing art in terms of tricks, craftsmanship, and expertise. What art was for, how it engaged the emotions – these were issues that, for all their appeal to modern philosophers, hardly perplexed Greek and Roman thinkers, even those who recurrently appealed to notions of 'the beautiful' (notably Plato and 'Neo-Platonists' such as Plotinus).

So we glean what we can from such records as there are: for the most part, anecdotal tales about artists and their methods. In themselves, these curious stories became formative influences upon the composition of 'artists' lives' in 16th-century Europe and beyond, by Giorgio Vasari and others – making characteristic archetypes of the skill and temperament one might expect any artistic 'genius' to manifest. But incidentally they also reveal some key truths about the function of art in Classical society.

Whoever starts reading the ancient literary sources relating to Classical art very soon realizes that this was an ambience in which the boundaries between 'art' and 'life' were so blurred as to be almost non-existent. It was a world where humans, animals, and images truly cohabited. Here is one well-known example. A successful Greek painter of the late 5th–early 4th century BC, called Zeuxis, painted a bunch of grapes: birds flew up to his picture, trying to peck the fruit, and Zeuxis was pleased. Then a rival painter, Parrhasios, challenged him – would Zeuxis like to see an even more realistic scene, concealed behind that curtain? Zeuxis went to part the curtain. And he was fooled: the curtain was a painting on the studio wall (Pliny the Elder, *Natural History* 35.64–65). Or consider the minor epic related by Pausanias with regard to the statue of an early 5th-century Olympic champion from Thasos called Theagenes (*Guide to Greece* 6.11.4). Theagenes

443 opposite Pygmalion and Galatea, *by the English artist Ernest Normand, 1886. The antique model for the body of Pygmalion's statue was the* Venus de Milo, *a figure of Aphrodite in the Louvre of c. 100 BC, which the painter had seen in Paris during his honeymoon. The facial features appear to be those of the artist's wife – suggesting that for Normand, at least, Pygmalion's fantasy really could come true . . .*

'Pygmalion's power': that is how E.H. Gombrich (see pp. 124–25) described the 'Greek Revolution' towards naturalistic art. It was a phenomenon, he argued, that was fuelled by the drive to close the gap between art and reality – quite literally, to bring art to life. Pygmalion was the bachelor king of Cyprus, disillusioned with the female courtesans of his native land. So, as vividly recounted here in the Metamorphoses *of Ovid (written in the late 1st century BC), Pygmalion made a statue of the most beautiful woman he could imagine:*

Meanwhile, with marvellous artistry, he skilfully carved a statue out of snowy ivory and made it more beautiful than any mortal-born woman. He fell in love with his creation: it had the appearance of a real girl – it seemed alive, to long to move (did its modesty not forbid). Thus did his art conceal its art. Pygmalion gaped in wonder, his heart set aflame for this semblance of a human form. He often ran his hands over the work, touching it to see whether it was made of flesh or still of ivory. He kissed it, and fantasized that his kisses were returned. He spoke to it. He embraced it. He thought he felt his fingers sink into the limbs that he touched; then he felt afraid – what if he bruised her limbs as he squeezed them . . .?

Pygmalion proceeded to court the figure with gifts, adorn it with jewelry, even to sleep beside it on his couch. All the while, he prayed to Aphrodite that his ideal idol might become reality beneath his sensuous touch – that his imitation of life might actually come to life. Sure enough, Aphrodite obliged:

When Pygmalion returned, he headed straight for the statue of his girl, leaned over the couch, and kissed her. She seemed warm. Again he put his mouth to hers, feeling her breast with his hands – the ivory had lost its hardness. It softened at his touch, yielding to his fingers, and gave way just as Hymettian wax softens in the sun and is shaped, as the thumb moulds it, into many forms so as to be rendered usable through use itself. The lover stood dumbfounded, joyful, and doubtful, afraid that he was mistaken. Again and again, he re-examined with his hands the object of his prayers. Yes, it was flesh! The veins throbbed beneath his probing finger.

Ovid, *Metamorphoses* 10.247–58, 280–89

triumphed in several athletic disciplines, gaining many prizes but also making enemies. When Theagenes died, one of these enemies came each night to flog his honorific statue, as if inflicting posthumous revenge. The statue eventually fell off its pedestal, killing the assailant: it was then prosecuted, convicted on a charge of homicide, and 'drowned' in the sea as punishment. But then the island of Thasos suffered a crop failure. Apollo's oracle at Delphi blamed this on the abuse of the *mnema* (commemorative statue) of Theagenes. In the end, fishermen recovered the statue, and the image was re-dedicated – and thereafter venerated respectfully.

444 opposite *Detail of 'Statue B', one of two bronze sculptures found in the sea off Riace in Calabria, South Italy, mid-5th century BC. Standing just under 2 metres (about 6½ feet) tall, the figure once held a shield in his left hand and a lowered spear in the right. The head – cast separately, and soldered into place – evidently also wore a tipped-back Corinthian-style helmet [cf. 262]. Lips and nipples are of copper inlay.*

Although bronze seems to have been the favourite medium for Greek sculpture, at least during the Classical period, only a handful of 5th-century BC bronze sculptures remain today [e.g. 41]. Very few of those that outlived the Roman conquest of Greece survived the later attacks on Rome by Goths and Vandals, destruction by Byzantine iconoclasts, and the fall of Constantinople in 1453.

445 right *Detail of an Attic red-figure kylix known as the Foundry Cup, the name-vase of the Foundry Painter, c. 490–480 BC [cf. 256, 585]. Two bronzeworkers are putting the finishing touches to an over-life-size statue of an advancing warrior. The tools they are using to smooth any tangs on the bronze surface closely resemble the strigils, or scrapers, used by athletes after a workout [52].*

Elsewhere in Pausanias, and evident from numerous other authors and inscriptions throughout the Graeco-Roman world (see p. 82), we read of statues being washed, perfumed, clothed, and adorned; statues apparently smiling, frowning, weeping, and sweating; statues moving around; and statues involved in sex. Was there ever such a society in which images enjoyed this extent of virtual reality? Not everyone regarded this equivalence of life and art with satisfaction. Principally, it was Plato who raised the alarm, and who tried to apply philosophical strictures on the devout illusionism of art in his time.

Plato actually had very little to say about artists and the making of images as such. What preoccupied him was the wider enterprise of *mimesis*, 'imitation'; and when he cites imitation as a practice or habit, Plato usually has poetry or diction in mind. A passage in the *Republic* (3.396b) castigates, for instance, the performer who thinks he is clever to conjure up a farmyard by imitating the barking of dogs and screeching of fowl. However, it is clear that Plato's suspicion of mimetic performance extended to the visual arts. So Plato has sometimes been caricatured as an enemy of art, on the basis of a logical chain or syllogism which runs as follows: 'Imitation is bad. All art is imitative [*mimetike*]. Therefore, all art is bad.' Plato, it is often asserted, would ban art and artists from his ideal polity. In fact the second stage of that sequential logic is unfair. Plato recognized that not all art was centred around imitation (*Republic* 607a). Where art was conceptual, predictable, and schematic, he admired its purpose and effect (*Laws* 656d): Plato praised Egyptian images, for example, because they were regulated by a set of diagrammatic forms and 'proper rules' (*kala schemata*) that had remained unchanged for

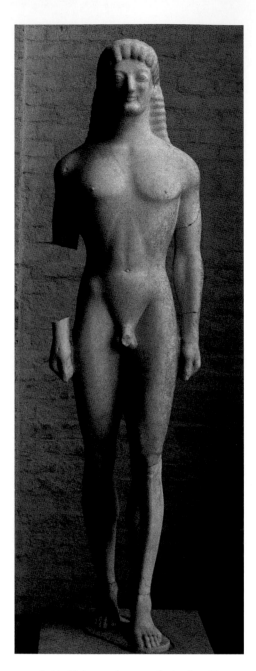

446 *Marble* kouros *known as the* Apollo of Tenea, *c. 550 BC. The bold nudity of this commemorative or votive statue-type gave Greek sculptors in the Archaic period repeated opportunities for studying the surface appearance of the male anatomy. The relative chronology of the kouroi has been constructed largely on the basis of anatomical 'accuracy' displayed within a highly schematic pose. The advanced leg is a stock component of this pose; so too (until the late 6th century BC) the fixed 'Archaic smile'.*

millennia. But as for the Greek artists of his own day, such as the celebrated Zeuxis who fooled birds with his picture of grapes, they were working to a very different ideal – of blurring the difference between truth and fiction, and thereby *deceiving* their viewers.

Unlike Plato, we seek to understand this aim of illusionism, not condemn it. It was clearly the main critical criterion by which the great Classical painters – Apelles, Parrhasios, Protogenes, and others – earned their reputation. The story was told about how Parrhasios, commissioned to paint the myth of how the Titan Prometheus was gruesomely punished by Zeus for the theft of fire [582], purchased a slave after the sack of Olynthos in 348 BC and put the man to slow and fatal torture in his studio in order to record 'convincingly' the expressions of someone in extreme distress (Seneca the Elder, *Controversies* 10.5). Or else an artist might achieve *mimesis* by sheer luck: Apelles, frustrated by his failure to depict the flecks of foam around a horse's mouth, in his enraged 'perplexity' (*aporia*) is said to have hurled a cleaning sponge at the picture – and the sponge made just the effect he had been trying to get (Sextus Empiricus, *Outlines of Pyrrhonism* 1.28). Philosophers outside the Platonic tradition also allowed that artists might not only 'copy' what they saw, but resort also to the power of the imagination (*phantasia*) – and thereby reveal things that could not be seen (this was one way of explaining how, for example, Pheidias created his wondrous image of Zeus at Olympia [126]: see Philostratos, *Life of Apollonius of Tyana* 6.19).

Painters were revered for investing their two-dimensional medium with depth – an illusionistic development that was probably accelerated by the rise in the 5th century BC of perspectival stage-painting (*skenographia*), in which, according to Vitruvius (*On Architecture* 1.2.2), 'some parts of a building, drawn on a vertical flat façade, may seem to be withdrawing into the background, others to be standing out in front'. With most Greek paintings now lost, the development of what, from the Renaissance onwards, would be known as 'pictorial perspective' and 'foreshortening' can only vaguely be charted – primarily from the distorted evidence of painted pottery and Roman wall-paintings from Pompeii and Herculaneum [e.g. 465, and cf. 243]. But sculpture, and in particular free-standing statuary, was the foremost medium for exploring the potential of illusionistic images in the ancient Greek *polis*. As forms projecting in three dimensions, statues were literally made honorary members of the community. They were like a second population.

The quantity of statues occupying certain sites in the Classical world is almost unimaginable. It has been estimated, for example, that the city of Rome once had some half a million statues on display – something like one statue for every two human beings. Some Greek sanctuaries had to be periodically cleared of votive figures, on account of a gross overcrowding by works of art. Given the testimonies of such quantity, it is not an exaggeration to say that relatively little survives of Classical art. Two important ancient categories of production, 'large-scale painting' (*megalographia*) and hollow bronze-casting, are notably absent from most museum collections today (with a few exceptions [e.g. 444]). On the other hand, some types of minor artefact have lasted more durably than their makers can ever have dreamed: this is certainly true of Greek painted vases. Today they fetch vast sums at auction; but their original market value was meagre.

The sheer quantity is gone, but the quality of what remains is telling. In the Western world, the artistic output of the Greeks, Romans, and Etruscans has been more or less systematically studied at least since the antiquarian J. J. Winckelmann [498] first published the original German edition of his *History of the Art of Antiquity* in 1764. From Winckelmann onwards, the general endeavour of scholars and

447 *Hades seizes Persephone: detail of a painting on the wall of a tomb at Vergina in northern Greece, third quarter of the 4th century BC. Tentatively attributed to a painter called Nikomachos, this scene offers a tantalizing sample of the range of colour and composition involved in the (mostly lost) Greek art of* megalographia *(or large-scale painting).*

connoisseurs has been to 'sort' and typologize the ancient production of art, whether by provenance and locality (e.g. 'Tanagra figurines', 'Fayum portraits'), presumed genre (e.g. '*kouroi*', 'funerary reliefs'), medium or craft specialization (e.g. 'engraved gems', 'alabaster sarcophagi'), chronological style (e.g. the 'four styles' of Pompeian painting [465]), or individual artists and workshops (e.g. 'Pheidias', 'The Aphrodisian School'). To compensate for the fact that most ancient art went unsigned, pieces must be attributed by idiosyncrasies of style (e.g. 'Polykleitan'), and sometimes assigned to artists whose names have had to be invented (e.g. 'Elbows-Out Painter', 'Master of the Olympia Pediments').

To those coming to it for the first time, such typologizing can seem an artificial and far-fetched enterprise. But for Sir John Beazley, who pioneered techniques of attribution in Greek vase-painting, the process of identifying an artist's hand was perceived as a quasi-scientific affair. Following the super-sleuth methods of late 19th-century connoisseurs of Italian art, especially Giovanni Morelli, Beazley scrutinized those figurative details of draughtsmanship that were executed with the least degree of conscious realization – anklebones, kneecaps, earlobes, and so on.

Whatever else this approach may reveal about the workshops and contexts in which Athenian potters worked, it does confirm the patently competitive drive of artistic production in the 6th and 5th centuries: pot-painters drew caricatures of their rivals and comrades, challenging them, in cheeky inscriptions, to outdo their virtuoso innovations. In the world of sculptural production too, such contests abounded, as when several contestants – including Pheidias and Polykleitos – each vied to make the best statue of an Amazon: as one might expect, each sculptor judged his own creation to be the finest (Pliny the Elder, *Natural History* 34.53).

Alongside or underpinning this sorting process has been the broad assumption that the prime concern of artists from *c*. 800 BC to *c*. AD 200 was to make images in 'naturalistic' fashion. The closer an image came to nature, the closer it came to 'perfection'. Winckelmann and his successors did not hesitate to use terms like 'perfect', in an absolute sense; entailing, of course, that a vocabulary must be found for the less-than-perfect ('degenerate', 'archaic', 'primitive', etc.: see p. 328). And it is ultimately from Winckelmann that the entrenched recourse to a chronological, linear, and evolutionary chain of ancient artistic development descends.

448 *Detail of the 'Married Couple' sarcophagus from Cerveteri, c. 520–500 BC. The medium of terracotta sculpture was a speciality of Etruscan art [cf. 177]: and though this couple are shown reclining on a couch as if at a Greek-style symposium – their hands once held drinking-cups and perhaps items of food – the aspect of male–female conviviality belongs very much to Etruscan ethnic identity [cf. 99, 406].*

A CHRONOLOGICAL SYNTHESIS

Modern art historians prefer not to discuss their subject in the argot of 'perfection', 'degeneracy', or other absolute terms; and most modern viewers of art accept that illusionistic naturalism is not art's only purpose, still less its evolutionary determinant (although many still wish it were). So is there any use in trying to construct a broad chronological summary of how art functioned in the Classical world? In some ways, any attempt is destined to be incomplete: it is near impossible to devise any universal scheme that will incorporate the arts of Etruria [448], or any other non-Greek and later non-Roman people, without imposing a model that sees one culture as the dominant producer, the other its passive consumer; and any chronological arrangement will invariably reflect our own artificial sense of historical order. We should point out too that the styles of different historical periods and places existed alongside each other, so that there was in fact an array of Classical traditions of art rather than any single monolithic tradition: in Rome, a melange of styles could be incorporated into a given monument to summon up a variety of cultural and political connotations, as we encountered, for example, on the Ara Pacis (pp. 182–84).

Still, for the sake of academic tidiness, the following scheme of development – roughly divided into the conventional epochs of 'Geometric', 'Archaic', 'Classical', 'Hellenistic', and 'Roman' – is offered for what it is worth as a broad outline of both the features and the developing functions of the visual arts.

I. Geometric period (9th–8th centuries BC)

This can be briefly summarized. Stylistically, Geometric art is so called because of its preference for rectilinear patterns: 'Protogeometric' mesmeric circles (which roughly characterize pot-painting between 1050 and 900 BC) gave way to symmetrical meandering lines and running crenellations. Figurative forms were relatively late to appear: heraldic horses, birds, deer, and goats are first rendered in the same decorative ways as other painted patterns, and human figures follow in the 8th century [16, 202–4]. In terms of functions, art appears

449 *Bronze statuette from Olympia, a votive figurine or cauldron attachment, late 8th century BC. Many thousands of small bronze figurines were recovered from the layers of 9th- and 8th-century cult practice at Olympia – before and around the time of the supposed beginning of the Olympic Games (776 BC).*

450 *Geometric bronze statuette of a horse, perhaps from Olympia, c. 750–700 BC.*

451 *Interior of a late Geometric cup from Attica, c. 730 BC. Grazing deer and birds appear amid a densely patterned decorative surface. The ring of highly stylized animal motifs is typical of the 'Orientalizing' phase of Greek art. Both the shape and decoration of this cup have been related to repoussé bronze bowls that were being imported from Phoenicia at the time – a phenomenon facilitated by increased trading by sea (see pp. 218–22).*

452 *Seated limestone figure from Prinias, Crete, c. 620–600 BC. This once formed part of a temple structure, probably the lintel of a ceremonial entrance.*

in this period essentially as a mode of gift-giving, and the core transactional principles of such exchange, as outlined by anthropological theorists (famously Marcel Mauss in his 1925 essay, *The Gift: Forms and Functions of Exchange in Archaic Societies*), are surely embodied in the early bronze votive offerings excavated at sanctuaries such as Olympia (see p. 36). Whether in the shape of large tripods or figurines, these are objects outside the scope of ordinary use, things either prized in themselves (tripods) or else symbolic of esteemed possessions (horses [cf. 450], chariots, cattle). In the terminology of Homeric epic, they count as *keimelia*, 'items to be treasured': Greeks and Etruscans alike, aristocrats across the Mediterranean 'networked' by exchanging such tokens of their status. In late Geometric Athens, large ceramic vessels, adorned with funerary and fantastic military scenes, were also used as markers on top of graves [16], sometimes with holes knocked through their bases to allow libations to be poured to the grave beneath.

2. Archaic period (7th–early 5th centuries BC)

The arts produced in the period straddling the late Geometric and early Archaic eras, roughly corresponding to the mid-8th to 7th centuries, are characterized by the conspicuous influence of the Near East (through increased trade with the Levant, Phoenicia, and Anatolia), and are therefore described as 'Orientalizing' [32, 451]. This formative phase of Classical iconography is chiefly marked by the influx of 'exotic' motifs – effectively familiarizing Mediterranean inhabitants with animals that they could never have hoped (or feared) to encounter in their own territory, such as lions and panthers. Statues too betray the influence of Syrian and Phoenician workshops. They are especially common on the island of Crete, a central trading-post between East and West, and today they are termed 'Daedalic', after the legendary Cretan craftsman Daedalus [573], to whom such statues were attributed in antiquity. They have flat backs, ornate almond-shaped eyes, and horizontal brows [257, 452]. Ivory and wood were the predominant media at first, but later artists became more confident at working limestone and marble.

453 Kouros *and* kore *as discovered at Merenda in Attica, c. 550 BC. Not a couple: an inscription on the* kore *defines her as a girl who died unmarried, and whose name was Phrasikleia ('well spoken-of').*

454 *Bronze mirror with Gorgon mask in repoussé relief, perhaps from South Italy, c. 500–480 BC. The Gorgon Medusa's head was 'apotropaic', having powers to 'turn away' evil; therefore it was often used as an emblem on temples [e.g. 132], shields, amulets – or, as here, on the reverse side of a mirror.*

The prevalent function of Orientalizing art and that of the Archaic period proper continues to be votive. However, we notice that art's symbolic purpose is undergoing a radical shift. It is not enough to offer a miniature model of an ox or a warrior. Archaic sculptors were now attempting to create an actual 'presence' in their art of 'representation'. Nowhere is this intention more evident than in the inscriptions incised (with the advent of literacy, *c.* 650 BC onwards) on the base or surface of certain statues. The statue becomes the subject of the verb 'I am' (*eimi*), as if calling for the attention of passers-by. It makes a claim upon space as a 'marker' or sign (*sema*). It also makes a claim upon time, as a solid reminder (*mnema*) of something that has passed away – particularly in the context of ceramic or sculpted funerary markers, which now begin to be one of art's primary manifestations (see pp. 16–17).

'I am the sign of Phrasikleia. Maiden [*kore*] I shall be called forever – the title I have been given by the gods in place of marriage.' The plangent message inscribed to accompany the statue of a girl from Attica in the mid-6th century BC [453] exemplifies the Archaic desire for an artefact to take the place of a flesh-and-blood person. Even while serving as witness or 'double' to an individual mortal, a statue was conceived as autonomous, with an existence of its own. And then we need to remember that the 'embodiment' imagined here was not that of a 'real being', but rather a figure beyond normality – heroized or immortalized (see p. 83). So when a *kouros* stands for a buried mortal, it may grow in stature in order to show the grand new ancestral status of the deceased. It is not fanciful, in this funerary context, to suppose that the advanced leg of the schematic *kouros* has the effect of making the image seem 'lively' and freed from *rigor mortis*. And when the 'Archaic smile' appears in Greek art from around the mid-6th century [446, 453] – when statues are adorned with cryptic smiles, even when consumed by the pangs of death – it must have been precisely with this desire to animate and invigorate the figure.

Another note from Pausanias confirms the essential faith in the power of images from the 6th century onwards (*Guide to Greece* 10.18.4). At Delphi he records that the people of Orneai in the Argolid, struggling in a war against Sicyon, vowed to Apollo that if they gained victory over the Sicyonians, they would offer daily processions to the god, and make abundant sacrifices too. Victory for Orneai ensued, and the city began paying its dues at Delphi. But soon the cost of such payment became a terrible economic burden: so, as Pausanias simply reports, 'they came up with the solution of dedicating to the god his procession and his sacrifice cast in bronze'. Representation was, therefore, not only honourable, but durably so.

Archaic artists richly extended the repertoire of the monstrous and fabulous: certain mythical motifs became especially popular, like that of the Gorgon staring out and 'petrifying' the viewer [454] (see p. 87). But Archaic figural representations remained stylized, with many details – ears, hair, musculature – still treated as surface patterns.

3. Classical period (early 5th–4th centuries BC)

In the Classical period, the human body became subject to a new and fetishistic reappraisal, with an increased awareness of its anatomical make-up and organic processes of movement [272]. As we have hinted, to say that Classical art became radically 'naturalistic' is slightly to misconstrue the case: it is impossible, for example, to recreate in the flesh the pose of Myron's *Diskobolos* [1] because this 'synoptic' statue incorporates several movements in a single representation.

455 *Marble* Winged Victory *by Paionios, from Olympia, c. 425 BC. The setting of this piece upon a lofty column within the statue-crowded Altis [47], was integral to its effect of swooping airborne descent.*

But what is important to grasp about the art of the Classical period is how 'the imitation of nature' encompassed an idealization of bodily beauty, both male [e.g. 37] and female [e.g. 457]. Precisely what lay behind that 'revolution', or to what extent we should rather see it as the natural evolution from 6th-century developments, remains (and has long remained) open to debate (see p. 174).

What of the function of Classical art? We described the *Tyrannicides* group originally erected in the Agora of Athens as 'a talismanic icon' of Athenian democracy (p. 173). We may go further, and claim that the figures of Harmodios and Aristogeiton are heralds of a new function for art in the Classical period: to make political statements [270, 271].

In Athens around 460 BC a sequence of large paintings was commissioned to hang in a colonnade off the Agora, not far from the *Tyrannicides*. This Stoa Poikile, or Painted Stoa [302:15], was a much-frequented place; many Athenian citizens must have passed by it every day. The paintings were all battle-related. One showed Theseus, the legendary early king of Athens, leading his people against an invasion by Amazons. Another depicted an encounter from recent history – the predominantly Athenian triumph over the Persians at Marathon in 490 BC. Marathon had been the first big military test of the Athenian democratic state, and was glorified accordingly, both in Athens and in the Panhellenic sanctuaries where citizens of Athens, and other states, participated. The entire colonnade of the Stoa Poikile can be seen as a political initiative, moved through assemblies and committees by Kimon, the son of Miltiades – and Miltiades was the general largely credited with strategic success at Marathon. But for centuries (certainly still in the time of Pausanias: *Guide to Greece* 1.15.1–4) the paintings enshrined more than that. They figured the semi-mythic ideals on which the Athenian constitution was founded.

Within the Greek democratic *polis*, opportunities for individual citizens to raise statues were limited (see pp. 174–75). Equality and collectivism inhibited personal patronage. Some posthumous commemoration was indulged, such as the statues of Pericles [cf. 262] and his father set up on the Athenian Acropolis, as if saying to those who entered through the great Propylaia, 'welcome to Periclean Athens'. But more often sculptors were commissioned to devise images of community-wide significance – perhaps mindful of Aristotle's appeal for 'ethical' art (*Politics* 1340a), or else simply following the wishes of the citizens' Assembly and Council.

Identifying the precise significance of these civic-sponsored images is not easy. No monument proves that more than the Parthenon frieze, to which we shall return in the next chapter (pp. 314–19). But there is no doubt whatsoever that this was an epoch in which sculpture was a key ideological instrument for expressing rivalry between city-states. It is sufficient to consider the commissions recorded at sanctuaries such as Delphi and Olympia. Did the ideal of Panhellenism at these sites restrict one Greek city from celebrating military victory over another? Apparently not. Pausanias tells us (*Guide to Greece* 5.24.3) that in the Altis (sacred 'grove') of the Temple of Zeus at Olympia [47] the Spartans erected a statue of Zeus as thank-offering for their success in quelling a rebellion by the Messenians – whom the Spartans had made their subjects – probably around 464–456 BC. A few decades later, in 425–424, there was revenge for Messene. With Athenian assistance, they captured an entire Spartan garrison on the island of Sphacteria, just off the coast from Pylos (Thucydides, *History of the Peloponnesian War* 4.2–41). What better place to commemorate the victory than in the Altis at Olympia? And what better way than the eye-catchingly airborne Nike of Paionios [455] – so clearly eclipsing or trumping the nearby Spartan votives?

456 above *Limestone and marble figure of a goddess, probably from South Italy, c. 424–400 BC. Missing from this over-life-size statue are the attributes she once held, but Aphrodite is a likely identity. The 'acrolithic' technique of combining marble (here, for the goddess's flesh) with other stones or media was favoured in the Greek colonies of Sicily and South Italy.*

457 above right *The* Winged Victory of Samothrace: *marble statue perhaps erected c. 300 BC in the 'Sanctuary of the Great Gods' on the island of Samothrace, in the eastern Aegean. The basis of the figure was set upon a sculpted prow which stood in a pool of water, in a naturally elevated and windswept position.*

4. Hellenistic period (323–31 BC)

'Hellenistic' is a relatively modern term, used to refer to a period of several centuries following the death of Alexander the Great in 323 BC. It was coined by J. G. Droysen in the 19th century, and delineates the era in which Greek language, literature, and art were diffused among non-Greek ethnic groups. For Droysen, the shift from the former 'Hellenic' (purely Greek) to the 'Hellenistic' world was an essentially positive one: the Hellenistic world facilitated the spread of *koine* (common dialect) Greek, the language of the Christian gospels, and thereby the diffusion of Christianity among Jews and gentiles. Throughout much of the late 19th and 20th century, however, Hellenistic art and literature were seen as something 'unoriginal', 'baroque', and 'over the top'; they reflected a supposed 'fall from grace' from earlier, and supposedly purer, Classical forms.

458–60 *The Great Altar of Zeus from Pergamon,* c. 165 BC. *The main altar base was covered with marble reliefs of the battle between gods and giants. On the east frieze (above) we see Athena wrenching the giant Alkyoneus away from his mother Gaia, who reaches out from her earthly domain to protect him: he is entwined by a serpent, and his pose recalls that of Laocoön [226]. On the north wing, beside the stairway (opposite, above), a clan of sea gods join in the fray against*

the giants. The depth, vigour, and exuberance of the relief carving are unparalleled in antiquity: notice how the combatants even appear to spill off the edge of the relief and to climb up the altar's steps.

A quieter frieze within the altar (opposite, below) shows episodes from the epic life of Telephos, mythical founder of Pergamon: carpenters are constructing the little boat in which Auge, mother of Telephos, is to be banished abroad [cf. 442].

Many scholars have tried to supply overall 'mentalities' for the Hellenistic period, stressing the 'theatricality' of its art, its 'individualism', or its new 'scholarly' and 'cosmopolitan' outlook. Stylistically, however, there is little break between the technical developments in Classical sculpture and painting in the 5th and 4th centuries and those in the 3rd, 2nd, and 1st; at the same time, it remains notoriously difficult to assign accurate dates for such emblematic 'Hellenistic' pieces as the *Winged Victory of Samothrace* [457] or the *Laocoön* group [226]. It is worth emphasizing that in this situation it is not only chronology that becomes uncertain; so too does our knowledge of the artists involved. (The most accomplished piece of sculpture in this period is the Great Altar of Zeus from Pergamon [458–60]: but we know nothing of the sixteen or so sculptors who signed it.) Most importantly of all, the art of this period tends to lose its function of specific reference.

Take another well-known Hellenistic 'masterpiece', the so-called *Uffizi Wrestlers* in Florence [461]. We do not know its maker. Nor do we know the names of the combatants. And, significantly, even if we were connoisseurs of the sport – probably the all-in fight (*pankration*), not wrestling – we could not tell which of them is going to win. They seem equally matched: the outcome is uncertain.

461 *The Uffizi Wrestlers: Roman marble copy, probably after a Hellenistic bronze original of c. 200 BC. (This group, discovered in Rome in 1583 and subsequently provided with heads, was one of the prize exhibits in the Tribuna of the Uffizi [479].)*

This is very different from any statue by Myron or Polykleitos heroizing an individual athletic victor [1, 37]. The Uffizi group cannot have been made with such a purpose. It was probably once placed as the crowning decoration of a *palaestra*. It served, then, to define an ambience, or characterize a space (and like many other Hellenistic sculptures, it seems to have been designed for viewing 'in the round').

We know that Hellenistic kings sometimes conceived of themselves as having Dionysian powers – including special erotic licence, which is why they might have commissioned groups of nymphs and satyrs, for example, or a sprawling 'rustic' figure such as the *Barberini Faun* [215]. Within the patronage of these kings, sculptors were of course required to produce larger-than-life, nude portraits – or at least Alexander-like stereotypes of a ruler's physiognomy [283, 462]. To call such sculptures evidence of ancient 'propaganda machines' would be to put the case too strongly (since ancient methods of image production and dissemination never matched those of 20th-century autocrats); but in the Hellenistic world, portraits that flaunted individual political power – on coins, in statuary, and even in the private home – became, for the first time, widely disseminated across cities, countries, and even continents. And it is probably this political aspect of Hellenistic art, together with a later distrust of the monarchic governments within which it was produced, that has been responsible for its dismissal as artistically 'decadent'.

Many other statues seem to have been made with no intention of representing (or glorifying) particular political individuals. The *Dying Gaul* [463] is one example of the Hellenistic generic interest in the exotic, not to mention the emotional plight of the conquered. Looking at the type of Hellenistic statue that has come to be known as the *Old Fisherman* [13], some may intuitively sense that it was, as it were, realistically modelled 'from life'; but it is not a named fisherman. Similarly the *Drunken Old Hag* attributed to Myron of Pergamon (not to be confused with the Athenian Myron) [11] may or may not have been related to a Dionysian festival of 'jug-carrying', but wherever the statue was once placed, surely no viewer recognized herself there. So Hellenistic art was, above all, atmospheric art.

Conventionally the Hellenistic period ends in 31 BC, with the victory of Octavian (Augustus) over the forces of Antony and Cleopatra at Actium. What next? Does Classical art end there – on the brink of the institutional formation of the Roman Empire?

462 The Terme Ruler, *3rd or 2nd century BC. The bronze figure is thought to represent a ruler of one of the Hellenistic kingdoms, posing as the heroic 'saviour' (soter) of his subjects, in the manner of Alexander the Great. The exaggerated musculature of the over-life-size body, which contrasts with the unnaturally small head, gives a sense of the figure's kingly* deinotes *('awesome forcefulness').*

463 The Dying Gaul: *Roman marble copy after a bronze statue set up in Pergamon c. 220 BC. The original is thought to have been part of the 'Greater Attalid Group', commemorating victory over the Galatians, or Gauls, by the Pergamene Attalids; some have (rather romantically) posited that this copy was commissioned by Julius Caesar in the mid-1st century BC, perhaps to celebrate his own military triumphs in Gaul. On rediscovery (around 1623) the statue was taken to represent a dying gladiator. The torque around his neck, moustache, and tousled hair (an effect reputedly achieved by applying limewater), however, were standard ways of signalling Galatian ethnic identity.*

5. The arts of Rome (31 BC–c. AD 330)

Of course not. Imperial Rome had plenty of uses for art, not least the maintenance of some unifying ideology throughout its constituent provinces. Yet there is no denying that by the late 1st century BC the 'Classical tradition of art' seemed to be at a formal end – if Romans thought about the matter at all. When, earlier in that century, the sculptor Pasiteles assembled his five volumes of *Great Masterpieces* (*Nobilia Opera*) it was tantamount to acknowledging this terminal situation. In certain areas of production, such as the casting of hollow bronze statues, there was (as Pliny the Elder recorded) a virtual cessation of output. True, new media were developed, such as the assemblage of floor and wall mosaics; and genres of art were explored that the Greeks had hardly known – such as landscape painting [465] (pioneered by one Studius or Ludius, see pp. 150–51) and 'veristic' portraiture [280]. But as far as Roman commentators and connoisseurs were concerned, the technical project of Classical art – the illusionistic mimesis of form that Plato so deplored – seemed largely to have been accomplished. Myron, Pheidias, Polykleitos, Parrhasios, Zeuxis, Lysippos, Apelles – these were some of the 'great names' of that achievement, whose works were eminently worth collecting. And rich Romans collected them with a vengeance – in the case of one late Republican politician, the notorious Gaius Verres, even to the point of illegality.

On the other hand, there was a vein of cultural hostility in Rome towards 'foreign' Greek art that can be traced back to the middle Republican period. In the eyes of traditionalists and Hellenophobes such as Cato the Elder, the Greek practice of nudity and its representation was one obvious sign of Greek 'corruption'. Even the more cosmopolitan-minded Pliny the Elder was inclined to regard art as a form of morally dubious *luxuria*. From the 3rd century BC onwards, however, a huge influx of sculptures and paintings, most of them Greek, entered Rome by way of war booty and triumphal processions [cf. 477]. Home-coming generals brought in the spoils of their success; the streets were lined by citizens eager to see proof of Rome's territorial expansion around the Mediterranean and beyond. Such trophies embellished the city and confirmed its status as a centre of power, so that the Romans became connoisseurs almost inadvertently. By Cicero's time, in the mid-1st century BC, the value of a Greek bronze statue lay not in its metal weight, but rather in its appeal to a collectors' market.

Suetonius (*Life of Augustus* 75) relates how Augustus played a dinner-party game that involved turning all the pictures on the wall back to front before the guests arrived. The host would then conduct a 'blind' auction: some guests ended up spending far too much money on a painting, while others got a bargain. Either way, the game could only have provided amusement if everyone present were able to recognize a picture's value at first sight. Becoming familiar with Greek art was, in elevated social circles, *de rigueur*. And because the stock of 'originals' was restricted, 'copies' abounded. The interior colonnades and gardens of Roman houses and villas served as congenial places for displaying such copies. The well-educated visitor would be able to relate or appreciate anecdotes about the originals and their makers; experts could certainly tell if this or that piece was in an archaizing style, or likely to have come from Periclean Athens, and so on.

Attributing Greek art to particular 'old masters', then, was important to the Romans. And so, ostensibly at least, was the degree of precision with which an original should be copied. 'All I ask is that you find the most attentive [*diligentissimum*] painter you can, for while it is hard enough to make a likeness from life, it is by far the most difficult of all to make an imitation of an imitation': thus Pliny the Younger instructed Vibius Severus, concerning some portraits he wished

464 *The* Apollo Belvedere, *Roman marble copy after a Greek bronze original of c. 330 BC. Displayed in the Belvedere Courtyard of the Vatican since 1511 (apart from its temporary removal by Napoleon in 1797), this figure of Apollo – once holding a bow – was a favourite of dilettanti for centuries. Winckelmann saluted it as 'the highest ideal of art among the works of antiquity', and the American painter Benjamin West more eccentrically praised it (c. 1760) for resembling 'a young Mohawk warrior'. Attitudes changed in the 19th century, coinciding with a preference for fragmentary Greek originals over restored Roman copies (see p. 318): indeed, as early as the end of the 18th century one French student dismissed the statue as a 'scraped turnip'.*

465 *Roman wall-painting showing a landscape scene, from Stabiae, on the bay of Naples near Pompeii, before AD 79. In the foreground, shaded by a tree, is a rustic sanctuary, with a tall gilded tripod in front of it. Beyond, fantastical colonnaded villas stretch off into the distance. The painting is a panel from a decorative scheme in the Third Style: it would have appeared in the centre of a plain-coloured panel, like a picture hanging on the wall.*

The system of classifying Pompeian painting into four styles was devised by August Mau in the 1880s. Mau's First Style, prevalent in the 2nd century BC, imitates masonry blocks, with no figurative scenes. The Second (c. 100–15 BC) is characterized by elaborate illusionistic schemes, featuring trompe-l'œil architectural vistas [296]. In the Third Style (c. 15 BC–AD 50), compositions with figures, like this one, are arranged as panels on the wall. The Fourth Style (AD 50–79) combines the Third Style with the Second, surrounding central panels with elaborate and fantastic architectural motifs.

to acquire for a friend; 'so please do not let the artist you choose deviate from the original, even to improve upon it' (*Letters* 4.28.3). Such talk has served to characterize Roman art as purely derivative and unoriginal – the 'Style of the Imitators', as Winckelmann summarily denounced all art unfortunate enough to come after his 'High' and 'Beautiful' (roughly corresponding to our 5th–4th-century Classical period).

Surviving Roman marble copies of lost Greek originals (with their telltale supporting struts [37] – a frequent necessity in marble, but not in the lighter medium of hollow-cast bronze) indicate that few artists took up Pliny's request. And our knowledge of the chronology of Greek and Roman art today has proved that many of Winckelmann's most prized ancient statues, such as the *Apollo Belvedere* [464] ('the most sublime of all statues of antiquity which escaped destruction') were, unbeknown to him, crafted in Roman, and not Classical Greek, times. In the absence of mechanical techniques of casting developed in the 19th century, the imitation of Greek *nobilia opera* proved to be a creative practice: hence the diversity of surviving Roman versions of such famous types as Polykleitos' *Doryphoros* [37], Praxiteles' *Aphrodite of Knidos* [83], and not least the range of re-workings of Greek 'master-paintings' [442].

But rather than being an art of pure plagiarism, Roman art was characterized by a new, and distinctly Roman, concern for aligning subject-matter with context (as in the dining-room at Sperlonga, menacingly adorned with – among other things – the archetype of the infamously dangerous dining host, Polyphemos: see pp. 127–30). In the Roman house, wall-paintings which alluded to Greek pictorial themes could certainly be harnessed to flex a patron's cultural muscle; but they could also, as Andrew Wallace-Hadrill has shown, demarcate a room's function, characterize different parts of the home as 'public' or 'private' spaces, and even direct viewers around the house.

Because pride of place was given to the Greek masterpieces of the past, the names of the painters, sculptors, and virtuoso mosaicists working in the Roman Empire went largely unheeded. Where their identities are known, they tend to indicate Greek ethnic origin (the same is true for Etruria). The poet Vergil was echoing a wide consensus when in his vision of Roman imperial greatness he has the shade of Anchises remark that 'others' (*alii*) would put 'breath into bronze, and coax living features from marble' (*Aeneid* 6.847–48). There was no doubt who those others were – the Greeks; and again it is in the wizardry of mimetic *techne* that the Greeks were deemed to excel.

As Anchises goes on to declare, the 'arts' in which the Romans would excel were those of government and war. And though modern art historians (beginning with Alois Riegl in the late 19th century) have striven to salvage some measure of *romanitas* from the substantial relics of art produced under Roman patronage, some have chosen to take Vergil at his word. As Riegl and his successors saw, the quintessentially 'Roman' contribution to the development of Classical art came in the creation of 'continuous narratives', typically the spiral-carved reliefs on the Columns of Trajan and Marcus Aurelius [314, 329, 466]. Such comprehensive visual storytelling, such documentary imaging of *res gestae*, 'things done', was never so much as attempted by the likes of Pheidias or Apelles. But was this art – or history?

Eventually, the canons of Classical forms and styles would be challenged and adapted by artists with priorities beyond the imitation of nature; a more pressing

466 *View of the Column of Marcus Aurelius, Rome, c. 193 AD [cf. 329]. In the words of one scholar (Ian Richmond), 'The scroll of an impressionist, interested rather in the tumult and horror of war than in the methods by which it was waged' – and as such, a contrast to its monumental precedent, the more meticulously detailed Column of Trajan [314].*

The tribulations encountered by Roman dignitaries in their race to acquire artistic kudos *are best attested by the private correspondence of Cicero. Cicero was an avid collector of art, seeking out appropriate pieces to adorn his villa at Tusculum (near modern Frascati, just outside Rome). In this letter, addressed in 61 BC to M. Fadius Gallus (as distinct from his earlier and more trusty agent in Athens, Titus Pomponius Atticus), Cicero hints at the Roman drive to match subject-matter with the function, and desired ambience, of a space. For Cicero at least, that consideration of suitability outweighed any concern for scale, medium, or even original Greek artist.*

Of all your purchases, Gallus, there is none that I really want. You, however, in ignorance of my principles, bought these four or five statues for more than I would pay for the whole collection of statuary in the world. You compare these Bacchantes to Metellus' Muses. What's the similarity, exactly? To begin with, I would never have reckoned those Muses worth so much (and all the Muses themselves would have agreed with me!). Still, at least the Muses would have been suitable for a library and in keeping with my literary pursuits. But these Bacchantes, where is there a place for them in my house? They are pretty little figures, I know – I am well acquainted with them and have often seen them before. Had I approved of them, I would have specifically commissioned you to buy statues that I had already known. For it is my custom to buy the sorts of statues that, decorating my palaestra, give the place the semblance of a gymnasium. But a statue of Mars? What good is that to me, the advocate of peace?

Cicero, *Letters to his Friends*, 7.23.2

467 *South side of the Arch of Constantine, Rome, c. AD 312–315. The arch notoriously 'cannibalized' earlier Roman imperial images: here, statues of Dacian prisoners probably came from Trajan's Forum; the panels between them were taken from an arch of Marcus Aurelius, and the roundels from a Hadrianic monument. The compressed horizontal registers show Constantine's siege of Verona, and his address (adlocutio) once he was established at Rome.*

requirement, with the onset of Christianity, would be to find symbols for the creeds and liturgies of Christian belief (see pp. 81–85). An 'anti-Classicism' of sorts was stylistically overt by the time of Constantine, and is evident enough on the triumphal arch in Rome that bears his name [467], itself a pastiche of earlier Classical styles. Nevertheless, when in the 2nd and 3rd centuries AD the great paintings and sculptures of Greece became the subject of set rhetorical descriptions – three such treatises survive, by Philostratos the Elder, his grandson, Philostratos the Younger, and a certain Callistratus – it is still the Classical tradition of mimetic illusionism and psychological depth that is most highly prized. But the medium of appreciation had changed: words had taken the place of images.

For Roman viewers in the 4th century and beyond, the Classical past had to be merged with the new myth-histories, narratives, and beliefs that stemmed from the eastern peripheries of the Empire in Palestine; Classical stories and styles were accordingly infused with Christian allegorical significance. That task of creating something meaningful out of the heritage of the Classical past, manipulating its various formal styles, was already an obligation in antiquity. And so begins the long-running process more generally known as 'the Classical tradition'.

THE PRESENT CLASSICAL PAST

468 *Titian's* Portrait of Jacopo Strada, *c. 1567–1568, captures the importance of Classical antiquity as a marker of culture and status in 16th-century Europe. Strada, a polymath and imperial antiquarian for the Emperor Rudolph II in Prague, holds a miniature copy of Praxiteles'* Aphrodite Pselioumene *('Aphrodite with Necklace'); on the table in front of him are ancient coins and a fragment of an ancient marble torso; on the cupboard behind are two books – perhaps two of Strada's several publications on Roman antiquities.*

469 opposite *Detail of* Roma Antica, *by G.P. Panini, c. 1757. The canonical art treasures of ancient Rome are collected in this imaginary gallery: on the right is the* Laocoön *[226; but here as first restored], and on the left the Apollo Belvedere [464]; the paintings show (among other things) the Column of Marcus Aurelius (far right) [466], the three columns of the Temple of Castor and Pollux in the Forum [303], the Pantheon [180], and the Colosseum [426]. Figures cluster around a copy of the 'Aldobrandini Wedding', a Roman wall-painting discovered at the beginning of the 17th century. While Panini's painting testifies to the cultural and social prestige of collecting in the 18th century – of literally surrounding oneself with the relics of the Classical past – it also anticipates Romantic movements which looked to antiquity as an ensemble of picturesque fragments.*

THE PAST is not all in the past. This is a truism recognized in the grammatical structures of a number of ancient languages (Greek, Latin, and Sanskrit among them), each of which allows its verbs to have an 'imperfect' tense. So a particular set of word-endings is reserved to describe an action or event of incomplete duration. 'Imperfect', in this linguistic mode, does not mean some deficiency or flaw. It simply implies an unfinished process – an open or ongoing sequence.

The Classical past is imperfect in just such a way. We have hinted as much in the foregoing chapters: that there is no neatly fixed or canonical parcel of what constitutes Classical history, rather a scattered assortment of literary, epigraphic, and archaeological *testimonia* which we tend to interpret very much according to our own interests and preoccupations. However earnestly impartial we may proclaim ourselves in seeking 'the truth', our view is always filtered through the various prisms of previous attempts to establish such clarity. And we should never forget that the 'facts' of antiquity come to us more or less by accident – bequeathed by the selective copying of pagan texts by medieval monks, a natural disaster such as the eruption that buried Pompeii, or the mundane deposit of 'rubbish' at Oxyrhynchus.

But the cognate terms grouped around the very word 'Classical' are enough to warn us that this fluid state of knowledge tends to go unnoticed or repressed. 'Class', 'classify', 'classic', 'classy' – whether in formal or more idiomatic usage, these words suggest a fixed and absolute standard, or at least some system of ranking that depends upon a distinction of the first-rate; a model of excellence by which other things are measured for their relative worthiness. In the royal courts and educational institutions of Europe from the 15th century on, the 'Classical authors' were those Greek and Latin writers held up for emulation in poetry and prose. University degrees in 'Classics' as such came later (in the early 19th century); but the understanding remained that across the various genres of literary effort – including lyric and epic poetry, tragic drama, political oratory, and the writing of history – the exemplary models were those that survived from the ancient world.

It is no radical exposé to reveal that interest in the Classical world has for centuries been bound up with class, social hierarchy, and cultural snobbery. In fact, even as early as the mid- to late 2nd century AD, Classicism seems to have denoted classism, as is evidenced by the Latin writings of Aulus Gellius. In his academic miscellany, he records a debate between an orator named Cornelius Fronto and a unnamed poet; the fastidious subject is whether or not singular words like *harena* ('sand') can have a plural form, or plural words like *arma* (military 'arms') can exist in the singular. 'Go and consult the orators and poets for yourself', comes Cornelius Fronto's response (*Attic Nights* 19.8.15); 'I mean from the earlier group – some proper first-class writer, not a vulgar hack' ('classicus adsiduusque aliquis scriptor, non proletarius').

Is the Classical world, then, inherently 'highbrow' and 'exclusive'? No one can deny that the Grand Tours around the Mediterranean, so modish by the late 18th century, were the preserve of a well-heeled élite; that trophies from those tours

served to furnish the stately homes of wealthy visitors from Europe (and later America) with Classical relics; and that, in the absence of the real thing, a variety of 'Neoclassical' motifs (from architectural and decorative allusions to fantastic evocations of Classical landscapes and myths) imitated Classical forms. To the highly successful English ceramics producer Josiah Wedgwood, the value of such Classicizing *objets d'art* was inseparable from the fact that they were expensive souvenirs ('a great price', he remarked to his partner Thomas Bentley, 'is at first necessary to make the vases esteemed ornaments for palaces'). Wedgwood could produce delicate replicas of Roman glassware [473, 474]; but his commercial genius lay in the confection of an 'Etruscan' decorative style whose motifs were drawn from Greek vases found in Italy, aimed at the aristocratic market. (The vases, supplied most famously by Sir William Hamilton, were – since they were discovered in Etruscan tombs – mistakenly thought to have been native Etruscan products, and Wedgwood's factory site was accordingly named 'Etruria'.) Wedgwood's contemporary, the Scottish-born architect Robert Adam, on the other hand, offered the gentry interiors based on a medley of patterns he had gathered from diverse Classical sources [470, 472] – including the site of Herculaneum (where excavations had begun in 1738) and Diocletian's Palace at Split on the Dalmatian coast.

It is equally undeniable that Classical art and literature have been wielded as weapons of presumed cultural superiority. In the case of the British Empire, Classicizing architecture functioned as a sign of cultural domination: it quashed indigenous forms, flaunting a 'civilized' identity that served to demonstrate (and legitimize) European imperial power [471]. Within that empire, the teaching of Latin and Greek contributed to the enshrining of a 'Western canon' of art and literature. It was part of a larger suppression of non-Western civilization – what the 20th-century Afro-Caribbean political theorist Frantz Fanon called the enforced conversion of 'black skin' into 'white masks'.

The category of the 'Classical' therefore denotes much more than an artistic style or period of history: it comes as a complex ideological package. The Classical world is not just the stuff of history books, something dead and gone; nor is 'Classicism' some aesthetic set in stone. Accepting that the discipline of 'Classics' is what bridges the gap between the ancient world and our own, our purpose in this final chapter is to suggest a peculiar, perhaps even paradoxical, point. The term 'Classical' indeed carries connotations of conservatism, exclusivity, and arch superiority. But what has ensured the 'imperfect', ongoing process of the Classical tradition is its durable capacity for change, flexibility, and tolerance – and an intellectual compass that reckons, in the famous phrase of the Latin playwright Terence, 'nothing human out of bounds'.

470 *In Robert Adam's 1766 design for the Great Staircase of Shelburne House (subsequently known as Lansdowne House) in London, every space is articulated with Neoclassical motifs in stucco, and a painting of antique ruins is set into the wall.*

471 *Government House, Calcutta, the residence of the British governor of Bengal, was designed by Charles Wyatt and built in 1798–1803. (It is seen here in a print after James Baillie Fraser, 1819.) The building is articulated with a number of Classical motifs, and, to emphasize the governor's authority, the grounds were entered through a grand triumphal arch.*

472 Osterley Park near London was converted into a Neoclassical country house by Robert Adam between 1765 and 1780. The hall's walls and ceilings were decorated with stucco designs based on the antique; the large panels on the walls are modelled on ones Adam had seen at Diocletian's Palace at Split, which he visited during a long spell of study on the Continent spent chiefly in Rome. At both ends of the hall, in exedras, are niches for Classical statues.

473, 474 The Portland Vase (right), and Josiah Wedgwood's copy of it (far right). The Roman vase (named after the Duke of Portland who acquired it in 1784) is a notable example of cameo glass [see 438]; it probably dates from the first quarter of the 1st century AD. Josiah Wedgwood's copy, displayed in 1790, consisted of black basalt 'dipped' into white basalt, which was in turn incised. Wedgwood later reminisced, 'I have endeavoured to preserve the style and spirit, or if you please, the elegant simplicity of the antique forms.'

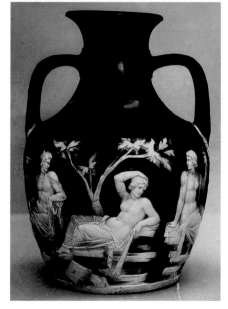

'DECLINE AND FALL' – OR THE STUFF OF DREAMS?

It was in autumn 1764, amid the ruins on Rome's Capitoline hill, that a portly Englishman by the name of Edward Gibbon conceived his plan of writing a narrative that he was to call *The Decline and Fall of the Roman Empire*. His basic theme was prompted not only by the visual spread of disintegrated magnificence around him, but by the sound he could hear coming from what had once been the ancient Capitoline Temple of Jupiter – the chanting of evening hymns, from a choir of barefooted friars. These Christians had colonized the ruins. And they, no less than the barbarian hordes that had descended on Rome in the early 5th century AD, were to be blamed for causing the collapse in the first place.

Gibbon's simple but grandiose thesis, completed in 1787, was conceived as a personal claim upon posterity. He wanted to write a 'classic' of historical synthesis; he belonged to an age of literary activity in English that aspired to be a second 'Augustan' epoch of genius and patronage. Few historians today would accept the broad outline that Gibbon imposed on the past. Quite apart from the question of how far Christianity was responsible for the 'decline' of the Roman Empire – and most today would argue that it was a matter of 'transformation', nothing else – it is no longer tenable to think of the 'end' of Classical antiquity as some terminal switch, plunging Europe into a gloom of 'Dark Ages' from which it was not relieved

475 *The capture of Troy, brought up to date for a 15th-century audience (note the city's medieval turrets). In this illumination from Raoul Le Febvre's* Recueil des histoires troyennes, *of 1464, the foolish Trojans have demolished their wall to let in the Horse and the invading Greeks [cf. 218].*

476 *The persistence of Classical literature into much later centuries is encapsulated in this detail from a 15th-century Italian manuscript of the* Divine Comedy. *Near the beginning of his poem, the 14th-century Florentine Dante hails the 1st-century BC Roman poet Vergil (*Inferno 1.85–87):*
> . . . My master thou and guide!
> Thou he from whom alone I have deriv'd
> That style, which for its beauty into fame
> Exalts me.

In this image Vergil introduces Dante to Homer, chief among the Virtuous Pagans – 'that lord of loftiest song who flies like an eagle above the rest'. Homer, the first poet to write about war, is shown carrying a sword. Behind him are Horace, Ovid, and Lucan. All are 'lofty' poets, like Vergil, and to Dante's delight they welcome him and make him 'sixth among those high intelligences' (4.82–105).

477 *A scene from* The Triumph of Caesar, *by Andrea Mantegna, c. 1485, which evokes the pageantry of a Roman triumph, as soldiers process with the spoils of conquest. Mantegna was trained in Padua, in North Italy, at a time of a new and zealous 'humanistic' interest in the arts of antiquity, and must have studied ancient accounts of such processions. His painting perhaps also implicitly compares the Roman conquest of Classical art with its triumphal renaissance in 15th-century Italy.*

until a 'rebirth' of Classical culture after *c.* 1400, 'the Renaissance' [372, 477, 512]. This melodrama eclipses too many bright spirits – from the 9th-century King Alfred the Great of England, a gifted Latinist, to Dante Alighieri, whose *Divine Comedy* written soon after 1300, along with the work of his junior fellow-Italian Petrarch, was so sweetly attuned to Classical values and voices (especially that of Vergil) [476]. It also overlooks the painstaking copying of pagan texts by medieval scribes, and the artistic engagement with those texts in the form of illuminated manuscripts [475].

478 above The Creation of Man, by Michelangelo, on the ceiling of the Sistine Chapel in the Vatican, c. 1508–1512. Adam has the sculptural bulk of a Classical Greek athlete, while the Creator's pose resembles that of the Victories on the Arch of Titus in Rome [318].

479 below *Crowded masterpieces of ancient and modern art jostle for attention in this detail of* The Tribuna of the Uffizi *by Johann Zoffany, c. 1772–1778. Centre left are the Uffizi Wrestlers [461]; in the foreground, Titian's Venus of Urbino (c. 1538); and on the right, the Medici Venus [cf. 70].*

480 above *The Temple of Saturn, with the Arch of Septimius Severus and Church of the Accademia di San Luca in the background, in an etching by G. B. Piranesi, c. 1774. Piranesi believed ancient Roman architecture to be exemplary, and superior to anything Greek. Here the magnificent relics of ancient Rome slide into romantic decay, superseded by the monuments of Christianity.*

481 opposite *Sigmund Freud at his desk, surrounded by a silent audience of ancient statuettes, in an etching by Max Pollock, 1914.*

It was a supreme officer of the Christian faith, Pope Pius II, who in 1462 sanctioned a protection order to be placed on the ruins of ancient Rome. Papal legislation anticipated what would become by 1800 a 'Romantic' response to prospects of architectural decay, by citing an 'exemplary frailty' as one reason to preserve the sight of so many toppled columns. But it was the founder of modern psychoanalysis, Sigmund Freud [481], who recognized how the 'Eternal City' of Rome might serve as an archaeological metaphor for the mechanics of the human mind. Rome was like a palimpsest – a manuscript covered with erasures, crossings-out, and second thoughts; and the human subconscious was like the stratified layers of ancient Rome. The task of the psychoanalyst, therefore, was to 'excavate' the significance concealed within previous phases of experience. With careful questioning – as Freud put it – 'stones speak'.

482 Athens, photographed from the south-west (on the slopes of Mouseion hill), c. 1865. The Parthenon rises on the Acropolis, with the Propylaia to the left (still encumbered by a tower from the time when the Acropolis was a Turkish fortress). Below is the Odeon of Herodes Atticus.

From the late Middle Ages until 1833, when the country gained independence, Greece was a remote backwater of the Ottoman Empire, and Athens was a small farming village with a few hundred houses mostly clustered over the site of the Agora [299]. It was hardly visited by 18th-century European Grand Tourists. Prominent pioneers were J.-D. Le Roy, who published his Ruins of the Most Beautiful Monuments of Greece in French in 1758; and James Stuart and Nicholas Revett, who began publishing their Antiquities of Athens in 1762.

'SPEAKING STONES': THE PARTHENON

Freud went to Athens, driven primarily by a desire to visit the Parthenon, in the summer of 1904. As he later recalled the experience, it was a revelation that moved him in a very peculiar way. Not only did he find the temple the most beautiful thing he had ever seen: he could hardly believe it really existed – or that he had actually made the pilgrimage to find it. It was not only a dream come true, but as if a mythical fantasy had suddenly materialized.

Freud would come up with his own psychological explanation for the overwhelming sensation of wonder and incredulity that struck him on the Athenian Acropolis [482]. But it was perhaps no accident that of all ancient buildings, it should have been the Parthenon that caused this minor trauma. For, as Mary Beard has recently concluded, 'the Parthenon belongs . . . to that élite band of monuments whose historical significance is overlaid by the fame of *being famous*'. However we engage with this building and its art [288, 486–88], our response can be contextualized within a lengthy and continuous timeline of previous engagements. The timeline at the back of this book (pp. 334–37) covers only a

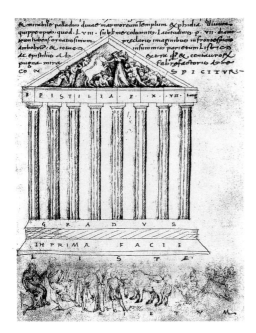

483 The earliest surviving visual record of the exterior of the Parthenon, made by the Italian merchant Cyriac of Ancona, who visited Athens between 1436 and 1444. It predates the gunpowder explosion during the Venetian siege of 1687, and the victorious general's disastrous attempt to take sculpture from the west pediment, seen here. Cyriac shows the building correctly with eight Doric columns (albeit strangely elongated). His note in Latin at the top calls the building a 'divine work by Pheidias' representing the 'Athenian victories in the time of Pericles'.

484, 485 Nashville, Tennessee, self-styled 'Athens of the South', built a replica of the Parthenon in wood, plaster, and brick as the centrepiece of the Tennessee Centennial Exposition of 1897. In 1931 a concrete replacement was finished (above), said to reproduce the venerable Greek building correctly to 'an eighth of an inch' (3 mm). 'The Classic Grandeur of Grecian Art' was called upon to promote the 'Parthenon Assortment' by the Standard Candy Co. of Nashville (right) – a nice example of Athenian Classicism quite literally meeting American consumerism.

brief span of that history: the history of the Parthenon's reception is far more expansive and multi-dimensional than could ever be conveyed in a temporal chart. It is a timeline that must include, for example, the procurement of a substantial portion of the Parthenon's metopes, frieze, and pediments by Thomas Bruce, 7th Earl of Elgin (a story subject to all manner of partisan colouring: see p. 317); numerous architectural reproductions, among them a full-size replica of the building and subsequently its cult statue in Nashville, Tennessee [484, 485]; and both modern Greek claims to cultural ownership and contemporary debates about a shared 'world heritage' under UNESCO auspices.

In fact, our reaction to the Parthenon forms part of a much larger response to ancient Greece, and likewise to ancient Rome. 'Poor old scrubby Rome sinks into nothing at the side of such beautiful magnificence', wrote the artist Edward Lear on approaching the Parthenon in 1848. For Lear, as for us, the Parthenon constitutes one of the key sites for negotiating the difference between the arts, and therefore cultures, of ancient Greece and Rome. 'The glory that was Greece' was how Edgar Allen Poe pitched the difference in 1829, as opposed to 'the grandeur that was Rome'; many 19th-century artists have used the Parthenon to evoke that Greek 'glory', not least Sir Lawrence Alma-Tadema in his *Pheidias and the Frieze of the Parthenon* [489].

Even as early as the early 2nd century AD, it is possible to detect a comparable reverence for the Athenian 'Classicism' embodied in the Parthenon. When the building programmes initiated by Pericles (see p. 175) were described by Plutarch, a language of 'classic' status was already being invoked. These monuments (of which the Parthenon was only one) are, according to Plutarch, 'eternally new': they are in a state of perpetual organic florescence, defying the wear of time. What is especially interesting about this relatively early construction of Classical art is the way in which its attributed timelessness is achieved through the suppression of the building's own temporality. Although the monument is located within the age of Pericles, that era is treated not as a chronologically determined historical period but rather as a mythical golden age (cf. pp. 168–70). The very attribute of timelessness serves to offset Plutarch's own cultural distance from the period that he describes, writing in the period today known as the 'Second Sophistic', when all things Greek

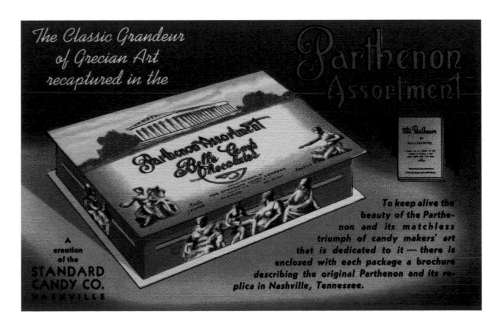

486 Cut-away reconstruction of a corner of the Parthenon [cf. 505], showing the position of the pediment, metopes, and inner frieze. The frieze was boxed in under the roof [cf. 489] and – at almost 12 metres (40 feet) above the ground – scarcely visible, it seems, to ancient visitors.

487 It remains a mystery why the sculptors of the Parthenon took special care to complete the backs of the statues in the pediments, which could never have been seen from the ground. This figure from the east pediment has been variously identified as Theseus, Herakles, and Dionysos.

488 Though the Parthenon frieze has been the subject of close scholarly scrutiny for over two hundred years, there is little consensus as to the narrative it represented. Is it some procession of the Greater Panathenaic festival? Were there 192 heroized youths on horseback, referring to the number of Athenians traditionally killed at the battle of Marathon in 490 BC? Or are we looking at the mustered forces of the mythical King Erechtheus of Athens, who after sacrificing his daughter has led his forces to success against a besieging enemy? This detail of the cavalcade comes from the frieze on the west end of the temple; bronze harnesses were attached to the small holes in the horses' heads.

enjoyed a revival within the Roman Empire. And his response constitutes one of the earliest and most fascinating examples of attempting to see ancient art 'as the ancients saw it'. It is the same cultural phenomenon that we witness a little later when Pausanias, ascending the Athenian Acropolis, discusses the Parthenon without a word about the more recent Temple of Rome and Augustus that flanked its east façade (*Guide to Greece* 1.24.5–7); or when, in the 15th century, the Italian traveller Cyriac of Ancona described the Parthenon while entirely overlooking its later history as a Christian church [483]. Indeed there is also a striking parallel with the 19th-century restoration of the Parthenon as a numinous Classical relic. The almost perpetual veil of present-day scaffolding is there for a purpose – to enable modern tourists to experience a frozen moment of history; a wishfully 'perfect' past.

489 *In his* Pheidias and the Frieze of the Parthenon *of 1868–1869, Lawrence Alma-Tadema imagines the men and women of Athens, like visitors to the British Museum, appreciating the frieze at close hand; Pheidias (in the centre) proudly stands behind the rope ready to answer questions. Although the painting is pure fantasy, Alma-Tadema adds one significant historical detail: the frieze was painted in bright colours, perhaps making its figures more readily legible from the ground.*

The rapturous response *of the poet John Keats to the Elgin Marbles in 1817 – a year after their purchase by the British government – captures something of their initial impact on contemporary British tastes.*

My spirit is too weak – mortality
　Weighs heavily on me like unwilling sleep,
　And each imagined pinnacle and steep
Of godlike hardship, tells me I must die
Like a sick Eagle looking at the sky.
　Yet 'tis a gentle luxury to weep
　That I have not the cloudy winds to keep,
Fresh for the opening of the morning's eye.
Such dim-conceived glories of the brain
　Bring round the heart an undescribable feud;
So do these wonders a most dizzy pain,
　That mingles Grecian grandeur with the rude
Wasting of old Time – with a billowy main –
A sun – a shadow of a magnitude.

　　John Keats, *On Seeing the Elgin Marbles*

More stridently, though, resounds a very different 'Romantic' engagement with the marbles – the outcry of Lord Byron. In The Curse of Minerva, *written some five years earlier, Byron imagined the Parthenon's goddess scorning her British plunderers ('Scaped from the ravage of the Turk and Goth,/ Thy country sends a spoiler worse than both'); faced with Athena's wrath against the British, Byron pinned the blame on Elgin's Scottish descent ('Frown not on England; England owns him not:/ Athena, no! thy plunderer was a Scot!'). But those who champion Lord Byron as the hero of responsible (and pro-Hellenic) archaeology should remember how far removed Byron's original cause was from modern ideologies of rescue excavation, scholarship, and display. If Byron had prevailed, after all, every ancient monument would long since have decayed through the picturesque ravages of time (including graffiti: Byron literally inscribed himself into the Classical past by scratching his name on one of the columns of the Temple of Poseidon at Sounion in Attica).*

490 left Perseus, by Antonio Canova.
Pope Pius VII acquired the marble statue in
1802 to replace the Apollo Belvedere [464]
that Napoleon had removed to France in 1797.
The subject is Perseus with the head of the
Gorgon Medusa [cf. 135], but the pose and
polished finish evoke the Apollo Belvedere
itself. Napoleon's régime was often personified
by its critics as the Medusa, so the change in
subject-matter seems highly symbolic.
  Canova both created statues closely based
on antique models and restored ancient pieces.
By the early 19th century, however, aesthetic
preferences shifted towards more fragmentary
Greek originals, as embodied in the marbles
from the Parthenon. Canova foreshadowed
that development when he declined Lord
Elgin's invitation to restore the pediment
figures: 'it would be a sacrilege . . .', he said,
'to presume to touch them with a chisel.'

491 opposite Sir Charles Townley's library
in his London house, as imagined by Johann
Zoffany, c. 1781–1783. The statues are Roman,
and have all been creatively 'restored'. The
collection was bought by the British Museum
in 1808 – eight years before the Parthenon
marbles were acquired. While the latter are
today the most famous collection in the
museum, Townley's sculptures are displayed
underground, and attract few visitors.

In 1808, just eight years before the British Government would purchase the
Elgin marbles, the British Museum had opened a gallery of restored, 'perfected'
and often prudishly 'fig-leafed' Roman sculptures, based on the collection of Sir
Charles Townley [491]; these were the sorts of statues that had previously been
admired and fervently imitated by the likes of Antonio Canova [490]. With the
installation of the Parthenon sculptures in the British Museum came a marked
shift of taste away from restored Roman statues (that patently adapted Greek
themes) in favour of Greek 'originals', albeit incomplete and damaged ones. The
'Elgin Marbles' were soon placed at the absolute pinnacle of artistic achievement
– a vertiginous level of admiration that was confirmed in the 1930s, when the
spacious gallery endowed by Joseph Duveen seemed to give them an unparalleled
status within the extensive holdings of the museum.

CLAIMS ON THE CLASSICAL

Does the Parthenon stand for democracy and political liberalism? It tends to be used as just such a signal in modern Greece. But in the mid-20th century the building was confidently claimed as the rightful property of the ideologues of National Socialism. Occupying Greece from 1941 to 1944, German troops took care to visit the Acropolis [493] and study local antiquities; they were exhorted to do so by certain distinguished Classicists at home (notably Ernst Buschor). Adolf Hitler himself declared Greek Classicizing aesthetics as the distinctive heritage of an 'Aryan' race descended from the Dorians; they were defined in opposition to the 'degenerate' Modernism that was deemed symptomatic of Russia's Bolshevik malaise ('if the creative spirit of the Periclean age be manifest in the Parthenon, the Bolshevik era is embodied in its cubist grimace', Hitler enthused in *Mein Kampf*). There was a long tradition of philhellenism in Germany, but it was the Nazi party that promised truly to reconnect the country with her latent – but timeless – ethnic roots. Classical styles were imitated and glorified, in the works of Arno Breker [494], Josef Thorak, Fritz Klimsch, and other artists, championed in the annual 'Great German Exhibition of Art'; Neoclassical forms were accordingly thought appropriate for huge gathering-places for the German *Volk* designed by Hitler's favourite Classicizing architect, Alfred Speer [492]; and a propagandist film of the 1936 Berlin Olympics had Myron's *Diskobolos* [1] magically melt into gleaming Aryan muscle [495].

In Italy, meanwhile, Benito Mussolini presented his Fascist régime as a continuation, and culmination, of Augustan Rome. 'Within five years,' he declared in 1925, 'Rome must appear marvellous to all the peoples of the world – vast, orderly, powerful, as in the time of Augustus'. Mussolini proceeded to celebrate the two-thousandth anniversary of the first Roman emperor's birth in 1937–1938 with a huge exhibition (*Mostra augustea della Romanità*, or 'Augustan Exhibition of Roman Culture'); to parade the connection in a specially constructed museum to Roman civilization [497]; and to forge physical links with an idealized Roman past by building the 'Via dell' Impero' between the centres of ancient and modern Rome, in addition to numerous other monuments [496].

492 *A detail of the Luitpoldarena, designed by Albert Speer as part of the Nazi rally-ground at Nuremberg built in 1934–1937. While Hitler stressed a spiritual connection with ancient Greece, the huge eagle and the standards held by the soldiers here associated Nazi Germany with the military discipline and imperial authority of ancient Rome.*

493 *Raising of the Nazi flag on the Acropolis in Athens, with the Parthenon in the distance, May 1941. The occupation of Greece provided a commemorative opportunity for the Nazi propaganda machinery: at last, it seemed, the monumental achievements of Classical Greece had been returned to their rightful heirs.*

494 right *Arno Breker's The Avenger was originally designed as one of twenty-four reliefs that would adorn a gigantic marble triumphal arch in Berlin, planned by Albert Speer. This plaster version was displayed in the 'Great German Exhibition of Art' in 1941: it takes up the iconography of the Laocoön [226], while transforming it into an allegory of the struggle between Aryan forces and such 'evils' as Bolshevism and Judaism.*

495 far right *At the end of the opening sequence of Leni Riefenstahl's film about the Berlin Olympics of 1936, a statue of Myron's Diskobolos [1] melts into real-life German flesh and blood – a powerful symbol of Nazi Germany's supposed re-awakening of the 'Hellenic spirit'.*

496 *The Stadio dei Marmi (Marble Stadium) in Rome was inaugurated in 1932. Sixty fig-leafed statues, with the hefty musculature of Classical statuary, surround the stadium, inspiring competitors and spectators alike to emulate their strength and virility.*

497 *The Museo della Civiltà Romana (Museum of Roman Civilization) in Rome was designed by P. Aschieri, D. Bernardini, and C. Pascoletti between 1939 and 1941 (though only finished after the Second World War, in 1955). Its purpose was to provide a permanent home for the exhibits of the 'Augustan Exhibition of Roman Culture' of 1937–1938. This is one of its two towering colonnaded entrances, their doorways surmounted by eagles – a direct allusion to Roman military insignia.*

But such claims to Classical heritage are not in themselves, of course, limited to totalitarian régimes. As previously noted (pp. 169–70), almost every Western country has, at one time or another, found in the Classical world a precedent for its own political sentiments. So Napoleon could celebrate his selfconscious identification with Roman antiquity by means of a distinctively *Roman* sort of monument [500]. And the capital of democratic America, Washington, D.C., was fitted out in the 19th and 20th centuries with a mélange of Classicizing monuments [501].

In fact, the Classical world has supplied models for an astonishing range of theories, opinions, and political leanings. Antiquity has certainly had its fair share of traditionalist, right-wing, and reactionary venerators. But Classical ideas and traditions have also been deployed in the service of radical reform and liberalism – the abolition of slavery, the resistance to empire, and the Suffragette movements

of the early 20th century among them. The Classical world has offered an alternative and precedent for all manner of social oppressions – and repressions. It is no secret that Johann Joachim Winckelmann, acclaimed by many as the founder of ancient art history (see pp. 290–92), could celebrate the sensuous 'perfections' of Classical art as a means of simultaneously fulfilling and sublimating his own homoerotic desires [498]. By the end of the 19th century, within a British society where homosexuality was only beginning to be termed as such, but was still deemed a criminal offence, the homoeroticism vaunted in canonical Greek and Latin works could offer very different social alternatives; likewise, the sculptures of Classical antiquity could provide acceptable models for the hetero- and homoerotic display of the male body [499].

The importance of the Classical world lies precisely in the pluralistic claims that have been made of it. Classical antiquity, and our response to its arts and literature, is always in a state of flux, as we compare its precedents with shifting aspects of our own cultures. To study it does not constitute a way of idolizing a petrified canon or embalming European prejudice; instead, it is a way of thinking about how and why certain aspects of the Classical world might still be relevant to our own.

498 *J. J. Winckelmann sits before a print of a relief of Antinous, the Emperor Hadrian's boyfriend, in this painting by A. von Maron, 1768; behind him is a bust of Homer. In his* History of the Art of Antiquity, *published in German in 1764, Winckelmann described another depiction of Antinous – a bust in the Vatican – as the 'most beautiful work that has come down to us'. The terms of approval were common enough (compare Winckelmann's response to the* Apollo Belvedere *[464]); underpinning his definition of 'beauty', however, was a barely disguised homoerotic interest.*

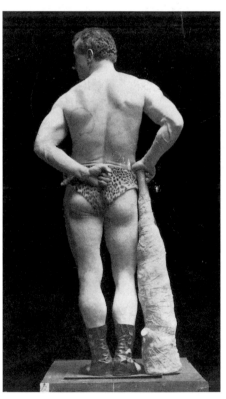

499 *Eugen Sandow, saluted as the 'father' of modern body-building, liked to imitate the attitudes of Graeco-Roman statuary, on occasion even covering himself with powder to evoke the appearance of white marble. In this photograph, of c. 1900, the large club and the arm twisted behind the back evoke the* Weary Herakles *type first created by Lysippos [142].*

500 *The Arc de Triomphe in Paris, designed in 1806 by J.-F. Chalgrin and completed by G.-A. Blouet in 1836, clearly alludes to the triumphal arches of Imperial Rome [e.g. 318, 467], while outdoing them in its unprecedented scale. The Emperor Napoleon planned it as a monument to the victories of the French army under his command.*

501 *The Jefferson Memorial in Washington, D.C., was designed by John Russell Pope and dedicated in 1943. Its Ionic façade and Pantheon-like dome befit the Classical ideals of Thomas Jefferson, President of the United States from 1801 to 1809, who enthused that the instruction of young citizens in Latin and Greek could 'impress their minds with useful facts and good principles'.*

CINEMATIC CLASSICS

502 below Russell Crowe plays Maximus, a successful Roman general turned enslaved gladiator who challenges the corrupt Emperor Commodus, in Gladiator. In this film, directed by Ridley Scott and released in 2000, the greatness of Rome becomes a 'vision', resurrected by state-of-the-art computer-generated graphics; Commodus, like the film's director, promises gladiatorial games that will give the people 'the greatest vision of their lives' so that 'they will soon forget the tedious sermonizing of a few dry old men'.

503 below right Peter Ustinov stars as the megalomaniac Emperor Nero in Mervyn LeRoy's Quo Vadis? of 1951. Developed from the pages of Henryk Sienkiewicz's novel (1896) and earlier films on the same subject, the film presents Nero as both an Antichrist thwarting the spread of early Christianity and a tyrant corrupted by absolute power.

504 opposite The spectacular chariot race in the Hollywood blockbuster Ben-Hur, directed by William Wyler, 1959, in which Judah Ben-Hur (played by Charlton Heston) challenges the supremacy of his Roman rival, Messala. Like earlier cinematic versions of the late 19th-century novel by General Lew Wallace, the film narrates the life and times of Christ through the eyes of Ben-Hur, a Jew who converts to Christianity and sets himself at odds with the ideology of empire. It proved an instant international success: this promotional still for its release in Germany markets it as William Wyler's 'Meisterwerk'.

'He who screens the history, makes the history', or so the screenwriter and essayist Gore Vidal opined in 1992. From the earliest days of the 'big screen', the popular cinematic reconstruction of antiquity has perhaps exerted the single most influential force on our attitudes towards the Classical world. These reconstructions include the epic blockbusters that took audiences by storm in the 1950s and early 1960s (such as Mervin LeRoy's *Quo Vadis?* in 1951 [503], William Wyler's *Ben-Hur* in 1959 [504], or Joseph K. Mankiewicz's *Cleopatra* in 1963 with its $62 million budget); but they also incorporate farcical comedies (*Carry on Cleo* in 1964, *A Funny Thing Happened on the Way to the Forum* in 1966, and *Monty Python's Life of Brian* in 1979) and hauntingly surrealist adaptations of Classical texts (Pier Paolo Pasolini's *Oedipus Rex* and *Medea* in 1967 and 1970 respectively, or Federico Fellini's *Fellini Satyricon* in 1969). The epic success of Ridley Scott's digitally enhanced *Gladiator* [502] in 2000 suggested that this genre was far from dead; and numerous films on subjects as diverse as the fall of Troy and the life of Alexander the Great are following in its wake.

On one hand, the cinematic resurrection of antiquity poses a different sort of historical challenge from those which we have encountered during the course of this book. Hollywood movies necessarily masquerade as a sort of time-travel or virtual reality; they are concerned with narrative viewing rather than secondary interpretation, discussion, and analysis. (We should note here that many of our impressions of antiquity ultimately stem from these cinematic realities: the official Roman 'salute', the fanfare music of the Roman army, the battle sequences in the gladiatorial arena, and so on.) On the other hand, both cinematic and academic interpretations of antiquity bring to the Classical world their own ideologies, values, and experiences: cinematic directors and academic scholars alike look to antiquity with both approval and disapproval. 'We were looking at Roman architecture and studying books and I began to realize how gracious and civilized

Rome was; at the same time, it was built on such blood and savagery', pondered Hans Zimmer, who composed the score for *Gladiator*; 'I wanted the music to reflect that sort of duality.'

According to Anthony Mann, director of an earlier portrayal of *Gladiator*'s historical period (*The Fall of the Roman Empire*, 1964), 'inaccuracies from a historical point of view are not important – the most important thing is that you get a *sense* of history'. To many Classical scholars, such talk constitutes a real source of tension; a number continue to dissociate themselves from 'condemnable' cinematic compromises of 'truth' and 'accuracy'. One historical advisor to *Gladiator*'s film script publicly despaired of the film's 'distortions and errors . . . that appal me and all other Classical scholars'; she contrasted it with her own 'responsible study of Antiquity'. 'I am deeply disillusioned by the final product,' she declared, 'which makes virtually no attempt to represent an authentic Roman past.' Others have welcomed such challenges to that very concept of a single authentic Roman past, and to the 'tedious sermonizing' (to apply the phrase used by the Emperor Commodus in *Gladiator*) of those who claim it as their own. Cinematic reconstructions of antiquity, in other words, have become a key battleground in the tussle between 'purists' and 'populists' over the cultural ownership of the Classics.

KNOCKING THE RUINS

Detractors of the Classical tradition have characterized the authorities of Greek and Latin culture as so many 'Dead White European Males'. To certain defenders of the same tradition, this 'canon-busting' is itself tantamount to a national, and even international, crisis ('Dumbing-down'; 'The Closing of the American Mind', 'Killing Homer'). But as early as the 17th century, following the publication of Sir William Temple's controversial 'Essay upon the Ancient and Modern Learning' in 1692, the question of antiquity's canonical status was a subject that was violently disputed in Britain and elsewhere. The satirist Jonathan Swift imagined the conflict between the 'Ancients' and the 'Moderns' as coming to a head in the King's Library at St James's Palace in London, when modern books threatened to invade the top-shelf 'Parnassus' which had previously been reserved for Classical authors. Swift's account, which appeared in 1704, narrates the all-out war – the 'Battle of the Books' – that ensued. The works of Classical writers come to life, embody their authors, and pitch themselves against those written by modern thinkers. Apart from the farcical characterization of the authors themselves, the humour lies in Swift's presentation of the epic battle as an Iliadic feud (for example, in his invocation of the Muses); his text even masquerades as an ancient fragmentary manuscript (complete with the odd 'ingens hiatus', signalling a 'large gap' in the surviving sources).

505 *The central covered atrium of the École des Beaux-Arts, Paris, 1863–1874. Like most fine art institutes by the late 19th century, the school contained a whole gallery of plaster casts, used as models to instruct students. A corner of the Parthenon, complete with its metopes and part of its pediment [cf. 486], stood at the far end of the gallery – the ultimate embodiment of a Classical artistic tradition that young artists were taught to emulate.*

By the early 20th century the situation had changed dramatically. In his Manifesto to the Young People of Greece *(1933) Filippo Marinetti had the Parthenon come to life and denounce itself as 'the prison of futile wisdom': Greek students should turn their backs on the Acropolis, and 'assassinate melancholy and nostalgia by means of original discoveries'.*

506 opposite *Busts of twenty-eight famous orators, poets, philosophers, and other writers sit on top of a series of bookcases in the Wren Library at Trinity College, Cambridge, designed by Sir Christopher Wren and completed in 1695. On the left are shown Ancients (headed by Homer; the first seen here is Socrates), on the right Moderns (led by William Shakespeare; the first seen here is Francis Beaumont). Although these busts were not installed until later in the 18th century, the scheme had been part of the original designs for the library; the structural antithesis, with each ancient author facing a modern rival, corresponds very closely to the ideological battle between antiquity and modernity satirized by Swift's* Battle of the Books *in 1704.*

Jonathan Swift satirizes *a number of 17th-century writers, both English and French, lining them up against their Classical counterparts: the essayist and philosopher Sir Francis Bacon; the poets Sir William Davenant (alluded to through the main character of his epic* Gondibert)*, Sir John Denham, and Samuel Wesley (father of John Wesley); the philosopher René Descartes; the writer and cultural bureaucrat Claude Perrault; and the scientifically minded philosopher Bernard de Fontenelle.*

Then Aristotle, observing Bacon advance with a furious mien, drew his bow to the head, and let fly his arrow, which missed the valiant Modern and went whizzing over his head; but Descartes it hit; the steel point quickly found a defect in his head-piece; it pierced the leather and the pasteboard, and went in at his right eye. The torture of the pain whirled the valiant bow-man round till death, like a star of superior influence, drew him into his own vortex INGENS HIATUS . . . HIC IN MS . . . when Homer appeared at the head of the cavalry, mounted on a furious horse, with difficulty managed by the rider himself, but which no other mortal durst approach; he rode among the enemy's ranks, and bore down all before him. Say, goddess, whom he slew first and whom he slew last! First, Gondibert advanced against him, clad in heavy armour and mounted on a staid sober gelding, not so famed for his speed as his docility in kneeling whenever his rider would mount or alight . . . He had made a vow to Pallas that he would never leave the field till he had spoiled Homer of his armour: madman, who had never once seen the wearer, nor understood his strength! Him Homer overthrew, horse and man, to the ground, there to be trampled and choked in the dirt. Then with a long spear he slew Denham, a stout Modern, who from his father's side derived his lineage from Apollo, but his mother was of mortal race. He fell, and bit the earth. The celestial part Apollo took, and made it a star; but the terrestrial lay wallowing upon the ground. Then Homer slew Sam Wesley with a kick of his horse's heel; he took Perrault by mighty force out of his saddle, then hurled him at Fontenelle, with the same blow dashing out both their brains.

From Jonathan Swift, *The Battle of the Books*

Satire aside, however, we might easily replace the names of Swift's 'Moderns' with those of more recent poets and thinkers. The contest that Swift anticipated some three centuries ago is not over yet. In that respect, it is perhaps significant that Swift broke off his narrative before either side had achieved a decisive victory . . .

Artists, too, burdened by the influence and status of Classical art, have periodically rebelled against its vested authority. During the 20th century, numerous plaster casts of ancient sculptures – casts which 19th-century art schools had celebrated as 'masterpieces', using them to instruct their budding artists [505] – were exiled or smashed to pieces. Again, the protest was not entirely novel. 'We do not want either Greek or Roman models if we are but just and true to our imaginations', petitioned William Blake as early as 1804 – anticipating Futurism, Dadaism, and countless other artistic movements in the 20th century.

It is sometimes easy to overestimate how anti-Classical some of these 'revolutions' proved: the range of styles that can be found in different places, and at different times, within the Classical world makes its art resistant to modern changes in aesthetics and fashions. Just as the mid-19th century put the craggier (and more fragmentary) sculptures of the Parthenon firmly at the pinnacle of Classical art, by the mid-20th century 'primitivism' had become a virtue: prevailing taste shifted in favour of Archaic Greek *kouros* figures and artefacts from Etruria, Phoenician Iberia, and the indigenous inhabitants of regions in the Roman Empire, whose art was praised, rather than criticized, for its 'provincialism'. So while the 20th-century British sculptor Henry Moore resisted the legacy of Greek naturalism, deploring the reverence with which his teachers waxed lyrical over Athenian masters such as Praxiteles, he found a more acceptable precedent in the sculptures from the Cycladic islands of the 3rd millennium BC [436, 508]. For Moore, Cycladic art constituted a sort of proto-Modernism from which 'to start again from the beginnings of primitive art'. Others, like the Italian Alberto Giacometti, could look to Etruscan art for their inspiration [509, 510], enthusing over its supposed 'ethnic' originality, sensuous abstraction, and most importantly, perhaps, its distinctiveness from the arts of ancient Rome (then tainted by

In his eleven-point manifesto, published in a Parisian newspaper in 1909, a young Italian named Filippo Tommaso Marinetti proclaimed an age of 'Futurism'. The antiquarian, static, and shackling art of the past, Marinetti argued, should be abandoned in favour of the dynamic vitality of modern-day technology: 'a racing car is more beautiful than the Victory of Samothrace' [457]. But Marinetti's manifesto was much more than an aesthetic creed. It was a statement of national political revolution – an early 20th-century example of what Walter Benjamin would later term the 'aestheticization of politics'.

It is from Italy that we launch through the world this violently upsetting incendiary manifesto of ours. With it, today we establish Futurism, because we want to free this land from its smelly gangrene of professors, archaeologists, ciceroni, and antiquarians. For too long has Italy been a dealer in second-hand clothes. We mean to free her from the numberless museums that cover her like so many graveyards. Museums: cemeteries! . . . Identical, surely, in the sinister promiscuity of so many bodies unknown to one another. Museums: public dormitories where one lies forever beside hated or unknown beings. Museums: absurd abattoirs of painters and sculptors ferociously slaughtering each other with colour-blows and line-blows, the length of the fought-over walls! . . . Admiring an old picture is the same as pouring our sensibility into a funerary urn instead of hurtling it far off, in violent spasms of action and creation. Do you, then, wish to waste all your best powers in this eternal and futile worship of the past, from which you emerge fatally exhausted, shrunken, beaten down? In truth I tell you that daily visits to museums, libraries, and academies (cemeteries of empty exertion, Calvaries of crucified dreams, registries of aborted beginnings!) are, for artists, as damaging as the prolonged supervision by parents of certain young people drunk with their talent and their ambitious wills. When the future is barred to them, the admirable past may be a solace for the ills of the moribund, the sickly, the prisoner . . . But we want no part of it, the past, we the young and strong Futurists!

From Filippo Marinetti,
'The Futurist Manifesto',
Le Figaro, 20 February 1909

507 *Pablo Picasso created this Minotauromachy in 1935, a year before the outbreak of the Spanish Civil War. His characterization of the Minotaur offered an arresting prophesy of the inner bestiality of man that would so shortly be unleashed.*

508 right *The 20th-century English sculptor Henry Moore praised the 'great, elemental simplicity' of female marble figurines such as this one, of c. 2500–2400 BC, with their arms folded over their chest, unseparated legs, and straight profile. They were buried alongside the deceased in Cycladic tombs.*

509 centre *This votive offering from Nemi near Rome, of c. 350 BC, belongs to a type widespread in Etruria in the 4th–2nd centuries BC. The figure's head, with its central parting of the hair and diadem, remains close to contemporary Greek models; its sparsely detailed and elongated body was a new Etruscan departure.*

510 left *Alberto Giacometti found his inspiration in simple elongated Etruscan sculptures [509], most famously a statuette known as Evening Shadow. The bronze Standing Woman (Leoni), of 1947, is typical of his declared interest in rendering not the human figure 'but the shadow that it casts'.*

Mussolini's Fascist appropriations). Neither was the work of Pablo Picasso without its share of Classical allusion. 'The beauties of the Parthenon, Venuses, Nymphs, Narcissuses, are so many lies', he proclaimed; '. . . art is not the canon of beauty, but what the instinct and brain can conceive beyond any canon: when we love a woman, we don't start measuring her limbs.' Still, for Picasso (as for others), what icon could more poignantly evoke the political and cultural struggles in the late 1920s and 1930s, as well as the turmoil of his own private life, than that of the Cretan Minotaur, half man and half bull [507]?

Nowhere is this ambiguous relationship between the Classical and modern arts more evident than in the sphere of architecture. In the early 20th century, artistic rebellions against Classicism went hand in hand with a revolution against the appearance and function of 19th-century public buildings: generally speaking, designs which exploited modern materials and modern engineering methods and which supposedly met 'the needs of modern life' came into favour, while structures that merely paid homage to Classical prototypes were consigned to the past. This movement, as Louis Sullivan's *Kindergarten Chats* (1901) suggest, was part of a much broader attempt at effecting social and cultural change. It was concerned with building a new, progressive age that was reflected in (and brought about by) the skyscraper and tower-block; it was motivated, as Charles Jencks has put it, by the idea that 'a new, heroic, democratic society would emerge, led by a powerful race of supermen, the *avant-gardes*, the technicians and captains of industry, the enlightened scientists and teams of experts'.

No simple distinction exists between what has come to be termed 'Modern' architecture and the 'Postmodern' styles that subsequently emerged – except, that is, in books. (Some have even claimed that Modern buildings are the purest manifestation of Classical forms, embodying an idea of Classicism without being slave to its letter.) Broadly speaking, however, the late 20th century witnessed a reappraisal of Classical architectural forms – or at least a reappraisal of sorts. While many recent buildings allude to Classical motifs, they also self-consciously play upon those quotations. Take the case of Charles Moore's Piazza d'Italia in New Orleans (1976–1979) [511]. The scheme was immediately praised for initiating

511 *Piazza d'Italia, New Orleans, by Charles Moore, completed in 1979. A collage of temple fronts and colonnades, complete with grand-looking Latin inscriptions, provides a backdrop for a topographical map of Italy made of stepping stones.*

512 The Birth of Venus, *by Sandro Botticelli, c. 1485, fuses the myth of the goddess's birth from the sea (see p. 53) – famously depicted in a lost Greek painting attributed to Apelles – with that of her arrival on the island of Cyprus. Venus, riding on a shell, is driven to the shore by Zephyrus and Aura and greeted by an attendant, probably a personification of Spring. Her pose descends from the celebrated statue type of the 'Chaste Venus' (*Venus Pudica), *which ultimately stems from the cult statue of Aphrodite at Knidos, by Praxiteles [83].*

513 *In this mural, entitled* Venice Reconstituted, *of 1988–1989, Venice Beach in Los Angeles relates itself via Botticelli's painting [512] to a Classical artistic tradition. But the speech bubble and playful modern adaptation of the figure – Venus reconstituted, as much as Venice – remind us not to take that claim too seriously . . .*

514 The Louvre Venus de Milo *(the Greek statue of Aphrodite found on the island of Melos, probably dating to c. 100 BC) is here irreverently transformed into a kitsch novelty light, playing upon its status as one of the most imitated icons of Classical antiquity.*

a 'historical revival'; but its Classicizing forms were introduced only to have their coherence humorously questioned, recontextualized, and challenged. The piazza's central fountain is framed with walls adorned in the Doric, Tuscan, Ionic, Corinthian, and Composite orders (the mix in itself is significant). But these are empty façades, composed not only of marble but also of stainless steel; they are painted in bright colours and lit with neon lights; and their architraves are filled not with metopes or a sculpted frieze, but with square water jets – what the architect, with typical Postmodern wit, called 'wetopes'.

CLASSICAL PASTS, PRESENTS, AND FUTURES

'The past, since it cannot be destroyed, because its destruction leads to silence, must be revisited, but with irony, not innocently.' This statement of the cultural condition at the end of the 20th century (by the Italian scholar and novelist Umberto Eco) offers a broad insight into all manner of contemporary literary and artistic engagements with Classical antiquity. Strict Neoclassicism – paying complacent homage to the Classical past by imitating its forms – has been superseded. At the same time, all avant-garde efforts to jettison the past have also been challenged. What remains – Postmodernism – is no self-contained style or straightforward movement. It is a phenomenon that incorporates the past into the present by means of an artificial collage, an eclectic pastiche. It selectively puts together the fragments of cultural and artistic histories while self-consciously recognizing (and celebrating) its own fragmented state, and thereby the viewer's own cultural relativity. So Imperial Rome is resurrected as the Caesar's Palace casino on the plains of Las Vegas; the *Venus de Milo* becomes a light-up camp icon [514]; and a mural in California's Venice Beach transforms another Classicized Venus, the subject of Botticelli's Renaissance painting [512], into a modern-day beach-babe [513].

A fresh, banal, or irreverent form of Classicism? However we may view such contemporary references to the Classical past, they testify to the essential durability of a tradition. Whether we go to it as pilgrims or as vandals, the Classical world is still *there* – a past that is still present, as landmark, haven, or point of departure.

MAP

Aquilea

Po

Bologna • Ravenna
Marzabotto •

UMBRIA

Pisa • Florence
Arno

Arezzo

Roselle

ETRURIA
ELBA
Cosa
GIGLIO Tarquinia
Pyrgi Cerveteri • Veii
Ostia • Rome
Lavinium

Terracina

Ancona

Orvieto
Tiber

LATIUM

Palestrina

Sperlonga

Naples • Mt Vesuvius
Herculaneum • • Boscoreale
Pompeii
Paestum

CAMPANIA

SAMNIUM

LUCANIA

APULIA

Cannae

Brundisium

Taranto
Metapontum

Croton

Sybaris

Riace

Messina
Locri

Segesta
Selinus
Mt Etna ▲ Straits of Messina

Piazza Armerina
Agrigento •
Gela
Megara Hyblaea
Syracuse

HIBERNIA

CALEDONIA

Hadrian's
Wall

York •
• Chester

BRITANNIA

• Bath London •Colchester
Silchester • Thames

BELGIAN
GAUL

Seine

Paris

Loire

GAUL

Lyons

AQUITANIA

Garonne

La Graufesenque • Nîmes • Ora
PRO
Marseilles •
Rhône

Segovia •

Ampurias •

Tagus

Tarragona •

IBERIA

Ebro

M E D I

MAURETANIA   NUMIDIA

0   100   200   300   400   500 MILES
|———|———|———|———|———|———|———|———|———|———|

0   100 200 300 400 500 600 700 800 KILOMETRES
|——|——|——|——|——|——|——|——|——|——|——|——|——|——|——|——|——|

LESBOS

CHIOS

EUBOEA

Thermopylae
AETOLIA
PHOCIS
Mt Parnassus
Delphi
Chalkis
Eretria
Tanagra
BOEOTIA
Thebes
Rhamnous
Perachora
Eleusis
Marathon
Athens
ATTICA
Sicyon
Megara
Piraeus
Corinth
AEGINA
Laurium
Nemea
Mycenae
Tiryns
Sounion
Olympia
Argos
Epidauros
ELIS
ARCADIA
Bassae
Lerna
Phigaleia
LACONIA
Messene
Sparta
Pylos
MESSENIA

EPIRUS
ITHACA
KEPHALLONIA
ZAKYNTHOS

ANDROS
SAMOS
KEOS
MYKONOS
DELOS
PAROS
Apollonas
NAXOS
MELOS
THERA

KYTHERA

GERMANIA
Cologne
Rhine
Neumagen
Trier
Danube

DACIA
Adamklissi
Danube

BLACK SEA

ILLYRICUM
Split
DALMATIA
MOESIA

ADRIATIC SEA

Po
Arno
ELBA
Tiber
Rome
CORSICA

TYRRHENIAN SEA
SARDINIA
Naples
Nora

BITHYNIA
PONTUS
Constantinople (Byzantium)

THRACE
Philippi
MACEDONIA
Pella
Vergina
Olynthos
THASOS
SAMOTHRACE
Troy
Mt. Olympus
Dodona
EPIRUS
CORFU
THESSALY
AEGEAN
SEA
Athens

ASIA MINOR
PHRYGIA
GALATIA
CAPPADOCIA

Pergamon
Sardis
LYDIA
IONIA
Aphrodisias
CILICIA
Tyana
Ephesus
PAMPHYLIA
Priene
Miletos
ISAURIA
Seleucia
Al Mina
Antioch
Halicarnassus
Carrhae

PELOPONNESE
CYCLADES
Knidos
Palmyra
RHODES

SICILY
Syracuse
CYPRUS
Paphos
SYRIA
Baalbek
Damascus

MALTA
Knossos
CRETE
Sidon
Tyre
PHOENICIA
Caesarea
Jerusalem
PALESTINE

Carthage
Utthus

TERRA
MEDITERRANEAN SEA

AFRICA
Tripoli
Lepcis Magna
Cyrene
Alexandria
Naukratis
Petra
Fayum
Nile
EGYPT
Oxyrhynchus
Orontes

333

TIMELINE

Like all charts, this timeline is a selective one, but it aims to include the key moments in the history of the Classical world, as well as most of the people and events mentioned in this book. It also gives some impression of how literary and artistic activities fit chronologically with political developments in the ancient Mediterranean world, though the three-way thematic division here is purely for clarity of presentation. It is biased, of course, in both its geographical and its temporal scope, and even within the timeline some centuries have been 'stretched' and others 'squashed'. What we might call the high points of Athenian and Roman civilization, the 5th and 4th centuries BC and the 1st centuries BC and AD, receive the most space because these are the periods whose cultural achievements we know best. The conventional designation of Greek artistic 'periods' – Geometric, Archaic, Classical, and Hellenistic – despite its problems (see pp. 292–93), is retained here for convenience.

	900 BC	800	700	600

PEOPLE AND POWER

c. 900 Process of synoicism at Athens

8th C City-states arise in Greece

c. 750 Greeks begin to settle abroad

776 Traditional date of first Olympic Games

753 Traditional date of founding of Rome

c. 620 DRACO's penal code in Athens

c. 590 SOLON's reforms in Athens

7th/6th C (trad.) LYCURGUS lays down Spartan constitution

First gold and silver coins minted in Lydia during the reign of CROESUS (*c.* 560–547)

6th C Etruscan rule at Rome

PHILOSOPHY AND LITERATURE

c. 750 Introduction of Greek alphabet from a Phoenician source

c. 750–*c.* 650 HOMER's *Iliad* and *Odyssey* circulating as oral poems

7th C onwards *Homeric Hymns* in circulation

c. 700 HESIOD, *Theogony* and *Works and Days*

c. 600 SAPPHO and ALKAIOS writing lyric poetry on Lesbos

THALES OF MILETOS (b. 624), philosopher

ART AND ARCHITECTURE

'GEOMETRIC' (9th–8th C)   'ARCHAIC' (7th–6th C)

c. 750 Funerary amphoras and kraters at Dipylon cemetery in Athens

c. 650 Earliest Greek monumental statuary ('Daedalic')

late 7th–early 5th C Prevalence of *kouros/ko*

c. 630 Temple of Apollo, Thermon

c. 600–580 Temple of Artemis, Corfu

c. 7th C First paved Forum area in Rome

	900 BC	800	700	600

508/507 KLEISTHENES' political reorganization of Athens

450–429 PERICLES prominent in Athens

399 SOCRATES condemned to death in Athens

264–241 **First Punic War**

218–201 **Second Punic War** (HANNIBAL's campaigns in Italy)

546–527 PEISISTRATOS rules as tyrant of Athens

371 Spartans defeated by Thebes at ⚔Leuctra

338 PHILIP II of Macedon defeats the free Greek city-states at ⚔ Chaeronea

430–426 Plague in Athens

514 HARMODIOS and ARISTOGEITON assassinate HIPPARCHOS in Athens

336–323 ALEXANDER THE GREAT conquers the eastern Mediterranean and the Persian Empire as far as India

Persian Wars
490 Invading Persians repelled at ⚔ Marathon
480 Sack of Athens
479 Persians defeated at ⚔ Salamis and ⚔ Plataea

431–404 **Peloponnesian War** between Athens and Sparta

415–413 Athenian expedition to Sicily

323 Division of ALEXANDER's empire between his Successors (*Diadochoi*)

510 (trad.) Last king of Rome expelled; foundation of Roman Republic

396 fall of the Etruscan city of Veii to Rome

c. 300 PTOLEMY I SOTER founds the museum and library of Alexandria

---

Attic tragedians
AESCHYLUS (*c.* 525–456)
SOPHOCLES (*c.* 496–406)
EURIPIDES (*c.* 485–406)

427–386 ARISTOPHANES, 'Old Comedy' plays

324–*c.* 290 MENANDER, 'New Comedy' plays

mid–late 6th C PYTHAGORAS, scientist

late 5th C GORGIAS, *Encomium of Helen*

late 5th C HIPPOCRATES, physician

400–350s XENOPHON, writings

DEMOSTHENES (384–322), orator

Alexandrian scholars and poets
270s THEOCRITUS
270s–260s HERODAS
270s–*c.* 230 CALLIMACHUS
c. 270–215 APOLLONIUS OF RHODES

PINDAR (b. 518), lyric poet

440s–*c.* 430s HERODOTUS, *Histories*

c. 430–*c.* 400 THUCYDIDES, *History of the Peloponnesian War*

ZENO (335–263), founder of Stoicism

c. 300 THEOPHRASTUS, *Characters*

5th C 'Old Oligarch', *Constitution of Athens*

ARISTOTLE (384–322), philosopher

ARCHIMEDES (*c.* 287–212), mathematician

EMPEDOCLES (*c.* 493–*c.* 453), philosopher

CARNEADES (214–129), Sceptic philosopher

HERACLITUS (active *c.* 500), Ionian philosopher

PLATO (*c.* 429–347), philosopher

EPICURUS (341–270), philosopher

DEMOCRITUS (b. *c.* 460), philosopher

DIOGENES (*c.* 400–325), philosopher

'CLASSICAL' (early 5th–4th C)   **'HELLENISTIC' (323–31)**

---

509 ANTENOR, *Tyrannicides* (original group)

c. 460 Stoa Poikile, Athens

c. 370 Temple of Asklepios, Epidauros (theatre added in second half of 4th C)

c. 460 Temple of Zeus, Olympia

...tue types in Greece

c. 490 Treasury of Athenians, Delphi

447–432 Parthenon, Athens, including PHEIDIAS' *Athena Parthenos*

c. 360 PRAXITELES, *Aphrodite of Knidos*

c. 530–520 Change from black-figure to red-figure in Attic vase-painting

c. 480 *Kritian Boy*

c. 480–470 'Tomb of the Diver', Paestum

c. 450 MYRON, *Diskobolos*

LYSIPPOS (*c.* 370–315), *Weary Herakles*

c. 500 Portonaccio Temple, Veii

c. 450 POLYKLEITOS, *Doryphoros*

367–*c.* 350 Mausoleum of Halicarnassus

c. 520–500 'Married Couple' sarcophagus, Cerveteri

c. 510 Temple of Jupiter, Juno, and Minerva on the Capitoline Hill, Rome

c. 420 Temple of Apollo at Bassae begun

PEOPLE AND POWER

200–146 Roman conquest of Greece

149–146 Third Punic War
146 Sack of Carthage
146 Sack of Corinth

133 Proposed land reforms of TIBERIUS GRACCHUS

133 Pergamon 'bequeathed' to Rome

91–89 'Social War' in Italy

88–82 Civil war between SULLA and MARIUS

73–71 Slave revolt of SPARTACUS

50s JULIUS CAESAR'S campaigns in Gaul

49–48 CAESAR defeats POMPEY in Civil War
44 Assassination of CAESAR
43 Triumvirate of OCTAVIAN, MARK ANTONY, and LEPIDUS established
31 Actium: OCTAVIAN defeats MARK ANTONY and CLEOPATRA

Roman emperors until AD 200

2 AUGUSTUS receives the title 'pater patriae'

27 BC–AD 14 AUGUSTUS
14–37 TIBERIUS
37–41 CALIGULA
41–54 CLAUDIUS
54–68 NERO

c. **30** JESUS CHRIST executed in Judaea

50s Evangelism of ST PETER and ST PAUL

43 Invasion of Britain

69 Year of the Fou Emperors: GALBA, OTHO, VITELLIUS, VESPASIAN

69–7

PHILOSOPHY AND LITERATURE

c. **200–184** PLAUTUS, comedies

160s TERENCE, comedies

160 CATO THE ELDER, *On Agriculture*

167–*c.* **118** POLYBIUS, *Histories*

170s ENNIUS, *Annals*

CICERO (106–43), speeches, philosophy, letters

c. **50s** LUCRETIUS, *On the Nature of Things*

c. **60–54** CATULLUS, poems

50s–*c.* **30** DIODORUS SICULUS, *Library of History*

c. **35–19** VERGIL, *Georgics, Eclogues, Aeneid*

c. **38–8** HORACE, poems

c. **33–16** PROPERTIUS, *Elegies*

c. **26–19** TIBULLUS, *Elegies*

c. **20 BC–AD 17** OVID, poems

c. **30 BC–AD 17** LIVY, *History of Rome from its Foundation*

late 1st C VITRUVIUS, *On Architecture*

20s STRABO, *Geography*

SENECA (*c.* BC–AD 65), philosopher and dramatist

c. **50** COLUMELLA, *On Farming*

mid-1st C PETRONIUS, *Satyricon*

c. **20** CELSUS, *On Medicine*

?1st C LONGINUS, *On the Sublime*

62/63 LUCAN, *Pharsalia*

'HELLENISTIC' (323–31)

ART AND ARCHITECTURE

mid-2nd C Stoa of Attalos, Athens

c. **165** Great Altar of Pergamon built by EUMENES II

c. **100** 'Pseudo-Athlete', Delos

mid-1st C PASITELES writes *Great Masterpieces*

55 POMPEY builds first stone theatre in Rome

c. **28–27** Mausoleum of Augustus, Rome

27–25 Pantheon, Rome, built by AGRIPPA

9 BC Ara Pacis Augustae, Rome, dedicated

2 BC Forum of Augustus, Rome, dedicated

?early 1st C *Laocoön*

?early 1st C Installation of sculptural groups at Sperlonga

64–68 Golden House of Nero, Rome

64 Great fire of Rome

79 Eruption of Vesuvius: Pompeii and surrounding towns buried

70 Sack of Jerusalem

c. 122–126 HADRIAN'S WALL, Britain

130 Death of ANTINOUS

293 DIOCLETIAN establishes Tetrarchy

410 Sack of Rome by ALARIC the Goth

313 CONSTANTINE sanctions Christianity throughout the Roman Empire (Edict of Milan)

330 Constantinople founded

395 Division of Roman Empire between West and East

'ESPASIAN

79–81 TITUS

81–96 DOMITIAN

96–98 NERVA

98–117 TRAJAN

117–138 HADRIAN

138–161 ANTONINUS PIUS

161–180 MARCUS AURELIUS

180–192 COMMODUS

193–211 SEPTIMIUS SEVERUS

393 THEODOSIUS THE GREAT closes the Sanctuary at Olympia

70s PLINY THE ELDER, *Natural History*

80s–100s MARTIAL, *Epigrams*

90s STATIUS, poems

80s–110s DIO CHRYSOSTOM, Greek orator, at Rome

80s EPICTETUS (Stoic) teaching at Rome

c. 160 PAUSANIAS, *Guide to Greece*

100–120 PLUTARCH, *Lives*

c. 150–170 PTOLEMY, *Harmonics*

c. 100–112 PLINY THE YOUNGER, *Letters*

c. 120–160 ARRIAN, historical writings

c. 100 FRONTINUS, *On the Water-Supplies of Rome*

c. 120 SUETONIUS, *Lives of the Caesars*

120s JUVENAL, *Satires*

LUCIAN (b. 120), philosopher and satirist

98–120s TACITUS, historical works

mid-2nd C APULEIUS, *The Golden Ass*

c. 200 ATHENAEUS, *Intellectuals at the Table*

PORPHYRY (234–*c.* 305), Neo-Platonist philosopher

PLOTINUS (205–270), Neoplatonist philosopher

c. 170 MARCUS AURELIUS, *Meditations*

c. 160–*c.* 200 GALEN, physician, practising in Rome

c. 200–230 DIO CASSIUS, *Roman History*

c. 180 AULUS GELLIUS, *Attic Nights*

2nd–3rd C PHILOSTRATOS family, *Lives of the Sophists, Gymnastics, Life of Apollonius of Tyana*

?4th C 'APICIUS', *On Cookery*

360s AURELIUS VICTOR, *Lives of the Caesars*

ST AUGUSTINE (354–430), Christian philosopher

80 Colosseum, Rome, inaugurated

81 Arch of Titus, Rome

113 Trajan's Column, Rome

mid-2nd C Great Colonnade, Palmyra

c. 118 Pantheon rebuilt by HADRIAN

c. 125–138 Villa of Hadrian, Tivoli

c. 128–139 Mausoleum of Hadrian, Rome

c. 130–140 Sanctuary of Asklepios, Pergamon

c. 180–192 Column of Marcus Aurelius, Rome

c. 175 Bronze equestrian statue of Marcus Aurelius, Rome

c. 200 First catacombs, outside walls of Rome

212–217 Baths of Caracalla, Rome

c. 300–306 Diocletian's Palace, Split

c. 312–315 Arch of Constantine, Rome

c. 350 Dido and Aeneas mosaic, Low Ham, Britain

CLASSICAL LIVES

This section contains the epitomes of some two hundred individuals (and certain dynastic and political groups) whom we might deem the historical, or at least semi-historical, celebrities of the Classical world. It is selective – and unavoidably biased towards men.

515 *Aeschylus (Roman marble portrait after a Greek original made in the third quarter of the 4th century BC).*

516 *Agrippa (marble portrait, late 1st century BC).*

517 *Antinous (detail of an idealizing marble statue erected soon after his death in AD 130).*

Achaemenids Greek form of the dynastic name of the Persian royals, 7th–4th centuries BC. **Darius I** (r. 521–486 BC) was defeated by the Greeks at the battle of Marathon in 490 BC. His son, **Xerxes** (r. 486–465 BC), led the Persian invasion of Attica in 480 BC, which was defeated at Salamis by **Themistocles**.

Aeschines (*c.* 397–322 BC) Prominent Athenian advocate of compromise with **Philip II of Macedon**; as such, noted antagonist of **Demosthenes**.

Aeschylus (*c.* 525–456 BC) Athenian playwright, most esteemed for the *Oresteia* – the sole surviving trilogy of Athenian tragedies. His life spanned key events in the city: the fall of the tyrants, the rise of democracy, and the Persian wars. (Aeschylus himself is documented as having fought at both Marathon and Salamis, and his play, *The Persians*, includes what seem like eyewitness accounts of battle.) [515]

Aesop (probably early 6th century BC) Legendary composer of the 'Fables' – moralizing nuggets of homespun wisdom wrapped in brief tales about animals. Little is known of his life (the fables themselves only survive in the versions of other authors), although one tradition casts him as a slave on the island of Samos.

Agatharkos (5th century BC) Painter from Samos, said to have designed the first theatrical 'set', for a production of a play by **Aeschylus** (though not necessarily during the playwright's lifetime).

Agricola, Gnaeus Julius (AD 40–93) Roman governor of Britain, eulogized by his son-in-law **Tacitus** in a short biography.

Agrippa, Marcus Vipsanius (*c.* 64–12 BC) As right-hand man of **Augustus**, Agrippa masterminded several of the Emperor's military campaigns (most famously the defeat of **Mark Antony** at Actium in 31 BC); among his many public works were the reorganization of Rome's water supply, the erection of a new set of public baths, and the remodelling of the Campus Martius (to include a new temple 'to all the gods' – the Pantheon). [290, 516]

Agrippina Cognomen of two daughters of **Agrippa**, and the daughter of one of them: Vipsania Agrippina, first wife of the Emperor **Tiberius** (d. AD 20), and Vipsania Agrippina (*c.* 14 BC–AD 33), mother of **Caligula**, who was known as 'Agrippina the Elder' to distinguish

her from her daughter, Julia Agrippina 'the Younger' (AD 15–59). The latter was the mother of **Nero**; although her scheming brought about his succession, Nero reputedly ordered her murder at Baiae – after failing to drown her in a boat designed to sink.

Alaric (d. AD 410) Leader of the Visigoths from the Balkan region, whose 'Sack of Rome' in AD 410 is traditionally reckoned as an end-mark of Classical antiquity.

Alcibiades (*c.* 450–404 BC) Colourful protagonist of Athenian history, primed for political service by **Pericles** and famed for being a double-agent to Athens and Sparta; also an associate of **Socrates**.

Alexander the Great (356–323 BC) The name universally given to Alexander III of Macedon, son of **Philip II**, who was put in command of Macedonian forces while still crown prince. Dying young, Alexander generated a posthumous fame full of romance. But his image in literature and art consistently attests a highly charismatic figure, who led his army on a mission of conquest encompassing Persia, Bactria, Egypt, and the Hindu Kush. Though it was always part of his strategy to adopt and adapt to regional custom, Alexander undoubtedly fostered the ethos that characterizes the Hellenistic period – when the idioms of Greek art and language diffused around and far beyond the Mediterranean basin. [275–78, 374]

Alkaios (b. *c.* 620 BC) Greek poet from Mytilene in Lesbos, whose surviving lyrics (mostly in fragments) finely evoke the heroic-erotic aspirations of participants in the symposium.

Alkmaionids Powerful Athenian family, temporarily exiled by **Peisistratos**, and later instrumental in the reforms which led to a democratic constitution at Athens. **Kleisthenes** was the Alkmaionid who set up the Athenian voting districts in 508/7 BC. A later member of the family was **Pericles**.

Amasis (r. *c.* 569–525 BC) The Egyptian pharaoh Ahmose II ('Amasis' is how the Greeks rendered the name), who maintained an 'open door' policy to Greek traders.

Anacreon (b. *c.* 570 BC) Greek lyric poet, native of Teos on the coast of Asia Minor. His works, surviving mostly in fragments, largely concerned themselves with the

sympotic themes of love and convivial drinking.

Anaxagoras (*c.* 500–*c.* 428 BC) 'Pre-Socratic' philosopher at Athens (originally from Clazomenae in Ionia), whose interest was mainly in the physical micro-nature of things, and the way in which matter might animated by 'mind' (*nous*).

Antenor (fl. late 6th century BC) Athenian sculptor, credited with the first bronze group commemorating the **Tyrannicides**.

Antinous (d. AD 130) Bithynian-born boyfriend of the Emperor **Hadrian**. His premature death, by drowning in the Nile, set off a widespread cult to his memory, preserved by numerous portrait statues. Many show him in pseudo-divine guise. [517]

Antiochos The name of several of the Seleukid kings of Central Asia – foremost among them Antiochos I ('Soter', or 'Saviour', 324–261 BC) [362, 363], the son of **Seleukos I**, who restored control of his father's kingdom after his accession in 281 BC and founded many cities in the East.

Antoninus Pius (AD 86–161, r. 138–161) Adopted son and successor of the Emperor **Hadrian**. He gives his name to a series of 'Antonine' emperors in Rome (himself, then **Marcus Aurelius**, Lucius Verus, and **Commodus**). [148]

Antony see **Mark Antony**

Apelles (4th century BC) Greek painter (born at Colophon in Ionia) connected with the court of **Alexander the Great**, though his commissions are attested throughout the Aegean world. Ancient descriptions of his depictions of Calumny, Envy, Truth, and other abstract concepts, as well as the birth of Aphrodite [512], were highly influential in the Renaissance.

Apicius A byword for a Classical gourmet. The most celebrated 'Apicius' (Marcus Gavius Apicius) lived in the reign of the Emperor Tiberius, but the cognomen came to stand for culinary connoisseurship; hence a surviving 4th-century collection of recipes (*On Cookery*) was ascribed to a later chef of the same (pseudo-) name.

Apollonius of Rhodes (*c.* 295–215 BC) Hellenistic Greek poet based at Alexandria, and later Rhodes; author of the *Argonautica*, an epic saga in four books that retold the story of Jason and the Argonauts.

Apollonius of Tyana (1st century AD)
An itinerant Greek philosopher, born in Cappadocia, who claimed affiliation to the ideas of **Pythagoras**. His travels took him to the Indian subcontinent, and his remarkable experiences both as a Classical philosopher in Asia and an Asian-style 'shaman' in Classical territory are related in his biography by one of the writers called **Philostratos**.

Appian (AD *c*. 95–*c*. 165) Greek author of a *Roman History*, arranged according to the peoples that Rome conquered.

Apuleius, Lucius (b. *c*. AD 125) African-born author of *Metamorphoses*, or *The Golden Ass*, a rare intact example of the novel in Latin (cf. **Petronius**) – a burlesque tale of what happens when a dabbler in witchcraft named Lucius is turned into a donkey, then saved by the intervention of Isis. [518]

Archimedes (*c*. 287–212 BC) Greek physicist, mathematician, astronomer, and engineer, who gave his services to the ruler of the colony of Syracuse in Sicily, and died during the Roman siege of that city. He is traditionally said to have shouted 'Eureka, eureka!' ('I've found it!') while in the bath, having determined the relative proportions of gold and silver in a crown for the Syracusan king Hieron II.

Aristides (d. *c*. 467 BC) Athenian statesman and political rival of **Themistocles**; he was ostracized from Athens in 482 BC.

Aristogeiton see **Tyrannicides**

Aristophanes (*c*. 450–385 BC) Greek comic playwright, author of over forty plays (of which eleven survive in full). Acute in political satire, lyrical and bawdy, Aristophanes is the acknowledged master at Athens of 'Old Comedy' – more political and more fantastic than the 'New Comedy' of **Menander**.

Aristotle (384–322 BC) Greek philosopher, literary critic, and natural scientist. He was the pupil of **Plato**, then teacher of **Alexander the Great** before setting set up his own

518 *Apuleius* (*Roman contorniate, 4th century AD*).

519 *Aristotle* (*Roman marble portrait after a Greek original made in the last quarter of the 4th century BC*).

school *c*. 335 BC (ultimately known as the Lyceum). While his *Poetics* is not the most substantial of his many works (some five hundred were attributed to him), it is required reading for all those interested in Classical literature, especially the theory of tragedy. [519]

Arrian (Lucius Flavius Arrianus, *c*. AD 86–*c*. 160) Bithynian Greek, officer in the Roman army; in addition to publishing the lectures (*Discourses*) of **Epictetus**, he wrote a seven-book history of **Alexander the Great** (the *Anabasis of Alexander*).

Artemidoros (fl. late 2nd century AD) Greek author of *On the Interpretation of Dreams*.

Athenaeus (fl. *c*. 200 AD) Greek author, based in Egypt. *Intellectuals at the Table* (*Deipnosophistai*) records the imagined table-talk, covering topics from linguistics to anecdotes from daily life, of twenty-three men of learning.

Attalids Dynastic name of the rulers of Pergamon, beginning with Attalos I [520] as the first official 'king' in 241 BC. Attalos II sponsored a stoa in the Athenian Agora [300, 301]. Their wealth was derived from stocks of war booty deposited in the city by **Alexander the Great**: they used it to create a bastion of Classical culture, a 'second Athens' in the East, bequeathed to Rome on the death of Attalos III in 133 BC.

St Augustine (Aurelius Antoninus, AD 354–430) Christian theologian and bishop of Hippo (in North Africa), trained in Latin rhetoric and philosophy; his literary works include *On Christian Learning*, *On the Trinity*, and most famously his autobiographical *Confessions*.

Augustus (63 BC–AD 14, r. 27 BC–AD 14) The name (meaning 'consecrated one') assumed by Octavian in 27 BC after emerging as supreme ruler of Rome. On being

adopted by his great-uncle Julius **Caesar**, Augustus had earlier taken the name Gaius Julius Caesar Octavianus. All subsequent emperors would henceforth carry the title 'Caesar Augustus', as if acknowledging the two individuals who effectively transformed Rome from a Republican to an autocratic constitution. Augustus, however, took care to mask his political *coup* as a 'restitution' of peace, prosperity, and Republican ideals. He ordered that an autobiographical list of *The Achievements of the Deified Augustus* (*Res Gestae Divi Augusti*) be inscribed on bronze pillars at the entrance of his mausoleum after his death; it survives complete in a copy erected at Ancyra in Asia Minor. [286, 290, 291, 364]

Bacchylides (5th century BC) Greek poet from the island of Keos who, like **Pindar**, specialized in 'victory odes' for successful athletes.

Boethius, Anicius Manlius Severinus (*c*. AD 476–*c*. 524) Roman philosopher and Christian theologian, whose *Consolation of Philosophy* – written in prison before his execution on a charge of treason by Theodoric, Ostrogothic king of Italy under the emperor in Constantinople – epitomized a tradition of Greek philosophy in Latin and was influential throughout the Middle Ages.

Brutus Clan name of two 'anti-tyrannical' Romans:
• Lucius Junius (fl. late 6th century BC) assisted in the expulsion of the last **Tarquin** king, Tarquin the Proud, *c*. 510 BC. [521]
• Marcus Junius (*c*. 85–42 BC) headed the conspiracy to assassinate Julius **Caesar**; committed suicide after defeat by Octavian, **Mark Antony**, and **Lepidus** at Philippi.

Caesar, Gaius Julius (100–44 BC) General who extended Roman control over large parts of north-west Europe, and who waged a wide-ranging civil war against **Pompey**. After his eventual victory at the battle of Pharsalus in 48 BC, he assumed autocratic powers (and the title *dictator*), leading to his assassination by his own followers on the Ides (15th) of March. His *Commentaries* on how he conquered Gaul, written in the third person, remain a model of mechanically lucid Latin prose. [522]

Caligula (AD 12–41, r. 37–41) Nickname ('Little Boot') of the despotic Roman emperor Gaius Julius Caesar Germanicus, famed for the phrase 'Let them hate, so long as they fear' (**Suetonius**, *Life of Caligula* 30.1) – and his subsequent assassination. [292, 523]

Callimachus (*c*. 305–*c*. 240 BC) Greek poet and scholar at the library in

520 *Attalos I* (*marble portrait from Pergamon, 3rd century BC*).

521 *Lucius Brutus* (*bronze portrait, probably late 4th or 3rd century BC; the romantic identification was made in the 16th century*).

522 *Julius Caesar* (*marble portrait, mid-1st century BC*).

523 *Caligula* (*Roman marble portrait found in Asia Minor, crafted during his reign*).

524 *Caracalla (marble portrait, formerly inserted in a statue, said to be from Italy, first quarter of the 3rd century AD).*

525 *Claudius (gold aureus, c. AD 50).*

526 *Cleopatra (marble portrait, probably made for a Roman rather than an Egyptian context, c. 50–30 BC).*

527 *Constantine (colossal marble head from a seated statue in the Basilica of Maxentius in the Roman Forum, c. AD 315–325).*

Alexandria, a leading figure of the Hellenistic period, who was famed for his erudite, allusive, and often highly ironic tone, as well as his varied output. His six *Hymns* survive intact, but his most famous collection – the *Aetia* (*Causes*), written in four books – today survives only in fragments.

Caracalla (AD 188–217, r. 211–217) Nickname – derived from the hooded Celtic cloak that he supposedly introduced – of the Roman emperor Marcus Aurelius Antoninus, remembered equally for his despotism and his bath-buildings at Rome [67–69]. [524]

Carneades (*c.* 213–*c.* 129 BC) Philosopher from Cyrene in North Africa. As head of the Academy founded by **Plato** in Athens, *c.* 155–*c.* 137 BC, he ventured on a philosophical embassy to Rome (with **Diogenes**), and was also responsible for sceptically challenging Stoic and Epicurean dogmas (for which antiquity sometimes credited him with founding the 'New' Academy).

Catiline (Lucius Sergius Catilina, d. 62 BC) Rival of **Cicero**, defeated by him in the competition for consulship in 63 BC; famed for his conspiracy against Rome that led him to rebel openly against the state in 62 BC (as predicted in Cicero's four speeches *Against Catiline* and narrated in his **Sallust**'s *Catiline War*).

Cato the Elder (Marcus Porcius Cato, also known as 'The Censor', 234–149 BC) Roman statesman, proverbially austere, anti-Greek, and passionately committed to the smallholding basis of the Republic (as reflected in his *On Agriculture*).

Cato the Younger (Marcus Porcius Cato, 95–46 BC) Great-grandson of the above; loyal to the Roman Republican cause and senatorial modes of government to the end, he sided with **Pompey** during the Civil Wars, and committed an exemplary 'Stoic' suicide in defeat.

Catullus, Gaius Valerius (?84–?54 BC) Latin poet, whose urbane wit might seem scurrilous and bawdy, but whose lyrics (twenty-five addressed to his beloved 'Lesbia') combined Latin language with the themes and meters of Greek poetry.

Celsus, Aulus Cornelius (fl. first half of the 1st century AD) Roman author of an encyclopaedic book of *Arts*, of which only eight books dedicated to medicine survive.

Chrysippos (*c.* 280–207 BC) Pupil of Kleanthes (a follower of **Zeno**), whose (lost) Greek treatises did much to defend, and shape, Stoic philosophy.

Cicero, Marcus Tullius (106–43 BC) A skillful barrister, a controversial politician, a seasoned philosopher, as well as a fluent essayist and correspondent. The copious legacy of his writings (on subjects as diverse as the nature of the gods, rhetoric, and political theory), transcribed speeches (in all, fifty-seven survive), and extensive correspondence, has been a model of rhythmically articulated prose from antiquity to the present. [261]

Cincinnatus, Lucius Quintius (mid-5th century BC) The classic example of the smallholder-senator of the Roman Republic – interrupting his farming tasks to lead an army in 458 BC, and returning to the plough once victory was secured.

Claudius (Tiberius Claudius Nero Germanicus, 10 BC–AD 54, r. 41–54) Roman emperor, mocked as a stammering fool by historical tradition, but now often regarded as an astute and scholarly ruler (not least as reflected in his successful invasion of Britain, in AD 43). [525]

Cleon (d. 422 BC) Athenian politician and rival of **Pericles**, painted as antihero to the latter by **Thucydides**, and lampooned as a devious demagogue in the *Knights* of **Aristophanes**; he was purportedly responsible for ruthless Athenian foreign policies like the Mitylene Decree in 427 BC (which ordained that all male citizens of Mitylene should be executed following their attempted rebellion from their alliance with Athens).

Cleopatra (69–30 BC) Cleopatra VII of the dynasty founded by **Ptolemy** I. Her affairs with first Julius **Caesar** and then **Mark Antony** were probably led by diplomatic expediency: she committed suicide only after it became clear that the future **Augustus** wanted Egypt without her as its queen. [526]

Commodus, Lucius Aelius Aurelius (AD 161–192, r. 180–192) Son of **Marcus Aurelius** and his successor as emperor; infamous for associating himself with Herakles [145], for public performances as a gladiator, and for renaming Rome the 'colony of Commodus'.

Constantine (Flavius Valerius Constantinus, *c.* AD 285–337, r. 306–337) Roman emperor who converted to Christianity, and whose mother Helena made Jerusalem a site of Christian pilgrimage. Constantine dismantled the Tetrarchy (see **Diocletian**), becoming sole ruler in 323, and creating his capital, 'Constantinople' (modern Istanbul), on the site of Byzantium. [527]

Coriolanus, Gnaius Marcius (early 5th century BC) Roman Republican general who defected to enemy forces – the Volscians – and then threatened Rome: the city was only saved by a deputation of women

528 *The Tetrarchs: rulers of the West embrace rulers of the East. In the foreground,* **Diocletian** *with Maximian; behind, Constantius Chlorus and Galerius (Byzantine porphyry group at St Mark's, Venice, c. AD 305).*

(headed by Coriolanus' mother and wife), which moved him to withdraw his army, return to the Volscians, and resign himself to execution.

Crassus, Marcus Licinius (*c.* 115–53 BC) Immensely rich Roman consul and influential statesman. Defeated **Spartacus**; but at Carrhae in 53 BC was disastrously defeated by the Parthians: he was killed, and the Roman standards lost.

Croesus (*c.* 560–547 BC) Legendarily wealthy last king of Lydia, on the coast of Asia Minor, who made an unsuccessful expedition against Persia (see **Cyrus**).

Cyrus (559–529 BC) Founder of the **Achaemenid** dynasty, who initiated the Persian policy of conquest in Ionia after capturing **Croesus**.

Darius see **Achaemenids**.

Democritus (b. *c.* 460 BC) Greek philosopher, born in Abdera (in Thrace), most associated with 'Atomism' – the theory that all matter ultimately consists of tiny particles that are 'indivisible' (*atomos*).

Demosthenes (384–322 BC) Athenian orator, who performed with distinction in both the law-courts and the democratic Assembly. His tirades against **Philip II of Macedon** became classics of personal invective (hence our word 'Philippics'). [273, 274]

Dio Cassius (*c.* AD 150–235) Author of a year-by-year history of Rome, from Aeneas' landing in Italy to AD 229, written in Greek.

Dio Chrysostom (originally called Dio Cocceianus, *c.* AD 40–after 112) 'Golden-mouthed' Greek orator from Bithynia whose philosophical and political speeches brought him popularity.

Diocletian (Gaius Aurelius Valerius Diocletianus, *c.* AD 245–316, r. 284–305) Roman emperor, the last to conduct persecutions of the Christians. In AD 293, he devised the system of Roman imperial power-sharing known as the Tetrarchy [528], which essentially cut the Empire in half (roughly on a line due south from the Adriatic coast), with two further subdivisions east and west. The vast palace that he built for his retirement on the Adriatic coast in his native Dalmatia (now the town of Split, in modern Croatia) was a renowned destination for 18th-century Grand Tourists and an influential model for the revival of Classical architecture.

Diodorus Siculus (mid–late 1st century BC) Greek historian from Sicily who wrote a history of the world (*Library of History*) that reached its climax in the rise of Rome and the political struggles for power of his own time, *c.* 30 BC.

Diogenes (*c.* 400–*c.* 325 BC) Founder of the Greek philosophical sect known as the Cynics ('dogs'), who preached the pursuit of simple self-control (*autarkeia*). Many anecdotes refer to his own surly disregard for social convention. [374]

Domitian (Titus Flavius Domitianus, AD 51–96, r. 81–96) Roman emperor, son of **Vespasian** and last of the **Flavians**, with a reputation for cruelty in the pages of **Tacitus** and other writers (probably because of his disregard for the Senate). [529]

Empedocles (*c.* 493–*c.* 453 BC) Greek philosopher from Akragas (Agrigento) in Sicily, whose fragmentary writings (recently increased by a papyrus brought to light in Strasbourg) are the most eloquent of all the 'Pre-Socratic' collection. Empedocles founded the theory that there are four elements in the universe – earth, air, fire, and water – whose motions are 'Strife') or attraction (*Eros*, 'Love'). Legend has it that he thought he was divine – and died by leaping into the crater of Mount Etna.

Ennius, Quintus (*c.* 239–*c.* 169 BC) Early but deeply influential Roman poet, originally from Rudiae in Calabria, whose long narrative poem of the history of Rome (the *Annals*) was the first to introduce the dactylic hexameter to Latin verse.

Epictetus (mid-1st–2nd century AD) Influential teacher of Stoic philosophy in the Roman Empire, especially with the publication by **Arrian** of his *Discourses* after his death.

Epicurus (341–270 BC) Greek philosopher of the early Hellenistic period, who was born in Samos and

died in Athens. He gave his name to 'Epicureanism' – whose prime aim is a stress-free life; a contented existence which is not so much achieved by indulging one's sensuous appetite (as 'Epicurean' is sometimes understood today) as by renouncing ambitions and desire. [375]

Eratosthenes (*c.* 285–194 BC) Greek astronomer, and librarian at Alexandria. Pioneer of the notion that the earth was spherical, he also provided a near-accurate measure of the planet's circumference, and a mapping system using lines of longitude and latitude.

Euclid (fl. *c.* 300 BC) Greek mathematician based at the court of **Ptolemy** I in Alexandria. In addition to his treatise on music, thirteen books of his *Elements of Geometry* remain: up until the 19th century, the theorems collected by Euclid were the most systematic principles of geometry in circulation.

Euripides (*c.* 485–406 BC) Playwright, judged to be the most 'modern' of the classic Athenian tragedians, because of his capacity for psychologically sensitive characterization. Of the 92 plays ascribed to him, 19 survive whole (including *Medea*, *The Trojan Women*, and *The Bacchae*). [530]

Faustina Cognomen of two members of the Antonine imperial family: Annia Galeria Faustina 'the Elder' (d. AD 140), aunt of **Marcus Aurelius** and wife of **Antoninus Pius** [148, 303]; and Annia Galeria Faustina 'the Younger' (d. AD 175), daughter of the above, and wife (and cousin) of Marcus Aurelius [365].

Flavians Name of the family who ruled Rome AD 71–96 – **Vespasian**, then his sons **Titus** and **Domitian**.

Frontinus, Sextus Julius (*c.* AD 30–104) Energetic Roman soldier and administrator, best known for his treatise *On the Water-Supplies of Rome*, based on his own practical experience as curator of the water-supply to the Emperor **Nerva**.

Galen (AD 129–*c.* 200) Medical practitioner and writer, born at Pergamon, later physician to the Emperor **Marcus Aurelius** in Rome. His studies of anatomy and physiology remained influential in medieval Europe.

Gorgias (*c.* 483–*c.* 380 BC) Greek 'Sophist' from Sicily; an influential pioneer in the demonstration of the schematic word-play and stylistic devices that became the discipline of Classical rhetoric – preserved in his extant *Encomium of Helen* and *Defence of Palamedes*.

Gracchi Cognomen of two brothers: Tiberius Sempronius Gracchus (*c.* 169–133 BC) and Gaius Sempronius Gracchus (*c.* 160–121 BC). Both were

elected tribunes, and were notorious for their attempts at radical social legislation. Tiberius attempted to fix an upper limit on privately owned land and to distribute the surplus to the people – and was assassinated by his opponents; Gaius proposed measures subsidizing the distribution of corn to Roman citizens, reduced judicial corruption, and extended citizenship to all inhabitants of Italy.

Hadrian (Publius Aelius Hadrianus, AD 76–138, r. 117–138) Roman emperor, adoptive successor to **Trajan**, nicknamed 'Graeculus', 'Greekling', on account of his passion for Greek culture and learning. A tireless traveller, he made generous expression of this taste as he toured the empire, leaving a trail of endowed buildings and artworks. Athens and Rome in particular benefited from his patronage [e.g. 302:3]. 'Hadrian's Wall' in Britain [330] marks an imperial policy of containment instead of expansion. He personally designed his grandiose tomb in Rome (transformed into the Castel Sant'Angelo); also his extensive villa-retreat at Tivoli, a place of inspiration for Neoclassical musings since the 17th century. [149, 531]

Hannibal (247–183/182 BC) The general who took command of Carthaginian forces in 221 BC and led an army through Spain, across the Alps, and into Italy, where he campaigned unbeaten for sixteen years, but without taking Rome. Eventually he suffered defeat by **Scipio Africanus** at Zama (south of Carthage) in 202 BC. [532]

Harmodios see **Tyrannicides**

Hephaistion (d. 324 BC) Intimate friend, and bodyguard, of **Alexander the Great**.

Heraclitus (*c.* 540–*c.* 480 BC) Notoriously the most gnomic of the Greek 'Pre-Socratic' philosophers, his utterances – set down at Ephesus – are fragmentary, and highly elusive ('All is flux', 'Night and day are one', 'You cannot step into the same river twice', etc.).

Herod the Great (*c.* 73–4 BC, r. 40–4) Ruler of Roman Judaea; a great builder of aqueducts, roads, and fortresses in the region, and rebuilder of the Temple at Jerusalem (though he was deeply unpopular with the Jews). There is no evidence to corroborate the story in St Matthew's Gospel that Herod ordered mass infanticide at Bethlehem.

Herodas (*c.* 300–250 BC) Native of Kos or Miletos, whose *Mimiambs* drew on scenes of 'realistic' city life.

Herodes Atticus (*c.* AD 101–177) Roman consul, rhetorician, and friend of the Emperors **Hadrian** and

529 **Domitian** (marble portrait, crafted during his reign).

530 **Euripides** (Roman marble portrait after an original made in the third quarter of the 4th century BC).

531 **Hadrian** (bronze head, found in the River Thames at London, perhaps part of a statue erected in AD 122 to commemorate the Emperor's visit to Britain).

532 **Hannibal** (silver shekel struck by the Barcids in Spain, 237–209 BC).

533 *Julian the Apostate (marble statue, c. AD 362).*

534 *Justinian (mosaic in San Vitale, Ravenna, 6th century AD).*

535 *Leonidas (marble torso from Sparta, early 5th century BC).*

Antoninus Pius, 'Herod of Athens' was an individual of immense wealth who elegantly bridged the worlds of Roman politics and Athenian erudition. His benefactions are attested throughout Greece (e.g. the Odeon at Athens [482]).

Herodotus (early 5th century– *c.* 425 BC) Pioneer Greek historian, born at Halicarnassus in Ionia. His *Histories* remain a highly engaging account of the travels and interests of a good-natured and open-minded individual, with much vivid ethnographic data garnered from Egypt (book 2), Persia, and the Black Sea area. His narratives – read aloud to an Athenian audience *c.* 425 BC – also contain influential accounts of episodes in the Greek war against the Persians, such as the battle of Marathon (*Histories* 6.94–120).

Hesiod (fl. *c.* 700 BC) Greek poet from Boeotia, whose writings in hexameters, notably the *Works and Days* and the *Theogony*, deliver both rustic wisdom and some trenchant versions of Greek cosmic mythology.

Hipparchos (d. 514 BC) Younger son of **Peisistratos**, assassinated by the **Tyrannicides**.

Hippias (r. 527–510 BC) Elder son of **Peisistratos**. Ruler of Athens; after banishment in 510 BC, he sought exile with the Persians and fought on their side at the battle of Marathon in 490 BC.

Hippocrates (*c.* 460–*c.* 370 BC) Greek physician based on the island of Kos, the 'father' of clinical medicine. The 'Hippocratic Corpus' – some sixty medical treatises – is attributed to him. [114]

Hippodamos (b. *c.* 500 BC) Greek town-planner from Miletos on the Ionian coast, credited with the application, if not the invention, of the gridiron plan. His works are attested as late as 408 BC, and include the Piraeus area of Athens and the colony of Miletos.

Homer Despite his senior status in Greek literature, little is known about the supposed author of the two most important Classical epics, the *Iliad* and the *Odyssey*, who was also credited in antiquity with a motley collection of thirty-three *Homeric Hymns*. If any historical 'Homer' existed, he probably lived between the mid-8th and mid-7th centuries BC; but his two epics draw on much earlier oral traditions (conjuring up a heroic past vaguely located in what we would call the 'Mycenaean' world), and continued to develop before they were written down in the 6th century BC. An imaginary portrait type of the bard, probably created in the late 2nd century BC, reflects the tradition that he was blind. [184, 185, 476]

Horace (Quintus Horatius Flaccus, 65–8 BC) Of several Roman poets associated with **Augustus** and **Maecenas**, he enjoyed the most relaxed rapport with his patrons. In his *Odes* he celebrates a gentle hedonism and the pleasures of rural retreat; his *Satires* are rarely spiteful; and his *Art of Poetry* is a delicate stylish briefing about the delicacies of literary style. The Emperor's favour is reflected in Horace's *Hymn of the Century* (*Carmen Saeculare*), commissioned to accompany Augustus' Secular Games of 17 BC.

Ibykos (fl. second half of the 6th century BC) Lyric poet, originally from Rhegum in South Italy, who settled on Samos and wrote *encomia* of the Samian tyrant Polykrates.

Iktinos (fl. mid–late 5th century BC) Greek architect, credited (with Kallikrates) with the design of the Parthenon at Athens [482, 486]; also said to have designed the Temple of Apollo at Bassae [170–72].

Isokrates (436–338 BC) Athenian speech-writer and orator, who played a prominent part in the definition of a nationalistic, united, and self-consciously 'Greek' culture (reflected in his *Philippus*, which attempted to persuade **Philip II of Macedon** to lead a Greek expedition against the Persians). His theories on education are preserved in two essays, *Against the Sophists* and *On the Antidosis*.

Jesus Christ (d. ?AD 30) Itinerant preacher from Nazareth in Judaea; after his death by crucifixion in Jerusalem, the cult of 'Christianity' – primarily articulated by St **Paul** – spread rapidly around the Roman world, but was subject to periodic persecution until the time of **Constantine**. [cf. 128]

Josephus, Flavius (AD 37–after 93) Jewish historian of the Roman Middle East. Writing in Greek, he is the most impartial source of information for the period in which **Jesus Christ** and his apostles preached their new religion.

Julian the Apostate (Flavius Claudius Julianus, AD 332–366, r. 360–363) Roman emperor; he renounced Christianity and attempted to revive pagan cults. [533]

Julio-Claudians The Roman imperial family descended from **Julius Caesar**, claiming mythical origins from Iulus, an offspring of **Aeneas**. Their principal representatives include **Augustus** and **Livia**, **Tiberius**, **Caligula**, **Claudius**, and **Nero**.

Justinian (Flavius Petrus Sabbatius Justinianus, *c.* AD 482–565, r. 527–65) Byzantine-Roman emperor, who codified Roman law as we know it today. He was also an aggressively evangelical Christian, decreeing the final closure of pagan institutions such as the Academy at Athens with which **Plato** had been associated. [534]

Juvenal (Decimus Junius Juvenalis, fl. early 2nd century AD) Arguably the most 'biting' of Roman satirical poets, famously motivated by 'raw fury' (*saeva indignatio*), he remains the most influential Classical exponent of satire as a literary genre. Stand on any street corner, watch the people pass by – and who can resist (he asks in the first of his sixteen *Satires*) the urge to write about the postures and follies of civilized humanity?

Kallikrates (fl. mid-5th century BC) Athenian architect, who collaborated with **Iktinos** in building the Parthenon [482, 486].

Kimon (5th century BC) Athenian politician and general, son of **Miltiades**. He directed campaigns against the Persians (476–463 BC), in the course of which he brought back to Athens the alleged bones of Theseus from the island of Skyros. There is also a theory that Kimon initiated an earlier version of the Parthenon, which was then overtaken by his political rival **Pericles**.

Kleanthes see **Zeno**

Kleisthenes (fl. late 6th century BC) The presumed founder of democracy at Athens, due to the political reforms enacted during his magistracy of the city in 508–507 BC.

Lars Porsenna (fl. late 6th century BC?) Semi-legendary Etruscan warlord, who in the annals of Rome's early history is said to have unsuccessfully laid siege to the city in an attempt to restore **Tarquin** the Proud to power.

Leochares (fl. mid-4th-century BC) Greek sculptor, credited with portraits of **Philip II of Macedon** and family at Olympia; perhaps also responsible for parts of the Mausoleum at Halicarnassus [147], and the cult statue of Demeter at Knidos.

Leonidas (d. 480 BC) King of Sparta; leader of Spartan forces at the battle of Thermopylae, where he heroically (i.e. suicidally) held a mountain pass against the invading Persian army of **Xerxes**. [535]

Lepidus, Marcus Aemilius (d. 13/12 BC) A supporter of Julius **Caesar** and subsequently a member of the Triumvirate with **Mark Antony** and Octavian (the future **Augustus**) after Caesar's death. In 36 BC, after his troops had been persuaded to defect to Octavian, Lepidus was effectively banished from Rome.

Livia (58 BC–AD 29) Mother of **Tiberius** (by her first marriage) and wife of **Augustus**. She gave the early Roman imperial court its model *matrona* or *materfamilias*, a female bastion of power and respectability; with her villa at Prima Porta [243, 286] she also provided a good example of 'Augustan taste'. [294]

Livy (Titus Livius, 59 BC–AD 17) Roman historian. Chronicling the *History of Rome from its Foundation*, he did much to heroize the city's Republican beginnings and escape from Etruscan tyranny, while writing, poignantly, at the time of Rome's first emperor, **Augustus**. Only part of his work survives – including an important and dramatic account of the war with **Hannibal**.

Longinus Name given to the author of *On the Sublime*, a treatise in Greek on the achievement in literature of grandeur or greatness (literally, 'loftiness'). Of uncertain date AD, this survives in part. First translated in the 17th century (English 1652, French 1674), it became a major text for the Romantic movement of the 18th century: Longinus showed how certain natural phenomena (e.g. mountains, volcanoes) aroused awe and astonishment – the key aesthetic components of Romantic 'beauty'.

Longus (*c.* AD 200?) Greek writer of no fixed date or identity, but credited with the erotic, pastoral romance *Daphnis and Chloe*. This is one of five complete Greek romantic novels that survive from antiquity: others are Achilles Tatius' *Leukippe and Kleitophon*, Chariton's *Chareas and Kallirrhoe*, Heliodorus' *Theagenes and Chariclea*, and Xenophon of Ephesus' *Habrokomes and Antheia*.

Lucan (Marcus Annaeus Lucanus, AD 39–65) Roman author, born in Spain, whose *Pharsalia* turns the Civil War between **Pompey** and Julius **Caesar** into an epic poem.

Lucian (*c.* AD 120–after 180) Prolific Greek writer and intellectual, whose elegant essays and dialogues (some eighty are attributed to him) are rich in anecdotal detail and satiric swipes.

Lucretia Semi-legendary figure of the late 6th century BC, who committed suicide after being raped by Sextus, the son of **Tarquin** the Proud. The incident was said to have provided the impetus for Lucius Junius **Brutus'** expulsion of the Tarquins.

Lucretius (Titus Lucretius Carus, *c.* 94–55 BC) Roman philosopher-poet, whose *On the Nature of Things* is a powerful statement of Epicurean faith – and a poetic index of how physics and the cosmos might be understood in the 1st century BC.

Lycophron (fl. ?early 2nd century BC) Hellenistic poet, author of the *Alexandra* – a highly allusive, and elusive, monologue that purports to report Cassandra's demented ravings to her father, Priam.

Lycurgus (? fl. 7th century BC) Semi-legendary archaic ruler and lawgiver of Sparta.

Lysander (d. 395 BC) Spartan general, whose destruction of the Athenian fleet at Aegospotami in 405 BC marked the imminent close of the Peloponnesian War.

Lysias (*c.* 459/8–*c.* 380 BC) Famed Athenian orator, originally from Syracuse in Sicily and therefore a metic in Athens. Of an original output of over two hundred speeches, only thirty-five attributed to him survive.

Lysippos (*c.* 370–315 BC) 'Court sculptor' of **Alexander the Great** [cf. 283], and generally a prolific artist. His works included colossal statues [cf. 142], portraits (e.g. of **Socrates**), images of athletes, and imposing equestrian groups. He introduced a new system of proportions and was renowned for his realism.

Maecenas, Gaius (*c.* 70–8 BC) Wealthy and well-connected (the friend and adviser of **Augustus**), he was the literary patron *par excellence* at Rome, enabling **Horace**, **Propertius**, and **Vergil** (among others) to be full-time poets.

Marcus Aurelius (AD 121–180, r. 161–180) Roman emperor, best-remembered figure of the Antonine dynasty [158]. His equestrian statue in Rome [376] is a rare example of a Classical bronze surviving on view from antiquity to the present – thanks to its early misidentification by Christians as an image of **Constantine** – and conveys something of the person of Marcus as revealed by his Stoic *Meditations*: serene authority underpinned by a basic disregard of self.

Marius, Gaius (*c.* 157–*c.* 86 BC) Factional leader and general during the Roman Civil Wars, famed for his defeat of the Germanic tribes who invaded Gaul and Italy in 102–101 BC.

Mark Antony (Marcus Antonius, *c.* 82–30 BC) A distinguished supporter of Julius **Caesar**; a popular member of the Triumvirate (three-man alliance) with **Lepidus** and Octavian – the future **Augustus** – to avenge Caesar's assassination; the lover of **Cleopatra**; and ultimately the last serious opposition to the political ascendancy of Augustus. A swaggering soldier and extravagant drinker, Antony naturally played Dionysos [536] to the Apollo of Augustus. Defeated at Actium in 31 BC, he committed suicide in Alexandria before Octavian entered the city.

Martial (Marcus Valerius Martialis, *c.* AD 40–*c.* 104) Roman poet, born in Spain, known chiefly for his epigrams – pungent, topical verses, whose seasoned wit and vivid sensuality have ensured their appeal

down the ages. Also the author of a book of epigrams, *On the Spectacles*, which commemorated the opening games of the Colosseum in AD 80.

Mausolus (r. *c.* 377–353 BC) Satrap of the region of Caria on the coast of Asia Minor, and self-styled 'founder' of the city of Halicarnassus (modern Bodrum). His colossal tomb, the Mausoleum [147], was perhaps planned by him, but certainly brought into being by his wife Artemisia. [537]

Menander (*c.* 342–*c.* 290 BC) Leading exponent in Athens of 'New Comedy', characterized by its 'kitchen-sink' realism and interest in character, as distinct from the more political and fantastic 'Old Comedy' as written by **Aristophanes**. [423]

Miltiades (*c.* 550–489 BC) Athenian statesman and general. Though his political career was chequered, his role was decisive in achieving Athenian victory at the battle of Marathon in 490 BC.

Mithridates Name of six rulers of the area around the Black Sea known to the Romans as Pontus. The last, 'Mithridates the Great' (r. 120–63 BC), was at war with Rome for many years (the so-called Mithridatic Wars) until his final defeat by **Pompey**.

Mnesikles (5th century BC) Greek architect, responsible for the monumental gateway (Propylaia) on the Athenian Acropolis [482].

Moschus (fl. *c.* 150 BC) One of a triad of Hellenistic pastoral poets (the others being Bion and **Theocritus**); perhaps most famous is his *Europa*, a 'little epic' (*epyllion*)

Myron (fl. *c.* 480–445 BC) Greek bronze sculptor, famous in antiquity for his skills of naturalistic representation, and ability to catch movement in solid form (for example, the figure of a sprinter). Knowledge of his work comes solely from anecdotes about it, and Roman copies of statues such as the *Diskobolos* [1].

Nero (Nero Claudius Caesar, AD 37–68, r. 54–68) Probably Rome's most infamous emperor, last of the **Julio-Claudian** line that began with **Augustus**. If the remains of his lavish palace in Rome, the Domus Aurea ('Golden House'), appear to affirm literary traditions of his megalomania, other features of his notoriety – such as setting fire to Rome in AD 64 – are less readily proven beyond their mention in the pages of **Tacitus** and **Suetonius**, and Christian sources characterizing Nero as the Anti-Christ. He died by suicide. [538]

Nerva, Marcus Cocceius (*c.* AD 35–98, r. 96–98) Twice-serving Roman consul who was chosen by the Senate to succeed **Domitian** as emperor. His coinage – stamped with such slogans

536 *Mark Antony adorned with the ivy-leaf crown of Dionysos (silver cistophoros, c. 40 BC).*

537 *Colossal marble statue of a Carian noble, once identified as Mausolus himself (from the Mausoleum at Halicarnassus (c. 350 BC).*

538 *Nero (marble portrait crafted during his reign).*

539 *Philip II of Macedon (marble portrait, 2nd century AD, after a statue made in the ?4th century BC).*

540 *Plotinus (marble portrait, from Ostia, c. AD 260).*

541 *Posidonius (inscribed marble portrait from Pompeii, after an original made in the early 1st century BC).*

as 'public freedom', 'equity', 'salvation' – pronounced an end to imperial autocracy. After failing to win the support of the army, he began to transfer power to his successor, **Trajan**.

Nikias (*c.* 470–413 BC) Wealthy Athenian statesman and general. He reluctantly took charge of the ambitious Athenian naval expedition of 415–413 to attack Syracuse, and was blamed for its ultimate failure.

Octavian see **Augustus**.

Ovid (Publius Ovidius Naso, 43 BC–AD 17) Roman poet, whose works (including the *Metamorphoses*, *Love Affairs*, *Art of Love*, and *Festival Days*) reveal a writer of great inventive and stylistic facility. The *Metamorphoses*, in fifteen books, weave Greek stories around the theme of 'changing forms', and have provided a mythological treasury for writers and artists over centuries. Ovid also had an unlimited capacity for self-pity, as shown by the *Laments* (*Tristia*, literally 'Sorrows'). These were written during his exile to the Black Sea, imposed in AD 8 by **Augustus** for a 'poem and error' (*carmen et error*: see *Tristia* 2.207): the poem was probably *The Art of Love*, but the 'error' remains unclear.

Parrhasios (early 4th century BC) Celebrated Greek painter from Ephesus. None of his work – praised by **Pliny the Elder** for its subtlety of outline, perfect proportions and power of expression – survives, nor does his treatise on painting.

Pasiteles (fl. mid-1st century BC) Apparently one of the busiest and most diligent of Greek sculptors in Rome in his day, he is also said to have compiled a five-volume compendium of *Great Masterpieces*.

St Paul (fl. mid-1st century AD) Jewish tax-collector turned convert to Christianity, who nurtured early Christian communities across the Mediterranean (as testified both by the Acts of the Apostles and the thirteen letters ascribed to him). He died a martyr near Rome, probably during the reign of **Nero**. [128, 129]

Pausanias (fl. *c.* AD 160) Studious if gullible Greek traveller, author of the *Guide to Greece*, a proto-touristic account of many cities and sanctuaries of the Greek mainland. The descriptions of such sites as Delphi and Olympia remain valuable not only for the light shed upon archaeological remains, but because Pausanias witnessed them still active as places of ceremony and worship.

Peisistratos (*c.* 600–527 BC) Tyrant of Athens (in three different periods, the longest of which was 545–527 BC), and founder of the short-lived **Peisistratid** dynasty; his career is sketched in Herodotus, *Histories* 1.59–64. His civic works included the provision of public fountains, and in addition to establishing several Athenian cultic festivals, he funded a number of decorated temples on the Acropolis. It is cogently argued that he saw himself as a second Herakles – which might account for the prevalence of Heraklean images in 6th-century BC Athenian art.

Pericles (*c.* 495–429 BC) A political hero in the pages of **Thucydides**; the outstanding helmsman of democracy in mid-5th-century BC Athens, giving his name to an epoch of cultural achievement in the city; the monumental development of the Acropolis is owed to him. He is said to have been a personal friend to **Pheidias** and **Sophocles**; his mistress, Aspasia, a *hetaira* (courtesan) from Miletos, was also something of a celebrity – perhaps because Pericles' own Athenian citizenship law of *c.* 450 meant that the two could not be married. [262]

Petronius (Petronius Arbiter, d. *c.* AD 66) Roman writer, contemporary with **Nero**. His *Satyricon*, though it survives only piecemeal (its most complete episode narrates a dinner-party hosted by Trimalchio, a freed slave), is a convincing comic portrayal of snobbery and social climbing in early imperial Rome, as seen through the eyes of the novel's protagonist, Encolpius.

Pheidias (*c.* 490–*c.* 430 BC) Greek sculptor, probably the most renowned and industrious of Classical antiquity. He was born in Athens and may have died in Olympia. His best works were thought to be the chryselephantine statues of Athena in the Parthenon [122] and of Zeus at Olympia [126], now lost; but he was the acknowledged 'overseer' of the entire Parthenon project, and his style may be detected in what survives of the temple's sculptural programme [288, 487–89].

Philip II of Macedon (383/382–336 BC, r. 359–336 BC) Macedonian ruler, father of **Alexander the Great**. Victorious over a Greek alliance at the battle of Chaeronea in 338 BC, Philip laid down the effective strategy and foundation of the Macedonian empire, projecting the conquest of Persia at the time of his death (by assassination). A tomb excavated in the Macedonian royal cemetery at Vergina [cf. 28, 447] is thought by some to be his, by others to be that of his son, Philip III, half-brother of Alexander. [539]

Philostratos Shared cognomen of a family from Lemnos, borne by three or four different Greek writers who lived in the 2nd and 3rd centuries AD. Their works include the *Lives of the Sophists*, two sets of *Images*, *Gymnastics*, and the *Life of Apollonius of Tyana*.

Phryne (4th century BC) A renowned Greek *hetaira* (courtesan), mistress of the sculptor **Praxiteles** and model for his Aphrodite of Knidos [83].

Pindar (*c.* 518–after 446 BC) Greek lyric poet from Thebes who specialized in 'epinician' odes for victorious sportsmen (e.g. *Isthmian Odes, Pythian Odes, Olympian Odes, Nemean Odes*). Almost invariably a successful athlete is given a mythical pedigree, allowing the poet to enlarge his celebratory theme to epic scope.

Plato (*c.* 429–347 BC) Pupil of **Socrates**. His travels included time at Syracuse under the tyrant Dionysius II, whom he sought to educate as a 'philosopher-king'; then he was master of his own school at Athens, the Academy [cf. 371], founded *c.* 385 BC. Plato's range of philosophic interests was dominated by the quest for moral knowledge, but nevertheless astonishingly broad: all of his attributed works – some twenty-five philosophical dialogues (the *Republic* most famous among them) – survive. Later close adherents of Platonic ideas are usually defined as 'Neo-Platonists' (see **Plotinus**). [373]

Plautus, Titus Maccius (*c.* 250–184 BC) Comic playwright of Republican Rome, credited with 130 Latin plays (20 of which survive). His work imitated the Athenian models of **Menander** and his contemporaries, yet conveys a lively sense of Latin banter.

Pliny the Elder (Gaius Plinius Secundus, AD 23/24–79) Roman encyclopaedist, whose *Natural History*, completed in AD 77 but published posthumously *c.* 80, gathers (in thirty-seven volumes) diverse information about the structure and nature of the world as imperial Romans found (and ruled) it. It was typical of Pliny's curiosity that he went to see what happened when Vesuvius erupted in AD 79 – and nature's revenge that he was suffocated by its sulphurous fumes (as recounted by his nephew, **Pliny the Younger**, *Letters* 6.16).

Pliny the Younger (Gaius Plinius Caecilius Secundus, *c.* AD 61–*c.* 112) Adopted nephew of **Pliny the Elder**. A writer and politician whose letters are a source of much sane comment about Roman life and government of his time; a tenth book of letters contains his correspondence with the Emperor **Trajan** (including a valuable sketch of early Christianity, *Letters* 10.96).

Plotinus (AD 205–*c.* 270) Greek Neo-Platonist philosopher, based in

Alexandria and then Rome, whose main writings, the *Enneads* (groups of nine essays), develop Platonic ideas about the soul into a mystical set of doctrines that deeply influenced Christian thought. [540]

Plutarch (b. before AD 50, d. after AD 120) Greek writer, born in Chaeronea in Boeotia. In later life a priest serving at Delphi, he found time for a copious output character-ized by immense readability and sympathy for human affairs. His *Parallel Lives* (pairing notable Greeks and Romans) are not only model types of the genre of moralist biography, but attest the Classical penchant for 'twinning' myth and history. Translated into French (by Jacques Amyot) in 1559 and thence into English (by Thomas North) in 1579, the *Lives* also exerted a powerful influence upon European literature – supplying the plots and characters for several of Shakespeare's plays.

Polybius (*c.* 200–after 118 BC) Greek historian who chronicled the Punic Wars, fought between Carthage and Rome in the 3rd and 2nd centuries BC.

Polygnotos (fl. *c.* 475–447 BC) Greek painter from Thasos, whose works, now lost, were attested at Athens (in the Stoa Poikile, or Painted Stoa) and Delphi, and praised for the expressiveness of the subjects' faces.

Polykleitos (fl. mid-5th century BC) Greek sculptor from Argos. His work – all in bronze, apparently – was highly influential, perhaps because he enshrined its principles in a book, the *Canon*, which set out a predictable system of proportions for representing the human body, exemplified in the statue known as the *Doryphoros* [37].

Pompey (Gnaeus Pompeius, 106–48 BC) Roman soldier and politician, later styled 'the Great' [282]. His career was that of a highly successful general, whose most famous victory was over **Mithridates** in the eastern Mediterranean; but he ended his days as loser in the fight with his erstwhile father-in-law Julius **Caesar**.

Pontius Pilate (r. AD 26–36) Governor of the Roman province of Judaea, famed for condemning Jesus to death [128].

Porphyry (AD 234–*c.* 305) Student of **Plotinus** in Rome, and eventually editor of the latter's *Enneads*; also a prolific scholar in his own right (notably in the study of religion, philosophy, and philology).

Posidonius (*c.* 135–*c.* 51 BC) Polymath born in Syria, who learned Stoicism in Athens and settled in Rhodes. His diverse writings, now lost, were highly influential in Rome during the 1st century BC and beyond. [541]

Praxiteles (fl. mid-4th century BC) Celebrated Greek sculptor, born in Athens. Of his works, the *Aphrodite of Knidos* [83] (said to have been modelled on his mistress, **Phryne**) was most notorious in antiquity; this and others are known by copies [cf. 468], but some have seen the marble figure of Hermes cradling the infant Dionysos, discovered at Olympia [260], as one of his original surviving works.

Procoplus (*c.* AD 500–after 562) Greek historian, who served as secretary to Belisarius – commander-in-chief to the Emperor **Justinian** – and who wrote both an official *History* of Justinian's campaigns (as well as a panegyrical work *On Justinian's Buildings*) and a *Secret History* giving a very different (anti-imperial) slant on the same era and events.

Propertius, Sextus (*c.* 50–after 16 BC) Latin poet whose 'terse and elegant' output survives as four books of wide-ranging elegies, many of them about love and its frustrations at the hands of the poet's mistress ('Cynthia').

Protagoras (*c.* 485–*c.* 420 BC) Greek agnostic philosopher, an early 'Sophist', eventually charged with impiety at Athens – his motto that 'Man is the measure of all things' (quoted in Plato's *Theaetetus*) indicating a certain lack of faith in the Olympian deities.

Protogenes (fl. late 4th-century BC) Greek painter, and author of two lost books on painting, anecdotally remembered as a rival of **Apelles**.

Prudentius, Clemens Aurelius (AD 348–after 405) An administrator of Roman Spain, who gave up politics for poetry and succeeded in harnessing traditional Latin forms to express devoutly Christian sentiments (e.g. in his *Psychomachia*, or *Battle of the Soul*, an epic allegory of the spiritual struggle of the soul, highly influential in medieval times).

Ptolemy Dynastic name of rulers of Egypt, initiated by the general who took command after the death of **Alexander the Great** in 323 BC, Ptolemy I Soter ('Saviour') [542], and brought to an end with the death of **Cleopatra** in 30 BC.

Ptolemy (Claudius Ptolemaeus, *c.* AD 100–178) Classical antiquity's most influential geographer, mathematician, and astronomer, based at Alexandria. His *System of Mathematics* is more commonly known by its Arabic title, the *Amalgest*; he also wrote a three-book treatise on music, the *Harmonics*.

Pythagoras (mid–late 6th century BC) Greek philosopher and mathematician from Samos, who settled in the colony of Croton in South Italy. His followers, the 'Pythagoreans', believed that the entire universe could be explained by numbers and their ratios, and abstained from eating meat.

Pythios (4th century BC) Greek architect from Priene on the Ionian coast, who is said to have designed both the Mausoleum at Halicarnassus [147] and the Temple of Athena Polias at Priene, and thus pioneered an 'Ionic Renaissance' in Asia Minor.

Quintilian (Marcus Fabius Quintilianus, b. *c.* AD 35) Roman advocate and teacher, born in Spain; none of his speeches survives, but his magisterial handbook on the principles of rhetoric, the *Education of an Orator* (*Institutio Oratoria*), published in the 90s, is complete in ten books. Here Quintilian not only lays down the technical skills considered necessary for speaking and writing well, but also argues that to do so is a moral obligation.

Sallust (Gaius Sallustius Crispus, 86–35 BC) Political ally of Julius **Caesar**; Sallust then retired from public life to compose history. His account of the Roman war against the Berber territory of Numidia in North Africa, the *Jugurthine War* (Jugurtha was the Numidian king), is a model of clear, clipped Latin prose. He was also the author of a monograph on the **Catiline** War and of the annalistic *Historiae*.

Sappho (b. late 7th century BC) Only fragments remain of the lyrics attributed to this Greek poet, born on the island of Lesbos. Evidently she was part of an all-female social or cult circle (giving rise to the term 'lesbianism', though Sappho's verses celebrate heterosexual love as well as the beauty of girls). [543]

Scipio Distinguished Roman family name, with several historically notable representatives.
• Scipio Africanus 'the Elder' (Publius Cornelius Scipio Africanus, 236–184/183 BC) figured prominently in the Roman victory over **Hannibal** (thus earning his extra title, 'the African'). [544]
• Scipio Africanus 'the Younger' (Publius Cornelius Scipio Aemilianus Africanus, *c.* 185–129 BC), grandson of the above by adoption, enforced a blockade of Carthage leading to the city's erasure in 146 BC.

Seleukos I (*c.* 358–281 BC) Macedonian commander attached to the army of **Alexander the Great**. He went on to rule over tracts of Central Asia, though he (and his descendants, the Seleukids: see **Antiochos**) failed to hold territory beyond the Hindu Kush.

Seneca, Lucius Annaeus (*c.* 4 BC–AD 65) Philosophical tutor to the Emperor **Nero**, subsequently implicated in an anti-Neronian plot.

542 *Ptolemy I Soter (marble portrait from the Fayum in Egypt, probably a 1st-century BC copy after an original of c. 300–250 BC).*

543 *Sappho: this image of a bejewelled young woman wearing a gold hairnet and holding a wax tablet and stylus was first identified as a depiction of Sappho in the 18th century; it belongs to a type that seems to have been used to represent well-to-do Roman girls of learning in the 1st century AD (wall-painting from Pompeii, third quarter of the 1st century AD).*

544 *Scipio Africanus 'the Elder' (bronze portrait, found at Herculaneum, ?1st century BC).*

545 *Septimius Severus* (marble portrait, said to have been found on the Palatine, Rome, 3rd century AD).

546 *Socrates* (1st-century BC marble statuette from Alexandria, after a 4th-century BC Greek prototype).

547 *Tiberius* (marble portrait, c. AD 35).

Required to commit suicide, he calmly cut his wrists while standing in a bath – true to his Stoic convictions (reflected in his *Natural Questions*), and almost as bloodily dramatic as his nine tragedies, concerned with grim Greek themes (*Medea*, *Thyestes*, *Trojan Women*, etc.).

His father, of the same name (*c.* 55 BC–between AD 37 and 41), sometimes called **Seneca the Elder**, was a rhetorician, whose lessons and practice-pieces of debate (*Controversiae*) and advisory speeches (*Suasoriae*) are partly preserved.

Septimius Severus, Lucius (AD 145/146–211, r. 193–211) Roman emperor, the only one to die in Britain (at York). His birthplace at Lepcis Magna (on the coast of modern Libya) became, thanks to his patronage, the most elaborately urbanized of Roman settlements in North Africa. [545]

Severans Roman family who succeeded the **Antonines** as emperors AD 193–235: individually **Septimius Severus**, **Caracalla**, Elagabalus, and Alexander Severus.

Simonides (*c.* 556–466 BC) Greek poet from the island of Keos, author of many epigrams and verses (e.g. for the Spartan dead at the battle of Thermopylae in 480 BC), which survive only in fragments.

Skopas (4th century BC) Greek sculptor from the island of Paros, whose distinctively tortured expressive style has been identified on remains of figures from the Temple of Athena at Tegea. He is also attested as one of the sculptors working on the Mausoleum at Halicarnassus [147].

Socrates (469–399 BC) Greek philosopher, a cult figure in Athens He was caricatured by **Aristophanes** (in *The Clouds*) for his persistently inquiring and critical mind, yet revered by **Alcibiades**, **Plato**, and others. Because Plato so often uses Socrates as a character and mouthpiece, it can be difficult to tell where Socrates ends and Plato begins. Socrates was tried and condemned on a charge of corrupting the young and introducing new gods; his dignified death only made Socrates a martyr for his followers. [369, 370, 546]

Solon (fl. early 6th century BC) Leader (*archon*) of Athens, later celebrated as a wise reformer and lawgiver; also renowned in antiquity for his poetry.

Sophocles (*c.* 496–*c.* 406 BC) Athenian playwright. Only a small fraction of his output survives (7 out of some 120 plays), but that is sufficient to show why he was so respected by contemporaries and successors. Best-known of his plays are probably the dramatizations of the Oedipus myth; but for deft handling of a difficult plot, the *Ajax* is exemplary.

Spartacus (d. 71 BC) A slave and gladiator from Thrace, who led a slave revolt in 73–71 and was captured and killed by **Crassus**.

Spurinas Clan name of an important Etruscan family at Tarquinia, becoming 'Spurinna' in Roman times.

Statius, Publius Papinius (*c.* AD 45–before 96) Latin poet, whose fluency and facility characterize him as an exponent of 'Silver Latin' – writing his *Thebaid* in self-conscious epic mode, but with less *gravitas* and conviction than **Vergil**. His reputation suffers from the extravagance with which he praised the Emperor **Domitian** in his *Silvae* (literally 'Woods', therefore 'raw material', modestly implying that the poems are rough drafts).

Stesichoros (fl. first half of the 6th century BC) Greek poet, reputedly from South Italy. His work (of which very little remains) is thought to have contained a strong narrative element – derived from circulating epic sources – and so perhaps to have influenced early attempts at storytelling in Greek art [cf. 205].

Strabo (64/63 BC–*c.* AD 21) Greek topographer of the early Roman Empire and contingent territories; the seventeen books of his *Geography* diligently describe lands from Britain to Persia and India.

Suetonius (Gaius Suetonius Tranquillus, b. *c.* AD 70) At one time secretary to **Hadrian**, Suetonius wrote much that has been lost; but his *Lives of the Caesars* has long constituted a classic of moralizing biography. An apparently clinical concern with certain details (e.g. of physical appearance) blends with indiscriminate court gossip to give highly readable and partly credible Latin portraits of twelve Roman emperors from **Augustus** to **Nerva**.

Sulla, Lucius Cornelius (*c.* 138–78 BC) Ruthless Roman politician, legislator, and general, whose rule (as dictator 81–80 BC, following the civil war he fought against **Marius** in 88–82 BC) was famed in Rome for its conservatism and cruelty to its enemies, but temporarily served to increase the power of the Senate and curb the power of the *plebs*. [281]

Tacitus, Cornelius (*c.* AD 56–after 117) Chronicler of the early Roman Empire – in his *Annals* and *Histories*, both of which survive partially – Tacitus also left valuable literary sketches of Roman Britain (in his *Agricola*) and Celtic Germany (in his *Germania*). He was a distinguished orator (as reflected in his extant *Dialogue on Oratory*), and his Latin prose is hard to match for subtlety of eloquence, use of innuendo, and pessimistic tone.

Tarquins Clan of Etruscan aristocrats archaeologically attested in South Etruria and legendarily involved in Rome's early formation as a city-state (succeeding the mythical Romulus as kings of Rome, six in number). Historically, the Tarquins appear to have ruled and monumentalized Rome during the 6th century BC, building the earliest Capitoline Temple; the traditional date for their overthrow is 510 BC, after Lucius Junius **Brutus** expelled Lucius Tarquinius Superbus, Tarquin the Proud, who reigned 534–510 BC.

Terence (Publius Terentius Afer, *c.* 185–159 BC) Roman comic dramatist, said to have been born in Carthage and to have been a slave in Rome, whose short life was enough for six plays, all of which survive (e.g. *The Mother-in-Law*, *The Eunuch*, *The Girl from Andros*). These comedies are closer to their 'New Comedy' Greek sources (four are directly adapted from Menander) than those of **Plautus**, and their dialogue is packed with quick colloquial Latin.

Tertullian (Florens Quintus Septimius Tertullianus, *c.* AD 160–*c.* 240) Son of a Roman centurion, born in Carthage, an early convert to Christianity; his Latin *Apology* argued that Christianity posed no danger to the Roman Empire.

Thales (fl. *c.* 600 BC) One of the 'Seven Sages' of the 7th and 6th centuries BC who were renowned for their practical and proverbial wisdom. Thales, born in Miletos on the Ionian coast, holds the reputation as a Greek pioneer of 'scientific thinking' – though his various theories (e.g. that the world came about from water) are all reported secondhand.

Themistocles (*c.* 528–462 BC) Athenian statesman responsible for increasing the naval power of the *polis*, and commander of the successful fleet deployed against the Persians at the battle of Salamis in 480 BC; ostracized to Asia Minor in the late 470s BC [cf. 266].

Theocritus (first half of the 3rd century BC) Greek poet from Syracuse, who later moved to Alexandria; founder of the sophisticated literary genre known as the 'pastoral' or 'bucolic' – conjuring in his *Idylls* the half-mythic world of shepherds whiling away their hours with music and love (or, more frequently, wistful dreams of love).

Theophrastus (*c.* 370–*c.* 287 BC) Greek writer on philosophy, science, and especially botany, originally from Lesbos; pupil and successor of **Aristotle**, and his successor as head of the Lyceum. His *Characters* present waspish caricatures of 4th-century Athenian social types.

Theopompos (*c.* 377–*c.* 320 BC) Greek historian from Chios; friend of **Philip II** and **Alexander the Great**.

Thucydides (*c.* 460–*c.* 400 BC) Athenian general (exiled in 424 BC) and historian. His surviving work documents, with high aims of impartiality and accuracy, the causes and events of the protracted Peloponnesian War between Athens and Sparta from 431 BC; incomplete, it ends mid-sentence while narrating events of winter 411–410 BC.

Tiberius (Tiberius Claudius Nero Caesar, 42 BC–AD 37, r. AD 14–37) Roman emperor. Successor to his stepfather **Augustus** more by default than choice (he was the son of **Livia**), Tiberius was never popular at Rome – probably because of his 'treason'-trials and delegation of power to the sycophantic and unscrupulous prefect of the Praetorian guard, Sejanus. Archaeology remembers him for his private retreats (one on the island of Capri, the other probably at the coastal site of Sperlonga [212]). [316, 547]

Tibullus, Albius (*c.* 55–19 BC) Latin poet, normally counted as a lesser contemporary of **Horace** and the other 'Augustan' poets; he nonetheless wrote verses of durable charm (several addressed to his mistresses, Delia and Nemesis, and his beloved Marathus), including a succinct evocation of 'the Golden Age' – see *Elegies* 1.3.

Titus, Flavius Vespasianus (AD 39–81, r. 79–81) Roman emperor, son of **Vespasian**. In his short reign he completed the Flavian amphitheatre, – the Colosseum – and coped compassionately with the double disaster of the Vesuvian eruption in AD 79 and both fire and epidemic at Rome the following year. His military exploit of capturing Jerusalem in AD 70 and sacking the Temple is commemorated in the Arch of Titus [317, 318], erected by his brother and successor, **Domitian**. [549]

Trajan (Marcus Ulpius Trajanus, *c.* AD 53–117, r. 98–117) Roman emperor – the first to be born outside Italy, at Italica in Spain – saluted in his own time and by posterity as an effective soldier and conscientious ruler. His periodic campaigns against Decebalus in Dacia (modern Rumania) are visually chronicled in the marble Column that bears his name [314] – itself erected in a part of Rome 'typically improved by Trajan's urban development. [550]

Tyrannicides Honorary name given to the Athenians Harmodios and Aristogeiton, who in 514 BC

548 *Vercingetorix (silver denarius struck by Lucius Hostilius Saserna, 48 BC).*

assassinated **Hipparchos**, and were commemorated in an influential statue group first raised in the late 6th century [cf. 270, 271].

Ulpian (Domitius Ulpianus, d. AD 223) Authority on Roman law; active as a writer and legal adviser.

Varius Rufus, Lucius (fl. second half of the 1st century BC) Augustan poet, best known for preparing the *Aeneid* of **Vergil** for publication after the latter's death; his most famous work – a (lost) tragedy about Thyestes – is said to have been commissioned by Octavian (the future **Augustus**) and performed in 29 BC.

Varro, Marcus Terentius (116–27 BC) Roman scholar, librarian and politician. Of his copious works only two survive substantially: *On Farming*, and parts of a history of the Latin language.

Vegetius (Flavius Vegetius Renatus, fl. *c.* 400 AD) Official of the late Roman Empire who compiled a manual of Roman military organization and fieldcraft.

Velleius Paterculus (*c.* 19 BC–after AD 30) Roman author of a two-book *History of Rome*, notable for its 'official take' on contemporary events and its adulation of **Tiberius**.

Vercingetorix (d. 46 BC) Chief of one of the indigenous Celtic tribes challenged when Julius **Caesar** led the Roman conquest of Gaul; leader of a spirited uprising in 52 BC, he yielded six years later and was put to death in Rome. [548]

Vergil (Publius Vergilius Maro, 70–19 BC) The 'national poet' of Rome – at the behest of **Augustus**, who ultimately commissioned his epic of Rome's mythical prehistory, the *Aeneid*. Vergil himself was said to have been a reclusive type, whose rustic leanings are evident in his *Eclogues* (selections) and *Georgics* (versified farming wisdom). His writings became 'classics' within Vergil's own lifetime; and they have stayed in unbroken esteem, with European tradition – and in particular, the Italian poet Dante *c.*

1300 [476] – adopting him as a quasi-Christian prophet. [551]

Verres, Gaius (1st century BC) Roman provincial governor who abused his position (first in Asia Minor, then Sicily) to ransack sanctuaries and private residences for works of art. This was the prime charge eloquently (and successfully) prosecuted in 70–69 BC by **Cicero** in his *Verrine Orations*.

Vespasian (Titus Flavius Sabinus Vespasianus, AD 9–79, r. 69–79) Roman emperor, founder of the Flavian dynasty. Vespasian was an army commander, who emerged victorious during the 'Year of the Four Emperors' – the power vacuum left by the downfall of **Nero**. Among his public works in Rome were the Colosseum [426] (completed by **Titus**), and a short-lived reconstruction of the Capitoline Temple. Cynical but benign, his image evokes the virtuous hardheadedness of a Republican worthy (true to the ideology, emblazoned on his coinage, of ruling over 'the Republic restored'). [293]

Vitruvius (Vitruvius Pollio, fl. late 1st century BC) Self-confessedly a mediocre architect in Augustan Rome, Vitruvius remains our main source of information about the historical and technical development of Classical architecture – through his ten-book monograph *On Architecture*, dedicated to **Augustus**, which became generally known (and very influential) in Europe from the late 15th century.

Xenophanes (*c.* 570–*c.* 478 BC) Greek poet-philosopher from Colophon in Ionia, who settled in Sicily. In addition to his observations of fossils and natural history, he is renowned for his criticism of Greek polytheism and anthropomorphic conceptions of the gods.

Xenophon (*c.* 428–*c.* 354 BC) Athenian-born statesman, cavalry commander, and author. His historical writings include an affectionate memoir of his early mentor, **Socrates**; and important essays on education, military strategy, estate management, and constitutional affairs.

Xerxes see **Achaemenids**

Zeno (335–263 BC) Greek philosopher (one of several of that name), who *c.* 300 BC created the philosophical system of Stoicism (so called because the Painted Stoa in Athens was where he taught). The most fervent expression of Stoicism as a faith is to be found in the *Hymn to Zeus* by Zeno's disciple Kleanthes.

Zeuxis (fl. late 5th–early 4th century BC) Greek painter, from Heraclea in South Italy, famed for his illusionist skills.

549 *Titus (marble portrait crafted during his reign).*

550 *Trajan (marble portrait, c. AD 108–117).*

551 *Vergil seated between the Muses of Tragedy and Epic Poetry; he holds a scroll inscribed with Aeneid 1.11 (mosaic from Hadrumetum [modern Sousse] in Tunisia, late 2nd–early 3rd century AD).*

CLASSICAL MYTHOLOGY: A GUIDE

This section gives a checklist of the names most frequently encountered in Classical mythical narratives, with brief storylines attached. As we have emphasized (pp. 108–10), there is no such thing as a canonical 'bible' of Classical mythology: in antiquity, myths were reshaped according to different interests and concerns, with an endless array of intersections, versions, and outcomes. Although countless Greek and Latin authors attempted to collect – and sometimes reconcile – the different stories of deities, heroes, and monsters, none could manage to catalogue every variant, nor disentangle the historical from the fantastic. Images too broke down any distinction between the 'imaginary' spheres of higher powers and the 'real' worlds of human experience.

Names are given in their most commonly encountered forms – usually in Greek, but with Roman (Rom.) and Etruscan (Etr.) variants noted. In so doing, we do not mean to imply straightforward equivalences (cf. pp. 76–78) – rather, that academic shorthand is the only way of ordering the essentially chaotic, yet somehow coherent, web of Classical mythology.

552 *Achilles and Ajax playing dice (Attic black-figure amphora signed by Exekias, c. 550–540 BC).*

553 *The murder of Aegisthus by Orestes; Clytemnestra tries to stop him; behind her stands Electra (marble relief from Ariccia, south-east of Rome, probably a 1st-century BC Roman copy of a Greek relief of the late 6th century BC).*

Achaeus see **Hellen**
Achilles (Etr. Achle) Son of **Peleus** and **Thetis**. The outstanding young warrior of Greek legend, whose temperamental behaviour during the siege of Troy, after the seizure of **Briseis** [189], is the principal theme of Homer's *Iliad*. Artists often depicted his close relationship with **Patroklos** [189], duel with **Hector**, and various non-Trojan episodes, such as his upbringing by the **Centaurs**, and combats with **Amazons**. One story has it that his mother dipped him in the River Styx (in the Underworld) to make him invulnerable: she forgot to submerge his heel, leaving that his weak point – where he was shot with a poisoned arrow by **Paris**. [188, 224, 552, 585]
Actaeon A hunter who came across **Artemis** naked in a pool. The goddess punished him by setting his hounds to tear him apart. [559]
Adonis An eternally beautiful youth whose cult at Athens and Alexandria was associated with that of **Aphrodite**.
Adrastos King of Argos, who led the **Seven Against Thebes**.
Aegisthus Son of **Thyestes**. He seduced **Clytemnestra** and, with her, murdered her husband (his own cousin) **Agamemnon**, and was later killed by her son **Orestes**. [412, 553]
Aeneas Trojan, born of the union of **Aphrodite** with **Anchises**, who left Troy when the Greeks took the city. The legend of his journey westward via Carthage and romance with **Dido** became associated with the foundation of Rome; it was most famously elaborated in Vergil's *Aeneid*, in which he is presented as the founder of Lavinium, from which his son **Ascanius** would found Alba Longa. [205, 220–23]
Aeolus God of the winds [554]. Also the name of one of the sons of **Hellen**.
Aesculapius see **Asklepios**
Agamemnon Son of **Atreus**, and ruler of Mycenae. In the *Iliad*, the overall commander of the Greek expedition against Troy (the poem opens with his quarrel with **Achilles**). He was murdered on his return from Troy by **Clytemnestra** and **Aegisthus** – an act avenged by his son, **Orestes** [553].
Agave see **Pentheus**
Aithra Mother of **Theseus**. [220]
Ajax (Gr. Aias, Etr. Eivas) Second only to **Achilles** in the Greek contingent at Troy [552], the stalwart

554 *Aeolus shepherding the Clouds at the mouth of his cave (Attic 'knucklebone' pot attributed to the Sotades Painter, from Aegina, c. 460–440 BC).*

Ajax was the local hero of the island of Salamis. His madness and suicide after failing to inherit the arms of Achilles [267–69] were poignantly explored in Sophocles' *Ajax*, performed *c.* 441.
Distinct from him is the 'Lesser' Ajax, who raped **Cassandra** after the fall of Troy. [190, 205, 220]
Alkinous King of the Phaeacians, who entertains **Odysseus** at his court and gives him a magic ship in which to sail home (*Odyssey* 6–13).
Alkmene Wife of Amphitryon, by whom she gave birth to Iphikles. **Zeus** assumed her husband's appearance in order to sleep with her, begetting **Herakles** [413].
Amazons Tribe of female warriors, vaguely located in the East; Penthesileia and Hippolyta [145] were two of their queens; the former was killed in battle by **Achilles**, though he reputedly fell in love with her at the moment of her death. The Greek fascination with them has been related to male fear of a world with women in charge (hence the 'Amazonomachy', the battle between the Amazons and a cohort of mythical male heroes). Amazons rejected the stereotypical feminine roles of child-rearing and keeping house. In battle they fought (like the historical Persians) on horseback, with bows: to facilitate that, they supposedly cut off their right breasts (thus their name, meaning 'breastless'). [122, 147, 555]
Amphiaraos Key (but reluctant) member of the expedition known as the **Seven Against Thebes**. The oracular shrine at Oropos [cf. 113] was situated on the ground where **Zeus** ordered the earth to engulf him.
Amphitryon see **Alkmene**
Anchises Father of **Aeneas**, carried away from falling Troy on his son's back. [205, 220–22]
Andromache Wife and eventual widow of **Hector**. [220, 570]
Andromeda Daughter of the king of

Ethiopia, exposed on a rock by her father to protect his land against a sea monster; saved by **Perseus**. [130]
Antigone Daughter of **Oedipus**, who accompanied her father after his banishment from Thebes; after defying her uncle's royal decree and burying her brother Polyneikes (see **Seven against Thebes**), she was condemned to death.
Aphrodite (Etr. Turan, Rom. Venus) According to one genealogy, born near Cyprus from the marine foam (*aphros*) that rose around the severed genitals of **Ouranos**. Goddess of love, sex, beauty, and fertility in the Greek world and beyond (she relates to and perhaps derives from the Eastern goddess Astarte). [30, 70, 81–87, 182, 456, 556, 579]
Apollo Born (with his sister **Artemis**) of **Leto** on the island of Delos, which

555 *Amazons fighting Greeks (detail of the marble frieze from the Temple of Apollo at Bassae, c. 400 BC).*

556 *Aphrodite with Eros drawing back his bow (reverse of an engraved gilt bronze mirror, 4th century BC).*

557 *Apollo in his Doric temple at Delphi; before him stand a tripod and the omphalos – a monumental navel-stone that marked the mid-point of the earth (Attic red-figure volute krater by the Kleophon Painter, c. 440–430 BC).*

became one of his primary cult centres. Hailed by Homer as the 'far-shooter', armed with a bow, and patron of music, poetry, shepherds, and much else, Apollo was imagined as the paragon of manly excellence. His cult at Delphi centred round an oracle, where two mottoes ('Know thyself', and 'Nothing in excess') reminded visitors of an essentially civilizing concept of the god. His numerous love interests included **Cassandra** and **Daphne**. [163, 172, 177, 258, 363, 386, 391–93, 439, 464, 557]

558 *Ariadne and Dionysos (silver-gilt medallion set within a bowl from Asia Minor, late 2nd century BC).*

559 *Artemis and Actaeon, set upon by his hunting hounds (Attic red-figure krater attributed to the Pan Painter, c. 470 BC).*

Arachne Maiden who challenged **Athena** to a weaving contest, and was consequently turned into a spider.
Ares (Rom. Mars) The god of war, only son of **Zeus** and **Hera**.
Argonauts see **Jason**
Ariadne Daughter of King **Minos** of Crete; she assisted **Theseus** in his mission against the **Minotaur**, but was abandoned by him on the island of Naxos, where **Dionysos** found her. [203, 389, 440, 558]
Artemis (Rom. Diana) 'Mistress of Beasts', twin of **Apollo**. Patroness of hunting, promoter of fertility, and assistant at female puberty rites (e.g. at Brauron in Attica); her cult was often bloody (as reported of her temple at Sparta), yet in certain places, such as Ephesus [127], deeply rooted and syncretic. [559]
Ascanius The son of **Aeneas**; sometimes identified also as Iulus, and hence progenitor of the 'Julian' family; credited with having founded Alba Longa [225], from which **Romulus and Remus** founded Rome. [205, 220, 221, 223]
Asklepios (Rom. Aesculapius) Hero-god of healing and medicine [106]. His cult flourished and expanded in the 4th century BC, with the rise of large sanctuaries such as the one at Epidauros.
Astyanax Son of **Andromache** and **Hector**, killed by **Neoptolemos** [190].
Atalanta A fast-footed huntress, beloved of **Meleager**. According to one story, a would-be suitor defeats her in a foot-race by dropping golden apples for her to pick up.
Athena (Etr. Menerva, Rom. Minerva) Patron goddess of Athens; she had numerous other civic connections, and was worshipped throughout Greece. Of warlike aspect, yet she doubled as a protectress of women's work (especially spinning) and crafts generally. The story of her birth from the head of **Zeus** was popular with artists [560]; so too her relationship with **Herakles** [121, 138, 140]. [57, 119, 120, 122, 182, 207, 269, 569, 574]
Atlas One of the **Titans**, brother of **Prometheus**; condemned by **Zeus** to hold up the heavens [561, 582]. In one myth, he fetches the apples of the **Hesperides** for **Herakles** while Herakles shoulders his burden [140]. Turned to stone by **Perseus** wielding the head of **Medusa**, he gave his name to a mountain range in North Africa.
Atreus Brother of **Thyestes**, and son of **Pelops** – from whom he inherited a curse which haunted him and his descendants at Mycenae, including his son **Agamemnon**.
Auge Daughter of Aleos, an Arcadian king, and priestess of Athena; she bore **Herakles** a son, **Telephos**, for which she was banished by her father [460].
Bacchants see **maenads**

Bacchus see **Dionysos**
Bellerophon Corinth-based hero, whose deeds, assisted by harnessing the winged horse **Pegasus**, included the killing of the **Chimaera** [576].
Briseis Concubine of **Achilles**. Her seizure by **Agamemnon** at the beginning of the *Iliad* (after one of Agamemnon's own concubines, **Chryseis**, had been returned to her father) enraged Achilles, who withdrew from battle [189].
Calydonian Boar see **Meleager**
Cassandra Daughter of **Priam**; **Apollo** endowed her with the gift of unerring prophecy, but after she rejected his advances, she was condemned never to be believed. During the fall of Troy, she was raped [190, 205, 220], and later taken by **Agamemnon** to Mycenae, where she was murdered by **Clytemnestra**.
Castor and Pollux (Gr. Polydeukes) The twins known as the Dioskouroi (Rom. Dioscuri); sons of **Zeus** by **Leda**, brothers of **Helen** and **Clytemnestra**, usually envisaged as young horsemen. One myth identified them with the constellation of Gemini; another cast them as demi-gods, spending alternate days one in the Underworld and the other on Mount Olympus.
Catamitus, Catmit see **Ganymede**
Centaurs Half-human, half-equine tribe, usually disruptive and barbaric, and rarely identified as individuals (one respectable Centaur was Chiron, who educated the young **Achilles**). Most famous for attending the wedding feast of Hippodamia at the invitation of the king of the Lapiths, and attempting to rape the bride and Lapith women: the battle that ensued frequently featured on temple pediments and metopes in the 5th and 4th centuries BC. [122, 147, 391, 562]
Ceres see **Demeter**
Charon (Etr. Charun) Ferryman across the Styx, the main river of the Underworld [563]. In Etruscan imagery, a hideous axe-bearing sprite who comes to collect the dead [224].

560 *The birth of **Athena** from the head of **Zeus** (Attic black-figure amphora attributed to the Antimenes Painter, c. 510 BC).*

561 *Atlas holding up the heavens (marble copy after a Hellenistic original of the 3rd or 2nd century BC, late 1st–2nd century AD).*

562 *Centaurs attack the **Lapith** Kaineus (bronze relief from Olympia, c. 630 BC).*

563 *Charon in his boat, with* **Hermes** *and the soul of a woman (Attic white-ground lekythos attributed to the Thanatos Painter, c. 440 BC).*

564 *Circe with two of the companions of* **Odysseus** *transformed into swine (Attic black-figure lekythos attributed to the Daybreak Painter, late 6th century BC).*

565 *Chimaera (Etruscan bronze, from Arretium [modern Arezzo], late 5th century BC).*

Charybdis see **Scylla**

Chelidon see **Philomela**

Chimaera A monstrous hybrid of lion, goat, and snake, killed by **Bellerophon** with the help of **Pegasus**. [565, 576]

Chiron see **Centaurs**

Chronos 'Time' – an ancient etymology for **Kronos**

Chrysaor see **Medusa**

Chryseis (Rom. Cressida) A girl taken by **Agamemnon** during the Trojan campaign and then surrendered to her father, Chryses (a priest of Apollo); in her place Agamemnon demanded the concubine of **Achilles**, **Briseis**. The romance of 'Troilos and Cressida' is probably a later medieval invention.

Circe Island-dwelling sorceress who transformed the crew of **Odysseus** into pigs [564] but then hosted him and his men for a year (*Odyssey* 10).

Clytemnestra Daughter of **Leda**, wife of **Agamemnon**, mother of **Orestes**, **Iphigeneia**, and **Electra** [553]. The story of her murder of **Agamemnon** (aided by **Aegisthus**), and her own death at the hands of **Orestes**, is famously told in Aeschylus' *Oresteia* trilogy, and in other 5th-century BC tragedies.

Cressida see **Chryseis**

Cupid see **Eros**

Cyclopes (sing. Cyclops, 'round-eyed'; Etr. Cuclu) A race of cave-dwelling one-eyed giants (of whom **Polyphemos** is the most famous), later associated with Sicily.

Daedalus (Gr. Daidalos, Etr. Taitle) Archetypal inventor, artist, and technician, he became patron of many Classical craftsmen, and associated with the invention of sculpture (hence the 'Daedalic' style). Credited with designing the 'Labyrinth' for King **Minos**, he later took flight – literally – from Crete to Sicily with his son Icarus. [573]

Danaids, Danaos see **Io**

Daphne Virgin nymph who rejected the advances of **Apollo**; after praying to her father, the river-god Peneus, to protect her virginity, she was changed into a laurel tree.

Demeter (Rom. Ceres) Goddess of agricultural fertility, especially grain, and 'bringer of treasures', maternal in her image [150]. The most powerful story connected with her cult (especially at Eleusis) was that of her daughter **Persephone**, whose redemption from the Underworld was invested with the symbolism of rebirth and renewal. [566]

Diana see **Artemis**

Dido Phoenician princess; founder of the city of Carthage, where **Aeneas** had an affair with her *en route* to Italy. His departure was the cause of her suicide. [223]

Diomedes One of the leading Greek warriors who took part in the Trojan War; most famous for his night-raid on Troy (along with **Odysseus**), during which he killed the Trojan prince Rhesos and stole the Palladium – a heaven-sent image of Athena, which protected Troy from attack [212] and which Rome later claimed to possess [222].

Dionysos (Etr. Fufluns or Pachies, Rom. Bacchus or Liber) Son of **Zeus** and **Semele**, god of wine cultivation and drunkenness, also associated with death, ritual madness, and theatre. Often bearded [98, 225, 388, 390, 407] but also sometimes effeminate in appearance [387, 389], Dionysos had a large following in various sections of Greek society, as well as a mythical cohort of **satyrs** and **maenads**. A good index of his power is given in Euripides' play *The Bacchae* (see **Pentheus**), while a censorious view of the Bacchic cult in Italy is related by the Roman historian Livy (*History of Rome from its Foundation* 39.8–18). [558, 572, 580]

Dioskouroi see **Castor and Pollux**

Dis see **Hades**

Dorus see **Hellen**

Eilytheia (Rom. Lucina) Goddess associated with pregnancy and childbirth, sometimes considered the daughter of **Hera**.

Eivas see **Ajax**

Electra Daughter of **Agamemnon** and **Clytemnestra**. Her loyalties were lodged with her father: thus she aided her brother **Orestes** in murdering **Clytemnestra** and **Aegisthus** [553].

Epaphos see **Io**

Erebos see **Hesperides**

Erechtheus Early king of Athens, son of **Gaia** (and sometimes thought to be the grandson of **Erichthonios**),

566 *Statue from the Sanctuary of* **Demeter** *at Knidos (marble, with finer marble for the head, c. 330 BC).*

but adopted by **Athena**. His cult gave its name to the temple complex on the Athenian Acropolis known as the Erechtheion. One myth has him sacrifice his own daughter, on the instruction of the Delphic oracle, to ward off Thracian invaders.

Erichthonios 'Earth-born' hero and first king of Athens, often confused with and perhaps once identical with **Erechtheus**. When **Hephaistos** attempted to rape **Athena** she wiped his semen from her thigh with a rag, and when she threw the rag to the ground, Erichthonios appeared. Athenians claimed descent from Erichthonios, and his lack of human parents was key to their claims (in the 5th century BC) to be the original, native inhabitants of Attica.

Eris The divine personification of strife. In revenge for not having been invited to the wedding of Peleus and Thetis, she instigates the dispute between **Hera**, **Athena**, and **Aphrodite** as to which goddess is most beautiful, leading to the 'Judgment of **Paris**'.

567 *Eros playing the lyre (Greek bronze figure from the Mahdia shipwreck, off Tunisia, early 1st century AD).*

568 *Ganymede*, *holding a cockerel – a traditional love gift – is carried away by* **Zeus** *(terracotta statue from the Sanctuary of Zeus at Olympia, c. 470 BC).*

Eros (Rom. Cupid) 'Love' (sexual love): a divine spirit, armed with bow and arrows, often presented as the infant son of **Aphrodite** [556], and figuratively multiplied. Later he takes on an allegorical importance, appearing on sarcophagi as a symbol of life after death – hence the Christian winged cherub. [71, 286, 567, 579]

Europa Phoenician virgin-princess. **Zeus** took the form of a bull in order to abduct her; she climbed on his back [94, 95], and was carried away across the sea to 'Europe' (specifically Crete) where, after coupling with Zeus, she bore Rhadamanthys and **Minos**.

Euryale see **Gorgons**

Eurydice see **Orpheus**

Fates (Rom. Fatai, also Parcae; Gr. Moirai) Old women (often considered three sisters), some-times deemed daughters of **Zeus**, or else Nyx (see **Hesperides**), who spun, wove, and finally cut the threads of human beings' allocated lives.

Faunus see **Pan**

Fortuna see **Tyche**

Fufluns see **Dionysos**

Gaia (also Ge; Rom. Terra or Tellus) 'Earth' [98]: born from primeval Chaos, Gaia was the mother of all life on earth, including the giants [458], **Titans**, **Cyclopes**, and **Ouranos** (who was both her son and her husband).

Galatea ('Milk-white') Sea-nymph unsuccessfully wooed by **Polyphemos** [217]. On discovering that she loved another, Acis, Polyphemos cast a rock at him, but Galatea rescued her beloved by turning him into a river. Another myth has her accept Polyphemos' advances, and bear a son, Galas, from whom the Galatians claimed descent. Also a name given to the woman crafted by **Pygmalion** [443].

Ganymede (Etr. Catmit, Rom. Catamitus) The 'cup-bearer' of **Zeus** [93]: a lissom shepherd boy seized by the god – either in person [568] or in the form of an eagle [92, 212].

Geryon A triple-bodied monster in the western Mediterranean; to steal his cattle was one of the 'labours' assigned to **Herakles** [139].

giants Primal race of monsters who challenged the divine order. Among the named giants are Porphyrion, **Pallas**, and Ephialtes. Their battle with the Olympian deities (who were aided by **Herakles**), known as the 'Gigantomachy', was a favourite theme of Classical artists from the 6th century on. [43, 216, 458, 459]

Gorgons Three monstrous sisters: **Medusa** ('queen'), Sthenno ('strong'), and Euryale ('wide-wandering'). The latter two chased **Perseus** after his decapitation of Medusa [134, 569].

Hades (Rom. Dis; also Pluto, 'the rich') Brother of **Zeus** and **Poseidon**, and the presiding deity of the Greek Underworld, to which his name was also given: he won control of it after drawing lots with his two brothers, dividing the kingdom of their father, **Kronos**, between them (**Poseidon** was assigned the realm of the sea, and **Zeus** the heavens). His consort was **Persephone**.

Hector The principal Trojan hero; eldest son of **Priam**, husband of **Andromache**. His death at the hands of **Achilles**, avenging the death of **Patroklos** whom Hector had killed, dominates the later books of the *Iliad*. [188, 570]

Hecuba Wife of **Priam**.

Hekate Nether-world goddess, associated with spirits, magic, and witchcraft, often worshipped at crossroads.

Helen 'The face that launched a thousand ships'; beautiful offspring of **Zeus** and **Leda**, the wife of **Menelaus**. It is a moot point whether she willingly eloped to Troy

569 *The Gorgon* **Medusa** *beheaded by* **Perseus***; she clutches her child,* **Pegasus***; on the left stands* **Athena** *(limestone metope from Temple C at Selinus [modern Selinunte] in Sicily, c. 530–510 BC).*

with **Paris** or was passively abducted: either way, she was deemed the prime cause of the Trojan War. [91]

Helios (Rom. Sol) The sun god.

Hellen Ultimate ancestor of the 'Hellenes', i.e. Greeks: his sons (Dorus, Aeolus, and Xythos) and grandsons (**Ion** and Achaeus) gave their names to supposed Greek sub-ethnicities (Dorians, Ionians, etc.).

Hephaistos (Rom. Vulcan) The god of fire (hence 'volcanoes', named after Vulcan), craftsmanship, and metalworking; usually characterized as lame. [585]

Hera (Etr. Uni, Rom. Juno) Sister and wife of Zeus, concerning whose affairs she is constantly jealous and enraged. [182, 571]

Herakles (Etr. Herkle, Rom. Hercules) The most ubiquitous of Greek heroes, Herakles was a son of **Zeus** by the princess **Alkmene**, and began his life as a mortal. Later, with the support of **Athena** [121, 140], he was received on Olympus as a god. The cycle of his heroic adventures is long and complex [136–39]; the twelve Labours (a *dodekathlon*) chosen to decorate the Temple of Zeus at Olympia [140] became canonical. As a powerful man deified, he was also an obvious alter ego for political autocrats, including perhaps the Athenian tyrant Peisistratos, certainly Alexander the Great, and several Roman emperors. [9, 136–45, 442]

Hercules see **Herakles**

Hermes (Rom. Mercury) The messenger god, usually shown carrying a distinctive staff or wand (the *kerykeion*, or *caduceus*), wearing a felt cap, and with winged feet. As escort of souls (*Psychopompos*) he had connections with the Underworld [563]. The bearded heads mounted on columns sporting erect phalluses, known as 'herms', were originally meant as representations of the god (and often marked places of thoroughfare). [182, 186, 206, 260, 413, 572, 578]

Hesperides Daughters of Nyx ('night') and Erebos ('darkness') who guarded a tree of golden apples, a wedding gift from **Gaia** to **Hera**. Their garden was located on the western border of Ocean: **Herakles** was ordered to fetch its apples as his eleventh Labour.

Hestia see **Vesta**

Hippodamia Daughter of Oinomaos, king of Pisa (near Olympia). **Pelops** won her as his wife after cheating to defeat her father in a chariot race.

Hippolyta Queen of the **Amazons**, and mother of **Hippolytus**.

Hippolytus Son of **Theseus** and **Hippolyta**, devotee of **Artemis**, who spurned the sexual advances of his

570 *Hector taking leave of* **Andromache** *(Chalkidian black-figure krater attributed to the Inscription Painter, mid–end 6th century BC).*

571 *Hera unveils herself to* **Zeus** *(marble metope from the Temple of Hera at Selinus [modern Selinunte] in Sicily, c. 460 BC).*

572 *Hermes with the infant* **Dionysos** *(Attic white-ground kalyx krater attributed to the Phiale Painter, c. 430 BC).*

573 *Icarus with **Daedalus**, who is crafting the wax wings for their escape (marble relief, 2nd century AD, the upper part restored).*

574 *Jason finds the Golden Fleece; in the centre, helping, is **Athena**; to the right is one of the Argonauts, with the prow of their ship (Attic red-figure column krater attributed to the Orchard Painter, c. 470–460 BC).*

575 *Leda and the swan (marble relief from Brauron in Attica, 2nd century AD).*

stepmother, Phaedra. She hanged herself, after writing a letter to Theseus alleging that Hippolytus had molested her; Theseus cursed him, and he was dragged to death when his horses were frightened by a sea-monster sent by Poseidon.

Hygieia Personified goddess of health, daughter of **Asklepios**. [110]

Hypnos The god of sleep, twin brother of death (**Thanatos**).

Icarus Son of **Daedalus**. He plunged to his death while escaping Crete with his father, who had equipped them both with wings [573]. Icarus flew too high: the wax which held his wings together melted, and he fell headlong into the sea.

Io Daughter of Inachos, King of Thebes. **Zeus** fell in love with her and transformed her into a heifer; after wandering over the earth, she gave birth in Egypt to Epaphos, whose descendants included Danaos and his fifty daughters (the Danaids).

Ion Founder of the Ionian Greeks. Creusa was his mother, but different myths ascribed him different fathers: according to Euripides' *Ion*, his father was **Apollo**; other sources make him the son of Xythos (thus the grandson of **Hellen**).

Iphikles see **Alkmene**

Iphigeneia Daughter of **Agamemnon** and **Clytemnestra**, condemned to be sacrificed when the Greek fleet bound for Troy was becalmed at Aulis. Some versions of her story say that she was saved by **Artemis**, the goddess who had ordered the sacrifice – her place being taken by a deer or a bear.

Iphitos see **Neleus**

Iris Goddess of the rainbow.

Isis Egyptian 'mother' goddess, whose mystery cult became especially popular at Rome in the late 1st and 2nd centuries AD [124].

Iulus see **Ascanius**

Jason Displaced heir to the throne at Iolchos (Volos) in Thessaly, Jason went on a mission to prove his birthright, sailing eastward with a band of heroes known as the Argonauts, after their ship, the *Argo*, to recover a golden ram's fleece at Colchis – a task in which he was aided by **Athena** and **Medea** [203, 574].

Jocasta see **Oedipus**

Juno see **Hera**

Jupiter see **Zeus**

Kadmos Originally from Tyre (in Phoenicia), he later founded Thebes, and was credited with the introduction of the Phoenician alphabet to Boeotia.

Kapaneus One of the **Seven Against Thebes**, who assailed the walls of Thebes boasting that not even **Zeus** could stop him [425] – at which he was promptly struck by Zeus' thunderbolt.

Kronos (Rom. Saturn) A Titan, offspring of **Gaia** and **Ouranos**; father of **Zeus** and **Hera** (by his sister, **Rhea**). As Hesiod relates (*Theogony* 164–75), Gaia incited Kronos to castrate Ouranos, leading to the creation of **Aphrodite**. Later, aware that he was destined to be supplanted by one of his children, Kronos devoured each of them at birth: Zeus escaped, and later overthrew his father. The Greeks sometimes thought of Kronos as Chronos, 'Time'; Romans transmuted him into Saturn, and deemed 'the age of Saturn' an idyllic primal period of peace and agricultural prosperity.

Laius see **Oedipus**

Laocoön Aristocratic priest of Troy, who feared the Greeks 'even when they came bearing gifts' (namely the Wooden Horse, in which they were hiding, ready to enter the city). **Apollo** or **Athena** despatched two serpents which devoured him and his sons [226].

Lapiths Mythical tribe of north-west Greece, known mainly for their brawl with the **Centaurs** [122, 391, 562].

Leda Beloved of **Zeus**; after he visited her in the form of a swan [575], she was sometimes said to have produced two eggs – one containing **Clytemnestra** and **Helen**, the other **Castor and Pollux**.

Leto (Rom. Latona) Mother of **Apollo** and **Artemis**, who gave birth to them on Delos.

maenads Female followers of **Dionysos**, inspired by his ecstatic frenzy; also known as Bacchants. [394, 396]

Mars see **Ares**

Marsyas An impudent **satyr** who challenged **Apollo** to a musical contest, of which the loser was to be flayed alive; inevitably, despite being deemed the victor by **Midas**, Marsyas lost.

Medea Princess of Colchis. She appears in various stories, usually credited with magical powers and a murderous temper, at first harnessed to the cause of **Jason**. The *Medea* by Euripides shows she had reason to feel cruelly mistreated in love – though not, perhaps, to murder her own two sons in revenge for their father's desertion of her in Corinth.

Medusa The **Gorgon** whose gaze was so terrible that it turned onlookers to stone, decapitated by **Perseus** [132–35, 490, 569]. Her head or mask was widely used as a shield-blazon [119] and a symbol in decorating temples and elsewhere [399, 454]. At her death, **Pegasus** and Chrysaor emerged from her neck [132, 134].

Meleager Leader of the hunt to catch the wild boar which **Artemis** had

despatched to ravage his native Calydon [187]; aided in the quest by the virgin huntress **Atalanta**, with whom he fell in love.

Menelaus Younger brother of **Agamemnon**, and king of Sparta. The abduction of his wife **Helen** was the immediate cause for the Trojan War. His presumed palace at Sparta was the focus of a hero-cult from the 8th century BC onwards.

Menerva see **Athena**

Mercury see **Hermes**

Midas Semi-legendary king of Phrygia. According to Ovid's *Metamorphoses* 11, **Dionysos** granted him his wish that all he touched would turn to gold (with disastrous results); later he adjudicated the contest between **Marsyas** and **Apollo** (and was given donkey's ears for his indiscrete judgment in favour of Marsyas).

Minerva see **Athena**

Minos Legendary king of Crete, son of **Zeus** and **Europa**. He kept the **Minotaur** in a labyrinth (created by **Daedalus**) at his palace at Knossos.

Minotaur Half-man, half-bull monster, to which **Minos** sacrificed Athenian youths. **Theseus** despatched the beast [586].

Muses Daughters of **Zeus** and Mnemosyne (Memory), the Muses were saluted as patrons of poetry, music and dance – eventually the presiding deities of all creative and intellectual activity. Canonically they were nine in number, and in Roman times each was assigned her own sphere: epic poetry, history, tragedy, comedy, flute-playing, choral song and dance, lyric song and dance, hymns, and astronomy. A 'museum' is where their gifts are gathered, most famously in the Ptolemaic court at Alexandria. [432, 577]

Narcissus Beloved of the nymph Echo; to punish his callous rejection of Echo's advances, **Aphrodite** ordained that he fall in love with his own reflection.

Neleus Son of **Poseidon**, and king of Pylos. When **Herakles** beseeched Neleus for purification after his murder of Iphitos, Neleus refused; Herakles thereupon killed him, along with all his sons save **Nestor**.

Neoptolemos Son of **Achilles**, famed for killing **Priam** and **Astyanax** [190, 205, 220]; he later sacrificed Priam's daughter Polyxena at his father's grave.

Neptune see **Poseidon**

Nereids see **Nereus**

Nereus The 'Old man of the sea', father of sea-**nymphs** known as Nereids.

Nestor Son of **Neleus**; the most senior Greek warrior at Troy, reputed to have outlived two generations. Homer places his home at Pylos [194].

Nike Goddess or personification of Victory, usually shown as winged [59, 122, 126, 455, 457].

Niobe Daughter of **Tantalos**; she boasted that her twelve children were equal to or better than **Apollo** and **Artemis**: Apollo and Artemis showered the children with a rain of arrows, and turned Niobe to stone.

nymphs Female personifications of trees, rivers, mountains, and other natural phenomena; frequently wooed by male deities.

Nyx see **Hesperides**

Odysseus (Etr. Uthuste, Rom. Ulixes or Ulysses) Son of Laertes and Antikleia, husband of **Penelope**, and father of Telemachos; the 'many-turning' (*polytropos*) hero whose adventures are described chiefly in Homer's *Odyssey*, though he appears prominently in the *Iliad* too. A quick and inventive intelligence is his hallmark. Iconographically, from the 5th century BC onwards, he is often shown wearing a conical cap [191, 214] – referring to his initial reluctance to go to Troy, when he pretended to be a simple peasant. [207–12, 217, 267, 268]

Oedipus Abandoned in infancy by his father, King Laius of Thebes, Oedipus eventually fulfils a prophecy that he would kill his father and marry his mother. Arriving at Thebes, he rids the city of the **Sphinx** which was plaguing it, by solving her riddle [584]. After he has unwittingly married his widowed mother, Jocasta, the truth of their relationship emerges, and he blinds himself before going into impoverished exile.

Oinomaos see **Hippodamia**

Orestes Son of **Agamemnon** and **Clytemnestra**; with his sister **Electra** he avenged his father's murder [553].

Orion Giant hunter, identified with a group of stars in the earliest mythology. According to one myth, blinded by the father of a girl he loved, Orion recovered his sight by groping towards the sun's rays. According to another, he and the Pleiades (the virgin daughters of **Atlas** and Pleione), for whom he longed, were turned into stars – explaining why he seems to chase them in the sky.

Orpheus Erstwhile Argonaut (see **Jason**) and master-poet, capable of taming wild beasts with his songs, he gives his name to a shadowy religious system known as 'Orphism', whose devotees believed in an eventual redemption from the horrors of the Underworld. One tale has Orpheus try to reclaim his wife Eurydice from the Underworld: he charmed **Hades** with his music and obtained permission to fetch Eurydice, on condition that he not turn round to look at her before

reaching the upper world; at the last moment, Orpheus broke the condition – thus losing her forever. [434, 578]

Ouranos (Rom. Uranus) In primordial cosmology, 'the heavens' – who partnered with **Gaia** (Earth) to produce the **Titans**, but who was castrated by one of his sons, **Kronos**, creating **Aphrodite**.

Pachies see **Dionysos**

Pallas Name of a **giant** killed by **Athena**.

Pan Rustic deity usually associated with the region of Arcadia; cloven-hoofed and horned and generally shaggy in appearance. He can cause 'panic' when malevolent, but is a natural inhabitant of the pastoral world of flocks, caves, and piping. In Roman times, Pan was associated with two native deities: Silvanus (Etr. Selvans), the god of wild and uncultivated land [155]; and Faunus, a pastoral and oracular god with the legs of a goat, who headed a clan of rustic satyr-like fauns [215]. [440, 441, 579]

Pandora 'All-giving', or 'All-endowed' – the prototypical female presented by **Zeus** to Epimetheus ('he who thinks afterwards') as a way of punishing the latter's brother, **Prometheus**; for with her came a jar (later characterized as a box) from which, when it was opened, countless evils and diseases

576 *Pegasus helping **Bellerophon** kill the **Chimaera** (Lakonian black-figure kylix attributed to the Boreads Painter, c. 570–565 BC).*

were set loose: only Hope counterbalanced these – some small consolation for mankind. [122]

Paris One of the sons of **Priam** of Troy. **Hermes** paraded before him the three goddesses **Hera**, **Athena**, and **Aphrodite**, and he nominated Aphrodite as the most beautiful, gaining **Helen** as his prize (the episode known as the 'Judgment of Paris' [182, 186]). His abduction of Helen [203] was the cause of the Trojan War, in which he played little part; it was his arrow, however, that killed **Achilles**.

Patroklos In the *Iliad*, the best friend and beloved of **Achilles** [189]. His death at the hands of **Hector** was commemorated with elaborate funerary games [187]; it also spurred Achilles back into furious battle, as an event to be avenged [188].

Pegasus Winged horse, born from the decapitated **Medusa** [132, 134, 569]. Pegasus helped **Bellerophon** defeat the **Chimaera** [576].

Peleus King of Phthia in Thessaly; one-time Argonaut (see **Jason**), husband of **Thetis** [25, 187], and father of **Achilles**.

Pelops Son of **Tantalos**, who is sometimes reputed to have served him as a dish for the gods. At Pisa near Olympia, Pelops gained his wife, **Hippodamia**, at the cost of a curse on his descendants (the 'house of **Atreus**') – later manifested in the feud between two of his sons, Atreus and **Thyestes**. His tomb is traditionally located at Olympia, and he gives his name to the 'Peloponnese' region of Greece.

Penelope Wife of **Odysseus** and mother of Telemachos. A model of wifely patience and dutifulness: during the long absence of her husband she repels suitors by attending to her loom [192].

Penthesileia see **Amazons**

Pentheus Son of Agave, grandson of **Kadmos** and cousin of **Dionysos**; king of Thebes; protagonist of Euripides' *Bacchae*, in which he refuses to recognize Dionysos' divinity and prohibits his worship. Eventually he is punished: as he spies on the Theban women whom Dionysos had possessed, including his own mother, she is induced to

577 *The nine **Muses** (Roman marble sarcophagus, c. AD 150).*

578 *Orpheus (right) and **Eurydice** with **Hermes** (marble relief after a Greek original of c. 420–410 BC, found in a Roman villa outside Herculaneum).*

579 *Pan molesting **Aphrodite**, who is poised for her bath [cf. 83]: she defends herself with one of her sandals, and is protected by **Eros** (marble group from the House of the Poseidoniasts of Berytos [Beirut] on Delos, c. 100 BC).*

580 *Persephone and Dionysos: she holds wheat, and a cockerel; he a vine laden with grapes, and a kantharos (terracotta plaque from Locri in South Italy, c. 460 BC).*

581 *Poseidon (obverse of a silver stater from Poseidonia [Paestum] in South Italy, late 6th century BC).*

582 above *Prometheus (right) and his brother Atlas undergoing the afflictions imposed upon them by Zeus (Spartan black-figure kylix attributed to the Painter of Archesilas II, c. 560–550 BC).*

583 right *Romulus and Remus suckled by the she-wolf (a pious Renaissance reconstruction: the bronze wolf is Etruscan, 5th century BC; the children were added in the 15th century, probably by Antonio del Pollaiuolo).*

believe Pentheus is a wild beast and to tear him to pieces.

Persephone (Rom. Proserpina) Also known as Kore ('Maiden') [150]. Daughter of **Zeus** and **Demeter**, she was abducted by the god of the Underworld, **Hades**, while gathering flowers [447]. Demeter protested by causing a crop failure, and negotiated an agreement whereby her daughter would return annually for half the year (the story is rationalized as the onset of spring, and germination of plants). [580]

Perseus Slayer of the Gorgon **Medusa** [133, 135, 207, 490, 569]; he gave her head to **Athena**, who is often shown wearing it as an emblem on her *aegis* [119]. He also rescued **Andromeda** from a sea monster (aided by winged shoes given him by **Hermes**) [131].

Phaedra see **Hippolytus**

Philomela and Procne (also known in Greek as Khelidon and Aedon [166]) Tereus, the husband of Procne, fell in love with Procne's sister, Philomela, raped her, and cut out her tongue. By weaving a message, Philomela informed her sister of the crime, and together they exacted their revenge by butchering Procne's own child, Itys, and serving him to his father. The three adults were transformed into birds – a hoopoe, nightingale, and swallow.

Phoenix Childless exile from Thessaly who sought refuge with **Peleus** and accompanied **Achilles** to Troy [189].

Pleiades see **Orion**

Pluto see **Hades**

Pollux, Polydeukes see **Castor and Pollux**

Polyneikes see **Seven Against Thebes**

Polyphemos A goat-rearing **Cyclops**, son of **Poseidon**; famous for his encounter with **Odysseus** (narrated in *Odyssey* 9), by whom he was blinded while drunk [207, 209–11, 212, 214]; also for his unsuccessful

wooing of **Galatea** [217].

Polyxena see **Neoptolemos**

Pomona Minor Roman goddess, associated with autumn fruits. Ovid's *Metamorphoses* 14 tells how she was wooed by **Vertumnus**.

Poseidon (Rom. Neptune) Brother of **Hades** and **Zeus**. God of water generally, and the sea in particular; in the Greek world he was also deemed responsible for earthquakes. The trident is his usual attribute [581].

Priam Elderly king of Troy, husband of **Hecuba**, father of fifty Trojan sons (among them **Hector**, **Paris**, and **Troilos**) and many daughters (including **Cassandra** and **Polyxena**). [190, 205, 206, 220]

Priapus Roman guardian-spirit of fertility, gardens, and the countryside: generally figured as a florid and ithyphallic presence [241].

Procne see **Philomela**

Prometheus ('Forethinker') The **Titan** who in Hesiod's cosmology figures as progenitor of humankind, fire, and sacrifice to the gods. He tricked **Zeus** into accepting the fat and offal from animal sacrifice (keeping the best meat for himself), and also stole fire from the gods. Zeus punished him in various ways (see **Pandora**), not least by chaining him to a rock and having an eagle peck at his liver, which replenished itself as fast as it was consumed [582].

Proserpina see **Persephone**

Pygmalion King of Cyprus, who created a statue of his ideal woman (sometimes called **Galatea** [443]): he fell in love with the image, and successfully beseeched **Aphrodite** to bring the statue to life.

pygmies A race of dwarves, associated with Africa [297] and famed for an ongoing battle with the cranes (the 'Geranomachy').

Remus see **Romulus**

Rhadamanthys see **Europa**

Rhea Mother of **Zeus**, by **Kronos**.

Rhea Silvia see **Romulus and Remus**

Romulus and Remus Twin sons of

Rhea Silvia and **Mars**, credited with founding Rome. Cast into the river Tiber at birth, they were washed ashore and suckled by a she-wolf [583]. After founding a new settlement at the site where they were discovered, the brothers quarrelled as to who should be king: an omen settled the dispute in Romulus' favour, and he killed his brother. As the first of Rome's six kings, Romulus expanded his city, populating it with runaway slaves and even criminals, and most famously by the collective kidnapping of the **Sabine women**. He was deified upon his 'death' on the grounds that he rose to heaven, enveloped in a cloud.

Sabine women It was a ploy of **Romulus** to increase the population of his nascent Rome by inviting a neighbouring people, the Sabines, to a festival, and then seizing their womenfolk.

Sarpedon Son of **Zeus**; Lycian prince and ally of the Trojans: his death at the hands of **Patroklos**, and removal by **Hypnos** and **Thanatos**, is narrated in *Iliad* 16.

Saturn see **Kronos**

satyr Mythical male follower of **Dionysos**, notoriously mischievous, lustful and drunken. Depicted as an upright and recognizably human figure, but with pointed ears and a bushy equine tail; later also often with goatish legs (cf. **Pan**). [76, 215, 390, 394, 396, 398, 403, 424, 438, 440]

Scylla and Charybdis Twin perils of the passage between Italy and Sicily (the Straits of Messina) – Scylla envisaged in the *Odyssey* as a six-headed woman, with fierce dogs around her waist [212]; Charybdis as a whirlpool.

Semele Daughter of **Kadmos**. Pregnant with **Dionysos**, she requested his father, **Zeus**, to appear to her in full divine splendour, and was consumed by lightning during his apparition. Zeus then removed the embryo from her womb and stitched it into his own thigh for nine months.

Seven Against Thebes After **Oedipus** bequeathed Thebes to his sons Eteokles and Polyneikes, Eteokles refused to share the rule, provoking Polyneikes to gather six fellow warriors for an assault on the city [425]. It ended in disaster: apart from **Adrastos**, all perished. Royal decree deemed Polyneikes the aggressor, and forbade his burial (an order disobeyed by **Antigone**).

Sibyl General name for an oracular prophetess, used especially of the prophetess at Cumae in Campania, visited by **Aeneas** in *Aeneid* 6. The Sybilline books or 'leaves' were a corpus of prophetic literature, kept

584 The **Sphinx** putting her riddle to **Oedipus**, depicted as a traveller (Attic red-figure kylix, the name-vase of the Oedipus Painter, c. 480–470 BC).

under the Capitoline Temple of Jupiter in Rome.

Silenus Mythical male follower of **Dionysos**. Like a **satyr**, usually a composite of man and beast; normally represented, however, as a much older (and wiser) creature [389]. Silenus' sons, generically termed sileni, inherited their father's appearance, but not his wisdom.

Silvanus (Etr. Selvans) see **Pan**

Sirens Sisters, part-bird, part-human, whose singing could charm sailors and lure them to their deaths; encountered most famously by **Odysseus** [191]. One myth has it that at the sound of **Orpheus**' song they threw themselves into the sea [434].

Sisyphus One of the damned in the Greek Underworld: his punishment was to push a boulder up a hill, only for it to roll back down again.

Sphinx Monster with human head (usually female in Greek art) and lion's body, of Egyptian origin [124]; connected with transporting souls, hence often found in funerary imagery. Generally an effective marker of fear, reverence, and foreboding, but also credited with enigmatic wisdom. According to one set of myths, **Oedipus** put an end to the Sphinx's terrorizing of Thebes by solving her riddle [584], at which she fell dead.

Taitle see **Daedalus**

Tantalos King of Sipylus and the area of Lydia in Asia Minor, whose crime is variously described: according to one set of myths, he gave mortals a taste of divine food (nectar and ambrosia); to another, he tried to feed the gods mortal flesh – worse still, that of his own son, **Pelops**. His punishment in the Underworld was to go continually hungry, 'tantalized' with food and drink which he could never quite reach.

Teiresias Theban seer, granted the gift of infallible prophecy although sightless; according to one story, he

was blinded by **Hera**, after divulging that women enjoyed sex nine times more than men.

Telemachos Son of **Odysseus**.

Telephos Son of **Herakles** and **Auge**; after being abandoned at birth in Arcadia, then rescued by shepherds, he became king of Mysia. Since Pergamon was built over the ancient city of Mysia, the Attalid kings treated him as a particularly important local hero. [442, 460]

Thanatos Spirit or personification of Death. **Hypnos** (Sleep) is his twin.

Theseus Son of **Aegeus** and Aithra, credited with many adventures – most notably ridding Crete of the **Minotaur** [586] and escaping with **Ariadne** [203], whom he later abandoned. His popularity increased in the early 5th century BC, when he was moulded into a hero of the Athenian democracy, and his alleged bones recovered by Kimon.

Thetis Sea-nymph, daughter of **Nereus**, wife of **Peleus** [25, 187], and mother of **Achilles**. Famous for acquiring Achilles' divine armour from **Hephaistos** [585].

Thyestes Son of **Pelops** and brother of **Atreus**. He seduced the latter's wife, Aerope, after Atreus had become king of Mycenae; in revenge, Atreus prepared a feast, in which he served the flesh of Thyestes' two sons to their father. By his own daughter Thyestes fathered a third son, **Aegisthus**, who would avenge his brothers-cum-uncles.

Tinia see **Zeus**

Titans ('Strainers') Primal gods or forces of nature, the wayward offspring of Heaven (**Ouranos**) and Earth (**Gaia**); their numbers include **Atlas** and **Prometheus**.

Triptolemos The youth chosen by **Demeter** to teach humanity how to grow corn; thereby the first initiate of the Eleusinian Mysteries. [97, 150]

Triton Male equivalent of a mermaid – half-man, half-fish, commonly shown holding a conch shell.

585 **Thetis** receiving the armour of **Achilles** from **Hephaistos** (Attic red-figure kylix known as the Foundry Cup [cf. 256, 445], the name-vase of the Foundry Painter, c. 490–480 BC).

Troilos A son of **Priam**. He was fatally ambushed by **Achilles** as he watered his horses at a fountain. See also **Chryseis**.

Turan see **Aphrodite**

Tyche (Rom. Fortuna) 'Fortune'; her worship was especially prominent in the Hellenistic world, when she appears as a personified goddess [117].

Ulysses see **Odysseus**

Uni see **Hera**

Uranus see **Ouranos**

Venus see **Aphrodite**

Vertumnus Rustic Roman deity of Etruscan origin, credited with supervising the 'turning' (from the Lat. verb vertere) of the agricultural year; husband of **Pomona**.

Vesta Roman goddess of the hearth (equivalent to the Greek Hestia, but more widely worshipped at a domestic level). Her primary temple was in the Forum at Rome [303], where six priestesses, the Vestal Virgins [587], tended a flame said to have come to Rome as a burning brand from Troy.

Xythus see **Hellen**

Zeus (Etr. Tinia, Rom. Jupiter) In Homer's formula, 'father of gods and men', and 'cloud-gatherer': the supreme Olympian, guardian of law and justice, who overthrew and succeeded his father, **Kronos**. His most celebrated image was at Olympia – the colossal throned figure made c. 435 BC by **Pheidias** [126]. Although married to **Hera** [571], he was famous for his erotic escapades – with **Alkmene** [412], **Io**, **Europa** [94, 95], **Leda** [575], **Semele**, **Ganymede** [92, 93, 212, 568], etc. [560]

586 Deeds of **Theseus**: in the centre he is shown killing the **Minotaur**; other exploits include wrestling with Kerkyon, King of Eleusis (top), swinging an axe to cut Prokrustes down to the size of his own bed (top right: Prokrustes made his victims fit a bed by chopping off their extremities or stretching them out), capturing the wild bull of Marathon (bottom), and dispatching the sow Phaea (top left) (Attic red-figure kylix attributed to the Codrus Painter, c. 440–430 BC).

587 **Vestal Virgins** banqueting (detail of a marble relief from the Ara Pietatis Augustae [Altar of Augustan Piety] in the Roman Forum, dedicated in AD 43).

GLOSSARY

Throughout this book we have endeavoured to avoid specialized jargon, or else to explain its occurrence. Here, however, is a summary checklist of some of the terminology that might be encountered in Classical literature, history, and archaeology.

588 *Principal shapes of Greek vases: 1. amphora, 2. hydria, 3. dinos, 4. volute krater, 5. oinochoe, 6. kylix, 7. kantharos, 8. skyphos, 9. kyathos, 10. rhyton, 11. lekythos, 12. pyxis, 13. aryballos, 14. alabastron.*

abacus Uppermost part of a **capital**, supporting the **architrave** [167–69].

acropolis (Gr.) The 'high city', hence citadel; in most Greek cities, an elevated area reserved for sanctuaries [300, 302, 482].

acroteria (Gr.) 'Topmost' ornaments or statues, placed on the top and corners of a **pediment** [486].

adventus (Lat.) Literally, 'arrival'; invoked for Roman images showing an emperor or general gloriously entering a city [314].

adyton (Gr.) Literally, 'a place not to be entered'; a small inner shrine sometimes placed at the back of a temple **cella**.

aedes (Lat.) Literally, 'dwelling'; a temple building.

aedicula (Lat.) A small shrine.

agora (Gr.) Marketplace; but more than stalls and shops – the central civic area of a Greek city [300, 302].

alabastron (Gr.) Small, usually pear-shaped, flask used for perfumes and essences [33, 588:14].

amphitheatre Literally, 'theatre in the round'; an oval space for public Roman spectacles ringed by a tiered circle of seating [426, 427, 430].

amphora (Gr.) Large two-handled jar for wine or oil storage [59, 588:1].

apodyterium (Lat.; Gr. *apodyterion*) Changing-room of a bath complex or **gymnasium**.

apse Semicircular recess with half-domed roof.

Archaic Literally, 'old' (Gr. *archaios*); strictly, the period *c.* 650–480 BC.

Archaizing Imitating the stylistic tropes of the **Archaic** period, a phenomenon particularly widespread in the 1st century BC [386, 393].

architrave Beam above columns; lowest part of the **entablature** in a Classical building [167–69].

archon (Gr., 'ruler') A Greek civic official or magistrate. In 5th- and 4th-century BC Athens, ten *archontes* were elected annually, each with different administrative, judicial, and religious duties.

arena (from Lat. *harena*, 'sand') Central area of an **amphitheatre** [427, 430].

aryballos (Gr.) Small, usually round, perfume or oil flask [353, 588:13].

as see **sestertius**

askos (Gr.) A flask with a spout at one end and a handle across the top; like an **aryballos**, often used for carrying precious oils [35].

atrium (Lat.) Central hall of a Roman house, usually with an open skylight, and often with a sloping roof to feed water into an **impluvium** [338].

Attic Relating to the city and territory of Athens (the region of Attica).

augur (Lat.) Of Etruscan origin; a priest with powers to glean information from examining patterns of bird flight, animal entrails, and other omens or 'auspices' [159].

aulos (Gr.) A cylindrical pipe sounded with a reed (a cross between the modern oboe, clarinet, and flute), played in pairs [390, 418, 440].

barbarians (from Gr. *barbaroi*) Collective term for peoples from foreign lands, considered less 'civilized' than their Greek and Roman counterparts.

basilica (Lat.) In Roman architecture, a rectangular hall, usually serving a public purpose (e.g. law-courts) [295]; the type was adapted in the 4th century AD as a model for Christian places of worship, typically with a nave flanked by two aisles, and an **apse** at its end.

black-figure Greek technique of vase-painting, which developed from **Protoattic** styles in early 6th-century Athens [e.g. 43, 59]. Silhouettes were drawn directly on the surface of an unfired pot; inner details were then scratched out of the paint using a stylus, again before firing. (Some extra details might also be added in white and purple paint.)

boule (Gr.) Executive 'council' in Greek city-states.

Bronze Age In Europe, the period that follows the Neolithic Age: *c.* 3000–1000 BC.

bucchero Etruscan type of pottery, with a shiny black finish suggestive of polished metal.

Byzantine The period of the later Roman Empire, from the 4th century AD onwards, named after the city of Byzantium (refounded as Constantinople by the Emperor Constantine).

capital The upper part of a column [167–69].

cella (Lat.) The principal room of a temple; cf. **naos**.

chiton (Gr.) Woollen tunic or shirt, generally sleeveless, worn next to the skin [48, 77, 150].

chora (Gr.) 'Hinterland': rural territory of a Greek **polis**.

choregos (Gr.) 'Chorus-leader' or 'chorus-producer', called upon to fund a **chorus** at a dramatic festival [412].

chorus (Gr.) Generally, a dancing group; in the theatre, a band of commentators and involved spectators who performed in the **orchestra**.

chous (Gr.) Dumpy-shaped jug [380, 402], often decorated with scenes of children. (Greek children were given their first taste of wine from a *chous*.)

chryselephantine Term, from Gr. for 'gold' and 'ivory', used to describe statues made of those two precious materials [258]. The most famous examples were Pheidias' statues of Athena Parthenos in Athens [122] and Zeus at Olympia [126].

chthonian Pertaining to the earth (Gr. *chthon*) or Underworld, especially to deities such as Hades, Persephone, and Hekate.

Classical Used in many chronologies to define the art and literature of the early 5th–4th centuries BC (conventionally *c.* 480–323 BC); but otherwise, as in the title of this book, or the phrase 'Classical civilization', refers to Graeco-Roman antiquity at large.

collegium (Lat.) A 'guild' or 'club' – specifically used of groups of Roman priests or magistrates, but also of any private association.

colossus (Lat.) A statue of over-life-size scale.

comitia (Lat.) An assembly of the Roman **plebs**, whose functions included the election of magistrates. There were three *comitia*, made up of different constituent groups.

consuls In Rome, the two chief governors in the **Senate**, elected annually.

Corinthian Architectural order; its capital combines volutes with acanthus leaves and tendrils [169].

cryptoporticus (Lat.) Subterranean passageway or corridor.

cubiculum (Lat.) Bedroom of a Roman house.

Curia (Lat.) Meeting place of the Roman **Senate** or municipal council.

cursus honorum (Lat.) The progressive career 'ladder' of Roman political offices.

Cycladic Used to refer to the **Bronze Age** cultures that developed on the 'circular' group of islands called the Cyclades (between Greece and Asia Minor) between the 3rd and mid-2nd millennia BC.

Daedalic Used to describe early Greek sculpture, especially that of the 7th century BC (deriving from the ancient attribution of such sculptures to the mythical Cretan craftsman Daedalus) [257, 452].

damnatio memoriae (Lat.) Literally, 'erasure of the record'. A posthumous condemnation of someone deemed by the Roman **Senate** to have been an enemy of the State. It might entail the removal of his name from the official records and the destruction of his images.

Dark Age (or sometimes 'the Dark Ages') The period *c.* 1100–800 BC in Greece. (As more archaeological light is shed on those centuries, the term is losing its application.)

deme (from Gr. *demos*) A 'village' or 'district', used to organize Athenian citizens into topographical units.

denarius (Lat.) Roman silver coin, roughly equivalent to a Greek **drachma**.

dictator (Lat.) In Rome, a magistrate temporarily granted full powers during a time of crisis.

dinos (Gr.) Large, round-bottomed bowl, requiring a separate stand [588:3].

Doric Architectural order characterized by distinctive tapering columns topped with simple circular **capitals**, supporting a frieze composed of **triglyphs** and **metopes** [167].

Dorians An ethnically defined unit of Greek peoples, including those from the southern and western parts of mainland Greece, characterized by their dialect and customs.

drachma (Gr.) Greek monetary unit, a 'handful' of 6 **obols**. Common currency existed as multiples of drachma (2 = didrachm, 4 = tetradrachm, etc.); 100 drachmas were equal to 1 mina.

ekklesia (Gr.) 'Assembly' of adult male citizens, whose debates and decisions determined the policies of the Greek **polis**.

ekphora (Gr.) The 'carrying out' of the body to a cemetery [21], the stage of a Greek funeral that follows the **prothesis**.

emporion (Gr.) 'Trading-post'.

encaustic A painting technique using heated wax.

entablature Collective term for the part of a building above the columns, comprising the **architrave**, **frieze**, and **cornice** [167–69].

entasis (Gr.) Convex tapering of a column – a trick of Classical architectural practice, devised to offset a tendency for the column's sides to appear concave.

ephebes (Gr. *epheboi*) Adolescent boys; from the 4th century BC, used of members of a military training college in Athens.

euergetism An act of individual beneficence, most frequently the embellishment of a town with new public buildings.

fasces (Lat.) Bundle of rods bound around an axe, carried by Roman **lictors**; a symbol of the power of senior Roman magistrates who could (theoretically, at least) deal out capital punishment.

fibula (Lat.) A safety-pin brooch used for fastening a garment.

forum (Lat.) Principal civic area and/or marketplace of a Roman town [298, 303], comparable to the Greek **agora**.

frigidarium (Lat.) Cold room of a bath complex [69].

Geometric The period *c*. 900–750 BC.

gymnasium (Lat.; Gr. *gymnasion*) Literally, 'place where one goes naked'. As today, a place set aside for physical exercise and training.

Helladic Used of the Greek **Bronze Age**.

Hellenistic Fusing Greek and non-Greek styles, expressions, and language; conventionally the period 323–31 BC.

helots Collectively enslaved native serfs in Sparta.

herm Quadrangular stone pillar that functioned as a boundary marker; originally topped with a head of Hermes, later with that of other figures

heroön (Gr.) Shrine to a hero, usually considered his tomb.

hetaira (Gr.) 'Female companion'; professional escort or hostess, with sexual favours also implied [e.g. 74].

himation A rectangular cloak, of wool or linen, worn by both men and women in ancient Greece [181, 439].

hoplite Greek foot soldier, with full-face helmet and large circular shield [e.g. 326], fighting in the interlocked unit known as the **phalanx**.

hybris (Gr.) 'Overweening arrogance', with an act of transgression implied.

hydria (Gr.) Three-handled jar, used for carrying water [137, 588:2].

impluvium (Lat.) In the Roman house, a pool in the centre of the **atrium** that collected rainwater from an opening in the roof [253, 338].

Ionians An ethnically defined unit of Greek peoples characterized by their dialect and customs, and contrasted with the Dorians. Athens claimed to be the mother-city of the Ionian people.

Ionic Architectural order characterized by slim columns with moulded bases, and **capitals** with scroll-like volutes; usually also with a continuous sculpted **frieze** [168].

Iron Age The period characterized by the use of iron, as opposed to bronze, weapons and implements: in Europe, roughly the 1st millennium BC.

ithyphallic 'With erect phallus'.

kalpis (Gr.) Water-carrying jar – similar to a **hydria**.

kantharos (Gr.) Drinking-cup with two high handles [e.g. 388, 588:7].

kithara (Gr.) Type of stringed lyre, traditionally with sounding-box of tortoise-shell [e.g. 439].

kline (Gr.) Couch or bed.

kore (Gr., pl. *korai*) 'Young girl' or 'maiden'; used of a statue type dedicated in the **Archaic** period [154, 453].

kottabos (Gr.) Game played at a **symposium**, involving flicking wine from a kylix at a target [394, 408].

kouros (Gr., pl. *kouroi*) 'Young man'; usually denotes generic **Archaic** statue-type [446, 453].

krater (Gr.) Capacious vessel used for mixing wine with water [e.g. 394, 588:4]. Large examples hold around 45 litres (10 gallons). Volute, kalyx, column, and bell shapes are subdivisions.

kyathos (Gr.) One-handled drinking cup, especially popular in Etruria [588:9].

kylix (Gr.) Drinking-cup; wide and shallow in shape, with two side handles and a stemmed foot [e.g. 404, 588:6].

latifundium (Lat.) A large Roman rural estate that combined agricultural, industrial, and commercial enterprises [245].

lekythos (Gr.) Tall flask for carrying oil; often used for funerary observances [342, 588:11].

libation Liquid offering (wine, oil) made at an altar or tomb.

libertus (Lat.) An emancipated slave.

lictors Attendants of Roman magistrates, who carried the **fasces**.

liturgy (from Gr. *leitourgia*, 'work for the people') In Athens, a form of taxation which called upon the richest citizens to donate money for public spending – e.g. funding the annual costs of manning a **trireme** (*trierarchia*) or the production of

a **chorus** in musical and dramatic festivals (*choregia*).

ludi (Lat.) In the Roman world, public games, incorporating anything from wild animal combats (*venationes* [429]) to mock sea-battles (*naumachiae*). Also used of gladiatorial training-schools, like the Ludus Magnus constructed on the east side of the Colosseum in Rome by the Emperor Domitian.

macellum (Lat.) Market.

Magna Graecia (Lat.) 'Great Greece': the area of South Italy and Sicily colonized by the Greeks.

manumissio (Lat.) In Rome, the formal release from slavery of a slave, who thereupon became a **libertus**.

metic (Gr. *metoikos*) Resident alien in the Greek **polis**, who did not have the same rights as its citizens.

metope (Gr.) Rectangular panel inserted between **triglyphs** of a building in the **Doric** order; together they form its **frieze** [165, 486].

mimesis (Gr.) 'Imitation': in Greek philosophical discourse, the critical nexus between art and reality.

mina see **drachma**

Minoan Crete-based **Bronze Age** 'palatial' civilization of the Aegean, named after the legendary King Minos at Knossos, and archaeologically defined as *c.* 3500–1100 BC. Its other key sites include the volcanic island of Thera (Santorini).

mos maiorum (Lat.) 'Way of our forebears' (also used in the pl., *mores maiorum*). A byword for the traditions of the Roman Republic.

municipium (Lat.) Italian town given rights of Roman citizenship; or provincial self-governing town with citizen rights conferred on magistrates and councillors.

munus (Lat.) 'A gift'; usually something given by a Roman citizen out of a sense of civic duty; it could therefore encompass anything from individual military service to funding elaborate gladiatorial games.

Mycenaean The **Helladic** civilization overlapping with, then overtaking, **Minoan**, *c.* 1600–1150 BC. The name is taken from the walled city of Mycenae in the Peloponnese [198–200].

mystery religions Secret forms of worship, often pertaining to the afterlife, centering around rites of initiation. Perhaps most famous were those of Demeter and Persephone at Eleusis in Attica [150].

naos In Gr., 'temple'; also used to mean the inner sanctum of a temple (cf. **cella**).

naumachiae see **ludi**

necropolis (Gr.) Literally, 'city of the dead': a cemetery.

Neo-Platonism Doctrine that combined the philosophy of Plato with Eastern mystic religions – and later,

Christianity – originating in the 3rd century AD.

nymphaeum (Lat.) Shrine of the nymphs, usually with a fountain and decorated with elaborate mosaics and sculptures.

obelisk A tall tapering pillar with Egyptian associations; several were shipped and erected in Rome to celebrate the Roman conquest of Egypt [148].

obol (Gr. *obelos*, a 'spit') Greek monetary unit, a sixth of a **drachma**.

oikos (Gr.) Household.

oinochoe (Gr.) Wine jug with trefoil mouth [157, 588:5].

olpe (Gr.) Squat round-lipped jug.

Olympiad The interval between the Olympic games, a period of four years – consequently used as a unit for reckoning time, counting from the first 'Olympic Games' in 776 BC.

omphalos (Gr.) 'Navel'; used of the centre of a geographical area, and most famously as a title of Delphi (celebrated by a domed stone in the shape of a navel [363, 557]).

opus (Lat.) Literally, a 'work'; also used to describe styles of Roman wall-construction: *opus quadratum*, featuring large squared masonry; *opus incertum*, small irregular chunks of stone; *opus reticulatum*, a 'network' of small square blocks set diagonally, etc.

oracle Message or instructions understood to come from divine authority; also the medium transmitting that message.

orchestra (Gr.) Circular 'dancing-space' in the Greek theatre, below the stage [415, 417]; probably derived from an area set aside for the threshing of grain.

Orientalizing Showing Eastern influence; term applied to the arts from the mid-8th to mid-7th centuries BC [451].

ostracism The democratic process of exiling a citizen from Athens for ten years; name derived from the practice of inscribing nominees on potsherds (Gr. *ostraka*) [266].

palaestra (Lat.; Gr. *palaistra*) Literally, a 'wrestling-school'; often a separate precinct, or else the area of a **gymnasium** complex set aside specifically for wrestling.

Panathenaia Civic festival of Athens, involving sacrifices and a large procession in Athena's honour; the 'Greater Panathenaia' was held every four years, featuring musical and athletic competitions that rivalled those held at the major **Panhellenic** sanctuaries. Winners in the athletic events received oil in **black-figure** 'Panathenaic amphoras', with Athena on one side, and their athletic event on the other [e.g. 48, 57, 59].

panegyric (Gr. *panegyrikon*, something 'fit for a public assembly') Used of eulogistic poems or other declarations praising a particular individual.

Panhellenic Exclusively open to, or involving, the Greek-speaking world. The four great Panhellenic sanctuaries were at Delphi, Olympia, Isthmia, and Nemea.

papyrus A reed grown in the Nile Delta; its pith was turned into sheets of 'paper', pasted together to form a continuous roll [377, 384]. 'Papyrology' is the study of deciphering surviving fragments.

parodos (Gr.) Side-entrance to the **orchestra** of a theatre [415].

patera (Lat.) Saucer-like dish, sometimes with a raised central boss, often used for libations and sacrifice (cf. **phiale**); or an architectural decoration resembling such a dish.

patricians (Lat. *patricii*) Members of the Roman noble class.

patronage In the Roman world, a bilateral agreement between a patron and a client: it could be literary, whereby the patron sponsored and protected an author; or non-literary, whereby a client was promised legal and political aid by a patron in return for his social and electoral support.

pediment Triangular-shaped frontage of a building. Often, but not necessarily, filled with sculptured decoration [486].

pelike (Gr.) Variant form of **amphora**, with broad, sagging body.

peplos (Gr.) Long, sleeveless woollen robe, worn pinned at the shoulders and belted, the normal apparel of Greek women [122, 154].

perioikoi (Gr.) Literally, 'dwellers around'. Denotes the free inhabitants who lived in the towns and villages around Sparta. Despite serving Sparta – e.g. through military service and taxes – they lacked the rights of Spartan citizenship.

peripteral Used of a building with exterior columns supporting its roof on all four sides.

peristyle (Gr.) Columns surrounding a building or courtyard [334, 335]; in the Roman house, a colonnaded courtyard beyond the **atrium** [244, 338].

phalanx (Gr.) Close infantry formation made up of **hoplites** [310]. Its cohesion depended on each soldier partially shielding his neighbour.

phiale (Gr.) Flat libation bowl or saucer, without handles (cf. **patera**).

phlyax A type of 'farce' (Gr.; pl. *phlyakes*) which became popular in South Italy in the 4th and 3rd centuries BC, distinctive for the 'swollen' costumes of its actors (who were also called *phlyakes*) [411–13].

phyle (Gr.) 'Tribe'; an artificial sub-unit for organizing citizen groups within the **polis**.

pithos (Gr.) Large terracotta storage vessel [219, 374].

plebs (Lat.) The Roman 'common people', the non-patrician class of citizens.

podium (Lat.) Platform base of a building [147], specifically a Roman temple [162].

polis (Gr.) The Greek 'city-state', encompassing the sovereign, self-contained unit of the city and its hinterland (**chora**), each with its own sense of communal identity.

polychromy Use of many colours in decorating architecture and sculpture.

pomerium (Lat.) The sacred boundary of the city of Rome, and of other Latin cities.

pontifex (Lat.) In Rome, a 'priest' who advised the state on religious issues; the chief priest was called the *pontifex maximus* – a title held by the Roman emperors after the precedent of Augustus [158, 290].

porne (Gr.) A prostitute, working from a brothel; unlike a **hetaira**, who could usually offer a variety of services besides copulation, for a *porne*, sex was the only trade.

porticus (Lat.) Colonnade.

pronaos (Gr.) The front porch of a temple.

propylon (Gr.) Monumental roofed gateway; on the Athenian Acropolis, the Propylaia [482] was a more complex structure flanked by additional architectural wings and a ramp.

proskynesis (Gr.) 'Bowing down in worship', as if before a god. In the East, the practice was an accepted form of showing respect to a mortal ruler; in Greece, Alexander the Great was reputedly, and controversially, the first to demand it of his subjects.

prothesis (Gr.) The 'setting forth' of the body on a funerary pyre [16].

Protoattic Style of vase painting, developed in Athens in the 7th century BC [207].

Protocorinthian Style of vase painting, developed in Corinth in the late 8th century BC [310].

psykter (Gr.) Vase filled with ice and placed inside a **krater** to cool wine.

pyxis (Gr.) Lidded box for cosmetics or jewelry [588:12].

quadriga (Lat.) Chariot drawn by four horses abreast [48].

red-figure Greek technique of vase painting [e.g. 38], originating in Athens *c*. 530–520 BC, which reverses the **black-figure** technique. The figures were 'reserved' in the colour of the clay by painting the background black. Details were then added using a thin brush. The practice continued into the 4th century BC, taken over by workshops in South Italy, where other colours were often added [e.g. 94].

rhapsode (Gr.) Literally, 'song-stitcher': a bard, or reciter of poems [181].

rhyton (Gr.) Drinking-horn [397, 588:10].

salutatio (Lat.) A formal greeting between a Roman client and patron that took place in the **tablinum** of the Roman house.

sarcophagus (from Gr. *sarkophagos*, 'flesh-digester') A stone coffin in which the remains of the deceased were interred; especially popular in the Roman world when inhumation rather than cremation became the primary way of disposing of the body (from the early 2nd century AD onwards) [440].

satyr-play Semi-comic type of drama in which the members of the chorus are dressed up as **ithyphallic** satyrs. One satyr-play would close each day's trilogy of tragedies during the City Dionysia in Athens.

Second Sophistic see **Sophists**

Senate The governing council of the Roman Republic; during the Empire, its power lay chiefly in the hands of the emperor.

sestertius Two and a half 'asses' (an 'as' was a standard weight of bronze). Most commonly encountered Roman monetary unit.

skenographia (Gr.) 'Stage-painting'.

skyphos (Gr.) Drinking cup with small side handles [588:8].

Sophists Literally 'wise men', whose wisdom especially depended on their skills of public speaking. Often a pejorative term, used in particular of professional 5th-century BC Greek intellectuals, such as Protagoras and Gorgias, who could make large sums of money peddling their philosophies or techniques of rhetoric, among which was the skill of arguing both sides of a question (from which our word 'sophistry' descends).

Second Sophistic is a term used to describe the period *c*. late 1st–mid-3rd centuries AD, characterized by a revival of Greek culture (especially the teaching and practice of Greek rhetoric) within the Roman Empire.

stamnos (Gr.) Wide-mouthed, short-necked vessel for wine.

stele (Gr.) Upright stone slab, often a gravestone, or used to carry inscriptions [e.g. 15].

stereobate Base or substructure of a building, below the **stylobate**.

stoa (Gr.) Colonnade or portico [300–302].

strigil Curved scraping implement used by athletes after exercise for cleansing, toning, and depilating the skin [52].

stylobate The course of pavement above the **stereobate**, on which the columns of a temple rest.

symposium (Gr. *symposion*) Drinking party, with music, poetry, and formalized rules [394]. In Greece, an all-male occasion, save for the presence of courtesans (**hetairai**).

synoicism The 'coming together to live', when small groups of peoples formed into centralized communal settlements in Greece during the early 1st millennium BC.

syrinx (Gr.) Panpipes [441].

tabernae (Lat.) Shops.

tablinum (Lat.) Reception room of a Roman house [338].

talent Greek unit of weight, the equivalent of 6,000 silver **drachmas**.

techne (Gr.) 'Craft'; any skill or labour, from brick-laying to rhetoric or painting.

temenos (Gr.) Literally, something 'cut off' – hence sacred land, an enclosure reserved for the gods.

tessera (Gr., Lat.) A small piece of stone or glass, the basic component of a mosaic.

tetradrachm see **drachma**

tetrarchy A term (literally, a 'foursome of rulers') most often applied to the system devised by Diocletian in AD 293 [528], which cut the Roman Empire in half north-south, and further subdivided it east-west.

thiasos (Gr.) The 'train', or entourage, of Dionysos, including satyrs and maenads [390].

tholos (Gr.) Circular building or tomb [82, 108].

thyrsos (Gr.) Rustic wand wreathed in ivy and vine-leaves and topped with a pinecone, carried by devotees of Dionysos [390].

toga (Lat.) Outer garment worn by Roman men, consisting of a semi-circular piece of cloth draped over the left shoulder [12, 284].

tribunes (Lat. *tribuni*) Ten Roman magistrates entrusted with the task of protecting the **plebs** and granted special constitutional powers; in Imperial Rome, the position was held by the emperor following the precedent of Augustus.

triclinium (Lat.) Dining-room of a Roman house, literally entailing three couches (along side and rear walls) [410].

triglyph Panel with three vertical grooves or bars, alternating with **metopes** in a **Doric frieze** [165].

tripod Tall, three-footed bowl or cauldron, usually bronze, awarded as a prize in athletic competitions, or dedicated as a votive offering.

trireme A ship with three banks of oars, used in naval warfare [313].

triumph A Roman general or emperor's ritual procession into Rome after a major victory [316].

vault An arched masonry roof.

venationes see **ludi**

white-ground Greek technique of vase-painting in which the pot (most often, a **lekythos**) is covered with white paint and then decorated in a range of colours [319, 320].

xoanon (Gr.) Old-fashioned wooden statue, often representing a deity [cf. 257].

FURTHER READING

REFERENCE

Cambridge Ancient History (2nd edn, Cambridge 1961–); *Cambridge History of Classical Literature*, I (Greek literature), ed. P. E. Easterling and B. M. W. Knox (Cambridge 1985), II (Latin literature), ed. E. J. Kenney and W. V. Clausen (Cambridge 1982); J. Boardman, J. Griffin, and O. Murray, eds, *Oxford History of the Classical World* (Oxford 1986); S. Haynes, *Etruscan Civilisation: A Cultural History* (London 2000); S. Hornblower and A. Spawforth, eds, *The Oxford Classical Dictionary* (rev. 3rd edn, Oxford 2003); M. Howatson, ed., *Oxford Companion to Classical Literature* (Oxford 1989); M. Le Glay, J.-L. Voisin, and Y. Le Bohec, *A History of Rome* (2nd edn, Malden, Mass./Oxford 2001); R. Stillwell, W. L. MacDonald, and M. Holland McAllister, eds, *The Princeton Encyclopedia of Classical Sites* (Princeton 1996); R. J. A. Talbert, *Atlas of Classical History* (London/New York 1985); M. Torelli, ed., *The Etruscans* (Venice 2000); J. Whitley, *The Archaeology of Ancient Greece* (Cambridge 2001)

I · MORTALS: THE BODY IN CLASSICAL ANTIQUITY

From cradle to grave

E. Fantham et al., eds, *Women in the Classical World* (New York 1994); R. Garland, *The Greek Way of Death* (London 1985), and *The Greek Way of Life* (London 1990); M. Golden, *Children and Childhood in Classical Athens* (Baltimore 1990); S. C. Humphreys, *The Family, Women, and Death* (London 1983); J. Neils and J. H. Oakley, *Coming of Age in Ancient Greece* (New Haven/London 2003); T. G. Parkin, *Old Age in the Roman World* (Baltimore 2003); B. Rawson, *Children and Childhood in Roman Italy* (Oxford 2003); J. M. Toynbee, *Death and Burial in the Roman World* London/Ithaca, N.Y. 1971); E. Vermeule, *Aspects of Death in Early Greek Art and Poetry* (Berkeley 1979)

Cosmetics and the art of looking good

L. Bonfante, 'Nudity as a Costume in Classical Art', in *American Journal of Archaeology* 93 (1989), 543–70; E. Doxiadis, *The Mysterious Fayum Portraits: Faces from Ancient Egypt* (London/New York 1995); B. Grillet, *Les Femmes et les fards dans l'antiquité grecque* (Lyon 1975); G. Metraux, *Sculptors and Physicians in Fifth-Century Greece* (Montreal 1995); W. Moon, ed., *Polykleitos, the Doryphoros and Tradition* (Madison, Wis. 1995); A. F. Stewart, *Art, Desire and the Body in Ancient Greece* (Cambridge 1997); D. Williams and J. Ogden, *Greek Gold: Jewellery of the Classical World* (London 1994)

Athletics

A. Bernand, *The Road to Olympia: Artistic and Sporting Festivals in Ancient Greece* (London 2003); M. Golden, *Sport and Society in Ancient Greece* (Cambridge 1998); H. Mackie, *Graceful Errors: Pindar and the Performance of Praise* (Ann Arbor, Mich. 2003); S. G. Miller, *Ancient Greek Athletics* (New Haven/London 2004); C. Morgan, *Athletes and Oracles: The Transformation of Olympia and Delphi in the 8th century BC* (Cambridge 1990); W. Raschke, *The Archaeology of the Olympics* (Madison, Wis. 1988); N. J. Spivey, *The Ancient Olympics* (Oxford 2004)

Bathtime

J. DeLaine, *Baths of Caracalla: A Study in the Design, Construction, and Economics of Large-Scale Building Projects in Imperial Rome* (Portsmouth, N.H. 1997); G. G. Fagan, *Bathing in Public in the Roman World* (Ann Arbor, Mich. 1999); F. Yegül, *Baths and Bathing in Classical Antiquity* (New York 1992)

Erotics

J. N. Adams, *The Latin Sexual Vocabulary* (Baltimore 1990); C. Arscott and K. Scott, eds, *Manifestations of Venus: Art and Sexuality* (Manchester 2000); J. Clarke, *Roman Sex: 100 BC–AD 250* (New York 2003); J. Davidson, *Courtesans and Fishcakes: The Consuming Passions of Classical Athens* (London 1997); S. Deacy and K. Pierce, eds, *Rape in Antiquity: Sexual Violence in the Greek and Roman Worlds* (London 1997); K. Dover, *Greek Homosexuality* (London 1978); P. DuBois, *Sappho is Burning* (Chicago 1995), and *Sowing the Body: Psychoanalysis and Ancient Representations of Women* (Chicago 1988); M. Foucault, *The History of Sexuality*, III: *The Care of the Self* (New York 1986); D. Halperin, *The Construction of Erotic Experience in the Ancient Greek World* (Princeton 1990); D. Halperin, J. Winkler, and F. Zeitlin, eds, *Before Sexuality: The Construction of Erotic Experience in the Ancient Greek World* (Princeton 1990); C. Havelock, *The Aphrodite of Knidos and her Successors: A Historical Review of the Female Nude in Art* (Ann Arbor, Mich. 1995); J. Henderson, *The Maculate Muse* (New Haven/London 1975); E. Keuls, *The Reign of the Phallus* (Berkeley 1993); G. Luck, *The Latin Love Elegy* (2nd edn, London 1979); A. Richlin, ed., *Pornography and Representation in Greece and Rome* (New York 1992); J. Winkler, *The Constraints of Desire* (London 1990)

Diet

J. André, *L'Alimentation et la cuisine à Rome* (Paris 1981); N. Blanc and A. Nercessian, eds, *La Cuisine romaine antique* (Grenoble 1992); D. Braund and J. Wilkins, eds, *Athenaeus and his World* (Exeter 2001); A. Dalby and S. Grainger, *The Classical Cookbook* (London 1996); P. Garnsey, *Food and Society in Classical Antiquity* (Cambridge 1999); E. Gowers, *The Loaded Table* (Oxford 1993); W. J. Slater, ed., *Dining in a Classical Context* (Ann Arbor, Mich. 1996)

Medicine

L. Edelstein, *Ancient Medicine* (Baltimore 1987); M. Green, *Pilgrims in Stone: Stone Images from the Gallo-Roman Sanctuary of Fontes Sequanae* (Oxford 1999); R. Jackson, *Doctors and Diseases in the Roman Empire* (London 1988); H. King, *Hippocrates' Woman: Reading the Female Body in Ancient Greece* (London 1998); G. E. R. Lloyd, *In the Grip of Disease: Studies in the Greek Imagination* (Oxford 2003); J. N. Longrigg, *Greek Rational Medicine* (London 1993); B. Simon, *Mind and Madness in Ancient Greece* (London 1978)

II · HIGHER POWERS: GODS AND HEROES

Pantheons and pagans

M. Bernal, *Black Athena: The Afro-Asiatic Roots of Classical Civilization*, I: *The Fabrication of Ancient Greece 1785–1985* (London 1987); L. Bruit Zaidman and P. Schmitt Pantel, *Religion in the Ancient Greek City* (Cambridge 1992); W. Burkert, *Greek Religion: Archaic and Classical* (Cambridge, Mass. 1985); R. Buxton, ed., *Oxford Readings in Greek Religion* (Oxford 2000); K. Dowden, *Religion and the Romans* (London 1992); P. E. Easterling and J. Muir, eds, *Greek Religion and Society* (Cambridge 1985); S. Goldhill, ed., *Being Greek under Rome: Cultural Identity, the Second Sophistic and the Development of Empire* (Cambridge 2001); K. Hopkins, *A World Full of Gods: The Strange Triumph of Christianity* (New York 2000); R. Lane Fox, *Pagans and Christians* (Harmondsworth/New York 1986); R. Turcan, *The Gods of Ancient Rome: Religion in Everyday Life from Archaic to Imperial Times* (London 2001)

Imagining and imaging the divine

J. Boardman, *The Diffusion of Classical Art in Antiquity* (London 1995); J. Elsner, *Imperial Rome and Christian Triumph* (Oxford 1998); D. Freedberg, *The Power of Images: Studies in the History and Theory of Response* (Chicago 1989); R. Gordon, 'The Real and the Imaginary: Production and Religion in the Graeco-Roman World', in *Art History* 2.1 (1979), 5–34; N. J. Spivey, 'Bionic Statues', in A. Powell, ed., *The Greek World* (London 1995), 442–59

Heroic intermediaries

A. Blanshard, *Hercules: Scenes from a Heroic Life* (London, forthcoming 2005); I. Gradel, *Emperor Worship and Roman Religion* (Oxford 2002); K. Galinsky, *The Heracles Theme: The Adaptations of the Hero in Literature from Homer to the Twentieth Century* (Oxford 1972); S. Hornblower, *Mausolus* (Oxford 1982); G. Nagy, *The Best of the Achaeans: Concepts of the Hero in Archaic Greek Poetry* (Baltimore 1979); S. Price, *Rituals and Power: The Roman Imperial Cult in Asia Minor* (Cambridge 1984); J. Whitley, 'Early States and Hero-cults: a Reappraisal', in *Journal of Hellenic Studies* 108 (1988), 173–82

Cultic performance

M. Beard, J. North, and S. Price, *Religions of Rome* (Cambridge 1998); W. Burkert, *Homo Necans* (Berkeley 1972); M. Cosmopoulos, ed., *Greek Mysteries: The Archaeology and Ritual of Ancient Greek Secret Cults* (London 2003); M. Detienne and J.-P. Vernant, *The Cuisine of Sacrifice Among the Greeks* (Chicago 1989); S. Peirce, 'Death, Revelry and thysia', in *Classical Antiquity* 12 (1993), 219–66; F. T. van Straten, *Hiera kala: Images of Animal Sacrifice in Archaic and Classical Greece* (Leiden 1995); H. Versnel, ed., *Faith, Hope and Worship* (Leiden 1984)

A place for the gods

S. Alcock and R. Osborne, *Placing the Gods: Sanctuaries and Sacred Space in Ancient Greece* (Oxford 1994); A. Boethius, *Etruscan and Early Roman Architecture* (2nd edn, Harmondsworth/New York 1978); I. Edlund-Berry, *The Gods and the Place: The Location and Function of Sanctuaries in the Countryside of Etruria and Magna Graecia (700–400 BC)* (Stockholm 1987); A. W. Lawrence, *Greek Architecture* (5th edn, rev. R. A. Tomlinson, New Haven/London 1996); N. Marinatos and R. Hägg, eds, *Greek Sanctuaries: New Approaches* (London/New York 1993); F. de Polignac, *Cults, Territory and the Origins of the Greek City-State* (Chicago 1995)

III · MYTH IN THE MAKING

Myths about myth

J. Boardman, *The Archaeology of Nostalgia: How the Greeks Re-Created their Mythical Past* (London 2002); W. Burkert, *Structure and History in Greek Mythology* (Berkeley 1979); R. Buxton, *Imaginary Greece: The Contexts of Mythology* (Cambridge 1994); T. Carpenter, *Art and Myth in Ancient Greece* (London 1986); J. Davidson Reid, *The Oxford Guide to Classical Mythology in the Arts, 1300–1990s* (New York 1993); G. Lloyd, *Demystifying Mentalities* (Cambridge 1990); J.-P. Vernant, *Myth and Society in Ancient Greece* (London 1982); P. Veyne, *Did the Greeks believe in their Myths?* (Chicago 1988)

The Iliad and the Odyssey

M. Edwards, *Homer, Poet of the Iliad* (Baltimore 1987); A. Ford, *Homer: The Poetry of the Past* (Ithaca, N.Y. 1992); J. Griffin, *Homer on Life and Death* (Oxford 1980), and *Homer* (Bristol 1991); G. Nagy, *Homeric Questions* (Austin 1996)

Excavating Homer

J. Carter and S. Morris, eds, *The Ages of Homer* (Austin 1995); O. Dickinson, *The Aegean Bronze Age* (Cambridge 1994); E. Gombrich, *Art and Illusion: A Study in the Psychology of Pictorial Representation* (5th edn, London/New York 1977), 99–125; R. Higgins, *Minoan and Mycenaean Art* (3rd edn, London 1997); R. Kannicht, 'Homer and the Monuments Afresh', in *Classical Antiquity* 1 (1982), 70–86; J. Lowenstam, 'The Uses of Vase Depictions in Homeric Studies' in *Transactions and Proceedings of the American Philological Society* 122 (1992), 165–98; B. Powell, *Homer and the Origins of the Greek Alphabet* (Cambridge 1991); D. Preziosi and L. Hitchcock, *Aegean Art and Architecture* (Oxford

1999); A. Sadurska, *Les Tables iliaques* (Warsaw 1964); A. M. Snodgrass, *Homer and the Artists: Text and Picture in Early Greek Art* (Cambridge 1998); M. Stansbury-O'Donnell, *Pictorial Narrative in Ancient Greek Art* (Cambridge 1999); D. Traill, *Schliemann of Troy: Treasure and Deceit* (London 1995)

'Greek' myth abroad

B. Andreae, *Odysseus: Mythos und Erinnerung* (Mainz 1999); B. Andreae and C. Parisi Presicce, eds, *Ulisse: il mito e la memoria* (Rome 1996); R. Buxton, ed., *From Myth to Reason? Studies in the Development of Greek Thought* (Oxford 1999); N. de Grummond and B. S. Ridgway, eds, *From Pergamon to Sperlonga: Sculpture and Context* (Berkeley 2000); N. Hopkinson, *A Hellenistic Anthology* (Cambridge 1987); R. Hunter, *The Argonautica of Apollonius: Literary Studies* (Cambridge 1993); G. Hutchinson, *Hellenistic Poetry* (Oxford 1998); R. Osborne, 'Death Revisited: The Death of the Artist in Archaic and Classical Greece', in *Art History* 11.1 (1988), 1–16

Trojan aspirations and Roman receptions

J. Bremmer and N. Horsfall, *Roman Myth and Mythography* (London 1987); R. Brilliant, *My Laocoön: Alternative Claims in the Interpretation of Artworks* (Berkeley 2000); F. Cairns, *Virgil's Augustan Epic* (Cambridge 1990); D. Feeney, *Literature and Religion at Rome: Cultures, Contexts and Beliefs* (Cambridge 1998); P. Hardie, *Virgil's Aeneid: Cosmos and Imperium* (Oxford 1986); R. Thomas, *Virgil and the Augustan Reception* (Cambridge 2001)

IV · MANIPULATING NATURE

Managing the countryside

T. van Andel and C. Runnels, *Beyond the Acropolis: A Rural Greek Past* (Stanford, Calif. 1987); M. Beagon, *Roman Nature: The Thought of Pliny the Elder* (Oxford 1992); T. W. Gallant, *Risk and Survival in Ancient Greece* (Stanford, Calif. 1991); P. Hordern and N. Purcell, *The Corrupting Sea* (Oxford 2000), 175–341; R. Osborne, *Classical Landscape with Figures* (London 1987); J. Rich and A. Wallace-Hadrill, eds, *City and Country in the Ancient World* (London 1991); R. Sallares, *The Ecology of the Ancient Greek World* (London 1991); A. M. Snodgrass, *An Archaeology of Greece* (Berkeley 1987); K. D. White, *Roman Farming* (London 1970); C. R. Whittaker, ed., *Pastoral Economies in Classical Antiquity* (Cambridge 1988)

'Beyond the acropolis'

G. Barker, ed., *A Mediterranean Valley: Landscape Archaeology and Annales History in the Biferno Valley* (Leicester 1995); G. Barker and J. Lloyd, eds, *Roman Landcapes* (London 1991); A. Carandini, *Settefinestre* (Modena 1985); S. L. Dyson, *The Roman Countryside* (London 2003); J. Percival, *The Roman Villa* (Berkeley 1976); T. W. Potter, *The Changing Landscape of South Etruria* (London 1979)

Landscape and gardens

A. M. Ciarallo, *Gardens of Pompeii* (Los Angeles 2001); W. Jashemski,

The Gardens of Pompeii (New York 1979, 1993); E. Leach, *The Rhetoric of Space: Literary and Artistic Representations of Landscape in Republican and Augustan Rome* (Princeton 1988); W. L. MacDonald and J. Pinto, *Hadrian's Villa and its Legacy* (New Haven/London 1995); E. B. MacDougall and W. Jashemski, eds, *Ancient Roman Gardens* (Washington 1981); S. Settis, *Le pareti ingannevoli* (Milan 2002)

Natural resources

P. Aicher, *Guide to the Aqueducts of Ancient Rome* (Wauconda, Ill. 1995); S. Carey, *Pliny's Catalogue of Culture: Art and Empire in the Natural History* (Oxford 2003); D. P. Crouch, *Water Management in Ancient Greek Cities* (Oxford 1993); R. Gnoli, *Marmora romana* (Rome 1971); A. T. Hodge, *Roman Aqueducts and Water Supply* (London 1989); J. Landels, *Engineering in the Ancient World* (London 1978); R. Meiggs, *Trees and Timbers in the Ancient Mediterranean World* (Oxford 1982); O. Wikander, ed., *Handbook of Ancient Water Technology* (Leiden 2000)

Craft specialization

S. Adam, *The Technique of Greek Sculpture* (London 1966); B. Ashmole, *Architect and Sculptor in Ancient Greece* (New York 1972); C. Bluemel, *Greek Sculptors at Work* (London 1969); A. Burford, *Craftsmen in Greek and Roman Society* (London 1972); C. Mattusch, *Greek Bronze Statuary* (New York 1988); J. P. Uhlenbrock, *The Coroplast's Art* (New York 1990); P. Vidal-Naquet, *The Black Hunter* (Baltimore 1986), 224–45

V · POLITICAL ANIMALS

Founding fathers

M. Beard and M. Crawford, *Rome in the Late Republic: Problems and Interpretations* (2nd edn, London 1999); A. Bosworth, *Conquest and Empire: The Reign of Alexander the Great* (Cambridge 1988); J. Dunn, *Democracy: The Unfinished Journey 508 BC–AD 1993* (Oxford/New York 1992); M. I. Finley, *Democracy Ancient and Modern* (2nd edn, London 1985), and *Politics in the Ancient World* (Cambridge 1983); R. Meiggs, *The Athenian Empire* (2nd edn, Oxford 1979); O. Murray and S. Price, *The Greek City from Homer to Alexander* (Oxford 1990); J. Ober, *The Athenian Revolution: Essays on Ancient Greek Democracy and Political Theory* (Princeton 1996); J. Ober and C. Hedrick, eds, *Demokratia: A Conversation on Democracies, Ancient and Modern* (Princeton 1996); C. Richard, *The Founders and the Classics: Greece, Rome and the American Enlightenment* (Cambridge, Mass. 1995); W. Vance, *America's Rome* (New Haven/London 1989)

Mythologizing political origins

W. Forrest, *The Emergence of Greek Democracy 800–400 BC* (London 1966); N. Loraux, *The Invention of Athens: The Funeral Oration in the Classical City* (Cambridge, Mass. 1986); N. J. Spivey, 'Psephological Heroes', in R. Osborne and S. Hornblower, eds, *Ritual, Finance, Politics* (Oxford 1991) 39–51; M. Taylor, *The Tyrant Slayers: The Heroic Image in*

5th-century BC Athenian Art and Politics (New York 1981)

Styling civic power

D. Buitron-Oliver, ed., *The Greek Miracle: Classical Sculpture from the Dawn of Democracy* (Washington 1992); K. Galinsky, *Augustan Culture* (Princeton 1996); E. Gruen, *Culture and National Identity in Rome* (London 1993); S. Nodelmann, 'How to read a Roman Portrait', in E. D'Ambra, ed., *Roman Art in Context: An Anthology* (Englewood Cliffs, N.J. 1993), 10–26; J. Pollini, 'The Augustus from Prima Porta and the Transformation of the Polykleitan Heroic Ideal: The Rhetoric of Art', in W. Moon, ed., *Polykleitos, the Doryphoros and Tradition* (Madison, Wis. 1995), 262–82; A. F. Stewart, *Faces of Power: Alexander's Image and Hellenistic Politics* (Berkeley/London 1993); S. Walker, *Greek and Roman Portraits* (London 1995); P. Zanker, *The Power of Images in the Age of Augustus* (Ann Arbor, Mich. 1988)

Situating the city

S. Alcock, F. Cherry, and J. Elsner, eds, *Pausanias: Travel and Memory in Roman Greece* (Oxford 2001); J. Camp, *The Athenian Agora: Excavations in the Heart of Classical Athens* (London 1992), and *The Archaeology of Athens* (New Haven/London 2001); D. Favro, *The Urban Image of Augustan Rome* (Cambridge 1996); J. Huskinson, *Experiencing Rome: Culture, Identity and Power in the Roman Empire* (London 2000); M. Millett, *The Romanization of Britain: An Essay on Archaeological Interpretation* (Cambridge 1990); E. J. Owens, *The City in the Greek and Roman World* (London 1991)

Citizen right and military might

B. Campbell, *Warfare and Society in Imperial Rome* (London 2002); B. Cohen, ed., *Not the Classical Ideal: Athens and the Construction of the Other in Greek Art* (Leiden 2000); I. M. Ferris, *Enemies of Rome: Barbarians through Roman Eyes* (Stroud, Glos. 2000); Y. Garlan, *War in the Ancient World: A Social History* (London 1975); E. Hall, *Inventing the Barbarian: Greek Self-Definition through Tragedy* (Oxford 1989); V. Hanson, *The Western Way of War* (Oxford 1989); F. Hartog, *The Mirror of Herodotus: The Representation of the Other in the Writing of History* (Berkeley 1988); J. Rich and G. Shipley, eds, *War and Society in the Greek World* (London/New York 1993)

VI · OIKOS AND ECONOMY

House and home

I. M. Barton, ed., *Roman Domestic Buildings* (Exeter 1996); N. Cahill, *Household and City Organization at Olynthus* (New Haven/London 2002); F. Coarelli, ed., *Pompeii* (New York 2002); W. Hoepfner and E.-L. Schwandner, *Haus und Stadt im klassischen Griechenland* (Munich 1986); W. Jongman, *The Economy and Society of Pompeii* (Amsterdam 1988); L. Nevett, *House and Society in the Ancient Greek World* (Cambridge 1999); E. Reeder, ed., *Pandora: Women in Classical Greece* (Princeton 1995); A. Wallace-Hadrill, *Houses and Society in Pompeii and*

Herculaneum (Princeton 1994); E. Walter-Karydi, *The Greek House* (Athens 1994)

Slaves in the classical economy

P. DuBois, *Slaves and other Objects* (Chicago 2003); K. R. Bradley, *Slavery and Society at Rome* (Cambridge 1994); M. I. Finley, ed., *Slavery in Classical Antiquity* (Cambridge 1960); W. V. Harris, 'Towards a Study of the Roman Slave Trade', in *Memoirs of the American Academy in Rome* 36 (1980), 117–40; K. Hopkins, *Conquerors and Slaves* (Cambridge 1978); G. E. M. de Ste Croix, *The Class Struggle in the Ancient Greek World* (London 1981); F. Thompson, *The Archaeology of Greek and Roman Slavery* (London 2003)

Trading abroad

M. Bound, *The Giglio Wreck* (Athens 1991); M. I. Finley, *The Ancient Economy* (updated edn, Berkeley/London 1999); P. Garnsey, K. Hopkins, and C. Whittaker, eds, *Trade in the Ancient Economy* (London 1983); K. Greene, *The Archaeology of the Roman Economy* (London 1986); A. J. Parker, *Ancient Shipwrecks of the Mediterranean and the Roman Provinces* (Oxford 1992); H. M. Parkins and C. J. Smith, eds, *Trade, Traders and the Ancient City* (London 1998); D. Peacock, *Pottery in the Roman World* (London 1982)

A monetary system?

J. Andreau, *Banking and Business in the Roman World* (Cambridge 1999); R. P. Duncan-Jones, *Money and Government in the Roman Empire* (Cambridge 1994); C. Howgego, *Ancient History from Coins* (London 1995); C. M. Kraay, *Greek Coins* (London 1966)

VII · PHILOSOPHY AND EDUCATION

'The unexamined life is not worth living'

J. Annas, *Ancient Philosophy: A Very Short Introduction* (Oxford 2000); T. Irwin, ed., *Classical Philosophy* (Oxford 1999); M. Lane, *Plato's Progeny: How Plato and Socrates still captivate the Modern Mind* (London 2001); G. Vlastos, *Socrates* (Cambridge 1991); P. Zanker, *The Mask of Socrates* (Berkeley 1995)

The 'schools' of classical philosophy

J. Brunschwig and G. E. R. Lloyd, eds, *Greek Thought: A Guide to Classical Knowledge* (Cambridge, Mass. 2000); A. A. Long and D. N. Sedley, eds, *The Hellenistic Philosophers* (Cambridge 1987); D. N. Sedley, ed., *Cambridge Companion to Greek and Roman Philosophy* (Cambridge 2003)

Paideia and the principles of classical education

F. A. G. Beck, *Greek Education* (New York 1964); S. F. Bonner, *Education in Ancient Rome* (London 1977); W. Dominik, *Roman Eloquence: Rhetoric in Society and Literature* (London 1997); W. V. Harris, *Ancient Literacy* (Cambridge, Mass. 1989); R. MacLeod, *The Library of Alexandria: Centre of Learning in the Ancient World* (London/New York 2000); Y. L. Too, ed., *Education in Greek and Roman Antiquity* (Leiden 2001)

VIII · DIONYSOS : APOLLO

A philosopher's polarity

T. Carpenter and M. Faraone, eds, *Masks of Dionysus* (Ithaca, N.Y. 1993); A.-F. Jaccottet, *Choisir Dionysos: les associations dionysiaques ou la face cachée du dionysisme* (Kilchberg 2003); D. Mannsperger, 'Apollon gegen Dionysos: Numismatische Beiträge zu Octavians Rolle als *Vindex Libertatis*', in *Gymnasium* 80 (1973), 381–404; M. Silk and J. Stern, *Nietzsche on Tragedy* (Cambridge 1991); J. Solomon, ed., *Apollo: Origins and Influences* (Tucson 1994); A. F. Stewart, 'When is a *kouros* not an Apollo? The Tenea Apollo Revisited', in M. del Chiaro, ed., *Corinthiaca* (Columbia, Miss. 1986), 54–70

Wining, dining, and Dionysizing

L. Bonfante, ed., *Etruscan Life and Afterlife: A Handbook of Etruscan Studies* (Warminster, Wilts. 1986); K. Dunbabin, *The Roman Banquet: Images of Conviviality* (Cambridge 2003); F. Lissarrague, *The Aesthetics of the Greek Banquet* (Princeton 1990); O. Murray, ed., *Sympotica: A Symposium on the Symposion* (Oxford 1991); P. Schmitt Pantel, *La Cité au banquet: histoire des repas publics dans les cités grecques* (Rome 1992); N. J. Spivey, 'Greek Vases in Etruria', in T. Rasmussen and N. J. Spivey, eds, *Looking at Greek Vases* (Cambridge 1991), 131–50; M. Vickers and D. Gill, *Artful Crafts: Ancient Greek Silverware and Pottery* (Oxford 1994)

Acting out Dionysos

R. Beacham, *Spectacle Entertainments of Early Imperial Rome* (New York 1999); B. Bergmann and C. Kondoleon, eds, *The Art of Ancient Spectacle* (New Haven/London 1999); M. Bieber, *The History of the Greek and Roman Theater* (2nd edn, Princeton 1961); P. A. Cartledge, *Aristophanes and his Theatre of the Absurd* (London 1995); A. Futrell, *Blood in the Arena: The Spectacle of Roman Power* (Austin 1999); S. Goldhill, *Reading Greek Tragedy* (Cambridge 1986); S. Goldhill and R. Osborne, eds, *Performance Culture and Athenian Democracy* (Cambridge 1999); R. Green and E. Handley, *Images of the Greek Theatre* (Austin 1995); R. Hunter, *The New Comedy of Greece and Rome* (Cambridge 1985); O. Taplin, *Greek Tragedy in Action* (London 1985); J. Winkler and F. Zeitlin, eds, *Nothing to do with Dionysos? Athenian Drama in its Social Context* (Princeton 1990); J. Wise, *Dionysus writes: the Invention of Theatre in Ancient Greece* (Ithaca, N.Y. 1998)

Apollo and cosmic harmony

G. Comotti, *Music in Greek and Roman Culture* (Baltimore 1989); S. Cuomo, *Ancient Mathematics* (London 2001); J. Landels, *Music in Ancient Greece and Rome* (London 1999); T. Mathiesen, *Apollo's Lyre: Greek Music and Musical Theory in Antiquity and the Middle Ages* (Lincoln, Neb. 1999); M. West, *Ancient Greek Music* (Oxford 1992); P. Wilson, 'The *aulos* in Athens', in S. Goldhill and R. Osborne, eds, *Performance Culture and Athenian Democracy* (Cambridge 1999), 58–95

IX · THE CLASSICAL TRADITION OF ART

Classical aesthetika

C. Bérard, ed., *A City of Images: Iconography and Society in Ancient Greece* (Princeton 1989); O. Brendel, *Prolegomena to the Study of Roman Art* (New Haven/London 1979); R. G. Collingwood, *The Principles of Art* (Oxford 1938); R. Gordon, 'The Real and the Imaginary: Production and Religion in the Graeco-Roman World', in *Art History* 2.1 (1979), 5–34; S. Halliwell, *Plato: Republic 10* (Warminster, Wilts. 1988), and *The Aesthetics of Mimesis* (Princeton 2002); J. Isager, *Pliny on Art and Society* (London 1991); C. Janaway, *Images of Excellence: Plato's Critique of the Arts* (Oxford 1995); E. Kris and O. Kurz, *Legend, Myth, and Magic in the Image of the Artist* (New Haven/London 1979); J. J. Pollitt, *The Art of Ancient Greece: Sources and Documents* (Cambridge 1990), and *The Art of Rome, c. 753 BC–AD 337: Sources and Documents* (Cambridge 1983); T. Rasmussen and N. J. Spivey, eds, *Looking at Greek Vases* (Cambridge 1991); A. Schnapp, 'Are Images Animated: The Psychology of Statues in Ancient Greece', in C. Renfrew and E. Zubrow, eds, *The Ancient Mind: Elements of Cognitive Archaeology* (Cambridge 1994), 40–44; W. Steiner, *Images in Mind: Statues in Archaic and Classical Greek Literature and Thought* (New Haven/London 2001); A. F. Stewart, *Greek Sculpture: An Exploration* (New Haven/London 1990); J. Whitley, 'Beazley as Theorist', in *Antiquity* 71 (1997), 40–47

A chronological synthesis

1. *Geometric period*: J. N. Coldstream, *Geometric Greece* (London 1977); S. P. Morris, *Daidalos and the Origins of Greek Art* (Princeton 1992)

2. *Archaic period*: J. Boardman, *Greek Sculpture: The Archaic Period* (London 1978), and *Early Greek Vase Painting* (London 1998); J. M. Hurwit, *The Art and Culture of Early Greece 1100–480 BC* (Ithaca, N.Y. 1985); G. M. A. Richter with I. A. Richter, *Kouroi, Archaic Greek Youths* (3rd edn, London 1970); B. S. Ridgway, *The Archaic Style in Greek Sculpture* (Chicago 1993)

3. *Classical period*: J. Boardman, *Greek Sculpture: The Classical Period* (London 1985); C. Hallett, 'The Origins of the Classical Style in Sculpture', in *Journal of Hellenic Studies* 106 (1996), 71–84; R. Osborne, *Archaic and Classical Art* (Oxford 1998); M. Robertson, *The Art of Vase-Painting in Classical Athens* (Cambridge 1992)

4. *Hellenistic period*: B. H. Fowler, *The Hellenistic Aesthetic* (Bristol 1989); J. J. Pollitt, *Art in the Hellenistic Age* (Cambridge 1986); R. R. R. Smith, *Hellenistic Sculpture* (London 1991)

5. *The Arts of Rome*: M. Beard and J. Henderson, *Classical Art: From Greece to Rome* (Oxford 2001); R. Brilliant, *Gesture and Rank in Roman Art* (New Haven/London 1963); E. D'Ambra, *Art and Identity in the Roman World* (London 1998); J. Elsner, *Art and the Roman Viewer* (New York 1995); D. Kleiner, *Roman Sculpture* (New Haven/London 1992); R. Ling, *Roman Painting* (Cambridge 1991); M. Marvin, 'Copying in Roman Sculpture: The Replica Series', in E. D'Ambra, ed., *Roman Art in Context: An Anthology* (Englewood Cliffs, N.J. 1993), 161–88; J. J. Pollitt, 'The Impact of Greek Art on Rome', in *Transactions of the American Philological Association* 108 (1978), 155–74; N. H. Ramage and A. Ramage, *Roman Art: Romulus to Constantine* (2nd edn, London 1995), 50–55; I. A. Richmond, *Trajan's Army on Trajan's Column* (London 1982); P. Stewart, *Statues in Roman Society: Representation and Response* (Oxford 2003); A. Wallace-Hadrill, *Houses and Society in Pompeii and Herculaneum* (Princeton 1994)

X · THE PRESENT CLASSICAL PAST

M. Beard and J. Henderson, *Classics: A Very Short Introduction* (Oxford 1995); S. Goldhill, *Love, Sex and Tragedy: How the Ancient World Shapes our Lives* (London 2004); M. Greenhalgh, *The Classical Tradition in Art* (London 1978); E. Harris, *The Genius of Robert Adam* (New Haven/London 2001); C. Hornsby, ed., *The Impact of Italy: The Grand Tour and Beyond* (London 2000); A. Kelly, *The Story of Wedgwood* (London 1962); I. Morris, ed., *Classical Greece: Ancient Histories and Modern Archaeologies* (Cambridge 1994); M. Shanks, *Classical Archaeology of Greece: Experiences of a Discipline* (London/New York 1996); O. Taplin, *Greek Fire* (London 1989); A. Tsingarida, ed., *Appropriating Antiquity* (Brussels 2002)

'Decline and fall'

L. Barkan, *Unearthing the Past: Archaeology and Aesthetics in the Making of Renaissance Culture* (New Haven/London 1999); P. Bondanella, *The Eternal City: Roman Images in the Modern World* (Chapel Hill 1987); C. Edwards, ed., *Roman Presences: Receptions of Rome in European Culture, 1789–1945* (Cambridge 1999); A. Payne, A. Kuttner, and R. Smick, eds, *Antiquity and its Interpreters* (Cambridge 2000); F. de Polignac and J. Raspi Serra, eds, *La Fascination de l'antique, 1700–1770: Rome découverte, Rome inventée* (Paris 1998); P. Pray Bober and R. Rubinstein, *Renaissance Artists and Antique Sculpture* (London 1986); A. Schnapp, *The Discovery of the Past: The Origins of Archaeology* (London 1996); J. Wilton-Ely, *The Mind and Art of Giovanni Battista Piranesi* (London 1978)

'Speaking stones'

M. Beard, *The Parthenon* (London 2002); D. Constantine, *Early Greek Travellers and the Hellenic Ideal* (Cambridge 1984); B. Cook, *The Townley Marbles* (London 1985); W. Creighton and L. Johnson, *The Parthenon in Nashville: Pearl of the Tennessee Centennial Exposition* (Nashville 1989); F. Haskell and N. Penny, *Taste and the Antique: The Lure of Classical Sculpture 1500–1900* (New Haven/London 1981); C. Hitchens, ed., *The Elgin Marbles: Should they be returned to Greece?* (London 1998); D. Irwin, *Neoclassicism* (London 1997); I. Jenkins, *Archaeologists and Aesthetes in the Sculpture Galleries of the British Museum 1800–1939* (London 1992); R. Rhodes, *Architecture and Meaning on the Athenian Acropolis* (Cambridge 1995); W. St Clair, *Lord Elgin and the Marbles: The Controversial History of the Parthenon Sculptures* (3rd edn, Oxford 1998); P. Tournikotis, ed., *The Parthenon and its Impact in Modern Times* (Athens 1994)

Claims on the Classical

D. Ades, ed., *Art and Power: Europe under the Dictators 1930–45* (London 1995); R. Aldrich, *The Seduction of the Mediterranean: Writing, Art and Homosexual Fantasy* (London 1993); M. Biddiss and M. Wyke, eds, *The Uses and Abuses of Antiquity* (Bern/New York 1999); L. Canfora, *Le vie del classicismo* (Rome/Bari 1989); F. Liffran, ed., *Rome, 1920–1945: Le modèle fasciste, son Duce, sa mythologie* (Paris 1991); A. Potts, *Flesh and the Ideal: Winckelmann and the Origins of Art History* (New Haven/London 1994); A. Scobie, *Hitler's State Architecture: The Impact of Classical Antiquity* (University Park, Pa. 1990); M. Wyke, 'Herculean Muscle! The Classicizing Rhetoric of Bodybuilding', in *Arion* 4.3 (1996), 51–79

Cinematic classics

A. Arenas, 'Popcorn and Circuses: *Gladiator* and the Spectacle of Virtue', in *Arion* 9.1 (1993), 1–13; S. Joshel, M. Malamud, and D. McGuire, eds, *Imperial Projections: Ancient Rome and Modern Popular Culture* (Baltimore 2001); J. Solomon, *The Ancient World in the Cinema* (2nd edn, New Haven/London 2001); M. Winkler, ed., *Classical Myth and Culture in the Cinema* (Oxford 2001); M. Wyke, *Projecting the Past: Ancient Rome, Cinema and History* (London 1997)

Knocking the ruins

M. Beard, 'Casts and Cast-offs: The Origins of the Museum of Classical Archaeology', in *Proceedings of the Cambridge Philological Society* 39 (1993), 1–29; A. Bloom, *The Closing of the American Mind: How Higher Education has failed Democracy and impoverished the Souls of Today's Students* (New York 1987); E. Cowling and J. Mundy, eds, *On Classic Ground: Picasso, Léger, de Chirico and the New Classicism, 1910–1930* (London 1990); P. DuBois, *Trojan Horses: Saving the Classics from Conservatives* (New York 2001); M. Greenhalgh, *What is Classicism?* (London 1990); V. Hanson and J. Heath, *Who Killed Homer? The Demise of Classical Education and the Recovery of Greek Wisdom* (New York 1998); B. Knox, *The Oldest Dead White European Males and other Reflections on the Classics* (New York 1993); A. Papadakis and H. Watson, eds, *The New Classicism* (London 1990)

Classical pasts, presents, and futures

D. Harvey, *The Condition of Postmodernity* (Oxford 1990); C. Jencks, *Post-modernism: The New Classicism in Art and Architecture* (New York 1987); J. Lyotard, *The Postmodern Condition: A Report on Knowledge* (Minneapolis 1984)

ACKNOWLEDGMENTS FOR ILLUSTRATIONS

Measurements where known are given in centimetres, followed by inches (in parentheses); D = diameter, H = height, L = length, W = width

Berlin = Staatliche Museen zu Berlin, Preußischer Kulturbesitz, Antikensammlung
BM = British Museum, London
DAI = Deutsches Archäologisches Institut
JPGM = The J. Paul Getty Museum, Malibu, California
Louvre = Musée du Louvre, Paris
MJS = photo Michael Squire
NAM, Athens = National Archaeological Museum, Athens
Naples = Museo Nazionale, Naples
NJS = photo Nigel Spivey
RW = photo Roger Wilson

p. 1 JPGM, D 25.3 (10); pp. 2–3 École Nationale Supérieure des Beaux-Arts, Paris; 1 Museo delle Terme, Rome/Scala, H 155 (61); 2 Museo Nazionale Archeologico, Syracuse, H 78 (30³/4); 3 Staatliche Antikensammlungen und Glyptothek, Munich; 4 Scala; 5 Musées Royaux d'Art et d'Histoire, Brussels; 6 JPGM, Gift of David Collins, H 58.5 (23), W 29.5 (11⁵/8); 7 JPGM, L 116 (45⁵/8); 8 JPGM, H 55 (21⁵/8); 9 Louvre, H 35 (13 6/8), © Photo RMN – Hervé Lewandowski; 10 Louvre/photo Michael Duigan; 11 Staatliche Antikensammlungen und Glyptothek, Munich; 12 Barberini Gallery, Rome/DAI, Rome; 13 Archivi Alinari, Florence; 14 JPGM, 87 x 39 x 7 (31¹/4 x 15³/8 x 2³/4); 15 JPGM, H 172.8 (68); 16 NAM, Athens/Scala, H 155 (61); 17 RW; 18 NAM, Athens/Scala, 19 JPGM, H 58 (22⁷/8); 20 JPGM, H 112.4 (44¹/4); 21 Berlin/photo Johannes Laurentius; 22, 23 Egyptian Museum, Cairo; 24 Egypt Exploration Society, London; 25 BM; 26 JPGM, 48 x 36 x 12.8 (18⁷/8 x 14³/16 x 5¹/16); 27 Staatliche Antikensammlungen und Glyptothek, Munich; 28 BM; 29 Archaeological Museum, Thessaloniki; 30 JPGM, 21.5 x 8 x 7.5 (8¹/2 x 3¹/8 x 3); 31 JPGM, H 12.4–13 (4⁷/8–5¹/8), W 47.2 (18⁵/8); 32 JPGM, H 21.8 (8⁹/16), D (rim) 15.1 (6); 33 JPGM, H 23 (9¹/16); 34 JPGM, H 38 (15), W 56 (22); 35 JPGM, Gift of Vasek Polak, L 13.5 (5³/8); 36 JPGM, 77.5 x 38.1 x 30.5 (30¹/2 x 15 x 12); 37 Naples/Scala, H 212 (83¹/2); 38 BM; 39 JPGM, H 6.5 (2¹/2), W 25.1 (9⁷/8), D 18.9 (7¹/2); 40 Scala; 41 Delphi Museum/Scala, H 180 (70⁷/8); 42 NAM, Athens; 43 JPGM, Gift of Barbara and Lawrence Fleischman, H 51 (20¹/8), D 42 (16¹/2); 44 Hirmer;

45 Scala; 46 © Sonia Halliday Photographs; 47 RW; 48 JPGM, Gift of Nicolas Koutoulakis in memory of J. Paul Getty, H 65 (25⁵/8), D 17.9 (7); 49 JPGM, greatest extent 14.5 (5³/4); 50 JPGM, D 35.5 (14), H 11 (4³/8), W 38.1 (15); 51, 52 JPGM, H 21.1 (8¹/4); 53 JPGM, H 41 (16¹/8), D 30 (12); 54 JPGM, H 9.5 (3³/4), D 14 (5¹/2); 55 JPGM, Gift of Barbara and Lawrence Fleischman, H 11.1 (4³/8), W 4.24 (1⁵/8), D 2.78 (1¹/8); 56 JPGM, D 19.5–21.7 (7¹¹/16–8⁹/16); 57 JPGM, Gift of Nicolas Koutoulakis in memory of J. Paul Getty, H 65 (25⁵/8), D 17.9 (7); 58 JPGM, H 151.5 (59⁵/8); 59 JPGM, H 89.5 (35¹/4), D 38.3 (15¹/16); 60 JPGM, H 58 (22⁷/8), W 39.5 (15¹/2); 61 Scala; 62 JPGM, 208 x 208 (81⁷/8 x 81⁷/8) ; 63 JPGM, H 21.1 (8¹/4); 64 Hessisches Landesmuseum, Darmstadt/RW; 65, 66 RW; 67 Scala; 69 George Taylor, after G.-A. Blouet, Restauration des Thermes d'Antonin Caracalla, à Rome, Paris 1828; 70 JPGM, H 97 (38¹/4); 71 JPGM, H 13.5 (5 5/16), L 42 (16¹/2), W 26 (10¹/4); 72 JPGM, H 10.7–11.7 (4¹/4–4⁵/8), W 38.9 (15³/8); 73 JPGM, D 18.5 (7¹/4); 74 JPGM, Gift of Alan E. Salke, H 12.6 (5), W 39.1 (15³/8), D 30.8 (12¹/8); 75 JPGM, D 33.5 (13¹/4), H 11 (4³/8), W 38.1 (15); 76 JPGM, D 23.5 (9¹/4); 77 JPGM, H 9 (3¹/2), W 29.5 (11⁵/8), D 22.5 (8⁷/8); 78 JPGM, H 36 (14¹/8), D 24.8 (9³/4); 79 JPGM, H 9–9.4 (3¹/2–3³/4) W 30.5 (12), D 23.4–23.6 (9¹/4); 80 JPGM, H 5.1 (2), greatest extent 15.9 (6¹/4); 81 JPGM, H 184 (72¹/2); 82 Sian Francis; 83 I Musei Vaticani/Scala, H 205 (80³/4); 84 JPGM, Gift of Nicolas Koutoulakis, Geneva, H 24.4 (9⁵/8); 85 JPGM, H 8.5 (3³/8); 86 JPGM, H 115 (45¹/4); 87 BM; 88 Giovanni Lattanzi; 89 Scala; 90 École Française d'Athènes; 91 The Toledo Museum of Art, Toledo, O., Gift of Edward Drummond Libbey, H 32.5 (12¹³/16), D 37.5 (14³/4); 92 JPGM, 1.6 x 1.38 (5/8 x ¹/2); 93 JPGM, H 13.3 (5¹/4), W 40.7 (16), D 32.4 (12³/4); 94 JPGM, H 71.2 (28); 95 English Heritage Photo Library/photo Jonathan Bailey; 96 JPGM, Gift of Barbara and Lawrence Fleischman, H 13 (5¹/8), W 5 (2), D 8.3 (3¹/4); 97 JPGM, H 36.8 (14¹/2), D (body) 35.7 (14¹/16); 98 JPGM, H 43 (16¹⁵/16), D 54 (21¹/4); 99 Scala; 100 Foto della Soprintendenza ai Beni Archeologici per l'Etruria Meridionale; 101 RW; 102 JPGM, 68.5 x 127 (27 x 50); 103 BM; 104 JPGM, Gift of Barbara and Lawrence Fleischman, H 8.5 (3³/8), W 26.7 (10¹/2), D 19.7 (7³/4); 105 Scala; 106 JPGM, H 16.5 (6¹/2); 107 from P. Shatzmann and R. Herzog, Asklepion, Kos I, 1932;

108 NJS; 109 John Decopoulos; 110 JPGM, H 16.5 (6¹/2); 111 The Art Archive/Museo della Civiltà Romana, Rome/Dagli Orti; 112 Bildarchiv Foto Marburg; 113 NAM, Athens; 114 Louvre/akg-images/Erich Lessing; 115, 116 Musée Archéologique, Dijon/photo F. Perrodin; 117 JPGM, H 84.5 (33¹/4); 118 Scala; 119 JPGM, Gift of Barbara and Lawrence Fleischman, H 20.7 (8¹/8); 120 JPGM, H 32.5 (12³/4); 121 JPGM, H 11.3–11.37 (4¹/2), W 34.35 (13¹/2); 122 Royal Ontario Museum, Toronto; 123 Drawing by Mrs M. Gough; 124 Naples/Scala; 125 BM, H 24 (9¹/2); 126 Sian Francis; 127 Naples/Scala; 128 Museo del Tesoro, Vatican/Scala; 129 akg-images/Pirozzi; 130 JPGM, H 62.7 (24⁵/8), W 38 (15); 131 JPGM, H 87 (34¹/4), D 26.9 (10⁵/8); 132 Scala, H 315 (124); 133 JPGM, H 7.81–7.86 (3¹/4); 134 JPGM, Gift of Barbara and Lawrence Fleischman, H 35 (13³/4), D (mouth) 13 (5¹/8), (foot) 12 (4³/4); 135 JPGM, 1.75 x 1 (11/16 x ³/8); 136 JPGM, Gift of Barbara and Lawrence Fleischman, H 15 (5⁷/8), W 29 (11³/8), D 20.9 (8¹/4); 137 JPGM, H 44.6 (17¹/2), D 33 (13); 138 JPGM, H 43 (16⁷/8), D (rim) 20.1 (7⁷/8), (body) 28.4 (11¹/8); 139 JPGM, Gift of Barbara and Lawrence Fleischman, H 42 (16¹/2), D (body) 27.2 (10³/4); 140 Olympia Museum/Scala, H 160 (63); 141 JPGM, Gift of Stanley Ungar, 12 x 8.8 x 3.3 (4³/4 x 3¹/2 x 1¹/4); 142 JPGM, Gift of Barbara and Lawrence Fleischman, H 15.2 (6); 143 JPGM, H 24.3 (9⁵/8); 144 JPGM, Gift of J. Paul Getty, H 193.5 (76¹/8); 145 Musei Capitolini, Rome/Scala; 146 NAM, Athens (57¹/2); 147 Philip Winton after Byron Bell; 148 Scala; 149 Archaeological Museum, Pergamon (Bergama); 150 NAM, Athens; 151 Medelshavsmuseet, Stockholm; 152 JPGM, H 21.6 (8¹/2); 153 NAM, Athens; 154 RW; 155 JPGM, H 19.7 (7³/4); 156 JPGM, 17.14 x 9.14 x 4.06 (6⁷/8 x 3⁵/8 x 1⁵/8); 157 JPGM, H 28.8 (11³/8), D 12.7 (5); 158 Musei Capitolini, Rome/Scala; 159 Scala; 160 Museo Civico, Piacenza/Scala; 161 Cambridge Museum of Archaeology, Cambridge University/RW, H 120 (47¹/4); 162 Scala; 163 Allard Pierson Museum, Amsterdam; 164 RW; 166 Hirmer; 170 NJS; 171, 172 from C. R. Cockerell, The Temples of Jupiter Panhellenius at Ægina, and of Apollo Epicurius at Bassae, London 1860; 173 Martin Hürlimann; 174, 175 Scala; 176 akg-images/Pirozzi; 177 Museo di Villa Giulia, Rome/Scala; 178 RW; 179, 180 Scala; 181 BM; 182 JPGM, H 48.3 (19), D (rim) 28.1 (11¹/8), D (body) 27.2 (10³/4);

183 JPGM, H 11.43 (4¹/2); 184 Louvre/RW; 185 BM; 186 JPGM, H 35.8 (14), D 23.6 (9¹/8); 187 Museo Archeologico, Florence/Scala, H 66 (26); 188 JPGM, L 248.9 (98), H 134.6 (53), W 147.3 (58); 189 JPGM, H 217 (85³/8), W 227 (89³/8); 190 Museo di Villa Giulia, Rome, H 19 (7¹/2), D 46.6 (18³/8); 191 Berlin V.I 4532/photo Christa Begall, H 37 (14⁵/8); 192 Museo Archeologico, Chiusi/Scala; 193 DAI, Rome; 194 Alison Frantz; 195 Scala; 196, 197 akg-images; 198 Scala; 199 MJS; 200 Scala; 201 JPGM, H 30.8 (12¹/8), D 57.2 (22¹/2); 202 Staatliche Antikensammlungen und Glyptothek, Munich; 203 BM, H 30 (12); 204 Louvre; 205 Musei Capitolini, Rome/Scala; 207 Eleusis Museum/RW, H 142 (55⁷/8); 208 JPGM, Gift of Barbara and Lawrence Fleischman, H 33 (13), W 35.5 (14), D (rim) 30 (12); 209 JPGM, H 33 (13); 210 Musei Capitolini, Rome, H 36.3 (14¹/4); 211 T. Okamura; 212 Giovanni Lattanzi; 213 MJS; 214 Sperlonga Museum/RW, H c. 350 (137³/4); 215 Staatliche Antikensammlungen und Glyptothek, Munich; 216 Archivi Alinari, Florence; 217 The Metropolitan Museum of Art, New York, Rogers Fund, 1920 (20.192.17), H 188 (73 ³/4), W 119 (46⁷/8); 218 akg-images; 219 Archae-ological Receipts Fund, Athens; 220 Martin von Wagner Museum, Würzburg; 221 after John Boardman; 222 BM; 223 Somerset County Museum, Taunton; 224 Administrazione Torlonia; 225 Museo Nazionale, Rome/RW; 226 I Musei Vaticani/Scala, H 214 (84 ¹/4); 227 Naples/Scala; 228 Berlin F 1806/photo Ingrid Geske, D 19.5 (7⁵/8); 229 NJS; 230 BM; 231 Bardo Museum, Tunis/Scala; 232 Museo di Villa Giulia, Rome/Scala; 233, 234 NJS; 235 Sheila Gibson; 236 NJS; 237 Scala; 238 RW; 239, 240 Scala; 241 Museo Gregoriano Profano, Vatican/Scala; 242 Museo Pio-Clementino, Vatican/Scala; 243 Museo delle Terme, Rome/Scala; 244 JPGM; 245 Scala; 246 RW; 247 Museo Pio-Clementino, Vatican/RW; 248 JPGM, Gift of Barbara and Lawrence Fleischman, H 17 (6 ³/4), W 25.3 (10); D 6.5 (2 ¹/2); 249 JPGM, Gift of Barbara and Lawrence Fleischman, H 17.5 (6 ⁷/8), D 18.5 (7 ¹/4); 250 JPGM, H 12.6 (5), W 17.6 (6 ⁷/8); 251 Scala; 252 NJS; 253 after Angelo Valenti; 254 after M. Cristofani, 'Economia e società', in Rasenna, 1986; 255 NJS; 256 Berlin F 2294, D 30.5 (12); 257 Louvre/Scala, H 62 (24³/8); 258 The Art Archive/Archaeological Museum Delphi/Dagli Orti; 259 NJS; 260 Olympia Museum/Scala, H 215 (84⁵/8); 261 Galleria degli Uffizi,

Florence/Scala; 262 Museo Pio-Clementino, Vatican/Scala, H 48 (18 7/8); 263 Smithsonian American Art Museum, Washington, DC/Art Resource/Scala; 264 from J. M. Camp, *The Athenian Agora* (1986); 265 Agora Museum, Athens/akg-images; 266 Agora Museum, Athens/Scala; 267, 268 Kunsthistorisches Museum, Vienna; 269 JPGM, D 31.4 (12 3/8); 270 Naples/Scala, H 192 (75 5/8); 271 JPGM, H 81.5 (32 1/8); 272 Acropolis Museum, Athens/RW, H 86 (33 7/8); 273 JPGM, H 7.9 (3 1/8), W 3.4 (1 5/16); 274 JPGM, 1.9 x 1.39 (3/4 x 9/16); 275 JPGM, H 29.1 (11 1/2), W 25.9 (10 1/4); 276 Lehnert & Landrock, Cairo; 277 BM; 278 Naples/Scala, 272 x 513 (107 1/8 x 202); 279 The Art Archive/NAM, Athens/Dagli Orti; 280 JPGM, H 34.9 (13 3/4); 281 JPGM, H 29.5 (11 5/8); 282 Ny Carlsberg Glyptotek, Copenhagen; 283 JPGM, Gift of Barbara and Lawrence Fleischman, H 17.5 (6 7/8); 284 JPGM, H 26 (10 1/4), W 13.8 (5 3/8); 285 Museo Archaeologico, Florence/Scala; 286 I Musei Vaticani/Scala; 287 Scala; 288 Acropolis Museum, Athens/Scala; 289 NJS; 290 Scala; 291 JPGM, H 39 (15 3/8); 292 JPGM, H 43 (16 7/8); 293 Ny Carlsberg Glyptotek, Copenhagen; 294 JPGM, 40.5 x 20.3 x 20.3 (15 13/16 x 8 x 8); 295 BM; 296 JPGM, Gift of Barbara and Lawrence Fleischman, H 91 (35 7/8), W 80.5 (31 3/4); 297 JPGM, H 45.7 (18), W 38 (14 15/16); 298 JPGM, 70.8 x 87.8 (27 7/8 x 34 5/8); 299 RW; 300, 301 © Sonia Halliday Photographs; 302 after W. B. Dinsmoor, Jr; 303 akg-images/Erich Lessing; 304 Museo della Civiltà Romana, Rome; 305 akg-images; 306 A.F. Kersting; 307 Silchester Field School, University of Reading; 308 Museo Nazionale Romana, Rome/Scala; 309 Allard Pierson Museum, Amsterdam; 310 Museo di Villa Giulia, Rome/Scala; 311 JPGM, Gift of Barbara and Lawrence Fleischman, H 12.4–13 (4 7/8–5 1/8), W 23 (9), D 34 (13 3/8); 312 JPGM, H 7.7 (3), D 18.8 (7 3/8); 313 © Mike Andrews/Ancient Art & Architecture Collection Ltd; 314 Scala; 315 Adrian Goldsworthy; 316 © Photo RMN; 317 Hirmer; 318 Peter Clayton; 319, 320 JPGM, H 33.4 (13 1/8); 321 JPGM, H 27.9 (11); 322 JPGM, H 13.4–13.8 (5 1/4–5 3/8); 323 JPGM, W 7.3 (2 7/8), L 13.5 (5 1/4); 324 JPGM, H 153 (60 1/4), W 45.1 (17 3/4); 325 JPGM, H 102.2 (40 1/4), W 44.5 (17 1/2); 326, 327 JPGM, Gift of Barbara and Lawrence Fleischman, H 47 (18 1/2), D 18.9 (7 1/2); 328 Courtesy, Museum of Fine Arts, Boston, Purchased of E. P. Warren from the H. L. Pierce Fund, H 17.7 (7); 329 akg-images; 330 © Emily Lane; 331 Egypt Exploration Society, London; 332 Museo Civico, Albenga/Scala; 333 MJS; 336 Museo Nazionale, Chieti/Scala; 337 Royal Ontario Museum, Toronto; 338 Scala;

339, 340 The Metropolitan Museum of Art, New York, Fletcher Fund, 1931, H 17.1 (6 3/4); 341 Museo di Villa Giulia, Rome; 342 Museo Archaeologico Nazionale di Reggio Calabria, H 26 (10 1/4); 343 Giovanni Lattanzi; 344 Scala; 345 RW; 346, 347 The Art Archive/Dagli Orti; 348 Nationalmuseet, Copenhagen; 349 © Bates Littlehales/CORBIS; 350, 351 Giovanni Lattanzi; 352, 353 Maritime Archaeology Research and Excavation, Oxford; 354, 355 Scala; 356 RW; 357 NJS; 358 RW; 359–367 JPGM; 368 JPGM, H 34.9 (13 3/4); 369 akg-images/Erich Lessing; 370 Museo Pio-Clementino, Vatican/Scala; 371 Naples/Scala; 372 Scala; 373 Berlin; 374 Archivi Alinari, Florence; 375 Musei Capitolini, Rome/Scala, H 40.5 (16); 376 akg-images/Jürgen Sorges; 377 Rheinisches Landesmuseum, Trier; 378 Louvre; 379 JPGM, Gift of Barbara and Lawrence Fleischman, H 15.3 (6), W 5.25 (2 1/8); 380 BM; 381 JPGM, W 6.75 (2 11/16); 382 JPGM, H 11.9 (4 5/8), D 31.2 (12 1/4); 383 JPGM, H 17.3 (6 3/4), D 13.65 (5 3/8); 384 The Board of Trinity College, Dublin; 385 The Art Archive/Louvre/Dagli Orti; 386 JPGM, H 146.1 (57 1/2); 387 JPGM, H 21.6 (8 1/2); 388 Staatliche Antikensammlungen und Glyptothek, Munich; 389 Scala; 390 BM; 391 Olympia Museum/Scala; 392 Scala; 393 NAM, Athens/Scala; 394 JPGM, H 54 (21 1/4), D 40 (15 3/4); 395 JPGM, Gift of Barbara and Lawrence Fleischman, H 14.8 (5 7/8), D (mouth) 5.4 (2 1/8), (body) 8.2 (3 1/4); 396 JPGM, H 40.5 (16), W 172.5 (67 7/8), D 47 (18 1/2); 397 JPGM, H 27.4 (10 13/16), L 46 (18 1/8), D 12.6 (5); 398 JPGM, H 10 (3 7/8); 399 JPGM, H 13.6 (5 3/8), D 36.4 (14 3/8); 400 JPGM, H 10.3 (4), D 23.9 (9 3/8); 401 JPGM, H 7.5–7.9 (3–3 1/8); D 19.4 (7 5/8); 402 JPGM, H 23 (9), D 18.6 (7 3/8); 403 JPGM, Gift of Barbara and Lawrence Fleischman, H 12.4–13 (4 7/8–5 1/8), W 43 (16 7/8), D 34 (13 3/8); 404 JPGM, H 30.6 (12), D (mouth) 12.9 (5 1/8), (body) 17.2 (6 3/4); 405 JPGM, Partial Gift of Barbara and Lawrence Fleischman, 3.5 x 7.5 x 2.5 (1 3/8 x 3 x 1), 3.5 x 7.2 x 2.4 (1 3/8 x 2 7/8 x 1), 3.7 x 7.4 x 2.6 (1 1/2 x 2 7/8 x 1); 406 Scala; 407 Museo Nazionale, Tarquinia; 408, 409 Scala; 410 RW; 411 JPGM, Gift of Barbara and Lawrence Fleischman, H 21.9 (8 5/8), W 25.5 (10); 412 Museo Gregoriano Etrusco, Vatican/Scala; 413 JPGM, H 37 (14 9/16), D 45 (17 11/16); 414 A.F. Kersting; 416 Michael Jenner; 417 Scala; 418 JPGM, H 18.7 (7 3/8), D 23 (9); 419 JPGM, Gift of Barbara and Lawrence Fleischman, H 10.3 (4); 420 JPGM, Gift of Barbara and Lawrence Fleischman, H 10.1 (4); 421 Museo Nazionale, Naples/Scala; 422 JPGM, Gift of Barbara and Lawrence Fleischman, H 61 (24),

W 81 (31 7/8); 423 JPGM, H 17 (6 3/4), 424, 425 JPGM, H 63.5 (25), W (body) 24.89 (9 3/4); 426, 427 Scala; 428 akg-images/Gilles Mermet; 429 RW; 430 Naples/Scala; 431 Scala; 432 JPGM, 97 x 30.5 x 22.9 (38 3/16 x 12 x 9); 433 JPGM, D 21.6 (8 1/2); 434 JPGM, H 140 (55 1/8), H 104 (41), H 140 (55 1/8); 435 Museo Nazionale, Naples/Scala; 436 JPGM, H 35.8 (14 1/16), W 9.5 (3 3/4); 437 Berlin F 2285, D 28.5 (11 1/4); 438 JPGM, H 10.5 (4 1/8), W 17.6 (6 7/8), D 10.6 (4 1/8); 439 JPGM, H 10.7–11.7 (4 1/4–4 5/8); 440 JPGM, 40.5 x 172.5 x 47 (16 x 67 7/8 x 18 1/2); 441, 442 Naples/Scala; 443 Atkinson Art Gallery, Southport Arts and Cultural Services, Sefton M.B.C., Merseyside, 152.5 x 121 (60 x 47 5/8); 444 Museo Nazionale di Reggio Calabria/Scala, H 198 (78); 445 Berlin F 2294/photo Ingrid Geske, D 30.5 (12); 446 Staatliche Antikensammlungen und Glyptothek, Munich/RW; 447 Makis Skiadaressis; 448 Museo di Villa Giulia, Rome/Scala; 449 Olympia Museum/DAI, Athens; 450 JPGM, H 7.87 (3 1/8), W 3.55 (1 3/8); 451 JPGM, H 5.84 (2 1/4), W 19.30 (7 5/8); 452 Heraklion Museum; 453 NAM, Athens; 454 JPGM, H 220 (86 5/8); 455 Acropolis Museum, Athens/Scala; 456 DAI, Athens; 457 Louvre/Scala, H 200 (78 3/4); 458, 459 akg-images/Erich Lessing; 460 Berlin/photo Jürgen Liepe; 461 Galleria degli Uffizi, Florence/Scala; 462 Museo delle Terme, Rome/Scala; 463 Musei Capitolini, Rome/Scala; 464 Museo Pio-Clementino, Vatican/Scala, H 224 (88 1/4); 465 Naples/Scala; 466, 467 Scala; 468 Kunsthistorisches Museum, Vienna/akg-images; 469 akg-images; 470 The Trustees of Sir John Soane's Museum, London; 471 from James Baillie Fraser, *Views of Calcutta and its Environs*, London 1824–26; 472 The National Trust Photographic Library; 473, 474 BM; 475 Bibliothèque Nationale de France, Paris; 476 I Musei Vaticani; 477 Royal Collection Enterprises; 478 I Musei Vaticani; 479 Royal Collection Enterprises; 480 from G. B. Piranesi, *Vedute di Roma*, Rome 1748; 481 Freud Museum, London; 482 Research Library, The Getty Research Institute, Los Angeles; 483 Biblioteca Apostolica Vaticana; 484 © Mark E. Gibson/CORBIS; 485 © Lake County Museum/CORBIS; 486 Philip Winton; 487 David Finn; 488 BM; 489 Birmingham Museums and Art Gallery; 490 MJS; 491 Townley Hall Art Gallery and Museum, Burnley, Lancs/Bridgeman Art Library, 127 x 99.1 (50 x 39); 492 Associated Press; 493 C. G. Sweeting; 494 akg-images; 495 bfi Collections; 496 akg-images; 497 MJS; 498 akg-images; 499 from Graeme Mercer Adam, *Sandow on Physical Training:*

a Study in the Perfect Type of Human Form, London 1894; 500 John Tickner Photography; 501 akg-images; 502 Kobal Collection; 503, 504 akg-images; 505 Giraudon; 506 Courtesy of the Masters and Fellows of Trinity College, Cambridge; 507 The Museum of Modern Art, New York. © Succession Picasso/DACS 2004; 508 JPGM, H 28.5 (11 1/4); 509 Louvre; 510 Franz Meyer, Zurich. © ADAGP, Paris and DACS, London 2004; 511 MJS; 512 © Robert Holmes/CORBIS; 513 Galleria degli Uffizi, Florence/Scala; 514 John Borthwick/Lonely Planet Images; 515 Naples; 516 DAI, Rome; 517 Naples; 518 Bibliothèque Nationale de France, Paris; 519 Kunsthistorisches Museum, Vienna; 520 Berlin; 521 Archivi Alinari, Florence; 522 DAI, Rome; 523 Ny Carlsberg Glyptotek, Copenhagen; 524 The Metropolitan Museum of Art, New York, Samuel D. Lee Fund, 1940; 525 BM; 526 Berlin; 527 Palazzo dei Conservatori, Rome/Scala; 528 Hirmer; 529 DAI, Rome; 530 Naples; 531, 532 BM; 533 Louvre; 534 Hirmer; 535 Sparta Museum; 536 BM; 537 RW; 538 BM; 539 Ny Carlsberg Glyptotek, Copenhagen; 540 Museo Ostiense, Ostia; 541 Naples; 542 Ny Carlsberg Glyptotek, Copenhagen; 543 Naples/akg-images/Erich Lessing; 544 Naples; 545, 546 BM; 547 Archivi Alinari, Florence; 548 Cabinet des Médailles, Paris; 549 Archivi Alinari, Florence; 550 BM; 551 Bardo Museum, Tunis; 552 I Musei Vaticani; 553 Ny Carlsberg Glyptotek, Copenhagen; 554, 555 BM; 556 Louvre; 557 Hirmer; 558 JPGM, H 2.7 (1 1/8), D 16.2 (6 3/8); 559 Courtesy, Museum of Fine Arts, Boston, James Fund and Special Contribution, H 37 (14 5/8), D 42.5 (16 3/4); 560 BM; 561 Naples; 562 Olympia Museum; 563 Staatliche Antikensammlungen und Glyptothek, Munich; 564 Taranto Museum; 565 Scala; 566 BM; 567 DAI, Rome; 568 Olympia Museum; 569 Hirmer; 570 Martin von Wagner-Museum der Universität, Würzburg; 571 Museo Nazionale, Palermo; 572 I Musei Vaticani; 573 Villa Albani, Rome; 574 The Metropolitan Museum of Art, New York, Harris Brisbane Dick Fund, 1934; 575 NAM, Athens; 576 JPGM, H 12.5 (4 7/8), D 18.4–18.5 (7 1/4); 577, 578 Louvre; 579 NAM, Athens; 580 Soprintendenza dalle Antichità, Reggio di Calabria; 581 Leonard von Matt; 582 Museo Gregoriano Etrusco, Vatican/Scala; 583 Musei Capitolini, Rome; 584 I Musei Vaticani; 585 Berlin; 586 BM; 587 Musei Capitolini, Rome

Figures in *italic* type refer to illustrations and captions; 'a', 'b', 'c', and 'd' indicate columns in the Reference section. Spellings are those adopted throughout this book; it may be necessary to search for both Greek and Latin forms.

TVS·POPVL

ESAR·I·DIVI

IO·AVG·GE

OTP·IB·POT

APA·IDVMC

OCVSTA·PV